ROUTLEDGE
STUDENT STATUTES

....

Employment Law Statutes
2010–2011

Designed specifically for students, and responding to current market feedback, Routledge Student Statutes offer a comprehensive collection of statutory provisions un-annotated and therefore ideal for LLB and GDL course and exam use. In addition, an accompanying website offers extensive guidance on how to use and interpret statutes, providing valuable tutorial and exam preparation.

The Routledge Student Statutes series collect together, in each volume, all the legislation students need to pass their exams so it is comprehensive, clearly presented and easy to access.

Routledge Student Statutes provide extensive innovative features, vital in aiding LLB and GDL learning:

- Comprehensive content, with legislation carefully selected to match the common curriculum
- Written by leading experts in each field so students can feel confident in the experience and judgement behind each selection
- Un-annotated, making the series ideal for both course and exam use
- Each title contains alphabetical, chronological and thematic contents listings and is fully indexed making it easy to navigate
- A free Companion Website providing students with extra guidance and testing on how to use and interpret statutes
- Updated annually to incorporate all of the latest legislation covered in UK law syllabi
- Highly competitive price makes Routledge Student Statutes the statutes series of choice

Janice Nairns LLB (Hons), LLM, PGCE (HE), Barrister has over ten years experience in the teaching of employment law to business and LLB students. She has a particular interest in discrimination law issues.

ROUTLEDGE STUDENT STATUTES

http://cw.routledge.com/textbooks/statutes/

ROUTLEDGE
STUDENT STATUTES

Employment Law Statutes
2010–2011

JANICE NAIRNS

Barrister

LONDON AND NEW YORK

First published 2011
by Routledge
2 Park Square, Milton Park, Abingdon, Oxon, OX14 4RN

Simultaneously published in the USA and Canada
by Routledge
270 Madison Avenue, New York, NY 10016

Routledge is an imprint of the Taylor & Francis Group, an informa business

Typeset in Sabon by RefineCatch Limited, Bungay, Suffolk
Printed and bound in Great Britain by MPG Books Group, UK

British Library Cataloguing in Publication Data
A catalogue record for this book is available from the British Library

Parliamentary material is reproduced with the permission of the Controller of HMSO on behalf of Parliament.

ISBN13: 978–0–415–58239–1 (pbk)

Contents

Guide to the Companion Website

....

http://cw.routledge.com/textbooks/statutes

Visit the Companion Website for Routledge Student Statutes in order to:

- **Understand** how to use a statute book in tutorials and exams;

- **Learn** how to interpret statutes and other legislation to maximum effect;

- **Gain** essential practice in statute interpretation prior to your exams, through unique problem-based scenarios;

- **Test** your understanding of statutes through a set of Multiple Choice Questions for revision or to check your own progress;

- **Understand** how the law is developing with updates, additional information and links to useful websites.

Statutes

Equal Pay Act 1970
(c. 41)

1—

(1) If the terms of a contract under which a woman is employed at an establishment in Great Britain do not include (directly or by reference to a collective agreement or otherwise) an equality clause they shall be deemed to include one.

(2) An equality clause is a provision which relates to terms (whether concerned with pay or not) of a contract under which a woman is employed (the "woman's contract"), and has the effect that—

(a) where the woman is employed on like work with a man in the same employment—
  (i) if (apart from the equality clause) any term of the woman's contract is or becomes less favourable to the woman than a term of a similar kind in the contract under which that man is employed, that term of the woman's contract shall be treated as so modified as not to be less favourable, and
  (ii) if (apart from the equality clause) at any time the woman's contract does not include a term corresponding to a term benefiting that man included in the contract under which he is employed, the woman's contract shall be treated as including such a term;

(b) where the woman is employed on work rated as equivalent with that of a man in the same employment—
  (i) if (apart from the equality clause) any term of the woman's contract determined by the rating of the work is or becomes less favourable to the woman than a term of a similar kind in the contract under which that man is employed, that term of the woman's contract shall be treated as so modified as not to be less favourable, and
  (ii) if (apart from the equality clause) at any time the woman's contract does not include a term corresponding to a term benefiting that man included in the contract under which he is employed and determined by the rating of the work, the woman's contract shall be treated as including such a term.

(c) where a woman is employed on work which, not being work in relation to which paragraph (a) or (b) above applies, is, in terms of the demands made on her (for instance under such headings as effort, skill and decision), of equal value to that of a man in the same employment—
  (i) if (apart from the equality clause) any term of the woman's contract is or becomes less favourable to the woman than a term of a similar kind in the contract under which that man is employed, that term of the woman's contract shall be treated as so modified as not to be less favourable, and

(ii) if (apart from the equality clause) at any time the woman's contract does not include a term corresponding to a term benefiting that man included in the contract under which he is employed, the woman's contract shall be treated as including such a term.

(d) where—

    (i) any term of the woman's contract regulating maternity-related pay provides for any of her maternity-related pay to be calculated by reference to her pay at a particular time,

    (ii) after that time (but before the end of the statutory maternity leave period) her pay is increased, or would have increased had she not been on statutory maternity leave, and

    (iii) the maternity-related pay is neither what her pay would have been had she not been on statutory maternity leave nor the difference between what her pay would have been had she not been on statutory maternity leave and any statutory maternity pay to which she is entitled,

if (apart from the equality clause) the terms of the woman's contract do not provide for the increase to be taken into account for the purpose of calculating the maternity-related pay, the term mentioned in sub-paragraph (i) above shall be treated as so modified as to provide for the increase to be taken into account for that purpose;

(e) if (apart from the equality clause) the terms of the woman's contract as to—

    (i) pay (including pay by way of bonus) in respect of times before she begins to be on statutory maternity leave,

    (ii) pay by way of bonus in respect of times when she is absent from work in consequence of the prohibition in section 72(1) of the Employment Rights Act 1996 (compulsory maternity leave), or

    (iii) pay by way of bonus in respect of times after she returns to work following her having been on statutory maternity leave,

do not provide for such pay to be paid when it would be paid but for her having time off on statutory maternity leave, the woman's contract shall be treated as including a term providing for such pay to be paid when ordinarily it would be paid;

(f) if (apart from the equality clause) the terms of the woman's contract regulating her pay after returning to work following her having been on statutory maternity leave provide for any of that pay to be calculated without taking into account any amount by which her pay would have increased had she not been on statutory maternity leave, the woman's contract shall be treated as including a term providing for the increase to be taken into account in calculating that pay.

(3) An equality clause falling within subsection (2)(a), (b) or (c) above shall not operate in relation to a variation between the woman's contract and the man's contract if the employer proves that the variation is genuinely due to a material factor which is not the difference of sex and that factor—

(a) in the case of an equality clause falling within subsection (2)(a) or (b) above, must be a material difference between the woman's case and the man's; and

(b) in the case of an equality clause falling within subsection (2)(c) above, may be such a material difference.

(4) A woman is to be regarded as employed on like work with men if, but only if, her work and theirs is of the same or a broadly similar nature, and the differences (if any) between the things she does and the things they do are not of practical importance in relation to terms and conditions of employment; and accordingly in comparing her work with theirs regard shall be had to the frequency or otherwise with which any such differences occur in practice as well as to the nature and extent of the differences.

(5)　A woman is to be regarded as employed on work rated as equivalent with that of any men if, but only if, her job and their job have been given an equal value, in terms of the demand made on a worker under various headings (for instance effort, skill, decision), on a study undertaken with a view to evaluating in those terms the jobs to be done by all or any of the employees in an undertaking or group of undertakings, or would have been given an equal value but for the evaluation being made on a system setting different values for men and women on the same demand under any heading.

(5A)　For the purposes of subsection (2)(d) to (f) above—
  (a)　"maternity-related pay", in relation to a woman, means pay (including pay by way of bonus) to which she is entitled as a result of being pregnant or in respect of times when she is on statutory maternity leave, except that it does not include any statutory maternity pay to which she is entitled;
  (b)　"statutory maternity leave period", in relation to a woman, means the period during which she is on statutory maternity leave;
  (c)　an increase in an amount is taken into account in a calculation if in the calculation the amount as increased is substituted for the unincreased amount.

(5B)　For the purposes of subsections (2)(d) to (f) and (5A) above, "on statutory maternity leave" means absent from work—
  (a)　in exercise of the right conferred by section 71(1) or 73(1) of the Employment Rights Act 1996 (ordinary or additional maternity leave), or
  (b)　in consequence of the prohibition in section 72(1) of that Act (compulsory maternity leave).

(6)　Subject to the following subsections, for purposes of this section—
  (a)　"employed" means employed under a contract of service or of apprenticeship or a contract personally to execute any work or labour, and related expressions shall be construed accordingly;
  (c)　Two employers are to be treated as associated if one is a company of which the other (directly or indirectly) has control or if both are companies of which a third person (directly or indirectly) has control,
and men shall be treated as in the same employment with a woman if they are men employed by her employer or any associated employer at the same establishment or at establishments in Great Britain which include that one and at which common terms and conditions of employment are observed either generally or for employees of the relevant classes.

(6A)　This section applies to—
  (a)　the holding of an office or post to which persons are appointed to discharge functions personally under the direction of another person, and in respect of which they are entitled to remuneration, or
  (b)　any office or post to which appointments are made by (or on the recommendation of or subject to the approval of) a Minister of the Crown, a government department, the National Assembly for Wales or any part of the Scottish Administration,
as it applies to employment by a private person, and shall so apply as if references to a contract of employment included references to the terms of appointment, and as if references to the employer included references to the person responsible for paying any remuneration that a holder of the office or post is entitled to in respect of the office or post.

(6B)　For the purposes of subsection (6A), the holder of an office or post—
  (a)　is to be regarded as discharging her functions under the direction of another person if that other person is entitled to direct her as to when and where she discharges those functions;

    (b) is not to be regarded as entitled to remuneration merely because she is entitled to payments—
       (i) in respect of expenses incurred by her in carrying out the functions of the office or post, or
      (ii) by way of compensation for the loss of income or benefits she would or might have received from any person had she not been carrying out the functions of the office or post.

(6C) For the purposes of subsection (6A)—
    (a) "office or post" does not include a political office (see section 1A), and
    (b) appointment to an office or post does not include election to an office or post.

(8)   This section shall apply to—
    (a) service for purposes of a Minister of the Crown or government department, other than service of a person holding a statutory office, or
    (b) service on behalf of the Crown for purposes of a person holding a statutory office or purposes of a statutory body,
as it applies to employment by a private person, and shall so apply as if references to a contract of employment included references to the terms of service.

(10) In this section "statutory body" means a body set up by or in pursuance of an enactment (including an enactment comprised in, or in an instrument made under, an Act of the Scottish Parliament), and "statutory office" means an office so set up; and service "for purposes of" a Minister of the Crown or government department does not include service in any office in Schedule 2 (Ministerial offices) to the House of Commons Disqualification Act 1975 as for the time being in force.

(10A) This section applies in relation to service as a relevant member of the House of Commons staff as in relation to service for the purposes of a Minister of the Crown or government department, and accordingly applies as if references to a contract of employment included references to the terms of service of such a member.

In this subsection "relevant member of the House of Commons staff" has the same meaning as in section 195 of the Employment Rights Act 1996; and subsections (6) to (12) of that section (person to be treated as employer of House of Commons staff) apply, with any necessary modifications, for the purposes of this section.

(10B) This section applies in relation to employment as a relevant member of the House of Lords staff as in relation to other employment.

In this subsection "relevant member of the House of Lords staff" has the same meaning as in section 194 of the Employment Rights Act 1996 and subsection (7) of that section applies for the purposes of this section.

(11) For the purposes of this Act it is immaterial whether the law which (apart from this subsection) is the law applicable to a contract is the law of any part of the United Kingdom or not.

(12) In this Act "Great Britain" includes such of the territorial waters of the United Kingdom as are adjacent to Great Britain.

(13) Provisions of this section and sections 2 to 2A below framed with reference to women and their treatment relative to men are to be read as applying equally in a converse case to men and their treatment relative to women.

2 DISPUTES AS TO, AND ENFORCEMENT OF, REQUIREMENT OF EQUAL TREATMENT

(1)   Any claim in respect of the contravention of a term modified or included by virtue of an equality clause, including a claim for arrears of remuneration or damages in respect of the contravention, may be presented by way of a complaint to an employment tribunal.

(1A) Where a dispute arises in relation to the effect of an equality clause the employer may apply to an employment tribunal for an order declaring the rights of the employer and the employee in relation to the matter in question.

(2)   Where it appears to the Minister that there may be a question whether the employer of any women is or has been contravening a term modified or included by virtue of their equality clauses, but that it is not reasonable to expect them to take steps to have the question determined, the question may be referred by him as respects all or any of them to an employment tribunal and shall be dealt with as if the reference were of a claim by the women or woman against the employer.

(3)   Where it appears to the court in which any proceedings are pending that a claim or counterclaim in respect of the operation of an equality clause could more conveniently be disposed of separately by an employment tribunal, the court may direct that the claim or counterclaim shall be struck out; and (without prejudice to the foregoing) where in proceedings before any court a question arises as to the operation of an equality clause, the court may on the application of any party to the proceedings or otherwise refer that question, or direct it to be referred by a party to the proceedings, to an employment tribunal for determination by the tribunal, and may stay or sist the proceedings in the meantime.

(4)   No determination may be made by an employment tribunal in the following proceedings—
(a) on a complaint under subsection (1) above,
(b) on an application under subsection (1A) above, or
(c) on a reference under subsection (2) above,
unless the proceedings are instituted on or before the qualifying date (determined in accordance with section 2ZA below).

(5)   A woman shall not be entitled, in proceedings brought in respect of a contravention of a term modified or included by virtue of an equality clause (including proceedings before an employment tribunal), to be awarded any payment by way of arrears of remuneration or damages—
(a) in proceedings in England and Wales, in respect of a time earlier than the arrears date (determined in accordance with section 2ZB below), and
(b) in proceedings in Scotland, in respect of a time before the period determined in accordance with section 2ZC below.

(5A) In this section "employer", in relation to the holder of an office or post to which section 1 above applies by virtue of subsection (6A) of that section, shall be construed in accordance with that subsection.

2ZA "QUALIFYING DATE" UNDER SECTION 2(4)

(1)   This section applies for the purpose of determining the qualifying date, in relation to proceedings in respect of a woman's employment, for the purposes of section 2(4) above.

(2)   In this section—

"concealment case" means a case where–

(a) the employer deliberately concealed from the woman any fact (referred to in this section as a "qualifying fact")—

(i) which is relevant to the contravention to which the proceedings relate, and

(ii) without knowledge of which the woman could not reasonably have been expected to institute the proceedings, and

(b) the woman did not discover the qualifying fact (or could not with reasonable diligence have discovered it) until after—

(i) the last day on which she was employed in the employment, or

(ii) the day on which the stable employment relationship between her and the employer ended,

(as the case may be);

"disability case" means a case where the woman was under a disability at any time during the six months after—

(a) the last day on which she was employed in the employment,

(b) the day on which the stable employment relationship between her and the employer ended, or

(c) the day on which she discovered (or could with reasonable diligence have discovered) the qualifying fact deliberately concealed from her by the employer (if that day falls after the day referred to in paragraph (a) or (b) above, as the case may be),

(as the case may be);

"stable employment case" means a case where the proceedings relate to a period during which a stable employment relationship subsists between the woman and the employer, notwithstanding that the period includes any time after the ending of a contract of employment when no further contract of employment is in force;

"standard case" means a case which is not—

(a) a stable employment case,

(b) a concealment case,

(c) a disability case, or

(d) both a concealment and a disability case.

(3) In a standard case, the qualifying date is the date falling six months after the last day on which the woman was employed in the employment.

(4) In a case which is a stable employment case (but not also a concealment or a disability case or both), the qualifying date is the date falling six months after the day on which the stable employment relationship ended.

(5) In a case which is a concealment case (but not also a disability case), the qualifying date is the date falling six months after the day on which the woman discovered the qualifying fact in question (or could with reasonable diligence have discovered it).

(6) In a case which is a disability case (but not also a concealment case), the qualifying date is the date falling six months after the day on which the woman ceased to be under a disability.

(7) In a case which is both a concealment and a disability case, the qualifying date is the later of the dates referred to in subsections (5) and (6) above.

2ZB "ARREARS DATE" IN PROCEEDINGS IN ENGLAND AND WALES UNDER SECTION 2(5)

(1) This section applies for the purpose of determining the arrears date, in relation to an award of any payment by way of arrears of remuneration or damages in proceedings in

England and Wales in respect of a woman's employment, for the purposes of section 2(5) (a) above.

(2)   In this section—

"concealment case" means a case where—
(a)   the employer deliberately concealed from the woman any fact—
    (i)   which is relevant to the contravention to which the proceedings relate, and
    (ii)   without knowledge of which the woman could not reasonably have been expected to institute the proceedings, and
(b)   the woman instituted the proceedings within six years of the day on which she discovered the fact (or could with reasonable diligence have discovered it);
"disability case" means a case where—
(a)   the woman was under a disability at the time of the contravention to which the proceedings relate, and
(b)   the woman instituted the proceedings within six years of the day on which she ceased to be under a disability;
"standard case" means a case which is not—
(a)   a concealment case,
(b)   a disability case, or
(c)   both.

(3)   In a standard case, the arrears date is the date falling six years before the day on which the proceedings were instituted.

(4)   In a case which is a concealment or a disability case or both, the arrears date is the date of the contravention.

2A PROCEDURE BEFORE TRIBUNAL IN CERTAIN CASES

(1)   Where on a complaint or reference made to an employment tribunal under section 2 above, a dispute arises as to whether any work is of equal value as mentioned in section 1(2)(c) above the tribunal may either—
(a)   proceed to determine that question; or
(b)   require a member of the panel of independent experts to prepare a report with respect to that question;

(1A)   Subsections (1B) and (1C) below apply in a case where the tribunal has required a member of the panel of independent experts to prepare a report under paragraph (b) of subsection (1) above.

(1B)   The tribunal may—
(a)   withdraw the requirement, and
(b)   request the member of the panel of independent experts to provide it with any documentation specified by it or make any other request to him connected with the withdrawal of the requirement.

(1C)   If the requirement has not been withdrawn under paragraph (a) of subsection (1B) above, the tribunal shall not make any determination under paragraph (a) of subsection (1) above unless it has received the report.

(2)   Subsection (2A) below applies in a case where—
(a)   a tribunal is required to determine whether any work is of equal value as mentioned in section 1(2)(c) above, and
(b)   the work of the woman and that of the man in question have been given different values on a study such as is mentioned in section 1(5) above.

(2A) The tribunal shall determine that the work of the woman and that of the man are not of equal value unless the tribunal has reasonable grounds for suspecting that the evaluation contained in the study—

(a) was (within the meaning of subsection (3) below) made on a system which discriminates on grounds of sex, or

(b) is otherwise unsuitable to be relied upon.

(3) An evaluation contained in a study such as is mentioned in section 1(5) above is made on a system which discriminates on grounds of sex where a difference, or coincidence, between values set by that system on different demands under the same or different headings is not justifiable irrespective of the sex of the person on whom those demands are made.

(4) In this section a reference to a member of the panel of independent experts is a reference to a person who is for the time being designated by the Advisory, Conciliation and Arbitration Service for the purposes of that paragraph as such a member, being neither a member of the Council of that Service nor one of its officers or servants.

As amended by the Sex Discrimination Act 1975 s 8(6), Sch 1 Pt I; Social Security Pensions Act 1975 s 53(6)(a); Employment Protection (Consolidation) Act 1978 (c 44), Sch 17; Equal Pay (Amendment) Regulations 1983/1794, reg 2(1), reg 2(2), reg 3(1); Contracts (Applicable Law) Act 1990 (c 36), s 5, Sch 4 para 1; Trade Union and Labour Relations (Consolidation) Act 1992 Sch 2 para 3(2); Trade Union Reform and Employment Rights Act 1993 Sch 7 para 8; Armed Forces Act 1996 Sch 7(III) para 1; Employment Rights Act 1996 Sch 1 para 1(2)(a), Sch 1 para 1(2)(b), Sch 1 para 1(3)(b); Sex Discrimination and Equal Pay (Miscellaneous Amendments) Regulations 1996/438 reg 3(2); Employment Rights (Dispute Resolution) Act 1998 Pt I s 1(2), Pt I s 1(2)(a); Scotland Act 1998 (Consequential Modifications) Order 2000/2040 Sch 1(I) para 4; Equal Pay Act 1970 (Amendment) Regulations 2003/1656 reg 3(2), reg 3(3), reg 4, reg 5, reg 10; Equal Pay Act 1970 (Amendment) Regulations 2004/2352 reg 2(2)(a), reg 2(2)(b), reg 2(3), reg 2(4), reg 2(5), reg 2(6); Employment Equality (Sex Discrimination) Regulations 2005/2467 reg 35(2), reg 35(4), reg 36(2), reg 36(3), reg 36(4); Transfer of Functions (Equality) Order 2007/2914 Sch 1 para 3(a).

SEX DISCRIMINATION ACT 1975
(c. 65)

Part I DISCRIMINATION TO WHICH ACT APPLIES

1 DIRECT AND INDIRECT DISCRIMINATION AGAINST WOMEN

(1) In any circumstances relevant for the purposes of any provision of this Act, other than a provision to which subsection (2) applies, a person discriminates against a woman if—

(a) on the ground of her sex he treats her less favourably than he treats or would treat a man, or

(b) he applies to her a requirement or condition which he applies or would apply equally to a man but—
   (i) which is such that the proportion of women who can comply with it is considerably smaller than the proportion of men who can comply with it, and
   (ii) which he cannot show to be justifiable irrespective of the sex of the person to whom it is applied, and
   (iii) which is to her detriment because she cannot comply with it.

(2) In any circumstances relevant for the purposes of a provision to which this subsection applies, a person discriminates against a woman if—
   (a) on the ground of her sex, he treats her less favourably than he treats or would treat a man, or
   (b) he applies to her a provision, criterion or practice which he applies or would apply equally to a man, but—
      (i) which puts or would put women at a particular disadvantage when compared with men,
      (ii) which puts her at that disadvantage, and
      (iii) which he cannot show to be a proportionate means of achieving a legitimate aim.

(3) Subsection (2) applies to—
   (a) any provision of Part 2,
   (aa) sections 29 to 31, except in so far as they relate to an excluded matter,
   (b) sections 35A and 35B, and
   (c) any other provision of Part 3, so far as it applies to vocational training.

2 SEX DISCRIMINATION AGAINST MEN

(1) Section 1, and the provisions of Parts II and III relating to sex discrimination against women, are to be read as applying equally to the treatment of men, and for that purpose shall have effect with such modifications as are requisite.

(2) In the application of subsection (1) no account shall be taken of special treatment afforded to women in connection with pregnancy or childbirth.

2A DISCRIMINATION ON THE GROUNDS OF GENDER REASSIGNMENT

(1) A person ("A") discriminates against another person ("B") in any circumstances relevant for the purposes of—
   (a) any provision of Part II,
   (aa) section 29, 30 or 31, except in so far as it relates to an excluded matter,
   (b) section 35A or 35B, or
   (c) any other provision of Part III, so far as it applies to vocational training,
   if he treats B less favourably than he treats or would treat other persons, and does so on the ground that B intends to undergo, is undergoing or has undergone gender reassignment.

(2) Subsection (3) applies to arrangements made by any person in relation to another's absence from work or from vocational training.

(3) For the purposes of subsection (1), B is treated less favourably than others under such arrangements if, in the application of the arrangements to any absence due to B undergoing gender reassignment—
   (a) he is treated less favourably than he would be if the absence was due to sickness or injury, or

    (b) he is treated less favourably than he would be if the absence was due to some other cause and, having regard to the circumstances of the case, it is reasonable for him to be treated no less favourably.

(4) In subsections (2) and (3) "arrangements" includes terms, conditions or arrangements on which employment, a pupillage or tenancy or vocational training is offered.

(5) For the purposes of subsection (1), a provision mentioned in that subsection framed with reference to discrimination against women shall be treated as applying equally to the treatment of men with such modifications as are requisite.

3 DISCRIMINATION AGAINST MARRIED PERSONS AND CIVIL PARTNERS IN EMPLOYMENT FIELD

(1) In any circumstances relevant for the purposes of any provision of Part 2, a person discriminates against a person ("A") who fulfils the condition in subsection (2) if—
    (a) on the ground of the fulfilment of the condition, he treats A less favourably than he treats or would treat a person who does not fulfil the condition, or
    (b) he applies to A a provision, criterion or practice which he applies or would apply equally to a person who does not fulfil the condition, but—
        (i) which puts or would put persons fulfilling the condition at a particular disadvantage when compared with persons not fulfilling the condition, and
        (ii) which puts A at that disadvantage, and
        (iii) which he cannot show to be a proportionate means of achieving a legitimate aim.

(2) The condition is that the person is—
    (a) married, or
    (b) a civil partner.

(3) For the purposes of subsection (1), a provision of Part 2 framed with reference to discrimination against women is to be treated as applying equally to the treatment of men, and for that purpose has effect with such modifications as are requisite.

3A DISCRIMINATION ON THE GROUND OF PREGNANCY OR MATERNITY LEAVE

(1) In any circumstances relevant for the purposes of a provision to which this subsection applies, a person discriminates against a woman if—
    (a) at a time in a protected period, and on the ground of the woman's pregnancy, the person treats her less favourably; or
    (b) on the ground that the woman is exercising or seeking to exercise, or has exercised or sought to exercise, a statutory right to maternity leave, the person treats her less favourably.

(2) In any circumstances relevant for the purposes of a provision to which this subsection applies, a person discriminates against a woman if, on the ground that section 72(1) of the Employment Rights Act 1996 (compulsory maternity leave) has to be complied with in respect of the woman, he treats her less favourably.

(3) For the purposes of subsection (1)—
    (a) in relation to a woman, a protected period begins each time she becomes pregnant, and the protected period associated with any particular pregnancy of hers ends in accordance with the following rules—
        (i) if she is entitled to ordinary but not additional maternity leave in connection with the pregnancy, the protected period ends at the end of her period of ordinary

maternity leave connected with the pregnancy or, if earlier, when she returns to work after the end of her pregnancy;

    (ii) if she is entitled to ordinary and additional maternity leave in connection with the pregnancy, the protected period ends at the end of her period of additional maternity leave connected with the pregnancy or, if earlier, when she returns to work after the end of her pregnancy;

    (iii) if she is not entitled to ordinary maternity leave in respect of the pregnancy, the protected period ends at the end of the 2 weeks beginning with the end of the pregnancy;

(b) where a person's treatment of a woman is on grounds of illness suffered by the woman as a consequence of a pregnancy of hers, that treatment is to be taken to be on the ground of the pregnancy;

(c) a "statutory right to maternity leave" means a right conferred by section 71(1) or 73(1) of the Employment Rights Act 1996 (ordinary and additional maternity leave).

(4) In subsection (3) "ordinary maternity leave" and "additional maternity leave" shall be construed in accordance with sections 71 and 73 of the Employment Rights Act 1996.

(5) Subsections (1) and (2) apply to—
(a) any provision of Part 2,
(b) sections 35A and 35B, and
(c) any other provision of Part 3, so far as it applies to vocational training.

3B DISCRIMINATION ON THE GROUND OF PREGNANCY OR MATERNITY: GOODS, FACILITIES, SERVICES OR PREMISES

(1) In any circumstances relevant for the purposes of a provision to which this subsection applies, a person discriminates against a woman if he treats her less favourably—
(a) on the ground of her pregnancy, or
(b) within the period of 26 weeks beginning on the day on which she gives birth, on the ground that she has given birth.

(2) A person (P) is taken to discriminate against a woman on the ground of her pregnancy if—
(a) P refuses to provide her with goods, facilities or services because P thinks that providing them would, because of her pregnancy, create a risk to her health or safety, or
(b) P provides or offers to provide them on conditions intended to remove or reduce such a risk because P thinks that provision of them without the conditions would create such a risk.

(3) Subsection (2) does not apply if—
(a) it is reasonable for P to think as mentioned in paragraph (a) or (b), and
(b) P applies an equivalent policy.

(4) An equivalent policy is—
(a) for the purposes of subsection (2)(a), refusing to provide the goods, facilities or services to persons with other physical conditions because P thinks that to do so would, because of such physical conditions, create a risk to the health or safety of such persons;
(b) for the purposes of subsection (2)(b), imposing conditions on the provision of goods, facilities or services to such persons which are intended to remove or reduce the risk to their health or safety because P thinks that the provision without the conditions would create such a risk.

(5)   Subsection (1) applies to sections 29 to 31, except in so far as they relate to an excluded matter.

4 DISCRIMINATION BY WAY OF VICTIMISATION

(1)   A person ("the discriminator") discriminates against another person ("the person victimised") in any circumstances relevant for the purposes of any provision of this Act if he treats the person victimised less favourably than in those circumstances he treats or would treat other persons, and do so by reason that the person victimised has—

(a)   brought proceedings against the discriminator or any other person under this Act or the Equal Pay Act 1970 or sections 62 to 65 of the Pensions Act 1995, or

(b)   given evidence or information in connection with proceedings brought by any person against the discriminator or any other person under this Act or the Equal Pay Act 1970 or sections 62 to 65 of the Pensions Act 1995, or

(c)   otherwise done anything under or by reference to this Act or the Equal Pay Act 1970 or sections 62 to 65 of the Pensions Act 1995 in relation to the discriminator or any other person, or

(d)   alleged that the discriminator or any other person has committed an act which (whether or not the allegation so states) would amount to a contravention of this Act or give rise to a claim under the Equal Pay Act 1970 or under sections 62 to 65 of the Pensions Act 1995,

or by reason that the discriminator knows the person victimised intends to do any of those things, or suspects the person victimised has done, or intends to do, any of them.

(2)   Subsection (1) does not apply to treatment of a person by reason of any allegation made by him if the allegation was false and not made in good faith.

(3)   For the purposes of subsection (1), a provision of Part II or III framed with reference to discrimination against women shall be treated as applying equally to the treatment of men and for that purpose shall have effect with such modifications as are requisite.

4A HARASSMENT, INCLUDING SEXUAL HARASSMENT

(1)   For the purposes of this Act, a person subjects a woman to harassment if—

(a)   he engages in unwanted conduct that is related to her sex or that of another person and has the purpose or effect—
     (i)   of violating her dignity, or
     (ii)   of creating an intimidating, hostile, degrading, humiliating or offensive environment for her,

(b)   he engages in any form of unwanted verbal, non-verbal or physical conduct of a sexual nature that has the purpose or effect—
     (i)   of violating her dignity, or
     (ii)   of creating an intimidating, hostile, degrading, humiliating or offensive environment for her, or

(c)   on the ground of her rejection of or submission to unwanted conduct of a kind mentioned in paragraph (a) or (b), he treats her less favourably than he would treat her had she not rejected, or submitted to, the conduct.

(2)   Conduct shall be regarded as having the effect mentioned in sub-paragraph (i) or (ii) of subsection (1)(a) or (b) only if, having regard to all the circumstances, including in particular the perception of the woman, it should reasonably be considered as having that effect.

(3)   For the purposes of this Act, a person ("A") subjects another person ("B") to harassment if—

    (a) A, on the ground that B intends to undergo, is undergoing or has undergone gender reassignment, engages in unwanted conduct that has the purpose or effect—
        (i) of violating B's dignity, or
        (ii) of creating an intimidating, hostile, degrading, humiliating or offensive environment for B, or
    (b) A, on the ground of B's rejection of or submission to unwanted conduct of a kind mentioned in paragraph (a), treats B less favourably than A would treat B had B not rejected, or submitted to, the conduct.

(4) Conduct shall be regarded as having the effect mentioned in sub-paragraph (i) or (ii) of subsection (3)(a) only if, having regard to all the circumstances, including in particular the perception of B, it should reasonably be considered as having that effect.

(5) Subsection (1) is to be read as applying equally to the harassment of men, and for that purpose shall have effect with such modifications as are requisite.

(6) For the purposes of subsections (1) and (3), a provision of Part 2 or 3 framed with reference to harassment of women shall be treated as applying equally to the harassment of men, and for that purpose will have effect with such modifications as are requisite.

Part II EMPLOYMENT FIELD

6 APPLICANTS AND EMPLOYEES

(1) It is unlawful for a person, in relation to employment by him at an establishment in Great Britain, to discriminate against a woman—
    (a) in the arrangements he makes for the purpose of determining who should be offered that employment, or
    (b) in the terms on which he offers her that employment, or
    (c) by refusing or deliberately omitting to offer her that employment.

(2) It is unlawful for a person, in the case of a woman employed by him at an establishment in Great Britain, to discriminate against her—
    (a) in the way he affords her access to opportunities for promotion, transfer or training, or to any other benefits, facilities or services, or by refusing or deliberately omitting to afford her access to them, or
    (b) by dismissing her, or subjecting her to any other detriment.

(2A) It is unlawful for an employer, in relation to employment by him at an establishment in Great Britain, to subject to harassment—
    (a) a woman whom he employs, or
    (b) a woman who has applied to him for employment.

(2B) For the purposes of subsection (2A), the circumstances in which an employer is to be treated as subjecting a woman to harassment shall include those where—
    (a) a third party subjects the woman to harassment in the course of her employment, and
    (b) the employer has failed to take such steps as would have been reasonably practicable to prevent the third party from doing so.

(2C) Subsection (2B) does not apply unless the employer knows that the woman has been subject to harassment in the course of her employment on at least two other occasions by a third party.

(2D) In subsections (2B) and (2C), "third party" means a person other than—
    (a) the employer, or
    (b) a person whom the employer employs,

and for the purposes of those subsections it is immaterial whether the third party is the same or a different person on each occasion.

(4)   Subsections (1)(b) and (2) do not render it unlawful for a person to discriminate against a woman in relation to her membership of, or rights under, an occupational pension scheme in such a way that, were any term of the scheme to provide for discrimination in that way, then, by reason only of any provision made by or under sections 62 to 64 of the Pensions Act 1995 (equal treatment), an equal treatment rule would not operate in relation to that term.

(4A) In subsection (4), "occupational pension scheme" has the same meaning as in the Pension Schemes Act 1993 and "equal treatment rule" has the meaning given by section 62 of the Pensions Act 1995.

(5)   Subject to section 8(3), subsection (1)(b) does not apply to any provision for the payment of money which, if the woman in question were given the employment, would be included (directly or otherwise) in the contract under which she was employed.

(6)   Subsection (2) does not apply to benefits consisting of the payment of money when the provision of those benefits is regulated by the woman's contract of employment.

(7)   Subsection (2) does not apply to benefits, facilities or services of any description if the employer is concerned with the provision (for payment or not) of benefits, facilities or services of that description to the public, or to a section of the public comprising the woman in question, unless—
(a) that provision differs in a material respect from the provision of the benefits, facilities or services by the employer to his employees, or
(b) the provision of the benefits, facilities or services to the woman in question is regulated by her contract of employment, or
(c) the benefits, facilities or services relate to training.

(8)   In its application to any discrimination falling within section 2A, this section shall have effect with the omission of subsections (4) to (6).

6A EXCEPTION RELATING TO TERMS AND CONDITIONS DURING MATERNITY LEAVE

(1)   Subject to subsection (2), section 6(1)(b) and (2) does not make it unlawful to deprive a woman who is on maternity leave of any benefit from the terms and conditions of her employment relating to remuneration.

(2)   The reference in subsection (1) to benefit from the terms and conditions of a woman's employment relating to remuneration does not include a reference to—
(a) maternity-related remuneration (including maternity-related remuneration that is increase-related),
(b) remuneration (including increase-related remuneration) in respect of times when the woman is not on maternity leave, or
(c) remuneration by way of bonus in respect of times when a woman is on compulsory maternity leave.

(3)   For the purposes of subsection (2), remuneration is increase-related so far as it falls to be calculated by reference to increases in remuneration that the woman would have received had she not been on maternity leave.

(4)   In this section—

"maternity-related remuneration", in relation to a woman, means remuneration to which she is entitled as a result of being pregnant or being on maternity leave;

"on compulsory maternity leave" means absent from work in consequence of the prohibition in section 72(1) of the Employment Rights Act 1996;

"on maternity leave" means—
(a) on compulsory maternity leave,
(b) absent from work in exercise of the right conferred by section 71(1) of the Employment Rights Act 1996 (ordinary maternity leave), or
(c) absent from work in exercise of the right conferred by section 73(1) of that Act (additional maternity leave); and

"remuneration" means benefits—
(a) that consist of the payment of money to an employee by way of wages or salary, and
(b) that are not benefits whose provision is regulated by the employee's contract of employment.

7 EXCEPTION WHERE SEX IS A GENUINE OCCUPATIONAL QUALIFICATION

(1) In relation to sex discrimination—
   (a) section 6(1)(a) or (c) does not apply to any employment where being a man is a genuine occupational qualification for the job, and
   (b) section 6(2)(a) does not apply to opportunities for promotion or transfer to, or training for, such employment.

(2) Being a man is a genuine occupational qualification for a job only where—
   (a) the essential nature of the job calls for a man for reasons of physiology (excluding physical strength or stamina) or, in dramatic performances or other entertainment, for reasons of authenticity, so that the essential nature of the job would be materially different if carried out by a woman; or
   (b) the job needs to be held by a man to preserve decency or privacy because—
      (i) it is likely to involve physical contact with men in circumstances where they might reasonably object to its being carried out by a woman, or
      (ii) the holder of the job is likely to do his work in circumstances where men might reasonably object to the presence of a woman because they are in a state of undress or are using sanitary facilities; or
   (ba) the job is likely to involve the holder of the job doing his work, or living, in a private home and needs to be held by a man because objection might reasonably be taken to allowing to a woman—
      (i) the degree of physical or social contact with a person living in the home, or
      (ii) the knowledge of intimate details of such a person's life,
      which is likely, because of the nature or circumstances of the job or of the home, to be allowed to, or available to, the holder of the job; or
   (c) the nature or location of the establishment makes it impracticable for the holder of the job to live elsewhere than in premises provided by the employer, and—
      (i) the only such premises which are available for persons holding that kind of job are lived in, or normally lived in, by men and are not equipped with separate sleeping accommodation for women and sanitary facilities which could be used by women in privacy from men, and
      (ii) it is not reasonable to expect the employer either to equip those premises with such accommodation and facilities or to provide other premises for women; or
   (d) the nature of the establishment, or of the part of it within which the work is done, requires the job to be held by a man because—
      (i) it is, or is part of, a hospital, prison or other establishment for persons requiring special care, supervision or attention, and

(ii) those persons are all men (disregarding any woman whose presence is exceptional), and

(iii) it is reasonable, having regard to the essential character of the establishment or that part, that the job should not be held by a woman; or

(e) the holder of the job provides individuals with personal services promoting their welfare or education, or similar personal services, and those services can most effectively be provided by a man, or

(g) the job needs to be held by a man because it is likely to involve the performance of duties outside the United Kingdom in a country whose laws or customs are such that the duties could not, or could not effectively, be performed by a woman, or

(h) the job is one of two to be held—

(i) by a married couple,

(ii) by a couple who are civil partners of each other, or

(iii) by a married couple or a couple who are civil partners of each other.

(3) Subsection (2) applies where some only of the duties of the job fall within paragraphs (a) to (g) as well as where all of them do.

(4) Paragraph (a), (b), (c), (d), (e)or (g) of subsection (2) does not apply in relation to the filling of a vacancy at a time when the employer already has male employees—

(a) who are capable of carrying out the duties falling within that paragraph, and

(b) whom it would be reasonable to employ on those duties, and

(c) whose numbers are sufficient to meet the employer's likely requirements in respect of those duties without undue inconvenience

7A CORRESPONDING EXCEPTION RELATING TO GENDER REASSIGNMENT

(1) In their application to discrimination falling within section 2A, subsections (1) and (2) of section 6 do not make unlawful an employer's treatment of another person if—

(a) in relation to the employment in question—

(i) being a man is a genuine occupational qualification for the job, or

(ii) being a woman is a genuine occupational qualification for the job, and

(b) the employer can show that the treatment is reasonable in view of the circumstances described in the relevant paragraph of section 7(2) and any other relevant circumstances.

(2) In subsection (1) the reference to the employment in question is a reference—

(a) in relation to any paragraph of section 6(1), to the employment mentioned in that paragraph;

(b) in relation to section 6(2)—

(i) in its application to opportunities for promotion or transfer to any employment or for training for any employment, to that employment;

(ii) otherwise, to the employment in which the person discriminated against is employed or from which that person is dismissed.

(3) In determining for the purposes of subsection (1) whether being a man or being a woman is a genuine occupational qualification for a job, section 7(4) applies in relation to dismissal from employment as it applies in relation to the filling of a vacancy.

(4) Subsection (1) does not apply in relation to discrimination against a person whose gender has become the acquired gender under the Gender Recognition Act 2004.

20A RELATIONSHIPS WHICH HAVE COME TO AN END

(1)   This section applies where—
    (a) there has been a relevant relationship between a woman and another person ("the relevant person"), and
    (b) the relationship has come to an end (whether before or after the commencement of this section).

(2)   In this section, a "relevant relationship" is a relationship during the course of which an act of discrimination by one party to the relationship against the other party to it is unlawful under any preceding provision of this Part.

(3)   It is unlawful for the relevant person to discriminate against the woman by subjecting her to a detriment where the discrimination arises out of and is closely connected to the relevant relationship.

(4)   It is unlawful for the relevant person to subject a woman to harassment where that treatment arises out of or is closely connected to the relevant relationship.

Part IV OTHER UNLAWFUL ACTS

37 DISCRIMINATORY PRACTICES

(1)   In this section "discriminatory practice" means—
    (a) the application of a provision, criterion or practice which results in an act of discrimination which is unlawful by virtue of any provision of Part 2 or 3 taken with section 1(2)(b) or 3(1)(b) or which would be likely to result in such an act of discrimination if the persons to whom it is applied were not all of one sex, or
    (b) the application of a requirement or condition which results in an act of discrimination which is unlawful by virtue of any provision of Part 3 taken with section 1(1)(b) or which would be likely to result in such an act of discrimination if the persons to whom it is applied were not all of one sex.

(2)   A person acts in contravention of this section if and so long as—
    (a) he applies a discriminatory practice, or
    (b) he operates practices or other arrangements which in any circumstances would call for the application by him of a discriminatory practice.

(3)   Proceedings in respect of a contravention of this section shall be brought only by the

38 DISCRIMINATORY ADVERTISEMENTS

(1)   It is unlawful to publish or cause to be published an advertisement which indicates, or might reasonably be understood as indicating, an intention by a person to do any act which is or might be unlawful by virtue of Part II or III.

(2)   Subsection (1) does not apply to an advertisement if the intended act would not in fact be unlawful.

(3)   For the purposes of subsection (1), use of a job description with a sexual connotation (such as "waiter", "salesgirl", "postman" or "stewardess") shall be taken to indicate an intention to discriminate, unless the advertisement contains an indication to the contrary.

(4)   The publisher of an advertisement made unlawful by subsection (1) shall not be subject to any liability under that subsection in respect of the publication of the advertisement if he proves—

(a) that the advertisement was published in reliance on a statement made to him by the person who caused it to be published to the effect that, by reason of the operation of subsection (2), the publication would not be unlawful, and

(b) that it was reasonable for him to rely on the statement.

(5) A person who knowingly or recklessly makes a statement such as is referred to in subsection (4) which in a material respect is false or misleading commits an offence, and shall be liable on summary conviction to a fine not exceeding level 5 on the standard scale.

(6) Proceedings in respect of a contravention of subsection (1) may be brought only—
(a) by the Commission, and
(b) in accordance with section 25 of the Equality Act 2006.

39 INSTRUCTIONS TO DISCRIMINATE

(1) It is unlawful for a person—
(a) who has authority over another person, or
(b) in accordance with whose wishes that other person is accustomed to act,
to instruct him to do any act which is unlawful by virtue of Part II or III, or procure or attempt to procure the doing by him of any such act.

(2) Proceedings in respect of a contravention of subsection (1) may be brought only—
(a) by the Commission, and
(b) in accordance with section 25 of the Equality Act 2006.

40 PRESSURE TO DISCRIMINATE

(1) It is unlawful to induce, or attempt to induce, a person to do any act which contravenes Part II or III by—
(a) providing or offering to provide him with any benefit, or
(b) subjecting or threatening to subject him to any detriment.

(2) An offer or threat is not prevented from falling within subsection (1) because it is not made directly to the person in question, if it is made in such a way that he is likely to hear of it.

(3) Proceedings in respect of a contravention of subsection (1) may be brought only—
(a) by the Commission, and
(b) in accordance with section 25 of the Equality Act 2006.

41 LIABILITY OF EMPLOYERS AND PRINCIPALS

(1) Anything done by a person in the course of his employment shall be treated for the purposes of this Act as done by his employer as well as by him, whether or not it was done with the employer's knowledge or approval.

(2) Anything done by a person as agent for another person with the authority (whether express or implied, and whether precedent or subsequent) of that other person shall be treated for the purposes of this Act as done by that other person as well as by him.

(3) In proceedings brought under this Act against any person in respect of an act alleged to have been done by an employee of his it shall be a defence for that person to prove that he took such steps as were reasonably practicable to prevent the employee from doing that act, or from doing in the course of his employment acts of that description.

42   AIDING UNLAWFUL ACTS

(1)   A person who knowingly aids another person to do an act made unlawful by this Act shall be treated for the purposes of this Act as himself doing an unlawful act of the like description.

(2)   For the purposes of subsection (1) an employee or agent for whose act the employer or principal is liable under section 41 (or would be so liable but for section 41(3)) shall be deemed to aid the doing of the act by the employer or principal.

(3)   A person does not under this section knowingly aid another to do an unlawful act if—
(a)   he acts in reliance on a statement made to him by that other person that, by reason of any provision of this Act, the act which he aids would not be unlawful, and
(b)   it is reasonable for him to rely on the statement.

(4)   A person who knowingly or recklessly makes a statement such as is referred to in subsection (3)(a) which in a material respect is false or misleading commits an offence, and shall be liable on summary conviction to a fine not exceeding level 5 on the standard scale.

Part VII ENFORCEMENT

63   JURISDICTION OF EMPLOYMENT TRIBUNALS

(1)   A complaint by any person ("the complainant") that another person ("the respondent")—
(a)   has committed an act of discrimination or harassment against the complainant which is unlawful by virtue of Part II or section 35A or 35B, or
(b)   is by virtue of section 41 or 42 to be treated as having committed such an act of discrimination or harassment against the complainant,
may be presented to an employment tribunal.

(2)   Subsection (1) does not apply to a complaint under section 13(1) of an act in respect of which an appeal, or proceedings in the nature of an appeal, may be brought under any enactment.

63A   BURDEN OF PROOF: EMPLOYMENT TRIBUNALS

(1)   This section applies to any complaint presented under section 63 to an employment tribunal.

(2)   Where, on the hearing of the complaint, the complainant proves facts from which the tribunal could, apart from this section, conclude in the absence of an adequate explanation that the respondent—
(a)   has committed an act of discrimination or harassment against the complainant which is unlawful by virtue of Part 2 or section 35A or 35B, or
(b)   is by virtue of section 41 or 42 to be treated as having committed such an act of discrimination or harassment against the complainant,
the tribunal shall uphold the complaint unless the respondent proves that he did not commit, or, as the case may be, is not to be treated as having committed, that act.

65   REMEDIES ON COMPLAINT UNDER SECTION 63

(1)   Where an employment tribunal finds that a complaint presented to it under section 63 is well-founded the tribunal shall make such of the following as it considers just and equitable—

(a) an order declaring the rights of the complainant and the respondent in relation to the act to which the complaint relates;

(b) an order requiring the respondent to pay to the complainant compensation of an amount corresponding to any damages he could have been ordered by a county court or by a sheriff court to pay to the complainant if the complaint had fallen to be dealt with under section 66;

(c) a recommendation that the respondent take within a specified period action appearing to the tribunal to be practicable for the purpose of obviating or reducing the adverse effect on the complainant of any act of discrimination to which the complaint relates.

(1A) In applying section 66 for the purposes of subsection (1)(b), no account shall be taken of subsection (3) of that section.

(1B) As respects an unlawful act of discrimination falling within section 1(2)(b) or section 3(1)(b), if the respondent proves that the provision, criterion or practice in question was not applied with the intention of treating the complainant unfavourably on the ground of his sex or (as the case may be) fulfilment of the condition in section 3(2), an order may be made under subsection (1)(b) only if the employment tribunal—

(a) makes such order under subsection (1)(a) and such recommendation under subsection (1)(c) (if any) as it would have made if it had no power to make an order under subsection (1)(b); and

(b) (where it makes an order under subsection (1)(a) or a recommendation under subsection (1)(c) or both) considers that it is just and equitable to make an order under subsection (1)(b) as well.

(3) If without reasonable justification the respondent to a complaint fails to comply with a recommendation made by an employment tribunal under subsection (1)(c), then, if they think it just and equitable to do so—

(a) the tribunal may increase the amount of compensation required to be paid to the complainant in respect of the complaint by an order made under subsection (1)(b), or

(b) if an order under subsection (1)(b) was not made, the tribunal may make such an order.

76 PERIOD WITHIN WHICH PROCEEDINGS TO BE BROUGHT

(1) An employment tribunal shall not consider a complaint under section 63 unless it is presented to the tribunal before the end of—

(a) the period of three months beginning when the act complained of was done; or

(b) in a case to which section 85(9A) applies, the period of six months so beginning.

(2) A county court or a sheriff court shall not consider a claim under section 66 unless proceedings in respect of the claim are instituted before the end of—

(a) the period of six months beginning when the act complained of was done; or

(b) in a case to which section 66(5) applies, the period of eight months so beginning.

(2A) Where in England and Wales—

(a) proceedings or prospective proceedings under section 66 relate to the act or omission of a qualifying institution, and

(b) the dispute concerned is referred as a complaint under the student complaints scheme before the end of the period of six months mentioned in subsection (2)(a),

the period allowed by subsection (2)(a) shall be extended by three months.

(2B) In subsection (2A)—

"qualifying institution" has the meaning given by section 11 of the Higher Education Act 2004;

"the student complaints scheme" means a scheme for the review of qualifying complaints, as defined by section 12 of that Act, that is provided by the designated operator, as defined by section 13(5)(b) of that Act.

(2C) The period allowed by subsection (2)(a) or (b) shall be extended by three months in the case of a dispute which is referred for conciliation in pursuance of arrangements under section 27 of the Equality Act 2006 (unless the period is extended under subsection (2A)).

(5) A court or tribunal may nevertheless consider any such complaint or claim which is out of time if, in all the circumstances of the case, it considers that it is just and equitable to do so.

(6) For the purposes of this section—
   (a) where the inclusion of any term in a contract renders the making of the contract an unlawful act that act shall be treated as extending throughout the duration of the contract, and
   (b) any act extending over a period shall be treated as done at the end of that period, and
   (c) a deliberate omission shall be treated as done when the person in question decided upon it,
   and in the absence of evidence establishing the contrary a person shall be taken for the purposes of this section to decide upon an omission when he does an act inconsistent with doing the omitted act or, if he has done no such inconsistent act, when the period expires within which he might reasonably have been expected to do the omitted act if it was to be done.

As amended by the Employment Protection Act 1975, s 122(2); Race Relations Act 1976, Sch 4 para 8(a); Criminal Justice Act 1982, ss 38, 46 and (Scotland) by Criminal Procedure (Scotland) Act 1975 (c 21), ss 289F, 289G; Sex Discrimination Act 1986, ss 1(1), s 1(2), 9, Sch Pt II; Employment Act 1989, ss 3(2), 4(1)(c), 5(1)(2)(b)(3)(4)(7), 6(1)(2), 29(4), Sch 7 Pt II; Sex Discrimination and Equal Pay (Remedies) Regulations 1993/2798 reg 2, Sch 1 para 1; Pensions Act 1995 Pt I s 66(2)(a), Pt I s 66(2)(b), Pt I s 66(3); Armed Forces Act 1996, s 21(6); Sex Discrimination and Equal Pay (Miscellaneous Amendments) Regulations 1996/438 reg 2(2), reg 2(3); Employment Rights (Dispute Resolution) Act 1998, Pt I s 1(2); Sex Discrimination (Gender Reassignment) Regulations 1999/1102 reg 2(1), reg 3(1), reg 4(1); Sex Discrimination (Indirect Discrimination and Burden of Proof) Regulations 2001/2660 reg 3, reg 5, reg 8(2), reg 8(3); Sex Discrimination Act 1975 (Amendment) Regulations 2003/1657 reg 3; Gender Recognition Act 2004 Sch 6(1) para 2; Civil Partnership Act 2004, Pt 7 s 251(2), Pt 7 s 251(4), Pt 7 s 251(5), Sch 30 para 1; Higher Education Act 2004, Pt 2 s 19(1); Employment Equality (Sex Discrimination) Regulations 2005/2467 reg 3(1),, reg 4, reg 5, reg 7(3), reg 7(4), reg 21, reg 28(2), reg 28(3), reg 29(2), reg 29(3); Employment Equality (Sex Discrimination) Regulations 2005/2467; Equality Act 2006 Sch 3 para 7, Sch 3 para 8, Sch 3 para 9, Sch 3 para 10, Sch 3 para 14(2), Sch 3 para 14(3), Sch 3 para 14(5), Sch 4 para 1; Sex Discrimination (Amendment of Legislation) Regulations 2008/963 Sch 1 para 3(1); Sex Discrimination Act 1975 (Amendment) Regulations 2008/656 reg 2(2), reg 2(3), reg 2(4), reg 3, reg 4, reg 5(1); Sex Discrimination (Amendment of Legislation) Regulations 2008/963 Sch 1 para 1, Sch 1 para 2.

RACE RELATIONS ACT 1976
(c. 74)

Part I DISCRIMINATION TO WHICH ACT APPLIES

1 RACIAL DISCRIMINATION

(1) A person discriminates against another in any circumstances relevant for the purposes of any provision of this Act if—
 (a) on racial grounds he treats that other less favourably than he treats or would treat other persons; or
 (b) he applies to that other a requirement or condition which he applies or would apply equally to persons not of the same racial group as that other but—
  (i) which is such that the proportion of persons of the same racial group as that other who can comply with it is considerably smaller than the proportion of persons not of that racial group who can comply with it; and
  (ii) which he cannot show to be justifiable irrespective of the colour, race, nationality or ethnic or national origins of the person to whom it is applied; and
  (iii) which is to the detriment of that other because he cannot comply with it.

(1A) A person also discriminates against another if, in any circumstances relevant for the purposes of any provision referred to in subsection (1B), he applies to that other a provision, criterion or practice which he applies or would apply equally to persons not of the same race or ethnic or national origins as that other, but—
 (a) which puts or would put persons of the same race or ethnic or national origins as that other at a particular disadvantage when compared with other persons,
 (b) which puts or would put that other at that disadvantage, and
 (c) which he cannot show to be a proportionate means of achieving a legitimate aim.

(1B) The provisions mentioned in subsection (1A) are—
 (a) Part II;
 (b) sections 17 to 18D;
 (c) section 19B, so far as relating to—
  (i) any form of social security;
  (ii) health care;
  (iii) any other form of social protection; and
  (iv) any form of social advantage;
  which does not fall within section 20;
 (d) sections 20 to 24;
 (e) sections 26A and 26B;
 (f) sections 76 and 76ZA; and
 (g) Part IV, in its application to the provisions referred to in paragraphs (a) to (f).

(1C) Where, by virtue of subsection (1A), a person discriminates against another, subsection (1)(b) does not apply to him.

(2) It is hereby declared that, for the purposes of this Act, segregating a person from other persons on racial grounds is treating him less favourably than they are treated.

2 DISCRIMINATION BY WAY OF VICTIMISATION

(1) A person ("the discriminator") discriminates against another person ("the person victimised") in any circumstances relevant for the purposes of any provision of this Act if he treats the person victimised less favourably than in those circumstances he treats or would treat other persons, and does so by reason that the person victimised has—
   (a) brought proceedings against the discriminator or any other person under this Act; or
   (b) given evidence or information in connection with proceedings brought by any person against the discriminator or any other person under this Act; or
   (c) otherwise done anything under or by reference to this Act in relation to the discriminator or any other person; or
   (d) alleged that the discriminator or any other person has committed an act which (whether or not the allegation so states) would amount to a contravention of this Act, or by reason that the discriminator knows that the person victimised intends to do any of those things, or suspects that the person victimised has done, or intends to do, any of them.

(2) Subsection (1) does not apply to treatment of a person by reason of any allegation made by him if the allegation was false and not made in good faith.

3 MEANING OF "RACIAL GROUNDS", "RACIAL GROUP" ETC

(1) In this Act, unless the context otherwise requires—

"racial grounds" means any of the following grounds, namely colour, race, nationality or ethnic or national origins;

"racial group" means a group of persons defined by reference to colour, race, nationality or ethnic or national origins, and references to a person's racial group refer to any racial group into which he falls.

(2) The fact that a racial group comprises two or more distinct racial groups does not prevent it from constituting a particular racial group for the purposes of this Act.

(3) In this Act—
   (a) references to discrimination refer to any discrimination falling within section 1 or 2; and
   (b) references to racial discrimination refer to any discrimination falling within section 1, and related expressions shall be construed accordingly.

(4) A comparison of the case of a person of a particular racial group with that of a person not of that group under section 1(1) or (1A) must be such that the relevant circumstances in the one case are the same, or not materially different, in the other.

3A HARASSMENT

(1) A person subjects another to harassment in any circumstances relevant for the purposes of any provision referred to in section 1(1B) where, on grounds of race or ethnic or national origins, he engages in unwanted conduct which has the purpose or effect of—
   (a) violating that other person's dignity, or
   (b) creating an intimidating, hostile, degrading, humiliating or offensive environment for him.

(2) Conduct shall be regarded as having the effect specified in paragraph (a) or (b) of subsection (1) only if, having regard to all the circumstances, including in particular the perception of that other person, it should reasonably be considered as having that effect.

Part II DISCRIMINATION IN THE EMPLOYMENT FIELD

4 APPLICANTS AND EMPLOYEES

(1)   It is unlawful for a person, in relation to employment by him at an establishment in Great Britain, to discriminate against another—
> (a)   in the arrangements he makes for the purpose of determining who should be offered that employment; or
> (b)   in the terms on which he offers him that employment; or
> (c)   by refusing or deliberately omitting to offer him that employment.

(2)   It is unlawful for a person, in the case of a person employed by him at an establishment in Great Britain, to discriminate against that employee—
> (a)   in the terms of employment which he affords him; or
> (b)   in the way he affords him access to opportunities for promotion, transfer or training, or to any other benefits, facilities or services, or by refusing or deliberately omitting to afford him access to them; or
> (c)   by dismissing him, or subjecting him to any other detriment.

(2A)   It is unlawful for an employer, in relation to employment by him at an establishment in Great Britain, to subject to harassment a person whom he employs or who has applied to him for employment.

(3)   Except in relation to discrimination falling within section 2 or discrimination on grounds of race or ethnic or national origins, subsections (1) and (2) do not apply to employment for the purposes of a private household.

(4)   Subsection (2) does not apply to benefits, facilities or services of any description if the employer is concerned with the provision (for payment or not) of benefits, facilities or services of that description to the public, or to a section of the public comprising the employee in question, unless—
> (a)   that provision differs in a material respect from the provision of the benefits, facilities or services by the employer to his employees; or
> (b)   the provision of the benefits, facilities or services to the employee in question is regulated by his contract of employment; or
> (c)   the benefits, facilities or services relate to training.

(4A)   In subsection (2)(c) reference to the dismissal of a person from employment includes, where the discrimination is on grounds of race or ethnic or national origins, reference—
> (a)   to the termination of that person's employment by the expiration of any period (including a period expiring by reference to an event or circumstance), not being a termination immediately after which the employment is renewed on the same terms; and
> (b)   to the termination of that person's employment by any act of his (including the giving of notice) in circumstances such that he is entitled to terminate it without notice by reason of the conduct of the employer.

4A EXCEPTION FOR GENUINE OCCUPATIONAL REQUIREMENT

(1)   In relation to discrimination on grounds of race or ethnic or national origins—
> (a)   section 4(1)(a) or (c) does not apply to any employment; and
> (b)   section 4(2)(b) does not apply to promotion or transfer to, or training for, any employment; and
> (c)   section 4(2)(c) does not apply to dismissal from any employment;
> where subsection (2) applies.

(2) This subsection applies where, having regard to the nature of the employment or the context in which it is carried out—

   (a) being of a particular race or of particular ethnic or national origins is a genuine and determining occupational requirement;

   (b) it is proportionate to apply that requirement in the particular case; and

   (c) either—

      (i) the person to whom that requirement is applied does not meet it, or

      (ii) the employer is not satisfied, and in all the circumstances it is reasonable for him not to be satisfied, that that person meets it.

5 EXCEPTIONS FOR GENUINE OCCUPATIONAL QUALIFICATIONS

(1) In relation to racial discrimination in cases where section 4A does not apply—

   (a) section 4(1)(a) or (c) does not apply to any employment where being of a particular racial group is a genuine occupational qualification for the job; and

   (b) section 4(2)(b) does not apply to opportunities for promotion or transfer to, or training for, such employment.

(2) Being of a particular racial group is a genuine occupational qualification for a job only where—

   (a) the job involves participation in a dramatic performance or other entertainment in a capacity for which a person of that racial group is required for reasons of authenticity; or

   (b) the job involves participation as an artist's or photographic model in the production of a work of art, visual image or sequence of visual images for which a person of that racial group is required for reasons of authenticity; or

   (c) the job involves working in a place where food or drink is (for payment or not) provided to and consumed by members of the public or a section of the public in a particular setting for which, in that job, a person of that racial group is required for reasons of authenticity; or

   (d) the holder of the job provides persons of that racial group with personal services promoting their welfare, and those services can most effectively be provided by a person of that racial group.

(3) Subsection (2) applies where some only of the duties of the job fall within paragraph (a), (b), (c) or (d) as well as where all of them do.

(4) Paragraph (a), (b), (c) or (d) of subsection (2) does not apply in relation to the filling of a vacancy at a time when the employer already has employees of the racial group in question—

   (a) who are capable of carrying out the duties falling within that paragraph; and

   (b) whom it would be reasonable to employ on those duties; and

   (c) whose numbers are sufficient to meet the employer's likely requirements in respect of those duties without undue inconvenience.

7 CONTRACT WORKERS

(1) This section applies to any work for a person ("the principal") which is available for doing by individuals ("contract workers") who are employed not by the principal himself but by another person, who supplies, them under a contract made with the principal.

(2) It is unlawful for the principal, in relation to work to which this section applies, to discriminate against a contract worker—

   (a) in the terms on which he allows him to do that work; or

   (b) by not allowing him to do it or continue to do it; or

(c) in the way he affords him access to any benefits, facilities or services or by refusing or deliberately omitting to afford him access to them; or

(d) by subjecting him to any other detriment.

(3) The principal does not contravene subsection (2)(b) by doing any act in relation to a person not of a particular racial group, or not of a particular race or particular ethnic or national origins, at a time when, if the work were to be done by a person taken into the principal's employment, being of that racial group or of that race or those origins would be a genuine occupational qualification or, as the case may be, that act would be lawful by virtue of section 4A for the job.

(3A) It is unlawful for the principal, in relation to work to which this section applies, to subject a contract worker to harassment.

(4) Nothing in this section shall render unlawful any act done by the principal on grounds other than those of race or ethnic or national origins, for the benefit of a contract worker not ordinarily resident in Great Britain in or in connection with allowing him to do work to which this section applies, where the purpose of his being allowed to do that work is to provide him with training in skills which he appears to the principal to intend to exercise wholly outside Great Britain.

(5) Subsection (2)(c) does not apply to benefits, facilities or services of any description if the principal is concerned with the provision (for payment or not) of benefits, facilities or services of that description to the public, or to a section of the public to which the contract worker in question belongs, unless that provision differs in a material respect from the provision of the benefits, facilities or services by the principal to his contract workers.

11 TRADE UNIONS, ETC.

(1) This section applies to an organisation of workers, an organisation of employers, or any other organisation whose members carry on a particular profession or trade for the purposes of which the organisation exists.

(2) It is unlawful for an organisation to which this section applies, in the case of a person who is not a member of the organisation, to discriminate against him—
(a) in the terms on which it is prepared to admit him to membership; or
(b) by refusing or deliberately omitting to accept, his application for membership.

(3) It is unlawful for an organisation to which this section applies, in the case of a person who is a member of the organisation, to discriminate against him—
(a) in the way it affords him access to any benefits, facilities or services, or by refusing or deliberately omitting to afford him access to them; or
(b) by depriving him of membership, or varying the terms on which he is a member; or
(c) by subjecting him to any other detriment.

(4) It is unlawful for an organisation to which this section applies, in relation to a person's membership or application for membership of that organisation, to subject him to harassment.

Part IV OTHER UNLAWFUL ACTS

27A RELATIONSHIPS WHICH HAVE COME TO AN END

(1) In this section a "relevant relationship" is a relationship during the course of which, by virtue of any provision referred to in section 1(1B), taken with section 1(1) or (1A), or (as the case may be) by virtue of section 3A—

(a) an act of discrimination by one party to the relationship ("the relevant party") against another party to the relationship, on grounds of race or ethnic or national origins, or

(b) harassment of another party to the relationship by the relevant party,

is unlawful.

(2) Where a relevant relationship has come to an end it is unlawful for the relevant party—

(a) to discriminate against another party, on grounds of race or ethnic or national origins, by subjecting him to a detriment, or

(b) to subject another party to harassment,

where the discrimination or harassment arises out of and is closely connected to that relationship.

(3) In subsection (1) reference to an act of discrimination or harassment which is unlawful includes, in the case of a relationship which has come to an end before 19th July 2003, reference to such an act which would, after that date, be unlawful.

(4) For the purposes of any proceedings in respect of an unlawful act under subsection (2), that act shall be treated as falling within circumstances relevant for the purposes of such of the provisions, or Parts, referred to in subsection (1) as determine most closely the nature of the relevant relationship.

28 DISCRIMINATORY PRACTICES

(1) In this section "discriminatory practice" means—

(a) the application of a requirement or condition which results in an act of discrimination which is unlawful by virtue of any provision of Part II or III taken with section 1(1) (b), or which would be likely to result in such an act of discrimination if the persons to whom it is applied included persons of any particular racial group as regards which there has been no occasion for applying it or

(b) the application of a provision, criterion or practice which results in an act of discrimination which is unlawful by virtue of any provision referred to in section 1(1B), taken with section 1(1A), or which would be likely to result in such an act of discrimination, if the persons to whom it is applied included persons of any particular race or of any particular ethnic or national origins, as regards which there has been no occasion for applying it.

(2) A person acts in contravention of this section if and so long as—

(a) he applies a discriminatory practice; or

(b) he operates practices or other arrangements which in any circumstances would call for the application by him of a discriminatory practice.

(3) Proceedings in respect of a contravention of this section shall be brought only by the Commission in accordance with sections 20 to 24 of the Equality Act 2006.

30 INSTRUCTIONS TO COMMIT UNLAWFUL ACTS

(1) It is unlawful for a person—

(a) who has authority over another person; or

(b) in accordance with whose wishes that other person is accustomed to act,

to instruct him to do any act which is unlawful by virtue of Part II or III, section 76ZA or, where it renders an act unlawful on grounds of race or ethnic or national origins, section 76, or procure or attempt to procure the doing by him of any such act.

(2)   Proceedings in respect of a contravention of subsection (1) may be brought only—
       (a) by the Commission, and
       (b) in accordance with section 25 of the Equality Act 2006.

31 PRESSURE TO COMMIT UNLAWFUL ACTS

(1)   It is unlawful to induce, or attempt to induce, a person to do any act which contravenes Part II or IIIsection 76ZA or, where it renders an act unlawful on grounds of race or ethnic or national origins, section 76.

(2)   An attempted inducement is not prevented from falling within subsection (1) because it is not made directly to the person in question, if it is made in such a way that he is likely to hear of it.

(3)   Proceedings in respect of a contravention of subsection (1) may be brought only—
       (a) by the Commission, and
       (b) in accordance with section 25 of the Equality Act 2006.

32 LIABILITY OF EMPLOYERS AND PRINCIPALS

(1)   Anything done by a person in the course of his employment shall be treated for the purposes of this Act (except as regards offences thereunder) as done by his employer as well as by him, whether or not it was done with the employer's knowledge or approval.

(2)   Anything done by a person as agent for another person with the authority (whether express or implied, and whether precedent or subsequent) of that other person shall be treated for the purposes of this Act (except as regards offences thereunder) as done by that other person as well as by him.

(3)   In proceedings brought under this Act against any person in respect of an act alleged to have been done by an employee of his it shall be a defence for that person to prove that he took such steps as were reasonably practicable to prevent the employee from doing that act, or from doing in the course of his employment acts of that description.

33 AIDING UNLAWFUL ACTS

(1)   A person who knowingly aids another person to do an act made unlawful by this Act shall be treated for the purposes of this Act as himself doing an unlawful act of the like description.

(2)   For the purposes of subsection (1) an employee or agent for whose act the employer or principal is liable under section 32 (or would be so liable but for section 32(3)) shall be deemed to aid the doing of the act by the employer or principal.

(3)   A person does not under this section knowingly aid another to do an unlawful act if—
       (a) he acts in reliance on a statement made to him by that other person that, by reason of any provision of this Act, the act which he aids would not be unlawful; and
       (b) it is reasonable for him to rely on the statement.

(4)   A person who knowingly or recklessly makes a statement such as is mentioned in subsection (3)(a) which in a material respect is false or misleading commits an offence, and shall be liable on summary conviction to a fine not exceeding level 5 on the standard scale.

Amended by the Criminal Justice Act 1982, ss 38, 46 and Criminal Procedure (Scotland) Act 1975, ss 289F, 289G; Employment Act 1989, s 12(2);Employment Protection Act 1975, s 122(2);Race Relations Act 1976 (Amendment) Regulations 2003/1626 reg 3, reg 4, reg 5, reg 6(1), reg 6(2)(a), reg 6(2)(b), reg 6(2)(c), reg 7, reg 8, reg 10(1), reg 10(2)(a)(i), reg 10(2)(a)(ii), reg 10(2)(a)(iii), reg 10(2)(b), reg 10(2)(c), reg 13, reg 29, reg 30, reg 31(1), reg 32(1), reg 32(2);Equality Act 2006, Sch 3 para 22, Sch 3 para 24, Sch 3 para 25;Race Relations Act 1976 (Amendment) Regulations 2008/3008 reg 2.

TRADE UNION AND LABOUR RELATIONS CONSOLIDATION ACT 1992
(c. 52)

Part I TRADE UNIONS

Chapter I INTRODUCTORY

1 MEANING OF "TRADE UNION"

In this Act a "trade union" means an organisation (whether temporary or permanent)—
(a) which consists wholly or mainly of workers of one or more descriptions and whose principal purposes include the regulation of relations between workers of that description or those descriptions and employers or employers' associations; or

(b) which consists wholly or mainly of—
  (i) constituent or affiliated organisations which fulfil the conditions in paragraph (a) (or themselves consist wholly or mainly of constituent or affiliated organisations which fulfil those conditions), or
  (ii) representatives of such constituent or affiliated organisations,
  and whose principal purposes include the regulation of relations between workers and employers or between workers and employers' associations, or the regulation of relations between its constituent or affiliated organisations.

2 THE LIST OF TRADE UNIONS

(1) The Certification Officer shall keep a list of trade unions containing the names of—
  (a) the organisations whose names were, immediately before the commencement of this Act, duly entered in the list of trade unions kept by him under section 8 of the Trade Union and Labour Relations Act 1974, and
  (b) the names of the organisations entitled to have their names entered in the list in accordance with this Part.

(2) The Certification Officer shall keep copies of the list of trade unions, as for the time being in force, available for public inspection at all reasonable hours free of charge.

(3) A copy of the list shall be included in his annual report.

(4)   The fact that the name of an organisation is included in the list of trade unions is evidence (in Scotland, sufficient evidence) that the organisation is a trade union.

(5)   On the application of an organisation whose name is included in the list, the Certification Officer shall issue it with a certificate to that effect.

(6)   A document purporting to be such a certificate is evidence (in Scotland, sufficient evidence) that the name of the organisation is entered in the list.

5   MEANING OF "INDEPENDENT TRADE UNION"

In this Act an "independent trade union" means a trade union which—

(a)   is not under the domination or control of an employer or group of employers or of one or more employers' associations, and

(b)   is not liable to interference by an employer or any such group or association (arising out of the provision of financial or material support or by any other means whatsoever) tending towards such control;

and references to "independence", in relation to a trade union, shall be construed accordingly.

6   APPLICATION FOR CERTIFICATE OF INDEPENDENCE

(1)   A trade union whose name is entered on the list of trade unions may apply to the Certification Officer for a certificate that it is independent.

The application shall be made in such form and manner as the Certification Officer may require and shall be accompanied by the prescribed fee.

(2)   The Certification Officer shall maintain a record showing details of all applications made to him under this section and shall keep it available for public inspection (free of charge) at all reasonable hours.

(3)   If an application is made by a trade union whose name is not entered on the list of trade unions, the Certification Officer shall refuse a certificate of independence and shall enter that refusal on the record.

(4)   In any other case, he shall not come to a decision on the application before the end of the period of one month after it has been entered on the record; and before coming to his decision he shall make such enquiries as he thinks fit and shall take into account any relevant information submitted to him by any person.

(5)   He shall then decide whether the applicant trade union is independent and shall enter his decision and the date of his decision on the record.

(6)   If he decides that the trade union is independent he shall issue a certificate accordingly; and if he decides that it is not, he shall give reasons for his decision

7   WITHDRAWAL OR CANCELLATION OF CERTIFICATE

(1)   The Certification Officer may withdraw a trade union's certificate of independence if he is of the opinion that the union is no longer independent.

(2)   Where he proposes to do so he shall notify the trade union and enter notice of the proposal in the record.

(3)   He shall not come to a decision on the proposal before the end of the period of one month after notice of it was entered on the record; and before coming to his decision he shall make such enquiries as he thinks fit and shall take into account any relevant information submitted to him by any person.

(4)   He shall then decide whether the trade union is independent and shall enter his decision and the date of his decision on the record.

(5)   He shall confirm or withdraw the certificate accordingly; and if he decides to withdraw it, he shall give reasons for his decision.

(6)   Where the name of an organisation is removed from the list of trade unions, the Certification Officer shall cancel any certificate of independence in force in respect of that organisation by entering on the record the fact that the organisation's name has been removed from that list and that the certificate is accordingly cancelled.

9 APPEAL AGAINST DECISION OF CERTIFICATION OFFICER

(1)   An organisation aggrieved by the refusal of the Certification Officer to enter its name in the list of trade unions, or by a decision of his to remove its name from the list, may appeal to the Employment Appeal Tribunal on any appealable question.

(2)   A trade union aggrieved by the refusal of the Certification Officer to issue it with a certificate of independence, or by a decision of his to withdraw its certificate, may appeal to the Employment Appeal Tribunal on any appealable question.

(4)   For the purposes of this section, an appealable question is any question of law arising in the proceedings before, or arising from the decision of, the Certification Officer.

20 LIABILITY OF TRADE UNION IN CERTAIN PROCEEDINGS IN TORT

(1)   Where proceedings in tort are brought against a trade union—
   (a) on the ground that an act—
      (i)   induces another person to break a contract or interferes or induces another person to interfere with its performance, or
      (ii) consists in threatening that a contract (whether one to which the union is a party or not) will be broken or its performance interfered with, or that the union will induce another person to break a contract or interfere with its performance, or
   (b) in respect of an agreement or combination by two or more persons to do or to procure the doing of an act which, if it were done without any such agreement or combination, would be actionable in tort on such a ground,
then, for the purpose of determining in those proceedings whether the union is liable in respect of the act in question, that act shall be taken to have been done by the union if, but only if, it is to be taken to have been authorised or endorsed by the trade union in accordance with the following provisions.

(2)   An act shall be taken to have been authorised or endorsed by a trade union if it was done, or was authorised or endorsed—
   (a) by any person empowered by the rules to do, authorise or endorse acts of the kind in question, or
   (b) by the principal executive committee or the president or general secretary, or
   (c) by any other committee of the union or any other official of the union (whether employed by it or not).

(3)   For the purposes of paragraph (c) of subsection (2)—
    (a)   any group of persons constituted in accordance with the rules of the union is a committee of the union; and
    (b)   an act shall be taken to have been done, authorised or endorsed by an official if it was done, authorised or endorsed by, or by any member of, any group of persons of which he was at the material time a member, the purposes of which included organising or co-ordinating industrial action.

(4)   The provisions of paragraphs (b) and (c) of subsection (2) apply notwithstanding anything in the rules of the union, or in any contract or rule of law, but subject to the provisions of section 21 (repudiation by union of certain acts).

(5)   Where for the purposes of any proceedings an act is by virtue of this section taken to have been done by a trade union, nothing in this section shall affect the liability of any other person, in those or any other proceedings, in respect of that act.

(6)   In proceedings arising out of an act which is by virtue of this section taken to have been done by a trade union, the power of the court to grant an injunction or interdict includes power to require the union to take such steps as the court considers appropriate for ensuring—
    (a)   that there is no, or no further, inducement of persons to take part or to continue to take part in industrial action, and
    (b)   that no person engages in any conduct after the granting of the injunction or interdict by virtue of having been induced before it was granted to take part or to continue to take part in industrial action.
The provisions of subsections (2) to (4) above apply in relation to proceedings for failure to comply with any such injunction or interdict as they apply in relation to the original proceedings.

(7)   In this section "rules", in relation to a trade union, means the written rules of the union and any other written provision forming part of the contract between a member and the other members.

22 LIMIT ON DAMAGES AWARDED AGAINST TRADE UNIONS IN ACTIONS IN TORT

(1)   This section applies to any proceedings in tort brought against a trade union, except—
    (a)   proceedings for personal injury as a result of negligence, nuisance or breach of duty;
    (b)   proceedings for breach of duty in connection with the ownership, occupation, possession, control or use of property;
    (c)   proceedings brought by virtue of Part I of the Consumer Protection Act 1987 (product liability).

(2)   In any proceedings in tort to which this section applies the amount which may awarded against the union by way of damages shall not exceed the following limit—

Number of members of union	Maximum award of damages
Less than 5,000	£10,000
5,000 or more but less than 25,000	£50,000
25,000 or more but less than 100,000	£125,000
100,000 or more	£250,000

(3)   The Secretary of State may by order amend subsection (2) so as to vary any of the sums specified; and the order may make such transitional provision as the Secretary of State considers appropriate.

(4)   Any such order shall be made by statutory instrument which shall be subject to annulment in pursuance of a resolution of either House of Parliament.

(5)   In this section—

"breach of duty" means breach of a duty imposed by any rule of law or by or under any enactment;

"personal injury" includes any disease and any impairment of a person's physical or mental condition; and

"property" means any property, whether real or personal (or in Scotland, heritable or moveable).

Chapter V RIGHTS OF TRADE UNION MEMBERS

62 RIGHT TO A BALLOT BEFORE INDUSTRIAL ACTION

(1)   A member of a trade union who claims that members of the union, including himself, are likely to be or have been induced by the union to take part or to continue to take part in industrial action which does not have the support of a ballot may apply to the court for an order under this section.

In this section "the relevant time" means the time when the application is made.

(2)   For this purpose industrial action shall be regarded as having the support of a ballot only if—
   (a) the union has held a ballot in respect of the action—
        (i)   in relation to which the requirements of section 226B so far as applicable before and during the holding of the ballot were satisfied,
        (ii) in relation to which the requirements of sections 227 to 231 were satisfied, and
        (iii) in which the majority voting in the ballot answered "Yes" to the question applicable in accordance with section 229(2) to industrial action of the kind which the applicant has been or is likely to be induced to take part in;
   (b) such of the requirements of the following sections as have fallen to be satisfied at the relevant time have been satisfied, namely—
        (i)   section 226B so far as applicable after the holding of the ballot, and
        (ii) section 231B ;
   (bb) section 232A does not prevent the industrial action from being regarded as having the support of the ballot; and
   (c) the requirements of section 233 (calling of industrial action with support of ballot) are satisfied.
Any reference in this subsection to a requirement of a provision which is disapplied or modified by section 232 has effect subject to that section.

(3)   Where on an application under this section the court is satisfied that the claim is well-founded, it shall make such order as it considers appropriate for requiring the union to take steps for ensuring—
   (a) that there is no, or no further, inducement of members of the union to take part or to continue to take part in the industrial action to which the application relates, and
   (b) that no member engages in conduct after the making of the order by virtue of having been induced before the making of the order to take part or continue to take part in the action.

(4)   Without prejudice to any other power of the court, the court may on an application under this section grant such interlocutory relief (in Scotland, such interim order) as it considers appropriate.

(5) For the purposes of this section an act shall be taken to be done by a trade union if it is authorised or endorsed by the union; and the provisions of section 20(2) to (4) apply for the purpose of determining whether an act is to be taken to be so authorised or endorsed.

Those provisions also apply in relation to proceedings for failure to comply with an order under this section as they apply in relation to the original proceedings.

(6) In this section—

"inducement" includes an inducement which is or would be ineffective, whether because of the member's unwillingness to be influenced by it or for any other reason; and

"industrial action" means a strike or other industrial action by persons employed under contracts of employment.

(7) Where a person holds any office or employment under the Crown on terms which do not constitute a contract of employment between that person and the Crown, those terms shall nevertheless be deemed to constitute such a contract for the purposes of this section.

(8) References in this section to a contract of employment include any contract under which one person personally does work or performs services for another; and related expressions shall be construed accordingly.

(9) Nothing in this section shall be construed as requiring a trade union to hold separate ballots for the purposes of this section and sections 226 to 234 (requirement of ballot before action by trade union).

64 RIGHT NOT TO BE UNJUSTIFIABLY DISCIPLINED

(1) An individual who is or has been a member of a trade union has the right not to be unjustifiably disciplined by the union.

(2) For this purpose an individual is "disciplined" by a trade union if a determination is made, or purportedly made, under the rules of the union or by an official of the union or a number of persons including an official that—
   (a) he should be expelled from the union or a branch or section of the union,
   (b) he should pay a sum to the union, to a branch or section of the union or to any other person;
   (c) sums tendered by him in respect of an obligation to pay subscriptions or other sums to the union, or to a branch or section of the union, should be treated as unpaid or paid for a different purpose,
   (d) he should be deprived to any extent of, or of access to, any benefits, services or facilities which would otherwise be provided or made available to him by virtue of his membership of the union, or a branch or section of the union,
   (e) another trade union, or a branch or section of it, should be encouraged or advised not to accept him as a member, or
   (f) he should be subjected to some other detriment;
and whether an individual is "unjustifiably disciplined" shall be determined in accordance with section 65.

(3) Where a determination made in infringement of an individual's right under this section requires the payment of a sum or the performance of an obligation, no person is entitled in any proceedings to rely on that determination for the purpose of recovering the sum or enforcing the obligation.

(4)   Subject to that, the remedies for infringement of the right conferred by this section are as provided by sections 66 and 67, and not otherwise.

(5)   The right not to be unjustifiably disciplined is in addition to (and not in substitution for) any right which exists apart from this section; and, subject to section 66(4), nothing in this section or sections 65 to 67 affects any remedy for infringement of any such right.

65   MEANING OF "UNJUSTIFIABLY DISCIPLINED"

(1)   An individual is unjustifiably disciplined by a trade union if the actual or supposed conduct which constitutes the reason, or one of the reasons, for disciplining him is—
(a)   conduct to which this section applies, or
(b)   something which is believed by the union to amount to such conduct;
but subject to subsection (6) (cases of bad faith in relation to assertion of wrongdoing).

(2)   This section applies to conduct which consists in—
(a)   failing to participate in or support a strike or other industrial action (whether by members of the union or by others), or indicating opposition to or a lack of support for such action;
(b)   failing to contravene, for a purpose connected with such a strike or other industrial action, a requirement imposed on him by or under a contract of employment;
(c)   asserting (whether by bringing proceedings or otherwise) that the union, any official or representative of it or a trustee of its property has contravened, or is proposing to contravene, a requirement which is, or is thought to be, imposed by or under the rules of the union or any other agreement or by or under any enactment (whenever passed) or any rule of law;
(d)   encouraging or assisting a person—
(i)   to perform an obligation imposed on him by a contract of employment, or
(ii)   to make or attempt to vindicate any such assertion as is mentioned in paragraph (c);
(e)   contravening a requirement imposed by or in consequence of a determination which infringes the individual's or another individual's right not to be unjustifiably disciplined.
(f)   failing to agree, or withdrawing agreement, to the making from his wages (in accordance with arrangements between his employer and the union) of deductions representing payments to the union in respect of his membership,
(g)   resigning or proposing to resign from the union or from another union, becoming or proposing to become a member of another union, refusing to become a member of another union, or being a member of another union,
(h)   working with, or proposing to work with, individuals who are not members of the union or who are or are not members of another union,
(i)   working for, or proposing to work for, an employer who employs or who has employed individuals who are not members of the union or who are or are not members of another union, or
(j)   requiring the union to do an act which the union is, by any provision of this Act, required to do on the requisition of a member.

(3)   This section applies to conduct which involves the Certification Officer being consulted or asked to provide advice or assistance with respect to any matter whatever, or which involves any person being consulted or asked to provide advice or assistance with respect to a matter which forms, or might form, the subject-matter of any such assertion as is mentioned in subsection (2)(c) above.

(4)   This section also applies to conduct which consists in proposing to engage, in or doing anything preparatory or incidental to, conduct falling within subsection (2) or (3).

(5)   This section does not apply to an act, omission or statement comprised in conduct falling within subsection (2), (3) or (4) above if it is shown that the act, omission or statement is one in respect of which individuals would be disciplined by the union irrespective of whether their acts, omissions or statements were in connection with conduct within subsection (2) or (3) above.

(6)   An individual is not unjustifiably disciplined if it is shown—
   (a) that the reason for disciplining him, or one of them, is that he made such an assertion as is mentioned in subsection (2)(c), or encouraged or assisted another person to make or attempt to vindicate such an assertion,
   (b) that the assertion was false, and
   (c) that he made the assertion, or encouraged or assisted another person to make or attempt to vindicate it, in the belief that it was false or otherwise in bad faith,
   and that there was no other reason for disciplining him or that the only other reasons were reasons in respect of which he does not fall to be treated as unjustifiably disciplined.

(7)   In this section—

   "conduct" includes statements, acts and omissions;

   "contract of employment", in relation to an individual, includes any agreement between that individual and a person for whom he works or normally works; "employer" includes such a person and related expressions shall be construed accordingly

   "representative", in relation to a union, means a person acting or purporting to act—
   (a) in his capacity as a member of the union, or
   (b) on the instructions or advice of a person acting or purporting to act in that capacity or in the capacity of an official of the union.
   "require" (on the part of an individual) includes request or apply for, and "requisition" shall be construed accordingly.

   and

   "wages" shall be construed in accordance with the definitions of "contract of employment", "employer" and related expressions.

(8)   Where a person holds any office or employment under the Crown on terms which do not constitute a contract of employment between him and the Crown, those terms shall nevertheless be deemed to constitute such a contract for the purposes of this section.

66 COMPLAINT OF INFRINGEMENT OF RIGHT

(1)   An individual who claims that he has been unjustifiably disciplined by a trade union may present a complaint against the union to an employment tribunal.

(2)   The tribunal shall not entertain such a complaint unless it is presented—
   (a) before the end of the period of three months beginning with the date of the making of the determination claimed to infringe the right, or
   (b) where the tribunal is satisfied—
      (i)   that it was not reasonably practicable for the complaint to be presented before the end of that period, or
      (ii) that any delay in making the complaint is wholly or partly attributable to a reasonable attempt to appeal against the determination or to have it reconsidered or reviewed,
   within such further period as the tribunal considers reasonable.

(3)   Where the tribunal finds the complaint well-founded, it shall make a declaration to that effect.

(4)   Where a complaint relating to an expulsion which is presented under this section is declared to be well-founded, no complaint in respect of the expulsion shall be presented or proceeded with under section 174 (right not to be excluded or expelled from trade union).

67 FURTHER REMEDIES FOR INFRINGEMENT OF RIGHT

(1)   An individual whose complaint under section 66 has been declared to be well-founded may make an application to an employment tribunal for one or both of the following—
(a) an award of compensation to be paid to him by the union;
(b) an order that the union pay him an amount equal to any sum which he has paid in pursuance of any such determination as is mentioned in section 64(2)(b).

(3)   An application under this section shall not be entertained if made before the end of the period of four weeks beginning with the date of the declaration or after the end of the period of six months beginning with that date.

(5)   The amount of compensation awarded shall, subject to the following provisions, be such as the employment tribunal considers just and equitable in all the circumstances.

(6)   In determining the amount of compensation to be awarded, the same rule shall be applied concerning the duty of a person to mitigate his loss as applies to damages recoverable under the common law in England and Wales or Scotland.

(7)   Where the employment tribunal finds that the infringement complained of was to any extent caused or contributed to by the action of the applicant, it shall reduce the amount of the compensation by such proportion as it considers just and equitable having regard to that finding.

(8)   The amount of compensation calculated in accordance with subsections (5) to (7) shall not exceed the aggregate of—
(a) an amount equal to 30 times the limit for the time being imposed by section 227(1)(a) of the Employment Rights Act 1996 (maximum amount of a week's pay for basic award in unfair dismissal cases), and
(b) an amount equal to the limit for the time being imposed by section 124(1) of that Act (maximum compensatory award in such cases).

(8A) If on the date on which the application was made—
(a) the determination infringing the applicant's right not to be unjustifiably disciplined has not been revoked, or
(b) the union has failed to take all the steps necessary for securing the reversal of anything done for the purpose of giving effect to the determination,
the amount of compensation shall be not less than the amount for the time being specified in section 176(6A).

69 RIGHT TO TERMINATE MEMBERSHIP OF UNION

In every contract of membership of a trade union, whether made before or after the passing of this Act, a term conferring a right on the member, on giving reasonable notice and complying with any reasonable conditions, to terminate his membership of the union shall be implied.

Part III **RIGHTS IN RELATION TO UNION MEMBERSHIP AND ACTIVITIES**

137 REFUSAL OF EMPLOYMENT ON GROUNDS RELATED TO UNION MEMBERSHIP

(1) It is unlawful to refuse a person employment—
  (a) because he is, or is not, a member of a trade union, or
  (b) because he is unwilling to accept a requirement—
    (i) to take steps to become or cease to be, or to remain or not to become, a member of a trade union, or
    (ii) to make payments or suffer deductions in the event of his not being a member of a trade union.

(2) A person who is thus unlawfully refused employment has a right of compliant to an employment tribunal.

(3) Where an advertisement is published which indicates, or might reasonably be understood as indicating—
  (a) that employment to which the advertisement relates is open only to a person who is, or is not, a member of a trade union, or
  (b) that any such requirement as is mentioned in subsection (1)(b) will be imposed in relation to employment to which the advertisement relates,
  a person who does not satisfy that condition or, as the case may be, is unwilling to accept that requirement, and who seeks and is refused employment to which the advertisement relates, shall be conclusively presumed to have been refused employment for that reason.

(4) Where there is an arrangement or practice under which employment is offered only to persons put forward or approved by a trade union, and the trade union puts forward or approves only persons who are members of the union, a person who is not a member of the union and who is refused employment in pursuance of the arrangement or practice shall be taken to have been refused employment because he is not a member of the trade union.

(5) A person shall be taken to be refused employment if he seeks employment of any description with a person and that person—
  (a) refuses or deliberately omits to entertain and process his application or enquiry, or
  (b) causes him to withdraw or cease to pursue his application or enquiry, or
  (c) refuses or deliberately omits to offer him employment of that description, or
  (d) makes him an offer of such employment the terms of which are such as no reasonable employer who wished to fill the post would offer and which is not accepted, or
  (e) makes him an offer of such employment but withdraws it or causes him not to accept it.

(6) Where a person is offered employment on terms which include a requirement that he is, or is not, a member of a trade union, or any such requirement as is mentioned in subsection (1)(b), and he does not accept the offer because he does not satisfy or, as the case may be, is unwilling to accept that requirement, he shall be treated as having been refused employment for that reason.

(7) Where a person may not be considered for appointment or election to an office in a trade union unless he is a member of the union, or of a particular branch or section of the union or of one of a number of particular branches or sections of the union, nothing in this section applies to anything done for the purpose of securing compliance with that condition although as holder of the office he would be employed by the union.

For this purpose an "office" means any position—
(a) by virtue of which the holder is an official of the union, or
(b) to which Chapter IV of Part I applies (duty to hold elections).

(8) The provisions of this section apply in relation to an employment agency acting, or purporting to act, on behalf of an employer as in relation to an employer

138 REFUSAL OF SERVICE OF EMPLOYMENT AGENCY ON GROUNDS RELATED TO UNION MEMBERSHIP

(1) It is unlawful for an employment agency to refuse a person any of its services—
(a) because he is, or is not, a member of a trade union, or
(b) because he is unwilling to accept a requirement to take steps to become or cease to be, or to remain or not to become, a member of a trade union.

(2) A person who is thus unlawfully refused any service of an employment agency has a right of complaint to an industrial tribunal.

(3) Where an advertisement is published which indicates, or might reasonably be understood as indicating—
(a) that any service of an employment agency is available only to a person who is, or is not, a member of a trade union, or
(b) that any such requirement as is mentioned in subsection (1)(b) will be imposed in relation to a service to which the advertisement relates,
a person who does not satisfy that condition or, as the case may be, is unwilling to accept that requirement, and who seeks to avail himself of and is refused that service, shall be conclusively presumed to have been refused it for that reason.

(4) A person shall be taken to be refused a service if he seeks to avail himself of it and the agency—
(a) refuses or deliberately omits to make the service available to him, or
(b) causes him not to avail himself of the service or to cease to avail himself of it, or
(c) does not provide the same service, on the same terms, as is provided to others.

(5) Where a person is offered a service on terms which include a requirement that he is, or is not, a member of a trade union, or any such requirement as is mentioned in subsection (1)(b), and he does not accept the offer because he does not satisfy or, as the case may be, is unwilling to accept that requirement, he shall be treated as having been refused the service for that reason.

139 TIME LIMIT FOR PROCEEDINGS

(1) An employment tribunal shall not consider a complaint under section 137 or 138 unless it is presented to the tribunal—
(a) before the end of the period of three months beginning with the date of the conduct to which the complaint relates, or
(b) where the tribunal is satisfied that it was not reasonably practicable for the complaint to be presented before the end of that period, within such further period as the tribunal considers reasonable.

(2) The date of the conduct to which a complaint under section 137 relates shall be taken to be—
(a) in the case of an actual refusal, the date of the refusal;
(b) in the case of a deliberate omission—
(i) to entertain and process the complainant's application or enquiry, or
(ii) to offer employment,
the end of the period within which it was reasonable to expect the employer to act;

(c) in the case of conduct causing the complainant to withdraw or cease to pursue his application or enquiry, the date of that conduct;

(d) in a case where an offer was made but withdrawn, the date when it was withdrawn;

(e) in any other case where an offer was made but not accepted, the date on which it was made.

(3)   The date of the conduct to which a complaint under section 138 relates shall be taken to be—

(a) in the case of an actual refusal, the date of the refusal;

(b) in the case of a deliberate omission to make a service available, the end of the period within which it was reasonable to expect the employment agency to act;

(c) in the case of conduct causing the complainant not to avail himself of a service or to cease to avail himself of it, the date of that conduct;

(d) in the case of failure to provide the same service, on the same terms, as is provided to others, the date or last date on which the service in fact provided was provided.

140   REMEDIES

(1)   Where the employment tribunal finds that a complaint under section 137 or 138 is well-founded, it shall make a declaration to that effect and may make such of the following as it considers just and equitable—

(a) an order requiring the respondent to pay compensation to the complainant of such amount as the tribunal may determine;

(b) a recommendation that the respondent take within a specified period action appearing to the tribunal to be practicable for the purpose of obviating or reducing the adverse effect on the complainant of any conduct to which the complaint relates.

(2)   Compensation shall be assessed on the same basis as damages for breach of statutory duty and may include compensation for injury to feelings.

(3)   If the respondent fails without reasonable justification to comply with a recommendation to take action, the tribunal may increase its award of compensation or, if it has not made such an award, make one.

(4)   The total amount of compensation shall not exceed the limit for the time being imposed by section 124(1) of the Employment Rights Act 1996 (limit on compensation for unfair dismissal).

146   DETRIMENT ON GROUNDS RELATED TO UNION MEMBERSHIP OR ACTIVITIES

(1)   A worker has the right not to be subjected to any detriment as an individual by any act, or any deliberate failure to act, by his employer if the act or failure takes place for the sole or main purpose of—

(a) preventing or deterring him from being or seeking to become a member of an independent trade union, or penalising him for doing so,

(b) preventing or deterring him from taking part in the activities of an independent trade union at an appropriate time, or penalising him for doing so,

(ba) preventing or deterring him from making use of trade union services at an appropriate time, or penalising him for doing so, or

(c) compelling him to be or become a member of any trade union or of a particular trade union or of one of a number of particular trade unions.

(2)   In subsection (1) "an appropriate time" means—

(a) a time outside the worker's working hours, or

(b) a time within his working hours at which, in accordance with arrangements agreed with or consent given by his employer, it is permissible for him to take part in the activities of a trade union or (as the case may be) make use of trade union services;

and for this purpose "working hours", in relation to a worker, means any time when, in accordance with his contract of employment (or other contract personally to do work or perform services), he is required to be at work.

(2A) In this section—
   (a) "trade union services" means services made available to the worker by an independent trade union by virtue of his membership of the union, and
   (b) references to a worker's "making use" of trade union services include his consenting to the raising of a matter on his behalf by an independent trade union of which he is a member.

(2B) If an independent trade union of which a worker is a member raises a matter on his behalf (with or without his consent), penalising the worker for that is to be treated as penalising him as mentioned in subsection (1)(ba).

(2C) A worker also has the right not to be subjected to any detriment as an individual by any act, or any deliberate failure to act, by his employer if the act or failure takes place because of the worker's failure to accept an offer made in contravention of section 145A or 145B.

(2D) For the purposes of subsection (2C), not conferring a benefit that, if the offer had been accepted by the worker, would have been conferred on him under the resulting agreement shall be taken to be subjecting him to a detriment as an individual (and to be a deliberate failure to act).

(3) A worker also has the right not to be subjected to any detriment as an individual by any act, or any deliberate failure to act, by his employer if the act or failure takes place for the sole or main purpose of enforcing a requirement (whether or not imposed by a contract of employment or in writing) that, in the event of his not being a member of any trade union or of a particular trade union or of one of a number of particular trade unions, he must make one or more payments.

(4) For the purposes of subsection (3) any deduction made by an employer from the remuneration payable to a worker in respect of his employment shall, if it is attributable to his not being a member of any trade union or of a particular trade union or of one of a number of particular trade unions, be treated as a detriment to which he has been subjected as an individual by an act of his employer taking place for the sole or main purpose of enforcing a requirement of a kind mentioned in that subsection.

(5) A worker or former worker may present a complaint to an employment tribunal on the ground that he has been subjected to a detriment by his employer in contravention of this section.

(5A) This section does not apply where—
   (a) the worker is an employee; and
   (b) the detriment in question amounts to dismissal.

147 TIME LIMIT FOR PROCEEDINGS

(1) An employment tribunal shall not consider a complaint under section 146 unless it is presented—
   (a) before the end of the period of three months beginning with the date of the act or

failure to which the complaint relates or, where that act or failure is part of a series of similar acts or failures (or both) the last of them or

(b) where the tribunal is satisfied that it was not reasonably practicable for the complaint to be presented before the end of that period, within such further period as it considers reasonable.

(2) For the purposes of subsection (1)—
(a) where an act extends over a period, the reference to the date of the act is a reference to the last day of that period;
(b) a failure to act shall be treated as done when it was decided on.

(3) For the purposes of subsection (2), in the absence of evidence establishing the contrary an employer shall be taken to decide on a failure to act—
(a) when he does an act inconsistent with doing the failed act, or
(b) if he has done no such inconsistent act, when the period expires within which he might reasonably have been expected to do the failed act if it was to be done.

149 REMEDIES

(1) Where the employment tribunal finds that a complaint under section 146 is well-founded, it shall make a declaration to that effect and may make an award of compensation to be paid by the employer to the complainant in respect of the act or failure complained of.

(2) The amount of the compensation awarded shall be such as the tribunal considers just and equitable in all the circumstances having regard to the infringement complained of and to any loss sustained by the complainant which is attributable to the act or failure which infringed his right.

(3) The loss shall be taken to include—
(a) any expenses reasonably incurred by the complainant in consequence of the act or failure complained of, and
(b) loss of any benefit which he might reasonably be expected to have had but for that act or failure.

(4) In ascertaining the loss, the tribunal shall apply the same rule concerning the duty of a person to mitigate his loss as applies to damages recoverable under the common law of England and Wales or Scotland.

(5) In determining the amount of compensation to be awarded no account shall be taken of any pressure which was exercised on the employer by calling, organising, procuring or financing a strike or other industrial action, or by threatening to do so; and that question shall be determined as if no such pressure had been exercised.

(6) Where the tribunal finds that the act or failure complained of was to any extent caused or contributed to by action of the complainant, it shall reduce the amount of the compensation by such proportion as it considers just and equitable having regard to that finding.

152 DISMISSAL OF EMPLOYEE ON GROUNDS RELATED TO UNION MEMBERSHIP OR ACTIVITIES

(1) For purposes of Part X of the Employment Rights Act 1996 (unfair dismissal) the dismissal of an employee shall be regarded as unfair if the reason for it (or, if more than one, the principal reason) was that the employee—
(a) was, or proposed to become, a member of an independent trade union,

(b) had taken part, or proposed to take part, in the activities of an independent trade union at an appropriate time,

(ba) had made use, or proposed to make use, of trade union services at an appropriate time,

(bb) had failed to accept an offer made in contravention of section 145A or 145B, or

(c) was not a member of any trade union, or of a particular trade union, or of one of a number of particular trade unions, or had refused, or proposed to refuse, to become or remain a member.

(2) In subsection (1) "an appropriate time" means—
(a) a time outside the employee's working hours, or
(b) a time within his working hours at which, in accordance with arrangements agreed with or consent given by his employer, it is permissible for him to take part in the activities of a trade union or (as the case may be) make use of trade union services;
and for this purpose "working hours", in relation to an employee, means any time when, in accordance with his contract of employment, he is required to be at work.

(2A) In this section—
(a) "trade union services" means services made available to the employee by an independent trade union by virtue of his membership of the union, and
(b) references to an employee's "making use" of trade union services include his consenting to the raising of a matter on his behalf by an independent trade union of which he is a member.

(2B) Where the reason or one of the reasons for the dismissal was that an independent trade union (with or without the employee's consent) raised a matter on behalf of the employee as one of its members, the reason shall be treated as falling within subsection (1)(ba).

(3) Where the reason, or one of the reasons, for the dismissal was—
(a) the employee's refusal, or proposed refusal, to comply with a requirement (whether or not imposed by his contract of employment or in writing) that, in the event of his not being a member of any trade union, or of a particular trade union, or of one of a number of particular trade unions, he must make one or more payments, or
(b) his objection, or proposed objection, (however expressed) to the operation of a provision (whether or not forming part of his contract of employment or in writing) under which, in the event mentioned in paragraph (a), his employer is entitled to deduct one or more sums from the remuneration payable to him in respect of his employment,
the reason shall be treated as falling within subsection (1)(c).

(4) References in this section to being, becoming or ceasing to remain a member of a trade union include references to being, becoming or ceasing to remain a member of a particular branch or section of that union or of one of a number of particular branches or sections of that trade union.

(5) References in this section—
(a) to taking part in the activities of a trade union, and
(b) to services made available by a trade union by virtue of membership of the union,
shall be construed in accordance with subsection (4).

153 SELECTION FOR REDUNDANCY ON GROUNDS RELATED TO UNION MEMBERSHIP OR ACTIVITIES

Where the reason or principal reason for the dismissal of an employee was that he was redundant, but it is shown—

(a) that the circumstances constituting the redundancy applied equally to one or more other employees in the same undertaking who held positions similar to that held by him and who have not been dismissed by the employer, and

(b) that the reason (or, if more than one, the principal reason) why he was selected for dismissal was one of those specified in section 152(1),

the dismissal shall be regarded as unfair for the purposes of Part X of the Employment Rights Act 1996 (unfair dismissal).

156 MINIMUM BASIC AWARD

(1) Where a dismissal is unfair by virtue of section 152(1) or 153, the amount of the basic award of compensation, before any reduction is made under section 122 of the Employment Rights Act 1996, shall be not less than £4,700.

(2) But where the dismissal is unfair by virtue of section 153, subsection (2) of that section (reduction for contributory fault) applies in relation to so much of the basic award as is payable because of subsection (1) above.

168 TIME OFF FOR CARRYING OUT TRADE UNION DUTIES

(1) An employer shall permit an employee of his who is an official of an independent trade union recognised by the employer to take time off during his working hours for the purpose of carrying out any duties of his, as such an official, concerned with—
   (a) negotiations with the employer related to or connected with matters falling within section 178(2) (collective bargaining) in relation to which the trade union is recognised by the employer, or
   (b) the performance on behalf of employees of the employer of functions related to or connected with matters falling within that provision which the employer has agreed may be so performed by the trade union,
   (c) receipt of information from the employer and consultation by the employer under section 188 (redundancies) or under the Transfer of Undertakings (Protection of Employment) Regulations 2006, or
   (d) negotiations with a view to entering into an agreement under regulation 9 of the Transfer of Undertakings (Protection of Employment) Regulations 2006 that applies to employees of the employer, or
   (e) the performance on behalf of employees of the employer of functions related to or connected with the making of an agreement under that regulation.

(2) He shall also permit such an employee to take time off during his working hours for the purpose of undergoing training in aspects of industrial relations—
   (a) relevant to the carrying out of such duties as are mentioned in subsection (1), and
   (b) approved by the Trades Union Congress or by the independent trade union of which he is an official.

(3) The amount of time off which an employee is to be permitted to take under this section and the purposes for which, the occasions on which and any conditions subject to which time off may be so taken are those that are reasonable in all the circumstances having regard to any relevant provisions of a Code of Practice issued by ACAS.

(4)   An employee may present a complaint to an employment tribunal that his employer has failed to permit him to take time off as required by this section.

168A   TIME OFF FOR UNION LEARNING REPRESENTATIVES

(1)   An employer shall permit an employee of his who is—
(a)   a member of an independent trade union recognised by the employer, and
(b)   a learning representative of the trade union,
to take time off during his working hours for any of the following purposes.

(2)   The purposes are—
(a)   carrying on any of the following activities in relation to qualifying members of the trade union—
(i)   analysing learning or training needs,
(ii)   providing information and advice about learning or training matters,
(iii)   arranging learning or training, and
(iv)   promoting the value of learning or training,
(b)   consulting the employer about carrying on any such activities in relation to such members of the trade union,
(c)   preparing for any of the things mentioned in paragraphs (a) and (b).

(3)   Subsection (1) only applies if—
(a)   the trade union has given the employer notice in writing that the employee is a learning representative of the trade union, and
(b)   the training condition is met in relation to him.

(4)   The training condition is met if—
(a)   the employee has undergone sufficient training to enable him to carry on the activities mentioned in subsection (2), and the trade union has given the employer notice in writing of that fact,
(b)   the trade union has in the last six months given the employer notice in writing that the employee will be undergoing such training, or
(c)   within six months of the trade union giving the employer notice in writing that the employee will be undergoing such training, the employee has done so, and the trade union has given the employer notice of that fact.

(5)   Only one notice under subsection (4)(b) may be given in respect of any one employee.

(6)   References in subsection (4) to sufficient training to carry out the activities mentioned in subsection (2) are to training that is sufficient for those purposes having regard to any relevant provision of a Code of Practice issued by ACAS or the Secretary of State.

(7)   If an employer is required to permit an employee to take time off under subsection (1), he shall also permit the employee to take time off during his working hours for the following purposes—
(a)   undergoing training which is relevant to his functions as a learning representative, and
(b)   where the trade union has in the last six months given the employer notice under subsection (4)(b) in relation to the employee, undergoing such training as is mentioned in subsection (4)(a).

(8)   The amount of time off which an employee is to be permitted to take under this section and the purposes for which, the occasions on which and any conditions subject to which time off may be so taken are those that are reasonable in all the circumstances having regard to any relevant provision of a Code of Practice issued by ACAS or the Secretary of State.

(9)   An employee may present a complaint to an employment tribunal that his employer has failed to permit him to take time off as required by this section.

(10)   In subsection (2)(a), the reference to qualifying members of the trade union is to members of the trade union—
(a)   who are employees of the employer of a description in respect of which the union is recognised by the employer, and
(b)   in relation to whom it is the function of the union learning representative to act as such.

(11)   For the purposes of this section, a person is a learning representative of a trade union if he is appointed or elected as such in accordance with its rules.

169 PAYMENT FOR TIME OFF UNDER SECTION 168

(1)   An employer who permits an employee to take time off under section 168 or 168A shall pay him for the time taken off pursuant to the permission.

(2)   Where the employee's remuneration for the work he would ordinarily have been doing during that time does not vary with the amount of work done, he shall be paid as if he had worked at that work for the whole of that time.

(3)   Where the employee's remuneration for the work he would ordinarily have been doing during that time varies with the amount of work done, he shall be paid an amount calculated by reference to the average hourly earnings for that work.

The average hourly earnings shall be those of the employee concerned or, if no fair estimate can be made of those earnings, the average hourly earnings for work of that description of persons in comparable employment with the same employer or, if there are no such persons, a figure of average hourly earnings which is reasonable in the circumstances.

(4)   A right to be paid an amount under this section does not affect any right of an employee in relation to remuneration under his contract of employment, but—
(a)   any contractual remuneration paid to an employee in respect of a period of time off to which this section applies shall go towards discharging any liability of the employer under this section in respect of that period, and
(b)   any payment under this section in respect of a period shall go towards discharging any liability of the employer to pay contractual remuneration in respect of that period.

(5)   An employee may present a complaint to an employment tribunal that his employer has failed to pay him in accordance with this section.

170 TIME OFF FOR TRADE UNION ACTIVITIES

(1)   An employer shall permit an employee of his who is a member of an independent trade union recognised by the employer in respect of that description of employee to take time off during his working hours for the purpose of taking part in—
(a)   any activities of the union, and
(b)   any activities in relation to which the employee is acting as a representative of the union.

(2)   The right conferred by subsection (1) does not extent to activities which themselves consist of industrial action, whether or not in contemplation or furtherance of a trade dispute.

(2A) The right conferred by subsection (1) does not extend to time off for the purpose of acting as, or having access to services provided by, a learning representative of a trade union.

(2B) An employer shall permit an employee of his who is a member of an independent trade union recognised by the employer in respect of that description of employee to take time off during his working hours for the purpose of having access to services provided by a person in his capacity as a learning representative of the trade union.

(2C) Subsection (2B) only applies if the learning representative would be entitled to time off under subsection (1) of section 168A for the purpose of carrying on in relation to the employee activities of the kind mentioned in subsection (2) of that section.

(3) The amount of time off which an employee is to be permitted to take under this section and the purposes for which, the occasions on which and any conditions subject to which time off may be so taken are those that are reasonable in all the circumstances having regard to any relevant provisions of a Code of Practice issued by ACAS.

(4) An employee may present a complaint to an employment tribunal that his employer has failed to permit him to take time off as required by this section.

(5) For the purposes of this section—
   (a) a person is a learning representative of a trade union if he is appointed or elected as such in accordance with its rules, and
   (b) a person who is a learning representative of a trade union acts as such if he carries on the activities mentioned in section 168A(2) in that capacity.

171 TIME LIMIT FOR PROCEEDINGS

An employment tribunal shall not consider a complaint under section 168, 168A, 169 or 170 unless it is presented to the tribunal—
(a) within three months of the date when the failure occurred, or

(b) where the tribunal is satisfied that it was not reasonably practicable for the complaint to be presented within that period, within such further period as the tribunal considers reasonable.

172 REMEDIES

(1) Where the tribunal finds a complaint under section 168, 168A or 170 is well-founded, it shall make a declaration to that effect and may make an award of compensation to be paid by the employer to the employee.

(2) The amount of the compensation shall be such as the tribunal considers just and equitable in all the circumstances having regard to the employer's default in failing to permit time off to be taken by the employee and to any loss sustained by the employee which is attributable to the matters complained of.

(3) Where on a complaint under section 169 the tribunal finds that the employer has failed to pay the employee in accordance with that section, it shall order him to pay the amount which it finds to be due.

174 RIGHT NOT TO BE EXCLUDED OR EXPELLED FROM UNION

(1) An individual shall not be excluded or expelled from a trade union unless the exclusion or expulsion is permitted by this section.

(2)   The exclusion or expulsion of an individual from a trade union is permitted by this section if (and only if)—

  (a) he does not satisfy, or no longer satisfies, an enforceable membership requirement contained in the rules of the union,

  (b) he does not qualify, or no longer qualifies, for membership of the union by reason of the union operating only in a particular part or particular parts of Great Britain,

  (c) in the case of a union whose purpose is the regulation of relations between its members and one particular employer or a number of particular employers who are associated, he is not, or is no longer, employed by that employer or one of those employers, or

  (d) the exclusion or expulsion is entirely attributable to conduct of his (other than excluded conduct) and the conduct to which it is wholly or mainly attributable is not protected conduct.

(3)   A requirement in relation to membership of a union is "enforceable" for the purposes of subsection (2)(a) if it restricts membership solely by reference to one or more of the following criteria—

  (a) employment in a specified trade, industry or profession,

  (b) occupational description (including grade, level or category of appointment), and

  (c) possession of specified trade, industrial or professional qualifications or work experience.

(4)   For the purposes of subsection (2)(d) "excluded conduct", in relation to an individual, means—

  (a) conduct which consists in his being or ceasing to be, or having been or ceased to be, a member of another trade union,

  (b) conduct which consists in his being or ceasing to be, or having been or ceased to be, employed by a particular employer or at a particular place, or

  (c) conduct to which section 65 (conduct for which an individual may not be disciplined by a union) applies or would apply if the references in that section to the trade union which is relevant for the purposes of that section were references to any trade union.

(4A) For the purposes of subsection (2)(d) "protected conduct" is conduct which consists in the individual's being or ceasing to be, or having been or ceased to be, a member of a political party.

(4B) Conduct which consists of activities undertaken by an individual as a member of a political party is not conduct falling within subsection (4A).

(4C) Conduct which consists in an individual's being or having been a member of a political party is not conduct falling within subsection (4A) if membership of that political party is contrary to—

  (a) a rule of the trade union, or

  (b) an objective of the trade union.

(4D) For the purposes of subsection (4C)(b) in the case of conduct consisting in an individual's being a member of a political party, an objective is to be disregarded—

  (a) in relation to an exclusion, if it is not reasonably practicable for the objective to be ascertained by a person working in the same trade, industry or profession as the individual;

  (b) in relation to an expulsion, if it is not reasonably practicable for the objective to be ascertained by a member of the union.

(4E) For the purposes of subsection (4C)(b) in the case of conduct consisting in an individual's having been a member of a political party, an objective is to be disregarded—

(a) in relation to an exclusion, if at the time of the conduct it was not reasonably practicable for the objective to be ascertained by a person working in the same trade, industry or profession as the individual;

(b) in relation to an expulsion, if at the time of the conduct it was not reasonably practicable for the objective to be ascertained by a member of the union.

(4F) Where the exclusion or expulsion of an individual from a trade union is wholly or mainly attributable to conduct which consists of an individual's being or having been a member of a political party but which by virtue of subsection (4C) is not conduct falling within subsection (4A), the exclusion or expulsion is not permitted by virtue of subsection (2)(d) if any one or more of the conditions in subsection (4G) apply.

(4G) Those conditions are—
(a) the decision to exclude or expel is taken otherwise than in accordance with the union's rules;
(b) the decision to exclude or expel is taken unfairly;
(c) the individual would lose his livelihood or suffer other exceptional hardship by reason of not being, or ceasing to be, a member of the union.

(4H) For the purposes of subsection (4G)(b) a decision to exclude or expel an individual is taken unfairly if (and only if)—
(a) before the decision is taken the individual is not given—
(i)   notice of the proposal to exclude or expel him and the reasons for that proposal, and
(ii) a fair opportunity to make representations in respect of that proposal, or
(b) representations made by the individual in respect of that proposal are not considered fairly.

(5) An individual who claims that he has been excluded or expelled from a trade union in contravention of this section may present a complaint to an employment tribunals.

175 TIME LIMIT FOR PROCEEDINGS

An employment tribunal shall not entertain a complaint under section 174 unless it is presented—
(a) before the end of the period of six months beginning with the date of the exclusion or expulsion, or

(b) where the tribunal is satisfied that it was not reasonably practicable for the complaint to be presented before the end of that period, within such further period as the tribunal considers reasonable.

176 REMEDIES

(1) Where the employment tribunal finds a complaint under section 174 is well-founded, it shall make a declaration to that effect.

(1A) If a tribunal makes a declaration under subsection (1) and it appears to the tribunal that the exclusion or expulsion was mainly attributable to conduct falling within section 174(4A) it shall make a declaration to that effect.

(1B) If a tribunal makes a declaration under subsection (1A) and it appears to the tribunal that the other conduct to which the exclusion or expulsion was attributable consisted wholly or mainly of conduct of the complainant which was contrary to—

(a) a rule of the union, or

(b) an objective of the union,

it shall make a declaration to that effect.

(1C) For the purposes of subsection (1B), it is immaterial whether the complainant was a member of the union at the time of the conduct contrary to the rule or objective.

(1D) A declaration by virtue of subsection (1B)(b) shall not be made unless the union shows that, at the time of the conduct of the complainant which was contrary to the objective in question, it was reasonably practicable for that objective to be ascertained—

(a) if the complainant was not at that time a member of the union, by a person working in the same trade, industry or profession as the complainant, and

(b) if he was at that time a member of the union, by a member of the union.

(2) An individual whose complaint has been declared to be well-founded may make an application to an employment tribunal for an award of compensation to be paid to him by the union.

(3) The application shall not be entertained if made—

(a) before the end of the period of four weeks beginning with the date of the declaration under subsection (1), or

(b) after the end of the period of six months beginning with that date.

(4) The amount of compensation awarded shall, subject to the following provisions, be such as the employment tribunal considers just and equitable in all the circumstances.

(5) Where the employment tribunal finds that the exclusion or expulsion complained of was to any extent caused or contributed to by the action of the applicant, it shall reduce the amount of the compensation by such proportion as it considers just and equitable having regard to that finding.

(6) The amount of compensation calculated in accordance with subsections (4) and (5) shall not exceed the aggregate of—

(a) an amount equal to thirty times the limit for the time being imposed by section 227(1)(a) of the Employment Rights Act 1996 (maximum amount of a week's pay for basic award in unfair dismissal cases), and

(b) an amount equal to the limit for the time being imposed by section 124(1) of that Act (maximum compensatory award in such cases).

(6A) on the date on which the application was made the applicant had not been admitted or re-admitted to the union, the award shall not be less than £7,200.

(6B) Subsection (6A) does not apply in a case where the tribunal which made the declaration under subsection (1) also made declarations under subsections (1A) and (1B).

Part IV INDUSTRIAL RELATIONS

Chapter I COLLECTIVE BARGAINING

178 COLLECTIVE AGREEMENTS AND COLLECTIVE BARGAINING

(1) In this Act "collective agreement" means any agreement or arrangement made by or on behalf of one or more trade unions and one or more employers or employers' associations and relating to one or more of the matters specified below; and "collective bargaining" means negotiations relating to or connected with one or more of those matters.

(2) The matters referred to above are—

(a) terms and conditions of employment, or the physical conditions in which any workers are required to work;

(b) engagement or non-engagement, or termination or suspension of employment or the duties of employment, of one or more workers;

(c) allocation of work or the duties of employment between workers or groups of workers;

(d) matters of discipline;

(e) a worker's membership or non-membership of a trade union;

(f) facilities for officials of trade unions; and

(g) machinery for negotiation or consultation, and other procedures, relating to any of the above matters, including the recognition by employers or employers' associations of the right of a trade union to represent workers in such negotiation or consultation or in the carrying out of such procedures.

(3) In this Act "recognition", in relation to a trade union, means the recognition of the union by an employer, or two or more associated employers, to any extent, for the purpose of collective bargaining; and "recognised" and other related expressions shall be construed accordingly.

181 GENERAL DUTY OF EMPLOYERS TO DISCLOSE INFORMATION

(1) An employer who recognises an independent trade union shall, for the purposes of all stages of collective bargaining about matters, and in relation to descriptions of workers, in respect of which the union is recognised by him, disclose to representatives of the union, on request, the information required by this section.

In this section and sections 182 to 185 "representative", in relation to a trade union, means an official or other person authorised by the union to carry on such collective bargaining.

(2) The information to be disclosed is all information relating to the employer's undertaking which is in his possession, or that of an associated employer, and is information—

(a) without which the trade union representatives would be to a material extent impeded in carrying on collective bargaining with him, and

(b) which it would be in accordance with good industrial relations practice that he should disclose to them for the purposes of collective bargaining.

(3) A request by trade union representatives for information under this section shall, if the employer so requests, be in writing or be confirmed in writing.

(4) In determining what would be in accordance with good industrial relations practice, regard shall be had to the relevant provisions of any Code of Practice issued by ACAS, but not so as to exclude any other evidence of what that practice is.

(5) Information which an employer is required by virtue of this section to disclose to trade union representatives shall, if they so request, be disclosed or confirmed in writing.

182 RESTRICTIONS ON GENERAL DUTY

(1) An employer is not required by section 181 to disclose information—

(a) the disclosure of which would be against the interests of national security, or

(b) which he could not disclose without contravening a prohibition imposed by or under an enactment, or

(c) which has been communicated to him in confidence, or which he has otherwise obtained in consequence of the confidence reposed in him by another person, or

(d) which relates specifically to an individual (unless that individual has consented to its being disclosed), or

(e) the disclosure of which would cause substantial injury to his undertaking for reasons other than its effect on collective bargaining, or

(f) obtained by him for the purpose of bringing, prosecuting or defending any legal proceedings.

In formulating the provisions of any Code of Practice relating to the disclosure of information, ACAS shall have regard to the provisions of this subsection.

(2) In the performance of his duty under section 181 an employer is not required—

(a) to produce, or allow inspection of, any document (other than a document prepared for the purpose of conveying or confirming the information) or to make a copy of or extracts from any document, or

(b) to compile or assemble any information where the compilation or assembly would involve an amount of work or expenditure out of reasonable proportion to the value of the information in the conduct of collective bargaining.

183 COMPLAINT OF FAILURE TO DISCLOSE INFORMATION

(1) A trade union may present a complaint to the Central Arbitration Committee that an employer has failed—

(a) to disclose to representatives of the union information which he was required to disclose to them by section 181, or

(b) to confirm such information in writing in accordance with that section.

The complaint must be in writing and in such form as the Committee may require.

(2) If on receipt of a complaint the Committee is of the opinion that it is reasonably likely to be settled by conciliation, it shall refer the complaint to ACAS and shall notify the trade union and employer accordingly, whereupon ACAS shall seek to promote a settlement of the matter.

If a complaint so referred is not settled or withdrawn and ACAS is of the opinion that further attempts at conciliation are unlikely to result in a settlement, it shall inform the Committee of its opinion.

(3) If the complaint is not referred to ACAS or, if it is so referred, on ACAS informing the Committee of its opinion that further attempts at conciliation are unlikely to result in a settlement, the Committee shall proceed to hear and determine the complaint and shall make a declaration stating whether it finds the complaint well-founded, wholly or in part, and stating the reasons for its findings.

(4) On the hearing of a complaint any person who the Committee considers has a proper interest in the complaint is entitled to be heard by the Committee, but a failure to accord a hearing to a person other than the trade union and employer directly concerned does not affect the validity of any decision of the Committee in those proceedings.

(5) If the Committee finds the complaint wholly or partly well-founded, the declaration shall specify—

(a) the information in respect of which the Committee finds that the complaint is well founded,

(b) the date (or, if more than one, the earliest date) on which the employer refused or failed to disclose or, as the case may be, to confirm in writing, any of the information in question, and

(c) a period (not being less than one week from the date of the declaration) within which the employer ought to disclose that information, or, as the case may be, to confirm it in writing.

(6) On a hearing of a complaint under this section a certificate signed by or on behalf of a Minister of the Crown and certifying that a particular request for information could not be complied with except by disclosing information the disclosure of which would have been against the interests of national security shall be conclusive evidence of that fact.

A document which purports to be such a certificate shall be taken to be such a certificate unless the contrary is proved.

Chapter II PROCEDURE FOR HANDLING REDUNDANCIES

188 DUTY OF EMPLOYER TO CONSULT REPRESENTATIVES

(1) Where an employer is proposing to dismiss as redundant 20 or more employees at one establishment within a period of 90 days or less, the employer shall consult about the dismissals all the persons who are appropriate representatives of any of the employees who may be affected by the proposed dismissals or may be affected by measures taken in connection with those dismissals.

(1A) The consultation shall begin in good time and in any event—
(a) where the employer is proposing to dismiss 100 or more employees as mentioned in subsection (1), at least 90 days, and
(b) otherwise, at least 30 days,
before the first of the dismissals takes effect.

(1B) For the purposes of this section the appropriate representatives of any affected employees are—
(a) if the employees are of a description in respect of which an independent trade union is recognised by their employer, representatives of the trade union, or
(b) in any other case, whichever of the following employee representatives the employer chooses:—
(i) employee representatives appointed re elected by the affected employees otherwise than for the purposes of this section, who (having regard to the purposes for and the method by which they were appointed or elected) have authority from those employees to receive information and to be consulted about the proposed dismissals on their behalf;
(ii) employee representatives elected by the affected employees, for the purposes of this section, in an election satisfying the requirements of section 188A(1).

(2) The consultation shall include consultation about ways of—
(a) avoiding the dismissals,
(b) reducing the numbers of employees to be dismissed, and
(c) mitigating the consequences of the dismissals,
and shall be undertaken by the employer with a view to reaching agreement with the appropriate representatives.

(3) In determining how many employees an employer is proposing to dismiss as redundant no account shall be taken of employees in respect of whose proposed dismissals consultation has already begun.

(4) For the purposes of the consultation the employer shall disclose in writing to the appropriate representatives—
(a) the reasons for his proposals,

(b)   the numbers and description of employees whom it is proposed to dismiss as redundant,

(c)   the total number of employees of any such description employed by the employer at the establishment in question,

(d)   the proposed method of selecting the employees who may be dismissed,

(e)   the proposed method of carrying out the dismissals, with due regard to any agreed procedure, including the period over which the dismissals are to take effect and,

(f)   the proposed method of calculating the amount of any redundancy payments to be made (otherwise than in compliance with an obligation imposed by or by virtue of any enactment) to employees who may be dismissed.

(5)   That information shall be given to each of the appropriate representatives by being delivered to them, or sent by post to an address notified by them to the employer, or (in the case of representatives of a trade union) sent by post to the union at the address of its head or main office.

(5A)   The employer shall allow the appropriate representatives access to the affected employees and shall afford to those representatives such accommodation and other facilities as may be appropriate.

(7)   If in any case there are special circumstances which render it not reasonably practicable for the employer to comply with a requirement of subsection (1A), (2) or (4), the employer shall take all such steps towards compliance with that requirement as are reasonably practicable in those circumstances.

Where the decision leading to the proposed dismissals is that of a person controlling the employer (directly or indirectly), a failure on the part of that person to provide information to the employer shall not constitute special circumstances rendering it not reasonably practicable for the employer to comply with such a requirement.

(7A)   Where—

(a)   the employer has invited any of the affected employees to elect employee representatives, and

(b)   the invitation was issued long enough before the time when the consultation is required by subsection (1A)(a) or (b) to begin to allow them to elect representatives by that time,

the employer shall be treated as complying with the requirements of this section in relation to those employees if he complies with those requirements as soon as is reasonably practicable after the election of the representatives.

(7B)   If, after the employer has invited affected employees to elect representatives, the affected employees fail to do so within a reasonable time, he shall give to each affected employee the information set out in subsection (4).

(8)   This section does not confer any rights on a trade union, a representative or an employee except as provided by sections 189 to 192 below.

Part V INDUSTRIAL ACTION

219 PROTECTION FROM CERTAIN TORT LIABILITIES

(1)   An act done by a person in contemplation or furtherance of a trade dispute is not actionable in tort on the ground only—

(a)   that it induces another person to break a contract or interferes or induces another person to interfere with its performance, or

(b) that it consists in his threatening that a contract (whether one to which he is a party or not) will be broken or its performance interfered with, or that he will induce another person to break a contract or interfere with its performance.

(2) An agreement or combination by two or more persons to do or procure the doing of an act in contemplation or furtherance of a trade dispute is not actionable in tort if the act is one which if done without any such agreement or combination would not be actionable in tort.

(3) Nothing in subsections (1) and (2) prevents an act done in the course of picketing from being actionable in tort unless it is done in the course of attendance declared lawful by section 220 (peaceful picketing)

(4) Subsections (1) and (2) have effect subject to sections 222 to 225 (action excluded from protection) and to sections 226 (requirement of ballot before action by trade union) and 234A (requirement of notice to employer of industrial action); and in those sections "not protected" means excluded from the protection afforded by this section or, where the expression is used with reference to a particular person, excluded from that protection as respects that person.

220 PEACEFUL PICKETING

(1) It is lawful for a person in contemplation or furtherance of a trade dispute to attend—
(a) at or near his own place of work, or
(b) if he is an official of a trade union, at or near the place of work of a member of the union whom he is accompanying and whom he represents,
for the purpose only of peacefully obtaining or communicating information, or peacefully persuading any person to work or abstain from working.

(2) If a person works or normally works—
(a) otherwise than at any one place, or
(b) at a place the location of which is such that attendance there for a purpose mentioned in subsection (1) is impracticable,
his place of work for the purposes of that subsection shall be any premises of his employer from which he works or from which his work is administered.

(3) In the case of a worker not in employment where—
(a) his last employment was terminated in connection with a trade dispute, or
(b) the termination of his employment was one of the circumstances giving rise to a trade dispute,
in relation to that dispute his former place of work shall be treated for the purposes of subsection (1) as being his place of work.

(4) A person who is an official of a trade union by virtue only of having been elected or appointed to be a representative of some of the members of the union shall be regarded for the purposes of subsection (1) as representing only those members; but otherwise an official of a union shall be regarded for those purposes as representing all its members.

224 SECONDARY ACTION

(1) An act is not protected if one of the facts relied on for the purpose of establishing liability is that there has been secondary action which is not lawful picketing.

(2) There is secondary action in relation to a trade dispute when, and only when, a person—

    (a) induces another to break a contract of employment or interferes or induces another to interfere with its performance, or

    (b) threatens that a contract of employment under which he or another is employed will be broken or its performance interfered with, or that he will induce another to break a contract of employment or to interfere with its performance,

and the employer under the contract of employment is not the employer party to the dispute.

(3)   Lawful picketing means acts done in the course of such attendance as is declared lawful by section 220 (peaceful picketing)—

    (a) by a worker employed (or, in the case of a worker not in employment, last employed) by the employer party to the dispute, or

    (b) by a trade union official whose attendance is lawful by virtue of subsection (1)(b) of that section.

(4)   For the purposes of this section an employer shall not be treated as party to a dispute between another employer and workers of that employer; and where more than one employer is in dispute with his workers, the dispute between each employer and his workers shall be treated as a separate dispute.

In this subsection "worker" has the same meaning as in section 244 (meaning of "trade dispute").

(5)   An act in contemplation or furtherance of a trade dispute which is primary action in relation to that dispute may not be relied on as secondary action in relation to another trade dispute.

Primary action means such action as is mentioned in paragraph (a) or (b) of subsection (2) where the employer under the contract of employment is the employer party to the dispute.

(6)   In this section "contract of employment" includes any contract under which one person personally does work or performs services for another, and related expressions shall be construed accordingly.

226   REQUIREMENT OF BALLOT BEFORE ACTION BY TRADE UNION

(1)   An act done by a trade union to induce a person to take part, or continue to take part, in industrial action—

    (a) is not protected unless the industrial action has the support of a ballot, and

    (b) where section 226A falls to be complied with in relation to the person's employer, is not protected as respects the employer unless the trade union has complied with section 226A in relation to him.

In this section "the relevant time", in relation to an act by a trade union to induce a person to take part, or continue to take part, in industrial action, means the time at which proceedings are commenced in respect of the act.

(2)   Industrial action shall be regarded as having the support of a ballot only if—

    (a) the union has held a ballot in respect of the action—

        (i)   in relation to which the requirements of section 226B so far as applicable before and during the holding of the ballot were satisfied,

        (ii) in relation to which the requirements of sections 227 to 231 were satisfied, and

        (iii) in which the majority voting in the ballot answered "Yes" to the question applicable in accordance with section 229(2) to industrial action of the kind to which the act of inducement relates;

(b) such of the requirements of the following sections as have fallen to be satisfied at the relevant time have been satisfied, namely—
  (i) section 226B so far as applicable after the holding of the ballot, and
  (ii) section 231B;
(bb) section 232A does not prevent the industrial action from being regarded as having the support of the ballot; and
(c) the requirements of section 233 (calling of industrial action with support of ballot) are satisfied.
Any reference in this subsection to a requirement of a provision which is disapplied or modified by section 232 has effect subject to that section.

(3) Where separate workplace ballots are held by virtue of section 228(1)—
  (a) industrial action shall be regarded as having the support of a ballot if the conditions specified in subsection (2) are satisfied, and
  (b) the trade union shall be taken to have complied with the requirements relating to a ballot imposed by section 226A if those requirements are complied with,
  in relation to the ballot for the place of work of the person induced to take part, or continue to take part, in the industrial action.

(3A) If the requirements of section 231A fall to be satisfied in relation to an employer, as respects that employer industrial action shall not be regarded as having the support of a ballot unless those requirements are satisfied in relation to that employer.

(4) For the purposes of this section an inducement, in relation to a person, includes an inducement which is or would be ineffective, whether because of his unwillingness to be influenced by it or for any other reason.

226A NOTICE OF BALLOT AND SAMPLE VOTING PAPER FOR EMPLOYERS

(1) The trade union must take such steps as are reasonably necessary to ensure that—
  (a) not later than the seventh day before the opening day of the ballot, the notice specified in subsection (2), and
  (b) not later than the third day before the opening day of the ballot, the sample voting paper specified in subsection (2F),
  is received by every person who it is reasonable for the union to believe (at the latest time when steps could be taken to comply with paragraph (a)) will be the employer of persons who will be entitled to vote in the ballot.

(2) The notice referred to in paragraph (a) of subsection (1) is a notice in writing—
  (a) stating that the union intends to hold the ballot,
  (b) specifying the date which the union reasonably believes will be the opening day of the ballot, and
  (c) containing—
    (i) the lists mentioned in subsection (2A) and the figures mentioned in subsection (2B), together with an explanation of how those figures were arrived at, or
    (ii) where some or all of the employees concerned are employees from whose wages the employer makes deductions representing payments to the union, either those lists and figures and that explanation or the information mentioned in subsection (2C).

(2A) The lists are—
  (a) a list of the categories of employee to which the employees concerned belong, and
  (b) a list of the workplaces at which the employees concerned work.

(2B) The figures are—
   (a) the total number of employees concerned,
   (b) the number of the employees concerned in each of the categories in the list mentioned in subsection (2A)(a), and
   (c) the number of the employees concerned who work at each workplace in the list mentioned in subsection (2A)(b).

(2C) The information referred to in subsection (2)(c)(ii) is such information as will enable the employer readily to deduce—
   (a) the total number of employees concerned,
   (b) the categories of employee to which the employees concerned belong and the number of the employees concerned in each of those categories, and
   (c) the workplaces at which the employees concerned work and the number of them who work at each of those workplaces.

(2D) The lists and figures supplied under this section, or the information mentioned in subsection (2C) that is so supplied, must be as accurate as is reasonably practicable in the light of the information in the possession of the union at the time when it complies with subsection (1)(a).

(2E) For the purposes of subsection (2D) information is in the possession of the union if it is held, for union purposes—
   (a) in a document, whether in electronic form or any other form, and
   (b) in the possession or under the control of an officer or employee of the union.

(2F) The sample voting paper referred to in paragraph (b) of subsection (1) is—
   (a) a sample of the form of voting paper which is to be sent to the employees concerned, or
   (b) where the employees concerned are not all to be sent the same form of voting paper, a sample of each form of voting paper which is to be sent to any of them.

(2G) Nothing in this section requires a union to supply an employer with the names of the employees concerned.

(2H) In this section references to the "employees concerned" are references to those employees of the employer in question who the union reasonably believes will be entitled to vote in the ballot.

(2I) For the purposes of this section, the workplace at which an employee works is—
   (a) in relation to an employee who works at or from a single set of premises, those premises, and
   (b) in relation to any other employee, the premises with which his employment has the closest connection.

(4) In this section references to the opening day of the ballot are references to the first day when a voting paper is sent to any person entitled to vote in the ballot.

(5) This section, in its application to a ballot in which merchant seamen to whom section 230(2A) applies are entitled to vote, shall have effect with the substitution in subsection (2F), for references to the voting paper which is to be sent to the employees, of references to the voting paper which is to be sent or otherwise provided to them.

227 ENTITLEMENT TO VOTE IN BALLOT

(1) Entitlement to vote in the ballot must be accorded equally to all the members of the trade union who it is reasonable at the time of the ballot for the union to believe will be induced

by the union to take part or, as the case may be, to continue to take part in the industrial action in question, and to no others.

228 SEPARATE WORKPLACE BALLOTS

(1) Subject to subsection (2), this section applies if the members entitled to vote in a ballot by virtue of section 227 do not all have the same workplace.

(2) This section does not apply if the union reasonably believes that all those members have the same workplace.

(3) Subject to section 228A, a separate ballot shall be held for each workplace; and entitlement to vote in each ballot shall be accorded equally to, and restricted to, members of the union who—
(a) are entitled to vote by virtue of section 227, and
(b) have that workplace.

(4) In this section and section 228A "workplace" in relation to a person who is employed means—
(a) if the person works at or from a single set of premises, those premises, and
(b) in any other case, the premises with which the person's employment has the closest connection.

230 CONDUCT OF BALLOT

(1) Every person who is entitled to vote in the ballot must—
(a) be allowed to vote without interference from, or constraint imposed by, the union or any of its members, officials or employees, and
(b) so far as is reasonably practicable, be enabled to do so without incurring any direct cost to himself.

(2) Except as regards persons falling within subsection (2A), so far as is reasonably practicable, every person who is entitled to vote in the ballot must—
(a) have a voting paper sent to him by post at his home address or any other address which he has requested the trade union in writing to treat as his postal address; and
(b) be given a convenient opportunity to vote by post.

(2A) Subsection (2B) applies to a merchant seaman if the trade union reasonably believes that—
(a) he will be employed in a ship either at sea or at a place outside Great Britain at some time in the period during which votes may be cast, and
(b) it will be convenient for him to receive a voting paper and to vote while on the ship or while at a place where the ship is rather than in accordance with subsection (2).

(2B) Where this subsection applies to a merchant seaman he shall, if it is reasonably practicable—
(a) have a voting paper made available to him while on the ship or while at a place where the ship is, and
(b) be given an opportunity to vote while on the ship or while at a place where the ship is.

(2C) In subsections (2A) and (2B) "merchant seaman" means a person whose employment, or the greater part of it, is carried out on board sea-going ships.

(4) A ballot shall be conducted so as to secure that—
(a) so far as is reasonably practicable, those voting do so in secret, and
(b) the votes given in the ballot are fairly and accurately counted.
For the purposes of paragraph (b) an inaccuracy in counting shall be disregarded if it is accidental and on a scale which could not affect the result of the ballot.

231 INFORMATION AS TO RESULT OF BALLOT

As soon as is reasonably practicable after the holding of the ballot, the trade union shall take such steps as are reasonably necessary to ensure that all persons entitled to vote in the ballot are informed of the number of—

(a)   votes cast in the ballot,

(b)   individuals answering "Yes" to the question, or as the case may be, to each question,

(c)   individuals answering "No" to the question, or, as the case may be, to each question, and

(d)   spoiled voting papers.

233 CALLING OF INDUSTRIAL ACTION WITH SUPPORT OF BALLOT

(1)   Industrial action shall not be regarded as having the support of a ballot unless it is called by a specified person and the conditions specified below are satisfied.

(2)   A "specified person" means a person specified or of a description specified in the voting paper for the ballot in accordance with section 229(3).

(3)   The conditions are that—
    (a) there must have been no call by the trade union to take part or continue to take part in industrial action to which the ballot relates, or any authorisation or endorsement by the union of any such industrial action, before the date of the ballot;
    (b) there must be a call for industrial action by a specified person, and industrial action to which it relates must begin, before the ballot ceases to be effective in accordance with section 234.

(4)   For the purposes of this section a call shall be taken to have been made by a trade union if it was authorised or endorsed by the union; and the provisions of section 20(2) to (4) apply for the purpose of determining whether a call, or industrial action, is to be taken to have been so authorised or endorsed.

234 PERIOD AFTER WHICH BALLOT CEASES TO BE EFFECTIVE

(1)   Subject to the following provisions, a ballot ceases to be effective for the purposes of section 233(3)(b) in relation to industrial action by members of a trade union at the end of the period, beginning with the date of the ballot—
    (a) of four weeks, or
    (b) of such longer duration not exceeding eight weeks as is agreed between the union and the members' employer."

(2)   Where for the whole or part of that period the calling or organising of industrial action is prohibited—
    (a) by virtue of a court order which subsequently lapses or is discharged, recalled or set aside, or
    (b) by virtue of an undertaking given to a court by any person from which he is subsequently released or by which he ceases to be bound,
the trade union may apply to the court for an order that the period during which the prohibition had effect shall not count towards the period referred to in subsection (1).

(3)   The application must be made forthwith upon the prohibition ceasing to have effect—
    (a) to the court by virtue of whose decision it ceases to have effect, or
    (b) where an order lapses or an undertaking ceases to bind without any such decision, to the court by which the order was made or to which the undertaking was given;

and no application may be made after the end of the period of eight weeks beginning with the date of the ballot.

(4)   The court shall not make an order if it appears to the court—
   (a)   that the result of the ballot no longer represents the views of the union members concerned, or
   (b)   that an event is likely to occur as a result of which those members would vote against industrial action if another ballot were to be held.

(5)   No appeal lies from the decision of the court to make or refuse an order under this section.

(6)   The period between the making of an application under this section and its determination does not count towards the period referred to in subsection (1).

But a ballot shall not by virtue of this subsection (together with any order of the court) be regarded as effective for the purposes of section 233(3)(b) after the end of the period of twelve weeks beginning with the date of the ballot.

234A NOTICE TO EMPLOYERS OF INDUSTRIAL ACTION

(1)   An act done by a trade union to induce a person to take part, or continue to take part, in industrial action is not protected as respects his employer unless the union has taken or takes such steps as are reasonably necessary to ensure that the employer receives within the appropriate period a relevant notice covering the act.

(2)   Subsection (1) imposes a requirement in the case of an employer only if it is reasonable for the union to believe, at the latest time when steps could be taken to ensure that he receives such a notice, that he is the employer of persons who will be or have been induced to take part, or continue to take part, in the industrial action.

(3)   For the purposes of this section a relevant notice is a notice in writing which—
   (a)   contains—
      (i)   the lists mentioned in subsection (3A) and the figures mentioned in subsection (3B), together with an explanation of how those figures were arrived at, or
      (ii)   where some or all of the affected employees are employees from whose wages the employer makes deductions representing payments to the union, either those lists and figures and that explanation or the information mentioned in subsection (3C), and
   (b)   states whether industrial action is intended to be continuous or discontinuous and specifies—
      (i)   where it is to be continuous, the intended date for any of the affected employees to begin to take part in the action,
      (ii)   where it is to be discontinuous, the intended dates for any of the affected employees to take part in the action.

(3A)   The lists referred to in subsection (3)(a) are—
   (a)   a list of the categories of employee to which the affected employees belong, and
   (b)   a list of the workplaces at which the affected employees work.

(3B)   The figures referred to in subsection (3)(a) are—
   (a)   the total number of the affected employees,
   (b)   the number of the affected employees in each of the categories in the list mentioned in subsection (3A)(a), and
   (c)   the number of the affected employees who work at each workplace in the list mentioned in subsection (3A)(b).

(3C) The information referred to in subsection (3)(a)(ii) is such information as will enable the employer readily to deduce—
    (a) the total number of the affected employees,
    (b) the categories of employee to which the affected employees belong and the number of the affected employees in each of those categories, and
    (c) the workplaces at which the affected employees work and the number of them who work at each of those workplaces.

(3D) The lists and figures supplied under this section, or the information mentioned in subsection (3C) that is so supplied, must be as accurate as is reasonably practicable in the light of the information in the possession of the union at the time when it complies with subsection (1).

(3E) For the purposes of subsection (3D) information is in the possession of the union if it is held, for union purposes—
    (a) in a document, whether in electronic form or any other form, and
    (b) in the possession or under the control of an officer or employee of the union.

(3F) Nothing in this section requires a union to supply an employer with the names of the affected employees.

(4) For the purposes of subsection (1) the appropriate period is the period—
    (a) beginning with the day when the union satisfies the requirement of section 231A in relation to the ballot in respect of the industrial action, and
    (b) ending with the seventh day before the day, or before the first of the days, specified in the relevant notice.

(5) For the purposes of subsection (1) a relevant notice covers an act done by the union if the person induced falls within a notified category of employee and the workplace at which he works is a notified workplace and—
    (a) where he is induced to take part or continue to take part in industrial action which the union intends to be continuous, if—
        (i)   the notice states that the union intends the industrial action to be continuous, and
        (ii) there is no participation by him in the industrial action before the date specified in the notice in consequence of any inducement by the union not covered by a relevant notice; and
    (b) where he is induced to take part or continue to take part in industrial action which the union intends to be discontinuous, if there is no participation by him in the industrial action on a day not so specified in consequence of any inducement by the union not covered by a relevant notice.

(5B) In subsection (5)—
    (a) a "notified category of employee" means—
        (i)   a category of employee that is listed in the notice, or
        (ii) where the notice contains the information mentioned in subsection (3C), a category of employee that the employer (at the time he receives the notice) can readily deduce from the notice is a category of employee to which some or all of the affected employees belong, and
    (b) a "notified workplace" means—
        (i)   a workplace that is listed in the notice, or
        (ii) where the notice contains the information mentioned in subsection (3C), a workplace that the employer (at the time he receives the notice) can readily deduce from the notice is the workplace at which some or all of the affected employees work.

(5C) In this section references to the "affected employees" are references to those employees of the employer who the union reasonably believes will be induced by the union, or have been so induced, to take part or continue to take part in the industrial action.

(5D) For the purposes of this section, the workplace at which an employee works is—
(a) in relation to an employee who works at or from a single set of premises, those premises, and
(b) in relation to any other employee, the premises with which his employment has the closest connection.

(6) For the purposes of this section—
(a) a union intends industrial action to be discontinuous if it intends it to take place only on some days on which there is an opportunity to take the action, and
(b) a union intends industrial action to be continuous if it intends it to be not so restricted.

(7) Subject to subsections (7A) and (7B) where—
(a) continuous industrial action which has been authorised or endorsed by a union ceases to be so authorised or endorsed, and
(b) the industrial action has at a later date again been authorised or endorsed by the union (whether as continuous or discontinuous action),
no relevant notice covering acts done to induce persons to take part in the earlier action shall operate to cover acts done to induce persons to take part in the action authorised or endorsed at the later date and this section shall apply in relation to an act to induce a person to take part, or continue to take part, in the industrial action after that date as if the references in subsection (3)(b)(i) to the industrial action were to the industrial action taking place after that date.

(7A) Subsection (7) shall not apply where industrial action ceases to be authorised or endorsed in order to enable the union to comply with a court order or an undertaking given to a court.

(7B) Subsection (7) shall not apply where—
(a) a union agrees with an employer, before industrial action ceases to be authorised or endorsed, that it will cease to be authorised or endorsed with effect from a date specified in the agreement ("the suspension date") and that it may again be authorised or endorsed with effect from a date not earlier than a date specified in the agreement ("the resumption date"),
(b) the action ceases to be authorised or endorsed with effect from the suspension date, and
(c) the action is again authorised or endorsed with effect from a date which is not earlier than the resumption date or such later date as may be agreed between the union and the employer.

(8) The requirement imposed on a trade union by subsection (1) shall be treated as having been complied with if the steps were taken by other relevant persons or committees whose acts were authorised or endorsed by the union and references to the belief or intention of the union in subsection (2) or, as the case may be, subsections (3), (5) (5C) and (6) shall be construed as references to the belief or the intention of the person or committee taking the steps.

(9) The provisions of section 20(2) to (4) apply for the purpose of determining for the purposes of subsection (1) who are relevant persons or committees and whether the trade union is to be taken to have authorised or endorsed the steps the person or committee took and for the purposes of subsections (7) to (7B) whether the trade union is to be taken to have authorised or endorsed the industrial action.

237 DISMISSAL OF THOSE TAKING PART IN UNOFFICIAL INDUSTRIAL ACTION

(1)   An employee has no right to complain of unfair dismissal if at the time of dismissal he was taking part in an unofficial strike or other unofficial industrial action.

(1A)   Subsection (1) does not apply to the dismissal of the employee if it is shown that the reason (or, if more than one, the principal reason) for the dismissal or, in a redundancy case, for selecting the employee for dismissal was one of those specified in or under—
    (a)   section 98B, 99, 100, 101A(d), 103, 103A or 104C of the Employment Rights Act 1996 (dismissal in jury service, family, health and safety, working time, employee representative, protected disclosure and flexible working cases),
    (b)   section 104 of that Act in its application in relation to time off under section 57A of that Act (dependants).
In this subsection "redundancy case" has the meaning given in section 105(9) of that Act; and a reference to a specified reason for dismissal includes a reference to specified circumstances of dismissal.

(2)   A strike or other industrial action is unofficial in relation to an employee unless—
    (a)   he is a member of a trade union and the action is authorised or endorsed by that union, or
    (b)   he is not a member of a trade union but there are among those taking part in the industrial action members of a trade union by which the action has been authorised or endorsed.
Provided that, a strike or other industrial action shall not be regarded as unofficial if none of those taking part in it are members of a trade union.

(3)   The provisions of section 20(2) apply for the purpose of determining whether industrial action is to be taken to have been authorised or endorsed by a trade union.

(4)   The question whether industrial action is to be so taken in any case shall be determined by reference to the facts as at the time of dismissal.

Provided that, where an act is repudiated as mentioned in section 21, industrial action shall not thereby be treated as unofficial before the end of the next working day after the day on which the repudiation takes place.

(5)   In this section the "time of dismissal" means—
    (a)   where the employee's contract of employment is terminated by notice, when the notice is given,
    (b)   where the employee's contract of employment is terminated without notice, when the termination takes effect, and
    (c)   where the employee is employed under a contract for a fixed term which expires without being renewed under the same contract, when that term expires;
and a "working day" means any day which is not a Saturday or Sunday, Christmas Day, Good Friday or a bank holiday under the Banking and Financial Dealings Act 1971.

(6)   For the purposes of this section membership of a trade union for purposes unconnected with the employment in question shall be disregarded; but an employee who was a member of a trade union when he began to take part in industrial action shall continue to be treated as a member for the purpose of determining whether that action is unofficial in relation to him or another notwithstanding that he may in fact have ceased to be a member.

238 DISMISSALS IN CONNECTION WITH OTHER INDUSTRIAL ACTION

(1) This section applies in relation to an employee who has a right to complain of unfair dismissal (the "complainant") and who claims to have been unfairly dismissed, where at the date of the dismissal—
(a) the employer was conducting or instituting a lock-out, or
(b) the complainant was taking part in a strike or other industrial action.

(2) In such a case an employment tribunal shall not determine whether the dismissal was fair or unfair unless it is shown—
(a) that one or more relevant employees of the same employer have not been dismissed, or
(b) that a relevant employee has before the expiry of the period of three months beginning with the date of his dismissal been offered re-engagement and that the complainant has not been offered re-engagement.

(2A) Subsection (2) does not apply to the dismissal of the employee if it is shown that the reason (or, if more than one, the principal reason) for the dismissal or, in a redundancy case, for selecting the employee for dismissal was one of those specified in or under—
(a) section 98B, 99, 100, 101A(d), 103 or 104C of the Employment Rights Act 1996 (dismissal in jury service, family, health and safety, working time, employee representative and flexible working cases),
(b) section 104 of that Act in its application in relation to time off under section 57A of that Act (dependants).
In this subsection "redundancy case" has the meaning given in section 105(9) of that Act; and a reference to a specified reason for dismissal includes a reference to specified circumstances of dismissal.

(2B) Subsection (2) does not apply in relation to an employee who is regarded as unfairly dismissed by virtue of section 238A below.

(3) For this purpose "relevant employees" means—
(a) in relation to a lock-out, employees who were directly interested in the dispute in contemplation or furtherance of which the lock-out occurred, and
(b) in relation to a strike or other industrial action, those employees at the establishment of the employer at or from which the complainant works who at the date of his dismissal were taking part in the action.
Nothing in section 237 (dismissal of those taking part in unofficial industrial action) affects the question who are relevant employees for the purposes of this section.

(4) An offer of re-engagement means an offer (made either by the original employer or by a successor of that employer or an associated employer) to re-engage an employee, either in the job which he held immediately before the date of dismissal or in a different job which would be reasonably suitable in his case.

(5) In this section "date of dismissal" means—
(a) where the employee's contract of employment was terminated by notice, the date on which the employer's notice was given, and
(b) in any other case, the effective date of termination.

SCHEDULE A1 COLLECTIVE BARGAINING RECOGNITION

Part I RECOGNITION

1

A trade union (or trade unions) seeking recognition to be entitled to conduct collective bargaining on behalf of a group or groups of workers may make a request in accordance with this Part of this Schedule.

2

(1) This paragraph applies for the purposes of this Part of this Schedule.

(2) References to the bargaining unit are to the group of workers concerned (or the groups taken together).

(3) References to the proposed bargaining unit are to the bargaining unit proposed in the request for recognition.

(3A) References to an appropriate bargaining unit's being decided by the CAC are to a bargaining unit's being decided by the CAC to be appropriate under paragraph 19(2) or (3) or 19A(2) or (3).

(4) References to the employer are to the employer of the workers constituting the bargaining unit concerned.

(5) References to the parties are to the union (or unions) and the employer.

3

(1) This paragraph applies for the purposes of this Part of this Schedule.

(2) The meaning of collective bargaining given by section 178(1) shall not apply.

(3) References to collective bargaining are to negotiations relating to pay, hours and holidays; but this has effect subject to sub-paragraph (4).

(4) If the parties agree matters as the subject of collective bargaining, references to collective bargaining are to negotiations relating to the agreed matters; and this is the case whether the agreement is made before or after the time when the CAC issues a declaration, or the parties agree, that the union is (or unions are) entitled to conduct collective bargaining on behalf of a bargaining unit.

(5) Sub-paragraph (4) does not apply in construing paragraph 31(3).

(6) Sub-paragraphs (2) to (5) do not apply in construing paragraph 35 or 44.

4

(1) The union or unions seeking recognition must make a request for recognition to the employer.

(2) Paragraphs 5 to 9 apply to the request.

5

The request is not valid unless it is received by the employer.

6

The request is not valid unless the union (or each of the unions) has a certificate of independence.

7

(1)   The request is not valid unless the employer, taken with any associated employer or employers, employs—
    (a)   at least 21 workers on the day the employer receives the request, or
    (b)   an average of at least 21 workers in the 13 weeks ending with that day.

(2)   To find the average under sub-paragraph (1)(b)—
    (a)   take the number of workers employed in each of the 13 weeks (including workers not employed for the whole of the week);
    (b)   aggregate the 13 numbers;
    (c)   divide the aggregate by 13.

(3)   For the purposes of sub-paragraph (1)(a) any worker employed by an associated company incorporated outside Great Britain must be ignored unless the day the request was made fell within a period during which he ordinarily worked in Great Britain.

(4)   For the purposes of sub-paragraph (1)(b) any worker employed by an associated company incorporated outside Great Britain must be ignored in relation to a week unless the whole or any part of that week fell within a period during which he ordinarily worked in Great Britain.

(5)   For the purposes of sub-paragraphs (3) and (4) a worker who is employed on board a ship registered in the register maintained under section 8 of the Merchant Shipping Act 1995 shall be treated as ordinarily working in Great Britain unless—
    (a)   the ship's entry in the register specifies a port outside Great Britain as the port to which the vessel is to be treated as belonging,
    (b)   the employment is wholly outside Great Britain, or
    (c)   the worker is not ordinarily resident in Great Britain.

(6)   The Secretary of State may by order—
    (a)   provide that sub-paragraphs (1) to (5) are not to apply, or are not to apply in specified circumstances, or
    (b)   vary the number of workers for the time being specified in sub-paragraph (1);
and different provision may be made for different circumstances.

(7)   An order under sub-paragraph (6)—
    (a)   shall be made by statutory instrument, and
    (b)   may include supplementary, incidental, saving or transitional provisions.

(8)   No such order shall be made unless a draft of it has been laid before Parliament and approved by a resolution of each House of Parliament.

10

(1)   If before the end of the first period the parties agree a bargaining unit and that the union is (or unions are) to be recognised as entitled to conduct collective bargaining on behalf of the unit, no further steps are to be taken under this Part of this Schedule.

(2)   If before the end of the first period the employer informs the union (or unions) that the employer does not accept the request but is willing to negotiate, sub-paragraph (3) applies

(3)   The parties may conduct negotiations with a view to agreeing a bargaining unit and that the union is (or unions are) to be recognised as entitled to conduct collective bargaining on behalf of the unit.

(4)   If such an agreement is made before the end of the second period no further steps are to be taken under this Part of this Schedule.

(5)   The employer and the union (or unions) may request ACAS to assist in conducting the negotiations.

(6)   The first period is the period of 10 working days starting with the day after that on which the employer receives the request for recognition.

(7)   The second period is—
(a)   the period of 20 working days starting with the day after that on which the first period ends, or
(b)   such longer period (so starting) as the parties may from time to time agree.

11

(1)   This paragraph applies if—
(a)   before the end of the first period the employer fails to respond to the request, or
(b)   before the end of the first period the employer informs the union (or unions) that the employer does not accept the request (without indicating a willingness to negotiate).

(2)   The union (or unions) may apply to the CAC to decide both these questions—
(a)   whether the proposed bargaining unit is appropriate;
(b)   whether the union has (or unions have) the support of a majority of the workers constituting the appropriate bargaining unit.

12

(1)   Sub-paragraph (2) applies if—
(a)   the employer informs the union (or unions) under paragraph 10(2), and
(b)   no agreement is made before the end of the second period.

(2)   The union (or unions) may apply to the CAC to decide both these questions—
(a)   whether the proposed bargaining unit is appropriate;
(b)   whether the union has (or unions have) the support of a majority of the workers constituting the appropriate bargaining unit.

(3)   Sub-paragraph (4) applies if—
(a)   the employer informs the union (or unions) under paragraph 10(2), and
(b)   before the end of the second period the parties agree a bargaining unit but not that the union is (or unions are) to be recognised as entitled to conduct collective bargaining on behalf of the unit.

(4)   The union (or unions) may apply to the CAC to decide the question whether the union has (or unions have) the support of a majority of the workers constituting the bargaining unit.

(5)   But no application may be made under this paragraph if within the period of 10 working days starting with the day after that on which the employer informs the union (or unions)

under paragraph 10(2) the employer proposes that ACAS be requested to assist in conducting the negotiations and—

(a) the union rejects (or unions reject) the proposal, or

(b) the union fails (or unions fail) to accept the proposal within the period of 10 working days starting with the day after that on which the employer makes the proposal.

13

The CAC must give notice to the parties of receipt of an application under 11 or 12.

14

(1) This paragraph applies if—

(a) two or more relevant applications are made,

(b) at least one worker falling within one of the relevant bargaining units also falls within the other relevant bargaining unit (or units), and

(c) the CAC has not accepted any of the applications.

(2) A relevant application is an application under paragraph 11 or 12.

(3) In relation to a relevant application, the relevant bargaining unit is—

(a) the proposed bargaining unit, where the application is under paragraph 11(2) or 12(2);

(b) the agreed bargaining unit, where the application is under paragraph 12(4).

(4) Within the acceptance period the CAC must decide, with regard to each relevant application, whether the 10 per cent test is satisfied.

(5) The 10 per cent test is satisfied if members of the union (or unions) constitute at least 10 per cent of the workers constituting the relevant bargaining unit.

(6) The acceptance period is—

(a) the period of 10 working days starting with the day after that on which the CAC receives the last relevant application, or

(b) such longer period (so starting) as the CAC may specify to the parties by notice containing reasons for the extension.

(7) If the CAC decides that—

(a) the 10 per cent test is satisfied with regard to more than one of the relevant applications, or

(b) the 10 per cent test is satisfied with regard to none of the relevant applications,

the CAC must not accept any of the relevant applications.

(8) If the CAC decides that the 10 per cent test is satisfied with regard to one only of the relevant applications the CAC—

(a) must proceed under paragraph 15 with regard to that application, and

(b) must not accept any of the other relevant applications.

(9) The CAC must give notice of its decision to the parties.

(10) If by virtue of this paragraph the CAC does not accept an application, no further steps are to be taken under this Part of this Schedule in relation to that application.

18

(1) If the CAC accepts an application under paragraph 11(2) or 12(2) it must try to help the parties to reach within the appropriate period an agreement as to what the appropriate bargaining unit is.

(2) The appropriate period is (subject to any notice under sub-paragraph (3), (4) or (5))—
  (a) the period of 20 working days starting with the day after that on which the CAC gives notice of acceptance of the application, or
  (b) such longer period (so starting) as the CAC may specify to the parties by notice containing reasons for the extension.

(3) If, during the appropriate period, the CAC concludes that there is no reasonable prospect of the parties' agreeing an appropriate bargaining unit before the time when (apart from this sub-paragraph) the appropriate period would end, the CAC may, by a notice given to the parties, declare that the appropriate period ends with the date of the notice.

(4) If, during the appropriate period, the parties apply to the CAC for a declaration that the appropriate period is to end with a date (specified in the application) which is earlier than the date with which it would otherwise end, the CAC may, by a notice given to the parties, declare that the appropriate period ends with the specified date.

(5) If the CAC has declared under sub-paragraph (4) that the appropriate period ends with a specified date, it may before that date by a notice given to the parties specify a later date with which the appropriate period ends.

(6) A notice under sub-paragraph (3) must contain reasons for reaching the conclusion mentioned in that sub-paragraph.

(7) A notice under sub-paragraph (5) must contain reasons for the extension of the appropriate period.

18A

(1) This paragraph applies if the CAC accepts an application under paragraph 11(2) or 12(2).

(2) Within 5 working days starting with the day after that on which the CAC gives the employer notice of acceptance of the application, the employer must supply the following information to the union (or unions) and the CAC—
  (a) a list of the categories of worker in the proposed bargaining unit,
  (b) a list of the workplaces at which the workers in the proposed bargaining unit work, and
  (c) the number of workers the employer reasonably believes to be in each category at each workplace.

(3) The lists and numbers supplied under this paragraph must be as accurate as is reasonably practicable in the light of the information in the possession of the employer at the time when he complies with sub-paragraph (2).

(4) The lists and numbers supplied to the union (or unions) and to the CAC must be the same.

(5) For the purposes of this paragraph, the workplace at which a worker works is—
  (a) if the person works at or from a single set of premises, those premises, and
  (b) in any other case, the premises with which the worker's employment has the closest connection.

19

(1) This paragraph applies if—
   (a) the CAC accepts an application under paragraph 11(2) or 12(2),
   (b) the parties have not agreed an appropriate bargaining unit at the end of the appropriate period (defined by paragraph 18), and
   (c) at the end of that period either no request under paragraph 19A(1)(b) has been made or such a request has been made but the condition in paragraph 19A(1)(c) has not been met.

(2) Within the decision period, the CAC must decide whether the proposed bargaining unit is appropriate.

(3) If the CAC decides that the proposed bargaining unit is not appropriate, it must also decide within the decision period a bargaining unit which is appropriate.

(4) The decision period is—
   (a) the period of 10 working days starting with the day after that with which the appropriate period ends, or
   (b) such longer period (so starting) as the CAC may specify to the parties by notice containing reasons for the extension.

19A

(1) This paragraph applies if—
   (a) the CAC accepts an application under paragraph 11(2) or 12(2),
   (b) during the appropriate period (defined by paragraph 18), the CAC is requested by the union (or unions) to make a decision under this paragraph, and
   (c) the CAC is, either at the time the request is made or at a later time during the appropriate period, of the opinion that the employer has failed to comply with the duty imposed by paragraph 18A.

(2) Within the decision period, the CAC must decide whether the proposed bargaining unit is appropriate.

(3) If the CAC decides that the proposed bargaining unit is not appropriate, it must also decide within the decision period a bargaining unit which is appropriate.

(4) The decision period is—
   (a) the period of 10 working days starting with the day after the day on which the request is made, or
   (b) such longer period (so starting) as the CAC may specify to the parties by notice containing reasons for the extension.

19B

(1) This paragraph applies if the CAC has to decide whether a bargaining unit is appropriate for the purposes of paragraph 19(2) or (3) or 19A(2) or (3).

(2) The CAC must take these matters into account—
   (a) the need for the unit to be compatible with effective management;
   (b) the matters listed in sub-paragraph (3), so far as they do not conflict with that need.

(3) The matters are—
   (a) the views of the employer and of the union (or unions);
   (b) existing national and local bargaining arrangements;

    (c) the desirability of avoiding small fragmented bargaining units within an undertaking;

    (d) the characteristics of workers falling within the bargaining unit under consideration and of any other employees of the employer whom the CAC considers relevant;

    (e) the location of workers.

(4)   In taking an employer's views into account for the purpose of deciding whether the proposed bargaining unit is appropriate, the CAC must take into account any view the employer has about any other bargaining unit that he considers would be appropriate.

(5)   The CAC must give notice of its decision to the parties.

20

(1)   This paragraph applies if—

    (a) the CAC accepts an application under paragraph 11(2) or 12(2),

    (b) the parties have agreed an appropriate bargaining unit at the end of the appropriate period (defined by paragraph 18), or the CAC has decided an appropriate bargaining unit, and

    (c) that bargaining unit differs from the proposed bargaining unit.

(2)   Within the decision period the CAC must decide whether the application is invalid within the terms of paragraphs 43 to 50.

(3)   In deciding whether the application is invalid, the CAC must consider any evidence which it has been given by the employer or the union (or unions).

(4)   If the CAC decides that the application is invalid—

    (a) the CAC must give notice of its decision to the parties,

    (b) the CAC must not proceed with the application, and

    (c) no further steps are to be taken under this Part of this Schedule.

(5)   If the CAC decides that the application is not invalid it must—

    (a) proceed with the application, and

    (b) give notice to the parties that it is so proceeding.

(6)   The decision period is—

    (a) the period of 10 working days starting with the day after that on which the parties agree an appropriate bargaining unit or the CAC decides an appropriate bargaining unit, or

    (b) such longer period (so starting) as the CAC may specify to the parties by notice containing reasons for the extension.

21

(1)   This paragraph applies if—

    (a) the CAC accepts an application under paragraph 11(2) or 12(2),

    (b) the parties have agreed an appropriate bargaining unit at the end of the appropriate period (defined by paragraph 18), or the CAC has decided an appropriate bargaining unit, and

    (c) that bargaining unit is the same as the proposed bargaining unit.

(2)   This paragraph also applies if the CAC accepts an application under paragraph 12(4).

(3)   The CAC must proceed with the application.

22

(1) This paragraph applies if—
  (a) the CAC proceeds with an application in accordance with paragraph 20 or 21 (and makes no declaration under paragraph 19F(5)), and
  (b) the CAC is satisfied that a majority of the workers constituting the bargaining unit are members of the union (or unions).

(2) The CAC must issue a declaration that the union is (or unions are) recognised as entitled to conduct collective bargaining on behalf of the workers constituting the bargaining unit.

(3) But if any of the three qualifying conditions is fulfilled, instead of issuing a declaration under sub-paragraph (2) the CAC must give notice to the parties that it intends to arrange for the holding of a secret ballot in which the workers constituting the bargaining unit are asked whether they want the union (or unions) to conduct collective bargaining on their behalf.

(4) These are the three qualifying conditions—
  (a) the CAC is satisfied that a ballot should be held in the interests of good industrial relations;
  (b) the CAC has evidence, which it considers to be credible, from a significant number of the union members within the bargaining unit that they do not want the union (or unions) to conduct collective bargaining on their behalf;
  (c) membership evidence is produced which leads the CAC to conclude that there are doubts whether a significant number of the union members within the bargaining unit want the union (or unions) to conduct collective bargaining on their behalf.

(5) The notification period is, in relation to notification by the union (or unions)—
  (a) the period of 10 working days starting with the day on which the union (or last of the unions) receives the CAC's notice under paragraph 22(3) or 23(2), or
  (b) such longer period so starting as the CAC may specify to the parties by notice.

(6) The notification period is, in relation to notification by the union (or unions) and the employer—
  (a) the period of 10 working days starting with the day on which the last of the parties receives the CAC's notice under paragraph 22(3) or 23(2), or
  (b) such longer period so starting as the CAC may specify to the parties by notice.

(7) The CAC may give a notice under sub-paragraph (5)(b) or (6)(b) only if the parties have applied jointly to it for the giving of such a notice.

23

(1) This paragraph applies if—
  (a) the CAC proceeds with an application in accordance with paragraph 20 or 21 (and makes no declaration under paragraph 19F(5)), and
  (b) the CAC is not satisfied that a majority of the workers constituting the bargaining unit are members of the union (or unions).

(2) The CAC must give notice to the parties that it intends to arrange for the holding of a secret ballot in which the workers constituting the bargaining unit are asked whether they want the union (or unions) to conduct collective bargaining on their behalf.

24

(1) This paragraph applies if the CAC gives notice under paragraph 22(3) or 23(2).

(2)   Within the notification period—
(a) the union (or unions), or
(b) the union (or unions) and the employer,
may notify the CAC that the party making the notification does not (or the parties making the notification do not) want the CAC to arrange for the holding of the ballot.

(3)   If the CAC is so notified—
(a) it must not arrange for the holding of the ballot,
(b) it must inform the parties that it will not arrange for the holding of the ballot, and why, and
(c) no further steps are to be taken under this Part of this Schedule.

(4)   If the CAC is not so notified it must arrange for the holding of the ballot.

(5)   The notification period is the period of 10 working days starting—
(a) for the purposes of sub-paragraph (2)(a), with the day on which the union (or last of the unions)receives the CAC's notice under paragraph 22(3) or 23(2), or
(b) for the purposes of sub-paragraph (2)(b), with that day or (if later) the day on which the employer receives the CAC's notice under paragraph 22(3) or 23(2).

25

(1)   This paragraph applies if the CAC arranges under paragraph 24 for the holding of a ballot.

(2)   The ballot must be conducted by a qualified independent person appointed by the CAC.

(3)   The ballot must be conducted within—
(a) the period of 20 working days starting with the day after that on which the qualified independent person is appointed, or
(b) such longer period (so starting) as the CAC may decide.

(4)   The ballot must be conducted—
(a) at a workplace or workplaces decided by the CAC,
(b) by post, or
(c) by a combination of the methods described in sub-paragraphs (a) and (b),
depending on the CAC's preference.

(5)   In deciding how the ballot is to be conducted the CAC must take into account—
(a) the likelihood of the ballot being affected by unfairness or malpractice if it were conducted at a workplace or workplaces;
(b) costs and practicality;
(c) such other matters as the CAC considers appropriate.

(6)   The CAC may not decide that the ballot is to be conducted as mentioned in sub-paragraph (4)(c) unless there are special factors making such a decision appropriate; and special factors include—
(a) factors arising from the location of workers or the nature of their employment;
(b) factors put to the CAC by the employer or the union (or unions).

(6A) If the CAC decides that the ballot must (in whole or in part) be conducted at a workplace (or workplaces), it may require arrangements to be made for workers—
(a) who (but for the arrangements) would be prevented by the CAC's decision from voting by post, and
(b) who are unable, for reasons relating to those workers as individuals, to cast their votes in the ballot at the workplace (or at any of them),

to be given the opportunity (if they request it far enough in advance of the ballot for this to be practicable) to vote by post; and the CAC's imposing such a requirement is not to be treated for the purposes of sub-paragraph (6) as a decision that the ballot be conducted as mentioned in sub-paragraph (4)(c).

(7) A person is a qualified independent person if—
   (a) he satisfies such conditions as may be specified for the purposes of this paragraph by order of the Secretary of State or is himself so specified, and
   (b) there are no grounds for believing either that he will carry out any functions conferred on him in relation to the ballot otherwise than competently or that his independence in relation to the ballot might reasonably be called into question.

(8) An order under sub-paragraph (7)(a) shall be made by statutory instrument subject to annulment in pursuance of a resolution of either House of Parliament.

(9) As soon as is reasonably practicable after the CAC is required under paragraph 24 to arrange for the holding of a ballot it must inform the parties—
   (a) that it is so required;
   (b) of the name of the person appointed to conduct the ballot and the date of his appointment;
   (c) of the period within which the ballot must be conducted;
   (d) whether the ballot is to be conducted by post or at a workplace or workplaces;
   (e) of the workplace or workplaces concerned (if the ballot is to be conducted at a workplace or workplaces).

26

(1) An employer who is informed by the CAC under paragraph 25(9) must comply with the following five duties.

(2) The first duty is to co-operate generally, in connection with the ballot, with the union (or unions) and the person appointed to conduct the ballot; and the second and third duties are not to prejudice the generality of this.

(3) The second duty is to give to the union (or unions) such access to the workers constituting the bargaining unit as is reasonable to enable the union (or unions) to inform the workers of the object of the ballot and to seek their support and their opinions on the issues involved.

(4) The third duty is to do the following (so far as it is reasonable to expect the employer to do so)—
   (a) to give to the CAC, within the period of 10 working days starting with the day after that on which the employer is informed under paragraph 25(9), the names and home address of the workers constituting the bargaining unit;
   (b) to give to the CAC, as soon as is reasonably practicable, the name and home address of any worker who joins the unit after the employer has complied with paragraph (a);
   (c) to inform the CAC, as soon as is reasonably practicable, of any worker whose name has been given to the CAC under paragraph 19D or paragraph (a) or (b) of this sub-paragraph and who ceases to be within the unit.

(4A) The fourth duty is to refrain from making any offer to any or all of the workers constituting the bargaining unit which—
   (a) has or is likely to have the effect of inducing any or all of them not to attend any relevant meeting between the union (or unions) and the workers constituting the bargaining unit, and
   (b) is not reasonable in the circumstances.

(4B) The fifth duty is to refrain from taking or threatening to take any action against a worker solely or mainly on the grounds that he—
   (a) attended or took part in any relevant meeting between the union (or unions) and the workers constituting the bargaining unit, or
   (b) indicated his intention to attend or take part in such a meeting.

(4C) A meeting is a relevant meeting in relation to a worker for the purposes of sub-paragraphs (4A) and (4B) if—
   (a) it is organised in accordance with any agreement reached concerning the second duty or as a result of a step ordered to be taken under paragraph 27 to remedy a failure to comply with that duty, and
   (b) it is one which the employer is, by such an agreement or order as is mentioned in paragraph (a), required to permit the worker to attend.

(4D) Without prejudice to the generality of the second duty imposed by this paragraph, an employer is to be taken to have failed to comply with that duty if—
   (a) he refuses a request for a meeting between the union (or unions) and any or all of the workers constituting the bargaining unit to be held in the absence of the employer or any representative of his (other than one who has been invited to attend the meeting) and it is not reasonable in the circumstances for him to do so,
   (b) he or a representative of his attends such a meeting without having been invited to do so,
   (c) he seeks to record or otherwise be informed of the proceedings at any such meeting and it is not reasonable in the circumstances for him to do so, or
   (d) he refuses to give an undertaking that he will not seek to record or otherwise be informed of the proceedings at any such meeting unless it is reasonable in the circumstances for him to do either of those things.

(4E) The fourth and fifth duties do not confer any rights on a worker; but that does not affect any other right which a worker may have.

(4F) Sub-paragraph (4)(a) does not apply to names and addresses that the employer has already given to the CAC under paragraph 19D.

(4G) Where (because of sub-paragraph (4F)) the employer does not have to comply with sub-paragraph (4)(a), the reference in sub-paragraph (4)(b) to the time when the employer complied with sub-paragraph (4)(a) is to be read as a reference to the time when the employer is informed under paragraph 25(9).

(4H) If—
   (a) a person was appointed on an application under paragraph 19C, and
   (b) the person appointed to conduct the ballot is not that person,
   the CAC must, as soon as is reasonably practicable, pass on to the person appointed to conduct the ballot the names and addresses given to it under paragraph 19D.

(5) As soon as is reasonably practicable after the CAC receives any information under sub-paragraph (4) it must pass it on to the person appointed to conduct the ballot.

(6) If asked to do so by the union (or unions) the person appointed to conduct the ballot must send to any worker—
   (a) whose name and home address have been passed on to him under paragraph 19D or this paragraph, and
   (b) who is still within the unit (so far as the person so appointed is aware),
   any information supplied by the union (or unions) to the person so appointed.

(7)   The duty under sub-paragraph (6) does not apply unless the union bears (or unions bear) the cost of sending the information.

(8)   Each of the powers specified in sub-paragraph (9) shall be taken to include power to issue Codes of Practice—
(a)   about reasonable access for the purposes of sub-paragraph (3), and
(b)   about the fourth duty imposed by this paragraph.

(9)   The powers are—
(a)   the power of ACAS under section 199(1);
(b)   the power of the Secretary of State under section 203(1)(a).

27

(1)   If the CAC is satisfied that the employer has failed to fulfil any of the duties imposed on him by paragraph 26, and the ballot has not been held, the CAC may order the employer—
(a)   to take such steps to remedy the failure as the CAC considers reasonable and specifies in the order, and
(b)   to do so within such period as the CAC considers reasonable and specifies in the order.

(2)   If the CAC is satisfied that the employer has failed to comply with an order under sub-paragraph (1), and the ballot has not been held, the CAC may issue a declaration that the union is (or unions are) recognised as entitled to conduct collective bargaining on behalf of the bargaining unit.

(3)   If the CAC issues a declaration under sub-paragraph (2) it shall take steps to cancel the holding of the ballot; and if the ballot is held it shall have no effect.

27A

(1)   Each of the parties informed by the CAC under paragraph 25(9) must refrain from using any unfair practice.

(2)   A party uses an unfair practice if, with a view to influencing the result of the ballot, the party—
(a)   offers to pay money or give money's worth to a worker entitled to vote in the ballot in return for the worker's agreement to vote in a particular way or to abstain from voting,
(b)   makes an outcome-specific offer to a worker entitled to vote in the ballot,
(c)   coerces or attempts to coerce a worker entitled to vote in the ballot to disclose—
(i)   whether he intends to vote or to abstain from voting in the ballot, or
(ii)   how he intends to vote, or how he has voted, in the ballot,
(d)   dismisses or threatens to dismiss a worker,
(e)   takes or threatens to take disciplinary action against a worker,
(f)   subjects or threatens to subject a worker to any other detriment, or
(g)   uses or attempts to use undue influence on a worker entitled to vote in the ballot.

(3)   For the purposes of sub-paragraph (2)(b) an "outcome-specific offer" is an offer to pay money or give money's worth which—
(a)   is conditional on the issuing by the CAC of a declaration that—
(i)   the union is (or unions are) recognised as entitled to conduct collective bargaining on behalf of the bargaining unit, or
(ii)   the union is (or unions are) not entitled to be so recognised, and
(b)   is not conditional on anything which is done or occurs as a result of the declaration in question.

(4)   The duty imposed by this paragraph does not confer any rights on a worker; but that does not affect any other right which a worker may have.

(5)   Each of the following powers shall be taken to include power to issue Codes of Practice about unfair practices for the purposes of this paragraph—
(a) the power of ACAS under section 199(1);
(b) the power of the Secretary of State under section 203(1)(a).

27B

(1)   A party may complain to the CAC that another party has failed to comply with paragraph 27A.

(2)   A complaint under sub-paragraph (1) must be made on or before the first working day after—
(a) the date of the ballot, or
(b) if votes may be cast in the ballot on more than one day, the last of those days.

(3)   Within the decision period the CAC must decide whether the complaint is well-founded.

(4)   A complaint is well-founded if—
(a) the CAC finds that the party complained against used an unfair practice, and
(b) the CAC is satisfied that the use of that practice changed or was likely to change, in the case of a worker entitled to vote in the ballot–
(i)   his intention to vote or to abstain from voting,
(ii) his intention to vote in a particular way, or
(iii) how he voted.

(5)   The decision period is—
(a) the period of 10 working days starting with the day after that on which the complaint under sub-paragraph (1) was received by the CAC, or
(b) such longer period (so starting) as the CAC may specify to the parties by a notice containing reasons for the extension.

(6)   If, at the beginning of the decision period, the ballot has not begun, the CAC may by notice to the parties and the qualified independent person postpone the date on which it is to begin until a date which falls after the end of the decision period.

27C

(1)   This paragraph applies if the CAC decides that a complaint under paragraph 27B is well-founded.

(2)   The CAC must, as soon as is reasonably practicable, issue a declaration to that effect.

(3)   The CAC may do either or both of the following—
(a) order the party concerned to take any action specified in the order within such period as may be so specified, or
(b) give notice to the employer and to the union (or unions) that it intends to arrange for the holding of a secret ballot in which the workers constituting the bargaining unit are asked whether they want the union (or unions) to conduct collective bargaining on their behalf.

(4)   The CAC may give an order or a notice under sub-paragraph (3) either at the same time as it issues the declaration under sub-paragraph (2) or at any other time before it acts under paragraph 29.

(5)   The action specified in an order under sub-paragraph (3)(a) shall be such as the CAC considers reasonable in order to mitigate the effect of the failure of the party concerned to comply with the duty imposed by paragraph 27A.

(6)   The CAC may give more than one order under sub-paragraph (3)(a).

27D

(1)   This paragraph applies if the CAC issues a declaration under paragraph 27C(2) and the declaration states that the unfair practice used consisted of or included—
(a)   the use of violence, or
(b)   the dismissal of a union official.

(2)   This paragraph also applies if the CAC has made an order under paragraph 27C(3)(a) and—
(a)   it is satisfied that the party subject to the order has failed to comply with it, or
(b)   it makes another declaration under paragraph 27C(2) in relation to a complaint against that party.

(3)   If the party concerned is the employer, the CAC may issue a declaration that the union is (or unions are) recognised as entitled to conduct collective bargaining on behalf of the bargaining unit.

(4)   If the party concerned is a union, the CAC may issue a declaration that the union is (or unions are) not entitled to be so recognised.

(5)   The powers conferred by this paragraph are in addition to those conferred by paragraph 27C(3).

27E

(1)   This paragraph applies if the CAC issues a declaration that a complaint under paragraph 27B is well-founded and—
(a)   gives a notice under paragraph 27C(3)(b), or
(b)   issues a declaration under paragraph 27D.

(2)   If the ballot in connection with which the complaint was made has not been held, the CAC shall take steps to cancel it.

(3)   If that ballot is held, it shall have no effect.

27F

(1)   This paragraph applies if the CAC gives a notice under paragraph 27C(3)(b).

(2)   Paragraphs 24 to 29 apply in relation to that notice as they apply in relation to a notice given under paragraph 22(3) or 23(2) but with the modifications specified in sub-paragraphs (3) to (6).

(3)   In each of sub-paragraphs (5)(a) and (6)(a) of paragraph 24 for "10 working days" substitute "5 working days".

(4)   An employer's duty under paragraph (a) of paragraph 26(4) is limited to—
(a)   giving the CAC the names and home addresses of any workers in the bargaining unit which have not previously been given to it in accordance with that duty;
(b)   giving the CAC the names and home addresses of those workers who have joined the bargaining unit since he last gave the CAC information in accordance with that duty;

(c) informing the CAC of any change to the name or home address of a worker whose name and home address have previously been given to the CAC in accordance with that duty; and

(d) informing the CAC of any worker whose name had previously been given to it in accordance with that duty who has ceased to be within the bargaining unit.

(5) Any order given under paragraph 27(1) or 27C(3)(a) for the purposes of the cancelled or ineffectual ballot shall have effect (to the extent that the CAC specifies in a notice to the parties) as if it were made for the purposes of the ballot to which the notice under paragraph 27C(3)(b) relates.

(6) The gross costs of the ballot shall be borne by such of the parties and in such proportions as the CAC may determine and, accordingly, sub-paragraphs (2) and (3) of paragraph 28 shall be omitted and the reference in sub-paragraph (4) of that paragraph to the employer and the union (or each of the unions) shall be construed as a reference to the party or parties which bear the costs in accordance with the CAC's determination.

28

(1) This paragraph applies if the holding of a ballot has been arranged under paragraph 24 whether or not it has been cancelled.

(2) The gross costs of the ballot shall be borne—
(a) as to half, by the employer, and
(b) as to half, by the union (or unions).

(3) If there is more than one union they shall bear their half of the gross costs—
(a) in such proportions as they jointly indicate to the person appointed to conduct the ballot, or
(b) in the absence of such an indication, in equal shares.

(4) The person appointed to conduct the ballot may send to the employer and the union (or each of the unions) a demand stating—
(a) the gross costs of the ballot, and
(b) the amount of the gross costs to be borne by the recipient.

(5) In such a case the recipient must pay the amount stated to the person sending the demand, and must do so within the period of 15 working days starting with the day after that on which the demand is received.

(6) In England and Wales, if the amount stated is not paid in accordance with sub-paragraph (5) it shall, if a county court so orders, be recoverable by execution issued from that court or otherwise as if it were payable under an order of that court.

(6A) Where an amount is recoverable from a union under sub-paragraph (6) execution may be carried out, to the same extent and in the same manner as if the union were a body corporate, against any property held in trust for the union other than protected property as defined in section 23(2).

(7) References to the costs of the ballot are to—
(a) the costs wholly, exclusively and necessarily incurred in connection with the ballot by the person appointed to conduct it,
(b) such reasonable amount as the person appointed to conduct the ballot charges for his services, and
(c) such other costs as the employer and the union (or unions) agree.

29

(1)   As soon as is reasonably practicable after the CAC is informed of the result of a ballot by the person conducting it, the CAC must act under this paragraph.

(1A) The duty in sub-paragraph (1) does not apply if the CAC gives a notice under paragraph 27C(3)(b).

(2)   The CAC must inform the employer and the union (or unions) of the result of the ballot.

(3)   If the result is that the union is (or unions are) supported by—
      (a) a majority of the workers voting, and
      (b) at least 40 per cent of the workers constituting the bargaining unit,
      the CAC must issue a declaration that the union is (or unions are)recognised as entitled to conduct collective bargaining on behalf of the bargaining unit.

(4)   If the result is otherwise the CAC must issue a declaration that the union is (or unions are) not entitled to be so recognised.

(5)   The Secretary of State may by order amend sub-paragraph (3) so as to specify a different degree of support; and different provision may be made for different circumstances.

(6)   An order under sub-paragraph (5) shall be made by statutory instrument.

(7)   No such order shall be made unless a draft of it has been laid before Parliament and approved by a resolution of each House of Parliament.

30

(1)   This paragraph applies if the CAC issues a declaration under this Part of this Schedule that the union is (or unions are) recognised as entitled to conduct collective bargaining on behalf of a bargaining unit.

(2)   The parties may in the negotiation period conduct negotiations with a view to agreeing a method by which they will conduct collective bargaining.

(3)   If no agreement is made in the negotiation period the employer or the union (or unions) may apply to the CAC for assistance.

(4)   The negotiation period is—
      (a) the period of 30 working days starting with the start day, or
      (b) such longer period (so starting) as the parties may from time to time agree.

(5)   The start day is the day after that on which the parties are notified of the declaration.

31

(1)   This paragraph applies if an application for assistance is made to the CAC under paragraph 30.

(2)   The CAC must try to help the parties to reach in the agreement period an agreement on a method by which they will conduct collective bargaining.

(3)   If at the end of the agreement period the parties have not made such an agreement the CAC must specify to the parties the method by which they are to conduct collective bargaining.

(4)   Any method specified under sub-paragraph (3) is to have effect as if it were contained in a legally enforceable contract made by the parties.

(5)   But if the parties agree in writing—
   (a) that sub-paragraph (4) shall not apply, or shall not apply to particular parts of the method specified by the CAC, or
   (b) to vary or replace the method specified by the CAC,
   the written agreement shall have effect as a legally enforceable contract made by the parties.

(6)   Specific performance shall be the only remedy available for breach of anything which is a legally enforceable contract by virtue of this paragraph.

(7)   If at any time before a specification is made under sub-paragraph (3) the parties jointly apply to the CAC requesting it to stop taking steps under this paragraph, the CAC must comply with the request.

(8)   The agreement period is—
   (a) the period of 20 working days starting with the day after that on which the CAC receives the application under paragraph 30, or
   (b) such longer period (so starting) as the CAC may decide with the consent of the parties.

32

(1)   This paragraph applies if—
   (a) the CAC issues a declaration under this Part of this Schedule that the union is (or unions are) recognised as entitled to conduct collective bargaining on behalf of a bargaining unit,
   (b) the parties agree a method by which they will conduct collective bargaining, and
   (c) one or more of the parties fails to carry out the agreement.

(2)   The employer or the union (or unions) may apply to the CAC for assistance.

(3)   Paragraph 31 applies as if "paragraph 30" (in each place) read "paragraph 30 or paragraph 32".

35

(1)   An application under paragraph 11 or 12 is not admissible if the CAC is satisfied that there is already in force a collective agreement under which a union is (or unions are) recognised as entitled to conduct collective bargaining on behalf of any workers falling within the relevant bargaining unit.

(2)   But sub-paragraph (1) does not apply to an application under paragraph 11 or 12 if—
   (a) the union (or unions) recognised under the collective agreement and the union (or unions)making the application under paragraph 11 or 12 are the same, and
   (b) the matters in respect of which the union is (or unions are) entitled to conduct collective bargaining do not include all of the following: pay, hours and holidays ("the core topics").

(3)   A declaration of recognition which is the subject of a declaration under paragraph 83(2) must for the purposes of sub-paragraph (1) be treated as ceasing to have effect to the extent specified in paragraph 83(2) on the making of the declaration under paragraph 83(2).

(4) In applying sub-paragraph (1) an agreement for recognition (the agreement in question) must be ignored if—

(a) the union does not have (or none of the unions has) a certificate of independence,

(b) at some time there was an agreement (the old agreement) between the employer and the union under which the union (whether alone or with other unions) was recognised as entitled to conduct collective bargaining on behalf of a group of workers which was the same or substantially the same as the group covered by the agreement in question, and

(c) the old agreement ceased to have effect in the period of three years ending with the date of the agreement in question.

(5) It is for the CAC to decide whether one group of workers is the same or substantially the same as another, but in deciding the CAC may take account of the views of any person it believes has an interest in the matter.

(6) The relevant bargaining unit is—

(a) the proposed bargaining unit, where the application is under paragraph 11(2) or 12(2);

(b) the agreed bargaining unit, where the application is under paragraph 12(4)

36

(1) An application under paragraph 11 or 12 is not admissible unless the CAC decides that—

(a) members of the union (or unions) constitute at least 10 per cent of the workers constituting the relevant bargaining unit, and

(b) a majority of the workers constituting the relevant bargaining unit would be likely to favour recognition of the union (or unions) as entitled to conduct collective bargaining on behalf of the bargaining unit.

(2) The relevant bargaining unit is—

(a) the proposed bargaining unit, where the application is under paragraph 11(2) or 12(2);

(b) the agreed bargaining unit, where the application is under paragraph 11(4).

(3) The CAC must give reasons for the decision.

37

(1) This paragraph applies to an application made by more than one union under paragraph 11 or 12.

(2) The application is not admissible unless—

(a) the unions show that they will co-operate with each other in a manner likely to secure and maintain stable and effective collective bargaining arrangements, and

(b) the unions show that, if the employer wishes, they will enter into arrangements under which collective bargaining is conducted by the unions acting together on behalf of the workers constituting the relevant bargaining unit.

(3) The relevant bargaining unit is—

(a) the proposed bargaining unit, where the application is under paragraph 11(2) or 12(2);

(b) the agreed bargaining unit, where the application is under paragraph 12(4).

38

(1)   This paragraph applies if—
   (a) the CAC accepts a relevant application relating to a bargaining unit or proceeds under paragraph 20 with an application relating to a bargaining unit,
   (b) the application has not been withdrawn,
   (c) no notice has been given under paragraph 17(2),
   (d) the CAC has not issued a declaration under paragraph 19F(5), 22(2), 27(2), 27D(3), 27D(4), 29(3) or 29(4) in relation to that bargaining unit, and
   (e) no notification has been made under paragraph 24(2).

(2)   Another relevant application is not admissible if—
   (a) at least one worker falling within the relevant bargaining unit also falls within the bargaining unit referred to in sub-paragraph (1), and
   (b) the application is made by a union (or unions) other than the union (or unions) which made the application referred to in sub-paragraph (1).

(3)   A relevant application is an application under paragraph 11 or 12.

(4)   The relevant bargaining unit is—
   (a) the proposed bargaining unit, where the application is under paragraph 11(2) or 12(2);
   (b) the agreed bargaining unit, where the application is under paragraph 12(4).

39

(1)   This paragraph applies if the CAC accepts a relevant application relating to a bargaining unit or proceeds under paragraph 20 with an application relating to a bargaining unit.

(2)   Another relevant application is not admissible if—
   (a) the application is made within the period of 3 years starting with the day after that on which the CAC gave notice of acceptance of the application mentioned in sub-paragraph (1).
   (b) the relevant bargaining unit is the same or substantially the same as the bargaining unit mentioned in sub-paragraph (1), and
   (c) the application is made by the union (or unions) which made the application mentioned in sub-paragraph (1).

(3)   A relevant application is an application under paragraph 11 or 12.

(4)   The relevant bargaining unit is—
   (a) the proposed bargaining unit, where the application is under paragraph 11(2) or 12(2);
   (b) the agreed bargaining unit, where the application is under paragraph 12(4).

(5)   This paragraph does not apply if paragraph 40 or 41 applies.

40

(1)   This paragraph applies if the CAC issues a declaration under paragraph 27D(4) or 29(4) that a union is (or unions are) not entitled to be recognised as entitled to conduct collective bargaining on behalf of a bargaining unit; and this is so whether the ballot concerned is arranged under this Part or Part III of this Schedule.

(2)   An application under paragraph 11 or 12 is not admissible if—
   (a) the application is made within the period of 3 years starting with the day after that on which the declaration was issued,

(b) the relevant bargaining unit is the same or substantially the same as the bargaining unit mentioned in sub-paragraph (1), and

(c) the application is made by the union (or unions) which made the application leading to the declaration.

(3) The relevant bargaining unit is—

(a) the proposed bargaining unit, where the application is under paragraph 11(2) or 12(2);

(b) the agreed bargaining unit, where the application is under paragraph 12(4).

41

(1) This paragraph applies if the CAC issues a declaration under paragraph 119D(4), 119H(5) or 121(3) that bargaining arrangements are to cease to have effect; and this is so whether the ballot concerned is arranged under Part IV or Part V of this Schedule.

(2) An application under paragraph 11 or 12 is not admissible if—

(a) the application is made within the period of 3 years starting with the day after that on which the declaration was issued,

(b) the relevant bargaining unit is the same or substantially the same as the bargaining unit to which the bargaining arrangements mentioned in sub-paragraph (1) relate, and

(c) the application is made by the union which was a party (or unions which were parties) to the proceedings leading to the declaration.

(3) The relevant bargaining unit is—

(a) the proposed bargaining unit, where the application is under paragraph 11(2) or 12(2);

(b) the agreed bargaining unit, where the application is under paragraph 12(4).

43

(1) Paragraphs 44 to 50 apply if the CAC has to decide under paragraph 20 whether an application is valid.

(2) In those paragraphs—

(a) references to the application in question are to that application, and

(b) references to the relevant bargaining unit are to the bargaining unit agreed by the parties or decided by the CAC.

44

(1) The application in question is invalid if the CAC is satisfied that there is already in force a collective agreement under which a union is (or unions are) recognised as entitled to conduct collective bargaining on behalf of any workers falling within the relevant bargaining unit.

(2) But sub-paragraph (1) does not apply to the application in question if—

(a) the union (or unions) recognised under the collective agreement and the union (or unions) making the application in question are the same, and

(b) the matters in respect of which the union is (or unions are) entitled to conduct collective bargaining do not include all of the following: pay, hours and holidays ("the core topics").

(3) A declaration of recognition which is the subject of a declaration under paragraph 83(2) must for the purposes of sub-paragraph (1) be treated as ceasing to have effect to the

extent specified in paragraph 83(2) on the making of the declaration under paragraph 83(2).

(4)   In applying sub-paragraph (1) an agreement for recognition (the agreement in question) must be ignored if—

(a)   the union does not have (or none of the unions has) a certificate of independence,

(b)   at some time there was an agreement (the old agreement) between the employer and the union under which the union (whether alone or with other unions) was recognised as entitled to conduct collective bargaining on behalf of a group of workers which was the same or substantially the same as the group covered by the agreement in question, and

(c)   the old agreement ceased to have effect in the period of three years ending with the date of the agreement in question.

(5)   It is for the CAC to decide whether one group of workers is the same or substantially the same an another, but in deciding the CAC may take account of the views of any person it believes has an interest in the matter.

45

The application in question is invalid unless the CAC decides that—

(a)   members of the union (or unions) constitute at least 10 per cent of the workers constituting the relevant bargaining unit, and

(b)   a majority of the workers constituting the relevant bargaining unit would be likely to favour recognition of the union (or unions) as entitled to conduct collective bargaining on behalf of the bargaining unit.

46

(1)   This paragraph applies if—

(a)   the CAC accepts an application under paragraph 11 or 12 relating to a bargaining unit or proceeds under paragraph 20 with an application relating to a bargaining unit,

(b)   the application has not been withdrawn,

(c)   no notice has been given under paragraph 17(2),

(d)   the CAC has not issued a declaration under paragraph 19F(5), 22(2), 27(2), 27D(3), 27D(4), 29(3) or 29(4) in relation to that bargaining unit, and

(e)   no notification has been made under paragraph 24(2).

(2)   The application in question is invalid if—

(a)   at least one worker falling within the relevant bargaining unit also falls within the bargaining unit referred to in sub-paragraph (1), and

(b)   the application in question is made by a union (or unions) other than the union (or unions) which made the application referred to in sub-paragraph (1).

47

(1)   This paragraph applies if the CAC accepts an application under paragraph 11 or 12 relating to a bargaining unit or proceeds under paragraph 20 with an application relating to a bargaining unit.

(2)   The application in question is invalid if—

(a)   the application is made within the period of 3 years starting with the day after that on which the CAC gave notice of acceptance of the application mentioned in sub-paragraph (1),

(b) the relevant bargaining unit is the same or substantially the same as the bargaining unit mentioned in sub-paragraph (1), and

(c) the application is made by the union (or unions) which made the application mentioned in sub-paragraph (1).

(3) This paragraph does not apply if paragraph 48 or 49 applies.

48

(1) This paragraph applies if the CAC issues a declaration under 27D(4) or paragraph 29(4) that a union is (or unions are) not entitled to be recognised as entitled to conduct collective bargaining on behalf of a bargaining unit; and this is so whether the ballot concerned is arranged under this Part or Part III of this Schedule.

(2) The application in question is invalid if—
(a) the application is made within the period of 3 years starting with the date of the declaration,
(b) the relevant bargaining unit is the same or substantially the same as the bargaining unit mentioned in sub-paragraph (1), and
(c) the application is made by the union (or unions) which made the application leading to the declaration.

49

(1) This paragraph applies if the CAC issues a declaration under paragraph 119D(4), 119H(5) or 121(3) that bargaining arrangements are to cease to have effect; and this is so whether the ballot concerned is arranged under Part IV or Part V of this Schedule.

(2) The application in question is invalid if—
(a) the application is made within the period of 3 years starting with the day after that on which the declaration was issued,
(b) the relevant bargaining unit is the same or substantially the same as the bargaining unit to which the bargaining arrangements mentioned in sub-paragraph (1) relate, and
(c) the application is made by the union which was a party (or unions which were parties) to the proceedings leading to the declaration.

Part II VOLUNTARY RECOGNITION

52

(1) This paragraph applies for the purposes of this Part of this Schedule.

(2) An agreement is an agreement for recognition if the following conditions are fulfilled in relation to it—
(a) the agreement is made in the permitted period between a union (or unions) and an employer in consequence of a request made under paragraph 4 and valid within the terms of paragraphs 5 to 9;
(b) under the agreement the union is (or unions are) recognised as entitled to conduct collective bargaining on behalf of a group or groups of workers employed by the employer;
(c) if sub-paragraph (5) applies to the agreement, it is satisfied.

(3) The permitted period is the period which begins with the day on which the employer receives the request and ends when the first of the following occurs—

(a) the union withdraws (or unions withdraw) the request;

(b) the union withdraws (or unions withdraw) any application under paragraph 11 or 12 made in consequence of the request;

(c) the CAC gives notice of a decision under paragraph 14(7) which precludes it from accepting such an application under paragraph 11 or 12;

(d) the CAC gives notice under paragraph 15(4)(a) or 20(4)(a) in relation to such an application under paragraph 11 or 12;

(e) the parties give notice to the CAC under paragraph 17(2) in relation to such an application under paragraph 11 or 12;

(f) the CAC issues a declaration under paragraph 19F(5) or 22(2) in consequence of such an application under paragraph 11 or 12;

(g) the CAC is notified under paragraph 24(2) in relation to such an application under paragraph 11 or 12;

(h) the last day of the notification period ends (the notification period being that defined by paragraph 24(6) and arising from such an application under paragraph 11 or 12);

(i) the CAC is required under paragraph 51(3) to cancel such an application under paragraph 11 or 12.

(4) Sub-paragraph (5) applies to an agreement if—

(a) at the time it is made the CAC has received an application under paragraph 11 or 12 in consequence of the request mentioned in sub-paragraph (2), and

(b) the CAC has not decided whether the application is admissible or it has decided that it is admissible.

(5) This sub-paragraph is satisfied if, in relation to the application under paragraph 11 or 12, the parties give notice to the CAC under paragraph 17 before the final event (as defined in paragraph 17) occurs.

53

(1) This paragraph applies for the purposes of this Part of this Schedule.

(2) In relation to an agreement for recognition, references to the bargaining unit are to the group of workers (or the groups taken together) to which the agreement for recognition relates.

(3) In relation to an agreement for recognition, references to the parties are to the union (or unions) and the employer who are parties to the agreement.

54

(1) This paragraph applies for the purposes of this Part of this Schedule.

(2) The meaning of collective bargaining given by section 178(1) shall not apply.

(3) Except in paragraph 63(2), in relation to an agreement for recognition references to collective bargaining are to negotiations relating to the matters in respect of which the union is (or unions are) recognised as entitled to conduct negotiations under the agreement for recognition.

(4) In paragraph 63(2) the reference to collective bargaining is to negotiations relating to pay, hours and holidays.

55

(1) This paragraph applies if one or more of the parties to an agreement applies to the CAC for a decision whether or not the agreement is an agreement for recognition.

(2) The CAC must give notice of receipt of an application under sub-paragraph (1) to any parties to the agreement who are not parties to the application.

(3) The CAC must within the decision period decide whether the agreement is an agreement for recognition.

(4) If the CAC decides that the agreement is an agreement for recognition it must issue a declaration to that effect.

(5) If the CAC decides that the agreement is not an agreement for recognition it must issue a declaration to that effect.

(6) The decision period is—
(a) the period of 10 working days starting with the day after that on which the CAC receives the application under sub-paragraph (1), or
(b) such longer period (so starting) as the CAC may specify to the parties to the agreement by notice containing reasons for the extension.

56

(1) The employer may not terminate an agreement for recognition before the relevant period ends.

(2) After that period ends the employer may terminate the agreement, with or without the consent of the union (or unions).

(3) The union (or unions) may terminate an agreement for recognition at any time, with or without the consent of the employer.

(4) Sub-paragraphs (1) to (3) have effect subject to the terms of the agreement or any other agreement of the parties.

(5) The relevant period is the period of three years starting with the day after the date of the agreement.

57

(1) If an agreement for recognition is terminated, as from the termination the agreement and any provisions relating to the collective bargaining method shall cease to have effect.

(2) For this purpose provisions relating to the collective bargaining method are—
(a) any agreement between the parties as to the method by which collective bargaining is to be conducted with regard to the bargaining unit, or
(b) anything effective as, or as if contained in, a legally enforceable contract and relating to the method by which collective bargaining is to be conducted with regard to the bargaining unit.

58

(1) This paragraph applies if the parties make an agreement for recognition.

(2) The parties may in the negotiation period conduct negotiations with a view to agreeing a method by which they will conduct collective bargaining.

(3)   If no agreement is made in the negotiation period the employer or the union (or unions) may apply to the CAC for assistance.

(4)   The negotiation period is—
     (a)   the period of 30 working days starting with the start day, or
     (b)   such longer period (so starting) as the parties may from time to time agree.

(5)   The start day is the day after that on which the agreement is made.

59

(1)   This paragraph applies if—
     (a)   the parties to an agreement for recognition agree a method by which they will conduct collective bargaining, and
     (b)   one or more of the parties fails to carry out the agreement as to a method.

(2)   The employer or the union (or unions) may apply to the CAC for assistance.

Part III   CHANGES AFFECTING BARGAINING UNIT

64

(1)   This Part of this Schedule applies if—
     (a)   the CAC has issued a declaration that a union is (or unions are) recognised as entitled to conduct collective bargaining on behalf of a bargaining unit, and
     (b)   provisions relating to the collective bargaining method apply in relation to the unit.

(2)   In such a case, in this Part of this Schedule—
     (a)   references to the original unit are to the bargaining unit on whose behalf the union is (or unions are) recognised as entitled to conduct collective bargaining, and
     (b)   references to the bargaining arrangements are to the declaration and to the provisions relating to the collective bargaining method which apply in relation to the original unit.

(3)   For this purpose provisions relating to the collective bargaining method are—
     (a)   the parties' agreement as to the method by which collective bargaining is to be conducted with regard to the original unit,
     (b)   anything effective as, or as if contained in, a legally enforceable contract and relating to the method by which collective bargaining is to be conducted with regard to the original unit, or
     (c)   any provision of this Part of this Schedule that a method of collective bargaining is to have effect with regard to the original unit.

65

References in this Part of this Schedule to the parties are to the employer and the union (or unions) concerned.

66

(1)   This paragraph applies if the employer believes or the union believes (or unions believe) that the original unit is no longer an appropriate bargaining unit.

(2)   The employer or union (or unions) may apply to the CAC to make a decision as to what is an appropriate bargaining unit.

67

(1) An application under paragraph 66 is not admissible unless the CAC decides that it is likely that the original unit is no longer appropriate by reason of any of the matters specified in sub-paragraph (2).

(2) The matters are—
(a) a change in the organisation or structure of the business carried on by the employer;
(b) a change in the activities pursued by the employer in the course of the business carried on by him;
(c) a substantial change in the number of workers employed in the original unit.

68

(1) The CAC must give notice to the parties of receipt of an application under paragraph 66.

(2) Within the acceptance period the CAC must decide whether the application is admissible within the terms of paragraphs 67 and 92.

(3) In deciding whether the application is admissible the CAC must consider any evidence which it has been given by the employer or the union (or unions).

(4) If the CAC decides that the application is not admissible—
(a) the CAC must give notice of its decision to the parties,
(b) the CAC must not accept the application, and
(c) no further steps are to be taken under this Part of this Schedule.

(5) If the CAC decides that the application is admissible it must—
(a) accept the application, and
(b) give notice of the acceptance to the parties.

(6) The acceptance period is—
(a) the period of 10 working days starting with the day after that on which the CAC receives the application, or
(b) such longer period (so starting) as the CAC may specify to the parties by notice containing reasons for the extension.

69

(1) This paragraph applies if—
(a) the CAC gives notice of acceptance of the application, and
(b) before the end of the first period the parties agree a bargaining unit or units (the new unit or units) differing from the original unit and inform the CAC of their agreement.

(2) If in the CAC's opinion the new unit (or any of the new units) contains at least one worker falling within an outside bargaining unit no further steps are to be taken under this Part of this Schedule.

(3) If sub-paragraph (2) does not apply—
(a) the CAC must issue a declaration that the union is (or unions are) recognised as entitled to conduct collective bargaining on behalf of the new unit or units;
(b) so far as it affects workers in the new unit (or units) who fall within the original unit, the declaration shall have effect in place of any declaration that the union is (or unions are) recognised as entitled to conduct collective bargaining on behalf of the original unit;
(c) the method of collective bargaining relating to the original unit shall have effect in relation to the new unit or units, with any modifications which the CAC considers

necessary to take account of the change of bargaining unit and specifies in the declaration.

(4)   The first period is—
(a)   the period of 10 working days starting with the day after that on which the CAC gives notice of acceptance of the application, or
(b)   such longer period (so starting) as the parties may from time to time agree and notify to the CAC.

(5)   An outside bargaining unit is a bargaining unit which fulfils these conditions—
(a)   it is not the original unit;
(b)   a union is (or unions are) recognised as entitled to conduct collective bargaining on its behalf;
(c)   the union (or at least one of the unions) is not a party referred to in paragraph 64.

70

(1)   This paragraph applies if—
(a)   the CAC gives notice of acceptance of the application, and
(b)   the parties do not inform the CAC before the end of the first period that they have agreed a bargaining unit or units differing from the original unit.

(2)   During the second period—
(a)   the CAC must decide whether or not the original unit continues to be an appropriate bargaining unit;
(b)   if the CAC decides that the original unit does not so continue, it must decide what other bargaining unit is or units are appropriate;
(c)   the CAC must give notice to the parties of its decision or decisions under paragraphs (a) and (b).

(3)   In deciding whether or not the original unit continues to be an appropriate bargaining unit the CAC must take into account only these matters—
(a)   any change in the organisation or structure of the business carried on by the employer;
(b)   any change in the activities pursued by the employer in the course of the business carried on by him;
(c)   any substantial change in the number of workers employed in the original unit.

(4)   In deciding what other bargaining unit is or units are appropriate the CAC must take these matters into account—
(a)   the need for the unit or units to be compatible with effective management;
(b)   the matters listed in sub-paragraph (5), so far as they do not conflict with that need.

(5)   The matters are—
(a)   the views of the employer and of the union (or unions);
(b)   existing national and local bargaining arrangements;
(c)   the desirability of avoiding small fragmented bargaining units within an undertaking;
(d)   the characteristics of workers falling within the original unit and of any other employees of the employer whom the CAC considers relevant;
(e)   the location of workers.

(6)   If the CAC decides that two or more bargaining units are appropriate its decision must be such that no worker falls within more than one of them.

(7) The second period is—
   (a) the period of 10 working days starting with the day after that on which the first period ends, or
   (b) such longer period (so starting) as the CAC may specify to the parties by notice containing reasons for the extension.

71

If the CAC gives notice under paragraph 70 of a decision that the original unit continues to be an appropriate bargaining unit no further steps are to be taken under this Part of this Schedule.

72

Paragraph 82 applies if the CAC gives notice under paragraph 70 of—
(a) a decision that the original unit is no longer an appropriate bargaining unit, and

(b) a decision as to the bargaining unit which is (or units which are) appropriate.

73

(1) This paragraph applies if—
   (a) the parties agree under paragraph 69 a bargaining unit or units differing from the original unit,
   (b) paragraph 69(2) does not apply, and
   (c) at least one worker falling within the original unit does not fall within the new unit (or any of the new units).

(2) In such a case—
   (a) the CAC must issue a declaration that the bargaining arrangements, so far as relating to the worker or workers mentioned in sub-paragraph (1)(c), are to cease to have effect on a date specified by the CAC in the declaration, and
   (b) the bargaining arrangements shall cease to have effect accordingly.

74

(1) If the employer—
   (a) believes that the original unit has ceased to exist, and
   (b) wishes the bargaining arrangements to cease to have effect,

   he must give the union (or each of the unions) a notice complying with sub-paragraph (2) and must give a copy of the notice to the CAC.

(2) A notice complies with this sub-paragraph if it—
   (a) identifies the unit and the bargaining arrangements,
   (b) states the date on which the notice is given,
   (c) states that the unit has ceased to exist, and
   (d) states that the bargaining arrangements are to cease to have effect on a date which is specified in the notice and which falls after the end of the period of 35 working days starting with the day after that on which the notice is given.

(3) Within the validation period the CAC must decide whether the notice complies with sub-paragraph (2).

(4) If the CAC decides that the notice does not comply with sub-paragraph (2)—
   (a) the CAC must give the parties notice of its decision, and
   (b) the employer's notice shall be treated as not having been given.

(5)   If the CAC decides that the notice complies with sub-paragraph (2) it must give the parties notice of the decision.

(6)   The bargaining arrangements shall cease to have effect on the date specified under sub-paragraph (2)(d) if—
       (a) the CAC gives notice under sub-paragraph (5), and
       (b) the union does not (or unions do not) apply to the CAC under paragraph 75.

(7)   The validation period is—
       (a) the period of 10 working days starting with the day after that on which the CAC receives the copy of the notice, or
       (b) such longer period (so starting) as the CAC may specify to the parties by notice containing reasons for the extension.

75

(1)   Paragraph 76 applies if—
       (a) the CAC gives notice under paragraph 74(5), and
       (b) within the period of 10 working days starting with the day after that on which the notice is given the union makes (or unions make) an application to the CAC for a decision on the questions specified in sub-paragraph (2).

(2)   The questions are—
       (a) whether the original unit has ceased to exist;
       (b) whether the original unit is no longer appropriate by reason of any of the matters specified in sub-paragraph (3).

(3)   The matters are—
       (a) a change in the organisation or structure of the business carried on by the employer;
       (b) a change in the activities pursued by the employer in the course of the business carried on by him;
       (c) a substantial change in the number of workers employed in the original unit.

76

(1)   The CAC must give notice to the parties of receipt of an application under paragraph 75.

(2)   Within the acceptance period the CAC must decide whether the application is admissible within the terms of paragraph 92.

(3)   In deciding whether the application is admissible the CAC must consider any evidence which it has been given by the employer or the union (or unions).

(4)   If the CAC decides that the application is not admissible—
       (a) the CAC must give notice of its decision to the parties,
       (b) the CAC must not accept the application, and
       (c) no further steps are to be taken under this Part of this Schedule.

(5)   If the CAC decides that the application is admissible it must—
       (a) accept the application, and
       (b) give notice of the acceptance to the parties.

(6)   The acceptance period is—
       (a) the period of 10 working days starting with the day after that on which the CAC receives the application, or

(b) such longer period (so starting) as the CAC may specify to the parties by notice containing reasons for the extension.

77

(1) If the CAC accepts an application it—
(a) must give the employer and the union (or unions) an opportunity to put their views on the questions in relation to which the application was made;
(b) must decide the questions before the end of the decision period.

(2) If the CAC decides that the original unit has ceased to exist—
(a) the CAC must give the parties notice of its decision, and
(b) the bargaining arrangements shall cease to have effect on the termination date.

(3) If the CAC decides that the original unit has not ceased to exist, and that it is not the case that the original unit is no longer appropriate by reason of any of the matters specified in paragraph 75(3)—
(a) the CAC must give the parties notice of its decision, and
(b) the employer's notice shall be treated as not having been given.

(4) If the CAC decides that the original unit has not ceased to exist, and that the original unit is no longer appropriate by reason of any of the matters specified in paragraph 75(3), the CAC must give the parties notice of its decision.

(5) The decision period is—
(a) the period of 10 working days starting with the day after that on which the CAC gives notice of acceptance of the application, or
(b) such longer period (so starting) as the CAC may specify to the parties by notice containing reasons for the extension.

(6) The termination date is the later of—
(a) the date specified under paragraph 74(2)(d), and
(b) the day after the last day of the decision period.

78

(1) This paragraph applies if—
(a) the CAC gives notice under paragraph 77(4), and
(b) before the end of the first period the parties agree a bargaining unit or units (the new unit or units) differing from the original unit and inform the CAC of their agreement.

(2) If in the CAC's opinion the new unit (or any of the new units) contains at least one worker falling within an outside bargaining unit no further steps are to be taken under this Part of this Schedule.

(3) If sub-paragraph (2) does not apply—
(a) the CAC must issue a declaration that the union is (or unions are) recognised as entitled to conduct collective bargaining on behalf of the new unit or units;
(b) so far as it affects workers in the new unit (or units) who fall within the original unit, the declaration shall have effect in place of any declaration that the union is (or unions are) recognised as entitled to conduct collective bargaining on behalf of the original unit;
(c) the method of collective bargaining relating to the original unit shall have effect in relation to the new unit or units, with any modifications which the CAC considers

necessary to take account of the change of bargaining unit and specifies in the declaration.

(4) The first period is—
   (a) the period of 10 working days starting with the day after that on which the CAC gives notice under paragraph 77(4), or
   (b) such longer period (so starting) as the parties may from time to time agree and notify to the CAC.

(5) An outside bargaining unit is a bargaining unit which fulfils these conditions—
   (a) it is not the original unit;
   (b) a union is (or unions are) recognised as entitled to conduct collective bargaining on its behalf;
   (c) the union (or at least one of the unions) is not a party referred to in paragraph 64.

79

(1) This paragraph applies if—
   (a) the CAC gives notice under paragraph 77(4), and
   (b) the parties do not inform the CAC before the end of the first period that they have agreed a bargaining unit or units differing from the original unit.

(2) During the second period the CAC—
   (a) must decide what other bargaining unit is or units are appropriate;
   (b) must give notice of its decision to the parties.

(3) In deciding what other bargaining unit is or units are appropriate, the CAC must take these matters into account—
   (a) the need for the unit or units to be compatible with effective management;
   (b) the matters listed in sub-paragraph (4), so far as they do not conflict with that need.

(4) The matters are—
   (a) the views of the employer and of the union (or unions);
   (b) existing national and local bargaining arrangements;
   (c) the desirability of avoiding small fragmented bargaining units within an undertaking;
   (d) the characteristics of workers falling within the original unit and of any other employees of the employer whom the CAC considers relevant;
   (e) the location of workers.

(5) If the CAC decides that two or more bargaining units are appropriate its decision must be such that no worker falls within more than one of them.

(6) The second period is—
   (a) the period of 10 working days starting with the day after that on which the first period ends, or
   (b) such longer period (so starting) as the CAC may specify to the parties by notice containing reasons for the extension.

80

Paragraph 82 applies if the CAC gives notice under paragraph 79 of a decision as to the bargaining unit which is (or units which are) appropriate.

81

(1) This paragraph applies if—
  (a) the parties agree under paragraph 78 a bargaining unit or units differing from the original unit,
  (b) paragraph 78(2) does not apply, and
  (c) at least one worker falling within the original unit does not fall within the new unit (or any of the new units).

(2) In such a case—
  (a) the CAC must issue a declaration that the bargaining arrangements, so far as relating to the worker or workers mentioned in sub-paragraph (1)(c), are to cease to have effect on a date specified by the CAC in the declaration, and
  (b) the bargaining arrangements shall cease to have effect accordingly.

82

(1) This paragraph applies if the CAC gives notice under paragraph 70 of—
  (a) a decision that the original unit is no longer an appropriate bargaining unit, and
  (b) a decision as to the bargaining unit which is (or units which are) appropriate.

(2) This paragraph also applies if the CAC gives notice under paragraph 79 of a decision as to the bargaining unit which is (or units which are) appropriate.

(3) The CAC—
  (a) must proceed as stated in paragraphs 83 to 89 with regard to the appropriate unit (if there is one only), or
  (b) must proceed as stated in paragraphs 83 to 89 with regard to each appropriate unit separately (if there are two or more).

(4) References in those paragraphs to the new unit are to the appropriate unit under consideration.

83

(1) This paragraph applies if in the CAC's opinion the new unit contains at least one worker falling within a statutory outside bargaining unit.

(2) In such a case—
  (a) the CAC must issue a declaration that the relevant bargaining arrangements, so far as relating to workers falling within the new unit, are to cease to have effect on a date specified by the CAC in the declaration, and
  (b) the relevant bargaining arrangements shall cease to have effect accordingly.

(3) The relevant bargaining arrangements are—
  (a) the bargaining arrangements relating to the original unit, and
  (b) the bargaining arrangements relating to each statutory outside bargaining unit containing workers who fall within the new unit.

(4) The bargaining arrangements relating to the original unit are the bargaining arrangements as defined in paragraph 64.

(5) The bargaining arrangements relating to an outside unit are—
  (a) the declaration recognising a union (or unions) as entitled to conduct collective bargaining on behalf of the workers constituting the outside unit, and
  (b) the provisions relating to the collective bargaining method.

(6)   For this purpose the provisions relating to the collective bargaining method are—
    (a)   any agreement by the employer and the union (or unions) as to the method by which collective bargaining is to be conducted with regard to the outside unit,
    (b)   anything effective as, or as if contained in, a legally enforceable contract and relating to the method by which collective bargaining is to be conducted with regard to the outside unit, or
    (c)   any provision of this Part of this Schedule that a method of collective bargaining is to have effect with regard to the outside unit.

(7)   A statutory outside bargaining unit is a bargaining unit which fulfils these conditions—
    (a)   it is not the original unit;
    (b)   a union is (or unions are) recognised as entitled to conduct collective bargaining on its behalf by virtue of a declaration of the CAC.
    (c)   the union (or at least one of the unions) is not a party referred to in paragraph 64.

(8)   The date specified under sub-paragraph (2)(a) must be—
    (a)   the date on which the relevant period expires, or
    (b)   if the CAC believes that to maintain the relevant bargaining arrangements would be impracticable or contrary to the interests of good industrial relations, the date after the date on which the declaration is issued;
    and the relevant period is the period of 65 working days starting with the day after that on which the declaration is issued.

84

(1)   This paragraph applies if in the CAC's opinion the new unit contains—
    (a)   at least one worker falling within a voluntary outside bargaining unit, but
    (b)   no worker falling within a statutory outside bargaining unit.

(2)   In such a case—
    (a)   the CAC must issue a declaration that the original bargaining arrangements, so far as relating to workers falling within the new unit, are to cease to have effect on a date specified by the CAC in the declaration, and
    (b)   the original bargaining arrangements shall cease to have effect accordingly.

(3)   The original bargaining arrangements are the bargaining arrangements as defined in paragraph 64.

(4)   A voluntary outside bargaining unit is a bargaining unit which fulfils these conditions—
    (a)   it is not the original unit;
    (b)   a union is (or unions are) recognised as entitled to conduct collective bargaining on its behalf by virtue of an agreement with the employer;
    (c)   the union (or at least one of the unions) is not a party referred to in paragraph 64.

(5)   The date specified under sub-paragraph (2)(a) must be—
    (a)   the date on which the relevant period expires, or
    (b)   if the CAC believes that to maintain the original bargaining arrangements would be impracticable or contrary to the interests of good industrial relations, the date after the date on which the declaration is issued;
    and the relevant period is the period of 65 working days starting with the day after that on which the declaration is issued.

85

(1) If the CAC's opinion is not that mentioned in paragraph 83(1) or 84(1) it must—
  (a) decide whether the difference between the original unit and the new unit is such that the support of the union (or unions) within the new unit needs to be assessed, and
  (b) inform the parties of its decision.

(2) If the CAC's decision is that such support does not need to be assessed—
  (a) the CAC must issue a declaration that the union is (or unions are) recognised as entitled to conduct collective bargaining on behalf of the new unit;
  (b) so far as it affects workers in the new unit who fall within the original unit, the declaration shall have effect in place of any declaration that the union is (or unions are) recognised as entitled to conduct collective bargaining on behalf of the original unit;
  (c) the method of collective bargaining relating to the original unit shall have effect in relation to the new unit, with any modifications which the CAC considers necessary to take account of the change of bargaining unit and specifies in the declaration.

86

(1) This paragraph applies if the CAC decides under paragraph 85(1) that the support of the union (or unions) within the new unit needs to be assessed.

(2) The CAC must decide these questions—
  (a) whether members of the union (or unions) constitute at least 10 per cent of the workers constituting the new unit;
  (b) whether a majority of the workers constituting the new unit would be likely to favour recognition of the union (or unions) as entitled to conduct collective bargaining on behalf of the new unit.

(3) If the CAC decides one or both of the questions in the negative—
  (a) the CAC must issue a declaration that the bargaining arrangements, so far as relating to workers falling within the new unit, are to cease to have effect on a date specified by the CAC in the declaration, and
  (b) the bargaining arrangements shall cease to have effect accordingly.

87

(1) This paragraph applies if—
  (a) the CAC decides both the questions in paragraph 86(2) in the affirmative, and
  (b) the CAC is satisfied that a majority of the workers constituting the new unit are members of the union (or unions).

(2) The CAC must issue a declaration that the union is (or unions are) recognised as entitled to conduct collective bargaining on behalf of the workers constituting the new unit.

(3) But if any of the three qualifying conditions is fulfilled, instead of issuing a declaration under sub-paragraph (2) the CAC must give notice to the parties that it intends to arrange for the holding of a secret ballot in which the workers constituting the new unit are asked whether they want the union (or unions) to conduct collective bargaining on their behalf.

(4) These are the three qualifying conditions—
  (a) the CAC is satisfied that a ballot should be held in the interests of good industrial relations;

(b) the CAC has evidence, which it considers to be credible, from a significant number of the union members within the new bargaining unit that they do not want the union (or unions) to conduct collective bargaining on their behalf;

(c) membership evidence is produced which leads the CAC to conclude that there are doubts whether a significant number of the union members within the new unit want the union (or unions) to conduct collective bargaining on their behalf.

(5) For the purposes of sub-paragraph (4)(c) membership evidence is—

(a) evidence about the circumstances in which union members became members;

(b) evidence about the length of time for which union members have been members, in a case where the CAC is satisfied that such evidence should be taken into account.

(6) If the CAC issues a declaration under sub-paragraph (2)—

(a) so far as it affects workers in the new unit who fall within the original unit, the declaration shall have effect in place of any declaration that the union is (or unions are) recognised as entitled to conduct collective bargaining on behalf of the original unit;

(b) the method of collective bargaining relating to the original unit shall have effect in relation to the new unit, with any modifications which the CAC considers necessary to take account of the change of bargaining unit and specifies in the declaration.

88

(1) This paragraph applies if—

(a) the CAC decides both the questions in paragraph 86(2) in the affirmative, and

(b) the CAC is not satisfied that a majority of the workers constituting the new unit are members of the union (or unions).

(2) The CAC must give notice to the parties that it intends to arrange for the holding of a secret ballot in which the workers constituting the new unit are asked whether they want the union (or unions) to conduct collective bargaining on their behalf.

89

(1) If the CAC gives notice under paragraph 87(3) or 88(2) the union (or unions) may within the notification period notify the CAC that the union does not (or unions do not) want the CAC to arrange for the holding of the ballot; and the notification period is the period of 10 working days starting with the day after that on which the union (or last of the unions) receives the CAC's notice.

(2) If the CAC is so notified—

(a) it must not arrange for the holding of the ballot,

(b) it must inform the parties that it will not arrange for the holding of the ballot, and why,

(c) it must issue a declaration that the bargaining arrangements, so far as relating to workers falling within the new unit, are to cease to have effect on a date specified by it in the declaration, and

(d) the bargaining arrangements shall cease to have effect accordingly.

(3) If the CAC is not so notified it must arrange for the holding of the ballot.

(4) Paragraph 25 applies if the CAC arranges under this paragraph for the holding of a ballot (as well as if the CAC arranges under paragraph 24 for the holding of a ballot).

(5) Paragraphs 26 to 29 apply accordingly, but as if—

(a) references to the bargaining unit were references to the new unit, and

(b) paragraph 26(4F) to (4H), and the references in paragraph 26(4) and (6) to paragraph 19D, were omitted.

(6) If as a result of the ballot the CAC issues a declaration that the union is (or unions are) recognised as entitled to conduct collective bargaining on behalf of the new unit—
  (a) so far as it affects workers in the new unit who fall within the original unit, the declaration shall have effect in place of any declaration that the union is (or unions are) recognised as entitled to conduct collective bargaining on behalf of the original unit;
  (b) the method of collective bargaining relating to the original unit shall have effect in relation to the new unit, with any modifications which the CAC considers necessary to take account of the change of bargaining unit and specifies in the declaration.

(7) If as a result of the ballot the CAC issues a declaration that the union is (or unions are) not entitled to be recognised as entitled to conduct collective bargaining on behalf of the new unit—
  (a) the CAC must state in the declaration the date on which the bargaining arrangements, so far as relating to workers falling within the new unit, are to cease to have effect, and
  (b) the bargaining arrangements shall cease to have effect accordingly.

(8) Paragraphs (a) and (b) of sub-paragraph (6) also apply if the CAC issues a declaration under paragraph 27(2) or 27D(3).

(9) Paragraphs (a) and (b) of sub-paragraph (7) also apply if the CAC issues a declaration under paragraph 27D(4).

90

(1) This paragraph applies if—
  (a) the CAC decides an appropriate bargaining unit or units under paragraph 70 or 79, and
  (b) at least one worker falling within the original unit does not fall within the new unit (or any of the new units).

(2) In such a case—
  (a) the CAC must issue a declaration that the bargaining arrangements, so far as relating to the worker or workers mentioned in sub-paragraph (1)(b), are to cease to have effect on a date specified by the CAC in the declaration, and
  (b) the bargaining arrangements shall cease to have effect accordingly.

91

(1) This paragraph applies if—
  (a) the CAC has proceeded as stated in paragraphs 83 to 89 with regard to the new unit (if there is one only) or with regard to each new unit (if there are two or more), and
  (b) in so doing the CAC has issued one or more declarations under paragraph 83.

(2) The CAC must—
  (a) consider each declaration issued under paragraph 83, and
  (b) in relation to each declaration, identify each statutory outside bargaining unit which contains at least one worker who also falls within the new unit to which the declaration relates;
and in this paragraph each statutory outside bargaining unit so identified is referred to as a parent unit.

(3)   The CAC must then—
    (a)   consider each parent unit, and
    (b)   in relation to each parent unit, identify any workers who fall within the parent unit but who do not fall within the new unit (or any of the new units);
    and in this paragraph the workers so identified in relation to a parent unit are referred to as a residual unit.

(4)   In relation to each residual unit, the CAC must issue a declaration that the outside union is (or outside unions are) recognised as entitled to conduct collective bargaining on its behalf.

(5)   But no such declaration shall be issued in relation to a residual unit if the CAC has received an application under paragraph 66 or 75 in relation to its parent unit.

(6)   In this paragraph references to the outside union (or to outside unions) in relation to a residual unit are to the union which is (or unions which are) recognised as entitled to conduct collective bargaining on behalf of its parent unit.

(7)   If the CAC issues a declaration under sub-paragraph (4)—
    (a)   the declaration shall have effect in place of the existing declaration that the outside union is (or outside unions are) recognised as entitled to conduct collective bargaining on behalf of the parent unit, so far as the existing declaration relates to the residual unit;
    (b)   if there is a method of collective bargaining relating to the parent unit, it shall have effect in relation to the residual unit with any modifications which the CAC considers necessary to take account of the change of bargaining unit and specifies in the declaration.

92

(1)   An application to the CAC under this Part of this Schedule is not admissible unless—
    (a)   it is made in such form as the CAC specifies, and
    (b)   it is supported by such documents as the CAC specifies.

(2)   An application which is made by a union (or unions) to the CAC under this Part of this Schedule is not admissible unless the union gives (or unions give) to the employer—
    (a)   notice of the application, and
    (b)   a copy of the application and any documents supporting it.

(3)   An application which is made by an employer to the CAC under this Part of this Schedule is not admissible unless the employer gives to the union (or each of the unions)—
    (a)   notice of the application, and
    (b)   a copy of the application and any documents supporting it.

93

(1)   If an application under paragraph 66 or 75 is accepted by the CAC, the applicant (or applicants) may not withdraw the application—
    (a)   after the CAC issues a declaration under paragraph 69(3) or 78(3),
    (b)   after the CAC decides under paragraph 77(2) or 77(3),
    (c)   after the CAC issues a declaration under paragraph 83(2), 85(2), 86(3) or 87(2) in relation to the new unit (where there is only one) or a declaration under any of those paragraphs in relation to any of the new units (where there is more than one),

(d) after the union has (or unions have) notified the CAC under paragraph 89(1) in relation to the new unit (where there is only one) or any of the new units (where there is more than one), or

(e) after the end of the notification period referred to in paragraph 89(1) and relating to the new unit (where there is only one) or any of the new units (where there is more than one).

(2) If an application is withdrawn by the applicant (or applicants)—

(a) the CAC must give notice of the withdrawal to the other party (or parties), and

(b) no further steps are to be taken under this Part of this Schedule.

94

(1) This paragraph applies for the purposes of this Part of this Schedule.

(2) Except in relation to paragraphs 69(5), 78(5) and 83(6), the meaning of collective bargaining given by section 178(1) shall not apply.

(3) In relation to a new unit references to collective bargaining are to negotiations relating to the matters which were the subject of collective bargaining in relation to the corresponding original unit; and the corresponding original unit is the unit which was the subject of an application under paragraph 66 or 75 in consequence of which the new unit was agreed by the parties or decided by the CAC.

(4) But if the parties agree matters as the subject of collective bargaining in relation to the new unit, references to collective bargaining in relation to that unit are to negotiations relating to the agreed matters; and this is the case whether the agreement is made before or after the time when the CAC issues a declaration that the union is (or unions are) recognised as entitled to conduct collective bargaining on behalf of the new unit.

(5) In relation to a residual unit in relation to which a declaration is issued under paragraph 91, references to collective bargaining are to negotiations relating to the matters which were the subject of collective bargaining in relation to the corresponding parent unit.

(6) In construing paragraphs 69(3)(c), 78(3)(c), 85(2)(c), 87(6)(b) and 89(6)(b)—

(a) sub-paragraphs (3) and (4) do not apply, and

(b) references to collective bargaining are to negotiations relating to pay, hours and holidays.

95

(1) This paragraph applies for the purposes of this Part of this Schedule.

(2) Where a method of collective bargaining has effect in relation to a new unit, that method shall have effect as if it were contained in a legally enforceable contract made by the parties.

(3) But if the parties agree in writing—

(a) that sub-paragraph (2) shall not apply, or shall not apply to particular parts of the method, or

(b) to vary or replace the method,

the written agreement shall have effect as a legally enforceable contract made by the parties.

(4) Specific performance shall be the only remedy available for breach of anything which is a legally enforceable contract by virtue of this paragraph.

As amended by the Trade Union Reform and Employment Rights Act 1993, Pt I s 14, Pt I s 16(1), Pt I s 16(2), Pt I s 17, Pt I s 18(1), Pt I s 18(2), Pt I s 21, Pt II s 34(2)(a), Pt II s 34(2)(c), Sch 8 para 47(a), Sch 8 para 47(b), Sch 8 para 48, Sch 8 para 49(a), Sch 8 para 49(b), Sch 8 para 50, Sch 8 para 51(a)(i), Sch 8 para 51(b), Sch 8 para 72, Sch 8 para 73(a), Sch 8 para 73(b), Sch 8 para 73(c), Sch 8 para 77, Sch 10 para 1; Collective Redundancies and Transfer of Undertakings (Protection of Employment) (Amendment) Regulations 1995/2587 reg 3(2), reg 3(3), reg 3(4)(a), reg 3(4)(b), reg 3(5), reg 3(6), reg 3(7), reg 3(8), reg 3(9), reg 3(10); Employment Rights Act 1996 c 18 Sch 1 para 56(2)(a), Sch 1 para 56(2)(b), Sch 1 para 56(6), Sch 1 para 56(7)(a), Sch 1 para 56(7)(b), Sch 1 para 56(9)(a), Sch 1 para 56(9)(b), Sch 1 para 56(13)(a), Sch 1 para 56(13) (b), Sch 1 para 56(15)(a), Sch 1 para 56(15)(b); Employment Rights (Dispute Resolution) Act 1998, Pt I s 1(2), Pt I s 1(2)(a); Employment Relations Act 1999 c 26 Sch 1 para 1, Sch 2 para 2(2), Sch 2 para 2(3), Sch 2 para 2(4), Sch 2 para 2(5), Sch 2 para 3(2), Sch 2 para 3(3), Sch 2 para 3(4), Sch 2 para 5(a), Sch 2 para 5(b), Sch 3 para 2(2), Sch 3 para 2(3), Sch 3 para 5, Sch 3 para 7, Sch 3 para 10, Sch 3 para 11(4)(a), Sch 3 para 11(5), Sch 3 para 11(6), Sch 4(III) para 2(a), Sch 4(III) para 3(a), Sch 4(III) para 3(b), Sch 5 para 2, Sch 9 para 1; Collective Redundancies and Transfer of Undertakings (Protection of Employment) (Amendment) Regulations 1999/1925 reg 3(2), reg 3(3), reg 3(4), reg 3(5), reg 3(6), reg 14; Employment Act 2002, Pt 4 s 43(2), Pt 4 s 43(3), Pt 4 s 43(4), Pt 4 s 43(5), Sch 7 para 19, Sch 7 para 20; Employment Relations Act 2004, Pt 1 s 1(1), Pt 1 s 1(2), Pt 1 s 2(2), Pt 1 s 3, Pt 1 s 4, Pt 1 s 5(2), Pt 1 s 5(3), Pt 1 s 5(4), Pt 1 s 5(5), Pt 1 s 8(1), Pt 1 s 8(2), Pt 1 s 9(2), Pt 1 s 9(3), Pt 1 s 9(4), Pt 1 s 9(5), Pt 1 s 9(7), Pt 1 s 9(8), Pt 1 s 9(9), Pt 1 s 9(10), Pt 1 s 10(1), Pt 1 s 10(2), Pt 1 s 11, Pt 1 s 12(8)(a), Pt 1 s 12(8)(b), Pt 1 s 12(8)(c), Pt 1 s 13(1), Pt 1 s 13(2), Pt 1 s 19, Pt 1 s 20, Pt 2 s 22(2), Pt 2 s 22(3), Pt 2 s 22(4), Pt 2 s 22(6), Pt 2 s 23, Pt 2 s 24(2), Pt 2 s 25(2)(a), Pt 2 s 25(3), Pt 2 s 25(4), Pt 2 s 25(5), Pt 2 s 25(6), Pt 3 s 30(2), Pt 3 s 30(3)(a), Pt 3 s 30(3)(b), Pt 3 s 30(4), Pt 3 s 30(5), Pt 3 s 30(6), Pt 3 s 30(7), Pt 3 s 30(10), Pt 3 s 31(2), Pt 3 s 31(3)(a), Pt 3 s 31(3)(b), Pt 3 s 31(4), Pt 3 s 32(2), Pt 3 s 32(3)(a), Pt 3 s 32(3)(b), Pt 3 s 32(4), Pt 3 s 32(6), Pt 3 s 33(2), Pt 3 s 33(3), Pt 3 s 33(4), Pt 3 s 33(5), Pt 3 s 33(6), Pt 3 s 34(2), Pt 3 s 34(6), Pt 3 s 34(8)(a), Pt 3 s 40(8)(b), Pt 3 s 40(9)(b), Pt 3 s 41(1)(b), Pt 3 s 41(2)(a), Pt 3 s 41(2)(b), Pt 3 s 41(1)(a), Pt 5 s 50(6), Pt 5 s 51(1)(a), Pt 5 s 51(1)(c), Sch 1 para 8, Sch 1 para 14, Sch 1 para 23(2), Sch 1 para 23(5), Sch 1 para 23(6), Sch 1 para 23(7), Sch 1 para 23(8), Sch 1 para 23(9), Sch 1 para 23(10)(a), Sch 1 para 23(10)(b), Sch 1 para 23(11)(a), Sch 1 para 23(11)(b), Sch 1 para 23(12), Sch 1 para 23(13)(a), Sch 1 para 23(13)(b), Sch 1 para 23(14)(a), Sch 1 para 23(14) (b), Sch 1 para 23(16)(a), Sch 1 para 23(16)(b), Sch 1 para 23(24), Sch 1 para 23(25), Sch 1 para 23(26)(a), Sch 1 para 23(26)(b), Sch 2 para 1; Transfer of Undertakings (Protection of Employment) Regulations 2006/246 Transfer of Undertakings (Protection of Employment) Regulations 2006/246 reg 9(4), Sch 2 para 1(e); Employment Act 2008, s 19(2), s 19(3); Employment Rights (Increase of Limits) Order 2008/3055 Sch 1 para 1. Employment Rights (Revision of Limits) Order 2009/3274, Sch 1 para 1.

DISABILITY DISCRIMINATION ACT 1995
(c. 50)

Part I DISABILITY

1 MEANING OF "DISABILITY" AND "DISABLED PERSON"

(1) Subject to the provisions of Schedule 1, a person has a disability for the purposes of this Act if he has a physical or mental impairment which has a substantial and long-term adverse effect on his ability to carry out normal day-to-day activities.

(2) In this Act "disabled person" means

2 PAST DISABILITIES

(1) The provisions of this Part and Parts II to 4 and 5A apply in relation to a person who has had a disability as they apply in relation to a person who has that disability.

(2) Those provisions are subject to the modifications made by Schedule 2

(3) Any regulations or order made under this Act by the Secretary of State, the Scottish Ministers or the Welsh Ministers may include provision with respect to persons who have had a disability.

(4) In any proceedings under Part 2, 3, 4 or 5A of this Act, the question whether a person had a disability at a particular time ("the relevant time") shall be determined, for the purposes of this section, as if the provisions of, or under, this Act in force when the act complained of was done had been in force at the relevant time.

(5) The relevant time may be a time before the passing

3 GUIDANCE

(A1) The Secretary of State may issue guidance about matters to be taken into account in determining whether a person is a disabled person.

(1) Without prejudice to the generality of subsection (A1), the Secretary of State may, in particular, issue guidance about the matters to be taken into account in determining—
  (a) whether an impairment has a substantial adverse effect on a person's ability to carry out normal day-to-day activities; or
  (b) whether such an impairment has a long-term effect.

(2) Without prejudice to the generality of subsection (A1), guidance about the matters mentioned in subsection (1) may, among other things, give examples of—
  (a) effects which it would be reasonable, in relation to particular activities, to regard for purposes of this Act as substantial adverse effects;
  (b) effects which it would not be reasonable, in relation to particular activities, to regard for such purposes as substantial adverse effects;
  (c) substantial adverse effects which it would be reasonable to regard, for such purposes, as long-term;
  (d) substantial adverse effects which it would not be reasonable to regard, for such purposes, as long-term.

(3) An adjudicating body determining, for any purpose of this Act, whether a person is a disabled person, shall take into account any guidance which appears to it to be relevant.

(3A) "Adjudicating body" means—
  (a) a court;
  (b) a tribunal; and
  (c) any other person who, or body which, may decide a claim under Part 4.

(4)   In preparing a draft of any guidance, the Secretary of State shall consult such persons as he considers appropriate.

(5)   Where the Secretary of State proposes to issue any guidance, he shall publish a draft of it, consider any representations that are made to him about the draft and, if he thinks it appropriate, modify his proposals in the light of any of those representations.

(6)   If the Secretary of State decides to proceed with any proposed guidance, he shall lay a draft of it before each House of Parliament.

(7)   If, within the 40-day period, either House resolves not to approve the draft, the Secretary of State shall take no further steps in relation to the proposed guidance.

(8)   If no such resolution is made within the 40-day period, the Secretary of State shall issue the guidance in the form of his draft.

(9)   The guidance shall come into force on such date as the Secretary of State may appoint by order.

(10)   Subsection (7) does not prevent a new draft of the proposed guidance from being laid before Parliament.

(11)   The Secretary of State may—
       (a) from time to time revise the whole or part of any guidance and re-issue it;
       (b) by order revoke any guidance.

(12)   In this section—

       "40-day period", in relation to the draft of any proposed guidance, means—
       (a) if the draft is laid before one House on a day later than the day on which it is laid before the other House, the period of 40 days beginning with the later of the two days, and
       (b) in any other case, the period of 40 days beginning with the day on which the draft is laid before each House,
       no account being taken of any period during which Parliament is dissolved or prorogued or during which both Houses are adjourned for more than 4 days; and

       "guidance" means guidance issued by the Secretary of State under this section and includes guidance which has been revised and re-issued.

Part II THE EMPLOYMENT FIELD

3A MEANING OF "DISCRIMINATION"

(1)   For the purposes of this Part, a person discriminates against a disabled person if—
       (a) for a reason which relates to the disabled person's disability, he treats him less favourably than he treats or would treat others to whom that reason does not or would not apply, and
       (b) he cannot show that the treatment in question is justified.

(2)   For the purposes of this Part, a person also discriminates against a disabled person if he fails to comply with a duty to make reasonable adjustments imposed on him in relation to the disabled person.

(3)   Treatment is justified for the purposes of subsection (1)(b) if, but only if, the reason for it is both material to the circumstances of the particular case and substantial.

(4)   But treatment of a disabled person cannot be justified under subsection (3) if it amounts to direct discrimination falling within subsection (5).

(5)   A person directly discriminates against a disabled person if, on the ground of the disabled person's disability, he treats the disabled person less favourably than he treats or would treat a person not having that particular disability whose relevant circumstances, including his abilities, are the same as, or not materially different from, those of the disabled person.

(6)   If, in a case falling within subsection (1), a person is under a duty to make reasonable adjustments in relation to a disabled person but fails to comply with that duty, his treatment of that person cannot be justified under subsection (3) unless it would have been justified even if he had complied with that duty.

3B MEANING OF "HARASSMENT"

(1)   For the purposes of this Part, a person subjects a disabled person to harassment where, for a reason which relates to the disabled person's disability, he engages in unwanted conduct which has the purpose or effect of—
(a) violating the disabled person's dignity, or
(b) creating an intimidating, hostile, degrading, humiliating or offensive environment for him.

(2)   Conduct shall be regarded as having the effect referred to in paragraph (a) or (b) of subsection (1) only if, having regard to all the circumstances, including in particular the perception of the disabled person, it should reasonably be considered as having that effect.

4 EMPLOYERS: DISCRIMINATION AND HARASSMENT

(1)   It is unlawful for an employer to discriminate against a disabled person—
(a) in the arrangements which he makes for the purpose of determining to whom he should offer employment;
(b) in the terms on which he offers that person employment; or
(c) by refusing to offer, or deliberately not offering, him employment.

(2)   It is unlawful for an employer to discriminate against a disabled person whom he employs—
(a) in the terms of employment which he affords him;
(b) in the opportunities which he affords him for promotion, a transfer, training or receiving any other benefit;
(c) by refusing to afford him, or deliberately not affording him, any such opportunity; or
(d) by dismissing him, or subjecting him to any other detriment.

(3)   It is also unlawful for an employer, in relation to employment by him, to subject to harassment—
(a) a disabled person whom he employs; or
(b) a disabled person who has applied to him for employment.

(4)   Subsection (2) does not apply to benefits of any description if the employer is concerned with the provision (whether or not for payment) of benefits of that description to the public, or to a section of the public which includes the employee in question, unless—
(a) that provision differs in a material respect from the provision of the benefits by the employer to his employees;
(b) the provision of the benefits to the employee in question is regulated by his contract of employment; or
(c) the benefits relate to training.

(5)   The reference in subsection (2)(d) to the dismissal of a person includes a reference—
    (a)   to the termination of that person's employment by the expiration of any period (including a period expiring by reference to an event or circumstance), not being a termination immediately after which the employment is renewed on the same terms; and
    (b)   to the termination of that person's employment by any act of his (including the giving of notice) in circumstances such that he is entitled to terminate it without notice by reason of the conduct of the employer.

(6)   This section applies only in relation to employment at an establishment in Great Britain.

4A EMPLOYERS: DUTY TO MAKE ADJUSTMENTS

(1)   Where—
    (a)   a provision, criterion or practice applied by or on behalf of an employer, or
    (b)   any physical feature of premises occupied by the employer,
places the disabled person concerned at a substantial disadvantage in comparison with persons who are not disabled, it is the duty of the employer to take such steps as it is reasonable, in all the circumstances of the case, for him to have to take in order to prevent the provision, criterion or practice, or feature, having that effect.

(2)   In subsection (1), "the disabled person concerned" means—
    (a)   in the case of a provision, criterion or practice for determining to whom employment should be offered, any disabled person who is, or has notified the employer that he may be, an applicant for that employment;
    (b)   in any other case, a disabled person who is—
       (i)   an applicant for the employment concerned, or
      (ii)   an employee of the employer concerned.

(3)   Nothing in this section imposes any duty on an employer in relation to a disabled person if the employer does not know, and could not reasonably be expected to know—
    (a)   in the case of an applicant or potential applicant, that the disabled person concerned is, or may be, an applicant for the employment; or
    (b)   in any case, that that person has a disability and is likely to be affected in the way mentioned in subsection (1).

16A RELATIONSHIPS WHICH HAVE COME TO AN END

(1)   This section applies where—
    (a)   there has been a relevant relationship between a disabled person and another person ("the relevant person"), and
    (b)   the relationship has come to an end.

(2)   In this section a "relevant relationship" is—
    (a)   a relationship during the course of which an act of discrimination against, or harassment of, one party to the relationship by the other party to it is unlawful under any preceding provision of this Part, other than sections 15B and 15C; or
    (b)   a relationship between a person providing employment services and a person receiving such services.

(3)   It is unlawful for the relevant person—
    (a)   to discriminate against the disabled person by subjecting him to a detriment, or
    (b)   to subject the disabled person to harassment,

where the discrimination or harassment arises out of and is closely connected to the relevant relationship.

(4)   This subsection applies where—
(a)   a provision, criterion or practice applied by the relevant person to the disabled person in relation to any matter arising out of the relevant relationship, or
(b)   a physical feature of premises which are occupied by the relevant person,
places the disabled person at a substantial disadvantage in comparison with persons who are not disabled, but are in the same position as the disabled person in relation to the relevant person.

(5)   Where subsection (4) applies, it is the duty of the relevant person to take such steps as it is reasonable, in all the circumstances of the case, for him to have to take in order to prevent the provision, practice or criterion, or feature, having that effect.

(6)   Nothing in subsection (5) imposes any duty on the relevant person if he does not know, and could not reasonably be expected to know, that the disabled person has a disability and is likely to be affected in the way mentioned in that subsection.

(7)   In subsection (2), reference to an act of discrimination or harassment which is unlawful includes, in the case of a relationship which has come to an end before the commencement of this section, reference to such an act which would, after the commencement of this section, be unlawful.

16B DISCRIMINATORY ADVERTISEMENTS

(1)   It is unlawful for a person to publish or cause to be published an advertisement which—
(a)   invites applications for a relevant appointment or benefit; and
(b)   indicates, or might reasonably be understood to indicate, that an application will or may be determined to any extent by reference to–
(i)   the applicant not having any disability, or any particular disability,
(ii)   the applicant not having had any disability, or any particular disability, or
(iii) any reluctance of the person determining the application to comply with a duty to make reasonable adjustments or (in relation to employment services) with the duty imposed by section 21(1) as modified by section 21A(6).

(2)   Subsection (1) does not apply where it would not in fact be unlawful under this Part or, to the extent that it relates to the provision of employment services, Part 3 for an application to be determined in the manner indicated (or understood to be indicated) in the advertisement.

(2A)   A person who publishes an advertisement of the kind described in subsection (1) shall not be subject to any liability under subsection (1) in respect of the publication of the advertisement if he proves—
(a)   that the advertisement was published in reliance on a statement made to him by the person who caused it to be published to the effect that, by reason of the operation of subsection (2), the publication would not be unlawful; and
(b)   that it was reasonable for him to rely on the statement.

(2B)   A person who knowingly or recklessly makes a statement such as is mentioned in subsection (2A)(a) which in a material respect is false or misleading commits an offence, and shall be liable on summary conviction to a fine not exceeding level 5 on the standard scale.

(2C) Subsection (1) does not apply in relation to an advertisement so far as it invites persons to apply, in their capacity as members of an authority to which sections 15B and 15C apply, for a relevant appointment or benefit which the authority is intending to make or confer.

(3) In this section, "relevant appointment or benefit" means—
  (a) any employment, promotion or transfer of employment;
  (b) membership of, or a benefit under, an occupational pension scheme;
  (c) an appointment to any office or post to which section 4D applies;
  (d) any partnership in a firm (within the meaning of section 6A);
  (e) any tenancy or pupillage (within the meaning of section 7A or 7C);
  (f) any membership of a trade organisation (within the meaning of section 13);
  (g) any professional or trade qualification (within the meaning of section 14A);
  (h) any work placement (within the meaning of section 14C);
  (i) any employment services.

(4) In this section, "advertisement" includes every form of advertisement or notice, whether to the public or not.

(5) Proceedings in respect of a contravention of subsection (1) may be brought only—
  (a) by the Commission for Equality and Human Rights, and
  (b) in accordance with section 25 of the Equality Act 2006.

16C INSTRUCTIONS AND PRESSURE TO DISCRIMINATE

(1) It is unlawful for a person—
  (a) who has authority over another person, or
  (b) in accordance with whose wishes that other person is accustomed to act,
  to instruct him to do any act which is unlawful under this Part or, to the extent that it relates to the provision of employment services, Part 3, or to procure or attempt to procure the doing by him of any such act.

(2) It is also unlawful to induce, or attempt to induce, a person to do any act which contravenes this Part or, to the extent that it relates to the provision of employment services, Part 3 by—
  (a) providing or offering to provide him with any benefit, or
  (b) subjecting or threatening to subject him to any detriment.

(3) An attempted inducement is not prevented from falling within subsection (2) because it is not made directly to the person in question, if it is made in such a way that he is likely to hear of it.

(4) Proceedings in respect of a contravention of this section may be brought only—
  (a) by the Commission for Equality and Human Rights, and
  (b) in accordance with section 25 of the Equality Act 2006.

17A ENFORCEMENT, REMEDIES AND PROCEDURE

(1) A complaint by any person that another person—
  (a) has discriminated against him, or subjected him to harassment, in a way which is unlawful under this Part, or
  (b) is, by virtue of section 57 or 58, to be treated as having done so,
  may be presented to an employment tribunal.

(1A) Subsection (1) does not apply to a complaint under section 14A(1) or (2) of an act in respect of which an appeal, or proceedings in the nature of an appeal, may be brought under any enactment.

(1C) Where, on the hearing of a complaint under subsection (1), the complainant proves facts from which the tribunal could, apart from this subsection, conclude in the absence of an adequate explanation that the respondent has acted in a way which is unlawful under this Part, the tribunal shall uphold the complaint unless the respondent proves that he did not so act.

(2) Where an employment tribunal finds that a complaint presented to it under this section is well-founded, it shall take such of the following steps as it considers just and equitable—
   (a) making a declaration as to the rights of the complainant and the respondent in relation to the matters to which the complaint relates;
   (b) ordering the respondent to pay compensation to the complainant;
   (c) recommending that the respondent take, within a specified period, action appearing to the tribunal to be reasonable, in all the circumstances of the case, for the purpose of obviating or reducing the adverse effect on the complainant of any matter to which the complaint relates.

(3) Where a tribunal orders compensation under subsection (2)(b), the amount of the compensation shall be calculated by applying the principles applicable to the calculation of damages in claims in tort or (in Scotland) in reparation for breach of statutory duty.

(4) For the avoidance of doubt it is hereby declared that compensation in respect of discrimination in a way which is unlawful under this Part may include compensation for injury to feelings whether or not it includes compensation under any other head.

(5) If the respondent to a complaint fails, without reasonable justification, to comply with a recommendation made by an employment tribunal under subsection (2)(c) the tribunal may, if it thinks it just and equitable to do so—
   (a) increase the amount of compensation required to be paid to the complainant in respect of the complaint, where an order was made under subsection (2)(b); or
   (b) make an order under subsection (2)(b).

(6) Regulations may make provision—
   (a) for enabling a tribunal, where an amount of compensation falls to be awarded under subsection (2)(b), to include in the award interest on that amount; and
   (b) specifying, for cases where a tribunal decides that an award is to include an amount in respect of interest, the manner in which and the periods and rate by reference to which the interest is to be determined.

(7) Regulations may modify the operation of any order made under section 14 of the Employment Tribunals Act 1996 (power to make provision as to interest on sums payable in pursuance of employment tribunal decisions) to the extent that it relates to an award of compensation under subsection (2)(b).

(8) Part I of Schedule 3 makes further provision about the enforcement of this Part and about procedure.

18B REASONABLE ADJUSTMENTS: SUPPLEMENTARY

(1) In determining whether it is reasonable for a person to have to take a particular step in order to comply with a duty to make reasonable adjustments, regard shall be had, in particular, to—

(a) the extent to which taking the step would prevent the effect in relation to which the duty is imposed;

(b) the extent to which it is practicable for him to take the step;

(c) the financial and other costs which would be incurred by him in taking the step and the extent to which taking it would disrupt any of his activities;

(d) the extent of his financial and other resources;

(e) the availability to him of financial or other assistance with respect to taking the step;

(f) the nature of his activities and the size of his undertaking;

(g) where the step would be taken in relation to a private household, the extent to which taking it would–
     (i) disrupt that household, or
     (ii) disturb any person residing there.

(2) The following are examples of steps which a person may need to take in relation to a disabled person in order to comply with a duty to make reasonable adjustments—

(a) making adjustments to premises;

(b) allocating some of the disabled person's duties to another person;

(c) transferring him to fill an existing vacancy;

(d) altering his hours of working or training;

(e) assigning him to a different place of work or training;

(f) allowing him to be absent during working or training hours for rehabilitation, assessment or treatment;

(g) giving, or arranging for, training or mentoring (whether for the disabled person or any other person);

(h) acquiring or modifying equipment;

(i) modifying instructions or reference manuals;

(j) modifying procedures for testing or assessment;

(k) providing a reader or interpreter;

(l) providing supervision or other support.

(3) For the purposes of a duty to make reasonable adjustments, where under any binding obligation a person is required to obtain the consent of another person to any alteration of the premises occupied by him—

(a) it is always reasonable for him to have to take steps to obtain that consent; and

(b) it is never reasonable for him to have to make that alteration before that consent is obtained.

(4) The steps referred to in subsection (3)(a) shall not be taken to include an application to a court or tribunal.

(5) In subsection (3), "binding obligation" means a legally binding obligation (not contained in a lease (within the meaning of section 18A(3)) in relation to the premises, whether arising from an agreement or otherwise.

(6) A provision of this Part imposing a duty to make reasonable adjustments applies only for the purpose of determining whether a person has discriminated against a disabled person; and accordingly a breach of any such duty is not actionable as such.

Part VII SUPPLEMENTAL

55 VICTIMISATION

(1) For the purposes of Part 2 or Part 4, or Part 3 other than sections 24A to 24L, a person ("A") discriminates against another person ("B") if—

(a) he treats B less favourably than he treats or would treat other persons whose circumstances are the same as B's; and

(b) he does so for a reason mentioned in subsection (2).

(2) The reasons are that—

(a) B has—

(i) brought proceedings against A or any other person under this Act; or

(ii) given evidence or information in connection with such proceedings brought by any person; or

(iii) otherwise done anything under, or by reference to, this Act in relation to A or any other person; or

(iv) alleged that A or any other person has (whether or not the allegation so states) contravened this Act; or

(b) A believes or suspects that B has done or intends to do any of those things.

(3) Where B is a disabled person, or a person who has had a disability, the disability in question shall be disregarded in comparing his circumstances with those of any other person for the purposes of subsection (1)(a).

(3A) For the purposes of Chapter 1 of Part 4—

(a) references in subsection (2) to B include references to—

(i) a person who is, for the purposes of that Chapter, B's parent; and

(ii) a sibling of B; and

(b) references in that subsection to this Act are, as respects a person mentioned in sub-paragraph (i) or (ii) of paragraph (a), restricted to that Chapter.

(4) Subsection (1) does not apply to treatment of a person because of an allegation made by him if the allegation was false and not made in good faith.

(5) In the case of an act which constitutes discrimination by virtue of this section, sections 4, 4B, 4D, 4G, 6A, 7A, 7C, 13, 14A, 14C, 15B and 16A also apply to discrimination against a person who is not disabled.

57 AIDING UNLAWFUL ACTS

(1) A person who knowingly aids another person to do an unlawful act is to be treated for the purposes of this Act as himself doing the same kind of unlawful act.

(2) For the purposes of subsection (1), an employee or agent for whose act the employer or principal is liable under section 58 (or would be so liable but for section 58(5)) shall be taken to have aided the employer or principal to do the act.

(3) For the purposes of this section, a person does not knowingly aid another to do an unlawful act if—

(a) he acts in reliance on a statement made to him by that other person that, because of any provision of this Act, the act would not be unlawful; and

(b) it is reasonable for him to rely on the statement.

(4) A person who knowingly or recklessly makes such a statement which is false or misleading in a material respect is guilty of an offence.

(5) Any person guilty of an offence under subsection (4) shall be liable on summary conviction to a fine not exceeding level 5 on the standard scale.

(6) "Unlawful act" means an act made unlawful by any provision of this Act other than a provision contained in Chapter 1 of Part 4.

58 LIABILITY OF EMPLOYERS AND PRINCIPALS

(1)   Anything done by a person in the course of his employment shall be treated for the purposes of this Act as also done by his employer, whether or not it was done with the employer's knowledge or approval.

(2)   Anything done by a person as agent for another person with the authority of that other person shall be treated for the purposes of this Act as also done by that other person.

(3)   Subsection (2) applies whether the authority was—
(a) express or implied; or
(b) given before or after the act in question was done.

(4)   Subsections (1) and (2) do not apply in relation to an offence under section 57(4).

(5)   In proceedings under this Act against any person in respect of an act alleged to have been done by an employee of his, it shall be a defence for that person to prove that he took such steps as were reasonably practicable to prevent the employee from—
(a) doing that act; or
(b) doing, in the course of his employment, acts of that description.

SCHEDULE 1 PROVISIONS SUPPLEMENTING SECTION 1

1 IMPAIRMENT

(2)   Regulations may make provision, for the purposes of this Act—
(a) for conditions of a prescribed description to be treated as amounting to impairments;
(b) for conditions of a prescribed description to be treated as not amounting to impairments.

(3)   Regulations made under sub-paragraph (2) may make provision as to the meaning of "condition" for the purposes of those regulations.

2 LONG-TERM EFFECTS

(1)   The effect of an impairment is a long-term effect if—
(a) if has lasted at least 12 months;
(b) the period for which it lasts is likely to be at least 12 months; or
(c) it is likely to last for the rest of the life of the person affected.

(2)   Where an impairment ceases to have a substantial adverse effect on a person's ability to carry out normal day-to-day activities, it is to be treated as continuing to have that effect if that effect is likely to recur.

(3)   For the purposes of sub-paragraph (2), the likelihood of an effect recurring shall be disregarded in prescribed circumstances.

(4)   Regulations may prescribe circumstances in which, for the purposes of this Act—
(a) an effect which would not otherwise be a long-term effect is to be treated as such an effect; or
(b) an effect which would otherwise be a long-term effect is to be treated as not being such an effect.

3 SEVERE DISFIGUREMENT

(1)   An impairment which consists of a severe disfigurement is to be treated as having a substantial adverse effect on the ability of the person concerned to carry out normal day-to-day activities.

(2)   Regulations may provide that in prescribed circumstances a severe disfigurement is not to be treated as having that effect.

(3)   Regulations under sub-paragraph (2) may, in particular, make provision with respect to deliberately acquired disfigurements.

4 NORMAL DAY-TO-DAY ACTIVITIES

(1)   An impairment is to be taken to affect the ability of the person concerned to carry out normal day-to-day activities only if it affects one of the following—
(a) mobility;
(b) manual dexterity;
(c) physical co-ordination;
(d) continence;
(e) ability to lift, carry or otherwise move everyday objects;
(f) speech, hearing or eyesight;
(g) memory or ability to concentrate, learn or understand; or
(h) perception of the risk of physical danger.

(2)   Regulations may prescribe—
(a) circumstances in which an impairment which does not have an effect falling within sub-paragraph (1) is to be taken to affect the ability of the person concerned to carry out normal day-to-day activities;
(b) circumstances in which an impairment which has an effect falling within sub-paragraph (1) is to be taken not to affect the ability of the person concerned to carry out normal day-to-day activities.

5 SUBSTANTIAL ADVERSE EFFECTS

Regulations may make provisions for the purposes of this Act—
(a)   for an effect of a prescribed kind on the ability of a person to carry out normal day-to-day activities to be treated as a substantial adverse effect;

(b)   for an effect of a prescribed kind on the ability of a person to carry out normal day-to-day activities to be treated as not being a substantial adverse effect.

6 EFFECT OF MEDICAL TREATMENT

(1)   An impairment which would be likely to have a substantial adverse effect on the ability of the person concerned to carry out normal day-to-day activities, but for the fact that measures are being taken to treat or correct it, is to be treated as having that effect.

(2)   In sub-paragraph (1) "measures" includes, in particular, medical treatment and the use of a prosthesis or other aid.

(3)   Sub-paragraph (1) does not apply—
(a) in relation to the impairment of a person's sight, to the extent that the impairment is, in his case, correctable by spectacles or contact lenses or in such other ways as may be prescribed; or

(b) in relation to such other impairments as may be prescribed, in such circumstances as may be prescribed.

6A PERSONS DEEMED TO BE DISABLED

(1) Subject to sub-paragraph (2), a person who has cancer, HIV infection or multiple sclerosis is to be deemed to have a disability, and hence to be a disabled person.

(2) Regulations may provide for sub-paragraph (1) not to apply in the case of a person who has cancer if he has cancer of a prescribed description.

(3) A description of cancer prescribed under sub-paragraph (2) may (in particular) be framed by reference to consequences for a person of his having it.

7 PERSONS DEEMED TO BE DISABLED

(1) Sub-paragraph (2) applies to any person whose name is, both on 12th January 1995 and on the date when this paragraph comes into force, in the register of disabled persons maintained under section 6 of the Disabled Persons (Employment) Act 1944.

(2) That person is to be deemed—
(a) during the initial period, to have disability, and hence to be a disabled person; and
(b) afterwards, to have had a disability and hence to have been a disabled person during that period.

(3) A certificate of registration shall be conclusive evidence, in relation to the person with respect to whom it was issued, of the matters certified.

(4) Unless the contrary is shown, any document purporting to be a certificate of registration shall be taken to be such a certificate and to have been validly issued.

(5) Regulations may provide for prescribed descriptions of person to be deemed to have disabilities, and hence to be disabled persons, for the purpose of this Act.

(5A) The generality of sub-paragraph (5) shall not be taken to be prejudiced by the other provisions of this Schedule.

(6) Regulations may prescribe circumstances in which a person who has been deemed to be a disabled person by the provisions of sub-paragraph (1) or regulations made under sub-paragraph (5) is to be treated as no longer being deemed to be such a person.

(7) In this paragraph—

"certificate of registration" means a certificate issued under regulations made under regulations made under section 6 of the Act of 1944; and

"initial period" means the period of three years beginning with the date on which this paragraph comes into force.

8 PROGRESSIVE CONDITIONS

(1) Where—
(a) a person has a progressive condition (such as cancer, multiple sclerosis or muscular dystrophy or HIV infection),
(b) as a result of that condition, he has an impairment which has (or had) an effect on his ability to carry out normal day-to-day activities, but
(c) that effect is not (or was not) a substantial adverse effect,

he shall be taken to have an impairment which has such a substantial adverse effect if the condition is likely to result in his having such an impairment.

(2) Regulations may make provision, for the purpose of this paragraph—
    (a) for conditions of a prescribed description to be treated as being progressive;
    (b) for conditions of a prescribed description to be treated as not being progressive.

SCHEDULE 3 ENFORCEMENT AND PROCEDURE

Part I EMPLOYMENT

3 PERIOD WITHIN WHICH PROCEEDINGS MUST BE BROUGHT

(1) An employment tribunal shall not consider a complaint under section 17A or 25(8) unless it presented before the end of the period of three months beginning when the act complained of was done.

(2) A tribunal may consider any such complaint which is out of time if, in all the circumstances of the case, if considers that it is just and equitable to do so.

(3) For the purpose of sub-paragraph (1)—
    (a) where an unlawful act is attributable to a term in a contract, that act is to be treated as extending throughout the duration of the contract;
    (b) any act extending over a period shall be treated as done at the end of that period; and
    (c) a deliberate omission shall be treated as done when the person in question decided upon it.

(4) In the absence of evidence establishing the contrary, a person shall be taken for the purpose of this paragraph to decide upon an omission—
    (a) when he does an act inconsistent with doing the omitted act; or
    (b) if he has done no such inconsistent act, when the period expires within which he might reasonably have been expected to do the omitted act if it was to be done.

As amended by the Employment Rights (Dispute Resolution) Act 1998, Pt I s 1(2); Special Educational Needs and Disability Act 2001, Pt 2 c.3 s 38(3), Pt 2 c.3 s 38(4), Pt 2 c.3 s 38(8), Pt 2 c.3 s 38(9), Pt 2 c.3 s 38(10); Disability Discrimination Act 1995 (Amendment) Regulations 2003/1673 Pt 2 reg 4(2), Pt 2 reg 5, Pt 2 reg 9(1), Pt 2 reg 9(2)(a), Pt 2 reg 9(2)(b), Pt 2 reg 9(2) (c), Pt 2 reg 15(1), Pt 2 reg 17(2), Pt 2 reg 21, Pt 2 reg 29(2)(c), Pt 2 reg 29(2)(d); Disability Discrimination Act 2005, s 10(2), s 10(3), s 10(4), s 18(3), s 18(4), Sch 1(1) para 2(2), Sch 1(1) para 2(3), Sch 1(1) para 2(4), Sch 1(1) para 3(2), Sch 1(1) para 3(3)(a), Sch 1(1) para 3(3)(b), Sch 1(1) para 3(4), Sch 1(1) para 3(5), Sch 1(1) para 7(a), Sch 1(1) para 8(2), Sch 1(1) para 29(2), Sch 1(1) para 29(3), Sch 1(1) para 29(4), Sch 1(1) para 36, Sch 2 para 1; Equality Act 2006, Sch 3 para 42, Sch 3 para 43; Government of Wales Act 2006 (Consequential Modifications and Transitional Provisions) Order 2007/1388 Sch 1 para 48.

EMPLOYMENT RIGHTS ACT 1996
(c. 18)

Part I EMPLOYMENT PARTICULARS

1 STATEMENT OF INITIAL EMPLOYMENT PARTICULARS

(1)   Where an employee begins employment with an employer, the employer shall give to the employee a written statement of particulars of employment.

(2)   The statement may (subject to section 2(4)) be given in instalments and (whether or not given in instalments) shall be given not later than two months after the beginning of the employment.

(3)   The statement shall contain particulars of—
(a)   the names of the employer and employee,
(b)   the date when the employment began, and
(c)   the date on which the employee's period of continuous employment began (taking into account any employment with a previous employer which counts towards that period).

(4)   The statement shall also contain particulars, as at a specified date not more than seven days before the statement (or the instalment containing them) is given, of—
(a)   the scale or rate of remuneration or the method of calculating remuneration,
(b)   the intervals at which remuneration is paid (that is, weekly, monthly or other specified intervals),
(c)   any terms and conditions relating to hours of work (including any terms and conditions relating to normal working hours),
(d)   any terms and conditions relating to any of the following—
(i)   entitlement to holidays, including public holidays, and holiday pay (the particulars given being sufficient to enable the employee's entitlement, including any entitlement to accrued holiday pay on the termination of employment, to be precisely calculated),
(ii)   incapacity for work due to sickness or injury, including any provision for sick pay, and
(iii)   pensions and pension schemes,
(e)   the length of notice which the employee is obliged to give and entitled to receive to terminate his contract of employment,
(f)   the title of the job which the employee is employed to do or a brief description of the work for which he is employed,

(g) where the employment is not intended to be permanent, the period for which it is expected to continue or, if it is for a fixed term, the date when it is to end,

(h) either the place of work or, where the employee is required or permitted to work at various places, an indication of that and of the address of the employer,

(j) any collective agreements which directly affect the terms and conditions of the employment including, where the employer is not a party, the persons by whom they were made, and

(k) where the employee is required to work outside the United Kingdom for a period of more than one month—

(i) the period for which he is to work outside the United Kingdom,

(ii) the currency in which remuneration is to be paid while he is working outside the United Kingdom,

(iii) any additional remuneration payable to him, and any benefits to be provided to or in respect of him, by reason of his being required to work outside the United Kingdom, and

(iv) any terms and conditions relating to his return to the United Kingdom.

(5) Subsection (4)(d)(iii) does not apply to an employee of a body or authority if—

(a) the employee's pension rights depend on the terms of a pension scheme established under any provision contained in or having effect under any Act, and

(b) any such provision requires the body or authority to give to a new employee information concerning the employee's pension rights or the determination of questions affecting those rights.

2 STATEMENT OF INITIAL PARTICULARS: SUPPLEMENTARY

(1) If, in the case of a statement under section 1, there are no particulars to be entered under any of the heads of paragraph (d) or (k) of subsection (4) of that section, or under any of the other paragraphs of subsection (3) or (4) of that section, that fact shall be stated.

(2) A statement under section 1 may refer the employee for particulars of any of the matters specified in subsection (4)(d)(ii) and (iii) of that section to the provisions of some other document which is reasonably accessible to the employee.

(3) A statement under section 1 may refer the employee for particulars of either of the matters specified in subsection (4)(e) of that section to the law or to the provisions of any collective agreement directly affecting the terms and conditions of the employment which is reasonably accessible to the employee.

(4) The particulars required by section 1(3) and (4)(a) to (c), (d)(i), (f) and (h) shall be included in a single document.

(5) Where before the end of the period of two months after the beginning of an employee's employment the employee is to begin to work outside the United Kingdom for a period of more than one month, the statement under section 1 shall be given to him not later than the time when he leaves the United Kingdom in order to begin so to work.

(6) A statement shall be given to a person under section 1 even if his employment ends before the end of the period within which the statement is required to be given.

3 NOTE ABOUT DISCIPLINARY PROCEDURES AND PENSIONS

(1) A statement under section 1 shall include a note—

(a) specifying any disciplinary rules applicable to the employee or referring the employee to the provisions of a document specifying such rules which is reasonably accessible to the employee,

(aa) specifying any procedure applicable to the taking of disciplinary decisions relating to the employee, or to a decision to dismiss the employee, or referring the employee to the provisions of a document specifying such a procedure which is reasonably accessible to the employee,

(b) specifying (by description or otherwise)—

(i)   a person to whom the employee can apply if dissatisfied with any disciplinary decision relating to him, or any decision to dismiss him, and

(ii) a person to whom the employee can apply for the purpose of seeking redress of any grievance relating to his employment,

and the manner in which any such application should be made, and

(c) where there are further steps consequent on any such application, explaining those steps or referring to the provisions of a document explaining them which is reasonably accessible to the employee.

(2) Subsection (1) does not apply to rules, disciplinary decisions, decisions to dismiss grievances or procedures relating to health or safety at work.

(5) The note shall also state whether there is in force a contracting-out certificate (issued in accordance with Chapter I of Part III of the Pension Schemes Act 1993) stating that the employment is contracted-out employment (for the purposes of that Part of that Act).

4 STATEMENT OF CHANGES

(1) If, after the material date, there is a change in any of the matters particulars of which are required by sections 1 to 3 to be included or referred to in a statement under section 1, the employer shall give to the employee a written statement containing particulars of the change.

(2) For the purposes of subsection (1)—

(a) in relation to a matter particulars of which are included or referred to in a statement given under section 1 otherwise than in instalments, the material date is the date to which the statement relates,

(b) in relation to a matter particulars of which—

(i)   are included or referred to in an instalment of a statement given under section 1, or

(ii) are required by section 2(4) to be included in a single document but are not included in an instalment of a statement given under section 1 which does include other particulars to which that provision applies,

the material date is the date to which the instalment relates, and

(c) in relation to any other matter, the material date is the date by which a statement under section 1 is required to be given.

(3) A statement under subsection (1) shall be given at the earliest opportunity and, in any event, not later than—

(a) one month after the change in question, or

(b) where that change results from the employee being required to work outside the United Kingdom for a period of more than one month, the time when he leaves the United Kingdom in order to begin so to work, if that is earlier.

(4)   A statement under subsection (1) may refer the employee to the provisions of some other document which is reasonably accessible to the employee for a change in any of the matters specified in sections 1(4)(d)(ii) and (iii) and 3(1)(a) and (c).

(5)   A statement under subsection (1) may refer the employee for a change in either of the matters specified in section 1(4)(e) to the law or to the provisions of any collective agreement directly affecting the terms and conditions of the employment which is reasonably accessible to the employee.

(6)   Where, after an employer has given to an employee a statement under section 1, either—
(a)   the name of the employer (whether an individual or a body corporate or partnership) is changed without any change in the identity of the employer, or
(b)   the identity of the employer is changed in circumstances in which the continuity of the employee's period of employment is not broken,
and subsection (7) applies in relation to the change, the person who is the employer immediately after the change is not required to give to the employee a statement under section 1; but the change shall be treated as a change falling within subsection (1) of this section.

(7)   This subsection applies in relation to a change if it does not involve any change in any of the matters (other than the names of the parties) particulars of which are required by sections 1 to 3 to be included or referred to in the statement under section 1.

(8)   A statement under subsection (1) which informs an employee of a change such as is referred to in subsection (6)(b) shall specify the date on which the employee's period of continuous employment began.

5 EXCLUSION FROM RIGHTS TO STATEMENTS

(1)   Sections 1 to 4 apply to an employee who at any time comes or ceases to come within the exceptions from those sections provided by section 199, and under section 209, as if his employment with his employer terminated or began at that time.

(2)   The fact that section 1 is directed by subsection (1) to apply to an employee as if his employment began on his ceasing to come within the exceptions referred to in that subsection does not affect the obligation under section 1(3)(b) to specify the date on which his employment actually began.

6 REASONABLY ACCESSIBLE DOCUMENT OR COLLECTIVE AGREEMENT

In sections 2 to 4 references to a document or collective agreement which is reasonably accessible to an employee are references to a document or collective agreement which—
(a)   the employee has reasonable opportunities of reading in the course of his employment, or
(b)   is made reasonably accessible to the employee in some other way.

7 POWER TO REQUIRE PARTICULARS OF FURTHER MATTERS

The Secretary of State may by order provide that section 1 shall have effect as if particulars of such further matters as may be specified in the order were included in the particulars required by that section; and, for that purpose, the order may include such provisions amending that section as appear to the Secretary of State to be expedient.

7A USE OF ALTERNATIVE DOCUMENTS TO GIVE PARTICULARS

(1) Subsections (2) and (3) apply where—
  (a) an employer gives an employee a document in writing in the form of a contract of employment or letter of engagement,
  (b) the document contains information which, were the document in the form of a statement under section 1, would meet the employer's obligation under that section in relation to the matters mentioned in subsections (3) and (4)(a) to (c), (d)(i), (f) and (h) of that section, and
  (c) the document is given after the beginning of the employment and before the end of the period for giving a statement under that section.

(2) The employer's duty under section 1 in relation to any matter shall be treated as met if the document given to the employee contains information which, were the document in the form of a statement under that section, would meet the employer's obligation under that section in relation to that matter.

(3) The employer's duty under section 3 shall be treated as met if the document given to the employee contains information which, were the document in the form of a statement under section 1 and the information included in the form of a note, would meet the employer's obligation under section 3.

(4) For the purposes of this section a document to which subsection (1)(a) applies shall be treated, in relation to information in respect of any of the matters mentioned in section 1(4), as specifying the date on which the document is given to the employee as the date as at which the information applies.

(5) Where subsection (2) applies in relation to any matter, the date on which the document by virtue of which that subsection applies is given to the employee shall be the material date in relation to that matter for the purposes of section 4(1).

(6) Where subsection (3) applies, the date on which the document by virtue of which that subsection applies is given to the employee shall be the material date for the purposes of section 4(1) in relation to the matters of which particulars are required to be given under section 3.

(7) The reference in section 4(6) to an employer having given a statement under section 1 shall be treated as including his having given a document by virtue of which his duty to give such a statement is treated as met.

7B GIVING OF ALTERNATIVE DOCUMENTS BEFORE START OF EMPLOYMENT

A document in the form of a contract of employment or letter of engagement given by an employer to an employee before the beginning of the employee's employment with the employer shall, when the employment begins, be treated for the purposes of section 7A as having been given at that time.

8 ITEMISED PAY STATEMENT

(1) An employee has the right to be given by his employer, at or before the time at which any payment of wages or salary is made to him, a written itemised pay statement.

(2) The statement shall contain particulars of—
  (a) the gross amount of the wages or salary,
  (b) the amounts of any variable, and (subject to section 9) any fixed, deductions from that gross amount and the purposes for which they are made,

(c) the net amount of wages or salary payable, and

(d) where different parts of the net amount are paid in different ways, the amount and method of payment of each part-payment.

11 REFERENCES TO EMPLOYMENT TRIBUNALS

(1) Where an employer does not give an employee a statement as required by section 1, 4 or 8 (either because he gives him no statement or because the statement he gives does not comply with what is required), the employee may require a reference to be made to an employment tribunal to determine what particulars ought to have been included or referred to in a statement so as to comply with the requirements of the section concerned.

(2) Where—

(a) a statement purporting to be a statement under section 1 or 4, or a pay statement or a standing statement of fixed deductions purporting to comply with section 8 or 9, has been given to an employee, and

(b) a question arises as to the particulars which ought to have been included or referred to in the statement so as to comply with the requirements of this Part,

either the employer or the employee may require the question to be referred to and determined by an employment tribunal.

(3) For the purposes of this section—

(a) a question as to the particulars which ought to have been included in the note required by section 3 to be included in the statement under section 1 does not include any question whether the employment is, has been or will be contracted-out employment (for the purposes of Part III of the Pension Schemes Act 1993), and

(b) a question as to the particulars which ought to have been included in a pay statement or standing statement of fixed deductions does not include a question solely as to the accuracy of an amount stated in any such particulars.

(4) An employment tribunal shall not consider a reference under this section in a case where the employment to which the reference relates has ceased unless an application requiring the reference to be made was made—

(a) before the end of the period of three months beginning with the date on which the employment ceased, or

(b) within such further period as the tribunal considers reasonable in a case where it is satisfied that it was not reasonably practicable for the application to be made before the end of that period of three months.

12 DETERMINATION OF REFERENCES

(1) Where, on a reference under section 11(1), an employment tribunal determines particulars as being those which ought to have been included or referred to in a statement given under section 1 or 4, the employer shall be deemed to have given to the employee a statement in which those particulars were included, or referred to, as specified in the decision of the tribunal.

(2) On determining a reference under section 11(2) relating to a statement purporting to be a statement under section 1 or 4, an employment tribunal may—

(a) confirm the particulars as included or referred to in the statement given by the employer,

(b) amend those particulars, or

(c) substitute other particulars for them,

as the tribunal may determine to be appropriate; and the statement shall be deemed to have been given by the employer to the employee in accordance with the decision of the tribunal.

(3)   Where on a reference under section 11 an employment tribunal finds—
   (a) that an employer has failed to give an employee any pay statement in accordance with section 8, or
   (b) that a pay statement or standing statement of fixed deductions does not, in relation to a deduction, contain the particulars required to be included in that statement by that section or section 9,
the tribunal shall make a declaration to that effect.

(4)   Where on a reference in the case of which subsection (3) applies the tribunal further finds that any unnotified deductions have been made from the pay of the employee during the period of thirteen weeks immediately preceding the date of the application for the reference (whether or not the deductions were made in breach of the contract of employment), the tribunal may order the employer to pay the employee a sum not exceeding the aggregate of the unnotified deductions so made.

(5)   For the purposes of subsection (4) a deduction is an unnotified deduction if it is made without the employer giving the employee, in any pay statement or standing statement of fixed deductions, the particulars of the deduction required by section 8 or 9.

Part II PROTECTION OF WAGES

13 RIGHT NOT TO SUFFER UNAUTHORISED DEDUCTIONS

(1)   An employer shall not make a deduction from wages of a worker employed by him unless—
   (a) the deduction is required or authorised to be made by virtue of a statutory provision or a relevant provision of the worker's contract, or
   (b) the worker has previously signified in writing his agreement or consent to the making of the deduction.

(2)   In this section "relevant provision", in relation to a worker's contract, means a provision of the contract comprised—
   (a) in one or more written terms of the contract of which the employer has given the worker a copy on an occasion prior to the employer making the deduction in question, or
   (b) in one or more terms of the contract (whether express or implied and, if express, whether oral or in writing) the existence and effect, or combined effect, of which in relation to the worker the employer has notified to the worker in writing on such an occasion.

(3)   Where the total amount of wages paid on any occasion by an employer to a worker employed by him is less than the total amount of the wages properly payable by him to the worker on that occasion (after deductions), the amount of the deficiency shall be treated for the purposes of this Part as a deduction made by the employer from the worker's wages on that occasion.

(4)   Subsection (3) does not apply in so far as the deficiency is attributable to an error of any description on the part of the employer affecting the computation by him of the gross amount of the wages properly payable by him to the worker on that occasion.

(5)   For the purposes of this section a relevant provision of a worker's contract having effect by virtue of a variation of the contract does not operate to authorise the making of a deduction on account of any conduct of the worker, or any other event occurring, before the variation took effect.

(6)   For the purposes of this section an agreement or consent signified by a worker does not operate to authorise the making of a deduction on account of any conduct of the worker, or any other event occurring, before the agreement or consent was signified.

(7)   This section does not affect any other statutory provision by virtue of which a sum payable to a worker by his employer but not constituting "wages" within the meaning of this Part is not to be subject to a deduction at the instance of the employer.

14   EXCEPTED DEDUCTIONS

(1)   Section 13 does not apply to a deduction from a worker's wages made by his employer where the purpose of the deduction is the reimbursement of the employer in respect of—
(a)   an overpayment of wages, or
(b)   an overpayment in respect of expenses incurred by the worker in carrying out his employment,
made (for any reason) by the employer to the worker.

(2)   Section 13 does not apply to a deduction from a worker's wages made by his employer in consequence of any disciplinary proceedings if those proceedings were held by virtue of a statutory provision.

(3)   Section 13 does not apply to a deduction from a worker's wages made by his employer in pursuance of a requirement imposed on the employer by a statutory provision to deduct and pay over to a public authority amounts determined by that authority as being due to it from the worker if the deduction is made in accordance with the relevant determination of that authority.

(4)   Section 13 does not apply to a deduction from a worker's wages made by his employer in pursuance of any arrangements which have been established—
(a)   in accordance with a relevant provision of his contract to the inclusion of which in the contract the worker has signified his agreement or consent in writing, or
(b)   otherwise with the prior agreement or consent of the worker signified in writing,
and under which the employer is to deduct and pay over to a third person amounts notified to the employer by that person as being due to him from the worker, if the deduction is made in accordance with the relevant notification by that person.

(5)   Section 13 does not apply to a deduction from a worker's wages made by his employer where the worker has taken part in a strike or other industrial action and the deduction is made by the employer on account of the worker's having taken part in that strike or other action.

(6)   Section 13 does not apply to a deduction from a worker's wages made by his employer with his prior agreement or consent signified in writing where the purpose of the deduction is the satisfaction (whether wholly or in part) of an order of a court or tribunal requiring the payment of an amount by the worker to the employer.

23   COMPLAINTS TO EMPLOYMENT TRIBUNALS

(1)   A worker may present a complaint to an employment tribunal—
(a)   that his employer has made a deduction from his wages in contravention of section 13 (including a deduction made in contravention of that section as it applies by virtue of section 18(2)),
(b)   that his employer has received from him a payment in contravention of section 15 (including a payment received in contravention of that section as it applies by virtue of section 20(1)),

(c) that his employer has recovered from his wages by means of one or more deductions falling within section 18(1) an amount or aggregate amount exceeding the limit applying to the deduction or deductions under that provision, or

(d) that his employer has received from him in pursuance of one or more demands for payment made (in accordance with section 20) on a particular pay day, a payment or payments of an amount or aggregate amount exceeding the limit applying to the demands or demands under section 21(1).

(2) Subject to subsection (4), an employment tribunal shall not consider a complaint under this section unless it is presented before the end of the period of three months beginning with—

(a) in the case of a complaint relating to a deduction by the employer, the date of payment of the wages from which the deduction was made, or

(b) in the case of a complaint relating to a payment received by the employer, the date when the payment was received.

(3) Where a complaint is brought under this section in respect of—

(a) a series of deductions or payments, or

(b) a number of payments falling within subsection (1)(d) and made in pursuance of demands for payment subject to the same limit under section 21(1) but received by the employer on different dates,

the references in subsection (2) to the deduction or payment are to the last deduction or payment in the series or to the last of the payments so received.

(4) Where the employment tribunal is satisfied that it was not reasonably practicable for a complaint under this section to be presented before the end of the relevant period of three months, the tribunal may consider the complaint if it is presented within such further period as the tribunal considers reasonable.

(5) No complaint shall be presented under this section in respect of any deduction made in contravention of section 86 of the Trade Union and Labour Relations (Consolidation) Act 1992 (deduction of political fund contribution where certificate of exemption or objection has been given).

24 DETERMINATION OF COMPLAINTS

(1) Where a tribunal finds a complaint under section 23 well-founded, it shall make a declaration to that effect and shall order the employer—

(a) in the case of a complaint under section 23(1)(a), to pay to the worker the amount of any deduction made in contravention of section 13,

(b) in the case of a complaint under section 23(1)(b), to repay to the worker the amount of any payment received in contravention of section 15,

(c) in the case of a complaint under section 23(1)(c), to pay to the worker any amount recovered from him in excess of the limit mentioned in that provision, and

(d) in the case of a complaint under section 23(1)(d), to repay to the worker any amount received from him in excess of the limit mentioned in that provision.

(2) Where a tribunal makes a declaration under subsection (1), it may order the employer to pay to the worker (in addition to any amount ordered to be paid under that subsection) such amount as the tribunal considers appropriate in all the circumstances to compensate the worker for any financial loss sustained by him which is attributable to the matter complained of.

27 MEANING OF "WAGES" ETC.

(1) In this Part "wages", in relation to a worker, means any sums payable to the worker in connection with his employment, including—

(a) any fee, bonus, commission, holiday pay or other emolument referable to his employment, whether payable under his contract or otherwise,

(b) statutory sick pay under Part XI of the Social Security Contributions and Benefits Act 1992,

(c) statutory maternity pay under Part XII of that Act,

(ca) ordinary statutory paternity pay or additional statutory paternity pay under Part 12ZA of that Act,

(cb) statutory adoption pay under Part 12ZB of that Act,

(d) a guarantee payment (under section 28 of this Act),

(e) any payment for time off under Part VI of this Act or section 169 of the Trade Union and Labour Relations (Consolidation) Act 1992 (payment for time off for carrying out trade union duties etc.),

(f) remuneration on suspension on medical grounds under section 64 of this Act and remuneration on suspension on maternity grounds under section 68 of this Act,

(g) any sum payable in pursuance of an order for reinstatement or re-engagement under section 113 of this Act,

(h) any sum payable in pursuance of an order for the continuation of a contract of employment under section 130 of this Act or section 164 of the Trade Union and Labour Relations (Consolidation) Act 1992, and

(j) remuneration under a protective award under section 189 of that Act,

but excluding any payments within subsection (2).

(2) Those payments are—

(a) any payment by way of an advance under an agreement for a loan or by way of an advance of wages (but without prejudice to the application of section 13 to any deduction made from the worker's wages in respect of any such advance),

(b) any payment in respect of expenses incurred by the worker in carrying out his employment,

(c) any payment by way of a pension, allowance or gratuity in connection with the worker's retirement or as compensation for loss of office,

(d) any payment referable to the worker's redundancy, and

(e) any payment to the worker otherwise than in his capacity as a worker.

(3) Where any payment in the nature of a non-contractual bonus is (for any reason) made to a worker by his employer, the amount of the payment shall for the purposes of this Part—

(a) be treated as wages of the worker, and

(b) be treated as payable to him as such on the day on which the payment is made.

(4) In this Part "gross amount", means in relation to any wages payable to a worker, the total amount of those wages before deductions of whatever nature.

(5) For the purposes of this Part any monetary value attaching to any payment or benefit in kind furnished to a worker by his employer shall not be treated as wages of the worker except in the case of any voucher, stamp or similar document which is—

(a) of a fixed value expressed in monetary terms, and

(b) capable of being exchanged (whether on its own or together with other vouchers, stamps or documents, and whether immediately or only after a time) for money, goods or services (or for any combination of two or more of those things).

Part IVA **PROTECTED DISCLOSURES**

43A MEANING OF "PROTECTED DISCLOSURE"

In this Act a "protected disclosure" means a qualifying disclosure (as defined by section 43B) which is made by a worker in accordance with any of sections 43C to 43H.

43B DISCLOSURES QUALIFYING FOR PROTECTION

(1)   In this Part a "qualifying disclosure" means any disclosure of information which, in the reasonable belief of the worker making the disclosure, tends to show one or more of the following—
    (a) that a criminal offence has been committed, is being committed or is likely to be committed,
    (b) that a person has failed, is failing or is likely to fail to comply with any legal obligation to which he is subject,
    (c) that a miscarriage of justice has occurred, is occurring or is likely to occur,
    (d) that the health or safety of any individual has been, is being or is likely to be endangered,
    (e) that the environment has been, is being or is likely to be damaged, or
    (f) that information tending to show any matter falling within any one of the preceding paragraphs has been, is being or is likely to be deliberately concealed.

(2)   For the purposes of subsection (1), it is immaterial whether the relevant failure occurred, occurs or would occur in the United Kingdom or elsewhere, and whether the law applying to it is that of the United Kingdom or of any other country or territory.

(3)   A disclosure of information is not a qualifying disclosure if the person making the disclosure commits an offence by making it.

(4)   A disclosure of information in respect of which a claim to legal professional privilege (or, in Scotland, to confidentiality as between client and professional legal adviser) could be maintained in legal proceedings is not a qualifying disclosure if it is made by a person to whom the information had been disclosed in the course of obtaining legal advice.

(5)   In this Part "the relevant failure", in relation to a qualifying disclosure, means the matter falling within paragraphs (a) to (f) of subsection (1).

43C DISCLOSURE TO EMPLOYER OR OTHER RESPONSIBLE PERSON

(1)   A qualifying disclosure is made in accordance with this section if the worker makes the disclosure in good faith—
    (a) to his employer, or
    (b) where the worker reasonably, believes that the relevant failure relates solely or mainly to—
        (i)   the conduct of a person other than his employer, or
        (ii) any other matter for which a person other than his employer has legal responsibility,
to that other person.

(2)   A worker who, in accordance with a procedure whose use by him is authorised by his employer, makes a qualifying disclosure to a person other than his employer, is to be treated for the purposes of this Part as making the qualifying disclosure to his employer.

43D DISCLOSURE TO LEGAL ADVISER

A qualifying disclosure is made in accordance with this section if it is made in the course of obtaining legal advice.

43E DISCLOSURE TO MINISTER OF THE CROWN

A qualifying disclosure is made in accordance with this section if—
(a) the worker's employer is—
    (i) an individual appointed under any enactment (including any enactment comprised in, or in an instrument made under, an Act of the Scottish Parliament) by a Minister of the Crown or a member of the Scottish Executive, or
    (ii) a body any of whose members are so appointed, and

(b) the disclosure is made in good faith to a Minister of the Crown or a member of the Scottish Executive.

43F DISCLOSURE TO PRESCRIBED PERSON

(1) A qualifying disclosure is made in accordance with this section if the worker—
    (a) makes the disclosure in good faith to a person prescribed by an order made by the Secretary of State for the purposes of this section, and
    (b) reasonably believes—
        (i) that the relevant failure falls within any description of matters in respect of which that person is so prescribed, and
        (ii) that the information disclosed, and any allegation contained in it, are substantially true.

(2) An order prescribing persons for the purposes of this section may specify persons or descriptions of persons, and shall specify the descriptions of matters in respect of which each person, or persons of each description, is or are prescribed.

43G DISCLOSURE IN OTHER CASES

(1) A qualifying disclosure is made in accordance with this section if—
    (a) the worker makes the disclosure in good faith,
    (b) he reasonably believes that the information disclosed, and any allegation contained in it, are substantially true,
    (c) he does not make the disclosure for purposes of personal gain,
    (d) any of the conditions in subsection (2) is met, and
    (e) in all the circumstances of the case, it is reasonable for him to make the disclosure.

(2) The conditions referred to in subsection (1)(d) are—
    (a) that, at the time he makes the disclosure, the worker reasonably believes that he will be subjected to a detriment by his employer if he makes a disclosure to his employer or in accordance with section 43F,
    (b) that, in a case where no person is prescribed for the purposes of section 43F in relation to the relevant failure, the worker reasonably believes that it is likely that evidence relating to the relevant failure will be concealed or destroyed if he makes a disclosure to his employer, or
    (c) that the worker has previously made a disclosure of substantially the same information—
        (i) to his employer, or
        (ii) in accordance with section 43F.

(3)   In determining for the purposes of subsection (1)(e) whether it is reasonable for the worker to make the disclosure, regard shall be had, in particular, to—

(a) the identity of the person to whom the disclosure is made,

(b) the seriousness of the relevant failure,

(c) whether the relevant failure is continuing or is likely to occur in the future,

(d) whether the disclosure is made in breach of a duty of confidentiality owed by the employer to any other person,

(e) in a case falling within subsection (2)(c)(i) or (ii), any action which the employer or the person to whom the previous disclosure in accordance with section 43F was made has taken or might reasonably be expected to have taken as a result of the previous disclosure, and

(f) in a case falling within subsection (2)(c)(i), whether in making the disclosure to the employer the worker complied with any procedure whose use by him was authorised by the employer.

(4)   For the purposes of this section a subsequent disclosure may be regarded as a disclosure of substantially the same information as that disclosed by a previous disclosure as mentioned in subsection (2)(c) even though the subsequent disclosure extends to information about action taken or not taken by any person as a result of the previous disclosure.

43H DISCLOSURE OF EXCEPTIONALLY SERIOUS FAILURE

(1)   A qualifying disclosure is made in accordance with this section if—

(a) the worker makes the disclosure in good faith,

(b) he reasonably believes that the information disclosed, and any allegation contained in it, are substantially true,

(c) he does not make the disclosure for purposes of personal gain,

(d) the relevant failure is of an exceptionally serious nature, and

(e) in all the circumstances of the case, it is reasonable for him to make the disclosure.

(2)   In determining for the purposes of subsection (1)(e) whether it is reasonable for the worker to make the disclosure, regard shall be had, in particular, to the identity of the person to whom the disclosure is made.

Part V PROTECTION FROM SUFFERING DETRIMENT IN EMPLOYMENT

44 HEALTH AND SAFETY CASES

(1)   An employee has the right not to be subjected to any detriment by any act, or any deliberate failure to act, by his employer done on the ground that—

(a) having been designated by the employer to carry out activities in connection with preventing or reducing risks to health and safety at work, the employee carried out (or proposed to carry out) any such activities,

(b) being a representative of workers on matters of health and safety at work or member of a safety committee—

(i) in accordance with arrangements established under or by virtue of any enactment, or

(ii) by reason of being acknowledged as such by the employer,

the employee performed (or proposed to perform) any functions as such a representative or a member of such a committee,

(ba) the employee took part (or proposed to take part) in consultation with the employer pursuant to the Health and Safety (Consultation with Employees) Regulations 1996 or in an election of representatives of employee safety within the meaning of those Regulations (whether as a candidate or otherwise),

(c) being an employee at a place where—

    (i) there was no such representative or safety committee, or

    (ii) there was such a representative or safety committee but it was not reasonably practicable for the employee to raise the matter by those means,

he brought to his employer's attention, by reasonable means, circumstances connected with his work which he reasonably believed were harmful or potentially harmful to health or safety,

(d) in circumstances of danger which the employee reasonably believed to be serious and imminent and which he could not reasonably have been expected to avert, he left (or proposed to leave) or (while the danger persisted) refused to return to his place of work or any dangerous part of his place of work, or

(e) in circumstances of danger which the employee reasonably believed to be serious and imminent, he took (or proposed to take) appropriate steps to protect himself or other persons from the danger.

(2) For the purposes of subsection (1)(e) whether steps which an employee took (or proposed to take) were appropriate is to be judged by reference to all the circumstances including, in particular, his knowledge and the facilities and advice available to him at the time.

(3) An employee is not to be regarded as having been subjected to any detriment on the ground specified in subsection (1)(e) if the employer shows that it was (or would have been) so negligent for the employee to take the steps which he took (or proposed to take) that a reasonable employer might have treated him as the employer did.

(4) This section does not apply where the detriment in question amounts to dismissal (within the meaning of Part X).

45A WORKING TIME CASES

(1) A worker has the right not to be subjected to any detriment by any Act, or any deliberate failure to act, by his employer done on the ground that the worker—

(a) refused (or proposed to refuse) to comply with a requirement which the employer imposed (or proposed to impose) in contravention of the Working Time Regulations 1998,

(b) refused (or proposed to refuse) to forgo a right conferred on him by those Regulations,

(c) failed to sign a workforce agreement for the purposes of those Regulations, or to enter into, or agree to vary or extend, any other agreement with his employer which is provided for in those Regulations,

(d) being—

    (i) a representative of members of the workforce for the purposes of Schedule 1 to those Regulations, or

    (ii) a candidate in an election in which any person elected will, on being elected, be such a representative,

performed (or proposed to perform) any functions or activities as such a representative or candidate,

(e) brought proceedings against the employer to enforce a right conferred on him by those Regulations, or

(f) alleged that the employer had infringed such a right.

(2)   It is immaterial for the purposes of subsection (1)(e) or (f)—

     (a)   whether or not the worker has the right, or

     (b)   whether or not the right has been infringed,

   but, for those provisions to apply, the claim to the right and that it has been infringed must be made in good faith.

(3)   It is sufficient for subsection (1)(f) to apply that the worker, without specifying the right, made it reasonably clear to the employer what the right claimed to have been infringed was.

(4)   This section does not apply where a worker is an employee and the detriment in question amounts to dismissal within the meaning of Part X.

47   EMPLOYEE REPRESENTATIVES

(1)   An employee has the right not to be subjected to any detriment by any act, or any deliberate failure to act, by his employer done on the ground that, being—

     (a)   an employee representative for the purposes of Chapter II of Part IV of the Trade Union and Labour Relations (Consolidation) Act 1992 (redundancies) or regulations 9, 13 and 15 of the Transfer of Undertakings (Protection of Employment) Regulations 2006, or

     (b)   a candidate in an election in which any person elected will, on being elected, be such an employee representative,

   he performed (or proposed to perform) any functions or activities as such an employee representative or candidate.

(1A)   An employee has the right not to be subjected to any detriment by any act, or by any deliberate failure to act, by his employer done on the ground of his participation in an election of employee representatives for the purposes of Chapter II of Part IV of the Trade Union and Labour Relations (Consolidation) Act 1992 (redundancies) or regulations 9, 13 and 15 of the Transfer of Undertakings (Protection of Employment) Regulations 2006.

(2)   This section does not apply where the detriment in question amounts to a dismissal (within the meaning of Part X).

47A   EMPLOYEES EXERCISING RIGHT TO TIME OFF WORK FOR STUDY OR TRAINING

(1)   An employee has the right not to be subjected to any detriment by any act, or any deliberate failure to act, by his employer or the principal (within the meaning of section 63A(3)) done on the ground that, being a person entitled to—

     (a)   time off under section 63A(1) or (3), and

     (b)   remuneration under section 63B(1) in respect of that time taken off,

   the employee exercised (or proposed to exercise) that right or received (or sought to receive) such remuneration.

(2)   This section does not apply where the detriment in question amounts to dismissal (within the meaning of Part X).

47B   PROTECTED DISCLOSURES

(1)   A worker has the right not to be subjected to any detriment by any act, or any deliberate failure to act, by his employer done on the ground that the worker has made a protected disclosure.

(2)   This section does not apply where—
(a) the worker is an employee, and
(b) the detriment in question amounts to dismissal (within the meaning of Part X).

(3)   For the purposes of this section, and of sections 48 and 49 so far as relating to this section, "worker" "worker's contract", "employment" and "employer" have the extended meaning given by section 43K.

47C LEAVE FOR FAMILY AND DOMESTIC REASONS

(1)   An employee has the right not to be subjected to any detriment by any act, or any deliberate failure to act, by his employer done for a prescribed reason.

(2)   A prescribed reason is one which is prescribed by regulations made by the Secretary of State and which relates to—
(a) pregnancy, childbirth or maternity,
(b) ordinary, compulsory or additional maternity leave,
(ba) ordinary or additional adoption leave,
(c) parental leave,
(ca) ordinary or additional paternity leave, or
(d) time off under section 57A.

(3)   A reason prescribed under this section in relation to parental leave may relate to action which an employee takes, agrees to take or refuses to take under or in respect of a collective or workforce agreement.

(4)   Regulations under this section may make different provision for different cases or circumstances.

47E FLEXIBLE WORKING

(1)   An employee has the right not to be subjected to any detriment by any act, or any deliberate failure to act, by his employer done on the ground that the employee—
(a) made (or proposed to make) an application under section 80F,
(b) exercised (or proposed to exercise) a right conferred on him under section 80G,
(c) brought proceedings against the employer under section 80H, or
(d) alleged the existence of any circumstance which would constitute a ground for bringing such proceedings.

(2)   This section does not apply where the detriment in question amounts to dismissal within the meaning of Part 10.

48 COMPLAINTS TO EMPLOYMENT TRIBUNALS

(1)   An employee may present a complaint to an employment tribunal that he has been subjected to a detriment in contravention of section 43M, 44, 45, 46, 47, 47A, 47C, 47E or 47F.

(1ZA) A worker may present a complaint to an employment tribunal that he has been subjected to a detriment in contravention of section 45A.

(1A)   A worker may present a complaint to an employment tribunal that he has been subjected to a detriment in contravention of section 47B.

(1B)   A person may present a complaint to an employment tribunal that he has been subjected to a detriment in contravention of section 47D.

(2)   On such a complaint it is for the employer to show the ground on which any act, or deliberate failure to act, was done.

(3)   An employment tribunal shall not consider a complaint under this section unless it is presented—
   (a) before the end of the period of three months beginning with the date of the act or failure to act to which the complaint relates or, where that act or failure is part of a series of similar acts or failures, the last of them, or
   (b) within such further period as the tribunal considers reasonable in a case where it is satisfied that it was not reasonably practicable for the complaint to be presented before the end of that period of three months.

(4)   For the purposes of subsection (3)—
   (a) where an act extends over a period, the "date of the act" means the last day of that period, and
   (b) a deliberate failure to act shall be treated as done when it was decided on;
   and, in the absence of evidence establishing the contrary, an employer shall be taken to decide on a failure to act when he does an act inconsistent with doing the failed act or, if he has done no such inconsistent act, when the period expires within which he might reasonably have been expected to do the failed act if it was to be done.

(5)   In this section and section 49 any reference to the employer includes, where a person complains that he has been subjected to a detriment in contravention of section 47A, the principal (within the meaning of section 63A(3)).

49 REMEDIES

(1)   Where an employment tribunal finds a complaint under section 48 well-founded, the tribunal—
   (a) shall make a declaration to that effect, and
   (b) may make an award of compensation to be paid by the employer to the complainant in respect of the act or failure to act to which the complaint relates.

(2)   Subject to subsections (5A) and (6) the amount of the compensation awarded shall be such as the tribunal considers just and equitable in all the circumstances having regard to—
   (a) the infringement to which the complaint relates, and
   (b) any loss which is attributable to the act, or failure to act, which infringed the complainant's right.

(3)   The loss shall be taken to include—
   (a) any expenses reasonably incurred by the complainant in consequence of the act, or failure to act, to which the complaint relates, and
   (b) loss of any benefit which he might reasonably be expected to have had but for that act or failure to act.

(4)   In ascertaining the loss the tribunal shall apply the same rule concerning the duty of a person to mitigate his loss as applies to damages recoverable under the common law of England and Wales or (as the case may be) Scotland.

(5)   Where the tribunal finds that the act, or failure to act, to which the complaint relates was to any extent caused or contributed to by action of the complainant, it shall reduce the amount of the compensation by such proportion as it considers just and equitable having regard to that finding.

(5A) Where—
   (a) the complaint is made under section 48 (1ZA),

(b)   the detriment to which the worker is subjected is the termination of his worker's contract, and

(c)   that contract is not a contract of employment,

any compensation must not exceed the compensation that would be payable under Chapter II of Part X if the worker had been an employee and had been dismissed for the reason specified in section 101A.

(6)   Where—

(a)   the complaint is made under section 48(1A),

(b)   the detriment to which the worker is subjected is the termination of his worker's contract, and

(c)   that contract is not a contract of employment,

any compensation must not exceed the compensation that would be payable under Chapter II of Part X if the worker had been an employee and had been dismissed for the reason specified in section 103A.

(7)   Where—

(a)   the complaint is made under section 48(1B) by a person who is not an employee, and

(b)   the detriment to which he is subjected is the termination of his contract with the person who is his employer for the purposes of section 25 of the Tax Credits Act 2002,

any compensation must not exceed the compensation that would be payable under Chapter 2 of Part 10 if the complainant had been an employee and had been dismissed for the reason specified in section 104B.

Part VI TIME OFF WORK

50 RIGHT TO TIME OFF FOR PUBLIC DUTIES

(1)   An employer shall permit an employee of his who is a justice of the peace to take time off during the employee's working hours for the purpose of performing any of the duties of his office.

(2)   An employer shall permit an employee of his who is a member of—

(a)   a local authority,

(b)   a statutory tribunal,

(c)   a police authority established under section 3 of the Police Act 1996 or the Metropolitan Police Authority,

(d)   an independent monitoring board for a prison or a prison visiting committee,

(e)   a relevant health body,

(f)   a relevant education body,

(g)   the Environment Agency or the Scottish Environment Protection Agency, [or]

(h)   Scottish Water or a Water Customer Consultation Panel,

to take time off during the employee's working hours for the purposes specified in subsection (3).

(3)   The purposes referred to in subsection (2) are—

(a)   attendance at a meeting of the body or any of its committees or sub-committees, and

(b)   the doing of any other thing approved by the body, or anything of a class so approved, for the purpose of the discharge of the functions of the body or of any of its committees or sub-committees, and

(c)   in the case of a local authority which are operating executive arrangements—

(i)   attendance at a meeting of the executive of that local authority or committee of that executive; and

(ii)   the doing of any other thing, by an individual member of that executive, for the purposes of the discharge of any function which is to any extent the responsibility of that executive.

(4)   The amount of time off which an employee is to be permitted to take under this section, and the occasions on which and any conditions subject to which time off may be so taken, are those that are reasonable in all the circumstances having regard, in particular, to—
   (a)   how much time off is required for the performance of the duties of the office or as a member of the body in question, and how much time off is required for the performance of the particular duty,
   (b)   how much time off the employee has already been permitted under this section or sections 168 and 170 of the Trade Union and Labour Relations (Consolidation) Act 1992 (time off for trade union duties and activities), and
   (c)   the circumstances of the employer's business and the effect of the employee's absence on the running of that business.

(5)   In subsection (2)(a) "a local authority" means—
   (a)   a local authority within the meaning of the Local Government Act 1972,
   (b)   a council constituted under section 2 of the Local Government etc. (Scotland) Act 1994,
   (c)   the Common Council of the City of London,
   (d)   a National Park authority, or
   (e)   the Broads Authority.

(7)   In subsection (2)(d)—
   (a)   "independent monitoring board" means a board appointed under section 6(2) of the Prison Act 1952, and
   (b)   "a prison visiting committee" means a visiting committee appointed under section 19(3) of the Prisons (Scotland) Act 1989 or constituted by virtue of rules made under section 39 (as read with section 8(1) of that Act.

(8)   In subsection (2)(e) "a relevant health body" means—
   (a)   a National Health Service trust established under section 25 of the National Health Service Act 2006, section 18 of the National Health Service (Wales) Act 2006 or the National Health Service (Scotland) Act 1978,
   (ab) an NHS foundation trust,
   (b)   a Strategic Health Authority established under section 13 of the National Health Service Act 2006, a Local Health Board established under section 11 of the National Health Service (Wales) Act 2006, a Special Health Authority established under section 28 of the National Health Service Act 2006 or section 22 of the National Health Service (Wales) Act 2006 or a Primary Care Trust established under section 18 of the National Health Service Act 2006, or
   (c)   a Health Board constituted under section 2 of the National Health Service (Scotland) Act 1978.

(9)   In subsection (2)(f) "a relevant education body" means—
   (a)   a managing or governing body of an educational establishment maintained by a local education authority,
   (b)   a governing body of a further education corporation or higher education corporation,
   (c)   a school council appointed under section 125(1) of the Local Government (Scotland) Act 1973,
   (d)   a parent council within the meaning of section 5(2) of the Scottish Schools (Parental Involvement) Act 2006,
   (f)   a board of management of a college of further education within the meaning of section 36(1) of the Further and Higher Education (Scotland) Act 1992,
   (g)   a governing body of a central institution within the meaning of section 135(1) of the Education (Scotland) Act 1980,
   (h)   a governing body of a designated institution within the meaning of Part II of the Further and Higher Education (Scotland) Act 1992.

(i)   the General Teaching Council for England, or

(j)   the General Teaching Council for Wales.

(9A) In subsection (3)(c) of this section "executive" and "executive arrangements" have the same meaning as in Part II of the Local Government Act 2000.

(10) The Secretary of State may by order—

(a)   modify the provisions of subsections (1) and (2) and (5) to (9) by adding any office or body, removing any office or body or altering the description of any office or body, or

(b)   modify the provisions of subsection (3).

(11) For the purposes of this section the working hours of an employee shall be taken to be any time when, in accordance with his contract of employment, the employee is required to be at work.

51 COMPLAINTS TO EMPLOYMENT TRIBUNALS

(1)   An employee may present a complaint to an employment tribunal that his employer has failed to permit him to take time off as required by section 50.

(2)   An employment tribunal shall not consider a complaint under this section that an employer has failed to permit an employee to take time off unless it is presented—

(a)   before the end of the period of three months beginning with the date on which the failure occurred, or

(b)   within such further period as the tribunal considers reasonable in a case where it is satisfied that it was not reasonably practicable for the complaint to be presented before the end of that period of three months.

(3)   Where an employment tribunal finds a complaint under this section well-founded, the tribunal—

(a)   shall make a declaration to that effect, and

(b)   may make an award of compensation to be paid by the employer to the employee.

(4)   The amount of the compensation shall be such as the tribunal considers just and equitable in all the circumstances having regard to—

(a)   the employer's default in failing to permit time off to be taken by the employee, and

(b)   any loss sustained by the employee which is attributable to the matters to which the complaint relates.

52 RIGHT TO TIME OFF TO LOOK FOR WORK OR ARRANGE TRAINING

(1)   An employee who is given notice of dismissal by reason of redundancy is entitled to be permitted by his employer to take reasonable time off during the employee's working hours before the end of his notice in order to—

(a)   look for new employment, or

(b)   make arrangements for training for future employment.

(2)   An employee is not entitled to take time off under this section unless, on whichever is the later of—

(a)   the date on which the notice is due to expire, and

(b)   the date on which it would expire were it the notice required to be given by section 86(1),

he will have been (or would have been) continuously employed for a period of two years or more.

(3)   For the purposes of this section the working hours of an employee shall be taken to be any time when, in accordance with his contract of employment, the employee is required to be at work.

53   RIGHT TO REMUNERATION FOR TIME OFF UNDER SECTION 52

(1)   An employee who is permitted to take time off under section 52 is entitled to be paid remuneration by his employer for the period of absence at the appropriate hourly rate.

(2)   The appropriate hourly rate, in relation to an employee, is the amount of one week's pay divided by the number of normal working hours in a week for that employee when employed under the contract of employment in force on the day when the notice of dismissal was given.

(3)   But where the number of normal working hours differs from week to week or over a longer period, the amount of one week's pay shall be divided instead by the average number of normal working hours calculated by dividing by twelve the total number of the employee's normal working hours during the period of twelve weeks ending with the last complete week before the day on which the notice was given.

(4)   If an employer unreasonably refuses to permit an employee to take time off from work as required by section 52, the employee is entitled to be paid an amount equal to the remuneration to which he would have been entitled under subsection (1) if he had been permitted to take the time off.

(5)   The amount of an employer's liability to pay remuneration under subsection (1) shall not exceed, in respect of the notice period of any employee, forty per cent. of a week's pay of that employee.

(6)   A right to any amount under subsection (1) or (4) does not affect any right of an employee in relation to remuneration under his contract of employment ("contractual remuneration").

(7)   Any contractual remuneration paid to an employee in respect of a period of time off under section 52 goes towards discharging any liability of the employer to pay remuneration under subsection (1) in respect of that period; and, conversely, any payment of remuneration under subsection (1) in respect of a period goes towards discharging any liability of the employer to pay contractual remuneration in respect of that period.

54   COMPLAINTS TO EMPLOYMENT TRIBUNALS

(1)   An employee may present a complaint to an employment tribunal that his employer—
   (a) has unreasonably refused to permit him to take time off as required by section 52, or
   (b) has failed to pay the whole or any part of any amount to which the employee is entitled under section 53(1) or (4).

(2)   An employment tribunal shall not consider a complaint under this section unless it is presented—
   (a) before the end of the period of three months beginning with the date on which it is alleged that the time off should have been permitted, or
   (b) within such further period as the tribunal considers reasonable in a case where it is satisfied that it was not reasonably practicable for the complaint to be presented before the end of that period of three months.

(3)   Where an employment tribunal finds a complaint under this section well-founded, the tribunal shall—
   (a) make a declaration to that effect, and
   (b) order the employer to pay to the employee the amount which it finds due to him.

(4)   The amount which may be ordered by a tribunal to be paid by an employer under subsection (3) (or, where the employer is liable to pay remuneration under section 53, the aggregate of that amount and the amount of that liability) shall not exceed, in respect of the notice period of any employee, forty per cent. of a week's pay of that employee.

55 RIGHT TO TIME OFF FOR ANTE-NATAL CARE

(1)   An employee who—
    (a) is pregnant, and
    (b) has, on the advice of a registered medical practitioner, registered midwife or registered nurse, made an appointment to attend at any place for the purpose of receiving ante-natal care,
is entitled to be permitted by her employer to take time off during the employee's working hours in order to enable her to keep the appointment.

(2)   An employee is not entitled to take time off under this section to keep an appointment unless, if her employer requests her to do so, she produces for his inspection—
    (a) a certificate from a registered medical practitioner, registered midwife or registered nurse stating that the employee is pregnant, and
    (b) an appointment card or some other document showing that the appointment has been made.

(3)   Subsection (2) does not apply where the employee's appointment is the first appointment during her pregnancy for which she seeks permission to take time off in accordance with subsection (1).

(4)   For the purposes of this section the working hours of an employee shall be taken to be any time when, in accordance with her contract of employment, the employee is required to be at work.

(5)   References in this section to a registered nurse are to such a nurse—
    (a) who is also registered in the Specialist Community Public Health Nurses' Part of the register maintained under article 5 of the Nursing and Midwifery Order 2001, and
    (b) whose entry in that Part of the register is annotated to show that he holds a qualification in health visiting.

56 RIGHT TO REMUNERATION FOR TIME OFF UNDER SECTION 55

(1)   An employee who is permitted to take time off under section 55 is entitled to be paid remuneration by her employer for the period of absence at the appropriate hourly rate.

(2)   The appropriate hourly rate, in relation to an employee, is the amount of one week's pay divided by the number of normal working hours in a week for that employee when employed under the contract of employment in force on the day when the time off is taken.

(3)   But where the number of normal working hours differs from week to week or over a longer period, the amount of one week's pay shall be divided instead by—
    (a) the average number of normal working hours calculated by dividing by twelve the total number of the employee's normal working hours during the period of twelve weeks ending with the last complete week before the day on which the time off is taken, or
    (b) where the employee has not been employed for a sufficient period to enable the calculation to be made under paragraph (a), a number which fairly represents the number of normal working hours in a week having regard to such of the considerations specified in subsection (4) as are appropriate in the circumstances.

(4)   The considerations referred to in subsection (3)(b) are—
  (a) the average number of normal working hours in a week which the employee could expect in accordance with the terms of her contract, and
  (b) the average number of normal working hours of other employees engaged in relevant comparable employment with the same employer.

(5)   A right to any amount under subsection (1) does not affect any right of an employee in relation to remuneration under her contract of employment ("contractual remuneration").

(6)   Any contractual remuneration paid to an employee in respect of a period of time off under section 55 goes towards discharging any liability of the employer to pay remuneration under subsection (1) in respect of that period; and, conversely, any payment of remuneration under subsection (1) in respect of a period goes towards discharging any liability of the employer to pay contractual remuneration in respect of that period.

57 COMPLAINTS TO EMPLOYMENT TRIBUNALS

(1)   An employee may present a complaint to an employment tribunal that her employer—
  (a) has unreasonably refused to permit her to take time off as required by section 55, or
  (b) has failed to pay the whole or any part of any amount to which the employee is entitled under section 56.

(2)   An employment tribunal shall not consider a complaint under this section unless it is presented—
  (a) before the end of the period of three months beginning with the date of the appointment concerned, or
  (b) within such further period as the tribunal considers reasonable in a case where it is satisfied that it was not reasonably practicable for the complaint to be presented before the end of that period of three months.

(3)   Where an employment tribunal finds a complaint under this section well-founded, the tribunal shall make a declaration to that effect.

(4)   If the complaint is that the employer has unreasonably refused to permit the employee to take time off, the tribunal shall also order the employer to pay to the employee an amount equal to the remuneration to which she would have been entitled under section 56 if the employer had not refused.

(5)   If the complaint is that the employer has failed to pay the employee the whole or part of any amount to which she is entitled under section 56, the tribunal shall also order the employer to pay to the employee the amount which it finds due to her.

57A TIME OFF FOR DEPENDANTS

(1)   An employee is entitled to be permitted by his employer to take a reasonable amount of time off during the employee's working hours in order to take action which is necessary—
  (a) to provide assistance on an occasion when a dependant falls ill, gives birth or is injured or assaulted,
  (b) to make arrangements for the provision of care for a dependant who is ill or injured,
  (c) in consequence of the death of a dependant,
  (d) because of the unexpected disruption or termination of arrangements for the care of a dependant, or
  (e) to deal with an incident which involves a child of the employee and which occurs unexpectedly in a period during which an educational establishment which the child attends is responsible for him.

(2)   Subsection (1) does not apply unless the employee—
    (a)   tells his employer the reason for his absence as soon as reasonably practicable, and
    (b)   except where paragraph (a) cannot be complied with until after the employee has returned to work, tells his employer for how long he expects to be absent.

(3)   Subject to subsections (4) and (5), for the purposes of this section "dependant" means, in relation to an employee—
    (a)   a spouse or civil partner,
    (b)   a child,
    (c)   a parent,
    (d)   a person who lives in the same household as the employee, otherwise than by reason of being his employee, tenant, lodger or boarder.

(4)   For the purposes of subsection (1)(a) or (b) "dependant" includes, in addition to the persons mentioned in subsection (3), any person who reasonably relies on the employee—
    (a)   for assistance on an occasion when the person falls ill or is injured or assaulted, or
    (b)   to make arrangements for the provision of care in the event of illness or injury.

(5)   For the purposes of subsection (1)(d) "dependant" includes, in addition to the persons mentioned in subsection (3), any person who reasonably relies on the employee to make arrangements for the provision of care.

(6)   A reference in this section to illness or injury includes a reference to mental illness or injury.

57B COMPLAINT TO EMPLOYMENT TRIBUNAL

(1)   An employee may present a complaint to an employment tribunal that his employer has unreasonably refused to permit him to take time off as required by section 57A.

(2)   An employment tribunal shall not consider a complaint under this section unless it is presented—
    (a)   before the end of the period of three months beginning with the date when the refusal occurred, or
    (b)   within such further period as the tribunal considers reasonable in a case where it is satisfied that it was not reasonably practicable for the complaint to be presented before the end of that period of three months.

(3)   Where an employment tribunal finds a complaint under subsection (1) well-founded, it—
    (a)   shall make a declaration to that effect, and
    (b)   may make an award of compensation to be paid by the employer to the employee.

(4)   The amount of compensation shall be such as the tribunal considers just and equitable in all the circumstances having regard to—
    (a)   the employer's default in refusing to permit time off to be taken by the employee, and
    (b)   any loss sustained by the employee which is attributable to the matters complained of.

61 RIGHT TO TIME OFF FOR EMPLOYEE REPRESENTATIVES

(1)   An employee who is—
    (a)   an employee representative for the purposes of Chapter II of Part IV of the Trade Union and Labour Relations (Consolidation) Act 1992 (redundancies) or regulations 9, 13 and 15 of the Transfer of Undertakings (Protection of Employment) Regulations 2006, or
    (b)   a candidate in an election in which any person elected will, on being elected, be such an employee representative,

is entitled to be permitted by his employer to take reasonable time off during the employee's working hours in order to perform his functions as such an employee representative or candidate or in order to undergo training to perform such functions.

(2)   For the purposes of this section the working hours of an employee shall be taken to be any time when, in accordance with his contract of employment, the employee is required to be at work.

62 RIGHT TO REMUNERATION FOR TIME OFF UNDER SECTION 61

(1)   An employee who is permitted to take time off under section 61 is entitled to be paid remuneration by his employer for the time taken off at the appropriate hourly rate.

(2)   The appropriate hourly rate, in relation to an employee, is the amount of one week's pay divided by the number of normal working hours in a week for that employee when employed under the contract of employment in force on the day when the time off is taken.

(3)   But where the number of normal working hours differs from week to week or over a longer period, the amount of one week's pay shall be divided instead by—
(a)   the average number of normal working hours calculated by dividing by twelve the total number of the employee's normal working hours during the period of twelve weeks ending with the last complete week before the day on which the time off is taken, or
(b)   where the employee has not been employed for a sufficient period to enable the calculation to be made under paragraph (a), a number which fairly represents the number of normal working hours in a week having regard to such of the considerations specified in subsection (4) as are appropriate in the circumstances.

(4)   The considerations referred to in subsection (3)(b) are—
(a)   the average number of normal working hours in a week which the employee could expect in accordance with the terms of his contract, and
(b)   the average number of normal working hours of other employees engaged in relevant comparable employment with the same employer.

(5)   A right to any amount under subsection (1) does not affect any right of an employee in relation to remuneration under his contract of employment ("contractual remuneration").

(6)   Any contractual remuneration paid to an employee in respect of a period of time off under section 61 goes towards discharging any liability of the employer to pay remuneration under subsection (1) in respect of that period; and, conversely, any payment of remuneration under subsection (1) in respect of a period goes towards discharging any liability of the employer to pay contractual remuneration in respect of that period.

63 COMPLAINTS TO EMPLOYMENT TRIBUNALS

(1)   An employee may present a complaint to an employment tribunal that his employer—
(a)   has unreasonably refused to permit him to take time off as required by section 61, or
(b)   has failed to pay the whole or any part of any amount to which the employee is entitled under section 62.

(2)   An employment tribunal shall not consider a complaint under this section unless it is presented—
(a)   before the end of the period of three months beginning with the day on which the time off was taken or on which it is alleged the time off should have been permitted, or

(b) within such further period as the tribunal considers reasonable in a case where it is satisfied that it was not reasonably practicable for the complaint to be presented before the end of that period of three months.

(3) Where an employment tribunal finds a complaint under this section well-founded, the tribunal shall make a declaration to that effect.

(4) If the complaint is that the employer has unreasonably refused to permit the employee to take time off, the tribunal shall also order the employer to pay to the employee an amount equal to the remuneration to which he would have been entitled under section 62 if the employer had not refused.

(5) If the complaint is that the employer has failed to pay the employee the whole or part of any amount to which he is entitled under section 62, the tribunal shall also order the employer to pay to the employee the amount which it finds due to him.

Part VII SUSPENSION FROM WORK

64 RIGHT TO REMUNERATION ON SUSPENSION ON MEDICAL GROUNDS

(1) An employee who is suspended from work by his employer on medical grounds is entitled to be paid by his employer remuneration while he is so suspended for a period not exceeding twenty-six weeks.

(2) For the purposes of this Part an employee is suspended from work on medical grounds if he is suspended from work in consequence of—
(a) a requirement imposed by or under a provision of an enactment or of an instrument made under an enactment, or
(b) a recommendation in a provision of a code of practice issued or approved under section 16 of the Health and Safety at Work etc. Act 1974,
and the provision is for the time being specified in subsection (3).

(3) The provisions referred to in subsection (2) are—

Regulation 16 of the Control of Lead at Work Regulations 1980,
Regulation 24 of the Ionising Radiations Regulations 1999 [S.I. 1999/3232], and
Regulation 11 of the Control of Substances Hazardous to Health Regulations 1988.

(4) The Secretary of State may by order add provisions to or remove provisions from the list of provisions specified in subsection (3).

(5) For the purposes of this Part an employee shall be regarded as suspended from work on medical grounds only if and for so long as he—
(a) continues to be employed by his employer, but
(b) is not provided with work or does not perform the work he normally performed before the suspension.

65 EXCLUSIONS FROM RIGHT TO REMUNERATION

(1) An employee is not entitled to remuneration under section 64 unless he has been continuously employed for a period of not less than one month ending with the day before that on which the suspension begins.

(3) An employee is not entitled to remuneration under section 64 in respect of any period during which he is incapable of work by reason of disease or bodily or mental disablement.

(4)   An employee is not entitled to remuneration under section 64 in respect of any period if—
    (a) his employer has offered to provide him with suitable alternative work during the period (whether or not it is work which the employee is under his contract, or was under the contract in force before the suspension, employed to perform) and the employee has unreasonably refused to perform that work, or
    (b) he does not comply with reasonable requirements imposed by his employer with a view to ensuring that his services are available.

66 MEANING OF SUSPENSION ON MATERNITY GROUNDS

(1)   For the purposes of this Part an employee is suspended from work on maternity grounds if, in consequence of any relevant requirement or relevant recommendation, she is suspended from work by her employer on the ground that she is pregnant, has recently given birth or is breastfeeding a child.

(2)   In subsection (1)—

"relevant requirement" means a requirement imposed by or under a specified provision of an enactment or of an instrument made under an enactment, and

"relevant recommendation" means a recommendation in a specified provision of a code of practice issued or approved under section 16 of the Health and Safety at Work etc. Act 1974;

and in this subsection "specified provision" means a provision for the time being specified in an order made by the Secretary of State under this subsection.

(3)   For the purposes of this Part an employee shall be regarded as suspended from work on maternity grounds only if and for so long as she—
    (a) continues to be employed by her employer, but
    (b) is not provided with work or (disregarding alternative work for the purposes of section 67) does not perform the work she normally performed before the suspension.

67 RIGHT TO OFFER OF ALTERNATIVE WORK

(1)   Where an employer has available suitable alternative work for an employee, the employee has a right to be offered to be provided with the alternative work before being suspended from work on maternity grounds.

(2)   For alternative work to be suitable for an employee for the purposes of this section—
    (a) the work must be of a kind which is both suitable in relation to her and appropriate for her to do in the circumstances, and
    (b) the terms and conditions applicable to her for performing the work, if they differ from the corresponding terms and conditions applicable to her for performing the work she normally performs under her contract of employment, must not be substantially less favourable to her than those corresponding terms and conditions.

68 RIGHT TO REMUNERATION

(1)   An employee who is suspended from work on maternity grounds is entitled to be paid remuneration by her employer while she is so suspended.

(2)   An employee is not entitled to remuneration under this section in respect of any period if—
    (a) her employer has offered to provide her during the period with work which is suitable alternative work for her for the purposes of section 67, and
    (b) the employee has unreasonably refused to perform that work.

70 COMPLAINTS TO EMPLOYMENT TRIBUNALS

(1)   An employee may present a complaint to an employment tribunal that his or her employer has failed to pay the whole or any part of remuneration to which the employee is entitled under section 64 or 68.

(2)   An employment tribunal shall not consider a complaint under subsection (1) relating to remuneration in respect of any day unless it is presented—
   (a)   before the end of the period of three months beginning with that day, or
   (b)   within such further period as the tribunal considers reasonable in a case where it is satisfied that it was not reasonably practicable for the complaint to be presented within that period of three months.

(3)   Where an employment tribunal finds a complaint under subsection (1) well-founded, the tribunal shall order the employer to pay the employee the amount of remuneration which it finds is due to him or her.

(4)   An employee may present a complaint to an employment tribunal that in contravention of section 67 her employer has failed to offer to provide her with work.

(5)   An employment tribunal shall not consider a complaint under subsection (4) unless it is presented—
   (a)   before the end of the period of three months beginning with the first day of the suspension, or
   (b)   within such further period as the tribunal considers reasonable in a case where it is satisfied that it was not reasonably practicable for the complaint to be presented within that period of three months.

(6)   Where an employment tribunal finds a complaint under subsection (4) well-founded, the tribunal may make an award of compensation to be paid by the employer to the employee.

(7)   The amount of the compensation shall be such as the tribunal considers just and equitable in all the circumstances having regard to—
   (a)   the infringement of the employee's right under section 67 by the failure on the part of the employer to which the complaint relates, and
   (b)   any loss sustained by the employee which is attributable to that failure.

Part VIII

Chapter 1 MATERNITY LEAVE

71 ORDINARY MATERNITY LEAVE

(1)   An employee may, provided that she satisfies any conditions which may be prescribed, be absent from work at any time during an ordinary maternity leave period.

(2)   An ordinary maternity leave period is a period calculated in accordance with regulations made by the Secretary of State.

(3)   Regulations under subsection (2)—
   (a)   shall secure that, where an employee has a right to leave under this section, she is entitled to an ordinary maternity leave period of at least 26 weeks;
   (b)   may allow an employee to choose, subject to prescribed restrictions, the date on which an ordinary maternity leave period starts;
   (c)   may specify circumstances in which an employee may work for her employer during an ordinary maternity leave period without bringing the period to an end.

(4)   Subject to section 74, an employee who exercises her right under subsection (1)—
- (a) is entitled, for such purposes and to such extent as may be prescribed, to the benefit of the terms and conditions of employment which would have applied if she had not been absent,
- (b) is bound, for such purposes and to such extent as may be prescribed by any obligations arising under those terms and conditions (except in so far as they are inconsistent with subsection (1)), and
- (c) is entitled to return from leave to a job of a prescribed kind.

(5)   In subsection (4)(a) "terms and conditions of employment"—
- (a) includes matters connected with an employee's employment whether or not they arise under her contract of employment, but
- (b) does not include terms and conditions about remuneration.

(6)   The Secretary of State may make regulations specifying matters which are, or are not, to be treated as remuneration for the purposes of this section.

(7)   The Secretary of State may make regulations making provision, in relation to the right to return under subsection (4)(c) above, about—
- (a) seniority, pension rights and similar rights;
- (b) terms and conditions of employment on return.

72 COMPULSORY MATERNITY LEAVE

(1)   An employer shall not permit an employee who satisfies prescribed conditions to work during a compulsory maternity leave period.

(2)   A compulsory maternity leave period is a period calculated in accordance with regulations made by the Secretary of State.

(3)   Regulations under subsection (2) shall secure—
- (a) that no compulsory leave period is less than two weeks, and
- (b) that every compulsory maternity leave period falls within an ordinary maternity leave period.

(4)   Subject to subsection (5), any provision of or made under the Health and Safety at Work etc. Act 1974 shall apply in relation to the prohibition under subsection (1) as if it were imposed by regulations under section 15 of that Act.

(5)   Section 33(1)(c) of the 1974 Act shall not apply in relation to the prohibition under subsection (1); and an employer who contravenes that subsection shall be—
- (a) guilty of an offence, and
- (b) liable on summary conviction to a fine not exceeding level 2 on the standard scale.

73 ADDITIONAL MATERNITY LEAVE

(1)   An employee who satisfies prescribed conditions may be absent from work at any time during an additional maternity leave period.

(2)   An additional maternity leave period is a period calculated in accordance with regulations made by the Secretary of State.

(3)   Regulations under subsection (2)—
- (a) may allow an employee to choose, subject to prescribed restrictions, the date on which an additional maternity leave period ends;

(b) may specify circumstances in which an employee may work for her employer during an additional maternity leave period without bringing the period to an end.

(4) Subject to section 74, an employee who exercises her right under subsection (1)—
(a) is entitled, for such purposes and to such extent as may be prescribed, to the benefit of the terms and conditions of employment which would have applied if she had not been absent,
(b) is bound, for such purposes and to such extent as may be prescribed, by obligations arising under those terms and conditions (except in so far as they are inconsistent with subsection (1)), and
(c) is entitled to return from leave to a job of a prescribed kind.

(5) In subsection (4)(a) "terms and conditions of employment"—
(a) includes matters connected with an employee's employment whether or not they arise under her contract of employment, but
(b) does not include terms and conditions about remuneration.

(5A) In subsection (4)(c), the reference to return from leave includes, where appropriate, a reference to a continuous period of absence attributable partly to additional maternity leave and partly to ordinary maternity leave.

(6) The Secretary of State may make regulations specifying matters which are, or are not, to be treated as remuneration for the purposes of this section.

(7) The Secretary of State may make regulations making provision, in relation to the right to return under subsection (4)(c), about—
(a) seniority, pension rights and similar rights;
(b) terms and conditions of employment on return.

Chapter 1A ADOPTION LEAVE

75A ORDINARY ADOPTION LEAVE

(1) An employee who satisfies prescribed conditions may be absent from work at any time during an ordinary adoption leave period.

(2) An ordinary adoption leave period is a period calculated in accordance with regulations made by the Secretary of State.

(2A) Regulations under subsection (2) may specify circumstances in which an employee may work for his employer during an ordinary adoption leave period without bringing the period to an end.

(3) Subject to section 75C, an employee who exercises his right under subsection (1)—
(a) is entitled, for such purposes and to such extent as may be prescribed, to the benefit of the terms and conditions of employment which would have applied if he had not been absent,
(b) is bound, for such purposes and to such extent as may be prescribed, by any obligations arising under those terms and conditions (except in so far as they are inconsistent with subsection (1)), and
(c) is entitled to return from leave to a job of a prescribed kind.

(4) In subsection (3)(a) "terms and conditions of employment"—
(a) includes matters connected with an employee's employment whether or not they arise under his contract of employment, but
(b) does not include terms and conditions about remuneration.

(5)   In subsection (3)(c), the reference to return from leave includes, where appropriate, a reference to a continuous period of absence attributable partly to ordinary adoption leave and partly to maternity leave.

(6)   The Secretary of State may make regulations specifying matters which are, or are not, to be treated as remuneration for the purposes of this section.

(7)   The Secretary of State may make regulations making provision, in relation to the right to return under subsection (3)(c), about—
(a) seniority, pension rights and similar rights;
(b) terms and conditions of employment on return.

75B ADDITIONAL ADOPTION LEAVE

(1)   An employee who satisfies prescribed conditions may be absent from work at any time during an additional adoption leave period.

(2)   An additional adoption leave period is a period calculated in accordance with regulations made by the Secretary of State.

(3)   Regulations under subsection (2)—
(a) may allow an employee to choose, subject to prescribed restrictions, the date on which an additional adoption leave period ends;
(b) may specify circumstances in which an employee may work for his employer during an additional adoption leave period without bringing the period to an end.

(4)   Subject to section 75C, an employee who exercises his right under subsection (1)—
(a) is entitled, for such purposes and to such extent as may be prescribed, to the benefit of the terms and conditions of employment which would have applied if he had not been absent,
(b) is bound, for such purposes and to such extent as may be prescribed, by obligations arising under those terms and conditions (except in so far as they are inconsistent with subsection (1)), and
(c) is entitled to return from leave to a job of a prescribed kind.

(5)   In subsection (4)(a) "terms and conditions of employment"—
(a) includes matters connected with an employee's employment whether or not they arise under his contract of employment, but
(b) does not include terms and conditions about remuneration.

(6)   In subsection (4)(c), the reference to return from leave includes, where appropriate, a reference to a continuous period of absence attributable partly to additional adoption leave and partly to—
(a) maternity leave, or
(b) ordinary adoption leave,
or to both.

(7)   The Secretary of State may make regulations specifying matters which are, or are not, to be treated as remuneration for the purposes of this section.

(8)   The Secretary of State may make regulations making provision, in relation to the right to return under subsection (4)(c), about—
(a) seniority, pension rights and similar rights;
(b) terms and conditions of employment on return.

Chapter 2 **PARENTAL LEAVE**

80 COMPLAINT TO EMPLOYMENT TRIBUNAL

(1) An employee may present a complaint to an employment tribunal that his employer—
   (a) has unreasonably postponed a period of parental leave requested by the employee, or
   (b) has prevented or attempted to prevent the employee from taking parental leave.

(2) An employment tribunal shall not consider a complaint under this section unless it is presented—
   (a) before the end of the period of three months beginning with the date (or last date) of the matters complained of, or
   (b) within such further period as the tribunal considers reasonable in a case where it is satisfied that it was not reasonably practicable for the complaint to be presented before the end of that period of three months.

(3) Where an employment tribunal finds a complaint under this section well-founded it—
   (a) shall make a declaration to that effect, and
   (b) may make an award of compensation to be paid by the employer to the employee.

(4) The amount of compensation shall be such as the tribunal considers just and equitable in all the circumstances having regard to—
   (a) the employer's behaviour, and
   (b) any loss sustained by the employee which is attributable to the matters complained of.

Part VIIIA **FLEXIBLE WORKING**

80F STATUTORY RIGHT TO REQUEST CONTRACT VARIATION

(1) A qualifying employee may apply to his employer for a change in his terms and conditions of employment if—
   (a) the change relates to—
      (i) the hours he is required to work,
      (ii) the times when he is required to work,
      (iii) where, as between his home and a place of business of his employer, he is required to work, or
      (iv) such other aspect of his terms and conditions of employment as the Secretary of State may specify by regulations, and
   (b) his purpose in applying for the change is to enable him to care for someone who, at the time of application, is—
      (i) a child who has not reached the prescribed age or falls within a prescribed description and in respect of whom (in either case) the employee satisfies prescribed conditions as to relationship, or
      (ii) a person aged 18 or over who falls within a prescribed description and in respect of whom the employee satisfies prescribed conditions as to relationship.

(2) An application under this section must—
   (a) state that it is such an application,
   (b) specify the change applied for and the date on which it is proposed the change should become effective,
   (c) explain what effect, if any, the employee thinks making the change applied for would have on his employer and how, in his opinion, any such effect might be dealt with, and
   (d) explain how the employee meets, in respect of the child or other person to be cared for, the conditions as to relationship mentioned in subsection (1)(b)(i) or (ii).

(4)   If an employee has made an application under this section, he may not make a further application under this section to the same employer before the end of the period of twelve months beginning with the date on which the previous application was made.

(5)   The Secretary of State may by regulations make provision about—
(a)   the form of applications under this section, and
(b)   when such an application is to be taken as made.

(8)   For the purposes of this section, an employee is—
(a)   a qualifying employee if he—
    (i)   satisfies such conditions as to duration of employment as the Secretary of State may specify by regulations, and
    (ii)   is not an agency worker;
(b)   an agency worker if he is supplied by a person ("the agent") to do work for another ("the principal") under a contract or other arrangement made between the agent and the principal.

(9)   Regulations under this section may make different provision for different cases.

(10)   In this section—

"child" means a person aged under 18;

"prescribed" means prescribed by regulations made by the Secretary of State.

80G   EMPLOYER'S DUTIES IN RELATION TO APPLICATION UNDER SECTION 80F

(1)   An employer to whom an application under section 80F is made—
(a)   shall deal with the application in accordance with regulations made by the Secretary of State, and
(b)   shall only refuse the application because he considers that one or more of the following grounds applies—
    (i)   the burden of additional costs,
    (ii)   detrimental effect on ability to meet customer demand,
    (iii)   inability to re-organise work among existing staff,
    (iv)   inability to recruit additional staff,
    (v)   detrimental impact on quality,
    (vi)   detrimental impact on performance,
    (vii)   insufficiency of work during the periods the employee proposes to work,
    (viii)   planned structural changes, and
    (ix)   such other grounds as the Secretary of State may specify by regulations.

(2)   Regulations under subsection (1)(a) shall include—
(a)   provision for the holding of a meeting between the employer and the employee to discuss an application under section 80F within twenty eight days after the date the application is made;
(b)   provision for the giving by the employer to the employee of notice of his decision on the application within fourteen days after the date of the meeting under paragraph (a);
(c)   provision for notice under paragraph (b) of a decision to refuse the application to state the grounds for the decision;
(d)   provision for the employee to have a right, if he is dissatisfied with the employer's decision, to appeal against it within fourteen days after the date on which notice under paragraph (b) is given;

(e) provision about the procedure for exercising the right of appeal under paragraph (d), including provision requiring the employee to set out the grounds of appeal;

(f) provision for notice under paragraph (b) to include such information as the regulations may specify relating to the right of appeal under paragraph (d);

(g) provision for the holding, within fourteen days after the date on which notice of appeal is given by the employee, of a meeting between the employer and the employee to discuss the appeal;

(h) provision for the employer to give the employee notice of his decision on any appeal within fourteen days after the date of the meeting under paragraph (g);

(i) provision for notice under paragraph (h) of a decision to dismiss an appeal to state the grounds for the decision;

(j) provision for a statement under paragraph (c) or (i) to contain a sufficient explanation of the grounds for the decision;

(k) provision for the employee to have a right to be accompanied at meetings under paragraph (a) or (g) by a person of such description as the regulations may specify;

(l) provision for postponement in relation to any meeting under paragraph (a) or (g) which a companion under paragraph (k) is not available to attend;

(m) provision in relation to companions under paragraph (k) corresponding to section 10(6) and (7) of the Employment Relations Act 1999 (c. 26) (right to paid time off to act as companion, etc.);

(n) provision, in relation to the rights under paragraphs (k) and (l), for the application (with or without modification) of sections 11 to 13 of the Employment Relations Act 1999 (provisions ancillary to right to be accompanied under section 10 of that Act).

(3) Regulations under subsection (1)(a) may include—
(a) provision for any requirement of the regulations not to apply where an application is disposed of by agreement or withdrawn;
(b) provision for extension of a time limit where the employer and employee agree, or in such other circumstances as the regulations may specify;
(c) provision for applications to be treated as withdrawn in specified circumstances;
and may make different provision for different cases.

(4) The Secretary of State may by order amend subsection (2).

80H COMPLAINTS TO EMPLOYMENT TRIBUNALS

(1) An employee who makes an application under section 80F may present a complaint to an employment tribunal—
(a) that his employer has failed in relation to the application to comply with section 80G(1), or
(b) that a decision by his employer to reject the application was based on incorrect facts.

(2) No complaint under this section may be made in respect of an application which has been disposed of by agreement or withdrawn.

(3) In the case of an application which has not been disposed of by agreement or withdrawn, no complaint under this section may be made until the employer—
(a) notifies the employee of a decision to reject the application on appeal, or
(b) commits a breach of regulations under section 80G(1)(a) of such description as the Secretary of State may specify by regulations.

(4) No complaint under this section may be made in respect of failure to comply with provision included in regulations under subsection (1)(a) of section 80G because of subsection (2)(k), (l) or (m) of that section.

(5)   An employment tribunal shall not consider a complaint under this section unless it is presented—
(a) before the end of the period of three months beginning with the relevant date, or
(b) within such further period as the tribunal considers reasonable in a case where it is satisfied that it was not reasonably practicable for the complaint to be presented before the end of that period of three months.

(6)   In subsection (5)(a), the reference to the relevant date is—
(a) in the case of a complaint permitted by subsection (3)(a), the date on which the employee is notified of the decision on the appeal, and
(b) in the case of a complaint permitted by subsection (3)(b), the date on which the breach concerned was committed.

80I REMEDIES

(1)   Where an employment tribunal finds a complaint under section 80H well-founded it shall make a declaration to that effect and may—
(a) make an order for reconsideration of the application, and
(b) make an award of compensation to be paid by the employer to the employee.

(2)   The amount of compensation shall be such amount, not exceeding the permitted maximum, as the tribunal considers just and equitable in all the circumstances.

(3)   For the purposes of subsection (2), the permitted maximum is such number of weeks' pay as the Secretary of State may specify by regulations.

(4)   Where an employment tribunal makes an order under subsection (1)(a), section 80G, and the regulations under that section, shall apply as if the application had been made on the date of the order.

Part IX TERMINATION OF EMPLOYMENT

86 RIGHTS OF EMPLOYER AND EMPLOYEE TO MINIMUM NOTICE

(1)   The notice required to be given by an employer to terminate the contract of employment of a person who has been continuously employed for one month or more—
(a) is not less than one week's notice if his period of continuous employment is less than two years,
(b) is not less than one week's notice for each year of continuous employment if his period of continuous employment is two years or more but less than twelve years, and
(c) is not less than twelve weeks' notice if his period of continuous employment is twelve years or more.

(2)   The notice required to be given by an employee who has been continuously employed for one month or more to terminate his contract of employment is not less than one week.

(3)   Any provision for shorter notice in any contract of employment with a person who has been continuously employed for one month or more has effect subject to subsections (1) and (2); but this section does not prevent either party from waiving his right to notice on any occasion or from accepting a payment in lieu of notice.

(4)   Any contract of employment of a person who has been continuously employed for three months or more which is a contract for a term certain of one month or less shall have effect as if it were for an indefinite period; and, accordingly, subsections (1) and (2) apply to the contract.

(6)   This section does not affect any right of either party to a contract of employment to treat the contract as terminable without notice by reason of the conduct of the other party.

87   RIGHTS OF EMPLOYEE IN PERIOD OF NOTICE

(1)   If an employer gives notice to terminate the contract of employment of a person who has been continuously employed for one month or more, the provisions of sections 88 to 91 have effect as respects the liability of the employer for the period of notice required by section 86(1).

(2)   If an employee who has been continuously employed for one month or more gives notice to terminate his contract of employment, the provisions of sections 88 to 91 have effect as respects the liability of the employer for the period of notice required by section 86(2).

(3)   In sections 88 to 91 "period of notice" means—
(a)   where notice is given by an employer, the period of notice required by section 86(1), and
(b)   where notice is given by an employee, the period of notice required by section 86(2).

(4)   This section does not apply in relation to a notice given by the employer or the employee if the notice to be given by the employer to terminate the contract must be at least one week more than the notice required by section 86(1).

92   RIGHT TO WRITTEN STATEMENT OF REASONS FOR DISMISSAL

(1)   An employee is entitled to be provided by his employer with a written statement giving particulars of the reasons for the employee's dismissal—
(a)   if the employee is given by the employer notice of termination of his contract of employment,
(b)   if the employee's contract of employment is terminated by the employer without notice, or
(c)   if the employee is employed under a limited-term contract and the contract terminates by virtue of the limiting event without being renewed under the same contract.

(2)   Subject to subsections (4) and (4A), an employee is entitled to a written statement under this section only if he makes a request for one; and a statement shall be provided within fourteen days of such a request.

(3)   Subject to subsections (4) and (4A), an employee is not entitled to a written statement under this section unless on the effective date of termination he has been, or will have been, continuously employed for a period of not less than one year ending with that date.

(4)   An employee is entitled to a written statement under this section without having to request it and irrespective of whether she has been continuously employed for any period if she is dismissed—
(a)   at any time while she is pregnant, or
(b)   after childbirth in circumstances in which her ordinary or additional maternity leave period ends by reason of the dismissal.

(4A)   An employee who is dismissed while absent from work during an ordinary or additional adoption leave period is entitled to a written statement under this section without having to request it and irrespective of whether he has been continuously employed for any period if he is dismissed in circumstances in which that period ends by reason of the dismissal.

(5)   A written statement under this section is admissible in evidence in any proceedings.

(6)   Subject to subsection (7), in this section "the effective date of termination"—

(a) in relation to an employee whose contract of employment is terminated by notice, means the date on which the notice expires,

(b) in relation to an employee whose contract of employment is terminated without notice, means the date on which the termination takes effect, and

(c) in relation to an employee who is employed under a limited-term contract which terminates by virtue of the limiting event without being renewed under the same contract, means the date on which the termination takes effect.

(7) Where—

(a) the contract of employment is terminated by the employer, and

(b) the notice required by section 86 to be given by an employer would, if duly given on the material date, expire on a date later than the effective date of termination (as defined by subsection (6)),

the later date is the effective date of termination.

(8) In subsection (7)(b) "the material date" means—

(a) the date when notice of termination was given by the employer, or

(b) where no notice was given, the date when the contract of employment was terminated by the employer.

93 COMPLAINTS TO EMPLOYMENT TRIBUNAL

(1) A complaint may be presented to an employment tribunal by an employee on the ground that—

(a) the employer unreasonably failed to provide a written statement under section 92, or

(b) the particulars of reasons given in purported compliance with that section are inadequate or untrue.

(2) Where an employment tribunal finds a complaint under this section well-founded, the tribunal—

(a) may make a declaration as to what it finds the employer's reasons were for dismissing the employee, and

(b) shall make an award that the employer pay to the employee a sum equal to the amount of two weeks' pay.

(3) An employment tribunal shall not consider a complaint under this section relating to the reasons for a dismissal unless it is presented to the tribunal at such a time that the tribunal would, in accordance with section 111, consider a complaint of unfair dismissal in respect of that dismissal presented at the same time.

Part X UNFAIR DISMISSAL

Chapter 1 RIGHT NOT TO BE UNFAIRLY DISMISSED

94 THE RIGHT

(1) An employee has the right not to be unfairly dismissed by his employer.

(2) Subsection (1) has effect subject to the following provisions of this Part (in particular sections 108 to 110) and to the provisions of the Trade Union and Labour Relations (Consolidation) Act 1992 (in particular sections 237 to 239).

95 CIRCUMSTANCES IN WHICH AN EMPLOYEE IS DISMISSED

(1) For the purposes of this Part an employee is dismissed by his employer if (and, subject to subsection (2), only if)—

(a) the contract under which he is employed is terminated by the employer (whether with or without notice),

(b) he is employed under a limited-term contract and that contract terminates by virtue of the limiting event without being renewed under the same contract, or

(c) the employee terminates the contract under which he is employed (with or without notice) in circumstances in which he is entitled to terminate it without notice by reason of the employer's conduct.

(2) An employee shall be taken to be dismissed by his employer for the purposes of this Part if—

(a) the employer gives notice to the employee to terminate his contract of employment, and

(b) at a time within the period of that notice the employee gives notice to the employer to terminate the contract of employment on a date earlier than the date on which the employer's notice is due to expire;

and the reason for the dismissal is to be taken to be the reason for which the employer's notice is given.

97 EFFECTIVE DATE OF TERMINATION

(1) Subject to the following provisions of this section, in this Part "the effective date of termination"—

(a) in relation to an employee whose contract of employment is terminated by notice, whether given by his employer or by the employee, means the date on which the notice expires,

(b) in relation to an employee whose contract of employment is terminated without notice, means the date on which the termination takes effect, and

(c) in relation to an employee who is employed under a limited-term contract which terminates by virtue of the limiting event without being renewed under the same contract, means the date on which the termination takes effect.

(2) Where—

(a) the contract of employment is terminated by the employer, and

(b) the notice required by section 86 to be given by an employer would, if duly given on the material date, expire on a date later than the effective date of termination (as defined by subsection (1)),

for the purposes of sections 108(1), 119(1) and 227(3) the later date is the effective date of termination.

(3) In subsection (2)(b) "the material date" means—

(a) the date when notice of termination was given by the employer, or

(b) where no notice was given, the date when the contract of employment was terminated by the employer.

(4) Where—

(a) the contract of employment is terminated by the employee,

(b) the material date does not fall during a period of notice given by the employer to terminate that contract, and

(c) had the contract been terminated not by the employee but by notice given on the material date by the employer, that notice would have been required by section 86 to expire on a date later than the effective date of termination (as defined by subsection (1)),

for the purposes of sections 108(1), 119(1) and 227(3) the later date is the effective date of termination.

(5)   In subsection (4) "the material date" means—
(a)   the date when notice of termination was given by the employee, or
(b)   where no notice was given, the date when the contract of employment was terminated by the employee.

98   GENERAL

(1)   In determining for the purposes of this Part whether the dismissal of an employee is fair or unfair, it is for the employer to show—
(a)   the reason (or, if more than one, the principal reason) for the dismissal, and
(b)   that it is either a reason falling within subsection (2) or some other substantial reason of a kind such as to justify the dismissal of an employee holding the position which the employee held.

(2)   A reason falls within this subsection if it—
(a)   relates to the capability or qualifications of the employee for performing work of the kind which he was employed by the employer to do,
(b)   relates to the conduct of the employee,
(ba) is retirement of the employee,
(c)   is that the employee was redundant, or
(d)   is that the employee could not continue to work in the position which he held without contravention (either on his part or on that of his employer) of a duty or restriction imposed by or under an enactment.

(2A)   Subsections (1) and (2) are subject to sections 98ZA to 98ZF.

(3)   In subsection (2)(a)—
(a)   "capability", in relation to an employee, means his capability assessed by reference to skill, aptitude, health or any other physical or mental quality, and
(b)   "qualifications", in relation to an employee, means any degree, diploma or other academic, technical or professional qualification relevant to the position which he held.

(3A)   In any case where the employer has fulfilled the requirements of subsection (1) by showing that the reason (or the principal reason) for the dismissal is retirement of the employee, the question whether the dismissal is fair or unfair shall be determined in accordance with section 98ZG.

(4)   In any other case where the employer has fulfilled the requirements of subsection (1), the determination of the question whether the dismissal is fair or unfair (having regard to the reason shown by the employer)—
(a)   depends on whether in the circumstances (including the size and administrative resources of the employer's undertaking) the employer acted reasonably or unreasonably in treating it as a sufficient reason for dismissing the employee, and
(b)   shall be determined in accordance with equity and the substantial merits of the case.

(6)   Subsection (4) is subject to—
(a)   sections 98A to 107 of this Act, and
(b)   sections 152, 153, 238 and 238A of the Trade Union and Labour Relations (Consolidation) Act 1992 (dismissal on ground of trade union membership or activities or in connection with industrial action).

98ZA   NO NORMAL RETIREMENT AGE: DISMISSAL BEFORE 65

(1)   This section applies to the dismissal of an employee if—
(a)   the employee has no normal retirement age, and

(b) the operative date of termination falls before the date when the employee reaches the age of 65.

(2) Retirement of the employee shall not be taken to be the reason (or a reason) for the dismissal.

98ZB NO NORMAL RETIREMENT AGE: DISMISSAL AT OR AFTER 65

(1) This section applies to the dismissal of an employee if—
  (a) the employee has no normal retirement age, and
  (b) the operative date of termination falls on or after the date when the employee reaches the age of 65.

(2) In a case where—
  (a) the employer has notified the employee in accordance with paragraph 2 of Schedule 6 to the 2006 Regulations, and
  (b) the contract of employment terminates on the intended date of retirement,
  retirement of the employee shall be taken to be the only reason for the dismissal by the employer and any other reason shall be disregarded.

(3) In a case where—
  (a) the employer has notified the employee in accordance with paragraph 2 of Schedule 6 to the 2006 Regulations, but
  (b) the contract of employment terminates before the intended date of retirement,
  retirement of the employee shall not be taken to be the reason (or a reason) for dismissal.

(4) In a case where—
  (a) the employer has not notified the employee in accordance with paragraph 2 of Schedule 6 to the 2006 Regulations, and
  (b) there is an intended date of retirement in relation to the dismissal, but
  (c) the contract of employment terminates before the intended date of retirement,
  retirement of the employee shall not be taken to be the reason (or a reason) for dismissal.

(5) In all other cases where the employer has not notified the employee in accordance with paragraph 2 of Schedule 6 to the 2006 Regulations, particular regard shall be had to the matters in section 98ZF when determining the reason (or principal reason) for dismissal.

98ZC NORMAL RETIREMENT AGE: DISMISSAL BEFORE RETIREMENT AGE

(1) This section applies to the dismissal of an employee if—
  (a) the employee has a normal retirement age, and
  (b) the operative date of termination falls before the date when the employee reaches the normal retirement age.

(2) Retirement of the employee shall not be taken to be the reason (or a reason) for the dismissal.

98ZD NORMAL RETIREMENT AGE 65 OR HIGHER: DISMISSAL AT OR AFTER RETIREMENT AGE

(1) This section applies to the dismissal of an employee if—
  (a) the employee has a normal retirement age,
  (b) the normal retirement age is 65 or higher, and

(c) the operative date of termination falls on or after the date when the employee reaches the normal retirement age.

(2) In a case where—
  (a) the employer has notified the employee in accordance with paragraph 2 of Schedule 6 to the 2006 Regulations, and
  (b) the contract of employment terminates on the intended date of retirement,
  retirement of the employee shall be taken to be the only reason for the dismissal by the employer and any other reason shall be disregarded.

(3) In a case where—
  (a) the employer has notified the employee in accordance with paragraph 2 of Schedule 6 to the 2006 Regulations, but
  (b) the contract of employment terminates before the intended date of retirement,
  retirement of the employee shall not be taken to be the reason (or a reason) for dismissal.

(4) In a case where—
  (a) the employer has not notified the employee in accordance with paragraph 2 of Schedule 6 to the 2006 Regulations, and
  (b) there is an intended date of retirement in relation to the dismissal, but
  (c) the contract of employment terminates before the intended date of retirement,
  retirement of the employee shall not be taken to be the reason (or a reason) for dismissal.

(5) In all other cases where the employer has not notified the employee in accordance with paragraph 2 of Schedule 6 to the 2006 Regulations, particular regard shall be had to the matters in section 98ZF when determining the reason (or principal reason) for dismissal.

98ZE NORMAL RETIREMENT AGE BELOW 65: DISMISSAL AT OR AFTER RETIREMENT AGE

(1) This section applies to the dismissal of an employee if—
  (a) the employee has a normal retirement age,
  (b) the normal retirement age is below 65, and
  (c) the operative date of termination falls on or after the date when the employee reaches the normal retirement age.

(2) If it is unlawful discrimination under the 2006 Regulations for the employee to have that normal retirement age, retirement of the employee shall not be taken to be the reason (or a reason) for dismissal.

(3) Subsections (4) to (7) apply if it is not unlawful discrimination under the 2006 Regulations for the employee to have that normal retirement age.

(4) In a case where—
  (a) the employer has notified the employee in accordance with paragraph 2 of Schedule 6 to the 2006 Regulations, and
  (b) the contract of employment terminates on the intended date of retirement,
  retirement of the employee shall be taken to be the only reason for dismissal by the employer and any other reason shall be disregarded.

(5) In a case where—
  (a) the employer has notified the employee in accordance with paragraph 2 of Schedule 6 to the 2006 Regulations, but
  (b) the contract of employment terminates before the intended date of retirement,
  retirement of the employee shall not be taken to be the reason (or a reason) for dismissal.

(6)   In a case where—
    (a)   the employer has not notified the employee in accordance with paragraph 2 of Schedule 6 to the 2006 Regulations, and
    (b)   there is an intended date of retirement in relation to the dismissal, but
    (c)   the contract of employment terminates before the intended date of retirement,
retirement of the employee shall not be taken to be the reason (or a reason) for dismissal.

(7)   In all other cases where the employer has not notified the employee in accordance with paragraph 2 of Schedule 6 to the 2006 Regulations, particular regard shall be had to the matters in section 98ZF when determining the reason (or principal reason) for dismissal.

98ZF   REASON FOR DISMISSAL: PARTICULAR MATTERS

(1)   These are the matters to which particular regard is to be had in accordance with section 98ZB(5), 98ZD(5) or 98ZE(7)—
    (a)   whether or not the employer has notified the employee in accordance with paragraph 4 of Schedule 6 to the 2006 Regulations;
    (b)   if the employer has notified the employee in accordance with that paragraph, how long before the notified retirement date the notification was given;
    (c)   whether or not the employer has followed, or sought to follow, the procedures in paragraph 7 of Schedule 6 to the 2006 Regulations.

(2)   In subsection (1)(b) "notified retirement date" means the date notified to the employee in accordance with paragraph 4 of Schedule 6 to the 2006 Regulations as the date on which the employer intends to retire the employee.

98ZG   RETIREMENT DISMISSALS: FAIRNESS

(1)   This section applies if the reason (or principal reason) for a dismissal is retirement of the employee.

(2)   The employee shall be regarded as unfairly dismissed if, and only if, there has been a failure on the part of the employer to comply with an obligation imposed on him by any of the following provisions of Schedule 6 to the 2006 Regulations—
    (a)   paragraph 4 (notification of retirement, if not already given under paragraph 2),
    (b)   paragraphs 6 and 7 (duty to consider employee's request not to be retired),
    (c)   paragraph 8 (duty to consider appeal against decision to refuse request not to be retired).

99   LEAVE FOR FAMILY REASONS

(1)   An employee who is dismissed shall be regarded for the purposes of this Part as unfairly dismissed if—
    (a)   the reason or principal reason for the dismissal is of a prescribed kind, or
    (b)   the dismissal takes place in prescribed circumstances.

(2)   In this section "prescribed" means prescribed by regulations made by the Secretary of State.

(3)   A reason or set of circumstances prescribed under this section must relate to—
    (a)   pregnancy, childbirth or maternity,
    (b)   ordinary, compulsory or additional maternity leave,
    (ba) ordinary or additional adoption leave,
    (c)   parental leave,

(ca) ordinary or additional paternity leave, or

(d) time off under section 57A;

and it may also relate to redundancy or other factors.

(4)   A reason or set of circumstances prescribed under subsection (1) satisfies subsection (3)(c) or (d) if it relates to action which an employee—

(a) takes,

(b) agrees to take, or

(c) refuses to take,

under or in respect of a collective or workforce agreement which deals with parental leave.

(5)   Regulations under this section may—

(a) make different provision for different cases or circumstances;

(b) apply any enactment, in such circumstances as may be specified and subject to any conditions specified, in relation to persons regarded as unfairly dismissed by reason of this section.

100 HEALTH AND SAFETY CASES

(1)   An employee who is dismissed shall be regarded for the purposes of this Part as unfairly dismissed if the reason (or, if more than one, the principal reason) for the dismissal is that—

(a) having been designated by the employer to carry out activities in connection with preventing or reducing risks to health and safety at work, the employee carried out (or proposed to carry out) any such activities,

(b) being a representative of workers on matters of health and safety at work or member of a safety committee—

(i) in accordance with arrangements established under or by virtue of any enactment, or

(ii) by reason of being acknowledged as such by the employer,

the employee performed (or proposed to perform) any functions as such a representative or a member of such a committee,

(ba) the employee took part (or proposed to take part) in consultation with the employer pursuant to the Health and Safety (Consultation with Employees) Regulations 1996 or in an election of representatives of employee safety within the meaning of those Regulations (whether as a candidate or otherwise),

(c) being an employee at a place where—

(i) there was no such representative or safety committee, or

(ii) there was such a representative or safety committee but it was not reasonably practicable for the employee to raise the matter by those means,

he brought to his employer's attention, by reasonable means, circumstances connected with his work which he reasonably believed were harmful or potentially harmful to health or safety,

(d) in circumstances of danger which the employee reasonably believed to be serious and imminent and which he could not reasonably have been expected to avert, he left (or proposed to leave) or (while the danger persisted) refused to return to his place of work or any dangerous part of his place of work, or

(e) in circumstances of danger which the employee reasonably believed to be serious and imminent, he took (or proposed to take) appropriate steps to protect himself or other persons from the danger.

(2)   For the purposes of subsection (1)(e) whether steps which an employee took (or proposed to take) were appropriate is to be judged by reference to all the circumstances including, in particular, his knowledge and the facilities and advice available to him at the time.

(3)   Where the reason (or, if more than one, the principal reason) for the dismissal of an employee is that specified in subsection (1)(e), he shall not be regarded as unfairly dismissed if the employer shows that it was (or would have been) so negligent for the employee to take the steps which he took (or proposed to take) that a reasonable employer might have dismissed him for taking (or proposing to take) them.

101A WORKING TIME CASES

(1)   An employee who is dismissed shall be regarded for the purposes of this Part as unfairly dismissed if the reason (or, if more than one, the principal reason) for the dismissal is that the employee—
   (a)   refused (or proposed to refuse) to comply with a requirement which the employer imposed (or proposed to impose) in contravention of the Working Time Regulations 1998,
   (b)   refused (or proposed to refuse) to forgo a right conferred on him by those Regulations,
   (c)   failed to sign a workforce agreement for the purposes of those Regulations, or to enter into, or agree to vary or extend, any other agreement with his employer which is provided for in those Regulations, or
   (d)   being—
      (i)   a representative of members of the workforce for the purposes of Schedule 1 to those Regulations, or
      (ii) a candidate in an election in which any person elected will, on being elected, be such a representative,
performed (or proposed to perform) any functions or activities as such a representative or candidate.

103 EMPLOYEE REPRESENTATIVES

(1)   An employee who is dismissed shall be regarded for the purposes of this Part as unfairly dismissed if the reason (or, if more than one, the principal reason) for the dismissal is that the employee, being—
   (a)   an employee representative for the purposes of Chapter II of Part IV of the Trade Union and Labour Relations (Consolidation) Act 1992 (redundancies) or regulations 9, 13 and 15 of the Transfer of Undertakings (Protection of Employment) Regulations 2006, or
   (b)   a candidate in an election in which any person elected will, on being elected, be such an employee representative,
performed (or proposed to perform) any functions or activities as such an employee representative or candidate.

(2)   An employee who is dismissed shall be regarded for the purposes of this Part as unfairly dismissed if the reason (or, if more than one, the principal reason) for the dismissal is that the employee took part in an election of employee representatives for the purposes of Chapter II of Part IV of the Trade Union and Labour Relations (Consolidation) Act 1992 (redundancies) or regulations 9, 13 and 15 of the Transfer of Undertakings (Protection of Employment) Regulations 2006.

103A PROTECTED DISCLOSURE

An employee who is dismissed shall be regarded for the purposes of this Part as unfairly dismissed if the reason (or, if more than one, the principal reason) for the dismissal is that the employee made a protected disclosure.

104 ASSERTION OF STATUTORY RIGHT

(1)   An employee who is dismissed shall be regarded for the purposes of this Part as unfairly dismissed if the reason (or, if more than one, the principal reason) for the dismissal is that the employee—

    (a) brought proceedings against the employer to enforce a right of his which is a relevant statutory right, or

    (b) alleged that the employer had infringed a right of his which is a relevant statutory right.

(2)   It is immaterial for the purposes of subsection (1)—

    (a) whether or not the employee has the right, or

    (b) whether or not the right has been infringed;

but, for that subsection to apply, the claim to the right and that it has been infringed must be made in good faith.

(3)   It is sufficient for subsection (1) to apply that the employee, without specifying the right, made it reasonably clear to the employer what the right claimed to have been infringed was.

(4)   The following are relevant statutory rights for the purposes of this section—

    (a) any right conferred by this Act for which the remedy for its infringement is by way of a complaint or reference to an employment tribunal,

    (b) the right conferred by section 86 of this Act,

    (c) the rights conferred by sections 68, 86, 145A, 145B, 146, 168, 168A, 169 and 170 of the Trade Union and Labour Relations (Consolidation) Act 1992 (deductions from pay, union activities and time off),

    (d) the rights conferred by the Working Time Regulations 1998, the Merchant Shipping (Working Time: Inland Waterway) Regulations 2003, the Fishing Vessels (Working Time: Sea-fisherman) Regulations 2004 or the Cross-border Railway Services (Working Time) Regulations 2008, and

    (e) the rights conferred by the Transfer of Undertakings (Protection of Employment) Regulations 2006.

(5)   In this section any reference to an employer includes, where the right in question is conferred by section 63A, the principal (within the meaning of section 63A(3)) or the Merchant Shipping (Working Time: Inland Waterways) Regulations 2003.

104A THE NATIONAL MINIMUM WAGE

(1)   An employee who is dismissed shall be regarded for the purposes of this Part as unfairly dismissed if the reason (or, if more than one, the principal reason) for the dismissal is that—

    (a) any action was taken, or was proposed to be taken, by or on behalf of the employee with a view to enforcing, or otherwise securing the benefit of, a right of the employee's to which this section applies; or

    (b) the employer was prosecuted for an offence under section 31 of the National Minimum Wage Act 1998 as a result of action taken by or on behalf of the employee for the purpose of enforcing, or otherwise securing the benefit of, a right of the employee's to which this section applies; or

    (c) the employee qualifies, or will or might qualify, for the national minimum wage or for a particular rate of national minimum wage.

(2)   It is immaterial for the purposes of paragraph (a) or (b) of subsection (1) above—

    (a) whether or not the employee has the right, or

    (b) whether or not the right has been infringed,

but, for that subsection to apply, the claim to the right and, if applicable, the claim that it has been infringed must be made in good faith.

(3)   The following are the rights to which this section applies—
    (a)   any right conferred by, or by virtue of, any provision of the National Minimum Wage Act 1998 for which the remedy for its infringement is by way of a complaint to an employment tribunal; and
    (b)   any right conferred by section 17 of the National Minimum Wage Act 1998 (worker receiving less than national minimum wage entitled to additional remuneration).

104C FLEXIBLE WORKING

An employee who is dismissed shall be regarded for the purposes of this Part as unfairly dismissed if the reason (or, if more than one, the principal reason) for the dismissal is that the employee—

(a)   made (or proposed to make) an application under section 80F,

(b)   exercised (or proposed to exercise) a right conferred on him under section 80G,

(c)   brought proceedings against the employer under section 80H, or

(d)   alleged the existence of any circumstance which would constitute a ground for bringing such proceedings.

105 REDUNDANCY

(1)   An employee who is dismissed shall be regarded for the purposes of this Part as unfairly dismissed if—
    (a)   the reason (or, if more than one, the principal reason) for the dismissal is that the employee was redundant,
    (b)   it is shown that the circumstances constituting the redundancy applied equally to one or more other employees in the same undertaking who held positions similar to that held by the employee and who have not been dismissed by the employer, and
    (c)   it is shown that any of subsections (2A) to (7M) applies.

(2A)   This subsection applies if the reason (or, if more than one, the principal reason) for which the employee was selected for dismissal was one of those specified in subsection (1) of section 98B (unless the case is one to which subsection (2) of that section applies).

(3)   This subsection applies if the reason (or, if more than one, the principal reason) for which the employee was selected for dismissal was one of those specified in subsection (1) of section 100 (read with subsections (2) and (3) of that section).

(4)   This subsection applies if either—
    (a)   the employee was a protected shop worker or an opted-out shop worker, or a protected betting worker or an opted-out betting worker, and the reason (or, if more than one, the principal reason) for which the employee was selected for dismissal was that specified in subsection (1) of section 101 (read with subsection (2) of that section), or
    (b)   the employee was a shop worker or a betting worker and the reason (or, if more than one, the principal reason) for which the employee was selected for dismissal was that specified in subsection (3) of that section.

(4A)   This subsection applies if the reason (or, if more than one, the principal reason) for which the employee was selected for dismissal was one of those specified in section 101A.

(5)   This subsection applies if the reason (or, if more than one, the principal reason) for which the employee was selected for dismissal was that specified in <u>section 102(1)</u>.

(6)   This subsection applies if the reason (or, if more than one, the principal reason) for which the employee was selected for dismissal was that specified in <u>section 103</u>.

(6A)   This subsection applies if the reason (or, if more than one, the principal reason) for which the employee was selected for dismissal was that specified in <u>section 103A</u>.

(7)   This subsection applies if the reason (or, if more than one, the principal reason) for which the employee was selected for dismissal was one of those specified in <u>subsection (1) of section 104</u> (read with <u>subsections (2) and (3)</u> of that section).

(7A)   This subsection applies if the reason (or, if more than one, the principal reason) for which the employee was selected for dismissal was one of those specified in <u>subsection (1) of section 104A</u> (read with <u>subsection (2)</u> of that section).

(7B)   This subsection applies if the reason (or, if more than one, the principal reason) for which the employee was selected for dismissal was one of those specified in <u>subsection (1) of section 104B</u> (read with <u>subsection (2)</u> of that section).

(7BA)   This subsection applies if the reason (or, if more than one, the principal reason) for which the employee was selected for dismissal was one of those specified in <u>section 104C</u>.

(7BB)   This subsection applies if the reason (or, if more than one, the principal reason) for which the employee was selected for dismissal was one of those specified in <u>section 104E</u>.

(7C)   This subsection applies if—
        (a) the reason (or, if more than one, the principal reason) for which the employee was selected for dismissal was the reason mentioned in <u>section 238A(2)</u> of the <u>Trade Union and Labour Relations (Consolidation) Act 1992</u> (participation in official industrial action), and
        (b) subsection (3), (4) or (5) of that section applies to the dismissal.

(7D)   This subsection applies if the reason (or, if more than one, the principal reason) for which the employee was selected for dismissal was one specified in paragraph (3) or (6) of <u>regulation 28</u> of the <u>Transnational Information and Consultation of Employees Regulations 1999</u> (read with paragraphs (4) and (7) of that regulation).

(7E)   This subsection applies if the reason (or, if more than one, the principal reason) for which the employee was selected for dismissal was one specified in <u>paragraph (3) of regulation 7</u> of the <u>Part-time Workers (Prevention of Less Favourable Treatment) Regulations 2000</u> (unless the case is one to which <u>paragraph (4)</u> of that regulation applies).

(7F)   This subsection applies if the reason (or, if more than one, the principal reason) for which the employee was selected for dismissal was one specified in <u>paragraph (3) of regulation 6</u> of the <u>Fixed-term Employees (Prevention of Less Favourable Treatment) Regulations 2002</u> (unless the case is one to which <u>paragraph (4)</u> of that regulation applies).

(7G)   This subsection applies if the reason (or, if more than one, the principal reason) for which the employee was selected for dismissal was one specified in <u>paragraph (3)</u> or <u>(6) of regulation 42</u> of the <u>European Public Limited-Liability Company Regulations 2004</u> (read with <u>paragraphs (4)</u> and <u>(7)</u> of that regulation).

(7H)   This subsection applies if the reason (or, if more than one, the principal reason) for which the employee was selected for dismissal was one specified in <u>paragraph (3)</u> or <u>(6) of regulation 30</u> of the <u>Information and Consultation of Employees Regulations 2004</u> (read with <u>paragraphs (4)</u> and <u>(7)</u> of that regulation).

(7I)   This subsection applies if the reason (or, if more than one, the principal reason) for which the employee was selected for dismissal was one specified in paragraph 5(3) or (5) of the Schedule to the Occupational and Personal Pension Schemes (Consultation by Employers and Miscellaneous Amendment) Regulations 2006 (read with paragraph 5(6) of that Schedule).

(7IA) This subsection applies if the reason (or, if more than one, the principal reason) for which the employee was selected for dismissal was that he—
   (a) exercised or sought to exercise his right to be accompanied in accordance with paragraph 9 of Schedule 6 to the Employment Equality (Age) Regulations 2006, or
   (b) accompanied or sought to accompany an employee pursuant to a request under that paragraph.

(7J)   This subsection applies if the reason (or, if more than one, the principal reason) for which the employee was selected for dismissal was one specified in paragraph (3) or (6) of regulation 31 of the European Cooperative Society (Involvement of Employees) Regulations 2006 (read with paragraphs (4) and (7) of that regulation).

(7K)   This subsection applies if the reason (or, if more than one, the principal reason) for which the employee was selected for dismissal was one specified in—
   (a) paragraph (2) of regulation 46 of the Companies (Cross-Border Mergers) Regulations 2007 (read with paragraphs (3) and (4) of that regulation); or
   (b) paragraph (2) of regulation 47 of the Companies (Cross-Border Mergers) Regulations 2007 (read with paragraph (3) of that regulation).

(7L)   This subsection applies if the reason (or, if more than one, the principal reason) for which the employee was selected for dismissal was one specified in paragraph (3) or (6) of regulation 29 of the European Public Limited-Liability Company (Employee Involvement) (Great Britain) Regulations 2009(S.I. 2009/2401) (read with paragraphs (4) and (7) of that regulation).

(7M) This subsection applies if—
   (a) the reason (or, if more than one, the principal reason) for which the employee was selected for dismissal was the one specified in the opening words of section 104F(1), and
   (b) the condition in paragraph (a) or (b) of that subsection was met.

(8)   For the purposes of section 36(2)(b) or 41(1)(b), the appropriate date in relation to this section is the effective date of termination.

(9)   In this Part "redundancy case" means a case where paragraphs (a) and (b) of subsection (1) of this section are satisfied.

108 QUALIFYING PERIOD OF EMPLOYMENT

(1)   Section 94 does not apply to the dismissal of an employee unless he has been continuously employed for a period of not less than one year ending with the effective date of termination.

(2)   If an employee is dismissed by reason of any such requirement or recommendation as is referred to in section 64(2), subsection (1) has effect in relation to that dismissal as if for the words "one year" there were substituted the words "one month".

(3)   Subsection (1) does not apply if—
   (aa) subsection (1) of section 98B (read with subsection (2) of that section) applies,
   (b) subsection (1) of section 99 (read with any regulations made under that section) applies,

(c) subsection (1) of section 100 (read with subsections (2) and (3) of that section applies,

(d) subsection (1) of section 101 (read with subsection (2) of that section) or subsection (3) of that section applies,

(dd) section 101A applies,

(e) section 102 applies,

(f) section 103 applies,

(ff) section 103A applies,

(g) subsection (1) of section 104 (read with subsections (2) and (3) of that section) applies,

(gg) subsection (1) of section 104A (read with subsection (2) of that section) applies,

(gh) subsection (1) of section 104B (read with subsection (2) of that section) applies,

(gi) section 104C applies,

(gk) section 104E applies,

(gk) subsection (1) of section 104F (read with subsection (2) of that section) applies,

(h) section 105 applies

(hh) paragraph (3) or (6) of regulation 28 of the Transnational Information and Consultation of Employees Regulations 1999 (read with paragraphs (4) and (7) of that regulation) applies

(i) paragraph (1) of regulation 7 of the Part-time Workers (Prevention of Less Favourable Treatment) Regulations 2000 applies

(j) paragraph (1) of regulation 6 of the Fixed-term Employees (Prevention of Less Favourable Treatment) Regulations 2002 applies

(k) paragraph (3) or (6) of regulation 42 of the European Public Limited-Liability Company Regulations 2004 applies

(l) paragraph (3) or (6) of regulation 30 of the Information and Consultation of Employees Regulations 2004 (read with paragraphs (4) and (7) of that regulation) applies

(m) paragraph 5(3) or (5) of the Schedule to the Occupational and Personal Pension Schemes (Consultation by Employers and Miscellaneous Amendment) Regulations 2006 (read with paragraph 5(6) of that Schedule) applies

(n) paragraph (a) or (b) of paragraph 13(5) of Schedule 6 to the Employment Equality (Age) Regulations 2006 applies;

(o) paragraph (3) or (6) of regulation 31 of the European Cooperative Society (Involvement of Employees) Regulations 2006 (read with paragraphs (4) and (7) of that regulation) applies;

(p) regulation 46 or 47 of the Companies (Cross-Border Mergers) Regulations 2007 applies, or

(q) paragraph (1)(a) or (b) of regulation 29 of the European Public Limited-Liability Company (Employee Involvement) (Great Britain) Regulations 2009(S.I. 2009/2401) applies

Chapter II REMEDIES FOR UNFAIR DISMISSAL

111 COMPLAINTS TO EMPLOYMENT TRIBUNAL

(1) A complaint may be presented to an employment tribunal against an employer by any person that he was unfairly dismissed by the employer.

(2) Subject to the following provisions of this section, an employment tribunal shall not consider a complaint under this section unless it is presented to the tribunal—

(a) before the end of the period of three months beginning with the effective date of termination, or

(b) within such further period as the tribunal considers reasonable in a case where it is satisfied that it was not reasonably practicable for the complaint to be presented before the end of that period of three months.

(3) Where a dismissal is with notice, an employment tribunal shall consider a complaint under this section if it is presented after the notice is given but before the effective date of termination.

(4) In relation to a complaint which is presented as mentioned in subsection (3), the provisions of this Act, so far as they relate to unfair dismissal, have effect as if—

(a) references to a complaint by a person that he was unfairly dismissed by his employer included references to a complaint by a person that his employer has given him notice in such circumstances that he will be unfairly dismissed when the notice expires,

(b) references to reinstatement included references to the withdrawal of the notice by the employer,

(c) references to the effective date of termination included references to the date which would be the effective date of termination on the expiry of the notice, and

(d) references to an employee ceasing to be employed included references to an employee having been given notice of dismissal.

(5) Where the dismissal is alleged to be unfair by virtue of section 104F (blacklists)—

(a) subsection (2)(b) does not apply, and

(b) an employment tribunal may consider a complaint that is otherwise out of time if, in all the circumstances of the case, it considers that it is just and equitable to do so.

112 THE REMEDIES: ORDERS AND COMPENSATION

(1) This section applies where, on a complaint under section 111, an employment tribunal finds that the grounds of the complaint are well-founded.

(2) The tribunal shall—

(a) explain to the complainant what orders may be made under section 113 and in what circumstances they may be made, and

(b) ask him whether he wishes the tribunal to make such an order.

(3) If the complainant expresses such a wish, the tribunal may make an order under section 113.

(4) If no order is made under section 113, the tribunal shall make an award of compensation for unfair dismissal (calculated in accordance with sections 118 to 126) to be paid by the employer to the employee.

(5) Where—

(a) an employee is regarded as unfairly dismissed by virtue of section 98ZG (whether or not his dismissal is unfair or regarded as unfair for any other reason), and

(b) an order is made in respect of the employee under section 113,
the employment tribunal shall, subject to subsection (6), also make an award of four weeks' pay to be paid by the employer to the employee.

(6) An employment tribunal shall not be required to make an award under subsection (5) if it considers that such an award would result in injustice to the employer.

113 THE ORDERS

An order under this section may be—

(a) an order for reinstatement (in accordance with section 114), or

(b) an order for re-engagement (in accordance with section 115), as the tribunal may decide.

114 ORDER FOR REINSTATEMENT

(1)   An order for reinstatement is an order that the employer shall treat the complainant in all respects as if he had not been dismissed.

(2)   On making an order for reinstatement the tribunal shall specify—

(a) any amount payable by the employer in respect of any benefit which the complainant might reasonably be expected to have had but for the dismissal (including arrears of pay) for the period between the date of termination of employment and the date of reinstatement,

(b) any rights and privileges (including seniority and pension rights) which must be restored to the employee, and

(c) the date by which the order must be complied with.

(3)   If the complainant would have benefited from an improvement in his terms and conditions of employment had he not been dismissed, an order for reinstatement shall require him to be treated as if he had benefited from that improvement from the date on which he would have done so but for being dismissed.

(4)   In calculating for the purposes of subsection (2)(a) any amount payable by the employer, the tribunal shall take into account, so as to reduce the employer's liability, any sums received by the complainant in respect of the period between the date of termination of employment and the date of reinstatement by way of—

(a) wages in lieu of notice or ex gratia payments paid by the employer, or

(b) remuneration paid in respect of employment with another employer,

and such other benefits as the tribunal thinks appropriate in the circumstances.

115 ORDER FOR RE-ENGAGEMENT

(1)   An order for re-engagement is an order, on such terms as the tribunal may decide, that the complainant be engaged by the employer, or by a successor of the employer or by an associated employer, in employment comparable to that from which he was dismissed or other suitable employment.

(2)   On making an order for re-engagement the tribunal shall specify the terms on which re-engagement is to take place, including—

(a) the identity of the employer,

(b) the nature of the employment,

(c) the remuneration for the employment,

(d) any amount payable by the employer in respect of any benefit which the complainant might reasonably be expected to have had but for the dismissal (including arrears of pay) for the period between the date of termination of employment and the date of re-engagement,

(e) any rights and privileges (including seniority and pension rights) which must be restored to the employee, and

(f) the date by which the order must be complied with.

(3)   In calculating for the purposes of subsection (2)(d) any amount payable by the employer, the tribunal shall take into account, so as to reduce the employer's liability, any sums received by the complainant in respect of the period between the date of termination of employment and the date of re-engagement by way of—

(a) wages in lieu of notice or ex gratia payments paid by the employer, or

(b) remuneration paid in respect of employment with another employer,

and such other benefits as the tribunal thinks appropriate in the circumstances.

116 CHOICE OF ORDER AND ITS TERMS

(1)   In exercising its discretion under section 113 the tribunal shall first consider whether to make an order for reinstatement and in so doing shall take into account—

(a)   whether the complainant wishes to be reinstated,

(b)   whether it is practicable for the employer to comply with an order for reinstatement, and

(c)   where the complainant caused or contributed to some extent to the dismissal, whether it would be just to order his reinstatement.

(2)   If the tribunal decides not to make an order for reinstatement it shall then consider whether to make an order for re-engagement and, if so, on what terms.

(3)   In so doing the tribunal shall take into account—

(a)   any wish expressed by the complainant as to the nature of the order to be made,

(b)   whether it is practicable for the employer (or a successor or an associated employer) to comply with an order for re-engagement, and

(c)   where the complainant caused or contributed to some extent to the dismissal, whether it would be just to order his re-engagement and (if so) on what terms.

(4)   Except in a case where the tribunal takes into account contributory fault under subsection (3)(c) it shall, if it orders re-engagement, do so on terms which are, so far as is reasonably practicable, as favourable as an order for reinstatement.

(5)   Where in any case an employer has engaged a permanent replacement for a dismissed employee, the tribunal shall not take that fact into account in determining, for the purposes of subsection (1)(b) or (3)(b), whether it is practicable to comply with an order for reinstatement or re-engagement.

(6)   Subsection (5) does not apply where the employer shows—

(a)   that it was not practicable for him to arrange for the dismissed employee's work to be done without engaging a permanent replacement, or

(b)   that—

(i)   he engaged the replacement after the lapse of a reasonable period, without having heard from the dismissed employee that he wished to be reinstated or re-engaged, and

(ii)   when the employer engaged the replacement it was no longer reasonable for him to arrange for the dismissed employee's work to be done except by a permanent replacement.

117 ENFORCEMENT OF ORDER AND COMPENSATION

(1)   An employment tribunal shall make an award of compensation, to be paid by the employer to the employee, if—

(a)   an order under section 113 is made and the complainant is reinstated or re-engaged, but

(b)   the terms of the order are not fully complied with.

(2)   Subject to section 124, the amount of the compensation shall be such as the tribunal thinks fit having regard to the loss sustained by the complainant in consequence of the failure to comply fully with the terms of the order.

(2A)   There shall be deducted from any award under subsection (1) the amount of any award made under section 112(5) at the time of the order under section 113.

(3)   Subject to subsections (1) and (2), if an order under section 113 is made but the complainant is not reinstated or re-engaged in accordance with the order, the tribunal shall make—

(a) an award of compensation for unfair dismissal (calculated in accordance with sections 118 to 126), and

(b) except where this paragraph does not apply, an additional award of compensation of an amount not less than twenty-six nor more than fifty-two weeks' pay,

to be paid by the employer to the employee.

(4) Subsection (3)(b) does not apply where—

(a) the employer satisfies the tribunal that it was not practicable to comply with the order,

(7) Where in any case an employer has engaged a permanent replacement for a dismissed employee, the tribunal shall not take that fact into account in determining for the purposes of subsection (4)(a) whether it was practicable to comply with the order for reinstatement or re-engagement unless the employer shows that it was not practicable for him to arrange for the dismissed employee's work to be done without engaging a permanent replacement.

(8) Where in any case an employment tribunal finds that the complainant has unreasonably prevented an order under section 113 from being complied with, in making an award of compensation for unfair dismissal it shall take that conduct into account as a failure on the part of the complainant to mitigate his loss.

118   GENERAL

(1) Where a tribunal makes an award of compensation for unfair dismissal under section 112(4) or 117(3)(a) the award shall consist of—

(a) a basic award (calculated in accordance with sections 119 to 122 and 126, and

(b) a compensatory award (calculated in accordance with sections 123, 124, 124A and 126).

119   BASIC AWARD

(1) Subject to the provisions of this section, sections 120 to 122 and section 126, the amount of the basic award shall be calculated by—

(a) determining the period, ending with the effective date of termination, during which the employee has been continuously employed,

(b) reckoning backwards from the end of that period the number of years of employment falling within that period, and

(c) allowing the appropriate amount for each of those years of employment.

(2) In subsection (1)(c) "the appropriate amount" means—

(a) one and a half weeks' pay for a year of employment in which the employee was not below the age of forty-one,

(b) one week's pay for a year of employment (not within paragraph (a)) in which he was not below the age of twenty-two, and

(c) half a week's pay for a year of employment not within paragraph (a) or (b).

(3) Where twenty years of employment have been reckoned under subsection (1), no account shall be taken under that subsection of any year of employment earlier than those twenty years.

120   BASIC AWARD: MINIMUM IN CERTAIN CASES

(1) The amount of the basic award (before any reduction under section 122) shall not be less than £4,700 where the reason (or, if more than one, the principal reason)—

(a) in a redundancy case, for selecting the employee for dismissal, or

(b) otherwise, for the dismissal,

is one of those specified in [section 100(1)(a) and (b), 101A(d), 102(1) or 103.

(1A) Where—

(a) an employee is regarded as unfairly dismissed by virtue of section 98ZG (whether or not his dismissal is unfair or regarded as unfair for any other reason),

(b) an award of compensation falls to be made under section 112(4), and

(c) the amount of the award under section 118(1)(a), before any reduction under section 122(3A) or (4), is less than the amount of four weeks' pay,

the employment tribunal shall, subject to subsection (1B), increase the award under section 118(1)(a) to the amount of four weeks' pay.

(1B) An employment tribunal shall not be required by subsection (1A) to increase the amount of an award if it considers that the increase would result in injustice to the employer.

(1C) Where an employee is regarded as unfairly dismissed by virtue of section 104F (blacklists) (whether or not the dismissal is unfair or regarded as unfair for any other reason), the amount of the basic award of compensation (before any reduction is made under section 122) shall not be less than £5,000.

122 BASIC AWARD: REDUCTIONS

(1) Where the tribunal finds that the complainant has unreasonably refused an offer by the employer which (if accepted) would have the effect of reinstating the complainant in his employment in all respects as if he had not been dismissed, the tribunal shall reduce or further reduce the amount of the basic award to such extent as it considers just and equitable having regard to that finding.

(2) Where the tribunal considers that any conduct of the complainant before the dismissal (or, where the dismissal was with notice, before the notice was given) was such that it would be just and equitable to reduce or further reduce the amount of the basic award to any extent, the tribunal shall reduce or further reduce that amount accordingly.

(3) Subsection (2) does not apply in a redundancy case unless the reason for selecting the employee for dismissal was one of those specified in section 100(1)(a) and (b), 101A(d), 102(1) or 103; and in such a case subsection (2) applies only to so much of the basic award as is payable because of section 120.

(3A) Where the complainant has been awarded any amount in respect of the dismissal under a designated dismissal procedures agreement, the tribunal shall reduce or further reduce the amount of the basic award to such extent as it considers just and equitable having regard to that award.

(4) The amount of the basic award shall be reduced or further reduced by the amount of—

(a) any redundancy payment awarded by the tribunal under Part XI in respect of the same dismissal, or

(b) any payment made by the employer to the employee on the ground that the dismissal was by reason of redundancy (whether in pursuance of Part XI or otherwise).

(5) Where a dismissal is regarded as unfair by virtue of section 104F (blacklists), the amount of the basic award shall be reduced or further reduced by the amount of any basic award in respect of the same dismissal under section 156 of the Trade Union and Labour Relations (Consolidation) Act 1992 (minimum basic award in case of dismissal on grounds related to trade union membership or activities).

123 COMPENSATORY AWARD

(1) Subject to the provisions of this section and sections 124, 124A and 126, the amount of the compensatory award shall be such amount as the tribunal considers just and equitable in all the circumstances having regard to the loss sustained by the complainant in consequence of the dismissal in so far as that loss is attributable to action taken by the employer.

(2) The loss referred to in subsection (1) shall be taken to include—
(a) any expenses reasonably incurred by the complainant in consequence of the dismissal, and
(b) subject to subsection (3), loss of any benefit which he might reasonably be expected to have had but for the dismissal.

(3) The loss referred to in subsection (1) shall be taken to include in respect of any loss of—
(a) any entitlement or potential entitlement to a payment on account of dismissal by reason of redundancy (whether in pursuance of Part XI or otherwise), or
(b) any expectation of such a payment,
only the loss referable to the amount (if any) by which the amount of that payment would have exceeded the amount of a basic award (apart from any reduction under section 122 in respect of the same dismissal.

(4) In ascertaining the loss referred to in subsection (1) the tribunal shall apply the same rule concerning the duty of a person to mitigate his loss as applies to damages recoverable under the common law of England and Wales or (as the case may be) Scotland.

(5) In determining, for the purposes of subsection (1), how far any loss sustained by the complainant was attributable to action taken by the employer, no account shall be taken of any pressure which by—
(a) calling, organising, procuring or financing a strike or other industrial action, or
(b) threatening to do so,
was exercised on the employer to dismiss the employee; and that question shall be determined as if no such pressure had been exercised.

(6) Where the tribunal finds that the dismissal was to any extent caused or contributed to by any action of the complainant, it shall reduce the amount of the compensatory award by such proportion as it considers just and equitable having regard to that finding.

(7) If the amount of any payment made by the employer to the employee on the ground that the dismissal was by reason of redundancy (whether in pursuance of Part XI or otherwise) exceeds the amount of the basic award which would be payable but for section 122(4), that excess goes to reduce the amount of the compensatory award.

(8) Where the amount of the compensatory award falls to be calculated for the purposes of an award under section 117(3)(a), there shall be deducted from the compensatory award any award made under section 112(5) at the time of the order under section 113.

124 LIMIT OF COMPENSATORY AWARD ETC.

(1) The amount of—
(a) any compensation awarded to a person under section 117(1) and (2), or
(b) a compensatory award to a person calculated in accordance with section 123,
shall not exceed £65,300.

(1A) Subsection (1) shall not apply to compensation awarded, or a compensatory award made, to a person in a case where he is regarded as unfairly dismissed by virtue of section 100, 103A, 105(3) or 105(6A).

(3) In the case of compensation awarded to a person under section 117(1) and (2), the limit imposed by this section may be exceeded to the extent necessary to enable the award fully to reflect the amount specified as payable under section 114(2)(a) or section 115(2)(d).

(4) Where—
(a) a compensatory award is an award under paragraph (a) of subsection (3) of section 117, and
(b) an additional award falls to be made under paragraph (b) of that subsection,
the limit imposed by this section on the compensatory award may be exceeded to the extent necessary to enable the aggregate of the compensatory and additional awards fully to reflect the amount specified as payable under section 114(2)(a) or section 115(2)(d).

(5) The limit imposed by this section applies to the amount which the [employment tribunal]⁴ would, apart from this section, award in respect of the subject matter of the complaint after taking into account—
(a) any payment made by the respondent to the complainant in respect of that matter, and
(b) any reduction in the amount of the award required by any enactment or rule of law.

130 ORDER FOR CONTINUATION OF CONTRACT OF EMPLOYMENT

(1) An order under section 129 for the continuation of a contract of employment is an order that the contract of employment continue in force—
(a) for the purposes of pay or any other benefit derived from the employment, seniority, pension rights and other similar matters, and
(b) for the purposes of determining for any purpose the period for which the employee has been continuously employed,
from the date of its termination (whether before or after the making of the order) until the determination or settlement of the complaint.

(2) Where the tribunal makes such an order it shall specify in the order the amount which is to be paid by the employer to the employee by way of pay in respect of each normal pay period, or part of any such period, falling between the date of dismissal and the determination or settlement of the complaint.

(3) Subject to the following provisions, the amount so specified shall be that which the employee could reasonably have been expected to earn during that period, or part, and shall be paid—
(a) in the case of a payment for any such period falling wholly or partly after the making of the order, on the normal pay day for that period, and
(b) in the case of a payment for any past period, within such time as may be specified in the order.

(4) If an amount is payable in respect only of part of a normal pay period, the amount shall be calculated by reference to the whole period and reduced proportionately.

(5) Any payment made to an employee by an employer under his contract of employment, or by way of damages for breach of that contract, in respect of a normal pay period, or part of any such period, goes towards discharging the employer's liability in respect of that period under subsection (2); and, conversely, any payment under that subsection in respect of a period goes towards discharging any liability of the employer under, or in respect of breach of, the contract of employment in respect of that period.

(6) If an employee, on or after being dismissed by his employer, receives a lump sum which, or part of which, is in lieu of wages but is not referable to any normal pay period, the

tribunal shall take the payment into account in determining the amount of pay to be payable in pursuance of any such order.

(7) For the purposes of this section, the amount which an employee could reasonably have been expected to earn, his normal pay period and the normal pay day for each such period shall be determined as if he had not been dismissed.

131 APPLICATION FOR VARIATION OR REVOCATION OF ORDER

(1) At any time between—
(a) the making of an order under section 129, and
(b) the determination or settlement of the complaint,
the employer or the employee may apply to an employment tribunal for the revocation or variation of the order on the ground of a relevant change of circumstances since the making of the order.

(2) Section 128 and 129 apply in relation to such an application as in relation to an original application for interim relief except that, in the case of an application by the employer, section 128(4) has effect with the substitution of a reference to the employee for the reference to the employer.

132 CONSEQUENCE OF FAILURE TO COMPLY WITH ORDER

(1) If, on the application of an employee, an employment tribunal is satisfied that the employer has not complied with the terms of an order for the reinstatement or re-engagement of the employee under section 129(5) or (7), the tribunal shall—
(a) make an order for the continuation of the employee's contract of employment, and
(b) order the employer to pay compensation to the employee.

(2) Compensation under subsection (1)(b) shall be of such amount as the tribunal considers just and equitable in all the circumstances having regard—
(a) to the infringement of the employee's right to be reinstated or reengaged in pursuance of the order, and
(b) to any loss suffered by the employee in consequence of the non-compliance.

(3) Section 130 applies to an order under subsection (1)(a) as in relation to an order under section 129.

(4) If on the application of an employee an employment tribunal is satisfied that the employer has not complied with the terms of an order for the continuation of a contract of employment subsection (5) or (6) applies.

(5) Where the non-compliance consists of a failure to pay an amount by way of pay specified in the order—
(a) the tribunal shall determine the amount owed by the employer on the date of the determination, and
(b) if on that date the tribunal also determines the employee's complaint that he has been unfairly dismissed, it shall specify that amount separately from any other sum awarded to the employee.

(6) In any other case, the tribunal shall order the employer to pay the employee such compensation as the tribunal considers just and equitable in all the circumstances having regard to any loss suffered by the employee in consequence of the non-compliance.

Part XI REDUNDANCY PAYMENTS ETC.

Chapter I RIGHT TO REDUNDANCY PAYMENT

135 THE RIGHT

(1) An employer shall pay a redundancy payment to any employee of his if the employee—
    (a) is dismissed by the employer by reason of redundancy, or
    (b) is eligible for a redundancy payment by reason of being laid off or kept on short-time.

(2) Subsection (1) has effect subject to the following provisions of this Part (including, in particular, sections 140 to 144, 149 to 152, 155 to 161 and 164).

136 CIRCUMSTANCES IN WHICH AN EMPLOYEE IS DISMISSED

(1) Subject to the provisions of this section and sections 137 and 138, for the purposes of this Part an employee is dismissed by his employer if (and only if)—
    (a) the contract under which he is employed by the employer is terminated by the employer (whether with or without notice),
    (b) he is employed under a limited term contract and that contract terminates by virtue of the limiting event without being renewed under the same contract, or
    (c) the employee terminates the contract under which he is employed (with or without notice) in circumstances in which he is entitled to terminate it without notice by reason of the employer's conduct.

(2) Subsection (1)(c) does not apply if the employee terminates the contract without notice in circumstances in which he is entitled to do so by reason of a lock-out by the employer.

(3) An employee shall be taken to be dismissed by his employer for the purposes of this Part if—
    (a) the employer gives notice to the employee to terminate his contract of employment, and
    (b) at a time within the obligatory period of notice the employee gives notice in writing to the employer to terminate the contract of employment on a date earlier than the date on which the employer's notice is due to expire.

(4) In this Part the "obligatory period of notice", in relation to notice given by an employer to terminate an employee's contract of employment, means—
    (a) the actual period of the notice in a case where the period beginning at the time when the notice is given and ending at the time when it expires is equal to the minimum period which (by virtue of any enactment or otherwise) is required to be given by the employer to terminate the contract of employment, and
    (b) the period which—
        (i) is equal to the minimum period referred to in paragraph (a), and
        (ii) ends at the time when the notice expires,
    in any other case.

(5) Where in accordance with any enactment or rule of law—
    (a) an act on the part of an employer, or
    (b) an event affecting an employer (including, in the case of an individual, his death),
operates to terminate a contract under which an employee is employed by him, the act or event shall be taken for the purposes of this Part to be a termination of the contract by the employer.

138 NO DISMISSAL IN CASES OF RENEWAL OF CONTRACT OR RE-ENGAGEMENT

(1)   Where—
    (a) an employee's contract of employment is renewed, or he is re-engaged under a new contract of employment in pursuance of an offer (whether in writing or not) made before the end of his employment under the previous contract, and
    (b) the renewal or re-engagement takes effect either immediately on, or after an interval of not more than four weeks after, the end of that employment,
the employee shall not be regarded for the purposes of this Part as dismissed by his employer by reason of the ending of his employment under the previous contract.

(2)   Subsection (1) does not apply if—
    (a) the provisions of the contract as renewed, or of the new contract, as to—
        (i) the capacity and place in which the employee is employed, and
        (ii) the other terms and conditions of his employment,
differ (wholly or in part) from the corresponding provisions of the previous contract, and
    (b) during the period specified in subsection (3)—
        (i) the employee (for whatever reason) terminates the renewed or new contract, or gives notice to terminate it and it is in consequence terminated, or
        (ii) the employer, for a reason connected with or arising out of any difference between the renewed or new contract and the previous contract, terminates the renewed or new contract, or gives notice to terminate it and it is in consequence terminated.

(3)   The period referred to in subsection (2)(b) is the period—
    (a) beginning at the end of the employee's employment under the previous contract, and
    (b) ending with—
        (i) the period of four weeks beginning with the date on which the employee starts work under the renewed or new contract, or
        (ii) such longer period as may be agreed in accordance with subsection (6) for the purpose of retraining the employee for employment under that contract;
and is in this Part referred to as the "trial period".

(4)   Where subsection (2) applies, for the purposes of this Part—
    (a) the employee shall be regarded as dismissed on the date on which his employment under the previous contract (or, if there has been more than one trial period, the original contract) ended, and
    (b) the reason for the dismissal shall be taken to be the reason for which the employee was then dismissed, or would have been dismissed had the offer (or original offer) of renewed or new employment not been made, or the reason which resulted in that offer being made.

(5)   Subsection (2) does not apply if the employee's contract of employment is again renewed, or he is again re-engaged under a new contract of employment, in circumstances such that subsection (1) again applies.

(6)   For the purposes of subsection (3)(b)(ii) a period of retraining is agreed in accordance with this subsection only if the agreement—
    (a) is made between the employer and the employee or his representative before the employee starts work under the contract as renewed, or the new contract,
    (b) is in writing,
    (c) specifies the date on which the period of retraining ends, and
    (d) specifies the terms and conditions of employment which will apply in the employee's case after the end of that period.

139 REDUNDANCY

(1) For the purposes of this Act an employee who is dismissed shall be taken to be dismissed by reason of redundancy if the dismissal is wholly or mainly attributable to—
   (a) the fact that his employer has ceased or intends to cease—
      (i)   to carry on the business for the purposes of which the employee was employed by him, or
      (ii) to carry on that business in the place where the employee was so employed, or
   (b) the fact that the requirements of that business—
      (i)   for employees to carry out work of a particular kind, or
      (ii) for employees to carry out work of a particular kind in the place where the employee was employed by the employer,
   have ceased or diminished or are expected to cease or diminish.

(2) For the purposes of subsection (1) the business of the employer together with the business or businesses of his associated employers shall be treated as one (unless either of the conditions specified in paragraphs (a) and (b) of that subsection would be satisfied without so treating them).

(3) For the purposes of subsection (1) the activities carried on by a local uthority with respect to the schools maintained by it, and the activities carried on by the governing bodies of those schools, shall be treated as one business (unless either of the conditions specified in paragraphs (a) and (b) of that subsection would be satisfied without so treating them).

(4) Where—
   (a) the contract under which a person is employed is treated by section 136(5) as terminated by his employer by reason of an act or event, and
   (b) the employee's contract is not renewed and he is not re-engaged under a new contract of employment,
   he shall be taken for the purposes of this Act to be dismissed by reason of redundancy if the circumstances in which his contract is not renewed, and he is not re-engaged, are wholly or mainly attributable to either of the facts stated in paragraphs (a) and (b) of subsection (1).

(5) In its application to a case within subsection (4), paragraph (a)(i) of subsection (1) has effect as if the reference in that subsection to the employer included a reference to any person to whom, in consequence of the act or event, power to dispose of the business has passed.

(6) In subsection (1) "cease" and "diminish" mean cease and diminish either permanently or temporarily and for whatever reason.

(7) In subsection (3) "local authority" has the meaning given by section 579(1) of the Education Act 1996.

140 SUMMARY DISMISSAL

(1) Subject to subsections (2) and (3), an employee is not entitled to a redundancy payment by reason of dismissal where his employer, being entitled to terminate his contract of employment without notice by reason of the employee's conduct, terminates it either—
   (a) without notice,
   (b) by giving shorter notice than that which, in the absence of conduct entitling the employer to terminate the contract without notice, the employer would be required to give to terminate the contract, or

(c) by giving notice which includes, or is accompanied by, a statement in writing that the employer would, by reason of the employee's conduct, be entitled to terminate the contract without notice.

(2)   Where an employee who—
   (a) has been given notice by his employer to terminate his contract of employment, or
   (b) has given notice to his employer under section 148(1) indicating his intention to claim a redundancy payment in respect of lay-off or short-time,
takes part in a strike at any relevant time in circumstances which entitle the employer to treat the contract of employment as terminable without notice, subsection (1) does not apply if the employer terminates the contract by reason of his taking part in the strike.

(3)   Where the contract of employment of an employee who—
   (a) has been given notice by his employer to terminate his contract of employment, or
   (b) has given notice to his employer under section 148(1) indicating his intention to claim a redundancy payment in respect of lay-off or short-time,
is terminated as mentioned in subsection (1) at any relevant time otherwise than by reason of his taking part in a strike, an employment tribunal may determine that the employer is liable to make an appropriate payment to the employee if on a reference to the tribunal it appears to the tribunal, in the circumstances of the case, to be just and equitable that the employee should receive it.

(4)   In subsection (3) "appropriate payment" means—
   (a) the whole of the redundancy payment to which the employee would have been entitled apart from subsection (1), or
   (b) such part of that redundancy payment as the tribunal thinks fit.

(5)   In this section "relevant time"—
   (a) in the case of an employee who has been given notice by his employer to terminate his contract of employment, means any time within the obligatory period of notice, and
   (b) in the case of an employee who has given notice to his employer under section 148(1), means any time after the service of the notice.

145 THE RELEVANT DATE

(1)   For the purposes of the provisions of this Act relating to redundancy payments "the relevant date" in relation to the dismissal of an employee has the meaning given by this section.

(2)   Subject to the following provisions of this section, "the relevant date"—
   (a) in relation to an employee whose contract of employment is terminated by notice, whether given by his employer or by the employee, means the date on which the notice expires,
   (b) in relation to an employee whose contract of employment is terminated without notice, means the date on which the termination takes effect, and
   (c) in relation to an employee who is employed under a limited-term contract which terminates by virtue of the limiting event without being renewed under the same contract, means the date on which the termination takes effect.

(3)   Where the employee is taken to be dismissed by virtue of section 136(3) the "relevant date" means the date on which the employee's notice to terminate his contract of employment expires.

(4)   Where the employee is regarded by virtue of section 138(4) as having been dismissed on the date on which his employment under an earlier contract ended, "the relevant date" means—

(a) for the purposes of section 164(1), the date which is the relevant date as defined by subsection (2) in relation to the renewed or new contract or, where there has been more than one trial period, the last such contract, and

(b) for the purposes of any other provision, the date which is the relevant date as defined by subsection (2) in relation to the previous contract or, where there has been more than one such trial period, the original contract.

(5) Where—
   (a) the contract of employment is terminated by the employer, and
   (b) the notice required by section 86 to be given by an employer would, if duly given on the material date, expire on a date later than the relevant date (as defined by the previous provisions of this section),
for the purposes of sections 155, 162(1) and 227(3) the later date is the relevant date.

(6) In subsection (5)(b) "the material date" means—
   (a) the date when notice of termination was given by the employer, or
   (b) where no notice was given, the date when the contract of employment was terminated by the employer.

150 RESIGNATION

(1) An employee is not entitled to a redundancy payment by reason of being laid off or kept on short-time unless he terminates his contract of employment by giving such period of notice as is required for the purposes of this section before the end of the relevant period.

(2) The period of notice required for the purposes of this section—
   (a) where the employee is required by his contract of employment to give more than one week's notice to terminate the contract, is the minimum period which he is required to give, and
   (b) otherwise, is one week.

(3) In subsection (1) "the relevant period"—
   (a) if the employer does not give a counter-notice within seven days after the service of the notice of intention to claim, is three weeks after the end of those seven days,
   (b) if the employer gives a counter-notice within that period of seven days but withdraws it by a subsequent notice in writing, is three weeks after the service of the notice of withdrawal, and
   (c) if—
      (i)   the employer gives a counter-notice within that period of seven days, and does not so withdraw it, and
      (ii) a question as to the right of the employee to a redundancy payment in pursuance of the notice of intention to claim is referred to an employment tribunal,
is three weeks after the tribunal has notified to the employee its decision on that reference.

(4) For the purposes of subsection (3)(c) no account shall be taken of—
   (a) any appeal against the decision of the tribunal, or
   (b) any proceedings or decision in consequence of any such appeal.

151 DISMISSAL

(1) An employee is not entitled to a redundancy payment by reason of being laid off or kept on short-time if he is dismissed by his employer.

(2) Subsection (1) does not prejudice any right of the employee to a redundancy payment in respect of the dismissal.

Chapter IV **GENERAL EXCLUSIONS FROM RIGHT**

155 QUALIFYING PERIOD OF EMPLOYMENT

An employee does not have any right to a redundancy payment unless he has been continuously employed for a period of not less than two years ending with the relevant date.

Chapter V **OTHER PROVISIONS ABOUT REDUNDANCY PAYMENTS**

162 AMOUNT OF A REDUNDANCY PAYMENT

(1)   The amount of a redundancy payment shall be calculated by—
    (a) determining the period, ending with the relevant date, during which the employee has been continuously employed,
    (b) reckoning backwards from the end of that period the number of years of employment falling within that period, and
    (c) allowing the appropriate amount for each of those years of employment.

(2)   In subsection (1)(c) "the appropriate amount" means—
    (a) one and a half weeks' pay for a year of employment in which the employee was not below the age of forty-one,
    (b) one week's pay for a year of employment (not within paragraph (a)) in which he was not below the age of twenty-two, and
    (c) half a week's pay for each year of employment not within paragraph (a) or (b).

(3)   Where twenty years of employment have been reckoned under subsection (1), no account shall be taken under that subsection of any year of employment earlier than those twenty years.

(6)   Subsections (1) to (3) apply for the purposes of any provision of this Part by virtue of which an employment tribunal may determine that an employer is liable to pay to an employee—
    (a) the whole of the redundancy payment to which the employee would have had a right apart from some other provision, or
    (b) such part of the redundancy payment to which the employee would have had a right apart from some other provision as the tribunal thinks fit,
as if any reference to the amount of a redundancy payment were to the amount of the redundancy payment to which the employee would have been entitled apart from that other provision.

165 WRITTEN PARTICULARS OF REDUNDANCY PAYMENT

(1)   On making any redundancy payment, otherwise than in pursuance of a decision of a tribunal which specifies the amount of the payment to be made, the employer shall give to the employee a written statement indicating how the amount of the payment has been calculated.

(2)   An employer who without reasonable excuse fails to comply with subsection (1) is guilty of an offence and liable on summary conviction to a fine not exceeding level 1 on the standard scale.

(3)   If an employer fails to comply with the requirements of subsection (1), the employee may by notice in writing to the employer require him to give to the employee a written statement complying with those requirements within such period (not being less than one week beginning with the day on which the notice is given) as may be specified in the notice.

(4)   An employer who without reasonable excuse fails to comply with a notice under subsection (3) is guilty of an offence and liable on summary conviction to a fine not exceeding level 3 on the standard scale.

Part XIV INTERPRETATION

Chapter I CONTINUOUS EMPLOYMENT

210 INTRODUCTORY

(1)   References in any provision of this Act to a period of continuous employment are (unless provision is expressly made to the contrary) to a period computed in accordance with this Chapter.

(2)   In any provision of this Act which refers to a period of continuous employment expressed in months or years—
  (a)   a month means a calendar month, and
  (b)   a year means a year of twelve calendar months.

(3)   In computing an employee's period of continuous employment for the purposes of any provision of this Act, any question—
  (a)   whether the employee's employment is of a kind counting towards a period of continuous employment, or
  (b)   whether periods (consecutive or otherwise) are to be treated as forming a single period of continuous employment,
shall be determined week by week; but where it is necessary to compute the length of an employee's period of employment it shall be computed in months and years of twelve months in accordance with section 211.

(4)   Subject to sections 215 to 217, a week which does not count in computing the length of a period of continuous employment breaks continuity of employment.

(5)   A person's employment during any period shall, unless the contrary is shown, be presumed to have been continuous.

211 PERIOD OF CONTINUOUS EMPLOYMENT

(1)   An employee's period of continuous employment for the purposes of any provision of this Act—
  (a)   (subject to subsection (3)) begins with the day on which the employee starts work, and
  (b)   ends with the day by reference to which the length of the employee's period of continuous employment is to be ascertained for the purposes of the provision.

(3)   If an employee's period of continuous employment includes one or more periods which (by virtue of section 215, 216 or 217) while not counting in computing the length of the period do not break continuity of employment, the beginning of the period shall be treated as postponed by the number of days falling within that intervening period, or the aggregate number of days falling within those periods, calculated in accordance with the section in question.

212 WEEKS COUNTING IN COMPUTING PERIOD

(1)   Any week during the whole or part of which an employee's relations with his employer are governed by a contract of employment counts in computing the employee's period of employment.

(3) Subject to subsection (4), any week (not within subsection (1)) during the whole or part of which an employee is—

(a) incapable of work in consequence of sickness or injury,

(b) absent from work on account of a temporary cessation of work, or

(c) absent from work in circumstances such that, by arrangement or custom, he is regarded as continuing in the employment of his employer for any purpose,

counts in computing the employee's period of employment.

(4) Not more than twenty-six weeks count under subsection (3)(a) between any periods falling under subsection (1).

As amended by the Health and Safety (Consultation with Employees) Regulations 1996/1513 reg 8; Employment Rights (Dispute Resolution) Act 1998 Pt I s 1(2), Sch 1 para 18, Sch 1 para 22, Sch 2 para 1; National Minimum Wage Act 1998 c. 39 s 25(3), Sch 3 para 1; Public Interest Disclosure Act 1998 s 1, s 2, s 3, s 4(2), s 4(3), s 7(1); School Standards and Framework Act 1998 Sch 31 para 1; Scotland Act 1998 (Consequential Modifications) Order 2000/2040 Sch 1(l) para 19(2), Sch 1(l) para 19(3); Teaching and Higher Education Act 1998 Sch 3 para 10, Sch 3 para 11(b); Working Time Regulations 1998/1833 Pt IV reg 31(1), Pt IV reg 31(2), Pt IV reg 31(3)(a), Pt IV reg 31(3)(b), Pt IV reg 32(4), Pt IV reg 32(5); Collective Redundancies and Transfer of Undertakings (Protection of Employment) (Amendment) Regulations 1999/1925 reg 12, reg 15; Employment Relations Act 1999 s 18(2)(b), s 33(2), s 37(1), Sch 4(I) para 1, Sch 4(II) para 1, Sch 4(III) para 8, Sch 4(III) para 12, Sch 4(III) para 15(b), Sch 4(III) para 38(3)(a), Sch 9 para 1; Ionising Radiations Regulations 1999/3232 Sch 9 para 2; Unfair Dismissal and Statement of Reasons for Dismissal (Variation of Qualifying Period) Order 1999/1436 art.2, art.3, art.4; Tax Credits Act 1999 Sch 6 para 1; Health Act 1999 (Supplementary, Consequential etc. Provisions) Order 2000/90 Sch 1 para 30(2); Standards in Scotland's Schools etc. Act 2000 asp 6 (Scottish Act) Sch 3 para.; Time Off for Public Duties Order 2000/1737 art.2(a), art.2(b); Time Off for Public Duties (No. 2) Order 2000/2463 art.2(2), art.2(3); Nursing and Midwifery Order (2001) 2002/253 Sch 5 para 13; Education Act 2002 c. 32 Sch 21 para 31; Employment Act 2002 s 18(2)(b), Pt 1 c.1 s 3, Pt 1 c.2 s 17(2)(a), Pt 1 c.2 s 17(2)(b), Pt 1 c.2 s 17(2)(c), Pt 1 c.2 s 17(3), Pt 1 c.2 s 17(4), Pt 3 s 34(4), Pt 3 s 34(5), Pt 3 s 35(2), Pt 3 s 35(3), Pt 3 s 35(4), Pt 3 s 36, Pt 3 s 37, Pt 4 s 47(2), Pt 4 s 47(3), Sch 7 para 26(2), Sch 7 para 26(3), Sch 7 para 25, Sch 7 para 31, Sch 7 para 32(a), Sch 7 para 32(b), Sch 7 para 36, Sch 7 para 37, Sch 7 para 38, Sch 7 para 39, Sch 8(1) para 1, Sch 9 para 1; Fixed-term Employees (Prevention of Less Favourable Treatment) Regulations 2002/2034 Sch 2(1) para 3(3), Sch 2(1) para 3(4), Sch 2(1) para 3(5), Sch 2(1) para 3(7), Sch 2(1) para 3(14), Sch 2(1) para 3(8), para 3(13); Local Authorities (Executive and Alternative Arrangements) (Modification of Enactments and Other Provisions) (Wales) Order 2002/808 art.29; Health and Social Care (Community Health and Standards) Act 2003 Sch 4 para 100; Merchant Shipping (Working Time: Inland Waterways) Regulations 2003/3049 Sch 2 para 3(2); Civil Partnership Act 2004 Sch 27 para 151; Employment Relations Act 2004 Pt 3 s 40(2), Pt 3 s 40(6), Sch 1 para 28, Sch 1 para 30, Sch 1 para 32, Sch 2 para 1; Fishing Vessels (Working Time: Sea-fishermen) Regulations 2004/1713 Sch 2 para 2(2); Health Act 1999 (Consequential Amendments) (Nursing and Midwifery) Order 2004/1771 Sch 1(1) para 3; Water Industry (Scotland) Act 2002 (Consequential Modifications) Order 2004/1822 Sch 1(1) para 18; Serious Organised Crime and Police Act 2005 Sch 17(2) para 1; Employment Equality (Age) Regulations 2006/1031 Sch 8(1) para 23, Sch 8(1) para 22(2), Sch 8(1) para 22(3), Sch 8(1) para 22(4), Sch 8(1) para 22(5), Sch 8(1) para 23, Sch 8(1) para 27(2), para 35(2), para 35(3); National Health Service (Consequential Provisions) Act 2006 Sch 1 para 179(a), Sch 1 para 179(b)(i), Sch 1 para 179(b)(ii), Sch 1 para 179(b)(iii), Sch 1 para 179(b)(iv); Work and Families Act 2006 s 12(2), s 12(3), s 12(5), Sch 1 para 29, Sch 1 para 30, Sch 1 para 31, Sch 1 para 32, Sch 1 para 33, Sch 1 para 34, Sch 1 para 41, Sch 2 para 1; Police and Justice Act 2006 Sch 14 para 31,

Sch 15(1)(B) para 1; Transfer of Undertakings (Protection of Employment) Regulations 2006/246 Sch 2 para 10(a), Sch 2 para 10(b); Companies (Cross-Border Mergers) Regulations 2007/2974 Pt 4(7) reg 48(1)(a), Pt 4(7) reg 48(1)(b); Employment Equality (Age) (Consequential Amendments) Regulations 2007/825 reg 3(2); Offender Management Act 2007 c. 21 Sch 3(2) para 8(a), Sch 3(2) para 8(b); References to Health Authorities Order 2007/961 Sch 1 para 27(3); Time Off for Public Duties (Parent Councils) Order 2007/1837 art.2; Cross-border Railway Services (Working Time) Regulations 2008/1660 Sch 3 para 2(2), Sch 3 para 2(3), Sch 3 para 2(4); Employment Act 2008 c. 24 s 7(1); Employment Rights (Increase of Limits) Order 2008/3055 Sch 1 para 1; Apprenticeships, Skills Children and Learning Act 2009 Sch 1 para 2, Sch 1 para 3, Sch 1 para 4; Local Education Authorities and Children's Services Authorities (Integration of Functions) Order 2010/1158 Sch 2(2) para 41(2), Sch 2(2) para 41(4); Employment Rights (Revision of Limits) Order 2009/3274 Sch 1 para 1; European Public Limited-Liability Company (Employee Involvement) (Great Britain) Regulations 2009/2401 Pt 8 reg. 30(1), Pt 8 reg. 30(2), Pt 8 reg. 30(3); Employment Relations Act 1999 (Blacklists) Regulations 2010/493, reg. 12(3)(a), reg. 12(3)(b), reg. 12(4), reg. 12(5)(a), reg. 12(5)(b), reg. 12(6), reg. 12(7).

National Minimum Wage Act 1998

(c. 39)

ENTITLEMENT TO THE NATIONAL MINIMUM WAGE

1 WORKERS TO BE PAID AT LEAST THE NATIONAL MINIMUM WAGE

(1) A person who qualifies for the national minimum wage shall be remunerated by his employer in respect of his work in any pay reference period at a rate which is not less than the national minimum wage.

(2) A person qualifies for the national minimum wage if he is an individual who—
(a) is a worker;
(b) is working, or ordinarily works, in the United Kingdom under his contract; and
(c) has ceased to be of compulsory school age.

(3) The national minimum wage shall be such single hourly rate as the Secretary of State may from time to time prescribe.

(4) For the purposes of this Act a "pay reference period" is such period as the Secretary of State may prescribe for the purpose.

(5) Subsections (1) to (4) above are subject to the following provisions of this Act.

REGULATIONS RELATING TO THE NATIONAL MINIMUM WAGE

2 DETERMINATION OF HOURLY RATE OF REMUNERATION

(1)   The Secretary of State may by regulations make provision for determining what is the hourly rate at which a person is to be regarded for the purposes of this Act as remunerated by his employer in respect of his work in any pay reference period.

(2)   The regulations may make provision for determining the hourly rate in cases where—
   (a) the remuneration, to the extent that it is at a periodic rate, is at a single rate;
   (b) the remuneration is, in whole or in part, at different rates applicable at different times or in different circumstances;
   (c) the remuneration is, in whole or in part, otherwise than at a periodic rate or rates;
   (d) the remuneration consists, in whole or in part, of benefits in kind.

(3)   The regulations may make provision with respect to—
   (a) circumstances in which, times at which, or the time for which, a person is to be treated as, or as not, working, and the extent to which a person is to be so treated;
   (b) the treatment of periods of paid or unpaid absence from, or lack of, work and of remuneration in respect of such periods.

(4)   The provision that may be made by virtue of paragraph (a) of subsection (3) above includes provision for or in connection with—
   (a) treating a person as, or as not, working for a maximum or minimum time, or for a proportion of the time, in any period;
   (b) determining any matter to which that paragraph relates by reference to the terms of an agreement.

(5)   The regulations may make provision with respect to—
   (a) what is to be treated as, or as not, forming part of a person's remuneration, and the extent to which it is to be so treated;
   (b) the valuation of benefits in kind;
   (c) the treatment of deductions from earnings;
   (d) the treatment of any charges or expenses which a person is required to bear.

(6)   The regulations may make provision with respect to—
   (a) the attribution to a period, or the apportionment between two or more periods, of the whole or any part of any remuneration or work, whether or not the remuneration is received or the work is done within the period or periods in question;
   (b) the aggregation of the whole or any part of the remuneration for different periods;
   (c) the time at which remuneration is to be treated as received or accruing.

(7)   Subsections (2) to (6) above are without prejudice to the generality of subsection (1) above.

(8)   No provision shall be made under this section which treats the same circumstances differently in relation to—
   (a) different areas;
   (b) different sectors of employment;
   (c) undertakings of different sizes;
   (d) persons of different ages; or
   (e) persons of different occupations.

9 DUTY OF EMPLOYERS TO KEEP RECORDS

For the purposes of this Act, the Secretary of State may by regulations make provision requiring employers—

(a)   to keep, in such form and manner as may be prescribed, such records as may be prescribed; and

(b)   to preserve those records for such period as may be prescribed.

RECORDS

10 WORKER'S RIGHT OF ACCESS TO RECORDS

(1)   A worker may, in accordance with the following provisions of this section,—
 (a) require his employer to produce any relevant records; and
 (b) inspect and examine those records and copy any part of them.

(2)   The rights conferred by subsection (1) above are exercisable only if the worker believes on reasonable grounds that he is or may be being, or has or may have been, remunerated for any pay reference period by his employer at a rate which is less than the national minimum wage.

(3)   The rights conferred by subsection (1) above are exercisable only for the purpose of establishing whether or not the worker is being, or has been, remunerated for any pay reference period by his employer at a rate which is less than the national minimum wage.

(4)   The rights conferred by subsection (1) above are exercisable—
 (a) by the worker alone; or
 (b) by the worker accompanied by such other person as the worker may think fit.

(5)   The rights conferred by subsection (1) above are exercisable only if the worker gives notice (a "production notice") to his employer requesting the production of any relevant records relating to such period as may be described in the notice.

(6)   If the worker intends to exercise the right conferred by subsection (4)(b) above, the production notice must contain a statement of that intention.

(7)   Where a production notice is given, the employer shall give the worker reasonable notice of the place and time at which the relevant records will be produced.

(8)   The place at which the relevant records are produced must be—
 (a) the worker's place of work; or
 (b) any other place at which it is reasonable, in all the circumstances, for the worker to attend to inspect the relevant records; or
 (c) such other place as may be agreed between the worker and the employer.

(9)   The relevant records must be produced—
 (a) before the end of the period of fourteen days following the date or receipt of the production notice; or
 (b) at such later time as may be agreed during that period between the worker and the employer.

(10) In this section—

"records" means records which the worker's employer is required to keep and, at the time of receipt of the production notice, preserve in accordance with section 9 above;

"relevant records" means such parts of, or such extracts from, any records as are relevant to establishing whether or not the worker has, for any pay reference period to which the records relate, been remunerated by the employer at a rate which is at least equal to the national minimum wage.

11 FAILURE OF EMPLOYER TO ALLOW ACCESS TO RECORDS

(1) A complaint may be presented to an employment tribunal by a worker on the ground that the employer—
  (a) failed to produce some or all of the relevant records in accordance with subsections (8) and (9) of section 10 above; or
  (b) failed to allow the worker to exercise some or all of the rights conferred by subsection (1)(b) or (4)(b) of that section.

(2) Where an employment tribunal finds a complaint under this section well-founded, the tribunal shall—
  (a) make a declaration to that effect; and
  (b) make an award that the employer pay to the worker a sum equal to 80 times the hourly amount of the national minimum wage (as in force when the award is made).

(3) An employment tribunal shall not consider a complaint under this section unless it is presented to the tribunal before the expiry of the period of three months following—
  (a) the end of the period of fourteen days mentioned in paragraph (a) of subsection (9) of section 10 above; or
  (b) in a case where a later day was agreed under paragraph (b) of that subsection, that later day.

(4) Where the employment tribunal is satisfied that it was not reasonably practicable for a complaint under this section to be presented before the expiry of the period of three months mentioned in subsection (3) above, the tribunal may consider the complaint if it is presented within such further period as the tribunal considers reasonable.

(5) Expressions used in this section and in section 10 above have the same meaning in this section as they have in that section.

ENFORCEMENT

17 NON-COMPLIANCE: WORKER ENTITLED TO ADDITIONAL REMUNERATION

(1) If a worker who qualifies for the national minimum wage is remunerated for any pay reference period by his employer at a rate which is less than the national minimum wage, the worker shall at any time ("the time of determination") be taken to be entitled under this contract to be paid, as additional remuneration in respect of that period, whichever is the higher of—
  (a) the amount described in subsection (2) below, and
  (b) the amount described in subsection (4) below.

(2) The amount referred to in subsection (1)(a) above is the difference between—
  (a) the relevant remuneration received by the worker for the pay reference period; and
  (b) the relevant remuneration which the worker would have received for that period had he been remunerated by the employer at a rate equal to the national minimum wage.

(3) In subsection (2) above, "relevant remuneration" means remuneration which falls to be brought into account for the purposes of regulations under section 2 above.

(4) The amount referred to in subsection (1)(b) above is the amount determined by the formula—

$$\frac{A}{R1} \times R2$$

where—

A is the amount described in subsection (2) above,

R1 is the rate of national minimum wage which was payable in respect of the worker during the pay reference period, and

R2 is the rate of national minimum wage which would have been payable in respect of the worker during that period had the rate payable in respect of him during that period been determined by reference to regulations under section 1 and 3 above in force at the time of determination.

(5)   Subsection (1) above ceases to apply to a worker in relation to any pay reference period when he is at any time paid the additional remuneration for that period to which he is at that time entitled under that subsection.

(6)   Where any additional remuneration is paid to the worker under this section in relation to the pay reference period but subsection (1) above has not ceased to apply in relation to him, the amounts described in subsections (2) and (4) above shall be regarded as reduced by the amount of that remuneration.

19 NOTICES OF UNDERPAYMENT: ARREARS

(1)   Subsection (2) below applies where an officer acting for the purposes of this Act is of the opinion that, on any day ("the relevant day"), a sum was due under section 17 above for any one or more pay reference periods ending before the relevant day to a worker who at any time qualified for the national minimum wage.

(2)   Where this subsection applies, the officer may, subject to this section, serve a notice requiring the employer to pay to the worker, within the 28-day period, the sum due to the worker under section 17 above for any one or more of the pay reference periods referred to in subsection (1) above.

(3)   In this Act, "notice of underpayment" means a notice under this section.

(4)   A notice of underpayment must specify, for each worker to whom it relates—
(a)   the relevant day in relation to that worker;
(b)   the pay reference period or periods in respect of which the employer is required to pay a sum to the worker as specified in subsection (2) above;
(c)   the amount described in section 17(2) above in relation to the worker in respect of each such period;
(d)   the amount described in section 17(4) above in relation to the worker in respect of each of such period;
(e)   the sum due under section 17 above to the worker for each such period.

(5)   Where a notice of underpayment relates to more than one worker, the notice may identify the workers by name or by description.

(6)   The reference in subsection (1) above to a pay reference period includes (subject to subsection (7) below) a pay reference period ending before the coming into force of this section.

(7)   A notice of underpayment may not relate to a pay reference period ending more than six years before the date of service of the notice.

(8)　In this section and sections 19A to 19C below "the 28-day period" means the period of 28 days beginning with the date of service of the notice of underpayment.

19A NOTICES OF UNDERPAYMENT: FINANCIAL PENALTY

(1)　A notice of underpayment must, subject to this section, require the employer to pay a financial penalty specified in the notice to the Secretary of State within the 28-day period.

(2)　The Secretary of State may by directions specify circumstances in which a notice of underpayment is not to impose a requirement to pay a financial penalty.

(3)　Directions under subsection (2) may be amended or revoked by further such directions.

(4)　The amount of any financial penalty is, subject as follows, to be 50% of the total of the amounts referred to in subsection (5) below.

(5)　Those amounts are the amounts specified under section 19(4)(c) above for all workers to whom the notice relates in respect of pay reference periods specified under section 19(4)(b) above which commence after the coming into force of this section.

(6)　If a financial penalty as calculated under subsection (4) above would be less than £100, the financial penalty specified in the notice shall be that amount.

(7)　If a financial penalty as calculated under subsection (4) above would be more than £5000, the financial penalty specified in the notice shall be that amount.

(8)　The Secretary of State may by regulations—
(a)　amend subsection (4) above so as to substitute a different percentage for the percentage at any time specified there;
(b)　amend subsection (6) or (7) above so as to substitute a different amount for the amount at any time specified there.

(9)　A notice of underpayment must, in addition to specifying the amount of any financial penalty, state how that amount was calculated.

(10)　In a case where a notice of underpayment imposes a requirement to pay a financial penalty, if the employer on whom the notice is served, within the period of 14 days beginning with the day on which the notice was served—
(a)　pays the amount required under section 19(2) above, and
(b)　pays at least half the financial penalty,
he shall be regarded as having paid the financial penalty.

(11)　A financial penalty paid to the Secretary of State pursuant to this section shall be paid by the Secretary of State into the Consolidated Fund.

19B SUSPENSION OF FINANCIAL PENALTY

(1)　This section applies in any case where it appears to the officer serving a notice of underpayment which imposes a requirement to pay a financial penalty that—
(a)　relevant proceedings have been instituted; or
(b)　relevant proceedings may be instituted.

(2)　In this section "relevant proceedings" means proceedings against the employer for an offence under section 31(1) below in relation to a failure to remunerate any worker to whom the notice relates for any ay reference period specified under section 19(4)(b) above in relation to that worker.

(3)   The notice of underpayment may contain provision suspending the requirement to pay the financial penalty payable under the notice until a notice terminating the suspension is served on the employer.

(4)   An officer acting for the purposes of this Act may serve on the employer a notice terminating the suspension ("a penalty activation notice") if it appears to the officer—

(a) in a case referred to in subsection (1)(a) above, that relevant proceedings have concluded without the employer having been convicted of an offence under section 31(1) below, or

(b) in a case referred to in subsection (1)(b) above—

(i)   that relevant proceedings will not be instituted; or

(ii) that relevant proceedings have been concluded without the employer having been convicted of an offence under section 31(1) below.

(5)   Where a penalty activation notice is served, the requirement to pay the financial penalty has effect as if the notice of underpayment had been served on the day on which the penalty activation notice was served.

(6)   An officer acting for the purposes of this Act must serve on the employer a notice withdrawing the requirement to pay the financial penalty if it appears to the officer that, pursuant to relevant proceedings, the employer has been convicted of an offence under section 31(1) below.

RIGHTS NOT TO SUFFER UNFAIR DISMISSAL OR OTHER DETRIMENT

23 THE RIGHT NOT TO SUFFER DETRIMENT

(1)   A worker has the right not to be subjected to any detriment by any act, or any deliberate failure to act, by his employer, done on the ground that—

(a) any action was taken, or was proposed to be taken, by or on behalf of the worker with a view to enforcing, or otherwise securing the benefit of, a right of the worker's to which this section applies; or

(b) the employer was prosecuted for an offence under section 31 below as a result of action taken by or on behalf of the worker for the purpose of enforcing, or otherwise securing the benefit of, a right of the worker's to which this section applies; or

(c) the worker qualifies, or will or might qualify, for the national minimum wage or for a particular rate of national minimum wage.

(2)   It is immaterial for the purposes of paragraph (a) or (b) of subsection (1) above—

(a) whether or not the worker has the right, or

(b) whether or not the right has been infringed,

but, for that subsection to apply, the claim to the right and, if applicable, the claim that it has been infringed must be made in good faith.

(3)   The following are the rights to which this section applies—

(a) any right conferred by, or by virtue of, any provision of this Act for which the remedy for its infringement is by way of a complaint to an employment tribunal; and

(b) any right conferred by section 17 above.

(4)   This section does not apply where the detriment in question amounts to dismissal within the meaning of—

(a) Part X of the Employment Rights Act 1996 (unfair dismissal), or

(b) Part XI of the Employment Rights (Northern Ireland) Order 1996 (corresponding provision for Northern Ireland), except where in relation to Northern Ireland the person in question is dismissed in circumstances in which, by virtue of Article 240 of that Order (fixed term contracts), Part XI does not apply to the dismissal.

24 ENFORCEMENT OF THE RIGHT

(1)   A worker may present a complaint to an employment tribunal that he has been subjected to a detriment in contravention of section 23 above.

(2)   Subject to the following provisions of this section, the provisions of—
   (a) sections 48(2) to (4) and 49 of the Employment Rights Act 1996 (complaints to employment tribunals and remedies), or
   (b) in relation to Northern Ireland, Articles 71(2) to (4) and 72 of the Employment Rights (Northern Ireland) Order 1996 (complaints to industrial tribunals and remedies),
shall apply in relation to a complaint under this section as they apply in relation to a complaint under section 48 of that Act or Article 71 of that Order (as the case may be), but taking references in those provisions to the employer as references to the employer within the meaning of section 23(1) above.

(3)   Where—
   (a) the detriment to which the worker is subjected is the termination of his worker's contract, but
   (b) that contract is not a contract of employment,
any compensation awarded under section 49 of the Employment Rights Act 1996 or Article 72 of the Employment Rights (Northern Ireland) Order 1996 by virtue of subsection (2) above must not exceed the limit specified in subsection (4) below.

(4)   The limit mentioned in subsection (3) above is the total of—
   (a) the sum which would be the basic award for unfair dismissal, calculated in accordance with section 119 of the Employment Rights Act 1996 or Article 153 of the Employment Rights (Northern Ireland) Order 1996 (as the case may be), if the worker had been an employee and the contract terminated had been a contract of employment; and
   (b) the sum for the time being specified in section 124(1) of that Act or Article 158(1) of that Order (as the case may be) which is the limit for a compensatory award to a person calculated in accordance with section 123 of that Act or Article 157 of that Order (as the case may be).

(5)   Where the worker has been working under arrangements which do not fall to be regarded as a worker's contract for the purposes of—
   (a) the Employment Rights Act 1996, or
   (b) in relation to Northern Ireland, the Employment Rights (Northern Ireland) Order 1996,
he shall be treated for the purposes of subsections (3) and (4) above as if any arrangements under which he has been working constituted a worker's contract falling within section 230(3)(b) of that Act or Article 3(3)(b) of that Order (as the case may be).

OFFENCES

31 OFFENCES

(1)   If the employer of a worker who qualifies for the national minimum wage refuses or wilfully neglects to remunerate the worker for any pay of reference period at a rate which is at least equal to the national minimum wage, that employer is guilty of an offence.

(2)   If a person who is required to keep or preserve any record in accordance with regulations under section 9 above fails to do so, that person in guilty of an offence.

(3)   If a person makes, or knowingly causes or allows to be made, in a record required to be kept in accordance with regulations under section 9 above any entry which he knows to be false in a material particular, that person is guilty of an offence.

(4)   If a person, for purposes connected with the provisions of this Act, produces or furnishes, or knowingly causes or allows to be produced or furnished, any record or information which he knows to be false in a material particular, that person is guilty of an offence.

(5)   If a person—
(a)   intentionally delays or obstructs an officer acting for the purposes of this Act in the exercise of any power conferred by this Act, or
(b)   refuses or neglects to answer any question, furnish any information or produce any document when required to do so under section 14(1) above,
that person is guilty of an offence.

(6)   Where the commission by any person of an offence under subsection (1) or (2) above is due to the act or default of some other person, that other person is also guilty of the offence.

(7)   A person may be charged with and convicted of an offence by virtue of subsection (6) above whether or not proceedings are taken against any other person.

(8)   In any proceedings for an offence under subsection (1) or (2) above it shall be a defence for the person charged to prove that he exercised all due diligence and took all reasonable precautions to secure that the provisions of this Act, and of any relevant regulations made under it, were complied with by himself and by any person under his control.

(9)   A person guilty of an offence under this section shall be liable
(a)   on conviction on indictment, to a fine, or
(b)   on summary conviction, to a fine not exceeding the statutory maximum.

As amended by the Employment Relations Act 1999, s 18(4); Employment Act 2008, s 8(2), s 8(3), s 8(4), s 8(5), s 9(1), s 11(1).

EMPLOYMENT RELATIONS ACT 1999
(c. 26)

DISCIPLINARY AND GRIEVANCE HEARINGS

10   RIGHT TO BE ACCOMPANIED

(1)   This section applies where a worker—
(a)   is required or invited by his employer to attend a disciplinary or grievance hearing, and
(b)   reasonably requests to be accompanied at the hearing.

(2A)   Where this section applies, the employer must permit the worker to be accompanied at the hearing by one companion who—
(a)   is chosen by the worker; and
(b)   is within subsection (3).

(2B)   The employer must permit the worker's companion to—

      (a) address the hearing in order to do any or all of the following—
          (i) put the worker's case;
          (ii) sum up that case;
          (iii) respond on the worker's behalf to any view expressed at the hearing;
      (b) confer with the worker during the hearing.

(2C) Subsection (2B) does not require the employer to permit the worker's companion to—
      (a) answer questions on behalf of the worker;
      (b) address the hearing if the worker indicates at it that he does not wish his companion to do so; or
      (c) use the powers conferred by that subsection in a way that prevents the employer from explaining his case or prevents any other person at the hearing from making his contribution to it.

(3) A person is within this subsection if he is—
      (a) employed by a trade union of which he is an official within the meaning of sections 1 and 119 of the Trade Union and Labour Relations (Consolidation) Act 1992,
      (b) an official of a trade union (within that meaning) whom the union has reasonably certified in writing as having experience of, or as having received training in, acting as a worker's companion at disciplinary or grievance hearings, or
      (c) another of the employer's workers.

(4) If—
      (a) a worker has a right under this section to be accompanied at a hearing,
      (b) his chosen companion will not be available at the time proposed for the hearing by the employer, and
      (c) the worker proposes an alternative time which satisfies subsection (5),
  the employer must postpone the hearing to the time proposed by the worker.

(5) An alternative time must—
      (a) be reasonable, and
      (b) fall before the end of the period of five working days beginning with the first working day after the day proposed by the employer.

(6) An employer shall permit a worker to take time off during working hours for the purpose of accompanying another of the employer's workers in accordance with a request under subsection (1)(b).

(7) Sections 168(3) and (4), 169 and 171 to 173 of the Trade Union and Labour Relations (Consolidation) Act 1992 (time off for carrying out trade union duties) shall apply in relation to subsection (6) above as they apply in relation to section 168(1) of that Act.

11 COMPLAINT TO EMPLOYMENT TRIBUNAL

(1) A worker may present a complaint to an employment tribunal that his employer has failed, or threatened to fail, to comply with section 10(2A), (2B) or (4).

(2) A tribunal shall not consider a complaint under this section in relation to a failure or threat unless the complaint is presented—
      (a) before the end of the period of three months beginning with the date of the failure or threat, or
      (b) within such further period as the tribunal considers reasonable in a case where it is satisfied that it was not reasonably practicable for the complaint to be presented before the end of that period of three months.

(3)   Where a tribunal finds that a complaint under this section is well-founded it shall order the employer to pay compensation to the worker of an amount not exceeding two weeks' pay.

(4)   Chapter II of Part XIV of the Employment Rights Act 1996 (calculation of a week's pay) shall apply for the purposes of subsection (3); and in applying that Chapter the calculation date shall be taken to be—

(a)   in the case of a claim which is made in the course of a claim for unfair dismissal, the date on which the employer's notice of dismissal was given or, if there was no notice, the effective date of termination, and

(b)   in any other case, the date on which the relevant hearing took place (or was to have taken place).

(5)   The limit in section 227(1) of the Employment Rights Act 1996 (maximum amount of week's pay) shall apply for the purposes of subsection (3) above.

12 DETRIMENT AND DISMISSAL

(1)   A worker has the right not to be subjected to any detriment by any act, or any deliberate failure to act, by his employer done on the ground that the—

(a)   exercised or sought to exercise the right under section 10(2A), (2B) or (4), or

(b)   accompanied or sought to accompany another worker (whether of the same employer or not) pursuant to a request under that section.

(2)   Section 48 of the Employment Rights Act 1996 shall apply in relation to contraventions of subsection (1) above as it applies in relation to contraventions of certain sections of that Act.

(3)   A worker who is dismissed shall be regarded for the purposes of Part X of the Employment Rights Act 1996 as unfairly dismissed if the reason (or, if more than one, the principal reason) for the dismissal is that he—

(a)   exercised or sought to exercise the right under section 10(2A), (2B) or (4), or

(b)   accompanied or sought to accompany another worker (whether of the same employer or not) pursuant to a request under that section.

(4)   Sections 108 and 109 of that Act (qualifying period of employment and upper age limit) shall not apply in relation to subsection(3) above.

(5)   Sections 128 to 132 of that Act (interim relief) shall apply in relation to dismissal for the reason specified in subsection (3)(a) or (b) above as they apply in relation to dismissal for a reason specified in section 128(1)(b) of that Act.

(6)   In the application of Chapter II of Part X of that Act in relation to subsection (3) above, a reference to an employee shall be taken as a reference to a worker.

(7)   References in this section to a worker having accompanied or sought to accompany another worker include references to his having exercised or sought to exercise any of the powers conferred by section 10(2A) or (2B).

13 INTERPRETATION

(1)   In sections 10 to 12 and this section "worker" means an individual who is—

(a)   a worker within the meaning of section 230(3) of the Employment Rights Act 1996,

(b)   an agency worker,

(c)   a home worker,

(d)   a person in Crown employment within the meaning of section 191 of that Act, other than a member of the naval, military, air or reserve forces of the Crown, or

(e) employed as a relevant member of the House of Lords staff or the House of Commons staff within the meaning of section 194(6) or 195(5) of that Act.

(2) In subsection (1) "agency worker" means an individual who—
  (a) is supplied by a person ("the agent") to do work for another ("the principal") by arrangement between the agent and the principal,
  (b) is not a party to a worker's contract, within the meaning of section 230(3) of that Act, relating to that work, and
  (c) is not a party to a contract relating to that work under which he undertakes to do the work for another party to the contract whose status is, by virtue of the contract, that of a client or customer of any professional or business undertaking carried on by the individual;
  and, for the purposes of sections 10 to 12, both the agent and the principal are employers of an agency worker.

(3) In subsection (1) "home worker" means an individual who—
  (a) contracts with a person, for the purposes of the person's business, for the execution of work to be done in a place not under the person's control or management, and
  (b) is not a party to a contract relating to that work under which the work is to be executed for another party to the contract whose status is, by virtue of the contract, that of a client or customer of any professional or business undertaking carried on by the individual;
  and, for the purposes of sections 10 to 12, the person mentioned in paragraph (a) is the home worker's employer.

(4) For the purposes of section 10 a disciplinary hearing is a hearing which could result in—
  (a) the administration of a formal warning to a worker by his employer,
  (b) the taking of some other action in respect of a worker by his employer, or
  (c) the confirmation of a warning issued or some other action taken.

(5) For the purposes of section 10 a grievance hearing is a hearing which concerns the performance of a duty by an employer in relation to a worker.

(6) For the purposes of section 10(5)(b) in its application to a part of Great Britain a working day is a day other than—
  (a) a Saturday or a Sunday,
  (b) Christmas Day or Good Friday, or
  (c) a day which is a bank holiday under the Banking and Financial Dealings Act 1971 in that part of Great Britain.

14 CONTRACTING OUT AND CONCILIATION

Sections 10 to 13 of this Act shall be treated as provisions of Part V of the Employment Rights Act 1996 for the purposes of—

(a) section 203(1), (2)(e) and (f), (3) and (4) of that Act (restrictions on contracting out), and

(b) section 18(1)(d) of the Employment Tribunals Act 1996 (conciliation).

As amended by the Employment Act 2002, Sch 8(1) para 1; Employment Relations Act 2004, Pt 3 s 37(1), Pt 3 s 37(2), Pt 3 s 37(3)(a), Pt 3 s 37(3)(b).

EMPLOYMENT ACT 2002
(c. 22)

....

38 FAILURE TO GIVE STATEMENT OF EMPLOYMENT PARTICULARS ETC.

(1)   This section applies to proceedings before an employment tribunal relating to a claim by an employee under any of the jurisdictions listed in Schedule 5.

(2)   If in the case of proceedings to which this section applies—
    (a)   the employment tribunal finds in favour of the employee, but makes no award to him in respect of the claim to which the proceedings relate, and
    (b)   when the proceedings were begun the employer was in breach of his duty to the employee under section 1(1) or 4(1) of the Employment Rights Act 1996 (c. 18) (duty to give a written statement of initial employment particulars or of particulars of change), the tribunal must, subject to subsection (5), make an award of the minimum amount to be paid by the employer to the employee and may, if it considers it just and equitable in all the circumstances, award the higher amount instead.

(3)   If in the case of proceedings to which this section applies—
    (a)   the employment tribunal makes an award to the employee in respect of the claim to which the proceedings relate, and
    (b)   when the proceedings were begun the employer was in breach of his duty to the employee under section 1(1) or 4(1) of the Employment Rights Act 1996,
the tribunal must, subject to subsection (5), increase the award by the minimum amount and may, if it considers it just and equitable in all the circumstances, increase the award by the higher amount instead.

(4)   In subsections (2) and (3)—
    (a)   references to the minimum amount are to an amount equal to two weeks' pay, and
    (b)   references to the higher amount are to an amount equal to four weeks' pay.

(5)   The duty under subsection (2) or (3) does not apply if there are exceptional circumstances which would make an award or increase under that subsection unjust or inequitable.

(6)   The amount of a week's pay of an employee shall—
    (a)   be calculated for the purposes of this section in accordance with Chapter 2 of Part 14 of the Employment Rights Act 1996 (c. 18), and
    (b)   not exceed the amount for the time being specified in section 227 of that Act (maximum amount of week's pay).

(7)   For the purposes of Chapter 2 of Part 14 of the Employment Rights Act 1996 as applied by subsection (6), the calculation date shall be taken to be—
    (a)   if the employee was employed by the employer on the date the proceedings were begun, that date, and
    (b)   if he was not, the effective date of termination as defined by section 97 of that Act.

(8)   The Secretary of State may by order—
    (a)   amend Schedule 5 for the purpose of—
        (i)   adding a jurisdiction to the list in that Schedule, or
        (ii)   removing a jurisdiction from that list;
    (b)   make provision, in relation to a jurisdiction listed in Schedule 5, for this section not to apply to proceedings relating to claims of a description specified in the order;
    (c)   make provision for this section to apply, with or without modifications, as if—

(i)   any individual of a description specified in the order who would not otherwise be an employee for the purposes of this section were an employee for those purposes, and

(ii) a person of a description specified in the order were, in the case of any such individual, the individual's employer for those purposes.

EQUALITY ACT 2006
(c. 3)

Part I THE COMMISSION FOR EQUALITY AND HUMAN RIGHTS

1 ESTABLISHMENT

There shall be a body corporate known as the Commission for Equality and Human Rights.

3 GENERAL DUTY

The Commission shall exercise its functions under this Part with a view to encouraging and supporting the development of a society in which—

(a)   people's ability to achieve their potential is not limited by prejudice or discrimination,

(b)   there is respect for and protection of each individual's human rights,

(c)   there is respect for the dignity and worth of each individual,

(d)   each individual has an equal opportunity to participate in society, and

(e)   there is mutual respect between groups based on understanding and valuing of diversity and on shared respect for equality and human rights

8 EQUALITY AND DIVERSITY

(1)   The Commission shall, by exercising the powers conferred by this Part—
      (a)   promote understanding of the importance of equality and diversity,
      (b)   encourage good practice in relation to equality and diversity,
      (c)   promote equality of opportunity,
      (d)   promote awareness and understanding of rights under the equality enactments,
      (e)   enforce the equality enactments,
      (f)   work towards the elimination of unlawful discrimination, and
      (g)   work towards the elimination of unlawful harassment.

(2)   In subsection (1)—

      "diversity" means the fact that individuals are different,

      "equality" means equality between individuals, and

      "unlawful" is to be construed in accordance with section 34.

(3)   In promoting equality of opportunity between disabled persons and others, the Commission may, in particular, promote the favourable treatment of disabled persons.

(4)   In this Part "disabled person" means a person who—

(a) is a disabled person within the meaning of the Disability Discrimination Act 1995 (c. 50), or

(b) has been a disabled person within that meaning (whether or not at a time when that Act had effect).

9 HUMAN RIGHTS

(1) The Commission shall, by exercising the powers conferred by this Part—
(a) promote understanding of the importance of human rights,
(b) encourage good practice in relation to human rights,
(c) promote awareness, understanding and protection of human rights, and
(d) encourage public authorities to comply with section 6 of the Human Rights Act 1998 (c. 42) (compliance with Convention rights).

(2) In this Part "human rights" means—
(a) the Convention rights within the meaning given by section 1 of the Human Rights Act 1998, and
(b) other human rights.

(3) In determining what action to take in pursuance of this section the Commission shall have particular regard to the importance of exercising the powers conferred by this Part in relation to the Convention rights.

(4) In fulfilling a duty under section 8 or 10 the Commission shall take account of any relevant human rights.

(5) A reference in this Part (including this section) to human rights does not exclude any matter by reason only of its being a matter to which section 8 or 10 relates.

10 GROUPS

(1) The Commission shall, by exercising the powers conferred by this Part—
(a) promote understanding of the importance of good relations—
(i)   between members of different groups, and
(ii) between members of groups and others,
(b) encourage good practice in relation to relations—
(i)   between members of different groups, and
(ii) between members of groups and others,
(c) work towards the elimination of prejudice against, hatred of and hostility towards members of groups, and
(d) work towards enabling members of groups to participate in society.

(2) In this Part "group" means a group or class of persons who share a common attribute in respect of any of the following matters—
(a) age,
(b) disability,
(c) gender,
(d) proposed, commenced or completed reassignment of gender (within the meaning given by section 82(1) of the Sex Discrimination Act 1975 (c. 65)),
(e) race,
(f) religion or belief, and
(g) sexual orientation.

(3) For the purposes of this Part a reference to a group (as defined in subsection (2)) includes a reference to a smaller group or smaller class, within a group, of persons

who share a common attribute (in addition to the attribute by reference to which the group is defined) in respect of any of the matters specified in subsection (2)(a) to (g).

(4)   In determining what action to take in pursuance of this section the Commission shall have particular regard to the importance of exercising the powers conferred by this Part in relation to groups defined by reference to race, religion or belief.

(5)   The Commission may, in taking action in pursuance of subsection (1) in respect of groups defined by reference to disability and others, promote or encourage the favourable treatment of disabled persons.

(6)   The Minister may by order amend the list in subsection (2) so as to—
(a)   add an entry, or
(b)   vary an entry.

(7)   This section is without prejudice to the generality of section 8.

16 INQUIRIES

(1)   The Commission may conduct an inquiry into a matter relating to any of the Commission's duties under sections 8, 9 and 10.

(2)   If in the course of an inquiry the Commission begins to suspect that a person may have committed an unlawful act—
(a)   in continuing the inquiry the Commission shall, so far as possible, avoid further consideration of whether or not the person has committed an unlawful act,
(b)   the Commission may commence an investigation into that question under section 20,
(c)   the Commission may use information or evidence acquired in the course of the inquiry for the purpose of the investigation, and
(d)   the Commission shall so far as possible ensure (whether by aborting or suspending the inquiry or otherwise) that any aspects of the inquiry which concern the person investigated, or may require his involvement, are not pursued while the investigation is in progress.

(3)   The report of an inquiry—
(a)   may not state (whether expressly or by necessary implication) that a specified or identifiable person has committed an unlawful act, and
(b)   shall not otherwise refer to the activities of a specified or identifiable person unless the Commission thinks that the reference—
(i)   will not harm the person, or
(ii)   is necessary in order for the report adequately to reflect the results of the inquiry.

(4)   Subsections (2) and (3) shall not prevent an inquiry from considering or reporting a matter relating to human rights (whether or not a necessary implication arises in relation to the equality enactments).

(5)   Before settling a report of an inquiry which records findings which in the Commission's opinion are of an adverse nature and relate (whether expressly or by necessary implication) to a specified or identifiable person the Commission shall—
(a)   send a draft of the report to the person,
(b)   specify a period of at least 28 days during which he may make written representations about the draft, and
(c)   consider any representations made.

(6)   Schedule 2 makes supplemental provision about inquiries.

20 INVESTIGATIONS

(1) The Commission may investigate whether or not a person—
    (a) has committed an unlawful act,
    (b) has complied with a requirement imposed by an unlawful act notice under section 21, or
    (c) has complied with an undertaking given under section 23.

(2) The Commission may conduct an investigation under subsection (1)(a) only if it suspects that the person concerned may have committed an unlawful act.

(3) A suspicion for the purposes of subsection (2) may (but need not) be based on the results of, or a matter arising during the course of, an inquiry under section 16.

(4) Before settling a report of an investigation recording a finding that a person has committed an unlawful act or has failed to comply with a requirement or undertaking the Commission shall—
    (a) send a draft of the report to the person,
    (b) specify a period of at least 28 days during which he may make written representations about the draft, and
    (c) consider any representations made.

(5) Schedule 2 makes supplemental provision about investigations.

21 UNLAWFUL ACT NOTICE

(1) The Commission may give a person a notice under this section (an "unlawful act notice") if—
    (a) he is or has been the subject of an investigation under section 20(1)(a), and
    (b) the Commission is satisfied that he has committed an unlawful act.

(2) A notice must specify—
    (a) the unlawful act, and
    (b) the provision of the equality enactments by virtue of which the act is unlawful.

(3) A notice must inform the recipient of the effect of—
    (a) subsections (5) to (7),
    (b) section 20(1)(b), and
    (c) section 24(1).

(4) A notice may—
    (a) require the person to whom the notice is given to prepare an action plan for the purpose of avoiding repetition or continuation of the unlawful act;
    (b) recommend action to be taken by the person for that purpose.

(5) A person who is given a notice may, within the period of six weeks beginning with the day on which the notice is given, appeal to the appropriate court or tribunal on the grounds—
    (a) that he has not committed the unlawful act specified in the notice, or
    (b) that a requirement for the preparation of an action plan imposed under subsection (4)(a) is unreasonable.

(6) On an appeal under subsection (5) the court or tribunal may—
    (a) affirm a notice;
    (b) annul a notice;
    (c) vary a notice;
    (d) affirm a requirement;
    (e) annul a requirement;
    (f) vary a requirement;
    (g) make an order for costs or expenses.

(7)   In subsection (5) "the appropriate court or tribunal" means—
      (a) an employment tribunal, if a claim in respect of the alleged unlawful act could be made to it, or
      (b) a county court (in England and Wales) or the sheriff (in Scotland), if a claim in respect of the alleged unlawful act could be made to it or to him.

22 ACTION PLANS

(1)   This section applies where a person has been given a notice under section 21 which requires him (under section 21(4)(a)) to prepare an action plan.

(2)   The notice must specify a time by which the person must give the Commission a first draft plan.

(3)   After receiving a first draft plan from a person the Commission shall—
      (a) approve it, or
      (b) give the person a notice which—
          (i)   states that the draft is not adequate,
          (ii) requires the person to give the Commission a revised draft by a specified time, and
          (iii) may make recommendations about the content of the revised draft.

(4)   Subsection (3) shall apply in relation to a revised draft plan as it applies in relation to a first draft plan.

(5)   An action plan comes into force—
      (a) if the period of six weeks beginning with the date on which a first draft or revised draft is given to the Commission expires without the Commission—
          (i)   giving a notice under subsection (3)(b), or
          (ii) applying for an order under subsection (6)(b), or
      (b) upon a court's declining to make an order under subsection (6)(b) in relation to a revised draft of the plan.

(6)   The Commission may apply to a county court (in England and Wales) or to the sheriff (in Scotland)—
      (a) for an order requiring a person to give the Commission a first draft plan by a time specified in the order,
      (b) for an order requiring a person who has given the Commission a revised draft plan to prepare and give to the Commission a further revised draft plan—
          (i)   by a time specified in the order, and
          (ii) in accordance with any directions about the plan's content specified in the order, or
      (c) during the period of five years beginning with the date on which an action plan prepared by a person comes into force, for an order requiring the person—
          (i)   to act in accordance with the action plan, or
          (ii) to take specified action for a similar purpose.

(7)   An action plan may be varied by agreement between the Commission and the person who prepared it.

(8)   Paragraphs 10 to 14 of Schedule 2 apply (but omitting references to oral evidence) in relation to consideration by the Commission of the adequacy of a draft action plan as they apply in relation to the conduct of an inquiry.

(9)   A person commits an offence if without reasonable excuse he fails to comply with an order under subsection (6); and a person guilty of an offence under this subsection shall be liable on summary conviction to a fine not exceeding level 5 on the standard scale.

23 AGREEMENTS

(1) The Commission may enter into an agreement with a person under which—
    (a) the person undertakes—
        (i)   not to commit an unlawful act of a specified kind, and
        (ii) to take, or refrain from taking, other specified action (which may include the preparation of a plan for the purpose of avoiding an unlawful act), and
    (b) the Commission undertakes not to proceed against the person under section 20 or 21 in respect of any unlawful act of the kind specified under paragraph (a)(i).

(2) The Commission may enter into an agreement with a person under this section only if it thinks that the person has committed an unlawful act.

(3) But a person shall not be taken to admit to the commission of an unlawful act by reason only of entering into an agreement under this section.

(4) An agreement under this section—
    (a) may be entered into whether or not the person is or has been the subject of an investigation under section 20,
    (b) may include incidental or supplemental provision (which may include provision for termination in specified circumstances), and
    (c) may be varied or terminated by agreement of the parties.

(5) This section shall apply in relation to the breach of a duty specified in section 34(2) as it applies in relation to the commission of an unlawful act; and for that purpose the reference in subsection.

24 APPLICATIONS TO COURT

(1) If the Commission thinks that a person is likely to commit an unlawful act, it may apply—
    (a) in England and Wales, to a county court for an injunction restraining the person from committing the act, or
    (b) in Scotland, to the sheriff for an interdict prohibiting the person from committing the act.

(2) Subsection (3) applies if the Commission thinks that a party to an agreement under section 23 has failed to comply, or is likely not to comply, with an undertaking under the agreement.

(3) The Commission may apply to a county court (in England and Wales) or to the sheriff (in Scotland) for an order requiring the person—
    (a) to comply with his undertaking, and
    (b) to take such other action as the court or the sheriff may specify.

28 LEGAL ASSISTANCE

(1) The Commission may assist an individual who is or may become party to legal proceedings if—
    (a) the proceedings relate or may relate (wholly or partly) to a provision of the equality enactments, and
    (b) the individual alleges that he has been the victim of behaviour contrary to a provision of the equality enactments.

(2) The Commission may assist an individual who is or may become party to legal proceedings in England and Wales if and in so far as the proceedings concern or may concern the question of a landlord's reasonableness in relation to consent to the making

of an improvement to a dwelling where the improvement would be likely to facilitate the enjoyment of the premises by the tenant or another lawful occupier having regard to a disability.

(3) The Commission may assist an individual who is or may become a party to legal proceedings in Scotland if and in so far as the proceedings concern or may concern the question whether—

  (a) it is unreasonable for a landlord to withhold consent to the carrying out of work in relation to a house (within the meaning of the Housing (Scotland) Act 2006 (asp 01)) for the purpose of making the house suitable for the accommodation, welfare or employment of any disabled person who occupies, or intends to occupy, the house as a sole or main residence, or

  (b) any condition imposed by a landlord on consenting to the carrying out of such work is unreasonable.

(4) In giving assistance under this section the Commission may provide or arrange for the provision of—

  (a) legal advice;
  (b) legal representation;
  (c) facilities for the settlement of a dispute;
  (d) any other form of assistance.

(5) Assistance may not be given under subsection (1) in relation to alleged behaviour contrary to a provision of Part V of the Disability Discrimination Act 1995 (c. 50) (public transport).

(6) Where proceedings relate or may relate partly to a provision of the equality enactments and partly to other matters—

  (a) assistance may be given under subsection (1) in respect of any aspect of the proceedings while they relate to a provision of the equality enactments, but

  (b) if the proceedings cease to relate to a provision of the equality enactments, assistance may not be continued under subsection (1) in respect of the proceedings (except in so far as it is permitted by virtue of subsection (7) or (8)).

(7) The Lord Chancellor may by order disapply subsection (6)(b), and enable the Commission to give assistance under subsection (1), in respect of legal proceedings which—

  (a) when instituted, related (wholly or partly) to a provision of the equality enactments,
  (b) have ceased to relate to the provision of the equality enactments, and
  (c) relate (wholly or partly) to any of the Convention rights within the meaning given by section 1 of the Human Rights Act 1998 (c. 42).

(8) The Minister may by order enable the Commission to give assistance under this section in respect of legal proceedings in the course of which an individual who is or has been a disabled person relies or proposes to rely on a matter relating to his disability; but an order under this subsection may not permit assistance in relation to alleged behaviour contrary to a provision of Part V of the Disability Discrimination Act 1995 (c. 50).

(9) An order under subsection (7) or (8) may make provision generally or only in relation to proceedings of a specified kind or description (which in the case of an order under subsection (7) may, in particular, refer to specified provisions of the equality enactments) or in relation to specified circumstances.

(10) This section is without prejudice to the effect of any restriction imposed, in respect of representation—

  (a) by virtue of an enactment (including an enactment in or under an Act of the Scottish Parliament), or
  (b) in accordance with the practice of a court.

(11) A legislative provision which requires insurance or an indemnity in respect of advice given in connection with a compromise contract or agreement shall not apply to advice provided by the Commission under this section.

(12) A reference in this section to a provision of the equality enactments includes a reference to a provision of Community law which—
   (a) relates to discrimination on grounds of sex (including reassignment of gender), racial origin, ethnic origin, religion, belief, disability, age or sexual orientation, and
   (b) confers rights on individuals.

(13) In its application by virtue of subsection (12), subsection (1)(b) shall have effect as if it referred to an allegation by an individual that he is disadvantaged by—
   (a) an enactment (including an enactment in or under an Act of the Scottish Parliament) which is contrary to a provision of Community law, or
   (b) a failure by the United Kingdom to implement a right as required by Community law.

As amended by the Transfer of Functions (Equality) Order 2007/2914, Sch 1 para 16(b), Sch 1 para 16(g).

EMPLOYMENT ACT 2008
(c. 24)

DISPUTE RESOLUTION

1 STATUTORY DISPUTE RESOLUTION PROCEDURES

In the Employment Act 2002 (c. 22), sections 29 to 33 and Schedules 2 to 4 (which make provision for statutory dispute resolution procedures) are repealed.

2 PROCEDURAL FAIRNESS

In the Employment Rights Act 1996 (c. 18), section 98A (procedural fairness) is repealed.

3 NON-COMPLIANCE WITH STATUTORY CODES OF PRACTICE

(1) The Trade Union and Labour Relations (Consolidation) Act 1992 (c. 52) is amended as specified in subsections (2) and (3).

(2) After section 207 there is inserted—

"207A Effect of failure to comply with Code: adjustment of awards
(1) This section applies to proceedings before an employment tribunal relating to a claim by an employee under any of the jurisdictions listed in Schedule A2.
(2) If, in the case of proceedings to which this section applies, it appears to the employment tribunal that—
   (a) the claim to which the proceedings relate concerns a matter to which a relevant Code of Practice applies,
   (b) the employer has failed to comply with that Code in relation to that matter, and
   (c) that failure was unreasonable,
the employment tribunal may, if it considers it just and equitable in all the circumstances to do so, increase any award it makes to the employee by no more than 25%.

(3) If, in the case of proceedings to which this section applies, it appears to the employment tribunal that—

(a) the claim to which the proceedings relate concerns a matter to which a relevant Code of Practice applies,

(b) the employee has failed to comply with that Code in relation to that matter, and

(c) that failure was unreasonable,

the employment tribunal may, if it considers it just and equitable in all the circumstances to do so, reduce any award it makes to the employee by no more than 25%.

(4) In subsections (2) and (3), "relevant Code of Practice" means a Code of Practice issued under this Chapter which relates exclusively or primarily to procedure for the resolution of disputes.

(5) Where an award falls to be adjusted under this section and under section 38 of the Employment Act 2002, the adjustment under this section shall be made before the adjustment under that section.

(6) The Secretary of State may by order amend Schedule A2 for the purpose of—

(a) adding a jurisdiction to the list in that Schedule, or

(b) removing a jurisdiction from that list.

(7) The power of the Secretary of State to make an order under subsection (6) includes power to make such incidental, supplementary, consequential or transitional provision as the Secretary of State thinks fit.

(8) An order under subsection (6) shall be made by statutory instrument.

(9) No order shall be made under subsection (6) unless a draft of the statutory instrument containing it has been laid before Parliament and approved by a resolution of each House."

(3) After Schedule A1 there is inserted—

"SCHEDULE A2 TRIBUNAL JURISDICTIONS TO WHICH SECTION 207A APPLIES

(Section 207A)

Section 2 of the Equal Pay Act 1970 (c. 41) (equality clauses)

Section 63 of the Sex Discrimination Act 1975 (c. 65) (discrimination in the employment field)

Section 54 of the Race Relations Act 1976 (c. 74) (discrimination in the employment field)

Section 145A of this Act (inducements relating to union membership or activities)

Section 145B of this Act (inducements relating to collective bargaining)

Section 146 of this Act (detriment in relation to union membership and activities)

Paragraph 156 of Schedule A1 to this Act (detriment in relation to union recognition rights)

Section 17A of the Disability Discrimination Act 1995 (c. 50) (discrimination in the employment field)

Section 23 of the Employment Rights Act 1996 (c. 18) (unauthorised deductions and payments)

Section 48 of that Act (detriment in employment)

Section 111 of that Act (unfair dismissal)

Section 163 of that Act (redundancy payments)

Section 24 of the National Minimum Wage Act 1998 (c. 39) (detriment in relation to national minimum wage)

The Employment Tribunal Extension of Jurisdiction (England and Wales) Order 1994 (SI 1994/1623) (breach of employment contract and termination)

The Employment Tribunal Extension of Jurisdiction (Scotland) Order 1994 (SI 1994/1624) (corresponding provision for Scotland)

Regulation 30 of the Working Time Regulations 1998 (SI 1998/1833) (breach of regulations)

Regulation 32 of the Transnational Information and Consultation of Employees Regulations 1999 (SI 1999/3323) (detriment relating to European Works Councils)

Regulation 28 of the Employment Equality (Sexual Orientation) Regulations 2003 (SI 2003/1660) (discrimination in the employment field)

Regulation 28 of the Employment Equality (Religion or Belief) Regulations 2003 (SI 2003/1661) (discrimination in the employment field)

Regulation 45 of the European Public Limited-Liability Company Regulations 2004 (SI 2004/2326) (detriment in employment)

Regulation 33 of the Information and Consultation of Employees Regulations 2004 (SI 2004/3426) (detriment in employment)

Paragraph 8 of the Schedule to the Occupational and Personal Pension Schemes (Consultation by Employers and Miscellaneous Amendment) Regulations 2006 (SI 2006/349) (detriment in employment)

Regulation 36 of the Employment Equality (Age) Regulations 2006 (SI 2006/1031) (discrimination in the employment field)

Regulation 34 of the European Cooperative Society (Involvement of Employees) Regulations 2006 (SI 2006/2059) (detriment in relation to involvement in a European Cooperative Society)

Regulation 17 of the Cross-border Railway Services (Working Time) Regulations 2008 (SI 2008/1660) (breach of regulations)."

(4) In section 124A of the Employment Rights Act 1996 (c. 18) (adjustments under the Employment Act 2002), in paragraph (a), for the words from "section 31" to "procedures)" there is substituted "section 207A of the Trade Union and Labour Relations (Consolidation) Act 1992 (effect of failure to comply with Code: adjustment of awards)".

4 DETERMINATION OF PROCEEDINGS WITHOUT HEARING

In the Employment Tribunals Act 1996 (c. 17), in section 7 (employment tribunal procedure regulations), after subsection (3A) there is inserted—

"(3AA) Employment tribunal procedure regulations under subsection (3A) may only authorise the determination of proceedings without any hearing in circumstances where—

(a) all the parties to the proceedings consent in writing to the determination without a hearing, or

(b) the person (or, where more than one, each of the persons) against whom the proceedings are brought—

(i)   has presented no response in the proceedings, or

(ii) does not contest the case.

(3AB) For the purposes of subsection (3AA)(b), a person does not present a response in the proceedings if he presents a response but, in accordance with provision made by the regulations, it is not accepted."

5 CONCILIATION BEFORE BRINGING OF PROCEEDINGS

(1) In the Employment Tribunals Act 1996, section 18 (conciliation) is amended as follows.

(2) In subsection (3), for the words from "shall act" to the end there is substituted "may endeavour to promote a settlement between the parties without proceedings being instituted".

(3) For subsection (5) there is substituted—

"(5) Where a conciliation officer acts pursuant to subsection (3) in a case where the person claiming as specified in paragraph (a) of that subsection has ceased to be employed by the employer and the proceedings which he claims could be brought by him are proceedings under section 111 of the Employment Rights Act 1996, the conciliation officer may in particular—

(a) seek to promote the reinstatement or re-engagement of that person by the employer, or by a successor of the employer or by an associated employer, on terms appearing to the conciliation officer to be equitable, or

(b) where the person does not wish to be reinstated or re-engaged, or where reinstatement or re-engagement is not practicable, seek to promote agreement between them as to a sum by way of compensation to be paid by the employer to that person."

6 CONCILIATION AFTER BRINGING OF PROCEEDINGS

(1) In the Employment Tribunals Act 1996 (c. 17), in section 18 (conciliation), subsection (2A) is repealed.

(2) In that Act, in section 19 (conciliation procedure), subsection (2) is repealed.

7 COMPENSATION FOR FINANCIAL LOSS

(1) In the Employment Rights Act 1996 (c. 18), in section 24 (determination of complaints relating to deductions from wages or payments to employer)—

(a) the existing provision becomes subsection (1), and

(b) after that provision there is inserted—

"(2) Where a tribunal makes a declaration under subsection (1), it may order the employer to pay to the worker (in addition to any amount ordered to be paid under that subsection) such amount as the tribunal considers appropriate in all the circumstances to compensate the worker for any financial loss sustained by him which is attributable to the matter complained of."

(2)   In that Act, in section 163 (determination of questions relating to redundancy payments), at the end there is inserted—

"(5) Where a tribunal determines under subsection (1) that an employee has a right to a redundancy payment it may order the employer to pay to the worker such amount as the tribunal considers appropriate in all the circumstances to compensate the worker for any financial loss sustained by him which is attributable to the non-payment of the redundancy payment."

Appendix
Equality Act 2010

At the time of writing, the Equality Act 2010 has yet to be implemented. However, the Act is due to be introduced in stages, beginning in October 2010. For this reason the most important provisions relating to employment law are reproduced in the following pages.

When using this text you should check whether the relevant provisions are currently in force.

EQUALITY ACT 2010

Part 2 EQUALITY: KEY CONCEPTS

Chapter 1 PROTECTED CHARACTERISTICS

4 THE PROTECTED CHARACTERISTICS

The following characteristics are protected characteristics—
age;
disability;
gender reassignment;
marriage and civil partnership;
pregnancy and maternity;
race;
religion or belief;
sex;
sexual orientation.

5 AGE

(1) In relation to the protected characteristic of age—
   (a) a reference to a person who has a particular protected characteristic is a reference to a person of a particular age group;
   (b) a reference to persons who share a protected characteristic is a reference to persons of the same age group.

(2) A reference to an age group is a reference to a group of persons defined by reference to age, whether by reference to a particular age or to a range of ages.

6 DISABILITY

(1) A person (P) has a disability if—
   (a) P has a physical or mental impairment, and
   (b) the impairment has a substantial and long-term adverse effect on P's ability to carry out normal day-to-day activities.

(2)   A reference to a disabled person is a reference to a person who has a disability.

(3)   In relation to the protected characteristic of disability—
   (a) a reference to a person who has a particular protected characteristic is a reference to a person who has a particular disability;
   (b) a reference to persons who share a protected characteristic is a reference to persons who have the same disability.

(4)   This Act (except Part 12 and section 190) applies in relation to a person who has had a disability as it applies in relation to a person who has the disability; accordingly (except in that Part and that section)—
   (a) a reference (however expressed) to a person who has a disability includes a reference to a person who has had the disability, and
   (b) a reference (however expressed) to a person who does not have a disability includes a reference to a person who has not had the disability.

(5)   A Minister of the Crown may issue guidance about matters to be taken into account in deciding any question for the purposes of subsection (1).

(6)   Schedule 1 (disability: supplementary provision) has effect.

7 GENDER REASSIGNMENT

(1)   A person has the protected characteristic of gender reassignment if the person is proposing to undergo, is undergoing or has undergone a process (or part of a process) for the purpose of reassigning the person's sex by changing physiological or other attributes of sex.

(2)   A reference to a transsexual person is a reference to a person who has the protected characteristic of gender reassignment.

(3)   In relation to the protected characteristic of gender reassignment—
   (a) a reference to a person who has a particular protected characteristic is a reference to a transsexual person;
   (b) a reference to persons who share a protected characteristic is a reference to transsexual persons.

8 MARRIAGE AND CIVIL PARTNERSHIP

(1)   A person has the protected characteristic of marriage and civil partnership if the person is married or is a civil partner.

(2)   In relation to the protected characteristic of marriage and civil partnership—
   (a) a reference to a person who has a particular protected characteristic is a reference to a person who is married or is a civil partner;
   (b) a reference to persons who share a protected characteristic is a reference to persons who are married or are civil partners.

9 RACE

(1)   Race includes—
   (a) colour;
   (b) nationality;
   (c) ethnic or national origins.

(2)   In relation to the protected characteristic of race—

(a) a reference to a person who has a particular protected characteristic is a reference to a person of a particular racial group;

(b) a reference to persons who share a protected characteristic is a reference to persons of the same racial group.

(3) A racial group is a group of persons defined by reference to race; and a reference to a person's racial group is a reference to a racial group into which the person falls.

(4) The fact that a racial group comprises two or more distinct racial groups does not prevent it from constituting a particular racial group.

(5) A Minister of the Crown may by order—
(a) amend this section so as to provide for caste to be an aspect of race;
(b) amend this Act so as to provide for an exception to a provision of this Act to apply, or not to apply, to caste or to apply, or not to apply, to caste in specified circumstances.

(6) The power under section 207(4)(b), in its application to subsection (5), includes power to amend this Act.

10　RELIGION OR BELIEF

(1) Religion means any religion and a reference to religion includes a reference to a lack of religion.

(2) Belief means any religious or philosophical belief and a reference to belief includes a reference to a lack of belief.

(3) In relation to the protected characteristic of religion or belief—
(a) a reference to a person who has a particular protected characteristic is a reference to a person of a particular religion or belief;
(b) a reference to persons who share a protected characteristic is a reference to persons who are of the same religion or belief.

11　SEX

In relation to the protected characteristic of sex—

(a) a reference to a person who has a particular protected characteristic is a reference to a man or to a woman;

(b) a reference to persons who share a protected characteristic is a reference to persons of the same sex.

12　SEXUAL ORIENTATION

(1) Sexual orientation means a person's sexual orientation towards—
(a) persons of the same sex,
(b) persons of the opposite sex, or
(c) persons of either sex.

(2) In relation to the protected characteristic of sexual orientation—
(a) a reference to a person who has a particular protected characteristic is a reference to a person who is of a particular sexual orientation;
(b) a reference to persons who share a protected characteristic is a reference to persons who are of the same sexual orientation.

Chapter 2 **PROHIBITED CONDUCT**

Discrimination

13 DIRECT DISCRIMINATION

(1)   A person (A) discriminates against another (B) if, because of a protected characteristic, A treats B less favourably than A treats or would treat others.

(2)   If the protected characteristic is age, A does not discriminate against B if A can show A's treatment of B to be a proportionate means of achieving a legitimate aim.

(3)   If the protected characteristic is disability, and B is not a disabled person, A does not discriminate against B only because A treats or would treat disabled persons more favourably than A treats B.

(4)   If the protected characteristic is marriage and civil partnership, this section applies to a contravention of Part 5 (work) only if the treatment is because it is B who is married or a civil partner.

(5)   If the protected characteristic is race, less favourable treatment includes segregating B from others.

(6)   If the protected characteristic is sex—
   (a) less favourable treatment of a woman includes less favourable treatment of her because she is breast-feeding;
   (b) in a case where B is a man, no account is to be taken of special treatment afforded to a woman in connection with pregnancy or childbirth.

(7)   Subsection (6)(a) does not apply for the purposes of Part 5 (work).

(8)   This section is subject to sections 17(6) and 18(7).

14 COMBINED DISCRIMINATION: DUAL CHARACTERISTICS

(1)   A person (A) discriminates against another (B) if, because of a combination of two relevant protected characteristics, A treats B less favourably than A treats or would treat a person who does not share either of those characteristics.

(2)   The relevant protected characteristics are—
   (a) age;
   (b) disability;
   (c) gender reassignment;
   (d) race
   (e) religion or belief;
   (f) sex;
   (g) sexual orientation.

(3)   For the purposes of establishing a contravention of this Act by virtue of subsection (1), B need not show that A's treatment of B is direct discrimination because of each of the characteristics in the combination (taken separately).

(4)   But B cannot establish a contravention of this Act by virtue of subsection (1) if, in reliance on another provision of this Act or any other enactment, A shows that A's treatment of B is not direct discrimination because of either or both of the characteristics in the combination.

(5) Subsection (1) does not apply to a combination of characteristics that includes disability in circumstances where, if a claim of direct discrimination because of disability were to be brought, it would come within section 116 (special educational needs).

(6) A Minister of the Crown may by order amend this section so as to—
 (a) make further provision about circumstances in which B can, or in which B cannot, establish a contravention of this Act by virtue of subsection (1);
 (b) specify other circumstances in which subsection (1) does not apply.

(7) The references to direct discrimination are to a contravention of this Act by virtue of section 13.

15 DISCRIMINATION ARISING FROM DISABILITY

(1) A person (A) discriminates against a disabled person (B) if—
 (a) A treats B unfavourably because of something arising in consequence of B's disability, and
 (b) A cannot show that the treatment is a proportionate means of achieving a legitimate aim.

(2) Subsection (1) does not apply if A shows that A did not know, and could not reasonably have been expected to know, that B had the disability.

16 GENDER REASSIGNMENT DISCRIMINATION: CASES OF ABSENCE FROM WORK

(1) This section has effect for the purposes of the application of Part 5 (work) to the protected characteristic of gender reassignment.

(2) A person (A) discriminates against a transsexual person (B) if, in relation to an absence of B's that is because of gender reassignment, A treats B less favourably than A would treat B if—
 (a) B's absence was because of sickness or injury, or
 (b) B's absence was for some other reason and it is not reasonable for B to be treated less favourably.

(3) A person's absence is because of gender reassignment if it is because the person is proposing to undergo, is undergoing or has undergone the process (or part of the process) mentioned in section 7(1).

18 PREGNANCY AND MATERNITY DISCRIMINATION: WORK CASES

(1) This section has effect for the purposes of the application of Part 5 (work) to the protected characteristic of pregnancy and maternity.

(2) A person (A) discriminates against a woman if, in the protected period in relation to a pregnancy of hers, A treats her unfavourably—
 (a) because of the pregnancy, or
 (b) because of illness suffered by her as a result of it.

(3) A person (A) discriminates against a woman if A treats her unfavourably because she is on compulsory maternity leave.

(4) A person (A) discriminates against a woman if A treats her unfavourably because she is exercising or seeking to exercise, or has exercised or sought to exercise, the right to ordinary or additional maternity leave.

(5)   For the purposes of subsection (2), if the treatment of a woman is in implementation of a decision taken in the protected period, the treatment is to be regarded as occurring in that period (even if the implementation is not until after the end of that period).

(6)   The protected period, in relation to a woman's pregnancy, begins when the pregnancy begins, and ends—
   (a) if she has the right to ordinary and additional maternity leave, at the end of the additional maternity leave period or (if earlier) when she returns to work after the pregnancy;
   (b) if she does not have that right, at the end of the period of 2 weeks beginning with the end of the pregnancy.

(7)   Section 13, so far as relating to sex discrimination, does not apply to treatment of a woman in so far as—
   (a) it is in the protected period in relation to her and is for a reason mentioned in paragraph (a) or (b) of subsection (2), or
   (b) it is for a reason mentioned in subsection (3) or (4).

19 INDIRECT DISCRIMINATION

(1)   A person (A) discriminates against another (B) if A applies to B a provision, criterion or practice which is discriminatory in relation to a relevant protected characteristic of B's.

(2)   For the purposes of subsection (1), a provision, criterion or practice is discriminatory in relation to a relevant protected characteristic of B's if—
   (a) A applies, or would apply, it to persons with whom B does not share the characteristic,
   (b) it puts, or would put, persons with whom B shares the characteristic at a particular disadvantage when compared with persons with whom B does not share it,
   (c) it puts, or would put, B at that disadvantage, and
   (d) A cannot show it to be a proportionate means of achieving a legitimate aim.

(3)   The relevant protected characteristics are—
   age;
   disability;
   gender reassignment;
   marriage and civil partnership;
   race;
   religion or belief;
   sex;
   sexual orientation.

Adjustments for Disabled Persons

20 DUTY TO MAKE ADJUSTMENTS

(1)   Where this Act imposes a duty to make reasonable adjustments on a person, this section, sections 21 and 22 and the applicable Schedule apply; and for those purposes, a person on whom the duty is imposed is referred to as A.

(2)   The duty comprises the following three requirements.

(3)   The first requirement is a requirement, where a provision, criterion or practice of A's puts a disabled person at a substantial disadvantage in relation to a relevant matter in

comparison with persons who are not disabled, to take such steps as it is reasonable to have to take to avoid the disadvantage.

(4)   The second requirement is a requirement, where a physical feature puts a disabled person at a substantial disadvantage in relation to a relevant matter in comparison with persons who are not disabled, to take such steps as it is reasonable to have to take to avoid the disadvantage.

(5)   The third requirement is a requirement, where a disabled person would, but for the provision of an auxiliary aid, be put at a substantial disadvantage in relation to a relevant matter in comparison with persons who are not disabled, to take such steps as it is reasonable to have to take to provide the auxiliary aid.

(6)   Where the first or third requirement relates to the provision of information, the steps which it is reasonable for A to have to take include steps for ensuring that in the circumstances concerned the information is provided in an accessible format.

(7)   A person (A) who is subject to a duty to make reasonable adjustments is not (subject to express provision to the contrary) entitled to require a disabled person, in relation to whom A is required to comply with the duty, to pay to any extent A's costs of complying with the duty.

(8)   A reference in section 21 or 22 or an applicable Schedule to the first, second or third requirement is to be construed in accordance with this section.

(9)   In relation to the second requirement, a reference in this section or an applicable Schedule to avoiding a substantial disadvantage includes a reference to—
        (a) removing the physical feature in question,
        (b) altering it, or
        (c) providing a reasonable means of avoiding it.

(10)   A reference in this section, section 21 or 22 or an applicable Schedule (apart from paragraphs 2 to 4 of Schedule 4) to a physical feature is a reference to—
        (a) a feature arising from the design or construction of a building,
        (b) a feature of an approach to, exit from or access to a building,
        (c) a fixture or fitting, or furniture, furnishings, materials, equipment or other chattels, in or on premises, or
        (d) any other physical element or quality.

21 FAILURE TO COMPLY WITH DUTY

(1)   A failure to comply with the first, second or third requirement is a failure to comply with a duty to make reasonable adjustments.

(2)   A discriminates against a disabled person if A fails to comply with that duty in relation to that person.

(3)   A provision of an applicable Schedule which imposes a duty to comply with the first, second or third requirement applies only for the purpose of establishing whether A has contravened this Act by virtue of subsection (2); a failure to comply is, accordingly, not actionable by virtue of another provision of this Act or otherwise.

22 REGULATIONS

(1)   Regulations may prescribe—
        (a) matters to be taken into account in deciding whether it is reasonable for A to take a step for the purposes of a prescribed provision of an applicable Schedule;
        (b) descriptions of persons to whom the first, second or third requirement does not apply.

(2)   Regulations may make provision as to—
    (a) circumstances in which it is, or in which it is not, reasonable for a person of a prescribed description to have to take steps of a prescribed description;
    (b) what is, or what is not, a provision, criterion or practice;
    (c) things which are, or which are not, to be treated as physical features;
    (d) things which are, or which are not, to be treated as alterations of physical features;
    (e) things which are, or which are not, to be treated as auxiliary aids.

(3)   Provision made by virtue of this section may amend an applicable Schedule.

Discrimination: Supplementary

23 COMPARISON BY REFERENCE TO CIRCUMSTANCES

(1)   On a comparison of cases for the purposes of section 13, 14, or 19 there must be no material difference between the circumstances relating to each case.

(2)   The circumstances relating to a case include a person's abilities if—
    (a) on a comparison for the purposes of section 13, the protected characteristic is disability;
    (b) on a comparison for the purposes of section 14, one of the protected characteristics in the combination is disability.

(3)   If the protected characteristic is sexual orientation, the fact that one person (whether or not the person referred to as B) is a civil partner while another is married is not a material difference between the circumstances relating to each case.

24 IRRELEVANCE OF ALLEGED DISCRIMINATOR'S CHARACTERISTICS

(1)   For the purpose of establishing a contravention of this Act by virtue of section 13(1), it does not matter whether A has the protected characteristic.

(2)   For the purpose of establishing a contravention of this Act by virtue of section 14(1), it does not matter—
    (a) whether A has one of the protected characteristics in the combination;
    (b) whether A has both.

25 REFERENCES TO PARTICULAR STRANDS OF DISCRIMINATION

(1)   Age discrimination is—
    (a) discrimination within section 13 because of age;
    (b) discrimination within section 19 where the relevant protected characteristic is age.

(2)   Disability discrimination is—
    (a) discrimination within section 13 because of disability;
    (b) discrimination within section 15;
    (c) discrimination within section 19 where the relevant protected characteristic is disability;
    (d) discrimination within section 21.

(3)   Gender reassignment discrimination is—
    (a) discrimination within section 13 because of gender reassignment;
    (b) discrimination within section 16;

(c) discrimination within section 19 where the relevant protected characteristic is gender reassignment.

(4) Marriage and civil partnership discrimination is—
(a) discrimination within section 13 because of marriage and civil partnership;
(b) discrimination within section 19 where the relevant protected characteristic is marriage and civil partnership.

(5) Pregnancy and maternity discrimination is discrimination within section 17 or 18.

(6) Race discrimination is—
(a) discrimination within section 13 because of race;
(b) discrimination within section 19 where the relevant protected characteristic is race.

(7) Religious or belief-related discrimination is—
(a) discrimination within section 13 because of religion or belief;
(b) discrimination within section 19 where the relevant protected characteristic is religion or belief.

(8) Sex discrimination is—
(a) discrimination within section 13 because of sex;
(b) discrimination within section 19 where the relevant protected characteristic is sex.

(9) Sexual orientation discrimination is—
(a) discrimination within section 13 because of sexual orientation;
(b) discrimination within section 19 where the relevant protected characteristic is sexual orientation.

Other Prohibited Conduct

26 HARASSMENT

(1) A person (A) harasses another (B) if—
(a) A engages in unwanted conduct related to a relevant protected characteristic, and
(b) the conduct has the purpose or effect of—
(i)   violating B's dignity, or
(ii) creating an intimidating, hostile, degrading, humiliating or offensive environment for B.

(2) A also harasses B if—
(a) A engages in unwanted conduct of a sexual nature, and
(b) the conduct has the purpose or effect referred to in subsection (1)(b).

(3) A also harasses B if—
(a) A or another person engages in unwanted conduct of a sexual nature or that is related to gender reassignment or sex,
(b) the conduct has the purpose or effect referred to in subsection (1)(b), and
(c) because of B's rejection of or submission to the conduct, A treats B less favourably than A would treat B if B had not rejected or submitted to the conduct.

(4) In deciding whether conduct has the effect referred to in subsection (1)(b), each of the following must be taken into account—
(a) the perception of B;
(b) the other circumstances of the case;
(c) whether it is reasonable for the conduct to have that effect.

(5) The relevant protected characteristics are—

age;
disability;
gender reassignment;
race;
religion or belief;
sex;
sexual orientation.

27 VICTIMISATION

(1) A person (A) victimises another person (B) if A subjects B to a detriment because—
  (a) B does a protected act, or
  (b) A believes that B has done, or may do, a protected act.

(2) Each of the following is a protected act—
  (a) bringing proceedings under this Act;
  (b) giving evidence or information in connection with proceedings under this Act;
  (c) doing any other thing for the purposes of or in connection with this Act;
  (d) making an allegation (whether or not express) that A or another person has contravened this Act.

(3) Giving false evidence or information, or making a false allegation, is not a protected act if the evidence or information is given, or the allegation is made, in bad faith.

(4) This section applies only where the person subjected to a detriment is an individual.

(5) The reference to contravening this Act includes a reference to committing a breach of an equality clause or rule.

Part 5 **WORK**

Chapter 1 **EMPLOYMENT, ETC.**

Employees

39 EMPLOYEES AND APPLICANTS

(1) An employer (A) must not discriminate against a person (B)—
  (a) in the arrangements A makes for deciding to whom to offer employment;
  (b) as to the terms on which A offers B employment;
  (c) by not offering B employment.

(2) An employer (A) must not discriminate against an employee of A's (B)—
  (a) as to B's terms of employment;
  (b) in the way A affords B access, or by not affording B access, to opportunities for promotion, transfer or training or for receiving any other benefit, facility or service;
  (c) by dismissing B;
  (d) by subjecting B to any other detriment.

(3) An employer (A) must not victimise a person (B)—
  (a) in the arrangements A makes for deciding to whom to offer employment;
  (b) as to the terms on which A offers B employment;
  (c) by not offering B employment.

(4) An employer (A) must not victimise an employee of A's (B)—
  (a) as to B's terms of employment;

(b) in the way A affords B access, or by not affording B access, to opportunities for promotion, transfer or training or for any other benefit, facility or service;

(c) by dismissing B;

(d) by subjecting B to any other detriment.

(5) A duty to make reasonable adjustments applies to an employer.

(6) Subsection (1)(b), so far as relating to sex or pregnancy and maternity, does not apply to a term that relates to pay—

(a) unless, were B to accept the offer, an equality clause or rule would have effect in relation to the term, or

(b) if paragraph (a) does not apply, except in so far as making an offer on terms including that term amounts to a contravention of subsection (1)(b) by virtue of section 13, 14 or 18.

(7) In subsections (2)(c) and (4)(c), the reference to dismissing B includes a reference to the termination of B's employment—

(a) by the expiry of a period (including a period expiring by reference to an event or circumstance);

(b) by an act of B's (including giving notice) in circumstances such that B is entitled, because of A's conduct, to terminate the employment without notice.

(8) Subsection (7)(a) does not apply if, immediately after the termination, the employment is renewed on the same terms.

40 EMPLOYEES AND APPLICANTS: HARASSMENT

(1) An employer (A) must not, in relation to employment by A, harass a person (B)—

(a) who is an employee of A's;

(b) who has applied to A for employment.

(2) The circumstances in which A is to be treated as harassing B under subsection (1) include those where—

(a) a third party harasses B in the course of B's employment, and

(b) A failed to take such steps as would have been reasonably practicable to prevent the third party from doing so.

(3) Subsection (2) does not apply unless A knows that B has been harassed in the course of B's employment on at least two other occasions by a third party; and it does not matter whether the third party is the same or a different person on each occasion.

(4) A third party is a person other than—

(a) A, or

(b) an employee of A's.

41 CONTRACT WORKERS

(1) A principal must not discriminate against a contract worker—

(a) as to the terms on which the principal allows the worker to do the work;

(b) by not allowing the worker to do, or to continue to do, the work;

(c) in the way the principal affords the worker access, or by not affording the worker access, to opportunities for receiving a benefit, facility or service;

(d) by subjecting the worker to any other detriment.

(2) A principal must not, in relation to contract work, harass a contract worker.

(3)   A principal must not victimise a contract worker—
    (a) as to the terms on which the principal allows the worker to do the work;
    (b) by not allowing the worker to do, or to continue to do, the work;
    (c) in the way the principal affords the worker access, or by not affording the worker access, to opportunities for receiving a benefit, facility or service;
    (d) by subjecting the worker to any other detriment.

(4)   A duty to make reasonable adjustments applies to a principal (as well as to the employer of a contract worker).

(5)   A "principal" is a person who makes work available for an individual who is—
    (a) employed by another person, and
    (b) supplied by that other person in furtherance of a contract to which the principal is a party (whether or not that other person is a party to it).

(6)   "Contract work" is work such as is mentioned in subsection (5).

(7)   A "contract worker" is an individual supplied to a principal in furtherance of a contract such as is mentioned in subsection (5)(b).

Partners

44 PARTNERSHIPS

(1)   A firm or proposed firm must not discriminate against a person—
    (a) in the arrangements it makes for deciding to whom to offer a position as a partner;
    (b) as to the terms on which it offers the person a position as a partner;
    (c) by not offering the person a position as a partner.

(2)   A firm (A) must not discriminate against a partner (B)—
    (a) as to the terms on which B is a partner;
    (b) in the way A affords B access, or by not affording B access, to opportunities for promotion, transfer or training or for receiving any other benefit, facility or service;
    (c) by expelling B;
    (d) by subjecting B to any other detriment.

(3)   A firm must not, in relation to a position as a partner, harass—
    (a) a partner;
    (b) a person who has applied for the position.

(4)   A proposed firm must not, in relation to a position as a partner, harass a person who has applied for the position.

(5)   A firm or proposed firm must not victimise a person—
    (a) in the arrangements it makes for deciding to whom to offer a position as a partner;
    (b) as to the terms on which it offers the person a position as a partner;
    (c) by not offering the person a position as a partner.

(6)   A firm (A) must not victimise a partner (B)—
    (a) as to the terms on which B is a partner;
    (b) in the way A affords B access, or by not affording B access, to opportunities for promotion, transfer or training or for receiving any other benefit, facility or service;
    (c) by expelling B;
    (d) by subjecting B to any other detriment.

(7)   A duty to make reasonable adjustments applies to—
    (a) a firm;
    (b) a proposed firm.

(8)   In the application of this section to a limited partnership within the meaning of the Limited Partnerships Act 1907, "partner" means a general partner within the meaning of that Act.

45 LIMITED LIABILITY PARTNERSHIPS

(1)   An LLP or proposed LLP must not discriminate against a person—
    (a) in the arrangements it makes for deciding to whom to offer a position as a member;
    (b) as to the terms on which it offers the person a position as a member;
    (c) by not offering the person a position as a member.

(2)   An LLP (A) must not discriminate against a member (B)—
    (a) as to the terms on which B is a member;
    (b) in the way A affords B access, or by not affording B access, to opportunities for promotion, transfer or training or for receiving any other benefit, facility or service;
    (c) by expelling B;
    (d) by subjecting B to any other detriment.

(3)   An LLP must not, in relation to a position as a member, harass—
    (a) a member;
    (b) a person who has applied for the position.

(4)   A proposed LLP must not, in relation to a position as a member, harass a person who has applied for the position.

(5)   An LLP or proposed LLP must not victimise a person—
    (a) in the arrangements it makes for deciding to whom to offer a position as a member;
    (b) as to the terms on which it offers the person a position as a member;
    (c) by not offering the person a position as a member.

(6)   An LLP (A) must not victimise a member (B)—
    (a) as to the terms on which B is a member;
    (b) in the way A affords B access, or by not affording B access, to opportunities for promotion, transfer or training or for receiving any other benefit, facility or service;
    (c) by expelling B;
    (d) by subjecting B to any other detriment.

(7)   A duty to make reasonable adjustments applies to—
    (a) an LLP;
    (b) a proposed LLP.

46 INTERPRETATION

(1)   This section applies for the purposes of sections 44 and 45.

(2)   "Partnership" and "firm" have the same meaning as in the Partnership Act 1890.

(3)   "Proposed firm" means persons proposing to form themselves into a partnership.

(4)   "LLP" means a limited liability partnership (within the meaning of the Limited Liability Partnerships Act 2000).

(5)   "Proposed LLP" means persons proposing to incorporate an LLP with themselves as members.

(6)   A reference to expelling a partner of a firm or a member of an LLP includes a reference to the termination of the person's position as such—

    (a) by the expiry of a period (including a period expiring by reference to an event or circumstance);

    (b) by an act of the person (including giving notice) in circumstances such that the person is entitled, because of the conduct of other partners or members, to terminate the position without notice;

    (c) (in the case of a partner of a firm) as a result of the dissolution of the partnership.

(7)   Subsection (6)(a) and (c) does not apply if, immediately after the termination, the position is renewed on the same terms.

Office Holders

49 PERSONAL OFFICES: APPOINTMENTS, ETC.

(1)   This section applies in relation to personal offices.

(2)   A personal office is an office or post—

    (a) to which a person is appointed to discharge a function personally under the direction of another person, and

    (b) in respect of which an appointed person is entitled to remuneration.

(3)   A person (A) who has the power to make an appointment to a personal office must not discriminate against a person (B)—

    (a) in the arrangements A makes for deciding to whom to offer the appointment;

    (b) as to the terms on which A offers B the appointment;

    (c) by not offering B the appointment.

(4)   A person who has the power to make an appointment to a personal office must not, in relation to the office, harass a person seeking, or being considered for, the appointment.

(5)   A person (A) who has the power to make an appointment to a personal office must not victimize a person (B)—

    (a) in the arrangements A makes for deciding to whom to offer the appointment;

    (b) as to the terms on which A offers B the appointment;

    (c) by not offering B the appointment.

(6)   A person (A) who is a relevant person in relation to a personal office must not discriminate against a person (B) appointed to the office—

    (a) as to the terms of B's appointment;

    (b) in the way A affords B access, or by not affording B access, to opportunities for promotion, transfer or training or for receiving any other benefit, facility or service;

    (c) by terminating B's appointment;

    (d) by subjecting B to any other detriment.

(7)   A relevant person in relation to a personal office must not, in relation to that office, harass a person appointed to it.

(8)   A person (A) who is a relevant person in relation to a personal office must not victimise a person (B) appointed to the office—

    (a) as to the terms of B's appointment;

    (b) in the way A affords B access, or by not affording B access, to opportunities for promotion, transfer or training or for receiving any other benefit, facility or service;

    (c) by terminating B's appointment;

    (d) by subjecting B to any other detriment.

(9)   A duty to make reasonable adjustments applies to—
    (a)   a person who has the power to make an appointment to a personal office;
    (b)   a relevant person in relation to a personal office.

(10)   For the purposes of subsection (2)(a), a person is to be regarded as discharging functions personally under the direction of another person if that other person is entitled to direct the person as to when and where to discharge the functions.

(11)   For the purposes of subsection (2)(b), a person is not to be regarded as entitled to remuneration merely because the person is entitled to payments—
    (a)   in respect of expenses incurred by the person in discharging the functions of the office or post, or
    (b)   by way of compensation for the loss of income or benefits the person would or might have received had the person not been discharging the functions of the office or post.

(12)   Subsection (3)(b), so far as relating to sex or pregnancy and maternity, does not apply to a term that relates to pay—
    (a)   unless, were B to accept the offer, an equality clause or rule would have effect in relation to the term, or
    (b)   if paragraph (a) does not apply, except in so far as making an offer on terms including that term amounts to a contravention of subsection (3)(b) by virtue of section 13, 14 or 18.

50   PUBLIC OFFICES: APPOINTMENTS, ETC.

(1)   This section and section 51 apply in relation to public offices.

(2)   A public office is—
    (a)   an office or post, appointment to which is made by a member of the executive;
    (b)   an office or post, appointment to which is made on the recommendation of, or subject to the approval of, a member of the executive;
    (c)   an office or post, appointment to which is made on the recommendation of, or subject to the approval of, the House of Commons, the House of Lords, the National Assembly for Wales or the Scottish Parliament.

(3)   A person (A) who has the power to make an appointment to a public office within subsection (2)(a) or (b) must not discriminate against a person (B)—
    (a)   in the arrangements A makes for deciding to whom to offer the appointment;
    (b)   as to the terms on which A offers B the appointment;
    (c)   by not offering B the appointment.

(4)   A person who has the power to make an appointment to a public office within subsection (2)(a) or (b) must not, in relation to the office, harass a person seeking, or being considered for, the appointment.

(5)   A person (A) who has the power to make an appointment to a public office within subsection (2)(a) or (b) must not victimise a person (B)—
    (a)   in the arrangements A makes for deciding to whom to offer the appointment;
    (b)   as to the terms on which A offers B the appointment;
    (c)   by not offering B the appointment.

(6)   A person (A) who is a relevant person in relation to a public office within subsection (2)(a) or (b) must not discriminate against a person (B) appointed to the office—
    (a)   as to B's terms of appointment;
    (b)   in the way A affords B access, or by not affording B access, to opportunities for promotion, transfer or training or for receiving any other benefit, facility or service;

(c) by terminating the appointment;

(d) by subjecting B to any other detriment.

(7) A person (A) who is a relevant person in relation to a public office within subsection (2)(c) must not discriminate against a person (B) appointed to the office—

(a) as to B's terms of appointment;

(b) in the way A affords B access, or by not affording B access, to opportunities for promotion, transfer or training or for receiving any other benefit, facility or service;

(c) by subjecting B to any other detriment (other than by terminating the appointment).

(8) A relevant person in relation to a public office must not, in relation to that office, harass a person appointed to it.

(9) A person (A) who is a relevant person in relation to a public office within subsection (2)(a) or (b) must not victimise a person (B) appointed to the office—

(a) as to B's terms of appointment;

(b) in the way A affords B access, or by not affording B access, to opportunities for promotion, transfer or training or for receiving any other benefit, facility or service;

(c) by terminating the appointment;

(d) by subjecting B to any other detriment.

(10) A person (A) who is a relevant person in relation to a public office within subsection (2)(c) must not victimise a person (B) appointed to the office—

(a) as to B's terms of appointment;

(b) in the way A affords B access, or by not affording B access, to opportunities for promotion, transfer or training or for receiving any other benefit, facility or service;

(c) by subjecting B to any other detriment (other than by terminating the appointment).

(11) A duty to make reasonable adjustments applies to—

(a) a relevant person in relation to a public office;

(b) a person who has the power to make an appointment to a public office within subsection (2)(a) or (b).

(12) Subsection (3)(b), so far as relating to sex or pregnancy and maternity, does not apply to a term that relates to pay—

(a) unless, were B to accept the offer, an equality clause or rule would have effect in relation to the term, or

(b) if paragraph (a) does not apply, except in so far as making an offer on terms including that term amounts to a contravention of subsection (3)(b) by virtue of section 13, 14 or 18.

51 PUBLIC OFFICES: RECOMMENDATIONS FOR APPOINTMENTS, ETC.

(1) A person (A) who has the power to make a recommendation for or give approval to an appointment to a public office within section 50(2)(a) or (b), must not discriminate against a person (B)—

(a) in the arrangements A makes for deciding who to recommend for appointment or to whose appointment to give approval;

(b) by not recommending B for appointment to the office;

(c) by making a negative recommendation of B for appointment to the office;

(d) by not giving approval to the appointment of B to the office.

(2)   A person who has the power to make a recommendation for or give approval to an appointment to a public office within section 50(2)(a) or (b) must not, in relation to the office, harass a person seeking or being considered for the recommendation or approval.

(3)   A person (A) who has the power to make a recommendation for or give approval to an appointment to a public office within section 50(2)(a) or (b), must not victimise a person (B)—
   (a) in the arrangements A makes for deciding who to recommend for appointment or to whose appointment to give approval;
   (b) by not recommending B for appointment to the office;
   (c) by making a negative recommendation of B for appointment to the office;
   (d) by not giving approval to the appointment of B to the office.

(4)   A duty to make reasonable adjustments applies to a person who has the power to make a recommendation for or give approval to an appointment to a public office within section 50(2)(a) or (b).

(5)   A reference in this section to a person who has the power to make a recommendation for or give approval to an appointment to a public office within section 50(2)(a) is a reference only to a relevant body which has that power; and for that purpose "relevant body" means a body established—
   (a) by or in pursuance of an enactment, or
   (b) by a member of the executive.

Qualifications

53 QUALIFICATIONS BODIES

(1)   A qualifications body (A) must not discriminate against a person (B)—
   (a) in the arrangements A makes for deciding upon whom to confer a relevant qualification;
   (b) as to the terms on which it is prepared to confer a relevant qualification on B;
   (c) by not conferring a relevant qualification on B.

(2)   A qualifications body (A) must not discriminate against a person (B) upon whom A has conferred a relevant qualification—
   (a) by withdrawing the qualification from B;
   (b) by varying the terms on which B holds the qualification;
   (c) by subjecting B to any other detriment.

(3)   A qualifications body must not, in relation to conferment by it of a relevant qualification, harass—
   (a) a person who holds the qualification, or
   (b) a person who applies for it.

(4)   A qualifications body (A) must not victimise a person (B)—
   (a) in the arrangements A makes for deciding upon whom to confer a relevant qualification;
   (b) as to the terms on which it is prepared to confer a relevant qualification on B;
   (c) by not conferring a relevant qualification on B.

(5)   A qualifications body (A) must not victimise a person (B) upon whom A has conferred a relevant qualification—
   (a) by withdrawing the qualification from B;
   (b) by varying the terms on which B holds the qualification;
   (c) by subjecting B to any other detriment.

(6)   A duty to make reasonable adjustments applies to a qualifications body.

(7)   The application by a qualifications body of a competence standard to a disabled person is not disability discrimination unless it is discrimination by virtue of section 19.

54 INTERPRETATION

(1)   This section applies for the purposes of section 53.

(2)   A qualifications body is an authority or body which can confer a relevant qualification.

(3)   A relevant qualification is an authorisation, qualification, recognition, registration, enrolment, approval or certification which is needed for, or facilitates engagement in, a particular trade or profession.

(4)   An authority or body is not a qualifications body in so far as—
(a)   it can confer a qualification to which section 96 applies,
(b)   it is the responsible body of a school to which section 85 applies,
(c)   it is the governing body of an institution to which section 91 applies,
(d)   it exercises functions under the Education Acts, or
(e)   it exercises functions under the Education (Scotland) Act 1980.

(5)   A reference to conferring a relevant qualification includes a reference to renewing or extending the conferment of a relevant qualification.

(6)   A competence standard is an academic, medical or other standard applied for the purpose of determining whether or not a person has a particular level of competence or ability.

Employment Services

55 EMPLOYMENT SERVICE-PROVIDERS

(1)   A person (an "employment service-provider") concerned with the provision of an employment service must not discriminate against a person—
(a)   in the arrangements the service-provider makes for selecting persons to whom to provide, or to whom to offer to provide, the service;
(b)   as to the terms on which the service-provider offers to provide the service to the person;
(c)   by not offering to provide the service to the person.

(2)   An employment service-provider (A) must not, in relation to the provision of an employment service, discriminate against a person (B)—
(a)   as to the terms on which A provides the service to B;
(b)   by not providing the service to B;
(c)   by terminating the provision of the service to B;
(d)   by subjecting B to any other detriment.

(3)   An employment service-provider must not, in relation to the provision of an employment service, harass—
(a)   a person who asks the service-provider to provide the service;
(b)   a person for whom the service-provider provides the service.

(4)   An employment service-provider (A) must not victimise a person (B)—
(a)   in the arrangements A makes for selecting persons to whom to provide, or to whom to offer to provide, the service;
(b)   as to the terms on which A offers to provide the service to B;
(c)   by not offering to provide the service to B.

(5) An employment service-provider (A) must not, in relation to the provision of an employment service, victimise a person (B)—
   (a) as to the terms on which A provides the service to B;
   (b) by not providing the service to B;
   (c) by terminating the provision of the service to B;
   (d) by subjecting B to any other detriment.

(6) A duty to make reasonable adjustments applies to an employment service-provider, except in relation to the provision of a vocational service.

(7) The duty imposed by section 29(7)(a) applies to a person concerned with the provision of a vocational service; but a failure to comply with that duty in relation to the provision of a vocational service is a contravention of this Part for the purposes of Part 9 (enforcement).

56 INTERPRETATION

(1) This section applies for the purposes of section 55.

(2) The provision of an employment service includes—
   (a) the provision of vocational training;
   (b) the provision of vocational guidance;
   (c) making arrangements for the provision of vocational training or vocational guidance;
   (d) the provision of a service for finding employment for persons;
   (e) the provision of a service for supplying employers with persons to do work;
   (f) the provision of a service in pursuance of arrangements made under section 2 of the Employment and Training Act 1973 (functions of the Secretary of State relating to employment);
   (g) the provision of a service in pursuance of arrangements made or a direction given under section 10 of that Act (careers services);
   (h) the exercise of a function in pursuance of arrangements made under section 2(3) of the Enterprise and New Towns (Scotland) Act 1990 (functions of Scottish Enterprise, etc. relating to employment);
   (i) an assessment related to the conferment of a relevant qualification within the meaning of section 53 above (except in so far as the assessment is by the qualifications body which confers the qualification).

(3) This section does not apply in relation to training or guidance in so far as it is training or guidance in relation to which another provision of this Part applies.

(4) This section does not apply in relation to training or guidance for pupils of a school to which section 85 applies in so far as it is training or guidance to which the responsible body of the school has power to afford access (whether as the responsible body of that school or as the responsible body of any other school at which the training or guidance is provided).

(5) This section does not apply in relation to training or guidance for students of an institution to which section 91 applies in so far as it is training or guidance to which the governing body of the institution has power to afford access.

(6) "Vocational training" means—
   (a) training for employment, or
   (b) work experience (including work experience the duration of which is not agreed until after it begins).

(7) A reference to the provision of a vocational service is a reference to the provision of an employment service within subsection (2)(a) to (d) (or an employment service within

subsection (2)(f) or (g) in so far as it is also an employment service within subsection (2) (a) to (d)); and for that purpose—

(a) the references to an employment service within subsection (2)(a) do not include a reference to vocational training within the meaning given by subsection (6)(b), and

(b) the references to an employment service within subsection (2)(d) also include a reference to a service for assisting persons to retain employment.

(8) A reference to training includes a reference to facilities for training.

57 TRADE ORGANISATIONS

(1) A trade organisation (A) must not discriminate against a person (B)—
(a) in the arrangements A makes for deciding to whom to offer membership of the organisation;
(b) as to the terms on which it is prepared to admit B as a member;
(c) by not accepting B's application for membership.

(2) A trade organisation (A) must not discriminate against a member (B)—
(a) in the way it affords B access, or by not affording B access, to opportunities for receiving a benefit, facility or service;
(b) by depriving B of membership;
(c) by varying the terms on which B is a member;
(d) by subjecting B to any other detriment.

(3) A trade organisation must not, in relation to membership of it, harass—
(a) a member, or
(b) an applicant for membership.

(4) A trade organisation (A) must not victimise a person (B)—
(a) in the arrangements A makes for deciding to whom to offer membership of the organisation;
(b) as to the terms on which it is prepared to admit B as a member;
(c) by not accepting B's application for membership.

(5) A trade organisation (A) must not victimise a member (B)—
(a) in the way it affords B access, or by not affording B access, to opportunities for receiving a benefit, facility or service;
(b) by depriving B of membership;
(c) by varying the terms on which B is a member;
(d) by subjecting B to any other detriment.

(6) A duty to make reasonable adjustments applies to a trade organisation.

(7) A trade organisation is—
(a) an organisation of workers,
(b) an organisation of employers, or
(c) any other organisation whose members carry on a particular trade or profession for the purposes of which the organisation exists.

Chapter 3 EQUALITY OF TERMS

Sex Equality

64 RELEVANT TYPES OF WORK

(1) Sections 66 to 70 apply where—

(a) a person (A) is employed on work that is equal to the work that a comparator of the opposite sex (B) does;

(b) a person (A) holding a personal or public office does work that is equal to the work that a comparator of the opposite sex (B) does.

(2) The references in subsection (1) to the work that B does are not restricted to work done contemporaneously with the work done by A.

65 EQUAL WORK

(1) For the purposes of this Chapter, A's work is equal to that of B if it is—
(a) like B's work,
(b) rated as equivalent to B's work, or
(c) of equal value to B's work.

(2) A's work is like B's work if—
(a) A's work and B's work are the same or broadly similar, and
(b) such differences as there are between their work are not of practical importance in relation to the terms of their work.

(3) So on a comparison of one person's work with another's for the purposes of subsection (2), it is necessary to have regard to—
(a) the frequency with which differences between their work occur in practice, and
(b) the nature and extent of the differences.

(4) A's work is rated as equivalent to B's work if a job evaluation study—
(a) gives an equal value to A's job and B's job in terms of the demands made on a worker, or
(b) would give an equal value to A's job and B's job in those terms were the evaluation not made on a sex-specific system.

(5) A system is sex-specific if, for the purposes of one or more of the demands made on a worker, it sets values for men different from those it sets for women.

(6) A's work is of equal value to B's work if it is—
(a) neither like B's work nor rated as equivalent to B's work, but
(b) nevertheless equal to B's work in terms of the demands made on A by reference to factors such as effort, skill and decision-making.

66 SEX EQUALITY CLAUSE

(1) If the terms of A's work do not (by whatever means) include a sex equality clause, they are to be treated as including one.

(2) A sex equality clause is a provision that has the following effect—
(a) if a term of A's is less favourable to A than a corresponding term of B's is to B, A's term is modified so as not to be less favourable;
(b) if A does not have a term which corresponds to a term of B's that benefits B, A's terms are modified so as to include such a term.

(3) Subsection (2)(a) applies to a term of A's relating to membership of or rights under an occupational pension scheme only in so far as a sex equality rule would have effect in relation to the term.

(4) In the case of work within section 65(1)(b), a reference in subsection (2) above to a term includes a reference to such terms (if any) as have not been determined by the rating of the work (as well as those that have).

69 DEFENCE OF MATERIAL FACTOR

(1)   The sex equality clause in A's terms has no effect in relation to a difference between A's terms and B's terms if the responsible person shows that the difference is because of a material factor reliance on which—

(a)   does not involve treating A less favourably because of A's sex than the responsible person treats B, and

(b)   if the factor is within subsection (2), is a proportionate means of achieving a legitimate aim.

(2)   A factor is within this subsection if A shows that, as a result of the factor, A and persons of the same sex doing work equal to A's are put at a particular disadvantage when compared with persons of the opposite sex doing work equal to A's.

(3)   For the purposes of subsection (1), the long-term objective of reducing inequality between men's and women's terms of work is always to be regarded as a legitimate aim.

(4)   A sex equality rule has no effect in relation to a difference between A and B in the effect of a relevant matter if the trustees or managers of the scheme in question show that the difference is because of a material factor which is not the difference of sex.

(5)   "Relevant matter" has the meaning given in section 67.

(6)   For the purposes of this section, a factor is not material unless it is a material difference between A's case and B's.

71 SEX DISCRIMINATION IN RELATION TO CONTRACTUAL PAY

(1)   This section applies in relation to a term of a person's work—

(a)   that relates to pay, but

(b)   in relation to which a sex equality clause or rule has no effect.

(2)   The relevant sex discrimination provision (as defined by section 70) has no effect in relation to the term except in so far as treatment of the person amounts to a contravention of the provision by virtue of section 13 or 14.

Pregnancy and Maternity Equality

72 RELEVANT TYPES OF WORK

Sections 73 to 76 apply where a woman—

(a)   is employed, or

(b)   holds a personal or public office.

73 MATERNITY EQUALITY CLAUSE

(1)   If the terms of the woman's work do not (by whatever means) include a maternity equality clause, they are to be treated as including one.

(2)   A maternity equality clause is a provision that, in relation to the terms of the woman's work, has the effect referred to in section 74(1), (6) and (8).

(3)   In the case of a term relating to membership of or rights under an occupational pension scheme, a maternity equality clause has only such effect as a maternity equality rule would have.

74 MATERNITY EQUALITY CLAUSE: PAY

(1) A term of the woman's work that provides for maternity-related pay to be calculated by reference to her pay at a particular time is, if each of the following three conditions is satisfied, modified as mentioned in subsection (5).

(2) The first condition is that, after the time referred to in subsection (1) but before the end of the protected period—
   (a) her pay increases, or
   (b) it would have increased had she not been on maternity leave.

(3) The second condition is that the maternity-related pay is not—
   (a) what her pay would have been had she not been on maternity leave, or
   (b) the difference between the amount of statutory maternity pay to which she is entitled and what her pay would have been had she not been on maternity leave.

(4) The third condition is that the terms of her work do not provide for the maternity-related pay to be subject to—
   (a) an increase as mentioned in subsection (2)(a), or
   (b) an increase that would have occurred as mentioned in subsection (2)(b).

(5) The modification referred to in subsection (1) is a modification to provide for the maternity-related pay to be subject to—
   (a) any increase as mentioned in subsection (2)(a), or
   (b) any increase that would have occurred as mentioned in subsection (2)(b).

(6) A term of her work that—
   (a) provides for pay within subsection (7), but
   (b) does not provide for her to be given the pay in circumstances in which she would have been given it had she not been on maternity leave, is modified so as to provide for her to be given it in circumstances in which it would normally be given.

(7) Pay is within this subsection if it is—
   (a) pay (including pay by way of bonus) in respect of times before the woman is on maternity leave,
   (b) pay by way of bonus in respect of times when she is on compulsory maternity leave, or
   (c) pay by way of bonus in respect of times after the end of the protected period.

(8) A term of the woman's work that—
   (a) provides for pay after the end of the protected period, but
   (b) does not provide for it to be subject to an increase to which it would have been subject had she not been on maternity leave, is modified so as to provide for it to be subject to the increase.

(9) Maternity-related pay is pay (other than statutory maternity pay) to which a woman is entitled—
   (a) as a result of being pregnant, or
   (b) in respect of times when she is on maternity leave.

(10) A reference to the protected period is to be construed in accordance with section 18.

Disclosure of Information

77 DISCUSSIONS ABOUT PAY

(1) A term of a person's work that purports to prevent or restrict the person (P) from disclosing or seeking to disclose information about the terms of P's work is unenforceable against P in so far as P makes or seeks to make a relevant pay disclosure.

(2)   A term of a person's work that purports to prevent or restrict the person (P) from seeking disclosure of information from a colleague about the terms of the colleague's work is unenforceable against P in so far as P seeks a relevant pay disclosure from the colleague; and "colleague" includes a former colleague in relation to the work in question.

(3)   A disclosure is a relevant pay disclosure if made for the purpose of enabling the person who makes it, or the person to whom it is made, to find out whether or to what extent there is, in relation to the work in question, a connection between pay and having (or not having) a particular protected characteristic.

(4)   The following are to be treated as protected acts for the purposes of the relevant victimisation provision—
   (a)   seeking a disclosure that would be a relevant pay disclosure;
   (b)   making or seeking to make a relevant pay disclosure;
   (c)   receiving information disclosed in a relevant pay disclosure.

78   GENDER PAY GAP INFORMATION

(1)   Regulations may require employers to publish information relating to the pay of employees for the purpose of showing whether, by reference to factors of such description as is prescribed, there are differences in the pay of male and female employees.

(2)   This section does not apply to—
   (a)   an employer who has fewer than 250 employees;
   (b)   a person specified in Schedule 19;
   (c)   a government department or part of the armed forces not specified in that Schedule.

(3)   The regulations may prescribe—
   (a)   descriptions of employer;
   (b)   descriptions of employee;
   (c)   how to calculate the number of employees that an employer has;
   (d)   descriptions of information;
   (e)   the time at which information is to be published;
   (f)   the form and manner in which it is to be published.

(4)   Regulations under subsection (3)(e) may not require an employer, after the first publication of information, to publish information more frequently than at intervals of 12 months.

(5)   The regulations may make provision for a failure to comply with the regulations—
   (a)   to be an offence punishable on summary conviction by a fine not exceeding level 5 on the standard scale;
   (b)   to be enforced, otherwise than as an offence, by such means as are prescribed.

(6)   The reference to a failure to comply with the regulations includes a reference to a failure by a person acting on behalf of an employer.

Supplementary

79   COMPARATORS

(1)   This section applies for the purposes of this Chapter.

(2)   If A is employed, B is a comparator if subsection (3) or (4) applies.

(3)   This subsection applies if—

    (a) B is employed by A's employer or by an associate of A's employer, and

    (b) A and B work at the same establishment.

(4)   This subsection applies if—

    (a) B is employed by A's employer or an associate of A's employer,

    (b) B works at an establishment other than the one at which A works, and

    (c) common terms apply at the establishments (either generally or as between A and B).

(5)   If A holds a personal or public office, B is a comparator if—

    (a) B holds a personal or public office, and

    (b) the person responsible for paying A is also responsible for paying B.

(6)   If A is a relevant member of the House of Commons staff, B is a comparator if—

    (a) B is employed by the person who is A's employer under subsection (6) of section 195 of the Employment Rights Act 1996, or

    (b) if subsection (7) of that section applies in A's case, B is employed by the person who is A's employer under that subsection.

(7)   If A is a relevant member of the House of Lords staff, B is a comparator if B is also a relevant member of the House of Lords staff.

(8)   Section 42 does not apply to this Chapter; accordingly, for the purposes of this Chapter only, holding the office of constable is to be treated as holding a personal office.

(9)   For the purposes of this section, employers are associated if—

    (a) one is a company of which the other (directly or indirectly) has control, or

    (b) both are companies of which a third person (directly or indirectly) has control.

80 INTERPRETATION AND EXCEPTIONS

(1)   This section applies for the purposes of this Chapter.

(2)   The terms of a person's work are—

    (a) if the person is employed, the terms of the person's employment that are in the person's contract of employment, contract of apprenticeship or contract to do work personally;

    (b) if the person holds a personal or public office, the terms of the person's appointment to the office.

(3)   If work is not done at an establishment, it is to be treated as done at the establishment with which it has the closest connection.

(4)   A person (P) is the responsible person in relation to another person if—

    (a) P is the other's employer;

    (b) P is responsible for paying remuneration in respect of a personal or public office that the other holds.

(5)   A job evaluation study is a study undertaken with a view to evaluating, in terms of the demands made on a person by reference to factors such as effort, skill and decision-making, the jobs to be done—

    (a) by some or all of the workers in an undertaking or group of undertakings, or

    (b) in the case of the armed forces, by some or all of the members of the armed forces.

(6)   In the case of Crown employment, the reference in subsection (5)(a) to an undertaking is to be construed in accordance with section 191(4) of the Employment Rights Act 1996.

(7)   "Civil partnership status" has the meaning given in section 124(1) of the Pensions Act 1995.

(8)   Schedule 7 (exceptions) has effect.

Part 8 PROHIBITED CONDUCT: ANCILLARY

108 RELATIONSHIPS THAT HAVE ENDED

(1)   A person (A) must not discriminate against another (B) if—
    (a) the discrimination arises out of and is closely connected to a relationship which used to exist between them, and
    (b) conduct of a description constituting the discrimination would, if it occurred during the relationship, contravene this Act.

(2)   A person (A) must not harass another (B) if—
    (a) the harassment arises out of and is closely connected to a relationship which used to exist between them, and
    (b) conduct of a description constituting the harassment would, if it occurred during the relationship, contravene this Act.

(3)   It does not matter whether the relationship ends before or after the commencement of this section.

(4)   A duty to make reasonable adjustments applies to A in so far as B continues to be placed at a substantial disadvantage as mentioned in section 20.

(5)   For the purposes of subsection (4), sections 20, 21 and 22 and the applicable Schedules are to be construed as if the relationship had not ended.

(6)   For the purposes of Part 9 (enforcement), a contravention of this section relates to the Part of this Act that would have been contravened if the relationship had not ended.

(7)   But conduct is not a contravention of this section in so far as it also amounts to victimisation of B by A.

109 LIABILITY OF EMPLOYERS AND PRINCIPALS

(1)   Anything done by a person (A) in the course of A's employment must be treated as also done by the employer.

(2)   Anything done by an agent for a principal, with the authority of the principal, must be treated as also done by the principal.

(3)   It does not matter whether that thing is done with the employer's or principal's knowledge or approval.

(4)   In proceedings against A's employer (B) in respect of anything alleged to have been done by A in the course of A's employment it is a defence for B to show that B took all reasonable steps to prevent A—
    (a) from doing that thing, or
    (b) from doing anything of that description.

(5)   This section does not apply to offences under this Act (other than offences under Part 12 (disabled persons: transport)).

110 LIABILITY OF EMPLOYEES AND AGENTS

(1)   A person (A) contravenes this section if—
    (a) A is an employee or agent,
    (b) A does something which, by virtue of section 109(1) or (2), is treated as having been done by A's employer or principal (as the case may be), and

(c) the doing of that thing by A amounts to a contravention of this Act by the employer or principal (as the case may be).

(2) It does not matter whether, in any proceedings, the employer is found not to have contravened this Act by virtue of section 109(4).

(3) A does not contravene this section if—
(a) A relies on a statement by the employer or principal that doing that thing is not a contravention of this Act, and
(b) it is reasonable for A to do so.

(4) A person (B) commits an offence if B knowingly or recklessly makes a statement mentioned in subsection (3)(a) which is false or misleading in a material respect.

(5) A person guilty of an offence under subsection (4) is liable on summary conviction to a fine not exceeding level 5 on the standard scale.

(6) Part 9 (enforcement) applies to a contravention of this section by A as if it were the contravention mentioned in subsection (1)(c).

(7) The reference in subsection (1)(c) to a contravention of this Act does not include a reference to disability discrimination in contravention of Chapter 1 of Part 6 (schools).

111 INSTRUCTING, CAUSING OR INDUCING CONTRAVENTIONS

(1) A person (A) must not instruct another (B) to do in relation to a third person (C) anything which contravenes Part 3, 4, 5, 6 or 7 or section 108(1) or (2) or 112(1) (a basic contravention).

(2) A person (A) must not cause another (B) to do in relation to a third person (C) anything which is a basic contravention.

(3) A person (A) must not induce another (B) to do in relation to a third person (C) anything which is a basic contravention.

(4) For the purposes of subsection (3), inducement may be direct or indirect.

(5) Proceedings for a contravention of this section may be brought—
(a) by B, if B is subjected to a detriment as a result of A's conduct;
(b) by C, if C is subjected to a detriment as a result of A's conduct;
(c) by the Commission.

(6) For the purposes of subsection (5), it does not matter whether—
(a) the basic contravention occurs;
(b) any other proceedings are, or may be, brought in relation to A's conduct.

(7) This section does not apply unless the relationship between A and B is such that A is in a position to commit a basic contravention in relation to B.

(8) A reference in this section to causing or inducing a person to do something includes a reference to attempting to cause or induce the person to do it.

(9) For the purposes of Part 9 (enforcement), a contravention of this section is to be treated as relating—
(a) in a case within subsection (5)(a), to the Part of this Act which, because of the relationship between A and B, A is in a position to contravene in relation to B;
(b) in a case within subsection (5)(b), to the Part of this Act which, because of the relationship between B and C, B is in a position to contravene in relation to C.

112 AIDING CONTRAVENTIONS

(1) A person (A) must not knowingly help another (B) to do anything which contravenes Part 3, 4, 5, 6 or 7 or section 108(1) or (2) or 111 (a basic contravention).

(2) It is not a contravention of subsection (1) if—
(a) A relies on a statement by B that the act for which the help is given does not contravene this Act, and
(b) it is reasonable for A to do so.

(3) B commits an offence if B knowingly or recklessly makes a statement mentioned in subsection (2)(a) which is false or misleading in a material respect.

(4) A person guilty of an offence under subsection (3) is liable on summary conviction to a fine not exceeding level 5 on the standard scale.

(5) For the purposes of Part 9 (enforcement), a contravention of this section is to be treated as relating to the provision of this Act to which the basic contravention relates.

(6) The reference in subsection (1) to a basic contravention does not include a reference to disability discrimination in contravention of Chapter 1 of Part 6 (schools).

Part 9 ENFORCEMENT

Chapter 3 EMPLOYMENT TRIBUNALS

120 JURISDICTION

(1) An employment tribunal has, subject to section 121, jurisdiction to determine a complaint relating to—
(a) a contravention of Part 5 (work);
(b) a contravention of section 108, 111 or 112 that relates to Part 5.

(2) An employment tribunal has jurisdiction to determine an application by a responsible person (as defined by section 61) for a declaration as to the rights of that person and a worker in relation to a dispute about the effect of a non-discrimination rule.

(3) An employment tribunal also has jurisdiction to determine an application by the trustees or managers of an occupational pension scheme for a declaration as to their rights and those of a member in relation to a dispute about the effect of a non-discrimination rule.

(4) An employment tribunal also has jurisdiction to determine a question that—
(a) relates to a non-discrimination rule, and
(b) is referred to the tribunal by virtue of section 122.

(5) In proceedings before an employment tribunal on a complaint relating to a breach of a non-discrimination rule, the employer—
(a) is to be treated as a party, and
(b) is accordingly entitled to appear and be heard.

(6) Nothing in this section affects such jurisdiction as the High Court, a county court, the Court of Session or the sheriff has in relation to a non-discrimination rule.

(7) Subsection (1)(a) does not apply to a contravention of section 53 in so far as the act complained of may, by virtue of an enactment, be subject to an appeal or proceedings in the nature of an appeal.

(8) In subsection (1), the references to Part 5 do not include a reference to section 60(1).

122 REFERENCES BY COURT TO TRIBUNAL, ETC.

(1)   If it appears to a court in which proceedings are pending that a claim or counter-claim relating to a non-discrimination rule could more conveniently be determined by an employment tribunal, the court may strike out the claim or counter-claim.

(2)   If in proceedings before a court a question arises about a non-discrimination rule, the court may (whether or not on an application by a party to the proceedings)—
   (a) refer the question, or direct that it be referred by a party to the proceedings, to an employment tribunal for determination, and
   (b) stay or sist the proceedings in the meantime.

123 TIME LIMITS

(1)   Proceedings on a complaint within section 120 may not be brought after the end of—
   (a) the period of 3 months starting with the date of the act to which the complaint relates, or
   (b) such other period as the employment tribunal thinks just and equitable.

(2)   Proceedings may not be brought in reliance on section 121(1) after the end of—
   (a) the period of 6 months starting with the date of the act to which the proceedings relate, or
   (b) such other period as the employment tribunal thinks just and equitable.

(3)   For the purposes of this section—
   (a) conduct extending over a period is to be treated as done at the end of the period;
   (b) failure to do something is to be treated as occurring when the person in question decided on it.

(4)   In the absence of evidence to the contrary, a person (P) is to be taken to decide on failure to do something—
   (a) when P does an act inconsistent with doing it, or
   (b) if P does no inconsistent act, on the expiry of the period in which P might reasonably have been expected to do it.

124 REMEDIES: GENERAL

(1)   This section applies if an employment tribunal finds that there has been a contravention of a provision referred to in section 120(1).

(2)   The tribunal may—
   (a) make a declaration as to the rights of the complainant and the respondent in relation to the matters to which the proceedings relate;
   (b) order the respondent to pay compensation to the complainant;
   (c) make an appropriate recommendation.

(3)   An appropriate recommendation is a recommendation that within a specified period the respondent takes specified steps for the purpose of obviating or reducing the adverse effect of any matter to which the proceedings relate—
   (a) on the complainant;
   (b) on any other person.

(4)   Subsection (5) applies if the tribunal—
   (a) finds that a contravention is established by virtue of section 19, but
   (b) is satisfied that the provision, criterion or practice was not applied with the intention of discriminating against the complainant.

(5)   It must not make an order under subsection (2)(b) unless it first considers whether to act under subsection (2)(a) or (c).

(6)   The amount of compensation which may be awarded under subsection (2)(b) corresponds to the amount which could be awarded by a county court or the sheriff under section 119.

(7)   If a respondent fails, without reasonable excuse, to comply with an appropriate recommendation in so far as it relates to the complainant, the tribunal may—
       (a) if an order was made under subsection (2)(b), increase the amount of compensation to be paid;
       (b) if no such order was made, make one.

Chapter 4 EQUALITY OF TERMS

127 JURISDICTION

(1)   An employment tribunal has, subject to subsection (6), jurisdiction to determine a complaint relating to a breach of an equality clause or rule.

(2)   The jurisdiction conferred by subsection (1) includes jurisdiction to determine a complaint arising out of a breach of an equality clause or rule; and a reference in this Chapter to a complaint relating to such a breach is to be read accordingly.

(3)   An employment tribunal also has jurisdiction to determine an application by a responsible person for a declaration as to the rights of that person and a worker in relation to a dispute about the effect of an equality clause or rule.

(4)   An employment tribunal also has jurisdiction to determine an application by the trustees or managers of an occupational pension scheme for a declaration as to their rights and those of a member in relation to a dispute about the effect of an equality rule.

(5)   An employment tribunal also has jurisdiction to determine a question that—
       (a) relates to an equality clause or rule, and
       (b) is referred to the tribunal by virtue of section 128(2).

(6)   This section does not apply to a complaint relating to an act done when the complainant was serving as a member of the armed forces unless—
       (a) the complainant has made a service complaint about the matter, and
       (b) the complaint has not been withdrawn.

(7)   Subsections (2) to (5) of section 121 apply for the purposes of subsection (6) of this section as they apply for the purposes of subsection (1) of that section.

(8)   In proceedings before an employment tribunal on a complaint relating to a breach of an equality rule, the employer—
       (a) is to be treated as a party, and
       (b) is accordingly entitled to appear and be heard.

(9)   Nothing in this section affects such jurisdiction as the High Court, a county court, the Court of Session or the sheriff has in relation to an equality clause or rule.

128 REFERENCES BY COURT TO TRIBUNAL, ETC.

(1)   If it appears to a court in which proceedings are pending that a claim or counter-claim relating to an equality clause or rule could more conveniently be determined by an employment tribunal, the court may strike out the claim or counter-claim.

(2)   If in proceedings before a court a question arises about an equality clause or rule, the court may (whether or not on an application by a party to the proceedings)—
   (a) refer the question, or direct that it be referred by a party to the proceedings, to an employment tribunal for determination, and
   (b) stay or sist the proceedings in the meantime.

129   TIME LIMITS

(1)   This section applies to—
   (a) a complaint relating to a breach of an equality clause or rule;
   (b) an application for a declaration referred to in section 127(3) or (4).

(2)   Proceedings on the complaint or application may not be brought in an employment tribunal after the end of the qualifying period.

(3)   If the complaint or application relates to terms of work other than terms of service in the armed forces, the qualifying period is, in a case mentioned in the first column of the table, the period mentioned in the second column.

Case	Qualifying period
A standard cased	The period of 6 months beginning with the last day of the employment or appointment
A stable work case (but not if it is also a concealment or incapacity case (or both))	The period of 6 months beginning with the day on which the stable working relationship ended
A concealment case (but not if it is also an incapacity case)	The period of 6 months beginning with the day on which the worker discovered (or could with reasonable diligence have discovered) the qualifying fact.
An incapacity case (but not if it is also a concealment case)	The period of 6 months beginning with the day on which the worker ceased to have the incapacity.
A case which is a concealment case and an incapacity case	The period of 6 months beginning with the later of the days on which the period would begin if the case were merely a concealment or incapacity case.

(4)   If the complaint or application relates to terms of service in the armed forces, the qualifying period is, in a case mentioned in the first column of the table, the period mentioned in the second column.

Case	Qualifying period
A standard case	The period of 9 months beginning with the last day of the period of service during which the complaint arose
A concealment case (but not if it is also an incapacity case)	The period of 9 months beginning with the day on which the worker discovered (or could with reasonable diligence have discovered) the qualifying fact
An incapacity case (but not if it is also a concealment case)	The period of 9 months beginning with the day on which the worker ceased to have the incapacity
A case which is a concealment case and an incapacity case.	The period of 9 months beginning with the later of the days on which the period would begin if the case were merely a concealment or incapacity case

130   SECTION 129: SUPPLEMENTARY

(1)   This section applies for the purposes of section 129.

(2)   A standard case is a case which is not—
    (a) a stable work case,
    (b) a concealment case,
    (c) an incapacity case, or
    (d) a concealment case and an incapacity case.

(3)   A stable work case is a case where the proceedings relate to a period during which there was a stable working relationship between the worker and the responsible person (including any time after the terms of work had expired).

(4)   A concealment case in proceedings relating to an equality clause is a case where—
    (a) the responsible person deliberately concealed a qualifying fact from the worker, and
    (b) the worker did not discover (or could not with reasonable diligence have discovered) the qualifying fact until after the relevant day.

(5)   A concealment case in proceedings relating to an equality rule is a case where—
    (a) the employer or the trustees or managers of the occupational pension scheme in question deliberately concealed a qualifying fact from the member, and
    (b) the member did not discover (or could not with reasonable diligence have discovered) the qualifying fact until after the relevant day.

(6)   A qualifying fact for the purposes of subsection (4) or (5) is a fact—
    (a) which is relevant to the complaint, and
    (b) without knowledge of which the worker or member could not reasonably have been expected to bring the proceedings.

(7)   An incapacity case in proceedings relating to an equality clause with respect to terms of work other than terms of service in the armed forces is a case where the worker had an incapacity during the period of 6 months beginning with the later of—

(a) the relevant day, or

(b) the day on which the worker discovered (or could with reasonable diligence have discovered) the qualifying fact deliberately concealed from the worker by the responsible person.

(8) An incapacity case in proceedings relating to an equality clause with respect to terms of service in the armed forces is a case where the worker had an incapacity during the period of 9 months beginning with the later of—

(a) the last day of the period of service during which the complaint arose, or

(b) the day on which the worker discovered (or could with reasonable diligence have discovered) the qualifying fact deliberately concealed from the worker by the responsible person.

(9) An incapacity case in proceedings relating to an equality rule is a case where the member of the occupational pension scheme in question had an incapacity during the period of 6 months beginning with the later of—

(a) the relevant day, or

(b) the day on which the member discovered (or could with reasonable diligence have discovered) the qualifying fact deliberately concealed from the member by the employer or the trustees or managers of the scheme.

(10) The relevant day for the purposes of this section is—

(a) the last day of the employment or appointment, or

(b) the day on which the stable working relationship between the worker and the responsible person ended.

131 ASSESSMENT OF WHETHER WORK IS OF EQUAL VALUE

(1) This section applies to proceedings before an employment tribunal on—

(a) a complaint relating to a breach of an equality clause or rule, or

(b) a question referred to the tribunal by virtue of section 128(2).

(2) Where a question arises in the proceedings as to whether one person's work is of equal value to another's, the tribunal may, before determining the question, require a member of the panel of independent experts to prepare a report on the question.

(3) The tribunal may withdraw a requirement that it makes under subsection (2); and, if it does so, it may—

(a) request the panel member to provide it with specified documentation;

(b) make such other requests to that member as are connected with the withdrawal of the requirement.

(4) If the tribunal requires the preparation of a report under subsection (2) (and does not withdraw the requirement), it must not determine the question unless it has received the report.

(5) Subsection (6) applies where—

(a) a question arises in the proceedings as to whether the work of one person (A) is of equal value to the work of another (B), and

(b) A's work and B's work have been given different values by a job evaluation study.

(6) The tribunal must determine that A's work is not of equal value to B's work unless it has reasonable grounds for suspecting that the evaluation contained in the study—

(a) was based on a system that discriminates because of sex, or

(b) is otherwise unreliable.

(7)   For the purposes of subsection (6)(a), a system discriminates because of sex if a difference (or coincidence) between values that the system sets on different demands is not justifiable regardless of the sex of the person on whom the demands are made.

(8)   A reference to a member of the panel of independent experts is a reference to a person—
(a)   who is for the time being designated as such by the Advisory, Conciliation and Arbitration Service (ACAS) for the purposes of this section, and
(b)   who is neither a member of the Council of ACAS nor one of its officers or members of staff.

(9)   "Job evaluation study" has the meaning given in section 80(5).

132   REMEDIES IN NON-PENSIONS CASES

(1)   This section applies to proceedings before a court or employment tribunal on a complaint relating to a breach of an equality clause, other than a breach with respect to membership of or rights under an occupational pension scheme.

(2)   If the court or tribunal finds that there has been a breach of the equality clause, it may—
(a)   make a declaration as to the rights of the parties in relation to the matters to which the proceedings relate;
(b)   order an award by way of arrears of pay or damages in relation to the complainant.

(3)   The court or tribunal may not order a payment under subsection (2)(b) in respect of a time before the arrears day.

(4)   In relation to proceedings in England and Wales, the arrears day is, in a case mentioned in the first column of the table, the day mentioned in the second column.

Case	Arrears Day
A standard case	The day falling 6 years before the day on which the proceedings were instituted
A concealment case or an incapacity case (or a case which is both)	The day on which the breach first occurred

(5)   In relation to proceedings in Scotland, the arrears day is the first day of—
(a)   the period of 5 years ending with the day on which the proceedings were commenced, or
(b)   if the case involves a relevant incapacity, or a relevant fraud or error, the period of 20 years ending with that day.

Chapter 5 MISCELLANEOUS

136 BURDEN OF PROOF

(1)   This section applies to any proceedings relating to a contravention of this Act.

(2)   If there are facts from which the court could decide, in the absence of any other explanation, that a person (A) contravened the provision concerned, the court must hold that the contravention occurred.

(3)   But subsection (2) does not apply if A shows that A did not contravene the provision.

(4)   The reference to a contravention of this Act includes a reference to a breach of an equality clause or rule.

(5)   This section does not apply to proceedings for an offence under this Act.

(6)   A reference to the court includes a reference to—
    (a)   an employment tribunal;
    (b)   the Asylum and Immigration Tribunal;
    (c)   the Special Immigration Appeals Commission;
    (d)   the First-tier Tribunal;
    (e)   the Special Educational Needs Tribunal for Wales;
    (f)   an Additional Support Needs Tribunal for Scotland.

137 PREVIOUS FINDINGS

(1)   A finding in relevant proceedings in respect of an act which has become final is to be treated as conclusive in proceedings under this Act.

(2)   Relevant proceedings are proceedings before a court or employment tribunal under any of the following—
    (a)   section 19 or 20 of the Race Relations Act 1968;
    (b)   the Equal Pay Act 1970;
    (c)   the Sex Discrimination Act 1975;
    (d)   the Race Relations Act 1976;
    (e)   section 6(4A) of the Sex Discrimination Act 1986;
    (f)   the Disability Discrimination Act 1995;
    (g)   Part 2 of the Equality Act 2006;
    (h)   the Employment Equality (Religion and Belief) Regulations 2003 (S.I. 2003/1660);
    (i)   the Employment Equality (Sexual Orientation) Regulations 2003 (S.I. 2003/1661);
    (j)   the Employment Equality (Age) Regulations 2006 (S.I. 2006/1031);
    (k)   the Equality Act (Sexual Orientation) Regulations 2007 (S.I. 2007/1263).

(3)   A finding becomes final—
    (a)   when an appeal against the finding is dismissed, withdrawn or abandoned, or
    (b)   when the time for appealing expires without an appeal having been brought.

Part 10 CONTRACTS, ETC.

Contracts and other agreements

142 UNENFORCEABLE TERMS

(1)   A term of a contract is unenforceable against a person in so far as it constitutes, promotes or provides for treatment of that or another person that is of a description prohibited by this Act.

(2)   A relevant non-contractual term is unenforceable against a person in so far as it constitutes, promotes or provides for treatment of that or another person that is of a description prohibited by this Act, in so far as this Act relates to disability.

(3)   A relevant non-contractual term is a term which—
    (a)   is a term of an agreement that is not a contract, and
    (b)   relates to the provision of an employment service within section 56(2)(a) to (e) or to the provision under a group insurance arrangement of facilities by way of insurance.

(4)   A reference in subsection (1) or (2) to treatment of a description prohibited by this Act does not include—

    (a)   a reference to the inclusion of a term in a contract referred to in section 70(2)(a) or 76(2), or

    (b)   a reference to the failure to include a term in a contract as referred to in section 70(2)(b).

(5)   Subsection (4) does not affect the application of section 148(2) to this section.

143 REMOVAL OR MODIFICATION OF UNENFORCEABLE TERMS

(1)   A county court or the sheriff may, on an application by a person who has an interest in a contract or other agreement which includes a term that is unenforceable as a result of section 142, make an order for the term to be removed or modified.

(2)   An order under this section must not be made unless every person who would be affected by it—

    (a)   has been given notice of the application (except where notice is dispensed with in accordance with rules of court), and

    (b)   has been afforded an opportunity to make representations to the county court or sheriff.

(3)   An order under this section may include provision in respect of a period before the making of the order.

144 CONTRACTING OUT

(1)   A term of a contract is unenforceable by a person in whose favour it would operate in so far as it purports to exclude or limit a provision of or made under this Act.

(2)   A relevant non-contractual term (as defined by section 142) is unenforceable by a person in whose favour it would operate in so far as it purports to exclude or limit a provision of or made under this Act, in so far as the provision relates to disability.

(3)   This section does not apply to a contract which settles a claim within section 114.

(4)   This section does not apply to a contract which settles a complaint within section 120 if the contract—

    (a)   is made with the assistance of a conciliation officer, or

    (b)   is a qualifying compromise contract.

(5)   A contract within subsection (4) includes a contract which settles a complaint relating to a breach of an equality clause or rule or of a non-discrimination rule.

(6)   A contract within subsection (4) includes an agreement by the parties to a dispute to submit the dispute to arbitration if—

    (a)   the dispute is covered by a scheme having effect by virtue of an order under section 212A of the Trade Union and Labour Relations (Consolidation) Act 1992, and

    (b)   the agreement is to submit the dispute to arbitration in accordance with the scheme.

Collective agreements and Rules of Undertaking

145 VOID AND UNENFORCEABLE TERMS

(1)   A term of a collective agreement is void in so far as it constitutes, promotes or provides for treatment of a description prohibited by this Act.

(2) A rule of an undertaking is unenforceable against a person in so far as it constitutes, promotes or provides for treatment of the person that is of a description prohibited by this Act.

Supplementary

147 MEANING OF "QUALIFYING COMPROMISE CONTRACT"

(1) This section applies for the purposes of this Part.

(2) A qualifying compromise contract is a contract in relation to which each of the conditions in subsection (3) is met.

(3) Those conditions are that—
 (a) the contract is in writing,
 (b) the contract relates to the particular complaint,
 (c) the complainant has, before entering into the contract, received advice from an independent adviser about its terms and effect (including, in particular, its effect on the complainant's ability to pursue the complaint before an employment tribunal),
 (d) on the date of the giving of the advice, there is in force a contract of insurance, or an indemnity provided for members of a profession or professional body, covering the risk of a claim by the complainant in respect of loss arising from the advice,
 (e) the contract identifies the adviser, and
 (f) the contract states that the conditions in paragraphs (c) and (d) are met.

(4) Each of the following is an independent adviser—
 (a) a qualified lawyer;
 (b) an officer, official, employee or member of an independent trade union certified in writing by the trade union as competent to give advice and as authorised to do so on its behalf;
 (c) a worker at an advice centre (whether as an employee or a volunteer) certified in writing by the centre as competent to give advice and as authorised to do so on its behalf;
 (d) a person of such description as may be specified by order.

(5) Despite subsection (4), none of the following is an independent adviser in relation to a qualifying compromise contract—
 (a) a person who is a party to the contract or the complaint;
 (b) a person who is connected to a person within paragraph (a);
 (c) a person who is employed by a person within paragraph (a) or (b);
 (d) a person who is acting for a person within paragraph (a) or (b) in relation to the contract or the complaint;
 (e) a person within subsection (4)(b) or (c), if the trade union or advice centre is a person within paragraph (a) or (b);
 (f) a person within subsection (4)(c) to whom the complainant makes a payment for the advice.

(6) A "qualified lawyer", for the purposes of subsection (4)(a), is—
 (a) in relation to England and Wales, a person who, for the purposes of the Legal Services Act 2007, is an authorised person in relation to an activity which constitutes the exercise of a right of audience or the conduct of litigation;
 (b) in relation to Scotland, an advocate (whether in practice as such or employed to give legal advice) or a solicitor who holds a practising certificate.

(7) "Independent trade union" has the meaning given in section 5 of the Trade Union and Labour Relations (Consolidation) Act 1992.

(8)   Two persons are connected for the purposes of subsection (5) if—
(a) one is a company of which the other (directly or indirectly) has control, or
(b) both are companies of which a third person (directly or indirectly) has control.

(9)   Two persons are also connected for the purposes of subsection (5) in so far as a connection between them gives rise to a conflict of interest in relation to the contract or the complaint.

SCHEDULE 1 DISABILITY: SUPPLEMENTARY PROVISION

Part 1: DETERMINATION OF DISABILITY

2 LONG-TERM EFFECTS

(1)   The effect of an impairment is long-term if—
(a) it has lasted for at least 12 months,
(b) it is likely to last for at least 12 months, or
(c) it is likely to last for the rest of the life of the person affected.

(2)   If an impairment ceases to have a substantial adverse effect on a person's ability to carry out normal day-to-day activities, it is to be treated as continuing to have that effect if that effect is likely to recur.

(3)   For the purposes of sub-paragraph (2), the likelihood of an effect recurring is to be disregarded in such circumstances as may be prescribed.

(4)   Regulations may prescribe circumstances in which, despite sub-paragraph (1), an effect is to be treated as being, or as not being, long-term.

3 SEVERE DISFIGUREMENT

(1)   An impairment which consists of a severe disfigurement is to be treated as having a substantial adverse effect on the ability of the person concerned to carry out normal day-to-day activities.

(2)   Regulations may provide that in prescribed circumstances a severe disfigurement is not to be treated as having that effect.

(3)   The regulations may, in particular, make provision in relation to deliberately acquired disfigurement.

6 CERTAIN MEDICAL CONDITIONS

(1)   Cancer, HIV infection and multiple sclerosis are each a disability.

(2)   HIV infection is infection by a virus capable of causing the Acquired Immune Deficiency Syndrome.

SCHEDULE 8 WORK: REASONABLE ADJUSTMENTS

Part 3 LIMITATIONS ON THE DUTY

20 LACK OF KNOWLEDGE OF DISABILITY, ETC.

(1)   A is not subject to a duty to make reasonable adjustments if A does not know, and could not reasonably be expected to know—
(a) in the case of an applicant or potential applicant, that an interested disabled person is or may be an applicant for the work in question;

(b) in any other case referred to in this Part of this Schedule, that an interested disabled person has a disability and is likely to be placed at the disadvantage referred to in the first, second or third requirement.

SCHEDULE 9 WORK: EXCEPTIONS

Part 1 OCCUPATIONAL REQUIREMENTS

1 GENERAL

(1) A person (A) does not contravene a provision mentioned in sub-paragraph (2) by applying in relation to work a requirement to have a particular protected characteristic, if A shows that, having regard to the nature or context of the work—
  (a) it is an occupational requirement,
  (b) the application of the requirement is a proportionate means of achieving a legitimate aim, and
  (c) the person to whom A applies the requirement does not meet it (or A has reasonable grounds for not being satisfied that the person meets it).

(2) The provisions are—
  (a) section 39(1)(a) or (c) or (2)(b) or (c);
  (b) section 41(1)(b);
  (c) section 44(1)(a) or (c) or (2)(b) or (c);
  (d) section 45(1)(a) or (c) or (2)(b) or (c);
  (e) section 49(3)(a) or (c) or (6)(b) or (c);
  (f) section 50(3)(a) or (c) or (6)(b) or (c);
  (g) section 51(1).

(3) The references in sub-paragraph (1) to a requirement to have a protected characteristic are to be read—
  (a) in the case of gender reassignment, as references to a requirement not to be a transsexual person (and section 7(3) is accordingly to be ignored);
  (b) in the case of marriage and civil partnership, as references to a requirement not to be married or a civil partner (and section 8(2) is accordingly to be ignored).

(4) In the case of a requirement to be of a particular sex, sub-paragraph (1) has effect as if in paragraph (c), the words from "or" to the end were omitted.

2 RELIGIOUS REQUIREMENTS RELATING TO SEX, MARRIAGE ETC., SEXUAL ORIENTATION

(1) A person (A) does not contravene a provision mentioned in sub-paragraph (2) by applying in relation to employment a requirement to which sub-paragraph (4) applies if A shows that—
  (a) the employment is for the purposes of an organised religion,
  (b) the application of the requirement engages the compliance or non-conflict principle, and
  (c) the person to whom A applies the requirement does not meet it (or A has reasonable grounds for not being satisfied that the person meets it).

(2) The provisions are—
  (a) section 39(1)(a) or (c) or (2)(b) or (c);
  (b) section 49(3)(a) or (c) or (6)(b) or (c);
  (c) section 50(3)(a) or (c) or (6)(b) or (c);
  (d) section 51(1).

(3) A person does not contravene section 53(1) or (2)(a) or (b) by applying in relation to a relevant qualification (within the meaning of that section) a requirement to which sub-paragraph (4) applies if the person shows that—
    (a) the qualification is for the purposes of employment mentioned in sub-paragraph (1)(a), and
    (b) the application of the requirement engages the compliance or non-conflict principle.

(4) This sub-paragraph applies to—
    (a) a requirement to be of a particular sex;
    (b) a requirement not to be a transsexual person;
    (c) a requirement not to be married or a civil partner;
    (d) a requirement not to be married to, or the civil partner of, a person who has a living former spouse or civil partner;
    (e) a requirement relating to circumstances in which a marriage or civil partnership came to an end;
    (f) a requirement related to sexual orientation.

(5) The application of a requirement engages the compliance principle if the requirement is applied so as to comply with the doctrines of the religion.

(6) The application of a requirement engages the non-conflict principle if, because of the nature or context of the employment, the requirement is applied so as to avoid conflicting with the strongly held religious convictions of a significant number of the religion's followers.

(7) A reference to employment includes a reference to an appointment to a personal or public office.

(8) In the case of a requirement within sub-paragraph (4)(a), sub-paragraph (1) has effect as if in paragraph (c) the words from "or" to the end were omitted.

3 OTHER REQUIREMENTS RELATING TO RELIGION OR BELIEF

A person (A) with an ethos based on religion or belief does not contravene a provision mentioned in paragraph 1(2) by applying in relation to work a requirement to be of a particular religion or belief if A shows that, having regard to that ethos and to the nature or context of the work—

(a) it is an occupational requirement,

(b) the application of the requirement is a proportionate means of achieving a legitimate aim, and

(c) the person to whom A applies the requirement does not meet it (or A has reasonable grounds for not being satisfied that the person meets it).

Part 2: EXCEPTIONS RELATING TO AGE

8 RETIREMENT

(1) It is not an age contravention to dismiss a relevant worker at or over the age of 65 if the reason for the dismissal is retirement.

(2) Each of the following is a relevant worker—
    (a) an employee within the meaning of section 230(1) of the Employment Rights Act 1996;
    (b) a person in Crown employment;
    (c) a relevant member of the House of Commons staff;
    (d) a relevant member of the House of Lords staff.

(3)   Retirement is a reason for dismissal only if it is a reason for dismissal by virtue of Part 10 of the Employment Rights Act 1996.

9 APPLICANTS AT OR APPROACHING RETIREMENT AGE

(1)   A person does not contravene section 39(1)(a) or (c), so far as relating to age, in a case where the other person—
  (a) has attained the age limit, or would have attained it before the end of six months beginning with the date on which the application for the employment had to be made, and
  (b) would, if recruited for the employment, be a relevant worker within the meaning of paragraph 8.

(2)   The age limit is whichever is the greater of—
  (a) the age of 65, and
  (b) the normal retirement age in the case of the employment concerned.

(3)   The reference to the normal retirement age is to be construed in accordance with section 98ZH of the Employment Rights Act 1996.

11 THE NATIONAL MINIMUM WAGE: YOUNG WORKERS

(1)   It is not an age contravention for a person to pay a young worker (A) at a lower rate than that at which the person pays an older worker (B) if—
  (a) the hourly rate for the national minimum wage for a person of A's age is lower than that for a person of B's age, and
  (b) the rate at which A is paid is below the single hourly rate.

(2)   A young worker is a person who qualifies for the national minimum wage at a lower rate than the single hourly rate; and an older worker is a person who qualifies for the national minimum wage at a higher rate than that at which the young worker qualifies for it.

(3)   The single hourly rate is the rate prescribed under section 1(3) of the National Minimum Wage Act 1998.

12 THE NATIONAL MINIMUM WAGE: APPRENTICES

(1)   It is not an age contravention for a person to pay an apprentice who does not qualify for the national minimum wage at a lower rate than the person pays an apprentice who does.

(2)   An apprentice is a person who—
  (a) is employed under a contract of apprenticeship, or
  (b) as a result of provision made by virtue of section 3(2)(a) of the National Minimum Wage Act 1998 (persons not qualifying), is treated as employed under a contract of apprenticeship.

13 REDUNDANCY

(1)   It is not an age contravention for a person to give a qualifying employee an enhanced redundancy payment of an amount less than that of an enhanced redundancy payment which the person gives to another qualifying employee, if each amount is calculated on the same basis.

(2)   It is not an age contravention to give enhanced redundancy payments only to those who are qualifying employees by virtue of sub-paragraph (3)(a) or (b).

(3)   A person is a qualifying employee if the person—
(a)   is entitled to a redundancy payment as a result of section 135 of the Employment Rights Act 1996,
(b)   agrees to the termination of the employment in circumstances where the person would, if dismissed, have been so entitled,
(c)   would have been so entitled but for section 155 of that Act (requirement for two years' continuous employment), or
(d)   agrees to the termination of the employment in circumstances where the person would, if dismissed, have been so entitled but for that section.

(4)   An enhanced redundancy payment is a payment the amount of which is, subject to sub-paragraphs (5) and (6), calculated in accordance with section 162(1) to (3) of the Employment Rights Act 1996.

(5)   A person making a calculation for the purposes of sub-paragraph (4)—
(a)   may treat a week's pay as not being subject to a maximum amount;
(b)   may treat a week's pay as being subject to a maximum amount above that for the time being specified in section 227(1) of the Employment Rights Act 1996;
(c)   may multiply the appropriate amount for each year of employment by a figure of more than one.

(6)   Having made a calculation for the purposes of sub-paragraph (4) (whether or not in reliance on sub-paragraph (5)), a person may multiply the amount calculated by a figure of more than one.

(7)   In sub-paragraph (5), "the appropriate amount" has the meaning given in section 162 of the Employment Rights Act 1996, and "a week's pay" is to be read with Chapter 2 of Part 14 of that Act.

(8)   For the purposes of sub-paragraphs (4) to (6), the reference to "the relevant date" in subsection (1)(a) of section 162 of that Act is, in the case of a person who is a qualifying employee by virtue of sub-paragraph (3)(b) or (d), to be read as reference to the date of the termination of the employment.

Part 3: OTHER EXCEPTIONS

17 NON-CONTRACTUAL PAYMENTS TO WOMEN ON MATERNITY LEAVE

(1)   A person does not contravene section 39(1)(b) or (2), so far as relating to pregnancy and maternity, by depriving a woman who is on maternity leave of any benefit from the terms of her employment relating to pay.

(2)   The reference in sub-paragraph (1) to benefit from the terms of a woman's employment relating to pay does not include a reference to—
(a)   maternity-related pay (including maternity-related pay that is increase-related),
(b)   pay (including increase-related pay) in respect of times when she is not on maternity leave, or
(c)   pay by way of bonus in respect of times when she is on compulsory maternity leave.

(3)   For the purposes of sub-paragraph (2), pay is increase-related in so far as it is to be calculated by reference to increases in pay that the woman would have received had she not been on maternity leave.

(4)   A reference to terms of her employment is a reference to terms of her employment that are not in her contract of employment, her contract of apprenticeship or her contract to do work personally.

(5)   "Pay" means benefits—
(a)   that consist of the payment of money to an employee by way of wages or salary, and
(b)   that are not benefits whose provision is regulated by the contract referred to in sub-paragraph (4).

(6)   "Maternity-related pay" means pay to which a woman is entitled—
(a)   as a result of being pregnant, or
(b)   in respect of times when she is on maternity leave.

Statutory Instruments

Employment Tribunals Extension of Jurisdiction (England and Wales) Order 1994/1623

3

Proceedings may be brought before an employment tribunal in respect of a claim of an employee for the recovery of damages or any other sum (other than a claim for damages, or for a sum due, in respect of personal injuries) if—

(a) the claim is one to which section 131(2) of the 1978 Act applies and which a court in England and Wales would under the law for the time being in force have jurisdiction to hear and determine;

(b) the claim is not one to which article 5 applies; and

(c) the claim arises or is outstanding on the termination of the employee's employment.

4

Proceedings may be brought before an employment tribunal in respect of a claim of an employer for the recovery of damages or any other sum (other than a claim for damages, or for a sum due, in respect of personal injuries) if—

(a) the claim is one to which section 131(2) of the 1978 Act applies and which a court in England and Wales would under the law for the time being in force have jurisdiction to hear and determine;

(b) the claim is not one to which article 5 applies;

(c) the claim arises or is outstanding on the termination of the employment of the employee against whom it is made; and

(d) proceedings in respect of a claim of that employee have been brought before an employment tribunal by virtue of this Order.

5

This article applies to a claim for breach of a contractual term of any of the following descriptions—

(a) a term requiring the employer to provide living accommodation for the employee;

(b) a term imposing an obligation on the employer or the employee in connection with the provision of living accommodation;

(c) a term relating to intellectual property;

(d)   a term imposing an obligation of confidence;

(e)   a term which is a covenant in restraint of trade.

In this article, "intellectual property" includes copyright, rights in performances, moral rights, design right, registered designs, patents and trade marks.

7

An employment tribunal shall not entertain a complaint in respect of an employee's contract claim unless it is presented—

(a)   within the period of three months beginning with the effective date of termination of the contract giving rise to the claim, or

(b)   where there is no effective date of termination, within the period of three months beginning with the last day upon which the employee worked in the employment which has terminated, or

(ba)   where the period within which a complaint must be presented in accordance with paragraph (a) or (b) is extended by regulation 15 of the Employment Act 2002 (Dispute Resolution) Regulations 2004, the period within which the complaint must be presented shall be the extended period rather than the period in paragraph (a) or (b).

(c)   where the tribunal is satisfied that it was not reasonably practicable for the complaint to be presented within whichever of those periods is applicable, within such further period as the tribunal considers reasonable.

8

An employment tribunal shall not entertain a complaint in respect of an employer's contract claim unless—

(a)   it is presented at a time when there is before the tribunal a complaint in respect of a contract claim of a particular employee which has not been settled or withdrawn;

(b)   it arises out of a contract with that employee; and

(c)   it is presented—
    (i)   within the period of six weeks beginning with the day, or if more than one the last of the days, on which the employer (or other person who is the respondent party to the employee's contract claim) received from the tribunal a copy of an originating application in respect of a contract claim of that employee; or
    (ii)   where the tribunal is satisfied that it was not reasonably practicable for the complaint to be presented within that period, within such further period as the tribunal considers reasonable.

10

An employment tribunal shall not in proceedings in respect of a contract claim, or in respect of a number of contract claims relating to the same contract, order the payment of an amount exceeding £25,000.

As amended by the Employment Rights (Dispute Resolution) Act 1998 c. 8 Pt I s 1(2); Employment Act 2002 (Dispute Resolution) Regulations 2004/752 reg 17(c).

EMPLOYMENT PROTECTION (CONTINUITY OF EMPLOYMENT) REGULATIONS 1996/3147

2 APPLICATION

These Regulations apply to any action taken in relation to the dismissal of an employee which consists of—

(a) his making a claim in accordance with a dismissal procedures agreement designated by an order under section 110 of the Employment Rights Act 1996,

(b) the presentation by him of a relevant complaint of dismissal,

(c) any action taken by a conciliation officer under section 18 of the Employment Tribunals Act 1996,

(d) the making of a relevant compromise contract,

(e) the making of an agreement to submit a dispute to arbitration in accordance with a scheme having effect by virtue of an order under section 212A of the Trade Union and Labour Relations (Consolidation) Act 1992,

(f) a decision taken arising out of the use of a statutory dispute resolution procedure contained in Schedule 2 to the Employment Act 2002 in a case where, in accordance with the Employment Act 2002 (Dispute Resolution) Regulations 2004, such a procedure applies, or

(g) a decision taken arising out of the use of the statutory duty to consider procedure contained in Schedule 6 to the Employment Equality (Age) Regulations 2006.

3 CONTINUITY OF EMPLOYMENT WHERE EMPLOYEE RE-ENGAGED

(1) The provisions of this regulation shall have effect to preserve the continuity of a person's period of employment for the purposes of—
  (a) Chapter I of Part XIV of the Employment Rights Act 1996 (continuous employment), and
  (b) that Chapter as applied by subsection (2) of section 282 of the Trade Union and Labour Relations (Consolidation) Act 1992 for the purposes of that section.

(2) If in consequence of any action to which these Regulations apply a dismissed employee is reinstated or re-employed by his employer or by a successor or associated employer of the employer–
  (a) the continuity of that employee's period of employment shall be preserved, and
  (b) the period beginning with the date on which the dismissal takes effect and ending with the date of reinstatement or re-engagement shall count in the computation of the employee's period of continuous employment.

4 EXCLUSION OF OPERATION OF SECTION 214 OF THE EMPLOYMENT RIGHTS ACT 1996 WHERE REDUNDANCY OR EQUIVALENT PAYMENT REPAID

(1) Section 214 of the Employment Rights Act 1996 (continuity broken where employee re-employed after the making of a redundancy payment or equivalent payment) shall not apply where—
  (a) in consequence of any action to which these Regulations apply a dismissed employee is reinstated or re-employed by his employer or by a successor or associated employer of the employer,

(b) the terms upon which he is so reinstated or re-engaged include provision for him to repay the amount of a redundancy payment or an equivalent payment paid in respect of the relevant dismissal, and

(c) that provision is complied with.

(2) For the purposes of this regulation the cases in which a redundancy payment shall be treated as having been paid are the cases mentioned in section 214(5) of the Employment Rights Act 1996.

> *As amended by the Employment Rights Act 1996, Schedule 1, para 56(18); Employment Rights (Dispute Resolution) Act 1998 c. 8 Pt I s 1(2); Employment Protection (Continuity of Employment) (Amendment) Regulations 2001/1188 reg 2(2)(a), reg 2(2)(b), reg 2(2)(c); Employment Act 2002 (Dispute Resolution) Regulations 2004/752 reg 17(e); Employment Equality (Age) Regulations 2006/1031 Sch 8(2) para 57(2)(b).*

WORKING TIME REGULATIONS 1998/1833

Part I GENERAL

3 INTERPRETATION

(1) In these Regulations—

"the 1996 Act" means the Employment Rights Act 1996;

"adult worker" means a worker who has attained the age of 18;

"the armed forces" means any of the naval, military and air forces of the Crown;

"calendar year" means the period of twelve months beginning with 1st January in any year;

"the civil protection services" includes the police, fire brigades and ambulance services, the security and intelligence services, customs and immigration officers, the prison service, the coastguard, and lifeboat crew and other voluntary rescue services;

"collective agreement" means a collective agreement within the meaning of section 178 of the Trade Union and Labour Relations (Consolidation) Act 1992, the trade union parties to which are independent trade unions within the meaning of section 5 of that Act;

"day" means a period of 24 hours beginning at midnight;

"employer", in relation to a worker, means the person by whom the worker is (or, where the employment has ceased, was) employed;

"employment", in relation to a worker, means employment under his contract, and"employed", shall be construed accordingly;

"fishing vessel" has the same meaning as in section 313 of the Merchant Shipping Act 1995;

"mobile worker" means any worker employed as a member of travelling or flying personnel by an undertaking which operates transport services for passengers or goods by road or air;

"night time", in relation to a worker, means a period—
(a) the duration of which is not less than seven hours, and
(b) which includes the period between midnight and 5 a.m.,
which is determined for the purposes of these Regulations by a relevant agreement, or, in default of such a determination, the period between 11 p.m. and 6 a.m.;

"night work" means work during night time;

"night worker" means a worker—
(a) who, as a normal course, works at least three hours of his daily working time during night time, or
(b) who is likely, during night time, to work at least such proportion of his annual working time as may be specified for the purposes of these Regulations in a collective agreement or a workforce agreement;
and, for the purpose of paragraph (a) of this definition, a person works hours as a normal course (without prejudice to the generality of that expression) if he works such hours on the majority of days on which he works;

"offshore work" means work performed mainly on or from offshore installations (including drilling rigs), directly or indirectly in connection with the exploration, extraction or exploitation of mineral resources, including hydrocarbons, and diving in connection with such activities, whether performed from an offshore installation or a vessel, including any such work performed in the territorial waters of the United Kingdom adjacent to Great Britain or in any area (except one or part of one in which the law of Northern Ireland applies) designated under section 1(7) of the Continental Shelf Act 1964;

"relevant agreement", in relation to a worker, means a workforce agreement which applies to him, any provision of a collective agreement which forms part of a contract between him and his employer, or any other agreement in writing which is legally enforceable as between the worker and his employer;

"relevant training" means work experience provided pursuant to a training course or programme, training for employment, or both, other than work experience or training—
(a) the immediate provider of which is an educational institution or a person whose main business is the provision of training, and
(b) which is provided on a course run by that institution or person;

"rest period", in relation to a worker, means a period which is not working time, other than a rest break or leave to which the worker is entitled under these Regulations;

"the restricted period", in relation to a worker, means the period between 10 p.m. and 6 a.m. or, where the worker's contract provides for him to work after 10 p.m., the period between 11 p.m. and 7 a.m.

"ship" has the same meaning as in section 313 of the Merchant Shipping Act 1995;

"worker" means an individual who has entered into or works under (or, where the employment has ceased, worked under)—
(a) a contract of employment; or
(b) any other contract, whether express or implied and (if it is express) whether oral or in writing, whereby the individual undertakes to do or perform personally any work or services for another party to the contract whose status is not by virtue of the contract

that of a client or customer of any profession or business undertaking carried on by the individual;

and any reference to a worker's contract shall be construed accordingly;

"worker employed in agriculture" has the same meaning as in the Agricultural Wages Act 1948 or the Agricultural Wages (Scotland) Act 1949, and a reference to a worker partly employed in agriculture is to a worker employed in agriculture whose employer also employs him for non-agricultural purposes;

"workforce agreement" means an agreement between an employer and workers employed by him or their representatives in respect of which the conditions set out in Schedule 1 to these Regulations are satisfied;

"working time", in relation to a worker, means—

(a) any period during which he is working, at his employer's disposal and carrying out his activity or duties,

(b) any period during which he is receiving relevant training, and

(c) any additional period which is to be treated as working time for the purpose of these Regulations under a relevant agreement;

and "work" shall be construed accordingly;

"Working Time Directive" means Council Directive 93/104/EC of 23rd November 1993 concerning certain aspects of the organization of working time;

"young worker" means a worker who has attained the age of 15 but not the age of 18 and who, as respects England and Wales, is over compulsory school age (construed in accordance with section 8 of the Education Act 1996) and, as respects Scotland, is over school age (construed in accordance with section 31 of the Education (Scotland) Act 1980), and

"Young Workers Directive" means Council Directive 94/33/EC of 22nd June 1994 on the protection of young people at work.

(2) In the absence of a definition in these Regulations, words and expressions used in particular provisions which are also used in corresponding provisions of the Working Time Directive or the Young Workers Directive have the same meaning as they have in those corresponding provisions.

(3) In these Regulations—

(a) a reference to a numbered regulation is to the regulation in these Regulations bearing that number;

(b) a reference in a regulation to a numbered paragraph is to the paragraph in that regulation bearing that number; and

(c) a reference in a paragraph to a lettered sub-paragraph is to the sub-paragraph in that paragraph bearing that letter.

Part II RIGHTS AND OBLIGATIONS CONCERNING WORKING TIME

3 GENERAL

(1) The provisions of this Part have effect subject to the exceptions provided for in Part III of these Regulations.

(2) Where, in this Part, separate provision is made as respects the same matter in relation to workers generally and to young workers, the provision relating to workers generally applies only to adult workers and those young workers to whom, by virtue of any exception in Part 3, the provision relating to young workers does not apply.

4 MAXIMUM WEEKLY WORKING TIME

(1)   Unless his employer has first obtained the worker's agreement in writing to perform such work, a worker's working time, including overtime, in any reference period which is applicable in his case shall not exceed an average of 48 hours for each seven days.

(2)   An employer shall take all reasonable steps, in keeping with the need to protect the health and safety of workers, to ensure that the limit specified in paragraph (1) is complied with in the case of each worker employed by him in relation to whom it applies and shall keep up-to-date records of all workers who carry out work to which it does not apply by reason of the fact that the employer has obtained the worker's agreement as mentioned in paragraph (1).

(3)   Subject to paragraphs (4) and (5) and any agreement under regulation 23(b), the reference periods which apply in the case of a worker are—

(a)   where a relevant agreement provides for the application of this regulation in relation to successive periods of 17 weeks, each such period, or

(b)   in any other case, any period of 17 weeks in the course of his employment.

(4)   Where a worker has worked for his employer for less than 17 weeks, the reference period applicable in his case is the period that has elapsed since he started work for his employer.

(5)   Paragraphs (3) and (4) shall apply to a worker who is excluded from the scope of certain provisions of these Regulations by regulation 21 as if for each reference to 17 weeks there were substituted a reference to 26 weeks.

(6)   For the purposes of this regulation, a worker's average working time for each seven days during a reference period shall be determined according to the formula—

$$\frac{A + B}{C}$$

where—

A is the aggregate number of hours comprised in the worker's working time during the course of the reference period;

B is the aggregate number of hours comprised in his working time during the course of the period beginning immediately after the end of the reference period and ending when the number of days in that subsequent period on which he has worked equals the number of excluded days during the reference period; and

C is the number of weeks in the reference period.

(7)   In paragraph (6), "excluded days" means days comprised in—
   (a)   any period of annual leave taken by the worker in exercise of his entitlement under regulation 13;
   (b)   any period of sick leave taken by the worker;
   (c)   any period of maternity paternity, adoption or parental leave taken by the worker; and
   (d)   any period in respect of which the limit specified in paragraph (1) did not apply in relation to the worker by reason of the fact that the employer has obtained the worker's agreement as mentioned in paragraph (1).

5 AGREEMENT TO EXCLUDE THE MAXIMUM

(2)   An agreement for the purposes of regulation 4—
 (a) may either relate to a specified period or apply indefinitely; and
 (b) subject to any provision in the agreement for a different period of notice, shall be terminable by the worker by giving not less than seven days' notice to his employer in writing.

(3)   Where an agreement for the purposes of regulation 4 makes provision for the termination of the agreement after a period of notice, the notice period provided for shall not exceed three months.

5A MAXIMUM WORKING TIME FOR YOUNG WORKERS

(1)   A young worker's working time shall not exceed—
 (a) eight hours a day, or
 (b) 40 hours a week.

(2)   If, on any day, or, as the case may be, during any week, a young worker is employed by more than one employer, his working time shall be determined for the purpose of paragraph (1) by aggregating the number of hours worked by him for each employer.

(3)   For the purposes of paragraphs (1) and (2), a week starts at midnight between Sunday and Monday.

(4)   An employer shall take all reasonable steps, in keeping with the need to protect the health and safety of workers, to ensure that the limits specified in paragraph (1) are complied with in the case of each worker employed by him in relation to whom they apply.

6 LENGTH OF NIGHT WORK

(1)   A night worker's normal hours of work in any reference period which is applicable in his case shall not exceed an average of eight hours for each 24 hours.

(2)   An employer shall take all reasonable steps, in keeping with the need to protect the health and safety or workers, to ensure that the limit specified in paragraph (1) is complied with in the case of each night worker employed by him.

(3)   The reference periods which apply in the case of a night worker are—
 (a) where a relevant agreement provides for the application of this regulation in relation to successive periods of 17 weeks, each such period, or
 (b) in any other case, any period of 17 weeks in the course of his employment.

(4)   Where a worker has worked for his employer for less than 17 weeks, the reference period applicable in his case is the period that has elapsed since he started work for his employer.

(5)   For the purposes of this regulation, a night worker's average normal hours of work for each 24 hours during a reference period shall be determined according to the formula—

$$\frac{A}{B-C}$$

where—

A is the number of hours during the reference period which are normal working hours for that worker;

B is the number of days during the reference period, and

C is the total number of hours during the reference period comprised in rest periods spent by the worker in pursuance of his entitlement under regulation 11, divided by 24.

(7) An employer shall ensure that no night worker employed by him whose work involves special hazards or heavy physical or mental strain works for more than eight hours in any 24-hour period during which the night worker performs night work.

(8) For the purposes of paragraph (7), the work of a night worker shall be regarded as involving special hazards or heavy physical or mental strain if—
   (a) it is identified as such in—
      (i)   a collective agreement, or
      (ii) a workforce agreement,
      which takes account of the specific effects and hazards of night work, or
   (b) it is recognised in a risk assessment made by the employer under regulation 3 of the Management of Health and Safety at Work Regulations 1999 as involving a significant risk to the health or safety of workers employed by him.

6A NIGHT WORK BY YOUNG WORKERS

An employer shall ensure that no young worker employed by him works during the restricted period.

8 PATTERN OF WORK

Where the pattern according to which an employer organizes work is such as to put the health and safety of a worker employed by him at risk, in particular because the work is monotonous or the work-rate is predetermined, the employer shall ensure that the worker is given adequate rest breaks.

9 RECORDS

An employer shall—
(a) keep records which are adequate to show whether the limits specified in regulations 4(1), 5A(1) and 6(1) and (7) and the requirements in regulations 6A and 7(1) and (2) are being complied with in the case of each worker employed by him in relation to whom they apply; and

(b) retain such records for two years from the date on which they were made.

10 DAILY REST

(1) A worker is entitled to a rest period of not less than eleven consecutive hours in each 24-hour period during which he works for his employer.

(2) Subject to paragraph (3), a young worker is entitled to a rest period of not less than twelve consecutive hours in each 24-hour period during which he works for his employer.

(3) The minimum rest period provided for in paragraph (2) may be interrupted in the case of activities involving periods of work that are split up over the day or of short duration.

11 WEEKLY REST PERIOD

(1) Subject to paragraph (2), a worker is entitled to an uninterrupted rest period of not less than 24 hours in each seven-day period during which he works for his employer.

(2) If his employer so determines, a worker shall be entitled to either—
   (a) two uninterrupted rest periods each of not less than 24 hours in each 14-day period during which he works for his employer; or
   (b) one uninterrupted rest period of not less than 48 hours in each such 14-day period,
   in place of the entitlement provided for in paragraph (1).

(3) Subject to paragraph (8), a young worker is entitled to a rest period of not less than 48 hours in each seven-day period during which he works for his employer.

(4) For the purpose of paragraphs (1) to (3), a seven-day period or (as the case may be) 14-day period shall be taken to begin—
   (a) at such times on such days as may be provided for for the purposes of this regulation in a relevant agreement; or
   (b) where there are no provisions of a relevant agreement which apply, at the start of each week or (as the case may be) every other week.

(5) In a case where, in accordance with paragraph (4), 14-day periods are to be taken to begin at the start of every other week, the first such period applicable in the case of a particular worker shall be taken to begin—
   (a) if the worker's employment began on or before the date on which these Regulations come into force, on 5th October 1998; or
   (b) if the worker's employment begins after the date on which these Regulations come into force, at the start of the week in which that employment begins.

(6) For the purposes of paragraphs (4) and (5), a week starts at midnight between Sunday and Monday.

(7) The minimum rest period to which a worker is entitled under paragraph (1) or (2) shall not include any part of a rest period to which the worker is entitled under regulation 10(1), except where this is justified by objective or technical reasons or reasons concerning the organization of work.

(8) The minimum rest period to which a young worker is entitled under paragraph (3)—
   (a) may be interrupted in the case of activities involving periods of work that are split up over the day or are of short duration; and
   (b) may be reduced where this is justified by technical or organization reasons, but not to less than 36 consecutive hours.

12 REST BREAKS

(1) Where a worker's working time is more than six hours, he is entitled to a rest break.

(2) The details of the rest break to which a worker is entitled under paragraph (1), including its duration and the terms on which it is granted, shall be in accordance with any provisions for the purposes of this regulation which are contained in a collective agreement or a workforce agreement.

(3) Subject to the provisions of any applicable collective agreement or workforce agreement, the rest break provided for in paragraph (1) is an uninterrupted period of not less than 20 minutes, and the worker is entitled to spend it away from his workstation if he has one.

(4) Where a young worker's daily working time is more than four and a half hours, he is entitled to a rest break of at least 30 minutes, which shall be consecutive if possible, and he is entitled to spend it away from his workstation if he has one.

(5) If, on any day, a young worker is employed by more than one employer, his daily working time shall be determined for the purpose of paragraph (4) by aggregating the number of hours worked by him for each employer.

13 ENTITLEMENT TO ANNUAL LEAVE

(1) Subject to paragraph (5), a worker is entitled to four weeks' annual leave in each leave year.

(3) A worker's leave year, for the purposes of this regulation, begins—
   (a) on such date during the calendar year as may be provided for in a relevant agreement; or
   (b) where there are no provisions of a relevant agreement which apply—
      (i)   if the worker's employment began on or before 1st October 1998, on that date and each subsequent anniversary of that date; or
      (ii) if the worker's employment begins after 1st October 1998, on the date on which that employment begins and each subsequent anniversary of that date.

(4) Paragraph (3) does not apply to a worker to whom Schedule 2 applies (workers employed in agriculture) except where, in the case of a worker partly employed in agriculture, a relevant agreement so provides.

(5) Where the date on which a worker's employment begins is later than the date on which (by virtue of a relevant agreement) his first leave year begins, the leave to which he is entitled in that leave year is a proportion of the period applicable under paragraph (1) equal to the proportion of that leave year remaining on the date on which his employment begins.

(9) Leave to which a worker is entitled under this regulation may be taken in instalments, but—
   (a) it may only be taken in the leave year in respect of which it is due, and
   (b) it may not be replaced by a payment in lieu except where the worker's employment is terminated.

13A ENTITLEMENT TO ADDITIONAL ANNUAL LEAVE

(1) Subject to regulation 26A and paragraphs (3) and (5), a worker is entitled in each leave year to a period of additional leave determined in accordance with paragraph (2).

(2) The period of additional leave to which a worker is entitled under paragraph (1) is—
   (a) in any leave year beginning on or after 1st October 2007 but before 1st April 2008, 0.8 weeks;
   (b) in any leave year beginning before 1st October 2007, a proportion of 0.8 weeks equivalent to the proportion of the year beginning on 1st October 2007 which would have elapsed at the end of that leave year;
   (c) in any leave year beginning on 1st April 2008, 0.8 weeks;
   (d) in any leave year beginning after 1st April 2008 but before 1st April 2009, 0.8 weeks and a proportion of another 0.8 weeks equivalent to the proportion of the year beginning on 1st April 2009 which would have elapsed at the end of that leave year;
   (e) in any leave year beginning on or after 1st April 2009, 1.6 weeks.

(3) The aggregate entitlement provided for in paragraph (2) and regulation 13(1) is subject to a maximum of 28 days.

(4) A worker's leave year begins for the purposes of this regulation on the same date as the worker's leave year begins for the purposes of regulation 13.

(5) Where the date on which a worker's employment begins is later than the date on which his first leave year begins, the additional leave to which he is entitled in that leave year is a proportion of the period applicable under paragraph (2) equal to the proportion of that leave year remaining on the date on which his employment begins.

(6)   Leave to which a worker is entitled under this regulation may be taken in instalments, but it may not be replaced by a payment in lieu except where—
   (a) the worker's employment is terminated; or
   (b) the leave is an entitlement that arises under paragraph (2)(a), (b) or (c); or
   (c) the leave is an entitlement to 0.8 weeks that arises under paragraph (2)(d) in respect of that part of the leave year which would have elapsed before 1st April 2009.

(7)   A relevant agreement may provide for any leave to which a worker is entitled under this regulation to be carried forward into the leave year immediately following the leave year in respect of which it is due.

(8)   This regulation does not apply to workers to whom the Agricultural Wages (Scotland) Act 1949 applies (as that Act had effect on 1 July 1999).

14 COMPENSATION RELATED TO ENTITLEMENT TO LEAVE

(1)   This regulation applies where—
   (a) a worker's employment is terminated during the course of his leave year, and
   (b) on the date on which the termination takes effect ("the termination date"), the proportion he has taken of the leave to which he is entitled in the leave year under regulation 13 and regulation 13A differs from the proportion of the leave year which has expired.

(2)   Where the proportion of leave taken by the worker is less than the proportion of the leave year which has expired, his employer shall make him a payment in lieu of leave in accordance with paragraph (3).

(3)   The payment due under paragraph (2) shall be—
   (a) such sum as may be provided for for the purposes of this regulation in a relevant agreement, or
   (b) where there are no provisions of a relevant agreement which apply, a sum equal to the amount that would be due to the worker under regulation 16 in respect of a period of leave determined according to the formula—

$(A \times B) - C$

where—

A is the period of leave to which the worker is entitled under regulation 13 and regulation 13A;

B is the proportion of the worker's leave year which expired before the termination date, and

C is the period of leave taken by the worker between the start of the leave year and the termination date.

(4)   A relevant agreement may provide that, where the proportion of leave taken by the worker exceeds the proportion of the leave year which has expired, he shall compensate his employer, whether by a payment, by undertaking additional work or otherwise.

15 DATES ON WHICH LEAVE IS TAKEN

(1)   A worker may take leave to which he is entitled under regulation 13 and regulation 13A on such days as he may elect by giving notice to his employer in accordance with paragraph (3), subject to any requirement imposed on him by his employer under paragraph (2).

(2)　A worker's employer may require the worker—
　　(a)　to take leave to which the worker is entitled under regulation 13 or regulation 13A; or
　　(b)　not to take such leave,
　　　　on particular days, by giving notice to the worker in accordance with paragraph (3).

(3)　A notice under paragraph (1) or (2)—
　　(a)　may relate to all or part of the leave to which a worker is entitled in a leave year;
　　(b)　shall specify the days on which leave is or (as the case may be) is not to be taken and, where the leave on a particular day is to be in respect of only part of the day, its duration; and
　　(c)　shall be given to the employer or, as the case may be, the worker before the relevant date.

(4)　The relevant date, for the purposes of paragraph (3), is the date—
　　(a)　in the case of a notice under paragraph (1) or (2)(a), twice as many days in advance of the earliest day specified in the notice as the number of days or part-days to which the notice relates, and
　　(b)　in the case of a notice under paragraph (2)(b), as many days in advance of the earliest day so specified as the number of days or part-days to which the notice relates.

(5)　Any right or obligation under paragraphs (1) to (4) may be varied or excluded by a relevant agreement.

(6)　This regulation does not apply to a worker to whom Schedule 2 applies (workers employed in agriculture) except where, in the case of a worker partly employed in agriculture, a relevant agreement so provides.

15A LEAVE DURING THE FIRST YEAR OF EMPLOYMENT

(1)　During the first year of his employment, the amount of leave a worker may take at any time in exercise of his entitlement under regulation 13 or regulation 13A is limited to the amount which is deemed to have accrued in his case at that time under paragraph (2) or (2A), as modified under paragraph (3) in a case where that paragraph applies, less the amount of leave (if any) that he has already taken during that year.

(2)　For the purposes of paragraph (1), in the case of workers to whom the Agricultural Wages (Scotland) Act 1949 applies, leave is deemed to accrue over the course of the worker's first year of employment, at the rate of one-twelfth of the amount specified in regulation 13(1) on the first day of each month of that year.

(2A)　Except where paragraph (2) applies, for the purposes of paragraph (1), leave is deemed to accrue over the course of the worker's first year of employment, at the rate of one-twelfth of the amount specified in regulation 13(1) and regulation 13A(2), subject to the limit contained in regulation 13A(3), on the first day of each month of that year.

(3)　Where the amount of leave that has accrued in a particular case includes a fraction of a day other than a half-day, the fraction shall be treated as a half-day if it is less than a half-day and as a whole day if it is more than a half-day.

(4)　This regulation does not apply to a worker whose employment began on or before 25th October 2001.

16 PAYMENT IN RESPECT OF PERIODS OF LEAVE

(1)　A worker is entitled to be paid in respect of any period of annual leave to which he is entitled under regulation 13 and regulation 13A, at the rate of a week's pay in respect of each week of leave.

(2)   Sections 221 to 224 of the 1996 Act shall apply for the purpose of determining the amount of a week's pay for the purposes of this regulation, subject to the modifications set out in paragraph (3).

(3)   The provisions referred to in paragraph (2) shall apply—
  (a)   as if references to the employee were references to the worker;
  (b)   as if references to the employee's contract of employment were references to the worker's contract;
  (c)   as if the calculation date were the first day of the period of leave in question; and
  (d)   as if the references to sections 227 and 228 did not apply.

(4)   A right to payment under paragraph (1) does not affect any right of a worker to remuneration under his contract ("contractual remuneration").

(5)   Any contractual remuneration paid to a worker in respect of a period of leave goes towards discharging any liability of the employer to make payments under this regulation in respect of that period; and, conversely, any payment of remuneration under this regulation in respect of a period goes towards discharging any liability of the employer to pay contractual remuneration in respect of that period.

17 ENTITLEMENTS UNDER OTHER PROVISIONS

Where during any period a worker is entitled to a rest period, rest break or annual leave both under a provisions of these Regulations and under a separate provision (including a provision of his contract), he may not exercise the two rights separately, but may, in taking a rest period, break or leave during that period, take advantage of whichever right is, in any particular respect, the more favourable.

Part III EXCEPTIONS

19 DOMESTIC SERVICE

Regulations 4(1) and (2), 5A(1) and (4),6(1), (2) and (7), 6A, 7(1), (2) and (6) and 8
do not apply in relation to a worker employed as a domestic servant in a private household.

20 UNMEASURED WORKING TIME

(1)   Regulations 4(1) and (2), 6(1), (2) and (7), 10(1), 11(1) and (2) and 12(1) do not apply in relation to a worker where, on account of the specific characteristics of the activity in which he is engaged, the duration of his working time is not measured or predetermined or can be determined by the worker himself, as may be the case for—
  (a)   managing executives or other persons with autonomous decision-taking powers;
  (b)   family workers; or
  (c)   workers officiating at religious ceremonies in churches and religious communities.

21 OTHER SPECIAL CASE

Subject to regulation 24, regulations 6(1), (2) and (7), 10(1), 11(1) and (2) and 12(1) do not apply in relation to a worker—
  (a)   where the worker's activities are such that his place of work and place of residence are distant from one another, including cases where the worker is employed in offshore work, or his different places of work are distant from one another;

(b)   where the worker is engaged in security and surveillance activities requiring a permanent presence in order to protect property and persons, as may be the case for security guards and caretakers or security firms;

(c)   where the worker's activities involve the need for continuity of service or production, as may be the case in relation to—
  (i)   services relating to the reception, treatment or care provided by hospitals or similar establishments (including the activities of doctors in training), residential institutions and prisons;
  (ii) work at docks or airports;
  (iii) press, radio, television, cinematographic production, postal and telecommunications services and civil protection services;
  (iv) gas, water and electricity production, transmission and distribution, household refuse collection and incineration;
  (v)   industries in which work cannot be interrupted on technical grounds;
  (vi) research and development activities;
  (vii) agriculture;
  (viii) the carriage of passengers on regular urban transport services;

(d)   where there is a foreseeable surge of activity, as may be the case in relation to—
  (i)   agriculture;
  (ii) tourism; and
  (iii) postal services;

(e)   where the worker's activities are affected by—
  (i)   an occurrence due to unusual and unforeseeable circumstances, beyond the control of the worker's employer;
  (ii) exceptional events, the consequences of which could not have been avoided despite the exercise of all due care by the employer; or
  (iii) an accident or the imminent risk of an accident;

(f)   where the worker works in railway transport and—
  (i)   his activities are intermittent;
  (ii) he spends his working time on board trains; or
  (iii) his activities are linked to transport timetables and to ensuring the continuity and regularity of traffic.

22 SHIFT WORKERS

(1)   Subject to regulation 24—
  (a)   regulation 10(1) does not apply in relation to a shift worker when he changes shift and cannot take a daily rest period between the end of one shift and the start of the next one;
  (b)   paragraphs (1) and (2) of regulation 11 do not apply in relation to a shift worker when he changes shift and cannot take a weekly rest period between the end of one shift and the start of the next one; and
  (c)   neither regulation 10(1) nor paragraphs (1) and (2) of regulation 11 apply to workers engaged in activities involving periods of work split up over the day, as may be the case for cleaning staff.

(2)   For the purposes of this regulation—

"shift worker" means any worker whose work schedule is part of shift work; and

"shift work" means any method of organizing work in shifts whereby workers succeed each other at the same workstations according to a certain pattern, including a rotating pattern, and which may be continuous or discontinuous, entailing the need for workers to work at different times over a given period of days or weeks.

23 COLLECTIVE AND WORKFORCE AGREEMENTS

A collective agreement or a workforce agreement may—

(a) modify or exclude the application of regulations 6(1) to (3) and (7), 10(1), 11(1) and (2) and 12(1), and

(b) for objective or technical reasons or reasons concerning the organization of work, modify the application of regulation 4(3) and (4) by the substitution, for each reference to 17 weeks, of a different period, being a period not exceeding 52 weeks,

in relation to particular workers or groups of workers.

24 COMPENSATORY REST

Where the application of any provision of these Regulations is excluded by regulation 21 or 22, or is modified or excluded by means of a collective agreement or a workforce agreement under regulation 23(a), and a worker is accordingly required by his employer to work during a period which would otherwise be a rest period or rest break—

(a) his employer shall wherever possible allow him to take an equivalent period of compensatory rest, and

(b) in exceptional cases in which it is not possible, for objective reasons, to grant such a period of rest, his employer shall afford him such protection as may be appropriate in order to safeguard the worker's health and safety.

24A MOBILE WORKERS

(1) Regulations 6(1), (2) and (7), 10(1), 11(1) and (2) and 12(1) do not apply to a mobile worker in relation to whom the application of those regulations is not excluded by any provision of regulation 18.

(2) A mobile worker, to whom paragraph (1) applies, is entitled to adequate rest, except where the worker's activities are affected by any of the matters referred to in regulation 21(e).

(3) For the purposes of this regulation, "adequate rest" means that a worker has regular rest periods, the duration of which are expressed in units of time and which are sufficiently long and continuous to ensure that, as a result of fatigue or other irregular working patterns, he does not cause injury to himself, to fellow workers or to others and that he does not damage his health, either in the short term or in the longer term.

26A ENTITLEMENT TO ADDITIONAL ANNUAL LEAVE UNDER A RELEVANT AGREEMENT

(1) Regulation 13A does not apply in relation to a worker whose employer, as at 1st October 2007 and by virtue of a relevant agreement, provides each worker employed by him with an annual leave entitlement of 1.6 weeks or 8 days (whichever is the lesser) in addition to each worker's entitlement under regulation 13, provided that such additional annual leave—

(a) may not be replaced by a payment in lieu except in relation to a worker whose employment is terminated;

   (b) may not be carried forward into a leave year other than that which immediately follows the leave year in respect of which the leave is due; and

   (c) is leave for which the worker is entitled to be paid at not less than the rate of a week's pay in respect of each week of leave, calculated in accordance with sections 221 to 224 of the 1996 Act, modified such that—

      (i) references to the employee are references to the worker;

     (ii) references to the employee's contract of employment are references to the worker's contract;

    (iii) the calculation date is the first day of the period of leave in question; and

    (iv) the references to sections 227 and 228 do not apply.

(2)   Notwithstanding paragraph (1), any additional annual leave in excess of 1.6 weeks or 8 days (whichever is the lesser) to which a worker is entitled, shall not be subject to the conditions of that paragraph.

(3)   This regulation shall cease to apply to a worker from the day when an employer ceases to provide additional annual leave in accordance with the conditions in paragraph (1).

(4)   This regulation does not apply to workers to whom the Agricultural Wages (Scotland) Act 1949 applies (as that Act had effect on 1 July 1999).

27 YOUNG WORKERS: FORCE MAJEURE

(1)   Regulations 5A, 6A, 10(2) and 12(4) do not apply in relation to a young worker where his employer requires him to undertake work which no adult worker is available to perform and which—

   (a) is occasioned by either—

      (i) an occurrence due to unusual and unforeseeable circumstances, beyond the employer's control, or

     (ii) exceptional events, the consequences of which could not have been avoided despite the exercise of all due care by the employer;

   (b) is of a temporary nature; and

   (c) must be performed immediately.

(2)   Where the application of regulation 5A, 6A, 10(2) or 12(4) is excluded by paragraph (1), and a young worker is accordingly required to work during a period which would otherwise be a rest period or rest break, his employer shall allow him to take an equivalent period of compensatory rest within the following three weeks.

27A OTHER EXCEPTIONS RELATING TO YOUNG WORKERS

(1)   Regulation 5A does not apply in relation to a young worker where—

   (a) the young worker's employer requires him to undertake work which is necessary either to maintain continuity of service or production or to respond to a surge in demand for a service or product;

   (b) no adult worker is available to perform the work, and

   (c) performing the work would not adversely affect the young worker's education or training.

(2)   Regulation 6A does not apply in relation to a young worker employed—

   (a) in a hospital or similar establishment, or

   (b) in connection with cultural, artistic, sporting or advertising activities,

in the circumstances referred to in paragraph (1).

(3)   Regulation 6A does not apply, except in so far as it prohibits work between midnight and 4 a.m., in relation to a young worker employed in—

(a) agriculture;

(b) retail trading;

(c) postal or newspaper deliveries;

(d) a catering business;

(e) a hotel, public house, restaurant, bar or similar establishment, or

(f) a bakery,

in the circumstances referred to in paragraph (1).

(4)   Where the application of regulation 6A is excluded by paragraph (2) or (3), and a young worker is accordingly required to work during a period which would otherwise be a rest period or rest break—

(a) he shall be supervised by an adult worker where such supervision is necessary for the young worker's protection, and

(b) he shall be allowed an equivalent period of compensatory rest.

Part IV MISCELLANEOUS

28 ENFORCEMENT

(1)   In this regulation, regulations 29—29E and Schedule 3—

"the 1974 Act" means the Health and Safety at Work etc. Act 1974;

"the Civil Aviation Authority" means the authority referred to in section 2(1) of the Civil Aviation Act 1982;

"code of practice" includes a standard, a specification and any other documentary form of practical guidance;

"enforcement authority" means the Executive, a local authority, the Civil Aviation Authority, VOSA or the Office of Rail Regulation;

"the Executive" means the Health and Safety Executive referred to in section 10(1) of the 1974 Act;

"local authority" means—

(a) in relation to England, a county council so far as they are the council for an area for which there are no district councils, a district council, a London borough council, the Common Council of the City of London, the Sub-Treasurer of the Inner Temple or the Under-Treasurer of the Middle Temple;

(b) in relation to Wales, a county council or a county borough council;

(c) in relation to Scotland, a council constituted under section 2 of the Local Government etc. (Scotland) Act 1994;

"premises" includes any place and, in particular, includes—

(a) any vehicle, vessel, aircraft or hovercraft;

(b) any installation on land (including the foreshore and other land intermittently covered by water), any offshore installation, and any other installation (whether floating, or resting on the seabed or the subsoil thereof, or resting on other land covered with water or the subsoil thereof) and

(c) any tent or movable structure;

"relevant civil aviation worker" means a mobile worker who works mainly on board civil aircraft, excluding any worker to whom regulation 18(2)(b) applies;

"the relevant requirements" means the following provisions—

(a) regulations 4(2), 5A(4), 6(2) and (7), 6A, 7(1), (2) and (6), 8, 9 and 27A(4)(a);
(b) regulation 24, in so far as it applies where regulation 6(1), (2) or (7) is modified or excluded, and
(c) regulation 24A(2), in so far as it applies where regulations 6(1), (2) or (7) is excluded;

"relevant road transport worker" means a mobile worker to whom one or more of the following applies—

(a) Council Regulation (EEC) 3820/85,
(b) the European Agreement concerning the Work of Crews of Vehicles engaged in International Road Transport (AETR) of 1st July 1970, and
(c) the United Kingdom domestic driver's hours code, which is set out in Part VI of the Transport Act 1968;

"the relevant statutory provisions" means—

(a) the provisions of the 1974 Act and of any regulations made under powers contained in that Act; and
(b) while and to the extent that they remain in force, the provisions of the Acts mentioned in Schedule 1 to the 1974 Act and which are specified in the third column of that Schedule and the regulations, orders or other instruments of a legislative character made or having effect under a provision so specified; and

"VOSA" means the Vehicle and Operator Services Agency.

(2) It shall be the duty of the Executive to make adequate arrangements for the enforcement of the relevant requirements except to the extent that—

(a) a local authority is made responsible for their enforcement by paragraph (3);
(b) the Civil Aviation Authority is made responsible for their enforcement by paragraph (5)
(c) VOSA is made responsible for their enforcement by paragraph (6); or
(d) the Office of Rail Regulation is made responsible for their enforcement by paragraph (3A).

(3) Where the relevant requirements apply in relation to workers employed in premises in respect of which a local authority is responsible, under the Health and Safety (Enforcing Authority) Regulations 1998, for enforcing any of the relevant statutory provisions, it shall be the duty of that authority to enforce those requirements.

(3A) Where the relevant requirements apply in relation to workers employed in the carrying out of any of the activities specified in regulation 3(2) of the Health and Safety (Enforcing Authority for Railways and Other Guided Transport Systems) Regulations 2006 it shall be the duty of the Office of Rail Regulation to enforce those requirements.

(4) The duty imposed on local authorities by paragraph (3) shall be performed in accordance with such guidance as may be given to them by the Executive.

(5) It shall be the duty of the Civil Aviation Authority to enforce the relevant requirements in relation to relevant civil aviation workers.

(6) It shall be the duty of VOSA to enforce the relevant requirements in relation to relevant road transport workers.

(7) The provisions of Schedule 3 shall apply in relation to the enforcement of the relevant requirements.

29 OFFENCES

(1)   An employer who fails to comply with any of the relevant requirements shall be guilty of an offence.

(2)   The provisions of paragraph (3) shall apply where an inspector is exercising or has exercised any power conferred by Schedule 3.

(3)   It is an offence for a person—
    (a) to contravene any requirement imposed by the inspector under paragraph 2 of Schedule 3;
    (b) to prevent or attempt to prevent any other person from appearing before the inspector or from answering any question to which the inspector may by virtue of paragraph 2(2)(e) of Schedule 3 require an answer;
    (c) to contravene any requirement or prohibition imposed by an improvement notice or a prohibition notice (including any such notice as is modified on appeal);
    (d) intentionally to obstruct the inspector in the exercise or performance of his powers or duties;
    (e) to use or disclose any information in contravention of paragraph 8 of Schedule 3;
    (f) to make a statement which he knows to be false or recklessly to make a statement which is false, where the statement is made in purported compliance with a requirement to furnish any information imposed by or under these Regulations.

(4)   An employer guilty of an offence under paragraph (1) shall be liable—
    (a) on summary conviction, to a fine not exceeding the statutory maximum;
    (b) on conviction on indictment, to a fine.

(5)   A person guilty of an offence under paragraph (3) shall be liable to the penalty prescribed in relation to that provision by paragraphs (6), (7) or (8) as the case may be.

(6)   A person guilty of an offence under sub-paragraph (3)(a), (b) or (d) shall be liable on summary conviction to a fine not exceeding level 5 on the standard scale.

(7)   A person guilty of an offence under sub-paragraph (3)(c) shall be liable—
    (a) on summary conviction, to imprisonment for a term not exceeding three months, or a fine not exceeding the statutory maximum;
    (b) on conviction on indictment, to imprisonment for a term not exceeding two years, or a fine, or both.

(8)   A person guilty of an offence under any of the sub-paragraphs of paragraph (3) not falling within paragraphs (6) or (7) above, shall be liable—
    (a) on summary conviction, to a fine not exceeding the statutory maximum;
    (b) on conviction on indictment—
        (i) if the offence is under sub-paragraph (3)(e), to imprisonment for a term not exceeding two years or a fine or both;
        (ii) if the offence is not one to which the preceding sub-paragraph applies, to a fine.

(9)   The provisions set out in regulations 29A–29E below shall apply in relation to the offences provided for in paragraphs (1) and (3).

29A OFFENCES DUE TO FAULT OF OTHER PERSON

Where the commission by any person of an offence is due to the act or default of some other person, that other person shall be guilty of the offence, and a person may be charged with and convicted of the offence by virtue of this paragraph whether or not proceedings are taken against the first-mentioned person.

29B OFFENCES BY BODIES CORPORATE

(1) Where an offence committed by a body corporate is proved to have been committed with the consent or connivance of, or to have been attributable to any neglect on the part of, any director, manager, secretary or other similar officer of the body corporate or a person who was purporting to act in any such capacity, he as well as the body corporate shall be guilty of that offence and shall be liable to be proceeded against and punished accordingly.

(2) Where the affairs of a body corporate are managed by its members, the preceding paragraph shall apply in relation to the acts and defaults of a member in connection with his functions of management as if he were a director of the body corporate.

29C RESTRICTION ON INSTITUTION OF PROCEEDINGS IN ENGLAND AND WALES

Proceedings for an offence shall not, in England and Wales, be instituted except by an inspector or by or with the consent of the Director of Public Prosecutions.

29 DPROSECUTIONS BY INSPECTORS

(1) An inspector, if authorised in that behalf by an enforcement authority, may, although not of counsel or a solicitor, prosecute before a magistrate's court proceedings for an offence under these Regulations.

(2) This regulation shall not apply to Scotland.

29 EPOWER OF COURT TO ORDER CAUSE OF OFFENCE TO BE REMEDIED

(1) Where a person is convicted of an offence in respect of any matters which appear to the court to be matters which it is in his power to remedy, the court may, in addition to or instead of imposing any punishment, order him, within such time as may be fixed by the order, to take such steps as may be specified in the order for remedying the said matters.

(2) The time fixed by an order under paragraph (1) may be extended or further extended by order of the court on an application made before the end of that time as originally fixed or as extended under this paragraph, as the case may be.

(3) Where a person is ordered under paragraph (1) to remedy any matters, that person shall not be liable under these Regulations in respect of those matters in so far as they continue during the time fixed by the order or any further time allowed under paragraph (2).

30 REMEDIES

(1) A worker may present a complaint to an employment tribunal that his employer—
   (a) has refused to permit him to exercise any right he has under—
       (i)   regulation 10(1) or (2), 11(1), (2) or (3), 12(1) or (4), 13 or 13A;
       (ii) regulation 24, in so far as it applies where regulation 10(1), 11(1) or (2) or 12(1) is modified or excluded;
       (iii) regulation 24A, in so far as it applies where regulation 10(1), 11(1) or (2) or 12(1) is excluded; or
       (iv) regulation 25(3), 27A(4)(b) or 27(2); or
   (b) has failed to pay him the whole or any part of any amount due to him under regulation 14(2) or 16(1).

(2)   An employment tribunal shall not consider a complaint under this regulation unless it is presented—

(a)   before the end of the period of three months (or, in a case to which regulation 38(2) applies, six months) beginning with the date on which it is alleged that the exercise of the right should have been permitted (or in the case of a rest period or leave extending over more than one day, the date on which it should have been permitted to begin) or, as the case may be, the payment should have been made;

(b)   within such further period as the tribunal considers reasonable in a case where it is satisfied that it was not reasonably practicable for the complaint to be presented before the end of that period of three or, as the case may be, six months.

(2A)   Where the period within which a complaint must be presented in accordance with paragraph (2) is extended by regulation 15 of the Employment Act 2002 (Dispute Resolution) Regulations 2004, the period within which the complaint must be presented shall be the extended period rather than the period in paragraph (2).

(3)   Where an employment tribunal finds a complaint under paragraph (1)(a) well-founded, the tribunal—

(a)   shall make a declaration to that effect, and

(b)   may make an award of compensation to be paid by the employer to the worker.

(4)   The amount of the compensation shall be such as the tribunal considers just and equitable in all the circumstances having regard to—

(a)   the employer's default in refusing to permit the worker to exercise his right, and

(b)   any loss sustained by the worker which is attributable to the matters complained of.

(5)   Where on a complaint under paragraph (1)(b) an employment tribunal finds that an employer has failed to pay a worker in accordance with regulation 14(2) or 16(1), it shall order the employer to pay to the worker the amount which it finds to be due to him.

35 RESTRICTIONS ON CONTRACTING OUT

(1)   Any provision in an agreement (whether a contract of employment or not) is void in so far as it purports—

(a)   to exclude or limit the operation of any provisions of these Regulations, save in so far as these Regulations provide for an agreement to have that effect, or

(b)   to preclude a person from bringing proceedings under these Regulations before an employment tribunal.

(2)   Paragraph (1) does not apply to—

(a)   any agreement to refrain from instituting or continuing proceedings where a conciliation officer has taken action under section 18 of the Employment Tribunals Act 1996 (conciliation); or

(b)   any agreement to refrain from instituting or continuing proceedings within section 18(1)(ff) of the Employment Tribunals Act 1996 (proceedings under these Regulations where conciliation is available), if the conditions regulating compromise agreements under these Regulations are satisfied in relation to the agreement.

(3)   For the purposes of paragraph (2)(b) the conditions regulating compromise agreements under these Regulations are that—

(a)   the agreement must be in writing,

(b)   the agreement must relate to the particular complaint,

(c)   the worker must have received advice from a relevant independent adviser as to the terms and effect of the proposed agreement and, in particular, its effect on his ability to pursue his rights before an employment tribunal,

(d) there must be in force, when the adviser gives the advice, a contract of insurance, or an indemnity provided for members of a profession or professional body, covering the risk of a claim by the worker in respect of loss arising in consequence of the advice,

(e) the agreement must identify the adviser, and

(f) the agreement must state that the conditions regulating compromise agreements under these Regulations are satisfied.

(4) A person is a relevant independent adviser for the purposes of paragraph (3)(c)—

(a) if he is a qualified lawyer,

(b) if he is an officer, official, employee or member of an independent trade union who has been certified in writing by the trade union as competent to give advice and as authorised to do so on behalf of the trade union, or

(c) if he works at an advice centre (whether as an employee or as a volunteer) and has been certified in writing by the centre as competent to give advice and as authorised to do so on behalf of the centre.

(5) But a person is not a relevant independent adviser for the purposes of paragraph (3)(c) in relation to the worker—

(a) if he is, is employed by or is acting in the matter for the employer or an associated employer,

(b) in the case of a person within paragraph (4)(b) or (c), if the trade union or advice centre is the employer or an associated employer, or

(c) in the case of a person within paragraph (4)(c), if the worker makes a payment for the advice received from him.

(6) In paragraph (4)(a), "qualified lawyer" means—

(a) as respects England and Wales, a person who, for the purposes of the Legal Services Act 2007), is an authorised person in relation to an activity which constitutes the exercise of a right of audience or the conduct of litigation (within the meaning of that Act); and

(b) as respects Scotland, an advocate (whether in practice as such or employed to give legal advice), or a solicitor who holds a practising certificate.

(6A) A person shall be treated as being a qualified lawyer within paragraph (6)(a) if he is a Fellow of the Institute of Legal Executives employed by a solicitors' practice.

(7) For the purposes of paragraph (5) any two employers shall be treated as associated if—

(a) one is a company of which the other (directly or indirectly) has control; or

(b) both are companies of which a third person (directly or indirectly) has control; and "associated employer" shall be construed accordingly.

Part V SPECIAL CLASSES OF PERSON

35 AGENCY WORKERS NOT OTHERWISE "WORKERS"

(1) This regulation applies in any case where an individual ("the agency worker")—

(a) is supplied by a person ("the agent") to do work for another ("the principal") under a contract or other arrangements made between the agent and the principal; but

(b) is not, as respects that work, a worker, because of the absence of a worker's contract between the individual and the agent or the principal; and

(c) is not a party to a contract under which he undertakes to do the work for another party to the contract whose status is, by virtue of the contract, that of a client or customer of any profession or business undertaking carried on by the individual.

(2)   In a case where this regulation applies, the other provisions of these Regulations shall have effect as if there were a worker's contract for the doing of the work by the agency worker made between the agency worker and—

(a)   whichever of the agent and the principal is responsible for paying the agency worker in respect of the work; or

(b)   if neither the agent nor the principal is so responsible, whichever of them pays the agency worker in respect of the work,

and as if that person were the agency worker's employer.

37 CROWN EMPLOYMENT

(1)   Subject to paragraph (4) and regulation 38, these Regulations have effect in relation to Crown employment and persons in Crown employment as they have effect in relation to other employment and other workers.

(2)   In paragraph (1) "Crown employment" means employment under or for the purposes of a government department or any officer or body exercising on behalf of the Crown functions conferred by a statutory provision.

(3)   For the purposes of the application of the provisions of these Regulations in relation to Crown employment in accordance with paragraph (1)—

(a)   references to a worker shall be construed as references to a person in Crown employment; and

(b)   references to a worker's contract shall be construed as references to the terms of employment of a person in Crown employment.

(4)   No act or omission by the Crown which is an offence under regulation 29 shall make the Crown criminally liable, but the High Court or, in Scotland, the Court of Session may, on the application of a person appearing to the Court to have an interest, declare any such act or omission unlawful.

42 NON-EMPLOYED TRAINEES

For the purposes of these Regulations, a person receiving relevant training, otherwise than under a contract of employment, shall be regarded as a worker, and the person whose undertaking is providing the training shall be regarded as his employer.

SCHEDULE 1 WORKFORCE AGREEMENTS

1

An agreement is a workforce agreement for the purposes of these Regulations if the following conditions are satisfied—

(a)   the agreement is in writing;

(b)   it has effect for a specified period not exceeding five years;

(c)   it applies either—

(i)   to all of the relevant members of the workforce, or

(ii)   to all of the relevant members of the workforce who belong to a particular group;

(d)   the agreement is signed—

(i)   in the case of an agreement of the kind referred to in sub-paragraph (c)(i), by the representatives of the workforce, and in the case of an agreement of the kind referred to in sub-paragraph (c)(ii) by the representatives of the group to which the agreement applies (excluding, in either case, any representative not a relevant member of the workforce on the date on which the agreement was first made available for signature), or

(ii) if the employer employed 20 or fewer workers on the date referred to in sub-paragraph (d)(i), either by the appropriate representatives in accordance with that sub-paragraph or by the majority of the workers employed by him;

(e) before the agreement was made available for signature, the employer provided all the workers to whom it was intended to apply on the date on which it came into effect with copies of the text of the agreement and such guidance as those workers might reasonably require in order to understand it fully.

2

For the purposes of this Schedule—

"a particular group" is a group of the relevant members of a workforce who undertake a particular function, work at a particular workplace or belong to a particular department or unit within their employer's business;

"relevant members of the workforce" are all of the workers employed by a particular employer, excluding any worker whose terms and conditions of employment are provided for, wholly or in part, in a collective agreement;

"representatives of the workforce" are workers duly elected to represent the relevant members of the workforce, "representatives of the group" are workers duly elected to represent the members of a particular group, and representatives are "duly elected" if the election at which they were elected satisfied the requirements of paragraph 3 of this Schedule.

3

The requirements concerning elections referred to in paragraph 2 are that—

(a) the number of representatives to be elected is determined by the employer;

(b) the candidates for election as representatives of the workforce are relevant members of the workforce, and the candidates for election as representatives of a group are members of the group;

(c) no worker who is eligible to be a candidate is unreasonably excluded from standing for election;

(d) all the relevant members of the workforce are entitled to vote for representatives of the workforce, and all the members of a particular group are entitled to vote for representatives of the group;

(e) the workers entitled to vote may vote for as many candidates as there are representatives to be elected;

(f) the election is conducted so as to secure that—
(i) so far as is reasonably practicable, those voting do so in secret, and
(ii) the votes given at the election are fairly and accurately counted.

As amended by the Working Time Regulations 1999/3372 reg 3(1)(a), reg 3(1)(b), reg 3(1)(c), reg 3(2)(a), reg 3(2)(b), reg 4; Management of Health and Safety at Work Regulations 1999/3242 Sch 2 para 1; Working Time (Amendment) Regulations 2001/3256 reg 2(2), reg 2(3), reg 2(4), reg 2(6), reg 3; Working Time (Amendment) Regulations 2002/3128 reg 3, reg 4, reg 5, reg 6, reg 7, reg 8, reg 10(a), reg 10(b), reg 11, reg 12, reg 13(a), reg 13(b), reg 14(b), reg 17, reg 18(a), reg 18(b); Employment Act 2002 (Dispute Resolution) Regulations 2004/752 reg 17(f); Working Time (Amendment) Regulations 2003/1684 reg 3(a), reg 3(b), reg 3(c), reg 5(a), reg 5(b), reg 5(c), reg 5(d), reg 6, reg 10, reg 11, Working Time Regulations 1998 (Amendment) Regulations 2004/2516 reg 2; Health and Safety (Enforcing Authority for Railways and Other Guided Transport Systems) Regulations 2006/557 Sch 1 para 7(a), Sch 1 para 7(b)(ii), Sch 1 para 7(c); Working Time (Amendment) Regulations 2006/99 reg 2; Working Time (Amendment) (No.2) Regulations 2006/2389 reg 2; Working Time (Amendment) Regulations 2007/2079 reg 2(2), reg 2(4), reg 2(5), reg 2(6), reg 2(7), reg 2(8), reg 2(9), reg 2(5), reg 2(3), reg 2(11); Legislative Reform (Health and Safety Executive) Order 2008/960 Sch 3 para 1; Legal Services Act 2007 (Consequential Amendments) Order 2009/3348 art 23.

MATERNITY AND PARENTAL LEAVE ETC. REGULATIONS 1999/3312

Part I GENERAL

2 INTERPRETATION

(1)   In these Regulations—

"the 1996 Act" means the Employment Rights Act 1996;

"additional adoption leave" means leave under section 75B of the 1996 Act;

"additional maternity leave" means leave under section 73 of the 1996 Act;

"business" includes a trade or profession and includes any activity carried on by a body of persons (whether corporate or unincorporated);

"child" means a person under the age of eighteen;

"childbirth" means the birth of a living child or the birth of a child whether living or dead after 24 weeks of pregnancy;

"collective agreement" means a collective agreement within the meaning of section 178 of the Trade Union and Labour Relations (Consolidation) Act 1992, the trade union parties to which are independent trade unions within the meaning of section 5 of that Act;

"contract of employment" means a contract of service or apprenticeship, whether express or implied, and (if it is express) whether oral or in writing;

"disability living allowance" means the disability living allowance provided for in Part III of the Social Security Contributions and Benefits Act 1992;

"employee" means an individual who has entered into or works under (or, where the employment has ceased, worked under) a contract of employment;

"employer" means the person by whom an employee is (or, where the employment has ceased, was) employed;

"expected week of childbirth" means the week, beginning with midnight between Saturday and Sunday, in which it is expected that childbirth will occur, and "week of childbirth" means the week, beginning with midnight between Saturday and Sunday, in which childbirth occurs;

"job", in relation to an employee returning after maternity leave or parental leave, means the nature of the work which she is employed to do in accordance with her contract and the capacity and place in which she is so employed;

"ordinary maternity leave" means leave under section 71 of the 1996 Act;

"parental leave" means leave under regulation 13(1);

"parental responsibility" has the meaning given by section 3 of the Children Act 1989, and "parental responsibilities" has the meaning given by section 1(3) of the Children (Scotland) Act 1995;

"statutory leave" means leave provided for in Part 8 of the 1996 Act;

"statutory maternity leave" means ordinary maternity leave and additional maternity leave;

"statutory maternity leave period" means the period during which the employee is on statutory maternity leave;

"workforce agreement" means an agreement between an employer and his employees or their representatives in respect of which the conditions set out in Schedule 1 to these Regulations are satisfied.

(2)   A reference in any provision of these Regulations to a period of continuous employment is to a period computed in accordance with Chapter I of Part XIV of the 1996 Act, as if that provision were a provision of that Act.

(3)   For the purposes of these Regulations any two employers shall be treated as associated if—
   (a) one is a company of which the other (directly or indirectly) has control; or
   (b) both are companies of which a third person (directly or indirectly) has control;
        and "associated employer" shall be construed accordingly.

(4)   In these Regulations, unless the context otherwise requires—
   (a) a reference to a numbered regulation or schedule is to the regulation or schedule in these Regulations bearing that number;
   (b) a reference in a regulation or schedule to a numbered paragraph is to the paragraph in that regulation or schedule bearing that number, and
   (c) a reference in a paragraph to a lettered sub-paragraph is to the sub-paragraph in that paragraph bearing that letter.

Part II MATERNITY LEAVE

4 ENTITLEMENT TO ORDINARY MATERNITY LEAVE AND TO ADDITIONAL MATERNITY LEAVE

(1)   An employee is entitled to ordinary maternity leave and to additional maternity leave provided that she satisfies the following conditions—

(a) no later than the end of the fifteenth week before her expected week of childbirth, or, if that is not reasonably practicable, as soon as is reasonably practicable, she notifies her employer of—
   (i)   her pregnancy;
   (ii) the expected week of childbirth, and
   (iii) the date on which she intends her ordinary maternity leave period to start, and
(b) if requested to do so by her employer, she produces for his inspection a certificate from—
   (i)   a registered medical practitioner, or
   (ii) a registered midwife,
        stating the expected week of childbirth.

(1A) An employee who has notified her employer under paragraph (1)(a)(iii) of the date on which she intends her ordinary maternity leave period to start may subsequently vary that date, provided that she notifies her employer of the variation at least—
(a) 28 days before the date varied, or
(b) 28 days before the new date,
whichever is the earlier, or, if that is not reasonably practicable, as soon as is reasonably practicable.

(2)   Notification under paragraph (1)(a)(iii) or (1A)—
(a) shall be given in writing, if the employer so requests, and
(b) shall not specify a date earlier than the beginning of the eleventh week before the expected week of childbirth.

(3)   Where, by virtue of regulation 6(1)(b), an employee's ordinary maternity leave period commences with the day which follows the first day after the beginning of the fourth week before the expected week of childbirth on which she is absent from work wholly or partly because of pregnancy—
(a) paragraph (1) does not require her to notify her employer of the date specified in that paragraph, but
(b) (whether or not she has notified him of that date) she is not entitled to ordinary maternity leave or to additional maternity leave unless she notifies him as soon as is reasonably practicable that she is absent from work wholly or partly because of pregnancy and of the date on which her absence on that account began.

(4)   Where, by virtue of regulation 6(2), an employee's ordinary maternity leave period commences on the day which follows the day on which childbirth occurs—
(a) paragraph (1) does not require her to notify her employer of the date specified in that paragraph, but
(b) (whether or not she has notified him of that date) she is not entitled to ordinary maternity leave or to additional maternity leave unless she notifies him as soon as is reasonably practicable after the birth that she has given birth and of the date on which the birth occurred.

(5)   The notification provided for in paragraphs (3)(b) and (4)(b) shall be given in writing, if the employer so requests.

6 COMMENCEMENT OF MATERNITY LEAVE PERIODS

(1)   Subject to paragraph (2), an employee's ordinary maternity leave period commences with the earlier of—

(a) the date which she notifies to her employer, in accordance with regulation 4, as the date on which she intends her ordinary maternity leave period to start, or, if by virtue of the provision for variation in that regulation she has notified more than one such date, the last date she notifies, and

(b) the day which follows the first day after the beginning of the fourth week before the expected week of childbirth on which she is absent from work wholly or partly because of pregnancy.

(2) Where the employee's ordinary maternity leave period has not commenced by virtue of paragraph (1) when childbirth occurs, her ordinary maternity leave period commences on the day which follows the day on which childbirth occurs.

(3) An employee's additional maternity leave period commences on the day after the last day of her ordinary maternity leave period.

7 DURATION OF MATERNITY LEAVE PERIODS

(1) Subject to paragraphs (2) and (5), an employee's ordinary maternity leave period continues for the period of 26 weeks from its commencement, or until the end of the compulsory maternity leave period provided for in regulation 8 if later.

(2) Subject to paragraph (5), where any requirement imposed by or under any relevant statutory provision prohibits the employee from working for any period after the end of the period determined under paragraph (1) by reason of her having recently given birth, her ordinary maternity leave period continues until the end of that later period.

(3) In paragraph (2), "relevant statutory provision" means a provision of—
(a) an enactment, or
(b) an instrument under an enactment,
other than a provision for the time being specified in an order under section 66(2) of the 1996 Act.

(4) Subject to paragraph (5), where an employee is entitled to additional maternity leave her additional maternity leave period continues until the end of the period of 26 weeks from the day on which it commenced.

(5) Where the employee is dismissed after the commencement of an ordinary or additional maternity leave period but before the time when (apart from this paragraph) that period would end, the period ends at the time of the dismissal.

(6) An employer who is notified under any provision of regulation 4 of the date on which, by virtue of any provision of regulation 6, an employee's ordinary maternity leave period will commence or has commenced shall notify the employee of the date on which her additional maternity leave period shall end.

(7) The notification provided for in paragraph (6) shall be given to the employee—
(a) where the employer is notified under regulation 4(1)(a)(iii), (3)(b) or (4)(b), within 28 days of the date on which he received the notification;
(b) where the employer is notified under regulation 4(1A), within 28 days of the date on which the employee's ordinary maternity leave period commenced.

8 COMPULSORY MATERNITY LEAVE

The prohibition in section 72 of the 1996 Act, against permitting an employee who satisfies prescribed conditions to work during a particular period (referred to as a "compulsory maternity leave period"), applies—

(a) in relation to an employee who is entitled to ordinary maternity leave, and

(b) in respect of the period of two weeks which commences with the day on which childbirth occurs.

9 APPLICATION OF TERMS AND CONDITIONS DURING ORDINARY MATERNITY LEAVE AND ADDITIONAL MATERNITY LEAVE

(1)   An employee who takes ordinary maternity leave or additional maternity leave—
    (a) is entitled, during the period of leave, to the benefit of all of the terms and conditions of employment which would have applied if she had not been absent, and
    (b) is bound, during that period, by any obligations arising under those terms and conditions, subject only to the exceptions in sections 71(4)(b) and 73(4)(b) of the 1996 Act.

(2)   In paragraph (1)(a), "terms and conditions" has the meaning given by sections 71(5) and 73(5) of the 1996 Act, and accordingly does not include terms and conditions about remuneration.

(3)   For the purposes of sections 71 and 73 of the 1996 Act, only sums payable to an employee by way of wages or salary are to be treated as remuneration.

(4)   In the case of accrual of rights under an employment-related benefit scheme within the meaning given by Schedule 5 to the Social Security Act 1989, nothing in paragraph (1)(a) concerning the treatment of additional maternity leave shall be taken to impose a requirement which exceeds the requirements of paragraph 5 of that Schedule.

10 REDUNDANCY DURING MATERNITY LEAVE

(1)   This regulation applies where, during an employee's ordinary or additional maternity leave period, it is not practicable by reason of redundancy for her employer to continue to employer her under her existing contract of employment.

(2)   Where there is a suitable available vacancy, the employee is entitled to be offered (before the end of her employment under her existing contract) alternative employment with her employer or his successor, or an associated employer, under a new contract of employment which complies with paragraph (3) (and takes effect immediately on the ending of her employment under the previous contract).

(3)   The new contract of employment must be such that—
    (a) the work to be done under it is of a kind which is both suitable in relation to the employee and appropriate for her to do in the circumstances, and
    (b) its provisions as to the capacity and place in which she is to be employed, and as to the other terms and conditions of her employment, are not substantially less favourable to her than if she had continued to be employed under the previous contract.

11 REQUIREMENT TO NOTIFY INTENTION TO RETURN DURING A MATERNITY LEAVE PERIOD

(1)   An employee who intends to return to work earlier than the end of her additional maternity leave period, shall give to her employer not less than 8 weeks' notice of the date on which she intends to return.

(2)   If an employee attempts to return to work earlier than the end of her additional maternity leave period without complying with paragraph (1), her employer is entitled to postpone her return to a date such as will secure, subject to paragraph (3), that he has 8 weeks' notice of her return.

(2A) An employee who complies with her obligations in paragraph (1) or whose employer has postponed her return in the circumstances described in paragraph (2), and who then decides to return to work—

    (a) earlier than the original return date, must give her employer not less than 8 weeks' notice of the date on which she now intends to return;

    (b) later than the original return date, must give her employer not less than 8 weeks' notice ending with the original return date.

(2B) In paragraph (2A) the "original return date" means the date which the employee notified to her employer as the date of her return to work under paragraph (1), or the date to which her return was postponed by her employer under paragraph (2).

(3) An employer is not entitled under paragraph (2) to postpone an employee's return to work to a date after the end of the relevant maternity leave period.

(4) If an employee whose return to work has been postponed under paragraph (2) has been notified that she is not to return to work before the date to which her return was postponed, the employer is under no contractual obligation to pay her remuneration until the date to which her return was postponed if she returns to work before that date.

(5) This regulation does not apply in a case where the employer did not notify the employee in accordance with regulation 7(6) and (7) of the date on which her additional maternity leave period would end.

12A WORK DURING MATERNITY LEAVE PERIOD

(1) Subject to paragraph (5), an employee may carry out up to 10 days' work for her employer during her statutory maternity leave period without bringing her maternity leave to an end.

(2) For the purposes of this regulation, any work carried out on any day shall constitute a day's work.

(3) Subject to paragraph (4), for the purposes of this regulation, work means any work done under the contract of employment and may include training or any activity undertaken for the purposes of keeping in touch with the workplace.

(4) Reasonable contact from time to time between an employee and her employer which either party is entitled to make during a maternity leave period (for example to discuss an employee's return to work) shall not bring that period to an end.

(5) Paragraph (1) shall not apply in relation to any work carried out by the employee at any time from childbirth to the end of the period of two weeks which commences with the day on which childbirth occurs.

(6) This regulation does not confer any right on an employer to require that any work be carried out during the statutory maternity leave period, nor any right on an employee to work during the statutory maternity leave period.

(7) Any days' work carried out under this regulation shall not have the effect of extending the total duration of the statutory maternity leave period.

Part III PARENTAL LEAVE

13 ENTITLEMENT TO PARENTAL LEAVE

(1) An employee who—

    (a) has been continuously employed for a period of not less than a year or is to be treated as having been so employed by virtue of paragraph (1A); and

    (b) has, or expects to have, responsibility for a child,

is entitled, in accordance with these Regulations, to be absent from work on parental leave for the purpose of caring for that child.

(1A) If, in a case where regulation 15(2) or (3) applies—
(a) the employee was employed, during the period between 15th December 1998 and 9th January 2002, by a person other than the person who was his employer on 9th January 2002, and
(b) the period of his employment by that person (or, if he was employed by more than one person during that period, any such person) was not less than a year, then, for the purposes of paragraph (1), he shall be treated as having been continuously employed for a period of not less than a year.;

(2) An employee has responsibility for a child, for the purpose of paragraph (1), if—
(a) he has parental responsibility or, in Scotland, parental responsibilities for the child; or
(b) he has been registered as the child's father under any provision of section 10(1) or 10A(1) of the Births and Deaths Registration Act 1953 or of section 18(1) or (2) of the Registration of Births, Deaths and Marriages (Scotland) Act 1965.

14 EXTENT OF ENTITLEMENT

(1) Except in the case referred to in paragraph (1A), an employee is entitled to thirteen weeks' leave in respect of any individual child.

(1A) An employee is entitled to eighteen weeks' leave in respect of a child who is entitled to a disability living allowance.

(2) Where the period for which an employee is normally required, under his contract of employment, to work in the course of a week does not vary, a week's leave for the employee is a period of absence from work which is equal in duration to the period for which he is normally required to work.

(3) Where the period for which an employee is normally required, under his contract of employment, to work in the course of a week varies from week to week or over a longer period, or where he is normally required under his contract to work in some weeks but not in others, a week's leave for the employee is a period of absence from work which is equal in duration to the period calculated by dividing the total of the periods for which he is normally required to work in a year by 52.

(4) Where an employee takes leave in periods shorter than the period which constitutes, for him, a week's leave under whichever of paragraphs (2) and (3) is applicable in his case, he completes a week's leave when the aggregate of the periods of leave he has taken equals the period constituting a week's leave for him under the applicable paragraph.

15

(1) Except in the cases referred to in paragraphs (2)–(4), an employee may not exercise any entitlement to parental leave in respect of a child after the date of the child's fifth birthday or, in the case of a child placed with the employee for adoption by him, on or after—
(a) the fifth anniversary of the date on which the placement began, or
(b) the date of the child's eighteenth birthday,
whichever is the earlier.

(2) In the case of child—
(a) born before 15th December 1999, whose fifth birthday was or is on or after that date, or
(b) placed with the employee for adoption by him before 15th December 1999, the fifth anniversary of whose placement was or is on or after that date,

not being a case to which paragraph (3) or (4) applies, any entitlement to parental leave may not be exercised after 31st March 2005.

(3) In the case of a child who is entitled to a disability living allowance, any entitlement to parental leave may not be exercised on or after the date of the child's eighteenth birthday.

(4) In a case where—
(a) the provisions set out in Schedule 2 apply, and
(b) the employee was unable to take leave in respect of a child within the time permitted in the case of that child under paragraphs (1) or (2) because the employer postponed the period of leave under paragraph 6 of that Schedule,
the entitlement to leave is exercisable until the end of the period to which the leave was postponed.

16 DEFAULT PROVISIONS IN RESPECT OF PARENTAL LEAVE

The provisions set out in Schedule 2 apply in relation to parental leave in the case of an employee whose contract of employment does not include a provision which—
(a) confers an entitlement to absence from work for the purpose of caring for a child, and

(b) incorporates or operates by reference to all or part of a collective agreement or workforce agreement.

Part IV PROVISIONS APPLICABLE IN RELATION TO MORE THAN ONE KIND OF ABSENCE

17 APPLICATION OF TERMS AND CONDITIONS DURING PERIODS OF LEAVE

An employee who takes parental leave—
(a) is entitled, during the period of leave, to the benefit of her employer's implied obligation to her of trust and confidence and any terms and conditions of her employment relating to—
(i) notice of the termination of the employment contract by her employer;
(ii) compensation in the event of redundancy, or
(iii) disciplinary or grievance procedures;

(b) is bound, during that period, by her implied obligation to her employer of good faith and any terms and conditions of her employment relating to—
(i) notice of the termination of the employment contract by her;
(ii) the disclosure of confidential information;
(iii) the acceptance of gifts or other benefits, or
(iv) the employee's participation in any other business.

18 RIGHT TO RETURN AFTER MATERNITY OR PARENTAL LEAVE

(1) An employee who returns to work after a period of ordinary maternity leave, or a period of parental leave of four weeks or less, which was—
(a) an isolated period of leave, or
(b) the last of two or more consecutive periods of statutory leave which did not include any period of additional maternity leave or additional adoption leave, or a period of parental leave of more than four weeks,
is entitled to return to the job in which she was employed before her absence.

(2) An employee who returns to work after—

    (a) a period of additional maternity leave, or a period of parental leave of more than four weeks, whether or not preceded by another period of statutory leave, or

    (b) a period of ordinary maternity leave, or a period of parental leave of four weeks or less, not falling within the description in paragraph (1)(a) or (b) above,

is entitled to return from leave to the job in which she was employed before her absence or, if it is not reasonably practicable for the employer to permit her to return to that job, to another job which is both suitable for her and appropriate for her to do in the circumstances.

(3) The reference in paragraphs (1) and (2) to the job in which an employee was employed before her absence is a reference to the job in which she was employed—

    (a) if her return is from an isolated period of statutory leave, immediately before that period began;

    (b) if her return is from consecutive periods of statutory leave, immediately before the first such period.

(4) This regulation does not apply where regulation 10 applies.

18A INCIDENTS OF THE RIGHT TO RETURN

(1) An employee's right to return under regulation 18(1) or (2) is a right to return—

    (a) with her seniority, pension rights and similar rights as they would have been if she had not been absent, and

    (b) on terms and conditions not less favourable than those which would have applied if she had not been absent.

(2) In the case of accrual of rights under an employment-related benefit scheme within the meaning given by Schedule 5 to the Social Security Act 1989, nothing in paragraph (1)(a) concerning the treatment of additional maternity leave shall be taken to impose a requirement which exceeds the requirements of paragraphs 5 and 6 of that Schedule.

(3) The provisions in paragraph (1) for an employee to be treated as if she had not been absent refer to her absence—

    (a) if her return is from an isolated period of statutory leave, since the beginning of that period;

    (b) if her return is from consecutive periods of statutory leave, since the beginning of the first such period.

19 PROTECTION FROM DETRIMENT

(1) An employee is entitled under section 47C of the 1996 Act not to be subjected to any detriment by any act, or any deliberate failure to act, by her employer done for any of the reasons specified in paragraph (2).

(2) The reasons referred to in paragraph (1) are that the employee—

    (a) is pregnant;

    (b) has given birth to a child;

    (c) is the subject of a relevant requirement, or a relevant recommendation, as defined by section 66(2) of the 1996 Act;

    (d) took, sought to take or availed herself of the benefits of, ordinary maternity leave or additional maternity leave;

    (e) took or sought to take—

        (ii) parental leave, or

        (iii) time off under section 57A of the 1996 Act;

(ee) failed to return after a period of ordinary or additional maternity leave in a case where—

(i) the employer did not notify her, in accordance with regulation 7(6) and (7) or otherwise, of the date on which the period in question would end, and she reasonably believed that that period had not ended, or

(ii) the employer gave her less than 28 days' notice of the date on which the period in question would end, and it was not reasonably practicable for her to return on that date;

(eee) undertook, considered undertaking or refused to undertake work in accordance with regulation 12A;

(f) declined to sign a workforce agreement for the purpose of these Regulations, or

(g) being—

(i) a representative of members of the workforce for the purpose of Schedule 1, or

(ii) a candidate in an election in which any person elected will, on being elected, become such a representative,

performed (or proposed to perform) any functions or activities as such a representative or candidate.

(3) For the purpose of paragraph (2)(d), a woman avails herself of the benefits of ordinary maternity leave if, during her ordinary maternity leave period, she avails herself of the benefit of any of the terms and conditions of her employment preserved by section 71 of the 1996 Act and regulation 9 during that period.

(3A) For the purposes of paragraph (2)(d), a woman avails herself of the benefits of additional maternity leave if, during her additional maternity leave period, she avails herself of the benefit of any of the terms and conditions of her employment preserved by section 73 of the 1996 Act and regulation 9 during that period.

(4) Paragraph (1) does not apply in a case where the detriment in question amounts to dismissal within the meaning of Part X of the 1996 Act.

(5) Paragraph (2)(b) only applies where the act or failure to act takes place during the employee's ordinary or additional maternity leave period.

(6) For the purpose of paragraph(5)—

(a) where an act extends over a period, the reference to the date of the act is a reference to the last day of that period, and

(b) a failure to act is to be treated as done when it was decided on.

(7) For the purposes of paragraph (6), in the absence of evidence establishing the contrary an employer shall be taken to decide on a failure act—

(a) when he does an act inconsistent with doing the failed act, or

(b) if he has done no such inconsistent act, when the period expires within which he might reasonably have been expected to do the failed act if it were to be done.

20 UNFAIR DISMISSAL

(1) An employee who is dismissed is entitled under section 99 of the 1996 Act to be regarded for the purposes of Part X of that Act as unfairly dismissed if—

(a) the reason or principal reason for the dismissal is of a kind specified in paragraph (3), or

(b) the reason or principal reason for the dismissal is that the employee is redundant, and regulation 10 has not been complied with.

(2) An employee who is dismissed shall also be regarded for the purposes of Part X of the 1996 Act as unfairly dismissed if—

(a) the reason (or, if more than one, the principal reason) for the dismissal is that the employee was redundant;

(b) it is shown that the circumstances constituting the redundancy applied equally to one or more employees in the same undertaking who held positions similar to that held by the employee and who have not been dismissed by the employer, and

(c) it is shown that the reason (or, if more than one, the principal reason) for which the employee was selected for dismissal was a reason of a kind specified in paragraph (3).

(3)   The kinds of reason referred to in paragraph (1) and (2) are reasons connected with—

(a)   the pregnancy of the employee;

(b)   the fact that the employee has given birth to a child;

(c)   the application of a relevant requirement, or a relevant recommendation, as defined by section 66(2) of the 1996 Act;

(d)   the fact that she took, sought to take or availed herself of the benefits of, ordinary maternity leave or additional maternity leave;

(e)   the fact that she took or sought to take—

(ii)   parental leave, or

(iii) time off under section 57A of the 1996 Act;

(ee) the fact that she failed to return after a period of ordinary or additional maternity leave in a case where—

(i)   the employer did not notify her, in accordance with regulation 7(6) and (7) or otherwise, of the date on which the period in question would end, and she reasonably believed that that period had not ended, or

(ii)   the employer gave her less than 28 days' notice of the date on which the period in question would end, and it was not reasonably practicable for her to return on that date;

(eee) the fact that she undertook, considered undertaking or refused to undertake work in accordance with regulation 12A;

(f)   the fact that she declined to sign a workforce agreement for the purposes of these Regulations, or

(g)   the fact that the employee, being—

(i)   a representative of members of the workforce for the purposes of Schedule 1, or

(ii)   a candidate in an election in which any person elected will, on being elected, become such a representative,

performed (or proposed to perform) any functions or activities as such a representative or candidate.

(4)   Paragraphs (1)(b) and (3)(b) only apply where the dismissal ends the employee's ordinary or additional maternity leave period.

(5)   Paragraphs (3) and (3A) of regulation 19 apply for the purposes of paragraph (3)(d) as they apply for the purposes of paragraph (2)(d) of that regulation.

(7)   Paragraph (1) does not apply in relation to an employee if—

(a)   it is not reasonably practicable for a reason other than redundancy for the employer (who may be the same employer or a successor of his) to permit her to return to a job which is both suitable for her and appropriate for her to do in the circumstances;

(b)   an associated employer offers her a job of that kind, and

(c)   she accepts or unreasonably refuses that offer.

(8)   Where on a complaint of unfair dismissal any question arises as to whether the operation of paragraph (1) is excluded by the provisions of paragraph (7), it is for the employer to show that the provisions in question were satisfied in relation to the complainant.

21 CONTRACTUAL RIGHTS TO MATERNITY OR PARENTAL LEAVE

(1) This regulation applies where an employee is entitled to—
   (a) ordinary maternity leave;
   (b) additional maternity leave, or
   (c) parental leave,
   (referred to in paragraph (2) as a "statutory right") and also to a right which corresponds to that right and which arises under the employee's contract of employment or otherwise.

(2) In a case where this regulation applies—
   (a) the employee may not exercise the statutory right and the corresponding right separately but may, in taking the leave for which the two rights provide, take advantage of whichever right is, in any particular respect, the more favourable, and
   (b) the provisions of the 1996 Act and of these Regulations relating to the statutory right apply, subject to any modifications necessary to give effect to any more favourable contractual terms, to the exercise of the composite right described in sub-paragraph (a) as they apply to the exercise of the statutory right

SCHEDULE 1 WORKFORCE AGREEMENTS

1

An agreement is a workforce agreement for the purposes of these Regulations if the following conditions are satisfied—

(a) the agreement is in writing;

(b) it has effect for a specified period not exceeding five years;

(c) it applies either—
   (i) to all of the relevant members of the workforce, or
   (ii) to all of the relevant members of the workforce who belong to a particular group;

(d) the agreement is signed—
   (i) in the case of an agreement of the kind referred to in sub-paragraph (c)(i), by the representatives of the workforce, and in the case of an agreement of the kind referred to in sub-paragraph (c)(ii), by the representatives of the group to which the agreement applies (excluding, in either case, any representative not a relevant member of the workforce on the date on which the agreement was first made available for signature), or
   (ii) if the employer employed 20 or fewer employees on the date referred to in sub-paragraph (d)(i), either by the appropriate representatives in accordance with that sub-paragraph or by the majority of the employees employed by him;
   and

(e) before the agreement was made available for signature, the employer provided all the employees to whom it was intended to apply on the date on which it came into effect with copies of the text of the agreement and such guidance as those employees might reasonably require in order to understand it in full.

2

For the purposes of this Schedule—

"a particular group" is a group of the relevant members of a workforce who undertake a particular function, work at a particular workplace or belong to a particular department or unit within their employer's business;

"relevant members of the workforce" are all of the employees employed by a particular employer, excluding any employee whose terms and conditions of employment are provided for, wholly or in part, in a collective agreement;

"representatives of the workforce" are employees duly elected to represent the relevant members of the workforce, "representatives of the group" are employees duly elected to represent the members of a particular group, and representatives are "duly elected" if the election at which they were elected satisfied the requirements of paragraph 3 of this Schedule.

3

The requirements concerning elections referred to in paragraph 2 are that—
(a)   the number of representatives to be elected is determined by the employer;

(b)   the candidates for election as representatives of the workforce are relevant members of the workforce, and the candidates for election as representatives of a group are members of the group;

(c)   no employee who is eligible to be a candidate is unreasonably excluded from standing for election;

(d)   all the relevant members of the workforce are entitled to vote for representatives of the workforce, and all the members of a particular group are entitled to vote for representatives of the group;

(e)   the employees entitled to vote may vote for as many candidates as there are representatives to be elected, and

(f)   the election is conducted so as to secure that—
(i)   so far as is reasonably practicable, those voting do so in secret, and
(ii)   the votes given at the election are fairly and accurately counted.

SCHEDULE 2 DEFAULT PROVISIONS IN RESPECT OF PARENTAL LEAVE

Conditions of entitlement

1

An employee may not exercise any entitlement to parental leave unless—
(a)   he has complied with any request made by his employer to produce for the employer's inspection evidence of his entitlement, of the kind described in paragraph 2;

(b)   he has given his employer notice, in accordance with whichever of paragraphs 3 to 5 is applicable, of the period of leave he proposes to take, and

(c)   in a case where paragraph 6 applies, his employer has not postponed the period of leave in accordance with that paragraph.

2

The evidence to be produced for the purpose of paragraph 1(a) is such evidence as may reasonably be required of—
(a)   the employee's responsibility or expected responsibility for the child in respect of whom the employee proposes to take parental leave;

(b)   the child's date of birth or, in the case of a child who was placed with the employee for adoption, the date on which the placement began, and

(c)   in a case where the employee's right to exercise an entitlement to parental leave under regulation 15, or to take a particular period of leave under paragraph 7, depends upon whether the child is entitled to a disability living allowance, the child's entitlement to that allowance.

2A

Where regulation 13(1A) applies, and the employee's entitlement to parental leave arises out of a period of employment by a person other than the person who was his employer on 9th January 2002, the employee may not exercise the entitlement unless he has given his employer notice of that period of employment, and provided him with such evidence of it as the employer may reasonably require.

Notice to be given to employer

3

Except in a case where paragraph 4 or 5 applies, the notice required for the purpose of paragraph 1(b) is notice which—
(a)   specifies the dates on which the period of leave is to begin and end, and

(b)   is given to the employer at least 21 days before the date on which that period is to begin.

4

Where the employee is the father of the child in respect of whom the leave is to be taken, and the period of leave is to begin on the date on which the child is born, the notice required for the purpose of paragraph 1(b) is notice which—
(a)   specifies the expected week of childbirth and the duration of the period of leave, and

(b)   is given to the employer at least 21 days before the beginning of the expected week of childbirth.

5

Where the child in respect of whom the leave is to be taken is to be placed with the employee for adoption by him and the leave is to begin on the date of the placement, the notice required for the purpose of paragraph 1(b) is notice which—
(a)   specifies the week in which the placement is expected to occur and the duration of the period of leave, and

(b)   is given to the employer at least 21 days before the beginning of that week, or, if that is not reasonably practicable, as soon as is reasonably practicable.

Postponement of leave

6

An employer may postpone a period of parental leave where—
(a)   neither paragraph 4 nor paragraph 5 applies, and the employee has accordingly given the employer notice in accordance with paragraph 3;

(b)   the employer considers that the operation of his business would be unduly disrupted if the employee took leave during the period identified in his notice;

(c)   the employer agrees to permit the employee to take a period of leave—
       (i)   of the same duration as the period identified in the employee's notice,
       (ii)   beginning on a date determined by the employer after consulting the employee, which is no later than six months after the commencement of that period; and
       (iii) ending before the date of the child's eighteenth birthday.

(d)   the employer gives the employee notice in writing of the postponement which—
       (i)   states the reason for it, and
       (ii)   specifies the dates on which the period of leave the employer agrees to permit the employee to take will begin and end,
    and

(e)   that notice is given to the employee not more than seven days after the employee's notice was given to the employer.

Minimum periods of leave

7

An employee may not take parental leave in a period other than the period which constitutes a week's leave for him under regulation 14 or a multiple of that period, except in a case where the child in respect of whom leave is taken is entitled to a disability living allowance.

Maximum annual leave allowance

8

An employee may not take more than four weeks' leave in respect of any individual child during a particular year.

9

For the purposes of paragraph 8, a year is the period of twelve months beginning—
(a)   except where sub-paragraph (b) applies, on the date on which the employee first became entitled to take parental leave in respect of the child in question, or

(b)   in a case where the employee's entitlement has been interrupted at the end of period of continuous employment, on the date on which the employee most recently became entitled to take parental leave in respect of that child,

    and each successive period of twelve months beginning on the anniversary of that date.

As amended by the Law Reform (Parent and Child) (Scotland) Act 1986; Family Law Reform Act 1987, s 24, s 25; Maternity and Parental Leave (Amendment) Regulations 2001/4010 reg 3(a), reg 3(b), reg 3(c), reg 4(a), reg 4(b), reg 5, reg 6(a), reg 6(b)(i), reg 6(b)(ii), reg 6(b)(iii); Maternity and Parental Leave (Amendment) Regulations 2002/2789 reg 4(a), reg 4(b), reg 4(c), reg 5(a), reg 5(b), reg 5(c), reg 5(d)(i), reg 5(d)(ii), reg 5(d)(iii), reg 5(e)(i), reg 5(e)(ii), reg 7(a)(i), reg 7(a)(ii), reg 7(a)(iii), reg 7(b)(i), reg 7(b)(ii), reg 7(c), reg 8(a), reg 8(b), reg 8(c), reg 9, reg 10(c), reg 12, reg 13(a), reg 13(b), reg 14; Pensions Act 2004, s 265(1); Maternity and Parental Leave etc. and the Paternity and Adoption Leave (Amendment) Regulations 2006/2014 reg 4, reg 5(a), reg 5(b), reg 7(a), reg 7(b), reg 8(a), reg 8(b)(i), reg 8(b)(ii), reg 8(c), reg 8(d), reg 9, reg 10, reg 11(a), reg 11(b), reg 11(c); Paternity and Adoption Leave (Amendment)

Regulations 2008/1966 reg 4(1)(a), reg 4(1)(b), reg 4(1)(c), reg 4(1)(d), reg 4(1)(e), reg 4(1)(f), reg 4(2), reg 5(a), reg 5(b), reg 5(c), reg 6(a), reg 6(b), reg 6(c), reg 7(a), reg 7(b), reg 7(c).

TRADE UNION RECOGNITION (METHOD OF COLLECTIVE BARGAINING) ORDER 2000/1300

2 SPECIFICATION OF METHOD

The method specified for the purposes of paragraphs 31(3) and 63(2) of Schedule A1 to the Trade Union and Labour Relations (Consolidation) Act 1992 is the method set out under the heading "the specified method" in the Schedule to this Order.

SCHEDULE 1 PREAMBLE

The method specified below ("the specified method") is one by which collective bargaining might be conducted in the particular, and possibly rare, circumstances discussed in the following paragraph. The specified method is not designed to be applied as a model for voluntary procedural agreements between employers and unions. Because most voluntary agreements are not legally binding and are usually concluded in a climate of trust and co-operation, they do not need to be as prescriptive as the specified method. However, the Central Arbitration Committee ("CAC") must take the specified method into account when exercising its powers to impose a method of collective bargaining under paragraphs 31(3) and 63(2) of Schedule A1 to the Trade Union and Labour Relations (Consolidation) Act 1992. In exercising those powers the CAC may depart from the specified method to such extent as it thinks appropriate in the circumstances of individual cases.

Paragraph 31(3) provides for the CAC to impose a method of collective bargaining in cases where a union (or unions, where two or more unions act jointly) has been recognised by an employer by means of an award of the CAC under Part I of Schedule A1, but the employer and union(s) have been unable to agree a method of bargaining between themselves, or have failed to follow an agreed method. Paragraph 63(2) provides for the CAC to impose a bargaining method in cases where an employer and a union (or unions) have entered an agreement for recognition, as defined by paragraph 52 of Part II of Schedule A1, but cannot agree a method of bargaining, or have failed to follow the agreed method.

The bargaining method imposed by the CAC has effect as if it were a legally binding contract between the employer and the union(s). If one party believes the other is failing to respect the method, the first party may apply to the court for an order of specific performance, ordering the other party to comply with the method. Failure to comply with such an order could constitute contempt of court.

Once the CAC has imposed a bargaining method, the parties can vary it, including the fact that it is legally binding, by agreement provided that they do so in writing.

The fact that the CAC has imposed a method does not affect the rights of individual workers under either statute or their contracts of employment. For example, it does not prevent or limit the rights of individual workers to discuss, negotiate or agree with their employer terms of their contract of employment, which differ from the terms of any collective agreement into which the employer and the union may enter as a result of collective bargaining conducted by this method. Nor does the imposed method affect an individual's statutory entitlement to time off for trade union activities or duties.

In cases where the CAC imposes a bargaining method on the parties, the employer is separately obliged, in accordance with Section 70B of the Trade Union and Labour Relations (Consolidation) Act 1992 (as inserted by section 5 of the Employment Relations Act 1999), to consult union representatives periodically on his policy, actions and plans on training. The specified method does not discuss how such consultations should be organised.

The law confers certain entitlements on independent trade unions which are recognised for collective bargaining purposes. For example, employers must disclose, on request, certain types of information to the representatives of the recognised unions. The fact that the CAC has imposed a bargaining method does not affect these existing statutory entitlements.

THE SPECIFIED METHOD

The Parties

1   The method shall apply in each case to two parties, who are referred to here as the "employer" and the "union". Unless the text specifies otherwise, the term "union" should be read to mean "unions" in cases where two or more unions are jointly recognised.

The Purpose

2   The purpose is to specify a method by which the employer and the union conduct collective bargaining concerning the pay, hours and holidays of the workers comprising the bargaining unit.

3   The employer shall not grant the right to negotiate pay, hours and holidays to any other union in respect of the workers covered by this method.

The Joint Negotiating Body

4   The employer and the union shall establish a Joint Negotiating Body (JNB) to discuss and negotiate the pay, hours and holidays of the workers comprising the bargaining unit. No other body or group shall undertake collective bargaining on the pay, hours and holidays of these workers, unless the employer and the union so agree.

JNB Membership

5   The membership of the JNB shall usually comprise three employer representatives (who together shall constitute the Employer Side of the JNB) and three union representatives (who together shall constitute the Union Side of the JNB). Each union recognised by the employer in respect of the bargaining unit shall be entitled to one seat at least. To meet this requirement, the Union Side may need to be larger than three and in this eventuality the employer shall be entitled to increase his representation on the JNB by the same number, if he wishes.

6   The employer shall select those individuals who comprise the Employer Side. The individuals must either be those who take the final decisions within the employer's organisation in respect of the pay, hours and holidays of the workers in the bargaining unit or who are expressly authorised by the employer to make recommendations directly to those who take such final decisions. Unless it would be unreasonable to do so, the employer shall select as a representative the most senior person responsible for employment relations in the bargaining unit.

7   The union shall select those individuals who comprise the Union Side in accordance with its own rules and procedures. The representatives must either be individuals employed by

the employer or individuals employed by the union who are officials of the union within the meaning of sections 1 and 119 of the Trade Union and Labour Relations (Consolidation) Act 1992 ("the 1992 Act").

8   The JNB shall determine their own rules in respect of the attendance at JNB meetings of observers and substitutes who deputise for JNB members.

Bargaining Procedure

14   The union's proposals for adjustments to pay, hours and holidays shall be dealt with on an annual basis, unless the two Sides agree a different bargaining period.

15   The JNB shall conduct these negotiations for each bargaining round according to the following staged procedure.

Step 1 — The union shall set out in writing, and send to the employer, its proposals (the "claim") to vary the pay, hours and holidays, specifying which aspects it wants to change. In its claim, the union shall set out the reasons for its proposals, together with the main supporting evidence at its disposal at the time. In cases where there is no established annual date when the employer reviews the pay, hours and holidays of all the workers in the bargaining unit, the union shall put forward its first claim within three months of this method being imposed (and by the same date in subsequent rounds). Where such a common review date is established, the union shall submit its first claim at least a month in advance of that date (and by the same date in subsequent rounds). In either case, the employer and the union may agree a different date by which the claim should be submitted each year. If the union fails to submit its claim by this date, then the procedure shall be ended for the bargaining round in question. Exceptionally, the union may submit a late claim without this penalty if its work on the claim was delayed while the Central Arbitration Committee considered a relevant complaint by the union of failure by the employer to disclose information for collective bargaining purposes.

Step 2 — Within ten working days of the Employer Side's receipt of the union's letter, a quorate meeting of the JNB shall be held to discuss the claim. At this meeting, the Union Side shall explain its claim and answer any reasonable questions arising to the best of its ability.

Step 3 — (a) Within fifteen working days immediately following the Step 2 meeting, the employer shall either accept the claim in full or write to the union responding to its claim. If the Employer Side requests it, a quorate meeting of the JNB shall be held within the fifteen day period to enable the employer to present this written response directly to the Union Side. In explaining the basis of his response, the employer shall set out in this written communication all relevant information in his possession. In particular, the written communication shall contain information costing each element of the claim and describing the business consequences, particularly any staffing implications, unless the employer is not required to disclose such information for any of the reasons specified in section 182(1) of the 1992 Act. The basis of these estimated costs and effects, including the main assumptions that the employer has used, shall be set out in the communication. In determining what information is disclosed as relevant, the employer shall be under no greater obligation that he is under the general duty imposed on him by sections 181 and 182 of the 1992 Act to disclose information for the purposes of collective bargaining.

(b) If the response contains any counter-proposals, the written communication shall set out the reasons for making them, together with the supporting evidence. The letter shall provide information estimating the costs and staffing consequences of implementing each element of the counter proposals, unless the employer is not required to disclose such information for any of the reasons specified in section 182(1) of the 1992 Act.

Step 4 — Within ten working days of the Union Side's receipt of the employer's written communication, a further quorate meeting of the JNB shall be held to discuss the employer's response. At this meeting, the Employer Side shall explain its response and answer any reasonable questions arising to the best of its ability.

Step 5 — If no agreement is reached at the Step 4 meeting (or the last of such meetings if more than one is held at that stage in the procedure), another quorate meeting of the JNB shall be held within ten working days. The union may bring to this meeting a maximum of two other individuals employed by the union who are officials within the meaning of the sections 1 and 119 of the 1992 Act. The employer may bring to the meeting a maximum of two other individuals who are employees or officials of an employer's organisation to which the employer belongs. These additional persons shall be allowed to contribute to the meeting, as if they were JNB members.

Step 6 — If no agreement is reached at the Step 5 meeting (or the last of such meetings if more than one meeting is held at that stage in the procedure), within five working days the employer and the union shall consider, separately or jointly, consulting ACAS about the prospect of ACAS helping them to find a settlement of their differences through conciliation. In the event that both parties agree to invite ACAS to conciliate, both parties shall give such assistance to ACAS as is necessary to enable it to carry out the conciliation efficiently and effectively.

16   The parties shall set aside half a working day for each JNB meeting, unless the Employer Side Chairman and the Union Side Chairman agree a different length of time for the meeting. Unless it is essential to do otherwise, meetings shall be held during the normal working time of most union members of the JNB. Meetings may be adjourned, if both Sides agree. Additional meetings at any point in the procedure may be arranged, if both Sides agree. In addition, if the Employer Side requests it, a meeting of the JNB shall be held before the union has submitted its claim or before the employer is required to respond, enabling the Employer Side to explain the business context within which the employer shall assess the claim.

17   The employer shall not vary the contractual terms affecting the pay, hours or holidays of workers in the bargaining unit, unless he has first discussed his proposals with the union. Such proposals shall normally be made by the employer in the context of his consideration of the union's claim at Steps 3 or 4. If, however, the employer has not tabled his proposals during that process and he wishes to make proposals before the next bargaining round commences, he must write to the union setting out his proposals and the reasons for making them, together with the supporting evidence. The letter shall provide information estimating the costs and staffing consequences of implementing each element of the proposals, unless the employer is not required to disclose such information for any of the reasons specified in section 182(1) of the 1992 Act. A quorate meeting of the JNB shall be held within five working days of the Union Side's receipt of the letter. If there is a failure to resolve the issue at that meeting, then meetings shall be arranged, and steps shall be taken, in accordance with Steps 5 and 6 of the above procedure.

18   Paragraph 17 does not apply to terms in the contract of an individual worker where that worker has agreed that the terms may be altered only by direct negotiation between the worker and the employer.

Collective Agreements

19   Any agreements affecting the pay, hours and holidays of workers in the bargaining unit, which the employer and the union enter following negotiations, shall be set down in writing and signed by the Chairman of the Employer Side and by the Chairman of the Union Side or, in their absence, by another JNB member on their respective Sides.

20   If either the employer or union consider that there has been a failure to implement the agreement, then that party can request in writing a meeting of the JNB to discuss the alleged failure. A quorate meeting shall be held within five working days of the receipt of the request by the JNB Secretary. If there is a failure to resolve the issue at that meeting, then meetings shall be arranged, and steps shall be taken, in accordance with Steps 5 and 6 of the above procedure.

Facilities and Time Off

21   If they are employed by the employer, union members of the JNB:
— shall be given paid time off by the employer to attend JNB meetings;
— shall be given paid time off by the employer to attend a two hour pre-meeting of the Union Side before each JNB meeting; and
— shall be given paid time off by the employer to hold a day-long meeting to prepare the claim at Step 1 in the bargaining procedure.
The union members of the JNB shall schedule such meetings at times which minimise the effect on production and services. In arranging these meetings, the union members of the JNB shall provide the employer and their line management with as much notice as possible and give details of the purpose of the time off, the intended location of the meeting and the timing and duration of the time off. The employer shall provide adequate heating and lighting for these meetings, and ensure that they are held in private.

22   If they are not employed by the employer, union members of the JNB or other union officials attending JNB meetings shall be given sufficient access to the employer's premises to allow them to attend Union Side pre-meetings, JNB meetings and meetings of the bargaining unit as specified in paragraph 23.

23   The employer shall agree to the union's reasonable request to hold meetings with members of the bargaining unit on company premises to discuss the Step 1 claim, the employer's offer or revisions to either. The request shall be made at least three working days in advance of the proposed meeting. However, the employer is not required to provide such facilities, if the employer does not possess available premises which can be used for meetings on the scale suggested by the union. The employer shall provide adequate heating and lighting for meetings, and ensure that the meeting is held in private. Where such meetings are held in working time, the employer is under no obligation to pay individuals for the time off. Where meetings take place outside normal working hours, they should be arranged at a time which is otherwise convenient for the workers.

24   Where resources permit, the employer shall make available to the Union Side of the JNB such typing, copying and word-processing facilities as it needs to conduct its business in private.

25   Where resources permit, the employer shall set aside a room for the exclusive use of the Union Side of the JNB. The room shall possess a secure cabinet and a telephone.

26   In respect of issues which are not otherwise specified in this method, the employer and the union shall have regard to the guidance issued in the ACAS Code of Practice on Time Off for Trade Union Duties and Activities and ensure that there is no unwarranted or unjustified failure to abide by it.

Disclosure of Information

27   The employer and the union shall have regard to the ACAS Code of Practice on the Disclosure of Information to Trade Unions for Collective Bargaining Purposes and ensure that there is no unwarranted or unjustified failure to abide by it in relation to the bargaining arrangements specified by this method.

Revision of the Method

28   The employer or the union may request in writing a meeting of the JNB to discuss revising any element of this method, including its status as a legally binding contract. A quorate meeting of the JNB shall be held within ten working days of the receipt of the request by the JNB Secretary. This meeting shall be held in accordance with the same arrangements for the holding of other JNB meetings.

General

29   The employer and the union shall take all reasonable steps to ensure that this method to conduct collective bargaining is applied efficiently and effectively.

30   The definition of a "working day" used in this method is any day other than a Saturday or a Sunday, Christmas Day or Good Friday, or a day which is a bank holiday.

31   All time limits mentioned in this method may be varied on any occasion, if both the employer and the union agree.

PART-TIME WORKERS (PREVENTION OF LESS FAVOURABLE TREATMENT) REGULATIONS 2000/1551

Part I   GENERAL AND INTERPRETATION

1   CITATION COMMENCEMENT AND INTERPRETATION

(1)   These Regulations may be cited as the Part-time Workers (Prevention of Less Favourable Treatment) Regulations 2000 and shall come into force on 1st July 2000.

(2)   In these Regulations—

"the 1996 Act" means the Employment Rights Act 1996;

"contract of employment" means a contract of service or of apprenticeship, whether express or implied, and (if it is express) whether oral or in writing;

"employee" means an individual who has entered into or works under or (except where a provision of these Regulations otherwise requires) where the employment has ceased, worked under a contract of employment;

"employer", in relation to any employee or worker, means the person by whom the employee or worker is or (except where a provision of these Regulations otherwise requires) where the employment has ceased, was employed;

"pro rata principle" means that where a comparable full-time worker receives or is entitled to receive pay or any other benefit, a part-time worker is to receive or be entitled to receive not less than the proportion of that pay or other benefit that the number of his weekly hours bears to the number of weekly hours of the comparable full-time worker;

"worker" means an individual who has entered into or works under or (except where a provision of these Regulations otherwise requires) where the employment has ceased, worked under—

(a) a contract of employment; or

(b) any other contract, whether express or implied and (if it is express) whether oral or in writing, whereby the individual undertakes to do or perform personally any work or services for another party to the contract whose status is not by virtue of the contract that of a client or customer of any profession or business undertaking carried on by the individual.

(3) In the definition of the pro rata principle and in regulations 3 and 4 "weekly hours" means the number of hours a worker is required to work under his contract of employment in a week in which he has no absences from work and does not work any overtime or, where the number of such hours varies according to a cycle, the average number of such hours.

2 MEANING OF FULL-TIME WORKER, PART-TIME WORKER AND COMPARABLE FULL-TIME WORKER

(1) A worker is a full-time worker for the purpose of these Regulations if he is paid wholly or in part by reference to the time he works and, having regard to the custom and practice of the employer in relation to workers employed by the worker's employer under the same type of contract, is identifiable as a full-time worker.

(2) A worker is a part-time worker for the purpose of these Regulations if he is paid wholly or in part by reference to the time he works and, having regard to the custom and practice of the employer in relation to workers employed by the worker's employer under the same type of contract, is not identifiable as a full-time worker.

(3) For the purposes of paragraphs (1), (2) and (4), the following shall be regarded as being employed under different types of contract—

(a) employees employed under a contract that is not a contract of apprenticeship;

(b) employees employed under a contract of apprenticeship;

(c) workers who are not employees;

(d) any other description of worker that it is reasonable for the employer to treat differently from other workers on the ground that workers of that description have a different type of contract.

(4) A full-time worker is a comparable full-time worker in relation to a part-time worker if, at the time when the treatment that is alleged to be less favourable to the part-time worker takes place—

(a) both workers are—

(i) employed by the same employer under the same type of contract, and

(ii) engaged in the same or broadly similar work having regard, where relevant, to whether they have a similar level of qualification, skills and experience; and

(b) the full-time worker works or is based at the same establishment as the part-time worker or, where there is no full-time worker working or based at that establishment who satisfies the requirements of sub-paragraph (a), works or is based at a different establishment and satisfies those requirements.

3 WORKERS BECOMING PART-TIME

(1)   This regulation applies to a worker who—
(a) was identifiable as a full-time worker in accordance with regulation 2(1); and
(b) following a termination or variation of his contract, continues to work under a new or varied contract, whether of the same type or not, that requires him to work for a number of weekly hours that is lower than the number he was required to work immediately before the termination or variation.

(2)   Notwithstanding regulation 2(4), regulation 5 shall apply to a worker to whom this regulation applies as if he were a part-time worker and as if there were a comparable full-time worker employed under the terms that applied to him immediately before the variation or termination.

(3)   The fact that this regulation applies to a worker does not affect any right he may have under these Regulations by virtue of regulation 2(4).

4 WORKERS RETURNING PART-TIME AFTER ABSENCE

(1)   This regulation applies to a worker who—
(a) was identifiable as a full-time worker in accordance with regulation 2(1) immediately before a period of absence (whether the absence followed a termination of the worker's contract or not);
(b) returns to work for the same employer within a period of less than twelve months beginning with the day on which the period of absence started;
(c) returns to the same job or to a job at the same level under a contract, whether it is a different contract or a varied contract and regardless of whether it is of the same type, under which he is required to work for a number of weekly hours that is lower than the number he was required to work immediately before the period of absence.

(2)   Notwithstanding regulation 2(4), regulation 5 shall apply to a worker to whom this regulation applies ("the returning worker") as if he were a part-time worker and as if there were a comparable full-time worker employed under—
(a) the contract under which the returning worker was employed immediately before the period of absence; or
(b) where it is shown that, had the returning worker continued to work under the contract mentioned in sub-paragraph (a) a variation would have been made to its term during the period of absence, the contract mentioned in that sub-paragraph including that variation.

(3)   The fact that this regulation applies to a worker does not affect any right he may have under these Regulations by virtue of regulation 2(4).

Part II RIGHTS AND REMEDIES

5 LESS FAVOURABLE TREATMENT OF PART-TIME WORKERS

(1)   A part-time worker has the right not to be treated by his employer less favourably than the employer treats a comparable full-time worker—
(a) as regards the terms of his contract; or
(b) by being subjected to any other detriment by any act, or deliberate failure to act, of his employer.

(2) The right conferred by paragraph (1) applies only if—
(a) the treatment is on the ground that the worker is a part-time worker, and
(b) the treatment is not justified on objective grounds.

(3) In determining whether a part-time worker has been treated less favourably than a comparable full-time worker the pro rata principle shall be applied unless it is inappropriate.

(4) A part-time worker paid at a lower rate for overtime worked by him in a period than a comparable full-time worker is or would be paid for overtime worked by him in the same period shall not, for that reason, be regarded as treated less favourably than the comparable full-time worker where, or to the extent that, the total number of hours worked by the part-time worker in the period, including overtime, does not exceed the number of hours the comparable full-time worker is required to work in the period, disregarding absences from work and overtime.

6 RIGHT TO RECEIVE A WRITTEN STATEMENT OF REASONS FOR LESS FAVOURABLE TREATMENT

(1) If a worker who considers that his employer may have treated him in a manner which infringes a right conferred on him by regulation 5 requests in writing from his employer a written statement giving particulars of the reasons for the treatment, the worker is entitled to be provided with such a statement within twenty-one days of his request.

(2) A written statement under this regulation is admissible as evidence in any proceedings under these Regulations.

(3) If it appears to the tribunal in any proceedings under these Regulations—
(a) that the employer deliberately, and without reasonable excuse, omitted to provide a written statement, or
(b) that the written statement is evasive or equivocal,
it may draw any inference which it considers it just and equitable to draw, including an inference that the employer has infringed the right in question.

(4) This regulation does not apply where the treatment in question consists of the dismissal of an employee, and the employee is entitled to a written statement of reasons for his dismissal under section 92 of the 1996 Act.

7 UNFAIR DISMISSAL AND THE RIGHT NOT TO BE SUBJECTED TO DETRIMENT

(1) An employee who is dismissed shall be regarded as unfairly dismissed for the purposes of Part X of the 1996 Act if the reason (or, if more than one, the principal reason) for the dismissal is a reason specified in paragraph (3).

(2) A worker has the right not to be subjected to any detriment by any act, or any deliberate failure to act, by his employer done on a ground specified in paragraph (3).

(3) The reasons or, as the case may be, grounds are—
(a) that the worker has—
(i)   brought proceedings against the employer under these Regulations;
(ii)   requested from his employer a written statement of reasons under regulation 6;
(iii) given evidence or information in connection with such proceedings brought by any worker;
(iv) otherwise done anything under these Regulations in relation to the employer or any other person;

      (v) alleged that the employer had infringed these Regulations; or

      (vi) refused (or proposed to refuse) to forgo a right conferred on him by these Regulations, or

    (b) that the employer believes or suspects that the worker has done or intends to do any of the things mentioned in sub-paragraph (a).

(4)   Where the reason or principal reason for dismissal or, as the case may be, ground for subjection to any act or deliberate failure to act, is that mentioned in paragraph (3)(a)(v), or (b) so far as it relates thereto, neither paragraph (1) nor paragraph (2) applies if the allegation made by the worker is false and not made in good faith.

(5)   Paragraph (2) does not apply where the determent in question amounts to the dismissal of an employee within the meaning of Part X of the 1996 Act.

8 COMPLAINTS TO EMPLOYMENT TRIBUNALS ETC.

(1)   Subject to regulation 7(5), a worker may present a complaint to an employment tribunal that his employer has infringed a right conferred on him by regulation 5 or 7(2).

(2)   Subject to paragraph (3), an employment tribunal shall not consider a complaint under this regulation unless it is presented before the end of the period of three months (or, in a case to which regulation 13 applies, six months) beginning with the date of the less favourable treatment or detriment to which the complaint relates or, where an act or failure to act is part of a series of similar acts or failures comprising the less favourable treatment or detriment, the last of them.

(3)   A tribunal may consider any such complaint which is out of time if, in all the circumstances of the case, it considers that it is just and equitable to do so.

(4)   For the purposes of calculating the date of the less favourable treatment or detriment under paragraph (2)—

    (a) where a term in a contract is less favourable, that treatment shall be treated, subject to paragraph (b), as taking place on each day of the period during which the term is less favourable;

    (b) where an application relies on regulation 3 or 4 the less favourable treatment shall be treated as occurring on, and only on, in the case of regulation 3, the first day on which the applicant worked under the new or varied contract and, in the case of regulation 4, the day on which the applicant returned; and

    (c) a deliberate failure to act contrary to regulation 5 or 7(2) shall be treated as done when it was decided on.

(5)   In the absence of evidence establishing the contrary, a person shall be taken for the purposes of paragraph (4)(c) to decide not to act—

    (a) when he does an act inconsistent with doing the failed act; or

    (b) if he has done no such inconsistent act, when the period expires within which he might reasonably have been expected to have done the failed act if it was to be done.

(6)   Where a worker presents a complaint under this regulation it is for the employer to identify the ground for the less favourable treatment or detriment.

(7)   Where an employment tribunal finds that a complaint presented to it under this regulation is well founded, it shall take such of the following steps as it considers just and equitable—

    (a) making a declaration as to the rights of the complainant and the employer in relation to the matters to which the complaint relates;

    (b) ordering the employer to pay compensation to the complainant;

(c) recommending that the employer take, within a specified period, action appearing to the tribunal to be reasonable, in all the circumstances of the case, for the purpose of obviating or reducing the adverse effect on the complainant of any matter to which the complaint relates.

(9) Where a tribunal orders compensation under paragraph (7)(b), the amount of the compensation awarded shall be such as the tribunal considers just and equitable in all the circumstances) having regard to—
(a) the infringement to which the complaint relates, and
(b) any loss which is attributable to the infringement having regard, in the case of an infringement of the right conferred by regulation 5, to the pro rata principle except where it is inappropriate to do so.

(10) The loss shall be taken to include—
(a) any expenses reasonably incurred by the complainant in consequence of the infringement, and
(b) loss of any benefit which he might reasonably be expected to have had but for the infringement.

(11) Compensation in respect of treating a worker in a manner which infringes the right conferred on him by regulation 5 shall not include compensation for injury to feelings.

(12) In ascertaining the loss the tribunal shall apply the same rule concerning the duty of a person to mitigate his loss as applies to damages recoverable under the common law of England and Wales or (as the case may be) Scotland.

(13) Where the tribunal finds that the act, or failure to act, to which the complaint relates was to any extent caused or contributed to by action of the complaint relates was to any extent caused or contributed to by action of the complainant, it shall reduce the amount of the compensation by such proportion as it considers just and equitable having regard to that finding.

(14) If the employer fails, without reasonable justification, to comply with a recommendation made by an employment tribunal under paragraph (7)(c) the tribunal may, if it thinks it just and equitable to do so—
(a) increase the amount of compensation required to be paid to the complainant in respect of the complaint, where an order was made under paragraph (7)(b); or
(b) make an order under paragraph (7)(b).

9 RESTRICTIONS ON CONTRACTING OUT

Section 203 of the 1996 Act1 (restrictions on contracting out) shall apply in relation to these Regulations as if they were contained in that Act.

Part III MISCELLANEOUS

11 LIABILITY OF EMPLOYERS AND PRINCIPALS

(1) Anything done by a person in the course of his employment shall be treated for the purposes of these Regulations as also done by his employer, whether or not it was done with the employer's knowledge or approval.

(2) Anything done by a person as agent for the employer with the authority of the employer shall be treated for the purposes of these Regulations as also done by the employer.

(3) In proceedings under these Regulations against any person in respect of an act alleged to have been done by a worker of his, it shall be a defence for that person to prove that he took such steps as were reasonably practicable to prevent the worker from—
(a) doing that act; or
(b) doing, in the course of his employment, acts of that discription.

Part IV SPECIAL CLASSES OF PERSON

12 CROWN EMPLOYMENT

(1) Subject to regulation 13, these Regulations have effect in relation to Crown employment and persons in Crown employment as they have effect in relation to other employment and other employees and workers.

(2) In paragraph (1) "Crown employment" means employment under or for the purposes of a government department or any officer or body exercising on behalf of the Crown functions conferred by a statutory provision.

(3) For the purposes of the application of the provisions of these Regulations in relation to Crown employment in accordance with paragraph (1)—
(a) references to an employee and references to a worker shall be construed as references to a person in Crown employment to whom the definition of employee or, as the case may be, worker is appropriate; and
(b) references to a contract in relation to an employee and references to a contract in relation to a worker shall be construed as references to the terms of employment of a person in Crown employment to whom the definition of employee or, as the case may be, worker is appropriate.

As amended by the Employment Rights (Dispute Resolution) Act 1998; Employment Relations Act 1999, s 9, s 44, Schedule 4 Part III para 1, para 5, Schedule 9.3; Unfair Dismissal and Statement of Reasons for Dismissal (Variation of Qualifying Period) Order 1999/1436, Article 3; Part-time Workers (Prevention of Less Favourable Treatment) Regulations 2000 (Amendment) Regulations 2002/2035 reg 2(a), reg 2(b)(i), reg 2(b)(ii).

FIXED-TERM EMPLOYEES (PREVENTION OF LESS FAVOURABLE TREATMENT) REGULATIONS 2002/2034

Part I GENERAL AND INTERPRETATION

1 CITATION, COMMENCEMENT AND INTERPRETATION

(1) These Regulations may be cited as the Fixed-term Employees (Prevention of Less Favourable Treatment) Regulations 2002 and shall come into force on 1st October 2002.

(2)   In these Regulations—

"the 1996 Act" means the Employment Rights Act 1996;

"collective agreement" means a collective agreement within the meaning of section 178 of the Trade Union and Labour Relations (Consolidation) Act 1992; the trade union parties to which are independent trade unions within the meaning of section 5 of that Act;

"employer", in relation to any employee, means the person by whom the employee is (or, where the employment has ceased, was) employed;

"fixed-term contract" means a contract of employment that, under its provisions determining how it will terminate in the normal course, will terminate—
(a) on the expiry of a specific term,
(b) on the completion of a particular task, or
(c) on the occurrence or non-occurrence of any other specific event other than the attainment by the employee of any normal and bona fide retiring age in the establishment for an employee holding the position held by him,

and any reference to "fixed-term" shall be construed accordingly;

"fixed-term employee" means an employee who is employed under a fixed-term contract;

"permanent employee" means an employee who is not employed under a fixed-term contract, and any reference to "permanent employment" shall be construed accordingly;

"pro rata principle" means that where a comparable permanent employee receives or is entitled to pay or any other benefit, a fixed-term employee is to receive or be entitled to such proportion of that pay or other benefit as is reasonable in the circumstances having regard to the length of his contract of employment and to the terms on which the pay or other benefit is offered;

"renewal" includes extension and references to renewing a contract shall be construed accordingly;

"workforce agreement" means an agreement between an employer and his employees or their representatives in respect of which the conditions set out in Schedule 1 to these Regulations are satisfied.

2 COMPARABLE EMPLOYEES

(1)   For the purposes of these Regulations, an employee is a comparable permanent employee in relation to a fixed-term employee if, at the time when the treatment that is alleged to be less favourable to the fixed-term employee takes place,
(a) both employees are—
(i)   employed by the same employer, and
(ii) engaged in the same or broadly similar work having regard, where relevant, to whether they have a similar level of qualification and skills; and
(b) the permanent employee works or is based at the same establishment as the fixed-term employee or, where there is no comparable permanent employee working or based at that establishment who satisfies the requirements of sub-paragraph (a), works or is based at a different establishment and satisfies those requirements.

(2)   For the purposes of paragraph (1), an employee is not a comparable permanent employee if his employment has ceased.

Part II **RIGHTS AND REMEDIES**

3 LESS FAVOURABLE TREATMENT OF FIXED-TERM EMPLOYEES

(1)   A fixed-term employee has the right not to be treated by his employer less favourably than the employer treats a comparable permanent employee—
(a) as regards the terms of his contract; or
(b) by being subjected to any other detriment by any act, or deliberate failure to act, of his employer.

(2)   Subject to paragraphs (3) and (4), the right conferred by paragraph (1) includes in particular the right of the fixed-term employee in question not to be treated less favourably than the employer treats a comparable permanent employee in relation to—
(a) any period of service qualification relating to any particular condition of service,
(b) the opportunity to receive training, or
(c) the opportunity to secure any permanent position in the establishment.

(3)   The right conferred by paragraph (1) applies only if—
(a) the treatment is on the ground that the employee is a fixed-term employee, and
(b) the treatment is not justified on objective grounds.

(4)   Paragraph (3)(b) is subject to regulation 4.

(5)   In determining whether a fixed-term employee has been treated less favourably than a comparable permanent employee, the pro rata principle shall be applied unless it is inappropriate.

(6)   In order to ensure that an employee is able to exercise the right conferred by paragraph (1) as described in paragraph (2)(c) the employee has the right to be informed by his employer of available vacancies in the establishment.

(7)   For the purposes of paragraph (6) an employee is "informed by his employer" only if the vacancy is contained in an advertisement which the employee has a reasonable opportunity of reading in the course of his employment or the employee is given reasonable notification of the vacancy in some other way.

4 OBJECTIVE JUSTIFICATION

(1)   Where a fixed-term employee is treated by his employer less favourably than the employer treats a comparable permanent employee as regards any term of his contract, the treatment in question shall be regarded for the purposes of regulation 3(3)(b) as justified on objective grounds if the terms of the fixed-term employee's contract of employment, taken as a whole, are at least as favourable as the terms of the comparable permanent employee's contract of employment.

(2)   Paragraph (1) is without prejudice to the generality of regulation 3(3)(b).

5 RIGHT TO RECEIVE A WRITTEN STATEMENT OF REASONS FOR LESS FAVOURABLE TREATMENT

(1)   If an employee who considers that his employer may have treated him in a manner which infringes a right conferred on him by regulation 3 requests in writing from his employer a written statement giving particulars of the reasons for the treatment, the employee is entitled to be provided with such a statement within twenty-one days of his request.

(2)   A written statement under this regulation is admissible as evidence in any proceedings under these Regulations.

(3)   If it appears to the tribunal in any proceedings under these Regulations—
(a) that the employer deliberately, and without reasonable excuse, omitted to provide a written statement, or
(b) that the written statement is evasive or equivocal,
it may draw any inference which it considers it just and equitable to draw, including an inference that the employer has infringed the right in question.

(4)   This regulation does not apply where the treatment in question consists of the dismissal of an employee, and the employee is entitled to a written statement of reasons for his dismissal under section 92 of the 1996 Act.

6 UNFAIR DISMISSAL AND THE RIGHT NOT TO BE SUBJECTED TO DETRIMENT

(1)   An employee who is dismissed shall be regarded as unfairly dismissed for the purposes of Part 10 of the 1996 Act 1 if the reason (or, if more than one, the principal reason) for the dismissal is a reason specified in paragraph (3).

(2)   An employee has the right not to be subjected to any detriment by any act, or any deliberate failure to act, of his employer done on a ground specified in paragraph (3).

(3)   The reasons or, as the case may be, grounds are—
(a) that the employee—
(i)   brought proceedings against the employer under these Regulations;
(ii)   requested from his employer a written statement under regulation 5 or regulation 9;
(iii) gave evidence or information in connection with such proceedings brought by any employee;
(iv)   otherwise did anything under these Regulations in relation to the employer or any other person;
(v)   alleged that the employer had infringed these Regulations;
(vi)   refused (or proposed to refuse) to forgo a right conferred on him by these Regulations;
(vii) declined to sign a workforce agreement for the purposes of these Regulations, or
(viii) being—
(aa) a representative of members of the workforce for the purposes of Schedule 1, or
(bb) a candidate in an election in which any person elected will, on being elected, become such a representative,
performed (or proposed to perform) any functions or activities as such a representative or candidate, or
(b) that the employer believes or suspects that the employee has done or intends to do any of the things mentioned in sub-paragraph (a).

(4)   Where the reason or principal reason for dismissal or, as the case may be, ground for subjection to any act or deliberate failure to act, is that mentioned in paragraph (3)(a)(v), or (b) so far as it relates thereto, neither paragraph (1) nor paragraph (2) applies if the allegation made by the employee is false and not made in good faith.

(5)   Paragraph (2) does not apply where the detriment in question amounts to dismissal within the meaning of Part 10 of the 1996 Act.

7 COMPLAINTS TO EMPLOYMENT TRIBUNALS ETC.

(1) An employee may present a complaint to an employment tribunal that his employer has infringed a right conferred on him by regulation 3, or (subject to regulation 6(5)), regulation 6(2).

(2) Subject to paragraph (3), an employment tribunal shall not consider a complaint under this regulation unless it is presented before the end of the period of three months beginning—
  (a) in the case of an alleged infringement of a right conferred by regulation 3(1) or 6(2), with the date of the less favourable treatment or detriment to which the complaint relates or, where an act or failure to act is part of a series of similar acts or failures comprising the less favourable treatment or detriment, the last of them;
  (b) in the case of an alleged infringement of the right conferred by regulation 3(6), with the date, or if more than one the last date, on which other individuals, whether or not employees of the employer, were informed of the vacancy.

(3) A tribunal may consider any such complaint which is out of time if, in all the circumstances of the case, it considers that it is just and equitable to do so.

(4) For the purposes of calculating the date of the less favourable treatment or detriment under paragraph (2)(a)—
  (a) where a term in a contract is less favourable, that treatment shall be treated, subject to paragraph (b), as taking place on each day of the period during which the term is less favourable;
  (b) a deliberate failure to act contrary to regulation 3 or 6(2) shall be treated as done when it was decided on.

(5) In the absence of evidence establishing the contrary, a person shall be taken for the purposes of paragraph (4)(b) to decide not to act—
  (a) when he does an act inconsistent with doing the failed act; or
  (b) if he has done no such inconsistent act, when the period expires within which he might reasonably have been expected to have done the failed act if it was to be done.

(6) Where an employee presents a complaint under this regulation in relation to a right conferred on him by regulation 3 or 6(2) it is for the employer to identify the ground for the less favourable treatment or detriment.

(7) Where an employment tribunal finds that a complaint presented to it under this regulation is well founded, it shall take such of the following steps as it considers just and equitable—
  (a) making a declaration as to the rights of the complainant and the employer in relation to the matters to which the complaint relates;
  (b) ordering the employer to pay compensation to the complainant;
  (c) recommending that the employer take, within a specified period, action appearing to the tribunal to be reasonable, in all the circumstances of the case, for the purpose of obviating or reducing the adverse effect on the complainant of any matter to which the complaint relates.

(8) Where a tribunal orders compensation under paragraph (7)(b), the amount of the compensation awarded shall be such as the tribunal considers just and equitable in all the circumstances having regard to—
  (a) the infringement to which the complaint relates, and
  (b) any loss which is attributable to the infringement.

(9) The loss shall be taken to include—

(a) any expenses reasonably incurred by the complainant in consequence of the infringement, and

(b) loss of any benefit which he might reasonably be expected to have had but for the infringement.

(10) Compensation in respect of treating an employee in a manner which infringes the right conferred on him by regulation 3 shall not include compensation for injury to feelings.

(11) In ascertaining the loss the tribunal shall apply the same rule concerning the duty of a person to mitigate his loss as applies to damages recoverable under the common law of England and Wales or (as the case may be) the law of Scotland.

(12) Where the tribunal finds that the act, or failure to act, to which the complaint relates was to any extent caused or contributed to by action of the complainant, it shall reduce the amount of the compensation by such proportion as it considers just and equitable having regard to that finding.

(13) If the employer fails, without reasonable justification, to comply with a recommendation made by an employment tribunal under paragraph (7)(c) the tribunal may, if it thinks it just and equitable to do so—

(a) increase the amount of compensation required to be paid to the complainant in respect of the complaint, where an order was made under paragraph (7)(b); or

(b) make an order under paragraph (7)(b).

8 SUCCESSIVE FIXED-TERM CONTRACTS

(1) This regulation applies where—

(a) an employee is employed under a contract purporting to be a fixed-term contract, and

(b) the contract mentioned in sub-paragraph (a) has previously been renewed, or the employee has previously been employed on a fixed-term contract before the start of the contract mentioned in sub-paragraph (a).

(2) Where this regulation applies then, with effect from the date specified in paragraph (3), the provision of the contract mentioned in paragraph (1)(a) that restricts the duration of the contract shall be of no effect, and the employee shall be a permanent employee, if—

(a) the employee has been continuously employed under the contract mentioned in paragraph 1(a), or under that contract taken with a previous fixed-term contract, for a period of four years or more, and

(b) the employment of the employee under a fixed-term contract was not justified on objective grounds—

(i) where the contract mentioned in paragraph (1)(a) has been renewed, at the time when it was last renewed;

(ii) where that contract has not been renewed, at the time when it was entered into.

(3) The date referred to in paragraph (2) is whichever is the later of—

(a) the date on which the contract mentioned in paragraph (1)(a) was entered into or last renewed, and

(b) the date on which the employee acquired four years' continuous employment.

(4) For the purposes of this regulation Chapter 1 of Part 14 of the 1996 Act shall apply in determining whether an employee has been continuously employed, and any period of continuous employment falling before the 10th July 2002 shall be disregarded.

(5) A collective agreement or a workforce agreement may modify the application of paragraphs (1) to (3) of this regulation in relation to any employee or specified description of employees, by substituting for the provisions of paragraph (2) or paragraph (3), or for

the provisions of both of those paragraphs, one or more different provisions which, in order to prevent abuse arising from the use of successive fixed-term contracts, specify one or more of the following—

(a) the maximum total period for which the employee or employees of that description may be continuously employed on a fixed-term contract or on successive fixed-term contracts;

(b) the maximum number of successive fixed-term contracts and renewals of such contracts under which the employee or employees of that description may be employed; or

(c) objective grounds justifying the renewal of fixed-term contracts, or the engagement of the employee or employees of that description under successive fixed-term contracts,

and those provisions shall have effect in relation to that employee or an employee of that description as if they were contained in paragraphs (2) and (3).

9   RIGHT TO RECEIVE WRITTEN STATEMENT OF VARIATION

(1) If an employee who considers that, by virtue of regulation 8, he is a permanent employee requests in writing from his employer a written statement confirming that his contract is no longer fixed-term or that he is now a permanent employee, he is entitled to be provided, within twenty-one days of his request, with either—

(a) such a statement, or

(b) a statement giving reasons why his contract remains fixed-term.

(2) If the reasons stated under paragraph (1)(b) include an assertion that there were objective grounds for the engagement of the employee under a fixed-term contract, or the renewal of such a contract, the statement shall include a statement of those grounds.

(3) A written statement under this regulation is admissible as evidence in any proceedings before a court, an employment tribunal and the Commissioners of the Inland Revenue.

(4) If it appears to the court or tribunal in any proceedings—

(a) that the employer deliberately, and without reasonable excuse, omitted to provide a written statement, or

(b) that the written statement is evasive or equivocal,

it may draw any inference which it considers it just and equitable to draw.

(5) An employee who considers that, by virtue of regulation 8, he is a permanent employee may present an application to an employment tribunal for a declaration to that effect.

(6) No application may be made under paragraph (5) unless—

(a) the employee in question has previously requested a statement under paragraph (1) and the employer has either failed to provide a statement or given a statement of reasons under paragraph (1)(b), and

(b) the employee is at the time the application is made employed by the employer.

Part III   MISCELLANEOUS

10   RESTRICTIONS ON CONTRACTING OUT

Section 203 of the 1996 Act (restrictions on contracting out) shall apply in relation to these Regulations as if they were contained in that Act.

12 LIABILITY OF EMPLOYERS AND PRINCIPALS

(1) Anything done by a person in the course of his employment shall be treated for the purposes of these Regulations as also done by his employer, whether or not it was done with the employer's knowledge or approval.

(2) Anything done by a person as agent for the employer with the authority of the employer shall be treated for the purposes of these Regulations as also done by the employer.

(3) In proceedings under these Regulations against any person in respect of an act alleged to have been done by an employee of his, it shall be a defence for that person to prove that he took such steps as were reasonably practicable to prevent the employee from—
(a) doing that act, or
(b) doing, in the course of his employment, acts of that description.

Part V EXCLUSIONS

19 AGENCY WORKERS

(1) Save in respect of paragraph 1 of Part 1 of Schedule 2, these Regulations shall not have effect in relation to employment under a fixed-term contract where the employee is an agency worker.

(2) In this regulation "agency worker" means any person who is supplied by an employment business to do work for another person under a contract or other arrangements made between the employment business and the other person.

(3) In this regulation "employment business" means the business (whether or not carried on with a view to profit and whether or not carried on in conjunction with any other business) of supplying persons in the employment of the person carrying on the business, to act for, and under the control of, other persons in any capacity.

SCHEDULE 1 WORKFORCE AGREEMENTS

1   An agreement is a workforce agreement for the purposes of these Regulations if the following conditions are satisfied—
(a) the agreement is in writing;
(b) it has effect for a specified period not exceeding five years;
(c) it applies either—
    (i)   to all of the relevant members of the workforce, or
    (ii) to all of the relevant members of the workforce who belong to a particular group;
(d) the agreement is signed—
    (i)   in the case of an agreement of the kind referred to in sub-paragraph (c)(i), by the representatives of the workforce, and in the case of an agreement of the kind referred to in sub-paragraph (c)(ii) by the representatives of the group to which the agreement applies (excluding, in either case, any representative not a relevant member of the workforce on the date on which the agreement was first made available for signature), or
    (ii) if the employer employed 20 or fewer employees on the date referred to in sub-paragraph (d)(i), either by the appropriate representatives in accordance with that sub-paragraph or by the majority of the employees employed by him;
(e) before the agreement was made available for signature, the employer provided all the employees to whom it was intended to apply on the date on which it came into effect

with copies of the text of the agreement and such guidance as those employees might reasonably require in order to understand it fully.

2   For the purposes of this Schedule—

"a particular group" is a group of the relevant members of a workforce who undertake a particular function, work at a particular workplace or belong to a particular department or unit within their employer's business;

"relevant members of the workforce" are all of the employees employed by a particular employer, excluding any employee whose terms and conditions of employment are provided for, wholly or in part, in a collective agreement;

"representatives of the workforce" are employees duly elected to represent the relevant members of the workforce, "representatives of the group" are employees duly elected to represent the members of a particular group, and representatives are "duly elected" if the election at which they were elected satisfied the requirements of paragraph 3 of this Schedule.

3   The requirements concerning elections referred to in paragraph 2 are that—
    (a) the number of representatives to be elected is determined by the employer;
    (b) the candidates for election as representatives of the workforce are relevant members of the workforce, and the candidates for election as representatives of a group are members of that group;
    (c) no employee who is eligible to be a candidate is unreasonably excluded from standing for election;
    (d) all the relevant members of the workforce are entitled to vote for representatives of the workforce, and all the members of a particular group are entitled to vote for representatives of the group;
    (e) the employees entitled to vote may vote for as many candidates as there are representatives to be elected;
    (f) the election is conducted so as to secure that—
        (i) so far as is reasonably practicable, those voting do so in secret, and
        (ii) the votes given at the election are fairly and accurately counted.

As amended by the Employment Rights (Dispute Resolution) Act 1998; Unfair Dismissal and Statement of Reasons for Dismissal (Variation of Qualifying Period) Order 1999/1436, Article 3; Employment Relations Act 1999, s 9, s 44, Schedule 4 Part 3 para 1, Schedule 4 Part 3 para 5, Schedule 9; Fixed-term Employees (Prevention of Less Favourable Treatment) (Amendment) Regulations 2008/2776 reg 2(2).

FLEXIBLE WORKING (ELIGIBILITY, COMPLAINTS AND REMEDIES) REGULATIONS 2002/3236

3 ENTITLEMENT TO REQUEST A CONTRACT VARIATION TO CARE FOR A CHILD

(1)   An employee is entitled to make an application to his employer for a contract variation to enable him, in accordance with section 80F(1)(b)(i) of the 1996 Act, to care for a child if he—
    (a) has been continuously employed for a period of not less than 26 weeks;
    (b) is either—

(i)   the mother, father, adopter, guardian, special guardian, foster parent or private foster carer of, or a person in whose favour a residence order is in force in respect of, the child; or

(ii) married to, the civil partner of or the partner of—

(aa) the child's mother, father, adopter, guardian, special guardian, foster parent or private foster carer, or

(bb) a person in whose favour a residence order is in force in respect of the child;

(c)   has, or expects to have responsibility for the upbringing of the child.

3A AGE OF CHILD

An application under regulation 3 must be made before the day on which the child concerned reaches the age of 17 or, if disabled, 18.

3B ENTITLEMENT TO REQUEST A CONTRACT VARIATION TO CARE FOR AN ADULT

An employee is entitled to make an application to his employer for a contract variation to enable him, in accordance with section 80F(1)(b)(ii) of the 1996 Act, to care for a person aged 18 or over if the employee—

(a)   has been continuously employed for a period of not less than 26 weeks;

(b)   is or expects to be caring for a person in need of care who is either—

(i)   married to or the partner or civil partner of the employee;

(ii) a relative of the employee; or

(iii) living at the same address as the employee.

7 COMPENSATION

The maximum amount of compensation that an employment tribunal may award under section 80I of the 1996 Act where it finds a complaint by an employee under section 80H of the Act well-founded is 8 weeks' pay.

As amended by the Flexible Working (Eligibility, Complaints and Remedies) (Amendment) Regulations 2006/3314 reg 4(2), reg 4(3), reg 4(5), reg 5; Flexible Working (Eligibility, Complaints and Remedies) (Amendment) (No. 2) Regulations 2007/2286 reg 4; Flexible Working (Eligibility, Complaints and Remedies) (Amendment) Regulations 2009/595 reg 2(2).

PATERNITY AND ADOPTION LEAVE REGULATIONS 2002/2788

Part I GENERAL

2 INTERPRETATION

(1)   In these Regulations—

"the 1996 Act" means the Employment Rights Act 1996;

"additional adoption leave" means leave under section 75B of the 1996 Act;

"additional maternity leave" means leave under section 73 of the 1996 Act;

"adopter", in relation to a child, means a person who has been matched with the child for adoption, or, in a case where two people have been matched jointly, whichever of them has elected to be the child's adopter for the purposes of these Regulations;

"adoption agency" has the meaning given, in relation to England and Wales, by section 1(4) of the Adoption Act 1976 and, in relation to Scotland, by section 1(4) of the Adoption (Scotland) Act 1978;

"adoption leave" means ordinary or additional adoption leave;

"child" means a person who is, or when placed with an adopter for adoption was, under the age of 18;

"contract of employment" means a contract of service or apprenticeship, whether express or implied, and (if it is express) whether oral or in writing;

"employee" means an individual who has entered into or works under (or, where the employment has ceased, worked under) a contract of employment;

"employer" means the person by whom an employee is (or, where the employment has ceased, was) employed;

"expected week", in relation to the birth of a child, means the week, beginning with midnight between Saturday and Sunday, in which it is expected that the child will be born;

"ordinary adoption leave" means leave under section 75A of the 1996 Act;

"parental leave" means leave under regulation 13(1) of the Maternity and Parental Leave etc. Regulations 1999;

"partner", in relation to a child's mother or adopter, means a person (whether of a different sex or the same sex) who lives with the mother or adopter and the child in an enduring family relationship but is not a relative of the mother or adopter of a kind specified in paragraph (2);

"paternity leave" means leave under regulation 4 or regulation 8 of these Regulations;

"statutory adoption leave" means ordinary adoption leave and additional adoption leave;

"statutory adoption leave period" means the period during which the adopter is on statutory adoption leave;

"statutory leave" means leave provided for in Part 8 of the 1996 Act.

(2)   The relatives of a child's mother or adopter referred to in the definition of "partner" in paragraph (1) are the mother's or adopter's parent, grandparent, sister, brother, aunt or uncle.

(3)   References to relationships in paragraph (2)—
(a) are to relationships of the full blood or half blood or, in the case of an adopted person, such of those relationships as would exist but for the adoption, and

(b) include the relationship of a child with his adoptive, or former adoptive, parents, but do not include any other adoptive relationships.

(4) For the purposes of these Regulations—
(a) a person is matched with a child for adoption when an adoption agency decides that that person would be a suitable adoptive parent for the child, either individually or jointly with another person, and
(b) a person is notified of having been matched with a child on the date on which he receives notification of the agency's decision, under regulation 11(2) of the Adoption Agencies Regulations 1983 or regulation 12(3) of the Adoption Agencies (Scotland) Regulations 1996;
(c) a person elects to be a child's adopter, in a case where the child is matched with him and another person jointly, if he and that person agree, at the time at which they are matched, that he and not the other person will be the adopter.

(5) A reference in any provision of these Regulations to a period of continuous employment is to a period computed in accordance with Chapter 1 of Part 14 of the 1996 Act, as if that provision were a provision of that Act.

(6) For the purposes of these Regulations, any two employers shall be treated as associated if—
(a) one is a company of which the other (directly or indirectly) has control; or
(b) both are companies of which a third person (directly or indirectly) has control;
and "associated employer" shall be construed accordingly.

Part II PATERNITY LEAVE

4 ENTITLEMENT TO PATERNITY LEAVE: BIRTH

(1) An employee is entitled to be absent from work for the purpose of caring for a child or supporting the child's mother if he—
(a) satisfies the conditions specified in paragraph (2), and
(b) has complied with the notice requirements in regulation 6 and, where applicable, the evidential requirements in that regulation.

(2) The conditions referred to in paragraph (1) are that the employee—
(a) has been continuously employed for a period of not less than 26 weeks ending with the week immediately preceding the 14th week before the expected week of the child's birth;
(b) is either—
(i) the father of the child or;
(ii) married to, the civil partner or the partner of the child's mother, but not the child's father;
(c) has, or expects to have—
(i) if he is the child's father, responsibility for the upbringing of the child;
(ii) if he is the mother's husband, civil partner or partner but not the child's father, the main responsibility (apart from any responsibility of the mother) for the upbringing of the child.

(3) An employee shall be treated as having satisfied the condition in paragraph (2)(a) on the date of the child's birth notwithstanding the fact that he has not then been continuously employed for a period of not less than 26 weeks, where—
(a) the date on which the child is born is earlier than the 14th week before the week in which its birth is expected, and
(b) the employee would have been continuously employed for such a period if his employment had continued until that 14th week.

(4)   An employee shall be treated as having satisfied the condition in paragraph (2)(b)(ii) if he would have satisfied it but for the fact that the child's mother has died.

(5)   An employee shall be treated as having satisfied the condition in paragraph (2)(c) if he would have satisfied it but for the fact that the child was stillborn after 24 weeks of pregnancy or has died.

(6)   An employee's entitlement to leave under this regulation shall not be affected by the birth, or expected birth, of more than one child as a result of the same pregnancy.

5   OPTIONS IN RESPECT OF LEAVE UNDER REGULATION 4

(1)   An employee may choose to take either one week's leave or two consecutive weeks' leave in respect of a child under regulation 4.

(2)   The leave may only be taken during the period which begins with the date on which the child is born and ends—
(a)   except in the case referred to in sub-paragraph (b), 56 days after that date;
(b)   in a case where the child is born before the first day of the expected week of its birth, 56 days after that day.

(3)   Subject to paragraph (2) and, where applicable, paragraph (4), an employee may choose to begin his period of leave on—
(a)   the date on which the child is born;
(b)   the date falling such number of days after the date on which the child is born as the employee may specify in a notice under regulation 6, or
(c)   a predetermined date, specified in a notice under that regulation, which is later than the first day of the expected week of the child's birth.

(4)   In a case where the leave is in respect of a child whose expected week of birth begins before 6th April 2003, an employee may choose to begin a period of leave only on a predetermined date, specified in a notice under regulation 6, which is at least 28 days after the date on which that notice is given.

6   NOTICE AND EVIDENTIAL REQUIREMENTS FOR LEAVE UNDER REGULATION 4

(1)   An employee must give his employer notice of his intention to take leave in respect of a child under regulation 4, specifying—
(a)   the expected week of the child's birth;
(b)   the length of the period of leave that, in accordance with regulation 5(1), the employee has chosen to take, and
(c)   the date on which, in accordance with regulation 5(3) or (4), the employee has chosen that his period of leave should begin.

(2)   The notice provided for in paragraph (1) must be given to the employer—
(a)   in or before the 15th week before the expected week of the child's birth, or
(b)   in a case where it was not reasonably practicable for the employee to give the notice in accordance with sub-paragraph (a), as soon as is reasonably practicable.

(3)   Where the employer requests it, an employee must also give his employer a declaration, signed by the employee, to the effect that the purpose of his absence from work will be that specified in regulation 4(1) and that he satisfies the conditions of entitlement in regulation 4(2)(b) and (c)

(4)   An employee who has given notice under paragraph (1) may vary the date he has chosen as the date on which his period of leave will begin, subject to paragraph (5) and provided that he gives his employer notice of the variation—

(a)   where the variation is to provide for the employee's period of leave to begin on the date on which the child is born, at least 28 days before the first day of the expected week of the child's birth;

(b)   where the variation is to provide for the employee's period of leave to begin on a date that is a specified number of days (or a different specified number of days) after the date on which the child is born, at least 28 days before the date falling that number of days after the first day of the expected week of the child's birth;

(c)   where the variation is to provide for the employee's period of leave to begin on a predetermined date (or a different predetermined date), at least 28 days before that date,

or, if it is not reasonably practicable to give the notice at least 28 days before whichever day or date is relevant, as soon as is reasonably practicable.

(5)   In a case where regulation 5(4) applies, an employee may only vary the date which he has chosen as the date on which his period of leave will begin by substituting a different predetermined date.

(6)   In a case where—

(a)   the employee has chosen to begin his period of leave on a particular predetermined date, and

(b)   the child is not born on or before that date,

the employee must vary his choice of date, by substituting a later predetermined date or (except in a case where regulation 5(4) applies) exercising an alternative option under regulation 5(3), and give his employer notice of the variation as soon as is reasonably practicable.

(7)   An employee must give his employer a further notice, as soon as is reasonably practicable after the child's birth, of the date on which the child was born.

(8)   Notice under paragraph (1), (4), (6) or (7) shall be given in writing, if the employer so requests.

8   ENTITLEMENT TO PATERNITY LEAVE: ADOPTION

(1)   An employee is entitled to be absent from work for the purpose of caring for a child or supporting the child's adopter if he—

(a)   satisfies the conditions specified in paragraph (2), and

(b)   has complied with the notice requirements in regulation 10 and, where applicable, the evidential requirements in that regulation.

(2)   The conditions referred to in paragraph (1) are that the employee—

(a)   has been continuously employed for a period of not less than 26 weeks ending with the week in which the child's adopter is notified of having been matched with the child;

(b)   is either married to, the civil partner or the partner of the child's adopter, and

(c)   has, or expects to have, the main responsibility (apart from the responsibility of the adopter) for the upbringing of the child.

(3)   In paragraph (2)(a), "week" means the period of seven days beginning with Sunday.

(4)   An employee shall be treated as having satisfied the condition in paragraph (2)(b) if he would have satisfied it but for the fact that the child's adopter died during the child's placement.

(5)   An employee shall be treated as having satisfied the condition in paragraph (2)(c) if he would have satisfied it but for the fact that the child's placement with the adopter has ended.

(6)   An employee's entitlement to leave under this regulation shall not be affected by the placement for adoption of more than one child as part of the same arrangement.

9 OPTIONS IN RESPECT OF LEAVE UNDER REGULATION 8

(1)   An employee may choose to take either one week's leave or two consecutive weeks' leave in respect of a child under regulation 8.

(2)   The leave may only be taken during the period of 56 days beginning with the date on which the child is placed with the adopter.

(3)   Subject to paragraph (2) and, where applicable, paragraph (4), an employee may choose to begin a period of leave under regulation 8 on—
       (a) the date on which the child is placed with the adopter;
       (b) the date falling such number of days after the date on which the child is placed with the adopter as the employee may specify in a notice under regulation 10, or
       (c) a predetermined date, specified in a notice under that regulation, which is later than the date on which the child is expected to be placed with the adopter.

(4)   In a case where the adopter was notified of having been matched with the child before 6th April 2003, the employee may choose to begin a period of leave only on a predetermined date, specified in a notice under regulation 10, which is at least 28 days after the date on which that notice is given.

10 NOTICE AND EVIDENTIAL REQUIREMENTS FOR LEAVE UNDER REGULATION 8

(1)   An employee must give his employer notice of his intention to take leave in respect of a child under regulation 8, specifying—
       (a) the date on which the adopter was notified of having been matched with the child;
       (b) the date on which the child is expected to be placed with the adopter;
       (c) the length of the period of leave that, in accordance with regulation 9(1), the employee has chosen to take, and
       (d) the date on which, in accordance with regulation 9(3) or (4), the employee has chosen that his period of leave should begin.

(2)   The notice provided for in paragraph (1) must be given to the employer—
       (a) no more than seven days after the date on which the adopter is notified of having been matched with the child, or
       (b) in a case where it was not reasonably practicable for the employee to give notice in accordance with sub-paragraph (a), as soon as is reasonably practicable.

(3)   Where the employer requests it, an employee must also give his employer a declaration, signed by the employee, to the effect that the purpose of his absence from work will be that specified in regulation 8(1) and that he satisfies the conditions of entitlement in regulation 8(2)(b) and (c).

(4)   An employee who has given notice under paragraph (1) may vary the date he has chosen as the date on which his period of leave will begin, subject to paragraph (5) and provided that he gives his employer notice of the variation—

(a) where the variation is to provide for the employee's period of leave to begin on the date on which the child is placed with the adopter, at least 28 days before the date specified in the employee's notice under paragraph (1) as the date on which the child is expected to be placed with the adopter;

(b) where the variation is to provide for the employee's period of leave to begin on a date that is a specified number of days (or a different specified number of days) after the date on which the child is placed with the adopter, at least 28 days before the date falling that number of days after the date specified in the employee's notice under paragraph (1) as the date on which the child is expected to be placed with the adopter;

(c) where the variation is to provide for the employee's period of leave to begin on a predetermined date, at least 28 days before that date, or, if it is not reasonably practicable to give the notice at least 28 days before whichever date is relevant, as soon as is reasonably practicable.

(5) In a case where regulation 9(4) applies, an employee may only vary the date which he has chosen as the date on which his period of leave will begin by substituting a different predetermined date.

(6) In a case where—
(a) the employee has chosen to begin his period of leave on a particular predetermined date, and
(b) the child is not placed with the adopter on or before that date,
the employee must vary his choice of date, by substituting a later predetermined date or (except in a case where regulation 9(4) applies) exercising an alternative option under regulation 9(3), and give his employer notice of the variation as soon as is reasonably practicable.

(7) An employee must give his employer a further notice, as soon as is reasonably practicable after the child's placement, of the date on which the child was placed.

(8) Notice under paragraph (1), (4), (6) or (7) shall be given in writing, if the employer so requests.

12 APPLICATION OF TERMS AND CONDITIONS DURING PATERNITY LEAVE

(1) An employee who takes paternity leave—
(a) is entitled, during the period of leave, to the benefit of all of the terms and conditions of employment which would have applied if he had not been absent, and
(b) is bound, during that period, by any obligations arising under those terms and conditions, subject only to the exception in section 80C(1)(b) of the 1996 Act.

(2) In paragraph (1)(a), "terms and conditions of employment" has the meaning given by section 80C(5) of the 1996 Act, and accordingly does not include terms and conditions about remuneration.

(3) For the purposes of section 80C of the 1996 Act, only sums payable to an employee by way of wages or salary are to be treated as remuneration.

13 RIGHT TO RETURN AFTER PATERNITY LEAVE

(1) An employee who returns to work after a period of paternity leave which was—
(a) an isolated period of leave, or

    (b) the last of two or more consecutive periods of statutory leave, which did not include any period of additional maternity leave or additional adoption leave or a period of parental leave of more than four weeks,

is entitled to return from leave to the job in which he was employed before his absence.

(2)   An employee who returns to work after a period of paternity leave not falling within the description in paragraph (1)(a) or (b) above is entitled to return from leave to the job in which he was employed before his absence, or, if it is not reasonably practicable for the employer to permit him to return to that job, to another job which is both suitable for him and appropriate for him to do in the circumstances.

(3)   The reference in paragraphs (1) and (2) to the job in which an employee was employed before his absence is a reference to the job in which he was employed—

    (a) if his return is from an isolated period of paternity leave, immediately before that period began;

    (b) if his return is from consecutive periods of statutory leave, immediately before the first such period.

14 INCIDENTS OF THE RIGHT TO RETURN AFTER PATERNITY LEAVE

(1)   An employee's right to return under regulation 13 is a right to return—

    (a) with his seniority, pension rights and similar rights—

        (i) in a case where the employee is returning from consecutive periods of statutory leave which included a period of additional adoption leave or additional maternity leave, as they would have been if the period or periods of his employment prior to the additional adoption leave or (as the case may be) additional maternity leave were continuous with the period of employment following it;

        (ii) in any other case, as they would have been if he had not been absent, and

    (b) on terms and conditions not less favourable than those which would have applied if he had not been absent.

(2)   The provision in paragraph (1)(a)(i) concerning the treatment of periods of additional maternity leave or additional adoption leave is subject to the requirements of paragraphs 5, 5B and 6 of Schedule 5 to the Social Security Act 1989 (equal treatment under pension schemes: maternity absence, adoption leave and family leave).

(3)   The provisions in paragraph (1)(a)(ii) and (b) for an employee to be treated as if he had not been absent refer to his absence—

    (a) if his return is from an isolated period of paternity leave, since the beginning of that period;

    (b) if his return is from consecutive periods of statutory leave, since the beginning of the first such period.

Part III ADOPTION LEAVE

15 ENTITLEMENT TO ORDINARY ADOPTION LEAVE

(1)   An employee is entitled to ordinary adoption leave in respect of a child if he—

    (a) satisfies the conditions specified in paragraph (2), and

    (b) has complied with the notice requirements in regulation 17 and, where applicable, the evidential requirements in that regulation.

(2)   The conditions referred to in paragraph (1) are that the employee—

(a) is the child's adopter;

(b) has been continuously employed for a period of not less than 26 weeks ending with the week in which he was notified of having been matched with the child, and

(c) has notified the agency that he agrees that the child should be placed with him and on the date of placement.

(3) In paragraph (2)(b), "week" means the period of seven days beginning with Sunday.

(4) An employee's entitlement to leave under this regulation shall not be affected by the placement for adoption of more than one child as part of the same arrangement.

16 OPTIONS IN RESPECT OF ORDINARY ADOPTION LEAVE

(1) Except in the case referred to in paragraph (2), an employee may choose to begin a period of ordinary adoption leave on—

(a) the date on which the child is placed with him for adoption, or

(b) a predetermined date, specified in a notice under regulation 17, which is no more than 14 days before the date on which the child is expected to be placed with the employee and no later than that date.

(2) In a case where the employee was notified of having been matched with the child before 6th April 2003, the employee may choose to begin a period of leave only on a predetermined date, specified in a notice under regulation 17, which is after 6th April 2003 and at least 28 days after the date on which that notice is given.

17 NOTICE AND EVIDENTIAL REQUIREMENTS FOR ORDINARY ADOPTION LEAVE

(1) An employee must give his employer notice of his intention to take ordinary adoption leave in respect of a child, specifying—

(a) the date on which the child is expected to be placed with him for adoption, and

(b) the date on which, in accordance with regulation 16(1) or (2), the employee has chosen that his period of leave should begin.

(2) The notice provided for in paragraph (1) must be given to the employer—

(a) no more than seven days after the date on which the employee is notified of having been matched with the child for the purposes of adoption, or

(b) in a case where it was not reasonably practicable for the employee to give notice in accordance with sub-paragraph (a), as soon as is reasonably practicable.

(3) Where the employer requests it, an employee must also provide his employer with evidence, in the form of one or more documents issued by the adoption agency that matched the employee with the child, of—

(a) the name and address of the agency;

(c) the date on which the employee was notified that he had been matched with the child, and

(d) the date on which the agency expects to place the child with the employee.

(4) An employee who has given notice under paragraph (1) may vary the date he has chosen as the date on which his period of leave will begin, subject to paragraph (5) and provided that he gives his employer notice of the variation—

(a) where the variation is to provide for the employee's period of leave to begin on the date on which the child is placed with him for adoption, at least 28 days before the date specified in his notice under paragraph (1) as the date on which the child is expected to be placed with him;

(b) where the variation is to provide for the employee's period of leave to begin on a predetermined date (or a different predetermined date), at least 28 days before that date,

or, if it is not reasonably practicable to give the notice 28 days before whichever date is relevant, as soon as is reasonably practicable.

(5) In a case where regulation 16(2) applies, an employee may only vary the date which he has chosen as the date on which his period of leave will begin by substituting a different predetermined date.

(6) Notice under paragraph (1) or (4) shall be given in writing, if the employer so requests.

(7) An employer who is given notice under paragraph (1) or (4) of the date on which an employee has chosen that his period of ordinary adoption leave should begin shall notify the employee, within 28 days of his receipt of the notice, of the date on which the period of additional adoption leave to which the employee will be entitled (if he satisfies the conditions in regulation 20(1)) after his period of ordinary adoption leave ends.

(8) The notification provided for in paragraph (7) shall be given to the employee—
(a) where the employer is given notice under paragraph (1), within 28 days of the date on which he received that notice;
(b) where the employer is given notice under paragraph (4), within 28 days of the date on which the employee's ordinary adoption leave period began.

18 DURATION AND COMMENCEMENT OF ORDINARY ADOPTION LEAVE

(1) Subject to regulations 22 and 24, an employee's ordinary adoption leave period is a period of 26 weeks.

(2) Except in the case referred to in paragraph (3), an employee's ordinary adoption leave period begins on the date specified in his notice under regulation 17(1), or, where he has varied his choice of date under regulation 17(4), on the date specified in his notice under that provision (or the last such date if he has varied his choice more than once).

(3) In a case where—
(a) the employee has chosen to begin his period of leave on the date on which the child is placed with him, and
(b) he is at work on that date,
the employee's period of leave begins on the day after that date.

19 APPLICATION OF TERMS AND CONDITIONS DURING ORDINARY ADOPTION LEAVE AND ADDITIONAL ADOPTION LEAVE

(1) An employee who takes ordinary adoption leave or additional adoption leave—
(a) is entitled, during the period of leave, to the benefit of all of the terms and conditions of employment which would have applied if he had not been absent, and
(b) is bound, during that period, by any obligations arising under those terms and conditions, subject only to the exceptions in section 75A(3)(b) and 75B(4)(b) of the 1996 Act.

(2) In paragraph (1)(a), "terms and conditions of employment" has the meaning given by section 75A(4) and 75B(5) of the 1996 Act, and accordingly does not include terms and conditions about remuneration.

(3)   For the purposes of sections 75A and 75B of the 1996 Act, only sums payable to an employee by way of wages or salary are to be treated as remuneration.

20 ADDITIONAL ADOPTION LEAVE: ENTITLEMENT, DURATION AND COMMENCEMENT

(1)   An employee is entitled to additional adoption leave in respect of a child if—
    (a) the child was placed with him for adoption,
    (b) he took ordinary adoption leave in respect of the child, and
    (c) his ordinary adoption leave period did not end prematurely under regulation 22(2)(a) or 24.

(2)   Subject to regulations 22 and 24, an employee's additional adoption leave period is a period of 26 weeks beginning on the day after the last day of his ordinary adoption leave period.

21A WORK DURING ADOPTION LEAVE PERIOD

(1)   An employee may carry out up to 10 days' work for his employer during his statutory adoption leave period without bringing his statutory adoption leave to an end.

(2)   For the purposes of this regulation, any work carried out on any day shall constitute a day's work.

(3)   Subject to paragraph (4),for the purposes of this regulation, work means any work done under the contract of employment and may include training or any activity undertaken for the purposes of keeping in touch with the workplace.

(4)   Reasonable contact from time to time between an employee and his employer which either party is entitled to make during an adoption leave period (for example to discuss an employee's return to work) shall not bring that period to an end.

(5)   This regulation does not confer any right on an employer to require that any work be carried out during the statutory adoption leave period, nor any right on an employee to work during the statutory adoption leave period.

(6)   Any days' work carried out under this regulation shall not have the effect of extending the total duration of the statutory adoption leave period

23 REDUNDANCY DURING ADOPTION LEAVE

(1)   This regulation applies where, during an employee's ordinary or additional adoption leave period, it is not practicable by reason of redundancy for his employer to continue to employ him under his existing contract of employment.

(2)   Where there is a suitable available vacancy, the employee is entitled to be offered (before the end of his employment under his existing contract) alternative employment with his employer or his employer's successor, or an associated employer, under a new contract of employment which complies with paragraph (3) and takes effect immediately on the ending of his employment under the previous contract.

(3)   The new contract of employment must be such that—
    (a) the work to be done under it is of a kind which is both suitable in relation to the employee and appropriate for him to do in the circumstances, and
    (b) its provisions as to the capacity and place in which he is to be employed, and as to the other terms and conditions of his employment, are not substantially less favourable to him than if he had continued to be employed under the previous contract.

24 DISMISSAL DURING ADOPTION LEAVE

Where an employee is dismissed after an ordinary or additional adoption leave period has begun but before the time when (apart from this regulation) that period would end, the period ends at the time of the dismissal.

26 RIGHT TO RETURN AFTER ADOPTION LEAVE

(1) An employee who returns to work after a period of ordinary adoption leave which was—
   (a) an isolated period of leave, or
   (b) the last of two or more consecutive periods of statutory leave, which did not include any period of additional maternity leave or additional adoption leave or a period of parental leave of more than four weeks,
   is entitled to return from leave to the job in which he was employed before his absence.

(2) An employee who returns to work after—
   (a) a period of additional adoption leave, whether or not preceded by another period of statutory leave, or
   (b) a period of ordinary adoption leave not falling within the description in paragraph (1) (a) or (b) above,
   is entitled to return from leave to the job in which he was employed before his absence, or, if it is not reasonably practicable for the employer to permit him to return to that job, to another job which is both suitable for him and appropriate for him to do in the circumstances.

(3) The reference in paragraphs (1) and (2) to the job in which an employee was employed before his absence is a reference to the job in which he was employed—
   (a) if his return is from an isolated period of adoption leave, immediately before that period began;
   (b) if his return is from consecutive periods of statutory leave, immediately before the first such period.

(4) This regulation does not apply where regulation 23 applies.

27 INCIDENTS OF THE RIGHT TO RETURN FROM ADOPTION LEAVE

(1) An employee's right to return under regulation 26 is to return—
   (a) with his seniority, pension rights and similar rights as they would have been if he had not been absent, and
   (b) on terms and conditions not less favourable than those which would have been applied to him if he had not been absent.

(2) In the case of accrual of rights under an employment-related benefit scheme within the meaning given by Schedule 5 to the Social Security Act 1989, nothing in paragraph (1)(a) concerning the treatment of additional adoption leave shall be taken to impose a requirement which exceeds the requirements of paragraphs 5, 5B and 6 of that Schedule.

(3) The provisions in paragraph (1) for an employee to be treated as if he had not been absent refer to his absence—
   (a) if his return is from an isolated period of ordinary adoption leave, since the beginning of that period;
   (b) if his return is from consecutive periods of statutory leave, since the beginning of the first such period.

Part IV **PROVISIONS APPLICABLE IN RELATION TO BOTH PATERNITY AND ADOPTION LEAVE**

28 PROTECTION FROM DETRIMENT

(1) An employee is entitled under section 47C of the 1996 Act not to be subjected to any detriment by any act, or any deliberate failure to act, by his employer because—
   (a) the employee took or sought to take paternity leave or ordinary or additional adoption leave;
   (b) the employer believed that the employee was likely to take ordinary or additional adoption leave,
   (bb) the employee undertook, considered undertaking or refused to undertake work in accordance with regulation 21A; or
   (c) the employee failed to return after a period of additional adoption leave in a case where—
      (i) the employer did not notify him, in accordance with regulation 17(7) and (8) or otherwise, of the date on which that period ended, and he reasonably believed that the period had not ended, or
      (ii) the employer gave him less than 28 days' notice of the date on which the period would end, and it was not reasonably practicable for him to return on that date.

(2) Paragraph (1) does not apply where the detriment in question amounts to dismissal within the meaning of Part 10 of the 1996 Act.

29 UNFAIR DISMISSAL

(1) An employee who is dismissed is entitled under section 99 of the 1996 Act to be regarded for the purpose of Part 10 of that Act as unfairly dismissed if—
   (a) the reason or principal reason for the dismissal is of a kind specified in paragraph (3), or
   (b) the reason or principal reason for the dismissal is that the employee is redundant, and regulation 23 has not been complied with.

(2) An employee who is dismissed shall also be regarded for the purposes of Part 10 of the 1996 Act as unfairly dismissed if—
   (a) the reason (or, if more than one, the principal reason) for the dismissal is that the employee was redundant;
   (b) it is shown that the circumstances constituting the redundancy applied equally to one or more employees in the same undertaking who had positions similar to that held by the employee and who have not been dismissed by the employer, and
   (c) it is shown that the reason (or, if more than one, the principal reason) for which the employee was selected for dismissal was a reason of a kind specified in paragraph (3).

(3) The kinds of reason referred to in paragraph (1) and (2) are reasons connected with the fact that—
   (a) the employee took, or sought to take, paternity or adoption leave;
   (b) the employer believed that the employee was likely to take ordinary or additional adoption leave,
   (bb) the employee undertook, considered undertaking or refused to undertake work in accordance with regulation 21A; or
   (c) the employee failed to return after a period of additional adoption leave in a case where—

(i) the employer did not notify him, in accordance with regulation 17(7) and (8) or otherwise, of the date on which that period would end, and he reasonably believed that the period had not ended, or

(ii) the employer gave him less than 28 days' notice of the date on which the period would end, and it was not reasonably practicable for him to return on that date.

(5) Paragraph (1) does not apply in relation to an employee if—

(a) it is not reasonably practicable for a reason other than redundancy for the employer (who may be the same employer or a successor of his) to permit the employee to return to a job which is both suitable for the employee and appropriate for him to do in the circumstances;

(b) an associated employer offers the employee a job of that kind, and

(c) the employee accepts or unreasonably refuses that offer.

(6) Where, on a complaint of unfair dismissal, any question arises as to whether the operation of paragraph (1) is excluded by the provisions of paragraph (5), it is for the employer to show that the provisions in question were satisfied in relation to the complainant.

30 CONTRACTUAL RIGHTS TO PATERNITY OR ADOPTION LEAVE

(1) This regulation applies where an employee is entitled to—

(a) paternity leave,

(b) ordinary adoption leave, or

(c) additional adoption leave,

(referred to in paragraph (2) as a "statutory right") and also to a right which corresponds to that right and which arises under the employee's contract of employment or otherwise.

(2) In a case where this regulation applies—

(a) the employee may not exercise the statutory right and the corresponding right separately but may, in taking the leave for which the two rights provide, take advantage of whichever right is, in any particular respect, the more favourable, and

(b) the provisions of the 1996 Act and of these Regulations relating to the statutory right apply, subject to any modifications necessary to give effect to any more favourable contractual terms, to the exercise of the composite right described in sub-paragraph (a) as they apply to the exercise of the statutory right.

As amended by the Social Security Act 1990, section 21(1), Schedule 6 para 29; Employment Relations Act 1999, Schedule 4 Part 3 para 8; Care Standards Act 2000, Schedule 4 para 5; Employment Act 2002, s 1, s 3, Schedule 7 para 26; Pensions Act 2004 (Commencement No. 2, Transitional Provisions and Consequential Amendments) Order 2005/275 art.5(2); Pensions Act 2004, s 265; Paternity and Adoption Leave (Amendment) Regulations 2004/923 reg 3, reg 4; Civil Partnership Act 2004 (Amendments to Subordinate Legislation) Order 2005/2114 Sch 17 para 1(2)(a), Sch 17 para 1(2)(b), Sch 17 para 1(3); Maternity and Parental Leave etc. and the Paternity and Adoption Leave (Amendment) Regulations 2006/2014 reg 13, reg 14, reg 16, reg 17(a), reg 17(b), reg 17(c); Maternity and Parental Leave etc. and the Paternity and Adoption Leave (Amendment) Regulations 2008/1966 reg 9(1)(a), reg 9(1)(b), reg 9(1)(c), reg 9(1)(d), reg 9(1)(e), reg 10(a), reg 10(b), reg 10(c).

Employment Equality (Religion or Belief) Regulations 2003/1660

Part I GENERAL

1 CITATION, COMMENCEMENT AND EXTENT

(1) These Regulations may be cited as the Employment Equality (Religion or Belief) Regulations 2003, and shall come into force on 2nd December 2003.

(2) These Regulations do not extend to Northern Ireland.

2 INTERPRETATION

(1) In these Regulations—
  (a) "religion" means any religion,
  (b) "belief" means any religious or philosophical belief,
  (c) a reference to religion includes a reference to lack of religion, and
  (d) a reference to belief includes a reference to lack of belief.

(2) In these Regulations, references to discrimination are to any discrimination falling within regulation 3 (discrimination on grounds of religion or belief) or 4 (discrimination by way of victimisation) and related expressions shall be construed accordingly, and references to harassment shall be construed in accordance with regulation 5 (harassment on grounds of religion or belief).

(3) In these Regulations—

"act" includes a deliberate omission;

"benefits", except in regulation 9A (trustees and managers of occupational pension schemes), includes facilities and services;

"detriment" does not include harassment within the meaning of regulation 5;

references to "employer", in their application to a person at any time seeking to employ another, include a person who has no employees at that time;

"employment" means employment under a contract of service or of apprenticeship or a contract personally to do any work, and related expressions shall be construed accordingly;

"Great Britain", except where the context otherwise requires in regulation 26 (protection of Sikhs from discrimination in connection with requirements as to wearing of safety helmets), includes such of the territorial waters of the United Kingdom as are adjacent to Great Britain;

"Minister of the Crown" includes the Treasury and the Defence Council;

"proprietor", in relation to a school in England and Wales, has the meaning given by section 579 of the Education Act 1996, and, in relation to a school in Scotland, means the governing body, trustees, or other person or body of persons responsible for the management of the school; and

"school", in England and Wales, has the meaning given by section 4 of the Education Act 1996, and, in Scotland, has the meaning given by section 135(1) of the Education (Scotland) Act 1980, and references to a school are to an institution in so far as it is engaged in the provision of education under those sections.

3 DISCRIMINATION ON GROUNDS OF RELIGION OR BELIEF

(1)   For the purposes of these Regulations, a person ("A") discriminates against another person ("B") if—
(a) on the grounds of the religion or belief of B or of any other person except A (whether or not it is also A's religion or belief) A treats B less favourably than he treats or would treat other persons; or
(b) A applies to B a provision, criterion or practice which he applies or would apply equally to persons not of the same religion or belief as B, but—
(i)   which puts or would put persons of the same religion or belief as B at a particular disadvantage when compared with other persons,
(ii) which puts B at that disadvantage, and
(iii) which A cannot show to be a proportionate means of achieving a legitimate aim.

(3)   A comparison of B's case with that of another person under paragraph (1) must be such that the relevant circumstances in the one case are the same, or not materially different, in the other.

4 DISCRIMINATION BY WAY OF VICTIMISATION

(1)   For the purposes of these Regulations, a person ("A") discriminates against another person ("B") if he treats B less favourably than he treats or would treat other persons in the same circumstances, and does so by reason that B has—
(a) brought proceedings against A or any other person under these Regulations;
(b) given evidence or information in connection with proceedings brought by any person against A or any other person under these Regulations;
(c) otherwise done anything under or by reference to these Regulations in relation to A or any other person; or
(d) alleged that A or any other person has committed an act which (whether or not the allegation so states) would amount to a contravention of these Regulations,
or by reason that A knows that B intends to do any of those things, or suspects that B has done or intends to do any of them.

(2)   Paragraph (1) does not apply to treatment of B by reason of any allegation made by him, or evidence or information given by him, if the allegation, evidence or information was false and not made (or, as the case may be, given) in good faith.

5 HARASSMENT ON GROUNDS OF RELIGION OR BELIEF

(1) For the purposes of these Regulations, a person ("A") subjects another person ("B") to harassment where, on grounds of religion or belief, A engages in unwanted conduct which has the purpose or effect of—
  (a) violating B's dignity; or
  (b) creating an intimidating, hostile, degrading, humiliating or offensive environment for B.

(2) Conduct shall be regarded as having the effect specified in paragraph (1)(a) or (b) only if, having regard to all the circumstances, including in particular the perception of B, it should reasonably be considered as having that effect.

Part II DISCRIMINATION IN EMPLOYMENT AND VOCATIONAL TRAINING

6 APPLICANTS AND EMPLOYEES

(1) It is unlawful for an employer, in relation to employment by him at an establishment in Great Britain, to discriminate against a person—
  (a) in the arrangements he makes for the purpose of determining to whom he should offer employment;
  (b) in the terms on which he offers that person employment; or
  (c) by refusing to offer, or deliberately not offering, him employment.

(2) It is unlawful for an employer, in relation to a person whom he employs at an establishment in Great Britain, to discriminate against that person—
  (a) in the terms of employment which he affords him;
  (b) in the opportunities which he affords him for promotion, a transfer, training, or receiving any other benefit;
  (c) by refusing to afford him, or deliberately not affording him, any such opportunity; or
  (d) by dismissing him, or subjecting him to any other detriment.

(3) It is unlawful for an employer, in relation to employment by him at an establishment in Great Britain, to subject to harassment a person whom he employs or who has applied to him for employment.

(4) Paragraph (2) does not apply to benefits of any description if the employer is concerned with the provision (for payment or not) of benefits of that description to the public, or to a section of the public which includes the employee in question, unless—
  (a) that provision differs in a material respect from the provision of the benefits by the employer to his employees; or
  (b) the provision of the benefits to the employee in question is regulated by his contract of employment; or
  (c) the benefits relate to training.

(5) In paragraph (2)(d) reference to the dismissal of a person from employment includes reference—
  (a) to the termination of that person's employment by the expiration of any period (including a period expiring by reference to an event or circumstance), not being a termination immediately after which the employment is renewed on the same terms; and
  (b) to the termination of that person's employment by any act of his (including the giving of notice) in circumstances such that he is entitled to terminate it without notice by reason of the conduct of the employer.

7 EXCEPTION FOR GENUINE OCCUPATIONAL REQUIREMENT

(1) In relation to discrimination falling within regulation 3 (discrimination on grounds of religion or belief)—

(a) regulation 6(1)(a) or (c) does not apply to any employment;

(b) regulation 6(2)(b) or (c) does not apply to promotion or transfer to, or training for, any employment; and

(c) regulation 6(2)(d) does not apply to dismissal from any employment,

where paragraph (2) or (3) applies.

(2) This paragraph applies where, having regard to the nature of the employment or the context in which it is carried out—

(a) being of a particular religion or belief is a genuine and determining occupational requirement;

(b) it is proportionate to apply that requirement in the particular case; and

(c) either—

(i) the person to whom that requirement is applied does not meet it, or

(ii) the employer is not satisfied, and in all the circumstances it is reasonable for him not to be satisfied, that that person meets it,

and this paragraph applies whether or not the employer has an ethos based on religion or belief.

(3) This paragraph applies where an employer has an ethos based on religion or belief and, having regard to that ethos and to the nature of the employment or the context in which it is carried out—

(a) being of a particular religion or belief is a genuine occupational requirement for the job;

(b) it is proportionate to apply that requirement in the particular case; and

(c) either—

(i) the person to whom that requirement is applied does not meet it, or

(ii) the employer is not satisfied, and in all the circumstances it is reasonable for him not to be satisfied, that that person meets it.

8 CONTRACT WORKERS

(1) It is unlawful for a principal, in relation to contract work at an establishment in Great Britain, to discriminate against a contract worker—

(a) in the terms on which he allows him to do that work;

(b) by not allowing him to do it or continue to do it;

(c) in the way he affords him access to any benefits or by refusing or deliberately not affording him access to them; or

(d) by subjecting him to any other detriment.

(2) It is unlawful for a principal, in relation to contract work at an establishment in Great Britain, to subject a contract worker to harassment.

(3) A principal does not contravene paragraph (1)(b) by doing any act in relation to a contract worker where, if the work were to be done by a person taken into the principal's employment, that act would be lawful by virtue of regulation 7 (exception for genuine occupational requirement).

(4) Paragraph (1) does not apply to benefits of any description if the principal is concerned with the provision (for payment or not) of benefits of that description to the public, or to a section of the public to which the contract worker in question belongs, unless that provision differs in a material respect from the provision of the benefits by the principal to his contract workers.

(5) In this regulation—

"principal" means a person ("A") who makes work available for doing by individuals who are employed by another person who supplies them under a contract made with A;

"contract work" means work so made available; and

"contract worker" means any individual who is supplied to the principal under such a contract.

21 RELATIONSHIPS WHICH HAVE COME TO AN END

(1) In this regulation a "relevant relationship" is a relationship during the course of which an act of discrimination against, or harassment of, one party to the relationship ("B") by the other party to it ("A") is unlawful by virtue of any preceding provision of this Part.

(2) Where a relevant relationship has come to an end, it is unlawful for A—
(a) to discriminate against B by subjecting him to a detriment; or
(b) to subject B to harassment,
where the discrimination or harassment arises out of and is closely connected to that relationship.

(3) In paragraph (1), reference to an act of discrimination or harassment which is unlawful includes, in the case of a relationship which has come to an end before the coming into force of these Regulations, reference to an act of discrimination or harassment which would, after the coming into force of these Regulations, be unlawful.

Part III OTHER UNLAWFUL ACTS

22 LIABILITY OF EMPLOYERS AND PRINCIPALS

(1) Anything done by a person in the course of his employment shall be treated for the purposes of these Regulations as done by his employer as well as by him, whether or not it was done with the employer's knowledge or approval.

(2) Anything done by a person as agent for another person with the authority (whether express or implied, and whether precedent or subsequent) of that other person shall be treated for the purposes of these Regulations as done by that other person as well as by him.

(3) In proceedings brought under these Regulations against any person in respect of an act alleged to have been done by an employee of his it shall be a defence for that person to prove that he took such steps as were reasonably practicable to prevent the employee from doing that act, or from doing in the course of his employment acts of that description.

23 AIDING UNLAWFUL ACTS

(1) A person who knowingly aids another person to do an act made unlawful by these Regulations shall be treated for the purpose of these Regulations as himself doing an unlawful act of the like description.

(2) For the purposes of paragraph (1) an employee or agent for whose act the employer or principal is liable under regulation 22 (or would be so liable but for regulation 22(3)) shall be deemed to aid the doing of the act by the employer or principal.

(3) A person does not under this regulation knowingly aid another to do an unlawful act if—
   (a) he acts in reliance on a statement made to him by that other person that, by reason of any provision of these Regulations, the act which he aids would not be unlawful; and
   (b) it is reasonable for him to rely on the statement.

(4) A person who knowingly or recklessly makes a statement such as is referred to in paragraph (3)(a) which in a material respect is false or misleading commits an offence, and shall be liable on summary conviction to a fine not exceeding level 5 on the standard scale.

Part IV GENERAL EXCEPTIONS FROM PARTS II AND III

24 EXCEPTION FOR NATIONAL SECURITY

Nothing in Part II or III shall render unlawful an act done for the purpose of safeguarding national security, if the doing of the act was justified by that purpose.

25 EXCEPTIONS FOR POSITIVE ACTION

(1) Nothing in Part II or III shall render unlawful any act done in or in connection with—
   (a) affording persons of a particular religion or belief access to facilities for training which would help fit them for particular work; or
   (b) encouraging persons of a particular religion or belief to take advantage of opportunities for doing particular work,
   where it reasonably appears to the person doing the act that it prevents or compensates for disadvantages linked to religion or belief suffered by persons of that religion or belief doing that work or likely to take up that work.

(2) Nothing in Part II or III shall render unlawful any act done by a trade organisation within the meaning of regulation 15 in or in connection with—
   (a) affording only members of the organisation who are of a particular religion or belief access to facilities for training which would help fit them for holding a post of any kind in the organisation; or
   (b) encouraging only members of the organisation who are of a particular religion or belief to take advantage of opportunities for holding such posts in the organisation,
   where it reasonably appears to the organisation that the act prevents or compensates for disadvantages linked to religion or belief suffered by those of that religion or belief holding such posts or likely to hold such posts.

(3) Nothing in Part II or III shall render unlawful any act done by a trade organisation within the meaning of regulation 15 in or in connection with encouraging only persons of a particular religion or belief to become members of the organisation where it reasonably appears to the organisation that the act prevents or compensates for disadvantages linked to religion or belief suffered by persons of that religion or belief who are, or are eligible to become, members.

26 PROTECTION OF SIKHS FROM DISCRIMINATION IN CONNECTION WITH REQUIREMENTS AS TO WEARING OF SAFETY HELMETS

(1) Where—
   (a) any person applies to a Sikh any provision, criterion or practice relating to the wearing by him of a safety helmet while he is on a construction site; and

(b) at the time when he so applies the provision, criterion or practice that person has no reasonable grounds for believing that the Sikh would not wear a turban at all times when on such a site,

then, for the purposes of regulation 3(1)(b)(iii), the provision, criterion or practice shall be taken to be one which cannot be shown to be a proportionate means of achieving a legitimate aim.

(2) Any special treatment afforded to a Sikh in consequence of section 11(1) or (2) of the Employment Act 1989 (exemption of Sikhs from requirements as to wearing of safety helmets on construction sites) shall not be regarded as giving rise, in relation to any other person, to any discrimination falling within regulation 3.

(3) In this regulation—

"construction site" means any place in Great Britain where any building operations or works of engineering construction are being undertaken, but does not include any site within the territorial sea adjacent to Great Britain unless there are being undertaken on that site such operations or works as are activities falling within Article 8(a) of the Health and Safety at Work etc Act 1974 (Application outside Great Britain) Order 2001; and

"safety helmet" means any form of protective headgear.

(4) In this regulation—
(a) any reference to a Sikh is a reference to a follower of the Sikh religion; and
(b) any reference to a Sikh being on a construction site is a reference to his being there whether while at work or otherwise.

Part V ENFORCEMENT

27 RESTRICTION OF PROCEEDINGS FOR BREACH OF REGULATIONS

(1) Except as provided by these Regulations no proceedings, whether civil or criminal, shall lie against any person in respect of an act by reason that the act is unlawful by virtue of a provision of these Regulations.

(2) Paragraph (1) does not prevent the making of an application for judicial review or the investigation or determination of any matter in accordance with Part X (investigations: the Pensions Ombudsman) of the Pension Schemes Act 1993 by the Pensions Ombudsman.

28 JURISDICTION OF EMPLOYMENT TRIBUNALS

(1) A complaint by any person ("the complainant") that another person ("the respondent")—
(a) has committed against the complainant an act to which this regulation applies; or
(b) is by virtue of regulation 22 (liability of employers and principals) or 23 (aiding unlawful acts) to be treated as having committed against the complainant such an act,
may be presented to an employment tribunal.

(2) This regulation applies to any act of discrimination or harassment which is unlawful by virtue of any provision of Part II other than—
(a) where the act is one in respect of which an appeal or proceedings in the nature of an appeal may be brought under any enactment, regulation 16 (qualifications bodies);
(b) regulation 20 (institutions of further and higher education); or
(c) where the act arises out of and is closely connected to a relationship between the complainant and the respondent which has come to an end but during the course of which an act of discrimination against, or harassment of, the complainant by the

respondent would have been unlawful by virtue of regulation 20, regulation 21 (relationships which have come to an end).

(3) In paragraph (2)(c), reference to an act of discrimination or harassment which would have been unlawful includes, in the case of a relationship which has come to an end before the coming into force of these Regulations, reference to an act of discrimination or harassment which would, after the coming into force of these Regulations, have been unlawful.

(4) In this regulation, "enactment" includes an enactment comprised in, or in an instrument made under, an Act of the Scottish Parliament.

29 BURDEN OF PROOF: EMPLOYMENT TRIBUNALS

(1) This regulation applies to any complaint presented under regulation 28 to an employment tribunal.

(2) Where, on the hearing of the complaint, the complainant proves facts from which the tribunal could, apart from this regulation, conclude in the absence of an adequate explanation that the respondent—
(a) has committed against the complainant an act to which regulation 28 applies; or
(b) is by virtue of regulation 22 (liability of employers and principals) or 23 (aiding unlawful acts) to be treated as having committed against the complainant such an act,
the tribunal shall uphold the complaint unless the respondent proves that he did not commit, or as the case may be, is not to be treated as having committed, that act.

30 REMEDIES ON COMPLAINTS IN EMPLOYMENT TRIBUNALS

(1) Where an employment tribunal finds that a complaint presented to it under regulation 28 is well-founded, the tribunal shall make such of the following as it considers just and equitable—
(a) an order declaring the rights of the complainant and the respondent in relation to the act to which the complaint relates;
(b) an order requiring the respondent to pay to the complainant compensation of an amount corresponding to any damages he could have been ordered by a county court or by a sheriff court to pay to the complainant if the complaint had fallen to be dealt with under regulation 31 (jurisdiction of county and sheriff courts);
(c) a recommendation that the respondent take within a specified period action appearing to the tribunal to be practicable for the purpose of obviating or reducing the adverse effect on the complainant of any act of discrimination or harassment to which the complaint relates.

(2) As respects an unlawful act of discrimination falling within regulation 3(1)(b), if the respondent proves that the provision, criterion or practice was not applied with the intention of treating the complainant unfavourably on grounds of religion or belief, an order may be made under paragraph (1)(b) only if the employment tribunal—
(a) makes such order under paragraph (1)(a) (if any) and such recommendation under paragraph (1)(c) (if any) as it would have made if it had no power to make an order under paragraph (1)(b); and
(b) (where it makes an order under paragraph (1)(a) or a recommendation under paragraph (1)(c) or both) considers that it is just and equitable to make an order under paragraph (1)(b) as well.

(3)   If without reasonable justification the respondent to a complaint fails to comply with a recommendation made by an employment tribunal under paragraph (1)(c), then, if it thinks it just and equitable to do so—
   (a) the tribunal may increase the amount of compensation required to be paid to the complainant in respect of the complaint by an order made under paragraph (1)(b); or
   (b) if an order under paragraph (1)(b) was not made, the tribunal may make such an order.

(4)   Where an amount of compensation falls to be awarded under paragraph (1)(b), the tribunal may include in the award interest on that amount subject to, and in accordance with, the provisions of the Employment Tribunals (Interest on Awards in Discrimination Cases) Regulations 1996.

(5)   This regulation has effect subject to paragraph 7 of Schedule 1A (occupational pension schemes).

31 JURISDICTION OF COUNTY AND SHERIFF COURTS

(1)   A claim by any person ("the claimant") that another person ("the respondent")—
   (a) has committed against the claimant an act to which this regulation applies; or
   (b) is by virtue of regulation 22 (liability of employers and principals) or 23 (aiding unlawful acts) to be treated as having committed against the claimant such an act,
   may be made the subject of civil proceedings in like manner as any other claim in tort or (in Scotland) in reparation for breach of statutory duty.

(2)   Proceedings brought under paragraph (1) shall—
   (a) in England and Wales, be brought only in a county court; and
   (b) in Scotland, be brought only in a sheriff court.

(3)   For the avoidance of doubt it is hereby declared that damages in respect of an unlawful act to which this regulation applies may include compensation for injury to feelings whether or not they include compensation under any other head.

(4)   This regulation applies to any act of discrimination or harassment which is unlawful by virtue of—
   (a) regulation 20 (institutions of further and higher education); or
   (b) where the act arises out of and is closely connected to a relationship between the claimant and the respondent which has come to an end but during the course of which an act of discrimination against, or harassment of, the claimant by the respondent would have been unlawful by virtue of regulation 20, regulation 21 (relationships which have come to an end).

(5)   In paragraph (4)(b), reference to an act of discrimination or harassment which would have been unlawful includes, in the case of a relationship which has come to an end before the coming into force of these Regulations, reference to an act of discrimination or harassment which would, after the coming into force of these Regulations, have been unlawful.

32 BURDEN OF PROOF: COUNTY AND SHERIFF COURTS

(1)   This regulation applies to any claim brought under regulation 31 in a county court in England and Wales or a sheriff court in Scotland.

(2)   Where, on the hearing of the claim, the claimant proves facts from which the court could, apart from this regulation, conclude in the absence of an adequate explanation that the respondent—

(a) has committed against the claimant an act to which regulation 31 applies; or

(b) is by virtue of regulation 22 (liability of employers and principals) or 23 (aiding unlawful acts) to be treated as having committed against the claimant such an act,

the court shall uphold the claim unless the respondent proves that he did not commit, or as the case may be, is not to be treated as having committed, that act.

33 HELP FOR PERSONS IN OBTAINING INFORMATION ETC.

(1) In accordance with this regulation, a person ("the person aggrieved") who considers he may have been discriminated against, or subjected to harassment, in contravention of these Regulations may serve on the respondent to a complaint presented under regulation 28 (jurisdiction of employment tribunals) or a claim brought under regulation 31 (jurisdiction of county and sheriff courts) questions in the form set out in Schedule 2 or forms to the like effect with such variation as the circumstances require; and the respondent may if he so wishes reply to such questions by way of the form set out in Schedule 3 or forms to the like effect with such variation as the circumstances require.

(2) Where the person aggrieved questions the respondent (whether in accordance with paragraph (1) or not)—

(a) the questions, and any reply by the respondent (whether in accordance with paragraph (1) or not) shall, subject to the following provisions of this regulation, be admissible as evidence in the proceedings;

(b) if it appears to the court or tribunal that the respondent deliberately, and without reasonable excuse, omitted to reply within eight weeks of service of the questions or that his reply is evasive or equivocal, the court or tribunal may draw any inference from that fact that it considers it just and equitable to draw, including an inference that he committed an unlawful act.

(3) In proceedings before a county court in England or Wales or a sheriff court in Scotland, a question shall only be admissible as evidence in pursuance of paragraph (2)(a)—

(a) where it was served before those proceedings had been instituted, if it was so served within the period of six months beginning when the act complained of was done;

(b) where it was served when those proceedings had been instituted, if it was served with the leave of, and within a period specified by, the court in question.

(4) In proceedings before an employment tribunal, a question shall only be admissible as evidence in pursuance of paragraph (2)(a)—

(a) where it was served before a complaint had been presented to a tribunal, if it was so served—

(i) within the period of three months beginning when the act complained of was done; or

(ii) where paragraph (1A) of regulation 34 applies, within the extended period;

(b) where it was served when a complaint had been presented to the tribunal, either—

(i) if it was so served within the period of twenty-one days beginning with the day on which the complaint was presented, or

(ii) if it was so served later with leave given, and within a period specified, by a direction of the tribunal.

(5) A question and any reply thereto may be served on the respondent or, as the case may be, on the person aggrieved—

(a) by delivering it to him;

(b) by sending it by post to him at his usual or last-known residence or place of business;

(c) where the person to be served is a body corporate or is a trade union or employers' association within the meaning of the Trade Union and Labour Relations

(Consolidation) Act 1992, by delivering it to the secretary or clerk of the body, union or association at its registered or principal office or by sending it by post to the secretary or clerk at that office;

(d) where the person to be served is acting by a solicitor, by delivering it at, or by sending it by post to, the solicitor's address for service; or

(e) where the person to be served is the person aggrieved, by delivering the reply, or sending it by post, to him at his address for reply as stated by him in the document containing the questions.

(6) This regulation is without prejudice to any other enactment or rule of law regulating interlocutory and preliminary matters in proceedings before a county court, sheriff court or employment tribunal, and has effect subject to any enactment or rule of law regulating the admissibility of evidence in such proceedings.

(7) In this regulation "respondent" includes a prospective respondent.

34 PERIOD WITHIN WHICH PROCEEDINGS TO BE BROUGHT

(1) An employment tribunal shall not consider a complaint under regulation 28 unless it is presented to the tribunal before the end of—
(a) the period of three months beginning when the act complained of was done; or
(b) in a case to which regulation 36(7) (armed forces) applies, the period of six months so beginning.

(1A) Where the period within which a complaint must be presented in accordance with paragraph (1) is extended by regulation 15 of the Employment Act 2002 (Dispute Resolution) Regulations 2004, the period within which the complaint must be presented shall be the extended period rather than the period in paragraph (1).

(2) A county court or a sheriff court shall not consider a claim brought under regulation 31 unless proceedings in respect of the claim are instituted before the end of the period of six months beginning when the act complained of was done.

(3) A court or tribunal may nevertheless consider any such complaint or claim which is out of time if, in all the circumstances of the case, it considers that it is just and equitable to do so.

(4) For the purposes of this regulation and regulation 33 (help for persons in obtaining information etc)—
(a) when the making of a contract is, by reason of the inclusion of any term, an unlawful act, that act shall be treated as extending throughout the duration of the contract; and
(b) any act extending over a period shall be treated as done at the end of that period; and
(c) a deliberate omission shall be treated as done when the person in question decided upon it,
and in the absence of evidence establishing the contrary a person shall be taken for the purposes of this regulation to decide upon an omission when he does an act inconsistent with doing the omitted act or, if he has done no such inconsistent act, when the period expires within which he might reasonably have been expected to do the omitted act if it was to be done.

SCHEDULE 4 VALIDITY OF CONTRACTS, COLLECTIVE AGREEMENT AND RULES OF UNDERTAKINGS

Part I VALIDITY AND REVISION OF CONTRACTS

1

(1)   A term of a contract is void where—
  (a) the making of the contract is, by reason of the inclusion of the term, unlawful by virtue of these Regulations;
  (b) it is included in furtherance of an act which is unlawful by virtue of these Regulations; or
  (c) it provides for the doing of an act which is unlawful by virtue of these Regulations.

(2)   Sub-paragraph (1) does not apply to a term the inclusion of which constitutes, or is in furtherance of, or provides for, unlawful discrimination against, or harassment of, a party to the contract, but the term shall be unenforceable against that party.

(3)   A term in a contract which purports to exclude or limit any provision of these Regulations is unenforceable by any person in whose favour the term would operate apart from this paragraph.

(4)   Sub-paragraphs (1), (2) and (3) shall apply whether the contract was entered into before or after the date on which these Regulations come into force; but in the case of a contract made before that date, those sub-paragraphs do not apply in relation to any period before that date.

2

(1)   Paragraph 1(3) does not apply—
  (a) to a contract settling a complaint to which regulation 28(1) (jurisdiction of employment tribunals) applies where the contract is made with the assistance of a conciliation officer within the meaning of section 211 of the Trade Union and Labour Relations (Consolidation) Act 1992;
  (b) to a contract settling a complaint to which regulation 28(1) applies if the conditions regulating compromise contracts under this Schedule are satisfied in relation to the contract; or
  (c) to a contract settling a claim to which regulation 31 (jurisdiction of county or sheriff courts) applies.

(2)   The conditions regulating compromise contracts under this Schedule are that—
  (a) the contract must be in writing;
  (b) the contract must relate to the particular complaint;
  (c) the complainant must have received advice from a relevant independent adviser as to the terms and effect of the proposed contract and in particular its effect on his ability to pursue a complaint before an employment tribunal;
  (d) there must be in force, when the adviser gives the advice, a contract of insurance, or an indemnity provided for members of a profession or professional body, covering the risk of a claim by the complainant in respect of loss arising in consequence of the advice;
  (e) the contract must identify the adviser; and
  (f) the contract must state that the conditions regulating compromise contracts under this Schedule are satisfied.

(3)   A person is a relevant independent adviser for the purposes of sub-paragraph (2)(c)—

(a) if he is a qualified lawyer;

(b) if he is an officer, official, employee or member of an independent trade union who has been certified in writing by the trade union as competent to give advice and as authorised to do so on behalf of the trade union; or

(c) if he works at an advice centre (whether as an employee or a volunteer) and has been certified in writing by the centre as competent to give advice and as authorised to do so on behalf of the centre.

(4) But a person is not a relevant independent adviser for the purposes of sub-paragraph (2)(c) in relation to the complainant—

(a) if he is, is employed by or is acting in the matter for the other party or a person who is connected with the other party;

(b) in the case of a person within sub-paragraph (3)(b) or (c), if the trade union or advice centre is the other party or a person who is connected with the other party; or

(c) in the case of a person within sub-paragraph (3)(c), if the complainant makes a payment for the advice received from him.

(5) In sub-paragraph (3)(a) "qualified lawyer" means—

(a) as respects England and Wales, a person who, for the purposes of the Legal Services Act 2007), is an authorised person in relation to an activity which constitutes the exercise of a right of audience or the conduct of litigation (within the meaning of that Act); and

(b) as respects Scotland, an advocate (whether in practice as such or employed to give legal advice), or a solicitor who holds a practising certificate.

(5A) A person shall be treated as being a qualified lawyer within sub-paragraph (5)(a) if he is a Fellow of the Institute of Legal Executives employed by a solicitors' practice.

(6) In sub-paragraph (3)(b) "independent trade union" has the same meaning as in the Trade Union and Labour Relations (Consolidation) Act 1992.

(7) For the purposes of sub-paragraph (4)(a) any two persons are to be treated as connected—

(a) if one is a company of which the other (directly or indirectly) has control; or

(b) if both are companies of which a third person (directly or indirectly) has control.

(8) An agreement under which the parties agree to submit a dispute to arbitration–

(a) shall be regarded for the purposes of sub-paragraph (1)(a) and (b) as being a contract settling a complaint if—

(i) the dispute is covered by a scheme having effect by virtue of an order under section 212A of the Trade Union and Labour Relations (Consolidation) Act 1992, and

(ii) the agreement is to submit it to arbitration in accordance with the scheme, but

(b) shall be regarded as neither being nor including such a contract in any other case.

3

(1) On the application of a person interested in a contract to which paragraph 1(1) or (2) applies, a county court or a sheriff court may make such order as it thinks fit for—

(a) removing or modifying any term rendered void by paragraph 1(1), or

(b) removing or modifying any term made unenforceable by paragraph 1(2);

but such an order shall not be made unless all persons affected have been given notice in writing of the application (except where under rules of court notice may be dispensed with) and have been afforded an opportunity to make representations to the court.

(2)   An order under sub-paragraph (1) may include provision as respects any period before the making of the order (but after the coming into force of these Regulations).

Part II COLLECTIVE AGREEMENTS AND RULES OF UNDERTAKINGS

4

(1)   This Part of this Schedule applies to—
   (a) any term of a collective agreement, including an agreement which was not intended, or is presumed not to have been intended, to be a legally enforceable contract;
   (b) any rule made by an employer for application to all or any of the persons who are employed by him or who apply to be, or are, considered by him for employment;
   (c) any rule made by a trade organisation (within the meaning of regulation 15) or a qualifications body (within the meaning of regulation 16) for application to—
      (i)   all or any of its members or prospective members; or
      (ii) all or any of the persons on whom it has conferred professional or trade qualifications (within the meaning of regulation 16) or who are seeking the professional or trade qualifications which it has power to confer.

(2)   Any term or rule to which this Part of this Schedule applies is void where—
   (a) the making of the collective agreement is, by reason of the inclusion of the term, unlawful by virtue of these Regulations;
   (b) the term or rule is included or made in furtherance of an act which is unlawful by virtue of these Regulations; or
   (c) the term or rule provides for the doing of an act which is unlawful by virtue of these Regulations.

(3)   Sub-paragraph (2) shall apply whether the agreement was entered into, or the rule made, before or after the date on which these Regulations come into force; but in the case of an agreement entered into, or a rule made, before the date on which these Regulations come into force, that sub-paragraph does not apply in relation to any period before that date.

5

A person to whom this paragraph applies may present a complaint to an employment tribunal that a term or rule is void by virtue of paragraph 4 if he has reason to believe—
(a)   that the term or rule may at some future time have effect in relation to him; and

(b)   where he alleges that it is void by virtue of paragraph 4(2)(c), that—
   (i)   an act for the doing of which it provides, may at some such time be done in relation to him, and
   (ii) the act would be unlawful by virtue of these Regulations if done in relation to him in present circumstances.

6

In the case of a complaint about—
(a)   a term of a collective agreement made by or on behalf of—
   (i)   an employer,
   (ii) an organisation of employers of which an employer is a member, or
   (iii) an association of such organisations of one of which an employer is a member, or

(b)   a rule made by an employer within the meaning of paragraph 4(1)(b), paragraph 5 applies to any person who is, or is genuinely and actively seeking to become, one of his employees.

7

In the case of a complaint about a rule made by an organisation or body to which paragraph 4(1)(c) applies, paragraph 5 applies to any person—

(a)   who is, or is genuinely and actively seeking to become, a member of the organisation or body;

(b)   on whom the organisation or body has conferred a professional or trade qualification (within the meaning of regulation 16); or

(c)   who is genuinely and actively seeking such a professional or trade qualification which the organisation or body has power to confer.

8

(1)   When an employment tribunal finds that a complaint presented to it under paragraph 5 is well-founded the tribunal shall make an order declaring that the term or rule is void.

(2)   An order under sub-paragraph (1) may include provision as respects any period before the making of the order (but after the coming into force of these Regulations).

9

The avoidance by virtue of paragraph 4(2) of any term or rule which provides for any person to be discriminated against shall be without prejudice to the following rights (except in so far as they enable any person to require another person to be treated less favourably than himself), namely—

(a)   such of the rights of the person to be discriminated against; and

(b)   such of the rights of any person who will be treated more favourably in direct or indirect consequence of the discrimination,

as are conferred by or in respect of a contract made or modified wholly or partly in pursuance of, or by reference to, that term or rule.

10

In this Schedule "collective agreement" means any agreement relating to one or more of the matters mentioned in section 178(2) of the Trade Union and Labour Relations (Consolidation) Act 1992 (meaning of trade dispute), being an agreement made by or on behalf of one or more employers or one or more organisations of employers or associations of such organisations with one or more organisations of workers or associations of such organisations.

As amended by Education Act 1997, s 51; Education Act 2002, Schedule 22, Part 3; Employment Equality (Religion or Belief) (Amendment) Regulations 2003/2828 reg 3(2), reg 3(4), reg 3(5); Employment Act 2002 (Dispute Resolution) Regulations 2004/752 reg 17(g)(i), reg 17(g)(ii); Employment Equality (Religion or Belief) Regulations 2003 (Amendment) (No.2) Regulations 2004/2520 reg 2; Equality Act 2006, Pt 2 s 77(1), Pt 2 s 77(2), Pt 2 s 77(3); Employment Equality (Sexual Orientation) (Religion or Belief) (Amendment) Regulations 2007/2269 reg 4(2); Legal Services Act 2007 (Consequential Amendments) Order 2009/3348 art 23.

EMPLOYMENT EQUALITY (SEXUAL ORIENTATION) REGULATIONS 2003/1661

Part I GENERAL

1 CITATION, COMMENCEMENT AND EXTENT

(1)   These Regulations may be cited as the Employment Equality (Sexual Orientation) Regulations 2003, and shall come into force on 1st December 2003.

(2)   These Regulations do not extend to Northern Ireland.

2 INTERPRETATION

(1)   In these Regulations, "sexual orientation" means a sexual orientation towards—
     (a)   persons of the same sex;
     (b)   persons of the opposite sex; or
     (c)   persons of the same sex and of the opposite sex.

(2)   In these Regulations, references to discrimination are to any discrimination falling within regulation 3 (discrimination on grounds of sexual orientation) or 4 (discrimination by way of victimisation) and related expressions shall be construed accordingly, and references to harassment shall be construed in accordance with regulation 5 (harassment on grounds of sexual orientation).

(3)   In these Regulations—

"act" includes a deliberate omission;

"benefits", except in regulation 9A (trustees and managers of occupational pension schemes), includes facilities and services;

"detriment" does not include harassment within the meaning of regulation 5;

references to "employer", in their application to a person at any time seeking to employ another, include a person who has no employees at that time;

"employment" means employment under a contract of service or of apprenticeship or a contract personally to do any work, and related expressions shall be construed accordingly;

"Great Britain" includes such of the territorial waters of the United Kingdom as are adjacent to Great Britain;

"Minister of the Crown" includes the Treasury and the Defence Council;

"proprietor", in relation to a school in England and Wales, has the meaning given by section 579 of the Education Act 1996, and, in relation to a school in Scotland, means the governing body, trustees, or other person or body of persons responsible for the management of the school; and

"school", in England and Wales, has the meaning given by section 4 of the Education Act 1996, and, in Scotland, has the meaning given by section 135(1) of the Education (Scotland) Act 1980, and references to a school are to an institution in so far as it is engaged in the provision of education under those sections.

3 DISCRIMINATION ON GROUNDS OF SEXUAL ORIENTATION

(1) For the purposes of these Regulations, a person ("A") discriminates against another person ("B") if—

(a) on grounds of sexual orientation, A treats B less favourably than he treats or would treat other persons; or

(b) A applies to B a provision, criterion or practice which he applies or would apply equally to persons not of the same sexual orientation as B, but—

(i) which puts or would put persons of the same sexual orientation as B at a particular disadvantage when compared with other persons,

(ii) which puts B at that disadvantage, and

(iii) which A cannot show to be a proportionate means of achieving a legitimate aim.

(2) A comparison of B's case with that of another person under paragraph (1) must be such that the relevant circumstances in the one case are the same, or not materially different, in the other.

(3) For the purposes of paragraph (2), in a comparison of B's case with that of another person the fact that one of the persons (whether or not B) is a civil partner while the other is married shall not be treated as a material difference between their respective circumstances.

4 DISCRIMINATION BY WAY OF VICTIMISATION

(1) For the purposes of these Regulations, a person ("A") discriminates against another person ("B") if he treats B less favourably than he treats or would treat other persons in the same circumstances, and does so by reason that B has—

(a) brought proceedings against A or any other person under these Regulations;

(b) given evidence or information in connection with proceedings brought by any person against A or any other person under these Regulations;

(c) otherwise done anything under or by reference to these Regulations in relation to A or any other person; or

(d) alleged that A or any other person has committed an act which (whether or not the allegation so states) would amount to a contravention of these Regulations,

or by reason that A knows that B intends to do any of those things, or suspects that B has done or intends to do any of them.

(2) Paragraph (1) does not apply to treatment of B by reason of any allegation made by him, or evidence or information given by him, if the allegation, evidence or information was false and not made (or, as the case may be, given) in good faith.

5 HARASSMENT ON GROUNDS OF SEXUAL ORIENTATION

(1) For the purposes of these Regulations, a person ("A") subjects another person ("B") to harassment where, on grounds of sexual orientation, A engages in unwanted conduct which has the purpose or effect of—

(a) violating B's dignity; or

(b) creating an intimidating, hostile, degrading, humiliating or offensive environment for B.

(2) Conduct shall be regarded as having the effect specified in paragraph (1)(a) or (b) only if, having regard to all the circumstances, including in particular the perception of B, it should reasonably be considered as having that effect.

Part II DISCRIMINATION IN EMPLOYMENT AND VOCATIONAL TRAINING

6 APPLICANTS AND EMPLOYEES

(1)   It is unlawful for an employer, in relation to employment by him at an establishment in Great Britain, to discriminate against a person—
   (a) in the arrangements he makes for the purpose of determining to whom he should offer employment;
   (b) in the terms on which he offers that person employment; or
   (c) by refusing to offer, or deliberately not offering, him employment.

(2)   It is unlawful for an employer, in relation to a person whom he employs at an establishment in Great Britain, to discriminate against that person—
   (a) in the terms of employment which he affords him;
   (b) in the opportunities which he affords him for promotion, a transfer, training, or receiving any other benefit;
   (c) by refusing to afford him, or deliberately not affording him, any such opportunity; or
   (d) by dismissing him, or subjecting him to any other detriment.

(3)   It is unlawful for an employer, in relation to employment by him at an establishment in Great Britain, to subject to harassment a person whom he employs or who has applied to him for employment.

(4)   Paragraph (2) does not apply to benefits of any description if the employer is concerned with the provision (for payment or not) of benefits of that description to the public, or to a section of the public which includes the employee in question, unless—
   (a) that provision differs in a material respect from the provision of the benefits by the employer to his employees; or
   (b) the provision of the benefits to the employee in question is regulated by his contract of employment; or
   (c) the benefits relate to training.

(5)   In paragraph (2)(d) reference to the dismissal of a person from employment includes reference—
   (a) to the termination of that person's employment by the expiration of any period (including a period expiring by reference to an event or circumstance), not being a termination immediately after which the employment is renewed on the same terms; and
   (b) to the termination of that person's employment by any act of his (including the giving of notice) in circumstances such that he is entitled to terminate it without notice by reason of the conduct of the employer.

7 EXCEPTION FOR GENUINE OCCUPATIONAL REQUIREMENT ETC.

(1)   In relation to discrimination falling within regulation 3 (discrimination on grounds of sexual orientation)—
   (a) regulation 6(1)(a) or (c) does not apply to any employment;
   (b) regulation 6(2)(b) or (c) does not apply to promotion or transfer to, or training for, any employment; and
   (c) regulation 6(2)(d) does not apply to dismissal from any employment,
   where paragraph (2) or (3) applies.

(2)   This paragraph applies where, having regard to the nature of the employment or the context in which it is carried out—
   (a) being of a particular sexual orientation is a genuine and determining occupational requirement;

(b) it is proportionate to apply that requirement in the particular case; and

(c) either—

    (i) the person to whom that requirement is applied does not meet it, or

    (ii) the employer is not satisfied, and in all the circumstances it is reasonable for him not to be satisfied, that that person meets it,

and this paragraph applies whether or not the employment is for purposes of an organised religion.

(3) This paragraph applies where—

(a) the employment is for purposes of an organised religion;

(b) the employer applies a requirement related to sexual orientation—

    (i) so as to comply with the doctrines of the religion, or

    (ii) because of the nature of the employment and the context in which it is carried out, so as to avoid conflicting with the strongly held religious convictions of a significant number of the religion's followers; and

(c) either—

    (i) the person to whom that requirement is applied does not meet it, or

    (ii) the employer is not satisfied, and in all the circumstances it is reasonable for him not to be satisfied, that that person meets it.

As amended by the Education Act 1997, s 51; School Standards and Framework Act 1998, section 140(1), Schedule 30, para 183(a)(iii); Education Act 2002, Schedule 22, Part 3; Education Act 2002 (Modification and Transitional Provisions) (England) Regulations 2003/2045; Employment Equality (Sexual Orientation) (Amendment) Regulations 2003/2827 reg 3(2); Civil Partnership Act 2004 (Amendments to Subordinate Legislation) Order 2005/2114 Sch 17 para 7(2); Education Act 2002 (Transitional Provisions and Consequential Amendments) (Wales) Regulations 2005/2913; Employment Equality (Sexual Orientation) (Religion or Belief) (Amendment) Regulations 2007/2269 reg 3(2)

INFORMATION AND CONSULTATION OF EMPLOYEES REGULATIONS 2004/3426

Part I GENERAL

2 INTERPRETATION

In these Regulations—

"the 1996 Act" means the Employment Rights Act 1996;

"Appeal Tribunal" means the Employment Appeal Tribunal;

"CAC" means the Central Arbitration Committee;

"consultation" means the exchange of views and establishment of a dialogue between—
(a) information and consultation representatives and the employer; or
(b) in the case of a negotiated agreement which provides as mentioned in regulation 16(1) (f)(ii), the employees and the employer;
"contract of employment" means a contract of service or apprenticeship, whether express or implied, and (if it is express) whether oral or in writing;

"date of the ballot" means the day or last day on which voting may take place and, where voting in different parts of the ballot is arranged to take place on different days or during periods ending on different days, the last of those days;

"employee" means an individual who has entered into or works under a contract of employment and in Part VIII and regulation 40 includes, where the employment has ceased, an individual who worked under a contract of employment;

"employee request" means a request by employees under regulation 7 for the employer to initiate negotiations to reach an agreement under these Regulations;

"employer notification" means a notification by an employer under regulation 11 that he wishes to initiate negotiations to reach an agreement under these Regulations;

"information" means data transmitted by the employer—
(a) to the information and consultation representatives; or
(b) in the case of a negotiated agreement which provides as mentioned in regulation 16(1) (f)(ii), directly to the employees,
in order to enable those representatives or those employees to examine and to acquaint themselves with the subject matter of the data;

"Information and Consultation Directive" means European Parliament and Council Directive 2002/14/EC of 11 March 2002 establishing a general framework for informing and consulting employees in the European Community;

"information and consultation representative" means—
(a) in the case of a negotiated agreement which provides as mentioned in regulation 16(1) (f)(i), a person appointed or elected in accordance with that agreement; or
(b) a person elected in accordance with regulation 19(1);

"negotiated agreement" means—
(a) an agreement between the employer and the negotiating representatives reached through negotiations as provided for in regulation 14 which satisfies the requirements of regulation 16(1); or
(b) an agreement between the employer and the information and consultation representatives referred to in regulation 18(2);

"negotiating representative" means a person elected or appointed pursuant to regulation 14(1)(a);

"parties" means the employer and the negotiating representatives or the information and consultation representatives, as the case may be;

"Pension Schemes Regulations" means the Occupational and Personal Pension Schemes (Consultation by Employers and Miscellaneous Amendment) Regulations 2006;

"pre-existing agreement" means an agreement between an employer and his employees or their representatives which—
(a) is made prior to the making of an employee request; and
(b) satisfies the conditions set out in regulation 8(1)(a) to (d),
but does not include an agreement concluded in accordance with regulations 17 or 42 to 45 of the Transnational Information and Consultation of Employees Regulations 1999 or a negotiated agreement;

"standard information and consultation provisions" means the provisions set out in regulation 20;

"undertaking" means a public or private undertaking carrying out an economic activity, whether or not operating for gain;

"valid employee request" means an employee request made to their employer by the employees of an undertaking to which these Regulations apply (under regulation 3) that satisfies the requirements of regulation 7 and is not prevented from being valid by regulation 12.

3 APPLICATION

(1)   These Regulations apply to undertakings—
(a) employing in the United Kingdom, in accordance with the calculation in regulation 4, at least the number of employees in column 1 of the table in Schedule 1 to these Regulations on or after the corresponding date in column 2 of that table; and
(b) subject to paragraph (2), whose registered office, head office or principal place of business is situated in Great Britain.

(2)   Where the registered office is situated in Great Britain and the head office or principal place of business is situated in Northern Ireland or vice versa, these Regulations shall only apply where the majority of employees are employed to work in Great Britain.

(3)   In these Regulations, an undertaking to which these Regulations apply is referred to, in relation to its employees, as "the employer".

Part II EMPLOYEE NUMBERS AND ENTITLEMENT TO DATA

4 CALCULATION OF NUMBER OF EMPLOYEES

(1)   Subject to paragraph (4), the number of employees for the purposes of regulation 3(1) shall be determined by ascertaining the average number of employees employed in the previous twelve months, calculated in accordance with paragraph (2).

(2)   Subject to paragraph (3), the average number of employees is to be ascertained by determining the number of employees employed in each month in the previous twelve months (whether they were employed throughout the month or not), adding together those monthly figures and dividing the number by 12.

(3)   For the purposes of the calculation in paragraph (2) if, for the whole of a month within the twelve month period, an employee works under a contract by virtue of which he would have worked for 75 hours or less in that month—
(i)   were the month to have contained 21 working days;
(ii) were the employee to have had no absences from work; and
(iii) were the employee to have worked no overtime,

the employee may be counted as representing half of a full-time employee for the month in question, if the employer so decides.

(4)   If the undertaking has been in existence for less than twelve months, the references to twelve months in paragraphs (1), (2) and (3), and the divisor of 12 referred to in paragraph (2), shall be replaced by the number of months the undertaking has been in existence.

Part III NEGOTIATED AGREEMENTS

7 EMPLOYEE REQUEST TO NEGOTIATE AN AGREEMENT IN RESPECT OF INFORMATION AND CONSULTATION

(1)   On receipt of a valid employee request, the employer shall, subject to paragraphs (8) and (9), initiate negotiations by taking the steps set out in regulation 14(1).

(2)   Subject to paragraph (3), an employee request is not a valid employee request unless it consists of—
(a) a single request made by at least 10% of the employees in the undertaking; or
(b) a number of separate requests made on the same or different days by employees which when taken together mean that at least 10% of the employees in that undertaking have made requests, provided that the requests are made within a period of six months.

(3)   Where the figure of 10% in paragraph (2) would result in less than 15 or more than 2,500 employees being required in order for a valid employee request to be made, that paragraph shall have effect as if, for the figure of 10%, there were substituted the figure of 15, or as the case may be, 2,500.

(4)   An employee request is not a valid employee request unless the single request referred to in paragraph (2)(a) or each separate request referred to in paragraph (2)(b)—
(a) is in writing;
(b) is sent to—
(i)   the registered office, head office or principal place of business of the employer; or
(ii) the CAC; and
(c) specifies the names of the employees making it and the date on which it is sent.

(5)   Where a request is sent to the CAC under paragraph (4)(b)(ii), the CAC shall—
(a) notify the employer that the request has been made as soon as reasonably practicable;
(b) request from the employer such information as it needs to verify the number and names of the employees who have made the request; and
(c) inform the employer and the employees who have made the request how many employees have made the request on the basis of the information provided by the employees and the employer.

(6)   Where the CAC requests information from the employer under paragraph (5)(b), the employer shall provide the information requested as soon as reasonably practicable.

(7)   The date on which an employee request is made is—
(a) where the request consists of a single request satisfying paragraph (2)(a) or of separate requests made on the same day satisfying paragraph (2)(b), the date on which the request is or requests are sent to the employer by the employees or the date on which the CAC informs the employer and the employees in accordance with paragraph (5)(c) of how many employees have made the request; and
(b) where the request consists of separate requests made on different days, the date on which—

> (i) the request which results in paragraph (2)(b) being satisfied is sent to the employer by the employees; or
>
> (ii) the CAC informs the employer and the employees in accordance with paragraph (5)(c) of how many employees have made the request where that request results in paragraph (2)(b) being satisfied.

(8) If the employer decides to hold a ballot under regulation 8 or 9, the employer shall not be required to initiate negotiations unless and until the outcome of the ballot is that in regulation 8(5)(b).

(9) If an application is made to the CAC under regulation 13, the employer shall not be required to initiate negotiations unless and until if the CAC declares that there was a valid employee request or that the employer's notification was valid.

11 EMPLOYER NOTIFICATION OF DECISION TO INITIATE NEGOTIATIONS

(1) The employer may start the negotiation process set out in regulation 14(1) on his own initiative by issuing a written notification satisfying the requirements of paragraph (2), and where the employer issues such a notification regulations 14 to 17 shall apply.

(2) The notification referred to in paragraph (1) must—
   (a) state that the employer intends to start the negotiating process and that the notification is given for the purpose of these Regulations;
   (b) state the date on which it is issued; and
   (c) be published in such a manner as to bring it to the attention of, so far as reasonably practicable, all the employees of the undertaking.

12 RESTRICTIONS ON EMPLOYEE REQUEST AND EMPLOYER NOTIFICATION

(1) Subject to paragraph (2), no employee request or employer notification is valid if it is made or issued, as the case may be,—
   (a) where a negotiated agreement applies, within a period of three years from the date of the agreement or, where the agreement is terminated within that period, before the date on which the termination takes effect;
   (b) where the standard information and consultation provisions apply within a period of three years from the date on which they started to apply; and
   (c) where the employer has held a ballot under regulation 8, or was one of the employers who held a ballot under regulation 9 and the result was that the employees did not endorse the valid employee request referred to in regulation 8(1), within a period of three years from the date of that request.

(2) Paragraph (1) does not apply where there are material changes in the undertaking during the applicable period having the result—
   (a) where a ballot held under regulation 8 or 9 had the result that the employees did not endorse the valid employee request, that there is no longer a pre-existing agreement which satisfies paragraph (1)(b) and (c) of regulation 8 or in the case of a ballot held under regulation 9, that there is no longer an agreement satisfying paragraph (1)(b) of that regulation; or
   (b) where a negotiated agreement exists, that the agreement no longer complies with the requirement in regulation 16(1) that it must cover all the employees of the undertaking.

13 DISPUTE ABOUT EMPLOYEE REQUEST, EMPLOYER NOTIFICATION OR WHETHER OBLIGATION IN REGULATION 7(1) APPLIES

(1) If the employer considers that there was no valid employee request—
  (a) because the employee request did not satisfy any requirement of regulation 7(2) to (4) or was prevented from being valid by regulation 12, or
  (b) because the undertaking was not one to which these Regulations applied (under Regulation 3) on the date on which the employee request was made,
  the employer may apply to the CAC for a declaration as to whether there was a valid employee request.

(2) If an employee or an employees' representative considers that an employer notification was not valid because it did not comply with one or more of the requirements in regulation 11(2) or was prevented from being valid by regulation 12, he may apply to the CAC for a declaration as to whether the notification was valid.

(3) The CAC shall only consider an application for a declaration made under paragraph (1) or (2) if the application is made within a one month period beginning on the date of the employee request or the date on which the employer notification is made.

14 NEGOTIATIONS TO REACH AN AGREEMENT

(1) In order to initiate negotiations to reach an agreement under these Regulations the employer must as soon as reasonably practicable—
  (a) make arrangements, satisfying the requirements of paragraph (2), for the employees of the undertaking to elect or appoint negotiating representatives; and thereafter
  (b) inform the employees in writing of the identity of the negotiating representatives; and
  (c) invite the negotiating representatives to enter into negotiations to reach a negotiated agreement.

(2) The requirements for the election or appointment of negotiating representatives under paragraph (1)(a) are that—
  (a) the election or appointment of the representatives must be arranged in such a way that, following their election or appointment, all employees of the undertaking are represented by one or more representatives; and
  (b) all employees of the undertaking must be entitled to take part in the election or appointment of the representatives and, where there is an election, all employees of the undertaking on the day on which the votes may be cast in the ballot, or if the votes may be cast on more than one day, on the first day of those days, must be given an entitlement to vote in the ballot.

(3) The negotiations referred to in paragraph (1)(c) shall last for a period not exceeding six months commencing at the end of the period of three months beginning with the date on which the valid employee request was made or the valid employer notification was issued; but the following periods shall not count towards the three month period—
  (a) where the employer holds a ballot pursuant to regulation 8 or 9, the period between the employer notifying the employees of his decision to hold such a ballot and whichever of the following dates is applicable—
    (i) where there is no complaint to the CAC under regulation 10, the date of the ballot;
    (ii) where there is a complaint to the CAC under regulation 10 and the complaint is dismissed by the CAC or on appeal, the date on which it is finally dismissed;

      (iii) where there is a complaint to the CAC and the outcome, whether of the complaint or of any appeal from it, is an order to hold the ballot under regulation 8 or 9 again, the date of the ballot that most recently took place;

      (iv) where there is a complaint to the CAC under regulation 10 and the outcome, whether of the complaint or of any appeal from it, is an order requiring the employer to initiate negotiations in accordance with regulation 7(1), the date on which the order is made;

(b) where an application for a declaration is made to the CAC pursuant to regulation 13, the period between the date of that application and the final decision of the CAC or any appeal from that decision; and

(c) where a complaint about the election or appointment of negotiating representatives is presented pursuant to regulation 15, the time between the date of the complaint and the determination of the complaint, including any appeal and, where the complaint is upheld, the further period until the negotiating representatives are re-elected or re-appointed.

(4)   Where a complaint about the ballot for employee approval of a negotiated agreement is presented pursuant to regulation 17, the time between the date the complaint is presented to the CAC and the determination of the complaint (including any appeal and, where the complaint is upheld, the further period until the re-holding of the ballot) shall not count towards the six month period mentioned in paragraph (3).

(5)   If, before the end of the six month period referred to in paragraph (3), the employer and a majority of the negotiating representatives agree that that period should be extended, it may be extended by such period as the parties agree and thereafter may be further extended by such period or periods as the parties agree.

(6)   Where one or more employers wish to initiate negotiations to reach an agreement to cover employees in more than one undertaking, any employer whose employees have not made a valid employee request and who has not issued a valid employer notification, shall issue such a notification.

(7)   Where paragraph (6) applies, the provisions of paragraphs (1) to (5) of this regulation and regulations 15 and 16 apply with the following modifications—

(a) the references to the employees of the undertaking refer to the employees of all the undertakings to be covered by any agreement negotiated; and

(b) references to employees refer to employees of all the undertakings to be covered by any agreement negotiated.

16 NEGOTIATED AGREEMENTS

(1)   A negotiated agreement must cover all employees of the undertaking and may consist either of a single agreement or of different parts (each being approved in accordance with paragraph (4)) which, taken together, cover all the employees of the undertaking. The single agreement or each part must—

(a) set out the circumstances in which the employer must inform and consult the employees to which it relates;

(b) be in writing;

(c) be dated;

(d) be approved in accordance with paragraphs (3) to (5);

(e) be signed by or on behalf of the employer; and

(f) either—

      (i) provide for the appointment or election of information and consultation representatives to whom the employer must provide the information and whom the employer must consult in the circumstances referred to in sub-paragraph (a); or

(ii) provide that the employer must provide information directly to the employees to which it relates and consult those employees directly in the circumstances referred to in sub-paragraph (a).

(2) Where a negotiated agreement consist of different parts they may provide differently in relation to the matters referred to in paragraph (1)(a) and (f).

(3) A negotiated agreement consisting of a single agreement shall be treated as being approved for the purpose of paragraph (1)(d) if—
   (a) it has been signed by all the negotiating representatives; or
   (b) it has been signed by a majority of negotiating representatives and either—
      (i) approved in writing by at least 50% of employees employed in the undertaking, or
      (ii) approved by a ballot of those employees, the arrangements for which satisfied the requirements set out in paragraph (5), in which at least 50% of the employees voting, voted in favour of approval.

(4) A part shall be treated as being approved for the purpose of paragraph (1)(d) if the part—
   (a) has been signed by all the negotiating representatives involved in negotiating the part; or
   (b) has been signed by a majority of those negotiating representatives and either—
      (i) approved in writing by at least 50% of employees (employed in the undertaking) to which the part relates, or
      (ii) approved by a ballot of those employees, the arrangements for which satisfied the requirements set out in paragraph (5), in which at least 50% of the employees voting, voted in favour of approving the part.

(5) The ballots referred to in paragraphs (3) and (4) must satisfy the following requirements—
   (a) the employer must make such arrangements as are reasonably practicable to ensure that the ballot is fair;
   (b) all employees of the undertaking or, as the case may be, to whom the part of the agreement relates, on the day on which the votes may be cast in the ballot, or if the votes may be cast on more than one day, on the first day of those days, must be given an entitlement to vote in the ballot; and
   (c) the ballot must be conducted so as to secure that—
      (i) so far as is reasonably practicable, those voting do so in secret; and
      (ii) the votes given in the ballot are accurately counted.

(6) Where the employer holds a ballot under this regulation he must, as soon as reasonably practicable after the date of the ballot, inform the employees entitled to vote of the result.

Part IV STANDARD INFORMATION AND CONSULTATION PROVISIONS

18 APPLICATION OF STANDARD INFORMATION AND CONSULTATION PROVISIONS

(1) Subject to paragraph (2)—
   (a) where the employer is under a duty, following the making of a valid employee request or issue of a valid employer notification, to initiate negotiations in accordance with regulation 14 but does not do so, the standard information and consultation provisions shall apply from the date—

       (i)   which is six months from the date on which the valid employee request was made or the valid employer notification was issued, or

       (ii) information and consultation representatives are elected under regulation 19, whichever is the sooner; and

  (b) if the parties do not reach a negotiated agreement within the time limit referred to in regulation 14(3) (or that period as extended by agreement under paragraph (5) of that regulation) the standard information and consultation provisions shall apply from the date—

       (i)   which is six months from the date on which that time limit expires; or

       (ii) information and consultation representatives are elected under regulation 19, whichever is the sooner.

(2)   Where the standard information and consultation provisions apply, the employer and the information and consultation representatives elected pursuant to regulation 19 may, at any time, reach an agreement that provisions other than the standard information and consultation provisions shall apply.

(3)   An agreement referred to in paragraph (2) shall only have effect if it covers all the employees of the undertaking, complies with the requirements listed in regulation 16(1)(a) to (c), (e) and (f), and is signed by a majority of the information and consultation representatives.

19 ELECTION OF INFORMATION AND CONSULTATION REPRESENTATIVES

(1)   Where the standard information and consultation provisions are to apply, the employer shall, before the standard information and consultation provisions start to apply, arrange for the holding of a ballot of its employees to elect the relevant number of information and consultation representatives.

(2)   The provisions in Schedule 2 to these Regulations apply in relation to the arrangements for and conduct of any such ballot.

(3)   In this regulation the "relevant number of information and consultation representatives" means one representative per fifty employees or part thereof, provided that that number is at least 2 and does not exceed 25.

(4)   An employee or an employee's representative may complain to the CAC that the employer has not arranged for the holding of a ballot in accordance with paragraph (1).

(5)   Where the CAC finds the complaint well-founded, it shall make an order requiring the employer to arrange, or re-arrange, and hold the ballot.

(6)   Where the CAC finds a complaint under paragraph (4) well-founded, the employee or the employee's representative may make an application to the Appeal Tribunal under regulation 22(6) and paragraphs (7) and (8) of that regulation shall apply to any such application.

20 STANDARD INFORMATION AND CONSULTATION PROVISIONS

(1)   Where the standard information and consultation provisions apply pursuant to regulation 18, the employer must provide the information and consultation representatives with information on—

  (a) the recent and probable development of the undertaking's activities and economic situation;

(b) the situation, structure and probable development of employment within the undertaking and on any anticipatory measures envisaged, in particular, where there is a threat to employment within the undertaking; and

(c) subject to paragraph (5), decisions likely to lead to substantial changes in work organisation or in contractual relations, including those referred to in—

    (i) sections 188 to 192 of the Trade Union and Labour Relations (Consolidation) Act 1992; and

    (ii) regulations 13 to 16 of the Transfer of Undertakings (Protection of Employment) Regulations 2006.

(2) The information referred to in paragraph (1) must be given at such time, in such fashion and with such content as are appropriate to enable, in particular, the information and consultation representatives to conduct an adequate study and, where necessary, to prepare for consultation.

(3) The employer must consult the information and consultation representatives on the matters referred to in paragraph (1)(b) and (c).

(4) The employer must ensure that the consultation referred to in paragraph (3) is conducted—

(a) in such a way as to ensure that the timing, method and content of the consultation are appropriate;

(b) on the basis of the information supplied by the employer to the information and consultation representatives and of any opinion which those representatives express to the employer;

(c) in such a way as to enable the information and consultation representatives to meet the employer at the relevant level of management depending on the subject under discussion and to obtain a reasoned response from the employer to any such opinion; and

(d) in relation to matters falling within paragraph (1)(c), with a view to reaching agreement on decisions within the scope of the employer's powers.

(5) The duties in this regulation to inform and consult the information and consultation representatives on decisions falling within paragraph (1)(c) cease to apply once the employer is under a duty under—

(a) section 188 of the Act referred to in paragraph (1)(c)(i) (duty of employer to consult representatives);

(b) regulation 13 of the Regulations referred to in paragraph (1)(c)(ii) (duty to inform and consult representatives), or

(c) any of regulations 11 to 13 of the Pension Schemes Regulations,

and he has notified the information and consultation representatives in writing that he will be complying with his duty under the legislation referred to in [sub-paragraph (a), (b) or (c)][3], as the case may be, instead of under these Regulations, provided that the notification is given on each occasion on which the employer has become or is about to become subject to the duty.

(6) Where there is an obligation in these Regulations on the employer to inform and consult his employees, a failure on the part of a person who controls the employer (either directly or indirectly) to provide information to the employer shall not constitute a valid reason for the employer failing to inform and consult.

Part V DUTY OF CO-OPERATION

21 CO-OPERATION

The parties are under a duty, when negotiating or implementing a negotiated agreement or when implementing the standard information and consultation provisions, to work in a spirit of co-operation and with due regard for their reciprocal rights and obligations, taking into account the interests of both the undertaking and the employees.

Part VI COMPLIANCE AND ENFORCEMENT

22 DISPUTES ABOUT OPERATION OF A NEGOTIATED AGREEMENT OR THE STANDARD INFORMATION AND CONSULTATION PROVISIONS

(1) Where—
(a) a negotiated agreement has been agreed; or
(b) the standard information and consultation provisions apply,
a complaint may be presented to the CAC by a relevant applicant who considers that the employer has failed to comply with the terms of the negotiated agreement or, as the case may be, one or more of the standard information and consultation provisions.

(2) A complaint brought under paragraph (1) must be brought within a period of three months commencing with the date of the alleged failure.

(3) In this regulation—

"failure" means an act or omission; and

"relevant applicant" means—
(a) in a case where information and consultation representatives have been elected or appointed, an information and consultation representative, or
(b) in a case where no information and consultation representatives have been elected or appointed, an employee or an employees' representative.

(4) Where the CAC finds the complaint well-founded it shall make a declaration to that effect and may make an order requiring the employer to take such steps as are necessary to comply with the terms of the negotiated agreement or, as the case may be, the standard information and consultation provisions.

(5) An order made under paragraph (4) shall specify—
(a) the steps which the employer is required to take; and
(b) the period within which the order must be complied with.

(6) If the CAC makes a declaration under paragraph (4) the relevant applicant may, within the period of three months beginning with the date on which the declaration is made, make an application to the Appeal Tribunal for a penalty notice to be issued.

(7) Where such an application is made, the Appeal Tribunal shall issue a written penalty notice to the employer requiring him to pay a penalty to the Secretary of State in respect of the failure unless satisfied, on hearing representations from the employer, that the failure resulted from a reason beyond the employer's control or that he has some other reasonable excuse for his failure.

(8) Regulation 23 shall apply in respect of a penalty notice issued under this regulation.

(9)   No order of the CAC under this regulation shall have the effect of suspending or altering the effect of any act done or of any agreement made by the employer or of preventing or delaying any act or agreement which the employer proposes to do or to make.

23 PENALTIES

(1)   A penalty notice issued under regulation 22 shall specify—
      (a) the amount of the penalty which is payable;
      (b) the date before which the penalty must be paid; and
      (c) the failure and period to which the penalty relates.

(2)   No penalty set by the Appeal Tribunal under this regulation may exceed £75,000.

(3)   Matters to be taken into account by the Appeal Tribunal when setting the amount of the penalty shall include—
      (a) the gravity of the failure;
      (b) the period of time over which the failure occurred;
      (c) the reason for the failure;
      (d) the number of employees affected by the failure; and
      (e) the number of employees employed by the undertaking or, where a negotiated agreement covers employees in more than one undertaking, the number of employees employed by both or all of the undertakings.

(4)   The date specified under paragraph (1)(b) must not be earlier than the end of the period within which an appeal against a declaration or order made by the CAC under regulation 22 may be made.

(5)   If the specified date in a penalty notice has passed and—
      (a) the period during which an appeal may be made has expired without an appeal having been made; or
      (b) such an appeal has been made and determined,
      the Secretary of State may recover from the employer, as a civil debt due to him, any amount payable under the penalty notice which remains outstanding.

(6)   The making of an appeal suspends the effect of a penalty notice.

(7)   Any sums received by the Secretary of State under regulation 22 or this regulation shall be paid into the Consolidated Fund.

24 EXCLUSIVITY OF REMEDY

The remedy for infringement of the rights conferred by Parts I to VI of these Regulations is by way of complaint to the CAC, and not otherwise.

Part VII CONFIDENTIAL INFORMATION

25 BREACH OF STATUTORY DUTY

(1)   A person to whom the employer, pursuant to his obligations under these Regulations, entrusts any information or document on terms requiring it to be held in confidence shall not disclose that information or document except, where the terms permit him to do so, in accordance with those terms.

(2)   In this regulation a person referred to in paragraph (1) to whom information or a document is entrusted is referred to as a "recipient".

(3)   The obligation to comply with paragraph (1) is a duty owed to the employer, and a breach of the duty is actionable accordingly (subject to the defences and other incidents applying to actions for breaches of statutory duty).

(4)   Paragraph (3) shall not affect any legal liability which any person may incur by disclosing the information or document, or any right which any person may have in relation to such disclosure otherwise than under this regulation.

(5)   No action shall lie under paragraph (3) where the recipient reasonably believed the disclosure to be a "protected disclosure" within the meaning given to that expression by section 43A of the 1996 Act.

(6)   A recipient to whom the employer has entrusted any information or document on terms requiring it to be held in confidence may apply to the CAC for a declaration as to whether it was reasonable for the employer to require the recipient to hold the information or document in confidence.

(7)   If the CAC considers, on an application under paragraph (6), that the disclosure of the information or document by the recipient would not, or would not be likely to, harm the legitimate interests of the undertaking, it shall make a declaration that it was not reasonable for the employer to require the recipient to hold the information or document in confidence.

(8)   If a declaration is made under paragraph (7), the information or document shall not at any time thereafter be regarded as having been entrusted to the recipient who made the application under paragraph (6), or to any other recipient, on terms requiring it to be held in confidence.

26 WITHHOLDING OF INFORMATION BY THE EMPLOYER

(1)   The employer is not required to disclose any information or document to a person for the purposes of these Regulations where the nature of the information or document is such that, according to objective criteria, the disclosure of the information or document would seriously harm the functioning of, or would be prejudicial to, the undertaking.

(2)   If there is a dispute between the employer and—
(a) where information and consultation representatives have been elected or appointed, such a representative; or
(b) where no information and consultation representatives have been elected or appointed, an employee or an employees' representative,
as to whether the nature of the information or document which the employer has failed to provide is such as is described in paragraph (1), the employer or a person referred to in sub-paragraph (a) or (b) may apply to the CAC for a declaration as to whether the information or document is of such a nature.

(3)   If the CAC makes a declaration that the disclosure of the information or document in question would not, according to objective criteria, be seriously harmful or prejudicial as mentioned in paragraph (1), the CAC shall order the employer to disclose the information or document.

(4)   An order under paragraph (3) shall specify—
(a) the information or document to be disclosed;
(b) the person or persons to whom the information or document is to be disclosed;
(c) any terms on which the information or document is to be disclosed; and
(d) the date before which the information or document is to be disclosed.

Part VIII **PROTECTIONS FOR INFORMATION AND CONSULTATION REPRESENTATIVES, ETC.**

27 RIGHT TO TIME OFF FOR INFORMATION AND CONSULTATION REPRESENTATIVES, ETC.

(1) An employee who is—
   (a) a negotiating representative; or
   (b) an information and consultation representative,
   is entitled to be permitted by his employer to take reasonable time off during the employee's working hours in order to perform his functions as such a representative.

(2) For the purposes of this regulation, the working hours of an employee shall be taken to be any time when, in accordance with his contract of employment, the employee is required to be at work.

28 RIGHT TO REMUNERATION FOR TIME OFF UNDER REGULATION 27

(1) An employee who is permitted to take time off under regulation 27 is entitled to be paid remuneration by his employer for the time taken off at the appropriate hourly rate.

(2) Chapter II of Part XIV of the 1996 Act (a week's pay) shall apply in relation to this regulation as it applies in relation to section 62 of the 1996 Act.

(3) The appropriate hourly rate, in relation to an employee, is the amount of one week's pay divided by the number of normal working hours in a week for that employee when employed under the contract of employment in force on the day when time is taken.

(4) But where the number of normal working hours differs from week to week or over a longer period, the amount of one week's pay shall be divided instead by—
   (a) the average number of normal working hours calculated by dividing by twelve the total number of the employee's normal working hours during the period of twelve weeks ending with the last complete week before the day on which the time is taken off; or
   (b) where the employee has not been employed for a sufficient period to enable the calculations to be made under sub-paragraph (a), a number which fairly represents the number of normal working hours in a week having regard to such of the considerations specified in paragraph (5) as are appropriate in the circumstances.

(5) The considerations referred to in paragraph (4)(b) are—
   (a) the average number of normal working hours in a week which the employee could expect in accordance with the terms of his contract; and
   (b) the average number of normal working hours of other employees engaged in relevant comparable employment with the same employer.

(6) A right to any amount under paragraph (1) does not affect any right of an employee in relation to remuneration under his contract of employment ("contractual remuneration").

(7) Any contractual remuneration paid to an employee in respect of a period of time off under regulation 27 goes towards discharging any liability of the employer to pay remuneration under paragraph (1) in respect of that period, and, conversely, any payment of remuneration under paragraph (1) in respect of a period goes towards discharging any liability of the employer to pay contractual remuneration in respect of that period.

29 RIGHT TO TIME OFF: COMPLAINT TO TRIBUNALS

(1) An employee may present a complaint to an employment tribunal that his employer—
  (a) has unreasonably refused to permit him to take time off as required by regulation 27; or
  (b) has failed to pay the whole or part of any amount to which the employee is entitled under regulation 28.

(2) A tribunal shall not consider a complaint under this regulation unless it is presented—
  (a) before the end of the period of three months beginning with the day on which the time off was taken or on which it is alleged the time off should have been permitted; or
  (b) within such further period as the tribunal considers reasonable in a case where it is satisfied that it was not reasonably practicable for the complaint to be presented before the end of that period of three months.

(3) Where a tribunal finds a complaint under this regulation well-founded, the tribunal shall make a declaration to that effect.

(4) If the complaint is that the employer has unreasonably refused to permit the employee to take time off, the tribunal shall also order the employer to pay to the employee an amount equal to the remuneration to which he would have been entitled under regulation 28 if the employer had not refused.

(5) If the complaint is that the employer has failed to pay the employee the whole or part of any amount to which he is entitled under regulation 28, the tribunal shall also order the employer to pay to the employee the amount it finds due to him.

30 UNFAIR DISMISSAL

(1) An employee who is dismissed and to whom paragraph (2) or (5) applies shall be regarded, if the reason (or, if more than one, the principal reason) for the dismissal is a reason specified in, respectively, paragraph (3) or (6), as unfairly dismissed for the purposes of Part 10 of the 1996 Act.

(2) This paragraph applies to an employee who is—
  (a) an employees' representative;
  (b) a negotiating representative;
  (c) an information and consultation representative; or
  (d) a candidate in an election in which any person elected will, on being elected, be such a representative.

(3) The reasons are that—
  (a) the employee performed or proposed to perform any functions or activities as such a representative or candidate;
  (b) the employee exercised or proposed to exercise an entitlement conferred on the employee by regulation 27 or 28; or
  (c) the employee (or a person acting on his behalf) made or proposed to make a request to exercise such an entitlement.

(4) Paragraph (1) does not apply in the circumstances set out in paragraph (3)(a) where the reason (or principal reason) for the dismissal is that in the performance, or purported performance, of the employee's functions or activities he has disclosed any information or document in breach of the duty in regulation 25, unless the employee reasonably believed the disclosure to be a "protected disclosure" within the meaning given to that expression by section 43A of the 1996 Act.

(5)   This paragraph applies to any employee whether or not he is an employee to whom paragraph (2) applies.

(6)   The reasons are that the employee—
    (a) took, or proposed to take, any proceedings before an employment tribunal to enforce a right or secure an entitlement conferred on him by these Regulations;
    (b) exercised, or proposed to exercise, any entitlement to apply or complain to the CAC or the Appeal Tribunal conferred by these Regulations or to exercise the right to appeal in connection with any rights conferred by these Regulations;
    (c) requested, or proposed to request, data in accordance with regulation 5;
    (d) acted with a view to securing that an agreement was or was not negotiated or that the standard information and consultation provisions did or did not become applicable;
    (e) indicated that he supported or did not support the coming into existence of a negotiated agreement or the application of the standard information and consultation provisions;
    (f) stood as a candidate in an election in which any person elected would, on being elected, be a negotiating representative or an information and consultation representative;
    (g) influenced or sought to influence by lawful means the way in which votes were to be cast by other employees in a ballot arranged under these Regulations;
    (h) voted in such a ballot;
    (i) expressed doubts, whether to a ballot supervisor or otherwise, as to whether such a ballot had been properly conducted; or
    (j) proposed to do, failed to do, or proposed to decline to do, any of the things mentioned in sub-paragraphs (d) to (i).

(7)   It is immaterial for the purpose of paragraph (6)(a)—
    (a) whether or not the employee has the right or entitlement; or
    (b) whether or not the right has been infringed;
    but for that sub-paragraph to apply, the claim to the right and, if applicable, the claim that it has been infringed must be made in good faith.

32 DETRIMENT

(1)   An employee to whom paragraph (2) or (5) applies has the right not to be subjected to any detriment by any act, or deliberate failure to act, by his employer, done on a ground specified in, respectively, paragraph (3) or (6).

(2)   This paragraph applies to an employee who is—
    (a) an employees' representative;
    (b) a negotiating representative;
    (c) an information and consultation representative; or
    (d) a candidate in an election in which any person elected will, on being elected, be such a representative.

(3)   The ground is that—
    (a) the employee performed or proposed to perform any functions or activities as such a representative or candidate;
    (b) the employee exercised or proposed to exercise an entitlement conferred on the employee by regulation 27 or 28; or
    (c) the employee (or a person acting on his behalf) made or proposed to make a request to exercise such an entitlement.

(4)   Paragraph (1) does not apply in the circumstances set out in paragraph (3)(a) where the ground (or principal ground) for the subjection to detriment is that in the performance, or

purported performance, of the employee's functions or activities he has disclosed any information or document in breach of the duty in regulation 25, unless the employee reasonably believed the disclosure to be a "protected disclosure" within the meaning given to that expression by section 43A of the 1996 Act.

(5)   This paragraph applies to any employee whether or not he is an employee to whom paragraph (2) applies.

(6)   The grounds are that the employee—
   (a) took, or proposed to take, any proceedings before an employment tribunal to enforce a right or secure an entitlement conferred on him by these Regulations;
   (b) exercised, or proposed to exercise, any entitlement to apply or complain to the CAC or the Appeal Tribunal conferred by these Regulations or to exercise the right to appeal in connection with any rights conferred by these Regulations;
   (c) requested, or proposed to request, data in accordance with regulation 5;
   (d) acted with a view to securing that an agreement was or was not negotiated or that the standard information and consultation provisions did or did not become applicable;
   (e) indicated that he supported or did not support the coming into existence of a negotiated agreement or the application of the standard information and consultation provisions;
   (f) stood as a candidate in an election in which any person elected would, on being elected, be a negotiating representative or an information and consultation representative;
   (g) influenced or sought to influence by lawful means the way in which votes were to be cast by other employees in a ballot arranged under these Regulations;
   (h) voted in such a ballot;
   (i) expressed doubts, whether to a ballot supervisor or otherwise, as to whether such a ballot had been properly conducted; or
   (j) proposed to do, failed to do, or proposed to decline to do, any of the things mentioned in sub-paragraphs (d) to (i).

(7)   It is immaterial for the purpose of paragraph (6)(a)—
   (a) whether or not the employee has the right or entitlement; or
   (b) whether or not the right has been infringed,
   but for that sub-paragraph to apply, the claim to the right and, if applicable, the claim that it has been infringed must be made in good faith.

(8)   This regulation does not apply where the detriment in question amounts to dismissal.

33 DETRIMENT: ENFORCEMENT AND SUBSIDIARY PROVISIONS

(1)   An employee may present a complaint to an employment tribunal that he has been subjected to a detriment in contravention of regulation 32.

(2)   The provisions of sections 48(2) to (4) and 49(1) to (5) of the 1996 Act (complaints to employment tribunals and remedies) shall apply in relation to a complaint under this regulation as they apply in relation to a complaint under section 48 of the Act but taking references to the employer as references to the employer within the meaning of regulation 32(1) above.

As amended by the Public Interest Disclosure Act 1998 (c. 23); Information and Consultation of Employees (Amendment) Regulations 2006/514 reg 3, reg 5(b), reg 5(c); Transfer of Undertakings (Protection of Employment) (Consequential Amendments) Regulations 2006/2405 reg 2.

TRANSFER OF UNDERTAKINGS (PROTECTION OF EMPLOYMENT) REGULATIONS 2006/246

2 INTERPRETATION

(1)   In these Regulations—

"assigned" means assigned other than on a temporary basis;

"collective agreement", "collective bargaining" and "trade union" have the same meanings respectively as in the 1992 Act;

"contract of employment" means any agreement between an employee and his employer determining the terms and conditions of his employment;

references to "contractor" in regulation 3 shall include a sub-contractor;

"employee" means any individual who works for another person whether under a contract of service or apprenticeship or otherwise but does not include anyone who provides services under a contract for services and references to a person's employer shall be construed accordingly;

"insolvency practitioner" has the meaning given to the expression by Part XIII of the Insolvency Act 1986;

references to "organised grouping of employees" shall include a single employee;

"recognised" has the meaning given to the expression by section 178(3) of the 1992 Act;

"relevant transfer" means a transfer or a service provision change to which these Regulations apply in accordance with regulation 3 and "transferor" and "transferee" shall be construed accordingly and in the case of a service provision change falling within regulation 3(1)(b), "the transferor" means the person who carried out the activities prior to the service provision change and "the transferee" means the person who carries out the activities as a result of the service provision change;

"the 1992 Act" means the Trade Union and Labour Relations (Consolidation) Act 1992;

"the 1996 Act" means the Employment Rights Act 1996;

"the 1996 Tribunals Act" means the Employment Tribunals Act 1996;

"the 1981 Regulations" means the Transfer of Undertakings (Protection of Employment) Regulations 1981.

(2)   For the purposes of these Regulations the representative of a trade union recognised by an employer is an official or other person authorised to carry on collective bargaining with that employer by that trade union.

(3)   In the application of these Regulations to Northern Ireland the Regulations shall have effect as set out in Schedule 1.

3 A RELEVANT TRANSFER

(1)   These Regulations apply to—
    (a) a transfer of an undertaking, business or part of an undertaking or business situated immediately before the transfer in the United Kingdom to another person where there is a transfer of an economic entity which retains its identity;

(b) a service provision change, that is a situation in which—
- (i) activities cease to be carried out by a person ("a client") on his own behalf and are carried out instead by another person on the client's behalf ("a contractor");
- (ii) activities cease to be carried out by a contractor on a client's behalf (whether or not those activities had previously been carried out by the client on his own behalf) and are carried out instead by another person ("a subsequent contractor") on the client's behalf; or
- (iii) activities cease to be carried out by a contractor or a subsequent contractor on a client's behalf (whether or not those activities had previously been carried out by the client on his own behalf) and are carried out instead by the client on his own behalf,

and in which the conditions set out in paragraph (3) are satisfied.

(2) In this regulation "economic entity" means an organised grouping of resources which has the objective of pursuing an economic activity, whether or not that activity is central or ancillary.

(3) The conditions referred to in paragraph (1)(b) are that—
- (a) immediately before the service provision change—
  - (i) there is an organised grouping of employees situated in Great Britain which has as its principal purpose the carrying out of the activities concerned on behalf of the client;
  - (ii) the client intends that the activities will, following the service provision change, be carried out by the transferee other than in connection with a single specific event or task of short-term duration; and
- (b) the activities concerned do not consist wholly or mainly of the supply of goods for the client's use.

(4) Subject to paragraph (1), these Regulations apply to—
- (a) public and private undertakings engaged in economic activities whether or not they are operating for gain;
- (b) a transfer or service provision change howsoever effected notwithstanding—
  - (i) that the transfer of an undertaking, business or part of an undertaking or business is governed or effected by the law of a country or territory outside the United Kingdom or that the service provision change is governed or effected by the law of a country or territory outside Great Britain;
  - (ii) that the employment of persons employed in the undertaking, business or part transferred or, in the case of a service provision change, persons employed in the organised grouping of employees, is governed by any such law;
- (c) a transfer of an undertaking, business or part of an undertaking or business (which may also be a service provision change) where persons employed in the undertaking, business or part transferred ordinarily work outside the United Kingdom.

(5) An administrative reorganisation of public administrative authorities or the transfer of administrative functions between public administrative authorities is not a relevant transfer.

(6) A relevant transfer—
- (a) may be effected by a series of two or more transactions; and
- (b) may take place whether or not any property is transferred to the transferee by the transferor.

(7) Where, in consequence (whether directly or indirectly) of the transfer of an undertaking, business or part of an undertaking or business which was situated immediately before the transfer in the United Kingdom, a ship within the meaning of the Merchant Shipping Act

1995 registered in the United Kingdom ceases to be so registered, these Regulations shall not affect the right conferred by section 29 of that Act (right of seamen to be discharged when ship ceases to be registered in the United Kingdom) on a seaman employed in the ship.

4   EFFECT OF RELEVANT TRANSFER ON CONTRACTS OF EMPLOYMENT

(1)   Except where objection is made under paragraph (7), a relevant transfer shall not operate so as to terminate the contract of employment of any person employed by the transferor and assigned to the organised grouping of resources or employees that is subject to the relevant transfer, which would otherwise be terminated by the transfer, but any such contract shall have effect after the transfer as if originally made between the person so employed and the transferee.

(2)   Without prejudice to paragraph (1), but subject to paragraph (6), and regulations 8 and 15(9), on the completion of a relevant transfer—
(a)   all the transferor's rights, powers, duties and liabilities under or in connection with any such contract shall be transferred by virtue of this regulation to the transferee; and
(b)   any act or omission before the transfer is completed, of or in relation to the transferor in respect of that contract or a person assigned to that organised grouping of resources or employees, shall be deemed to have been an act or omission of or in relation to the transferee.

(3)   Any reference in paragraph (1) to a person employed by the transferor and assigned to the organised grouping of resources or employees that is subject to a relevant transfer, is a reference to a person so employed immediately before the transfer, or who would have been so employed if he had not been dismissed in the circumstances described in regulation 7(1), including, where the transfer is effected by a series of two or more transactions, a person so employed and assigned or who would have been so employed and assigned immediately before any of those transactions.

(4)   Subject to regulation 9, in respect of a contract of employment that is, or will be, transferred by paragraph (1), any purported variation of the contract shall be void if the sole or principal reason for the variation is—
(a)   the transfer itself; or
(b)   a reason connected with the transfer that is not an economic, technical or organisational reason entailing changes in the workforce.

(5)   Paragraph (4) shall not prevent the employer and his employee, whose contract of employment is, or will be, transferred by paragraph (1), from agreeing a variation of that contract if the sole or principal reason for the variation is—
(a)   a reason connected with the transfer that is an economic, technical or organisational reason entailing changes in the workforce; or
(b)   a reason unconnected with the transfer.

(6)   Paragraph (2) shall not transfer or otherwise affect the liability of any person to be prosecuted for, convicted of and sentenced for any offence.

(7)   Paragraphs (1) and (2) shall not operate to transfer the contract of employment and the rights, powers, duties and liabilities under or in connection with it of an employee who informs the transferor or the transferee that he objects to becoming employed by the transferee.

(8)   Subject to paragraphs (9) and (11), where an employee so objects, the relevant transfer shall operate so as to terminate his contract of employment with the transferor but he shall not be treated, for any purpose, as having been dismissed by the transferor.

(9)   Subject to regulation 9, where a relevant transfer involves or would involve a substantial change in working conditions to the material detriment of a person whose contract of employment is or would be transferred under paragraph (1), such an employee may treat the contract of employment as having been terminated, and the employee shall be treated for any purpose as having been dismissed by the employer.

(10)   No damages shall be payable by an employer as a result of a dismissal falling within paragraph (9) in respect of any failure by the employer to pay wages to an employee in respect of a notice period which the employee has failed to work.

(11)   Paragraphs (1), (7), (8) and (9) are without prejudice to any right of an employee arising apart from these Regulations to terminate his contract of employment without notice in acceptance of a repudiatory breach of contract by his employer.

5 EFFECT OF RELEVANT TRANSFER ON COLLECTIVE AGREEMENTS

Where at the time of a relevant transfer there exists a collective agreement made by or on behalf of the transferor with a trade union recognised by the transferor in respect of any employee whose contract of employment is preserved by regulation 4(1) above, then—

(a)   without prejudice to sections 179 and 180 of the 1992 Act (collective agreements presumed to be unenforceable in specified circumstances) that agreement, in its application in relation to the employee, shall, after the transfer, have effect as if made by or on behalf of the transferee with that trade union, and accordingly anything done under or in connection with it, in its application in relation to the employee, by or in relation to the transferor before the transfer, shall, after the transfer, be deemed to have been done by or in relation to the transferee; and

(b)   any order made in respect of that agreement, in its application in relation to the employee, shall, after the transfer, have effect as if the transferee were a party to the agreement.

6 EFFECT OF RELEVANT TRANSFER ON TRADE UNION RECOGNITION

(1)   This regulation applies where after a relevant transfer the transferred organised grouping of resources or employees maintains an identity distinct from the remainder of the transferee's undertaking.

(2)   Where before such a transfer an independent trade union is recognised to any extent by the transferor in respect of employees of any description who in consequence of the transfer become employees of the transferee, then, after the transfer—
   (a)   the trade union shall be deemed to have been recognised by the transferee to the same extent in respect of employees of that description so employed; and
   (b)   any agreement for recognition may be varied or rescinded accordingly.

7 DISMISSAL OF EMPLOYEE BECAUSE OF RELEVANT TRANSFER

(1)   Where either before or after a relevant transfer, any employee of the transferor or transferee is dismissed, that employee shall be treated for the purposes of Part X of the 1996 Act (unfair dismissal) as unfairly dismissed if the sole or principal reason for his dismissal is—

(a) the transfer itself; or

(b) a reason connected with the transfer that is not an economic, technical or organisational reason entailing changes in the workforce.

(2) This paragraph applies where the sole or principal reason for the dismissal is a reason connected with the transfer that is an economic, technical or organisational reason entailing changes in the workforce of either the transferor or the transferee before or after a relevant transfer.

(3) Where paragraph (2) applies—

(a) paragraph (1) shall not apply;

(b) without prejudice to the application of section 98(4) of the 1996 Act (test of fair dismissal), the dismissal shall, for the purposes of sections 98(1) and 135 of that Act (reason for dismissal), be regarded as having been for redundancy where section 98(2)(c) of that Act applies, or otherwise for a substantial reason of a kind such as to justify the dismissal of an employee holding the position which that employee held.

(4) The provisions of this regulation apply irrespective of whether the employee in question is assigned to the organised grouping of resources or employees that is, or will be, transferred.

(5) Paragraph (1) shall not apply in relation to the dismissal of any employee which was required by reason of the application of section 5 of the Aliens Restriction (Amendment) Act 1919 to his employment.

(6) Paragraph (1) shall not apply in relation to a dismissal of an employee if the application of section 94 of the 1996 Act to the dismissal of the employee is excluded by or under any provision of the 1996 Act, the 1996 Tribunals Act or the 1992 Act.

8 INSOLVENCY

(1) If at the time of a relevant transfer the transferor is subject to relevant insolvency proceedings paragraphs (2) to (6) apply.

(2) In this regulation "relevant employee" means an employee of the transferor—

(a) whose contract of employment transfers to the transferee by virtue of the operation of these Regulations; or

(b) whose employment with the transferor is terminated before the time of the relevant transfer in the circumstances described in regulation 7(1).

(3) The relevant statutory scheme specified in paragraph (4)(b) (including that sub-paragraph as applied by paragraph 5 of Schedule 1) shall apply in the case of a relevant employee irrespective of the fact that the qualifying requirement that the employee's employment has been terminated is not met and for those purposes the date of the transfer shall be treated as the date of the termination and the transferor shall be treated as the employer.

(4) In this regulation the "relevant statutory schemes" are—

(a) Chapter VI of Part XI of the 1996 Act;

(b) Part XII of the 1996 Act.

(5) Regulation 4 shall not operate to transfer liability for the sums payable to the relevant employee under the relevant statutory schemes.

(6) In this regulation "relevant insolvency proceedings" means insolvency proceedings which have been opened in relation to the transferor not with a view to the liquidation of the assets of the transferor and which are under the supervision of an insolvency practitioner.

(7)   Regulations 4 and 7 do not apply to any relevant transfer where the transferor is the subject of bankruptcy proceedings or any analogous insolvency proceedings which have been instituted with a view to the liquidation of the assets of the transferor and are under the supervision of an insolvency practitioner.

9 VARIATIONS OF CONTRACT WHERE TRANSFERORS ARE SUBJECT TO RELEVANT INSOLVENCY PROCEEDINGS

(1)   If at the time of a relevant transfer the transferor is subject to relevant insolvency proceedings these Regulations shall not prevent the transferor or transferee (or an insolvency practitioner) and appropriate representatives of assigned employees agreeing to permitted variations.

(2)   For the purposes of this regulation "appropriate representatives" are—
(a) if the employees are of a description in respect of which an independent trade union is recognised by their employer, representatives of the trade union; or
(b) in any other case, whichever of the following employee representatives the employer chooses—
(i)   employee representatives appointed or elected by the assigned employees (whether they make the appointment or election alone or with others) otherwise than for the purposes of this regulation, who (having regard to the purposes for, and the method by which they were appointed or elected) have authority from those employees to agree permitted variations to contracts of employment on their behalf;
(ii) employee representatives elected by assigned employees (whether they make the appointment or election alone or with others) for these particular purposes, in an election satisfying requirements identical to those contained in regulation 14 except those in regulation 14(1)(d).

(3)   An individual may be an appropriate representative for the purposes of both this regulation and regulation 13 provided that where the representative is not a trade union representative he is either elected by or has authority from assigned employees (within the meaning of this regulation) and affected employees (as described in regulation 13(1)).

(4)   In section 168 of the 1992 Act (time off for carrying out trade union duties) in subsection (1), after paragraph (c) there is inserted—

", or

(d) negotiations with a view to entering into an agreement under regulation 9 of the Transfer of Undertakings (Protection of Employment) Regulations 2006 that applies to employees of the employer, or
(e) the performance on behalf of employees of the employer of functions related to or connected with the making of an agreement under that regulation.".

(5)   Where assigned employees are represented by non-trade union representatives—
(a) the agreement recording a permitted variation must be in writing and signed by each of the representatives who have made it or, where that is not reasonably practicable, by a duly authorised agent of that representative; and
(b) the employer must, before the agreement is made available for signature, provide all employees to whom it is intended to apply on the date on which it is to come into effect with copies of the text of the agreement and such guidance as those employees might reasonably require in order to understand it fully.

(6)   A permitted variation shall take effect as a term or condition of the assigned employee's contract of employment in place, where relevant, of any term or condition which it varies.

(7)   In this regulation—

"assigned employees" means those employees assigned to the organised grouping of resources or employees that is the subject of a relevant transfer;

"permitted variation" is a variation to the contract of employment of an assigned employee where—
(a) the sole or principal reason for it is the transfer itself or a reason connected with the transfer that is not an economic, technical or organisational reason entailing changes in the workforce; and
(b) it is designed to safeguard employment opportunities by ensuring the survival of the undertaking, business or part of the undertaking or business that is the subject of the relevant transfer;

"relevant insolvency proceedings" has the meaning given to the expression by regulation 8(6).

10 PENSIONS

(1)   Regulations 4 and 5 shall not apply—
(a) to so much of a contract of employment or collective agreement as relates to an occupational pension scheme within the meaning of the Pension Schemes Act 1993; or
(b) to any rights, powers, duties or liabilities under or in connection with any such contract or subsisting by virtue of any such agreement and relating to such a scheme or otherwise arising in connection with that person's employment and relating to such a scheme.

(2)   For the purposes of paragraphs (1) and (3), any provisions of an occupational pension scheme which do not relate to benefits for old age, invalidity or survivors shall not be treated as being part of the scheme.

(3)   An employee whose contract of employment is transferred in the circumstances described in regulation 4(1) shall not be entitled to bring a claim against the transferor for—
(a) breach of contract; or
(b) constructive unfair dismissal under section 95(1)(c) of the 1996 Act,
arising out of a loss or reduction in his rights under an occupational pension scheme in consequence of the transfer, save insofar as the alleged breach of contract or dismissal (as the case may be) occurred prior to the date on which these Regulations took effect.

11 NOTIFICATION OF EMPLOYEE LIABILITY INFORMATION

(1)   The transferor shall notify to the transferee the employee liability information of any person employed by him who is assigned to the organised grouping of resources or employees that is the subject of a relevant transfer—
(a) in writing; or
(b) by making it available to him in a readily accessible form.

(2)   In this regulation and in regulation 12 "employee liability information" means—
(a) the identity and age of the employee;
(b) those particulars of employment that an employer is obliged to give to an employee pursuant to section 1 of the 1996 Act;
(c) information of any—
    (i)   disciplinary procedure taken against an employee;
    (ii) grievance procedure taken by an employee,

within the previous two years, in circumstances where a Code of Practice issued under Part IV of the Trade Union and Labour Relations Act 1992 which relates exclusively or primarily to the resolution of disputes applies;

(d) information of any court or tribunal case, claim or action—

    (i) brought by an employee against the transferor, within the previous two years;

    (ii) that the transferor has reasonable grounds to believe that an employee may bring against the transferee, arising out of the employee's employment with the transferor; and

(e) information of any collective agreement which will have effect after the transfer, in its application in relation to the employee, pursuant to regulation 5(a).

(3) Employee liability information shall contain information as at a specified date not more than fourteen days before the date on which the information is notified to the transferee.

(4) The duty to provide employee liability information in paragraph (1) shall include a duty to provide employee liability information of any person who would have been employed by the transferor and assigned to the organised grouping of resources or employees that is the subject of a relevant transfer immediately before the transfer if he had not been dismissed in the circumstances described in regulation 7(1), including, where the transfer is effected by a series of two or more transactions, a person so employed and assigned or who would have been so employed and assigned immediately before any of those transactions.

(5) Following notification of the employee liability information in accordance with this regulation, the transferor shall notify the transferee in writing of any change in the employee liability information.

(6) A notification under this regulation shall be given not less than fourteen days before the relevant transfer or, if special circumstances make this not reasonably practicable, as soon as reasonably practicable thereafter.

(7) A notification under this regulation may be given—

(a) in more than one instalment;

(b) indirectly, through a third party.

12 REMEDY FOR FAILURE TO NOTIFY EMPLOYEE LIABILITY INFORMATION

(1) On or after a relevant transfer, the transferee may present a complaint to an employment tribunal that the transferor has failed to comply with any provision of regulation 11.

(2) An employment tribunal shall not consider a complaint under this regulation unless it is presented—

(a) before the end of the period of three months beginning with the date of the relevant transfer;

(b) within such further period as the tribunal considers reasonable in a case where it is satisfied that it was not reasonably practicable for the complaint to be presented before the end of that period of three months.

(3) Where an employment tribunal finds a complaint under paragraph (1) well-founded, the tribunal—

(a) shall make a declaration to that effect; and

(b) may make an award of compensation to be paid by the transferor to the transferee.

(4) The amount of the compensation shall be such as the tribunal considers just and equitable in all the circumstances, subject to paragraph (5), having particular regard to—

(a) any loss sustained by the transferee which is attributable to the matters complained of; and

(b) the terms of any contract between the transferor and the transferee relating to the transfer under which the transferor may be liable to pay any sum to the transferee in respect of a failure to notify the transferee of employee liability information.

(5) Subject to paragraph (6), the amount of compensation awarded under paragraph (3) shall be not less than £500 per employee in respect of whom the transferor has failed to comply with a provision of regulation 11, unless the tribunal considers it just and equitable, in all the circumstances, to award a lesser sum.

(6) In ascertaining the loss referred to in paragraph (4)(a) the tribunal shall apply the same rule concerning the duty of a person to mitigate his loss as applies to any damages recoverable under the common law of England and Wales, Northern Ireland or Scotland, as applicable.

(7) Section 18 of the 1996 Tribunals Act (conciliation) shall apply to the right conferred by this regulation and to proceedings under this regulation as it applies to the rights conferred by that Act and the employment tribunal proceedings mentioned in that Act.

13 DUTY TO INFORM AND CONSULT REPRESENTATIVES

(1) In this regulation and regulations 14 and 15 references to affected employees, in relation to a relevant transfer, are to any employees of the transferor or the transferee (whether or not assigned to the organised grouping of resources or employees that is the subject of a relevant transfer) who may be affected by the transfer or may be affected by measures taken in connection with it; and references to the employer shall be construed accordingly.

(2) Long enough before a relevant transfer to enable the employer of any affected employees to consult the appropriate representatives of any affected employees, the employer shall inform those representatives of—
(a) the fact that the transfer is to take place, the date or proposed date of the transfer and the reasons for it;
(b) the legal, economic and social implications of the transfer for any affected employees;
(c) the measures which he envisages he will, in connection with the transfer, take in relation to any affected employees or, if he envisages that no measures will be so taken, that fact; and
(d) if the employer is the transferor, the measures, in connection with the transfer, which he envisages the transferee will take in relation to any affected employees who will become employees of the transferee after the transfer by virtue of regulation 4 or, if he envisages that no measures will be so taken, that fact.

(3) For the purposes of this regulation the appropriate representatives of any affected employees are—
(a) if the employees are of a description in respect of which an independent trade union is recognised by their employer, representatives of the trade union; or
(b) in any other case, whichever of the following employee representatives the employer chooses—
(i) employee representatives appointed or elected by the affected employees otherwise than for the purposes of this regulation, who (having regard to the purposes for, and the method by which they were appointed or elected) have authority from those employees to receive information and to be consulted about the transfer on their behalf;
(ii) employee representatives elected by any affected employees, for the purposes of this regulation, in an election satisfying the requirements of regulation 14(1).

(4)   The transferee shall give the transferor such information at such a time as will enable the transferor to perform the duty imposed on him by virtue of paragraph (2)(d).

(5)   The information which is to be given to the appropriate representatives shall be given to each of them by being delivered to them, or sent by post to an address notified by them to the employer, or (in the case of representatives of a trade union) sent by post to the trade union at the address of its head or main office.

(6)   An employer of an affected employee who envisages that he will take measures in relation to an affected employee, in connection with the relevant transfer, shall consult the appropriate representatives of that employee with a view to seeking their agreement to the intended measures.

(7)   In the course of those consultations the employer shall—
(a)   consider any representations made by the appropriate representatives; and
(b)   reply to those representations and, if he rejects any of those representations, state his reasons.

(8)   The employer shall allow the appropriate representatives access to any affected employees and shall afford to those representatives such accommodation and other facilities as may be appropriate.

(9)   If in any case there are special circumstances which render it not reasonably practicable for an employer to perform a duty imposed on him by any of paragraphs (2) to (7), he shall take all such steps towards performing that duty as are reasonably practicable in the circumstances.

(10)   Where—
(a)   the employer has invited any of the affected employee to elect employee representatives; and
(b)   the invitation was issued long enough before the time when the employer is required to give information under paragraph (2) to allow them to elect representatives by that time,
the employer shall be treated as complying with the requirements of this regulation in relation to those employees if he complies with those requirements as soon as is reasonably practicable after the election of the representatives.

(11)   If, after the employer has invited any affected employees to elect representatives, they fail to do so within a reasonable time, he shall give to any affected employees the information set out in paragraph (2).

(12)   The duties imposed on an employer by this regulation shall apply irrespective of whether the decision resulting in the relevant transfer is taken by the employer or a person controlling the employer.

14 ELECTION OF EMPLOYEE REPRESENTATIVES

(1)   The requirements for the election of employee representatives under regulation 13(3) are that—
(a)   the employer shall make such arrangements as are reasonably practicable to ensure that the election is fair;
(b)   the employer shall determine the number of representatives to be elected so that there are sufficient representatives to represent the interests of all affected employees having regard to the number and classes of those employees;
(c)   the employer shall determine whether the affected employees should be represented either by representatives of all the affected employees or by representatives of particular classes of those employees;

(d)   before the election the employer shall determine the term of office as employee representatives so that it is of sufficient length to enable information to be given and consultations under regulation 13 to be completed;

(e)   the candidates for election as employee representatives are affected employees on the date of the election;

(f)   no affected employee is unreasonably excluded from standing for election;

(g)   all affected employees on the date of the election are entitled to vote for employee representatives;

(h)   the employees entitled to vote may vote for as many candidates as there are representatives to be elected to represent them or, if there are to be representatives for particular classes of employees, may vote for as many candidates as there are representatives to be elected to represent their particular class of employee;

(i)   the election is conducted so as to secure that—

    (i)   so far as is reasonably practicable, those voting do so in secret; and

    (ii)   the votes given at the election are accurately counted.

(2)   Where, after an election of employee representatives satisfying the requirements of paragraph (1) has been held, one of those elected ceases to act as an employee representative and as a result any affected employees are no longer represented, those employees shall elect another representative by an election satisfying the requirements of paragraph (1)(a), (e), (f) and (i).

15   FAILURE TO INFORM OR CONSULT

(1)   Where an employer has failed to comply with a requirement of regulation 13 or regulation 14, a complaint may be presented to an employment tribunal on that ground—

(a)   in the case of a failure relating to the election of employee representatives, by any of his employees who are affected employees;

(b)   in the case of any other failure relating to employee representatives, by any of the employee representatives to whom the failure related;

(c)   in the case of failure relating to representatives of a trade union, by the trade union; and

(d)   in any other case, by any of his employees who are affected employees.

(2)   If on a complaint under paragraph (1) a question arises whether or not it was reasonably practicable for an employer to perform a particular duty or as to what steps he took towards performing it, it shall be for him to show—

(a)   that there were special circumstances which rendered it not reasonably practicable for him to perform the duty; and

(b)   that he took all such steps towards its performance as were reasonably practicable in those circumstances.

(3)   If on a complaint under paragraph (1) a question arises as to whether or not an employee representative was an appropriate representative for the purposes of regulation 13, it shall be for the employer to show that the employee representative had the necessary authority to represent the affected employees.

(4)   On a complaint under paragraph (1)(a) it shall be for the employer to show that the requirements in regulation 14 have been satisfied.

(5)   On a complaint against a transferor that he had failed to perform the duty imposed upon him by virtue of regulation 13(2)(d) or, so far as relating thereto, regulation 13(9), he may not show that it was not reasonably practicable for him to perform the duty in question for the reason that the transferee had failed to give him the requisite information at the

requisite time in accordance with regulation 13(4) unless he gives the transferee notice of his intention to show that fact; and the giving of the notice shall make the transferee a party to the proceedings.

(6)   In relation to any complaint under paragraph (1), a failure on the part of a person controlling (directly or indirectly) the employer to provide information to the employer shall not constitute special circumstances rendering it not reasonably practicable for the employer to comply with such a requirement.

(7)   Where the tribunal finds a complaint against a transferee under paragraph (1) well-founded it shall make a declaration to that effect and may order the transferee to pay appropriate compensation to such descriptions of affected employees as may be specified in the award.

(8)   Where the tribunal finds a complaint against a transferor under paragraph (1) well-founded it shall make a declaration to that effect and may—
(a) order the transferor, subject to paragraph (9), to pay appropriate compensation to such descriptions of affected employees as may be specified in the award; or
(b) if the complaint is that the transferor did not perform the duty mentioned in paragraph (5) and the transferor (after giving due notice) shows the facts so mentioned, order the transferee to pay appropriate compensation to such descriptions of affected employees as may be specified in the award.

(9)   The transferee shall be jointly and severally liable with the transferor in respect of compensation payable under sub-paragraph (8)(a) or paragraph (11).

(10)   An employee may present a complaint to an employment tribunal on the ground that he is an employee of a description to which an order under paragraph (7) or (8) relates and that—
(a) in respect of an order under paragraph (7), the transferee has failed, wholly or in part, to pay him compensation in pursuance of the order;
(b) in respect of an order under paragraph (8), the transferor or transferee, as applicable, has failed, wholly or in part, to pay him compensation in pursuance of the order.

(11)   Where the tribunal finds a complaint under paragraph (10) well-founded it shall order the transferor or transferee as applicable to pay the complainant the amount of compensation which it finds is due to him.

(12)   An employment tribunal shall not consider a complaint under paragraph (1) or (10) unless it is presented to the tribunal before the end of the period of three months beginning with—
(a) in respect of a complaint under paragraph (1), the date on which the relevant transfer is completed; or
(b) in respect of a complaint under paragraph (10), the date of the tribunal's order under paragraph (7) or (8),
or within such further period as the tribunal considers reasonable in a case where it is satisfied that it was not reasonably practicable for the complaint to be presented before the end of the period of three months.

16 FAILURE TO INFORM OR CONSULT: SUPPLEMENTAL

(1)   Section 205(1) of the 1996 Act (complaint to be sole remedy for breach of relevant rights) and section 18 of the 1996 Tribunals Act (conciliation) shall apply to the rights conferred by regulation 15 and to proceedings under this regulation as they apply to the rights conferred by those Acts and the employment tribunal proceedings mentioned in those Acts.

(2)   An appeal shall lie and shall lie only to the Employment Appeal Tribunal on a question of law arising from any decision of, or arising in any proceedings before, an employment

tribunal under or by virtue of these Regulations; and section 11(1) of the Tribunals and Inquiries Act 1992 (appeals from certain tribunals to the High Court) shall not apply in relation to any such proceedings.

(3)   "Appropriate compensation" in regulation 15 means such sum not exceeding thirteen weeks' pay for the employee in question as the tribunal considers just and equitable having regard to the seriousness of the failure of the employer to comply with his duty.

(4)   Sections 220 to 228 of the 1996 Act shall apply for calculating the amount of a week's pay for any employee for the purposes of paragraph (3) and, for the purposes of that calculation, the calculation date shall be—

(a)   in the case of an employee who is dismissed by reason of redundancy (within the meaning of sections 139 and 155 of the 1996 Act) the date which is the calculation date for the purposes of any entitlement of his to a redundancy payment (within the meaning of those sections) or which would be that calculation date if he were so entitled;

(b)   in the case of an employee who is dismissed for any other reason, the effective date of termination (within the meaning of sections 95(1) and (2) and 97 of the 1996 Act) of his contract of employment;

(c)   in any other case, the date of the relevant transfer.

18   RESTRICTION ON CONTRACTING OUT

Section 203 of the 1996 Act (restrictions on contracting out) shall apply in relation to these Regulations as if they were contained in that Act, save for that section shall not apply in so far as these Regulations provide for an agreement (whether a contract of employment or not) to exclude or limit the operation of these Regulations.

As amended by the Former Enemy Aliens (Disabilities Removal) Act 1925 section 1, Schedule 2; Merchant Shipping Act 1970 section 100(3), Schedule 5; Transfer of Undertakings (Protection of Employment) (Amendment) Regulations 1987/442; Dock Work Act 1989, section 7(2); Sea Fish (Conservation) Act 1992, section 9; Trade Union Reform and Employment Rights Act 1993, sections 33, 51 and Schedule 10; Collective Redundancies and Transfer of Undertakings (Protection of Employment) (Amendment) Regulations 1995/2587; Merchant Shipping Act 1995 section 314, Schedule 12; Bankruptcy (Scotland) Act 1993 section 11(1); Employment Rights (Dispute Resolution) Act 1998, sections 1(2)(a), 11(1), 15 and Schedule 1, the National Minimum Wage Act 1998, sections 24 and 30(1); Employment Rights (Dispute Resolution) Act 1998 (Commencement No. 1 and Transitional and Saving Provisions) Order 1998/1658; Employment Rights (Dispute Resolution) Act 1998, section 1(2)(a); Working Time Regulations 1998/1833; Transfer of Undertakings (Protection of Employment) (Amendment) Regulations 1999/2402; Welfare Reform & Pensions Act 1999, section 18, Schedule 2; Transnational Information and Consultation of Employees Regulations 1999/3323; Scotland Act 1998 (Consequential Modifications) (No.2) Order 1999/1820; Collective Redundancies and Transfer of Undertakings (Protection of Employment; Employment Tribunals Act (Application of Conciliation Provisions) Order 2000/1299; Insolvency Act 2000, sections 4(1), 4(2)(a), 4(2)(b), 4(2)(c); Part-time Workers (Prevention of Less Favourable Treatment) Regulations 2000/1551; Part-time Workers (Prevention of Less Favourable Treatment) Regulations 2001/1107; Financial Services and Markets Act 2000 (Consequential Amendments and Repeals) Order 2001/3649; Special Educational Needs and Disability Act 2001, section 42(1), Schedule 8; Fixed-term Employees (Prevention of Less Favourable Treatment) Regulations 2002/2034; the Employment Act 2002, sections 24(2), 53 and Schedule 7; Employment Relations Act 2004 (c.24) section 57(1) and Schedule 1; Insolvency Act 1986 (Amendment) (No. 2) Regulations 2002/1240; Insolvent Partnerships (Amendment) (No. 2) Order 2002/2708; Employment Equality (Religion or Belief) Regulations 2003/1660;

Employment Equality (Sexual Orientation) Regulations 2003/1661; Disability Discrimination Act 1995 (Amendment) Regulations 2003/1673; Merchant Shipping (Working Time: Inland Waterways) Regulations 2003/3049; Pensions Act 2004, section 239; European Public Limited-Liability Company Regulations 2004/2326; Fishing Vessels (Working Time: Sea-fishermen) Regulations 2004/1713; Transfer of Undertakings (Protection of Employment) (Amendment) Regulations 2009/592 reg 2(2).

EMPLOYMENT EQUALITY (AGE) REGULATIONS 2006/1031

Part I GENERAL

2 INTERPRETATION

(1) In these Regulations, references to discrimination are to any discrimination falling within regulation 3 (discrimination on grounds of age), regulation 4 (discrimination by way of victimisation) or regulation 5 (instructions to discriminate) and related expressions shall be construed accordingly, and references to harassment shall be construed in accordance with regulation 6 (harassment on grounds of age).

(2) In these Regulations—

"1996 Act" means the Employment Rights Act 1996;

"act" includes a deliberate omission;

"benefit", except in regulation 11 and Schedule 2 (pension schemes), includes facilities and services;

"commencement date" means 1st October 2006;

"Crown employment" means—
(a) service for purposes of a Minister of the Crown or government department, other than service of a person holding a statutory office; or
(b) service on behalf of the Crown for purposes of a person holding a statutory office or purposes of a statutory body;
"detriment" does not include harassment within the meaning of regulation 6;

"employment" means employment under a contract of service or of apprenticeship or a contract personally to do any work, and related expressions (such as "employee" and "employer") shall be construed accordingly, but this definition does not apply in relation to regulation 30 (exception for retirement) or to Schedules 2, 6, 7 and 8;

"Great Britain" includes such of the territorial waters of the United Kingdom as are adjacent to Great Britain;

"Minister of the Crown" includes the Treasury and the Defence Council;

"proprietor", in relation to a school, has the meaning given by section 579 of the Education Act 1996;

"relevant member of the House of Commons staff" means any person who was appointed by the House of Commons Commission or who is a member of the Speaker's personal staff;

"relevant member of the House of Lords staff" means any person who is employed under a contract of employment with the Corporate Officer of the House of Lords;

"school", in England and Wales, has the meaning given by section 4 of the Education Act 1996, and, in Scotland, has the meaning given by section 135(1) of the Education (Scotland) Act 1980, and references to a school are to an institution in so far as it is engaged in the provision of education under those sections;

"service for purposes of a Minister of the Crown or government department" does not include service in any office mentioned in Schedule 2 (Ministerial offices) to the House of Commons Disqualification Act 1975;

"statutory body" means a body set up by or in pursuance of an enactment, and "statutory office" means an office so set up; and

"worker" in relation to regulations 32 and 34 and to Schedule 2, means, as the case may be—
(a) an employee;
(b) a person holding an office or post to which regulation 12 (office-holders etc) applies;
(c) a person holding the office of constable;
(d) a partner within the meaning of regulation 17 (partnerships);
(e) a member of a limited liability partnership within the meaning of that regulation;
(f) a person in Crown employment;
(g) a relevant member of the House of Commons staff;
(h) a relevant member of the House of Lords staff.

(3) In these Regulations references to "employer", in their application to a person at any time seeking to employ another, include a person who has no employees at that time.

3 DISCRIMINATION ON GROUNDS OF AGE

(1) For the purposes of these Regulations, a person ("A") discriminates against another person ("B") if—
(a) on grounds of B's age, A treats B less favourably than he treats or would treat other persons, or
(b) A applies to B a provision, criterion or practice which he applies or would apply equally to persons not of the same age group as B, but—
(i) which puts or would put persons of the same age group as B at a particular disadvantage when compared with other persons, and
(ii) which puts B at that disadvantage,

and A cannot show the treatment or, as the case may be, provision, criterion or practice to be a proportionate means of achieving a legitimate aim.

(2)   A comparison of B's case with that of another person under paragraph (1) must be such
       that the relevant circumstances in the one case are the same, or not materially different, in
       the other.

(3)   In this regulation—
       (a) "age group" means a group of persons defined by reference to age, whether by
            reference to a particular age or a range of ages; and
       (b) the reference in paragraph (1)(a) to B's age includes B's apparent age.

4 DISCRIMINATION BY WAY OF VICTIMISATION

(1)   For the purposes of these Regulations, a person ("A") discriminates against another
       person ("B") if he treats B less favourably than he treats or would treat other persons in
       the same circumstances, and does so by reason that B has—
       (a) brought proceedings against A or any other person under or by virtue of these
            Regulations;
       (b) given evidence or information in connection with proceedings brought by any person
            against A or any other person under or by virtue of these Regulations;
       (c) otherwise done anything under or by reference to these Regulations in relation to A
            or any other person; or
       (d) alleged that A or any other person has committed an act which (whether or not the
            allegation so states) would amount to a contravention of these Regulations,
       or by reason that A knows that B intends to do any of those things, or suspects that B has
       done or intends to do any of them.

(2)   Paragraph (1) does not apply to treatment of B by reason of any allegation made by him,
       or evidence or information given by him, if the allegation, evidence or information was
       false and not made (or, as the case may be, given) in good faith.

5 INSTRUCTIONS TO DISCRIMINATE

For the purposes of these Regulations, a person ("A") discriminates against another person
("B") if he treats B less favourably than he treats or would treat other persons in the same
circumstances, and does so by reason that—
(a)   B has not carried out (in whole or in part) an instruction to do an act which is unlawful
       by virtue of these Regulations, or

(b)   B, having been given an instruction to do such an act, complains to A or to any other
       person about that instruction.

6 HARASSMENT ON GROUNDS OF AGE

(1)   For the purposes of these Regulations, a person ("A") subjects another person ("B") to
       harassment where, on grounds of age, A engages in unwanted conduct which has the
       purpose or effect of—
       (a) violating B's dignity; or
       (b) creating an intimidating, hostile, degrading, humiliating or offensive environment
            for B.

(2)   Conduct shall be regarded as having the effect specified in paragraph (1)(a) or (b) only if,
       having regard to all the circumstances, including in particular the perception of B, it
       should reasonably be considered as having that effect.

Part II DISCRIMINATION IN EMPLOYMENT AND VOCATIONAL TRAINING

7 APPLICANTS AND EMPLOYEES

(1) It is unlawful for an employer, in relation to employment by him at an establishment in Great Britain, to discriminate against a person—
  (a) in the arrangements he makes for the purpose of determining to whom he should offer employment;
  (b) in the terms on which he offers that person employment; or
  (c) by refusing to offer, or deliberately not offering, him employment.

(2) It is unlawful for an employer, in relation to a person whom he employs at an establishment in Great Britain, to discriminate against that person—
  (a) in the terms of employment which he affords him;
  (b) in the opportunities which he affords him for promotion, a transfer, training, or receiving any other benefit;
  (c) by refusing to afford him, or deliberately not affording him, any such opportunity; or
  (d) by dismissing him, or subjecting him to any other detriment.

(3) It is unlawful for an employer, in relation to employment by him at an establishment in Great Britain, to subject to harassment a person whom he employs or who has applied to him for employment.

(4) Subject to paragraph (5), paragraph (1)(a) and (c) does not apply in relation to a person—
  (a) whose age is greater than the employer's normal retirement age or, if the employer does not have a normal retirement age, the age of 65; or
  (b) who would, within a period of six months from the date of his application to the employer, reach the employer's normal retirement age or, if the employer does not have a normal retirement age, the age of 65.

(5) Paragraph (4) only applies to a person to whom, if he was recruited by the employer, regulation 30 (exception for retirement) could apply.

(6) Paragraph (2) does not apply to benefits of any description if the employer is concerned with the provision (for payment or not) of benefits of that description to the public, or to a section of the public which includes the employee in question, unless—
  (a) that provision differs in a material respect from the provision of the benefits by the employer to his employees; or
  (b) the provision of the benefits to the employee in question is regulated by his contract of employment; or
  (c) the benefits relate to training.

(7) In paragraph (2)(d) reference to the dismissal of a person from employment includes reference—
  (a) to the termination of that person's employment by the expiration of any period (including a period expiring by reference to an event or circumstance), not being a termination immediately after which the employment is renewed on the same terms; and
  (b) to the termination of that person's employment by any act of his (including the giving of notice) in circumstances such that he is entitled to terminate it without notice by reason of the conduct of the employer.

(8) In paragraph (4) "normal retirement age" is an age of 65 or more which meets the requirements of section 98ZH of the 1996 Act1.

8 EXCEPTION FOR GENUINE OCCUPATIONAL REQUIREMENT ETC.

(1) In relation to discrimination falling within regulation 3 (discrimination on grounds of age)—

(a) regulation 7(1)(a) or (c) does not apply to any employment;

(b) regulation 7(2)(b) or (c) does not apply to promotion or transfer to, or training for, any employment; and

(c) regulation 7(2)(d) does not apply to dismissal from any employment,

where paragraph (2) applies.

(2) This paragraph applies where, having regard to the nature of the employment or the context in which it is carried out—

(a) possessing a characteristic related to age is a genuine and determining occupational requirement;

(b) it is proportionate to apply that requirement in the particular case; and

(c) either—

(i) the person to whom that requirement is applied does not meet it, or

(ii) the employer is not satisfied, and in all the circumstances it is reasonable for him not to be satisfied, that that person meets it.

9 CONTRACT WORKERS

(1) It is unlawful for a principal, in relation to contract work at an establishment in Great Britain, to discriminate against a contract worker—

(a) in the terms on which he allows him to do that work;

(b) by not allowing him to do it or continue to do it;

(c) in the way he affords him access to any benefits or by refusing or deliberately not affording him access to them; or

(d) by subjecting him to any other detriment.

(2) It is unlawful for a principal, in relation to contract work at an establishment in Great Britain, to subject a contract worker to harassment.

(3) A principal does not contravene paragraph (1)(b) by doing any act in relation to a contract worker where, if the work were to be done by a person taken into the principal's employment, that act would be lawful by virtue of regulation 8 (exception for genuine occupational requirement etc).

(4) Paragraph (1) does not apply to benefits of any description if the principal is concerned with the provision (for payment or not) of benefits of that description to the public, or to a section of the public to which the contract worker in question belongs, unless that provision differs in a material respect from the provision of the benefits by the principal to his contract workers.

(5) In this regulation—

"principal" means a person ("A") who makes work available for doing by individuals who are employed by another person who supplies them under a contract made with A;

"contract work" means work so made available; and

"contract worker" means any individual who is supplied to the principal under such a contract

18   TRADE ORGANISATIONS

(1)   It is unlawful for a trade organisation to discriminate against a person—
     (a)   in the terms on which it is prepared to admit him to membership of the organisation; or
     (b)   by refusing to accept, or deliberately not accepting, his application for membership.

(2)   It is unlawful for a trade organisation, in relation to a member of the organisation, to discriminate against him—
     (a)   in the way it affords him access to any benefits or by refusing or deliberately omitting to afford him access to them;
     (b)   by depriving him of membership, or varying the terms on which he is a member; or
     (c)   by subjecting him to any other detriment.

(3)   It is unlawful for a trade organisation, in relation to a person's membership or application for membership of that organisation, to subject that person to harassment.

(4)   In this regulation—

"trade organisation" means an organisation of workers, an organisation of employers, or any other organisation whose members carry on a particular profession or trade for the purposes of which the organisation exists;

"profession" includes any vocation or occupation; and

"trade" includes any business.

24   RELATIONSHIPS WHICH HAVE COME TO AN END

(1)   In this regulation a "relevant relationship" is a relationship during the course of which an act of discrimination against, or harassment of, one party to the relationship ("B") by the other party to it ("A") is unlawful by virtue of any preceding provision of this Part.

(2)   Where a relevant relationship has come to an end, it is unlawful for A—
     (a)   to discriminate against B by subjecting him to a detriment; or
     (b)   to subject B to harassment;
     where the discrimination or harassment arises out of and is closely connected to that relationship.

(3)   In paragraph (1), reference to an act of discrimination or harassment which is unlawful includes, in the case of a relationship which has come to an end before the date on which the act of discrimination or harassment became unlawful by virtue of these Regulations, reference to an act of discrimination or harassment which would, after that date, be unlawful.

Part III   OTHER UNLAWFUL ACTS

25   LIABILITY OF EMPLOYERS AND PRINCIPALS

(1)   Anything done by a person in the course of his employment shall be treated for the purposes of these Regulations as done by his employer as well as by him, whether or not it was done with the employer's knowledge or approval.

(2)   Anything done by a person as agent for another person with the authority (whether express or implied, and whether precedent or subsequent) of that other person shall be treated for the purposes of these Regulations as done by that other person as well as by him.

(3)   In proceedings brought under these Regulations against any person in respect of an act alleged to have been done by an employee of his it shall be a defence for that person to prove that he took such steps as were reasonably practicable to prevent the employee from doing that act, or from doing in the course of his employment acts of that description

26 AIDING UNLAWFUL ACTS

(1)   A person who knowingly aids another person to do an act made unlawful by these Regulations shall be treated for the purpose of these Regulations as himself doing an unlawful act of the like description.

(2)   For the purposes of paragraph (1) an employee or agent for whose act the employer or principal is liable under regulation 25 (or would be so liable but for regulation 25(3)) shall be deemed to aid the doing of the act by the employer or principal.

(3)   A person does not under this regulation knowingly aid another to do an unlawful act if—
(a)   he acts in reliance on a statement made to him by that other person that, by reason of any provision of these Regulations, the act which he aids would not be unlawful; and
(b)   it is reasonable for him to rely on the statement.

(4)   A person who knowingly or recklessly makes a statement such as is referred to in paragraph (3)(a) which in a material respect is false or misleading commits an offence, and shall be liable on summary conviction to a fine not exceeding level 5 on the standard scale.

Part IV GENERAL EXCEPTIONS FROM PARTS 2 AND 3

29 EXCEPTIONS FOR POSITIVE ACTION

(1)   Nothing in Part 2 or 3 shall render unlawful any act done in or in connection with—
(a)   affording persons of a particular age or age group access to facilities for training which would help fit them for particular work; or
(b)   encouraging persons of a particular age or age group to take advantage of opportunities for doing particular work;
where it reasonably appears to the person doing the act that it prevents or compensates for disadvantages linked to age suffered by persons of that age or age group doing that work or likely to take up that work.

(2)   Nothing in Part 2 or 3 shall render unlawful any act done by a trade organisation within the meaning of regulation 18 in or in connection with—
(a)   affording only members of the organisation who are of a particular age or age group access to facilities for training which would help fit them for holding a post of any kind in the organisation; or
(b)   encouraging only members of the organisation who are of a particular age or age group to take advantage of opportunities for holding such posts in the organisation,
where it reasonably appears to the organisation that the act prevents or compensates for disadvantages linked to age suffered by those of that age or age group holding such posts or likely to hold such posts.

(3)   Nothing in Part 2 or 3 shall render unlawful any act done by a trade organisation within the meaning of regulation 18 in or in connection with encouraging only persons of a particular age or age group to become members of the organisation where it reasonably appears to the organisation that the act prevents or compensates for disadvantages linked to age suffered by persons of that age or age group who are, or are eligible to become, members.

30 EXCEPTION FOR RETIREMENT

(1) This regulation applies in relation to an employee within the meaning of section 230(1) of the 1996 Act, a person in Crown employment, a relevant member of the House of Commons staff, and a relevant member of the House of Lords staff.

(2) Nothing in Part 2 or 3 shall render unlawful the dismissal of a person to whom this regulation applies at or over the age of 65 where the reason for the dismissal is retirement.

(3) For the purposes of this regulation, whether or not the reason for a dismissal is retirement shall be determined in accordance with sections 98ZA to 98ZF of the 1996 Act.

32 EXCEPTION FOR PROVISION OF CERTAIN BENEFITS BASED ON LENGTH OF SERVICE

(1) Subject to paragraph (2), nothing in Part 2 or 3 shall render it unlawful for a person ("A"), in relation to the award of any benefit by him, to put a worker ("B") at a disadvantage when compared with another worker ("C"), if and to the extent that the disadvantage suffered by B is because B's length of service is less than that of C.

(2) Where B's length of service exceeds 5 years, it must reasonably appear to A that the way in which he uses the criterion of length of service, in relation to the award in respect of which B is put at a disadvantage, fulfils a business need of his undertaking (for example, by encouraging the loyalty or motivation, or rewarding the experience, of some or all of his workers).

(3) In calculating a worker's length of service for these purposes, A shall calculate—
(a) the length of time the worker has been working for him doing work which he reasonably considers to be at or above a particular level (assessed by reference to the demands made on the worker, for example, in terms of effort, skills and decision making); or
(b) the length of time the worker has been working for him in total;
and on each occasion on which he decides to use the criterion of length of service in relation to the award of a benefit to workers, it is for him to decide which of these definitions to use to calculate their lengths of service.

(4) For the purposes of paragraph (3), in calculating the length of time a worker has been working for him—
(a) A shall calculate the length of time in terms of the number of weeks during the whole or part of which the worker was working for him;
(b) A may discount any period during which the worker was absent from work (including any period of absence which at the time it occurred was thought by A or the worker to be permanent) unless in all the circumstances (including the way in which other workers' absences occurring in similar circumstances are treated by A in calculating their lengths of service) it would not be reasonable for him to do so;
(c) A may discount any period of time during which the worker was present at work ("the relevant period") where—
  (i) the relevant period preceded a period during which the worker was absent from work, and
  (ii) in all the circumstances (including the length of the worker's absence, the reason for his absence, the effect his absence has had on his ability to discharge the duties of his work, and the way in which other workers are treated by A in similar circumstances) it is reasonable for A to discount the relevant period.

(5) For the purposes of paragraph (3)(b), a worker shall be treated as having worked for A during any period during which he worked for another if—

    (a) that period is treated as a period of employment with A for the purposes of the 1996 Act by virtue of the operation of section 218 of that Act;

    (b) were the worker to be made redundant by A, that period and the period he has worked for A would amount to "relevant service" within the meaning of section 155 of that Act; or,

    (c) in any case to which sub-paragraph (a) or (b) does not apply, that period is treated as a period of employment with A by or under an enactment pursuant to which his employment was transferred to A.

(6) In paragraph (5)—

    (a) the reference to being made redundant is a reference to being dismissed by reason of redundancy for the purposes of the 1996 Act;

    (b) the reference to section 155 of that Act is a reference to that section as modified by the Redundancy Payments (Continuity of Employment in Local Government, etc.) (Modification) Order 1999.

(7) In this regulation—

"benefit" does not include any benefit awarded to a worker by virtue of his ceasing to work for A;

"enactment" includes an enactment comprised in, or in an instrument made under, an Act of the Scottish Parliament; and

"year" means a year of 12 calendar months.

Part V ENFORCEMENT

35 RESTRICTION OF PROCEEDINGS FOR BREACH OF REGULATIONS

(1) Except as provided by these Regulations no proceedings, whether civil or criminal, shall lie against any person in respect of an act by reason that the act is unlawful by virtue of a provision of these Regulations.

(2) Paragraph (1) does not prevent the making of an application for judicial review or the investigation or determination of any matter in accordance with Part 10 (investigations: the Pensions Ombudsman) of the Pension Schemes Act 1993 by the Pensions Ombudsman.

36 JURISDICTION OF EMPLOYMENT TRIBUNALS

(1) A complaint by any person ("the complainant") that another person ("the respondent")—

    (a) has committed against the complainant an act to which this regulation applies; or

    (b) is by virtue of regulation 25 (liability of employers and principals) or 26 (aiding unlawful acts) to be treated as having committed against the complainant such an act;

may be presented to an employment tribunal.

(2) This regulation applies to any act of discrimination or harassment which is unlawful by virtue of any provision of Part 2 other than—

    (a) where the act is one in respect of which an appeal or proceedings in the nature of an appeal may be brought under any enactment, regulation 19 (qualifications bodies);

    (b) regulation 23 (institutions of further and higher education); or

    (c) where the act arises out of and is closely connected to a relationship between the complainant and the respondent which has come to an end but during the course of which an act of discrimination against, or harassment of, the complainant by the respondent would have been unlawful by virtue of regulation 23, regulation 24 (relationships which have come to an end).

(3) In paragraph (2)(c), reference to an act of discrimination or harassment which would have been unlawful includes, in the case of a relationship which has come to an end before the date on which the act of discrimination or harassment became unlawful by virtue of these Regulations, reference to an act of discrimination or harassment which would, after that date, have been unlawful.

(4) In this regulation, "enactment" includes an enactment comprised in, or in an instrument made under, an Act of the Scottish Parliament.

37 BURDEN OF PROOF: EMPLOYMENT TRIBUNALS

(1) This regulation applies to any complaint presented under regulation 36 to an employment tribunal.

(2) Where, on the hearing of the complaint, the complainant proves facts from which the tribunal could, apart from this regulation, conclude in the absence of an adequate explanation that the respondent—
    (a) has committed against the complainant an act to which regulation 36 applies; or
    (b) is by virtue of regulation 25 (liability of employers and principals) or 26 (aiding unlawful acts) to be treated as having committed against the complainant such an act,
the tribunal shall uphold the complaint unless the respondent proves that he did not commit, or as the case may be, is not to be treated as having committed, that act.

38 REMEDIES ON COMPLAINTS IN EMPLOYMENT TRIBUNALS

(1) Where an employment tribunal finds that a complaint presented to it under regulation 36 is well-founded, the tribunal shall make such of the following as it considers just and equitable—
    (a) an order declaring the rights of the complainant and the respondent in relation to the act to which the complaint relates;
    (b) an order requiring the respondent to pay to the complainant compensation of an amount corresponding to any damages he could have been ordered by a county court or by a sheriff court to pay to the complainant if the complaint had fallen to be dealt with under regulation 39 (jurisdiction of county and sheriff courts);
    (c) a recommendation that the respondent take within a specified period action appearing to the tribunal to be practicable for the purpose of obviating or reducing the adverse effect on the complainant of any act of discrimination or harassment to which the complaint relates.

(2) As respects an unlawful act of discrimination falling within regulation 3(1)(b) (discrimination on the grounds of age), if the respondent proves that the provision, criterion or practice was not applied with the intention of treating the complainant unfavourably on grounds of age, an order may be made under paragraph (1)(b) only if the employment tribunal—
    (a) makes such order under paragraph (1)(a) (if any) and such recommendation under paragraph (1)(c) (if any) as it would have made if it had no power to make an order under paragraph (1)(b); and

(b) (where it makes an order under paragraph (1)(a) or a recommendation under paragraph (1)(c) or both) considers that it is just and equitable to make an order under paragraph (1)(b) as well.

(3) If without reasonable justification the respondent to a complaint fails to comply with a recommendation made by an employment tribunal under paragraph (1)(c), then, if it thinks it just and equitable to do so—
  (a) the tribunal may increase the amount of compensation required to be paid to the complainant in respect of the complaint by an order made under paragraph (1)(b); or
  (b) if an order under paragraph (1)(b) was not made, the tribunal may make such an order.

(4) Where an amount of compensation falls to be awarded under paragraph (1)(b), the tribunal may include in the award interest on that amount subject to, and in accordance with, the provisions of the Employment Tribunals (Interest on Awards in Discrimination Cases) Regulations 1996.

(5) This regulation has effect subject to paragraph 6 of Schedule 2 (pension schemes).

39 JURISDICTION OF COUNTY AND SHERIFF COURTS

(1) A claim by any person ("the claimant") that another person ("the respondent")—
  (a) has committed against the claimant an act to which this regulation applies; or
  (b) is by virtue of regulation 25 (liability of employers and principals) or 26 (aiding unlawful acts) to be treated as having committed against the claimant such an act,
  may be made the subject of civil proceedings in like manner as any other claim in tort or (in Scotland) in reparation for breach of statutory duty.

(2) Proceedings brought under paragraph (1) shall—
  (a) in England and Wales, be brought only in a county court; and
  (b) in Scotland, be brought only in a sheriff court.

(3) For the avoidance of doubt it is hereby declared that damages in respect of an unlawful act to which this regulation applies may include compensation for injury to feelings whether or not they include compensation under any other head.

(4) This regulation applies to any act of discrimination or harassment which is unlawful by virtue of—
  (a) regulation 23 (institutions of further and higher education); or
  (b) where the act arises out of and is closely connected to a relationship between the claimant and the respondent which has come to an end but during the course of which an act of discrimination against, or harassment of, the claimant by the respondent would have been unlawful by virtue of regulation 23, regulation 24 (relationships which have come to an end).

(5) In paragraph (4)(b), reference to an act of discrimination or harassment which would have been unlawful includes, in the case of a relationship which has come to an end before the date on which the act of discrimination or harassment became unlawful by virtue of these Regulations, reference to an act of discrimination or harassment which would, after that date, have been unlawful.

42 PERIOD WITHIN WHICH PROCEEDINGS TO BE BROUGHT

(1) An employment tribunal shall not consider a complaint under regulation 36 unless it is presented to the tribunal before the end of the period of three months beginning when the act complained of was done.

(1A) Where the period within which a complaint must be presented in accordance with paragraph (1) is extended by regulation 15 of the Employment Act 2002 (Dispute Resolution) Regulations 2004, the period within which the complaint must be presented shall be the extended period rather than the period in paragraph (1).

(2) A county court or a sheriff court shall not consider a claim brought under regulation 39 unless proceedings in respect of the claim are instituted before the end of the period of six months beginning when the act complained of was done.

(3) A court or tribunal may nevertheless consider any such complaint or claim which is out of time if, in all the circumstances of the case, it considers that it is just and equitable to do so.

(4) For the purposes of this regulation and regulation 41 (help for persons in obtaining information etc)—
   (a) when the making of a contract is, by reason of the inclusion of any term, an unlawful act, that act shall be treated as extending throughout the duration of the contract; and
   (b) any act extending over a period shall be treated as done at the end of that period; and
   (c) a deliberate omission shall be treated as done when the person in question decided upon it,
   and in the absence of evidence establishing the contrary a person shall be taken for the purposes of this regulation to decide upon an omission when he does an act inconsistent with doing the omitted act or, if he has done no such inconsistent act, when the period expires within which he might reasonably have been expected to do the omitted act if it was to be done.

SCHEDULE 5 VALIDITY OF CONTRACTS, COLLECTIVE AGREEMENTS AND RULES OF UNDERTAKINGS

Part I VALIDITY AND REVISION OF CONTRACTS

1

(1) A term of a contract is void where—
   (a) the making of the contract is, by reason of the inclusion of the term, unlawful by virtue of these Regulations;
   (b) it is included in furtherance of an act which is unlawful by virtue of these Regulations; or
   (c) it provides for the doing of an act which is unlawful by virtue of these Regulations.

(2) Sub-paragraph (1) does not apply to a term the inclusion of which constitutes, or is in furtherance of, or provides for, unlawful discrimination against, or harassment of, a party to the contract, but the term shall be unenforceable against that party.

(3) A term in a contract which purports to exclude or limit any provision of these Regulations is unenforceable by any person in whose favour the term would operate apart from this paragraph.

(4) Sub-paragraphs (1), (2) and (3) shall apply whether the contract was entered into before or after the date on which any term of the contract became unlawful by virtue of these Regulations, but in the case of a contract made before the date on which a term became unlawful, those sub-paragraphs do not apply to that term in relation to any period before that date.

2

(1)   Paragraph 1(3) does not apply—

     (a)   to a contract settling a complaint to which regulation 36(1) (jurisdiction of employment tribunals) applies where the contract is made with the assistance of a conciliation officer within the meaning of section 211 of the Trade Union and Labour Relations (Consolidation) Act 1992;

     (b)   to a contract settling a complaint to which regulation 36(1) applies if the conditions regulating compromise contracts under this Schedule are satisfied in relation to the contract; or

     (c)   to a contract settling a claim to which regulation 39 (jurisdiction of county or sheriff courts) applies.

(2)   The conditions regulating compromise contracts under this Schedule are that—

     (a)   the contract must be in writing;

     (b)   the contract must relate to the particular complaint;

     (c)   the complainant must have received advice from a relevant independent adviser as to the terms and effect of the proposed contract and in particular its effect on his ability to pursue a complaint before an employment tribunal;

     (d)   there must be in force, when the adviser gives the advice, a contract of insurance, or an indemnity provided for members of a profession or professional body, covering the risk of a claim by the complainant in respect of loss arising in consequence of the advice;

     (e)   the contract must identify the adviser; and

     (f)   the contract must state that the conditions regulating compromise contracts under this Schedule are satisfied.

(3)   A person is a relevant independent adviser for the purposes of sub-paragraph (2)(c)—

     (a)   if he is a qualified lawyer;

     (b)   if he is an officer, official, employee or member of an independent trade union who has been certified in writing by the trade union as competent to give advice and as authorised to do so on behalf of the trade union; or

     (c)   if he works at an advice centre (whether as an employee or a volunteer) and has been certified in writing by the centre as competent to give advice and as authorised to do so on behalf of the centre.

(4)   But a person is not a relevant independent adviser for the purposes of sub-paragraph (2)(c) in relation to the complainant—

     (a)   if he is employed by, or is acting in the matter for the other party, or is a person who is connected with the other party;

     (b)   in the case of a person within sub-paragraph (3)(b) or (c), if the trade union or advice centre is the other party or a person who is connected with the other party; or

     (c)   in the case of a person within sub-paragraph (3)(c), if the complainant makes a payment for the advice received from him.

(5)   In sub-paragraph (3)(a) "qualified lawyer" means—

     (a)   as respects England and Wales, a person who, for the purposes of the Legal Services Act 2007, is an authorised person in relation to an activity which constitutes the exercise of a right of audience or the conduct of litigation (within the meaning of that Act); and

     (b)   as respects Scotland, an advocate (whether in practice as such or employed to give legal advice), or a solicitor who holds a practising certificate.

(6)   A person shall be treated as being a qualified lawyer within sub-paragraph (5)(a) if he is a Fellow of the Institute of Legal Executives employed by a solicitors' practice.

(7) In sub-paragraph (3)(b) "independent trade union" has the same meaning as in the Trade Union and Labour Relations (Consolidation) Act 1992.

(8) For the purposes of sub-paragraph (4)(a) any two persons are to be treated as connected—
(a) if one is a company of which the other (directly or indirectly) has control; or
(b) if both are companies of which a third person (directly or indirectly) has control.

(9) An agreement under which the parties agree to submit a dispute to arbitration—
(a) shall be regarded for the purposes of sub-paragraphs (1)(a) and (b) as being a contract settling a complaint if—
(i) the dispute is covered by a scheme having effect by virtue of an order under section 212A of the Trade Union and Labour Relations (Consolidation) Act 1992, and
(ii) the agreement is to submit it to arbitration in accordance with the scheme, but
(b) shall be regarded as neither being nor including such a contract in any other case.

3

(1) On the application of a person interested in a contract to which paragraph 1(1) or (2) applies, a county court or a sheriff court may make such order as it thinks fit for—
(a) removing or modifying any term rendered void by paragraph 1(1), or
(b) removing or modifying any term made unenforceable by paragraph 1(2);
but such an order shall not be made unless all persons affected have been given notice in writing of the application (except where under rules of court notice may be dispensed with) and have been afforded an opportunity to make representations to the court.

(2) An order under sub-paragraph (1) may include provision as respects any period before the making of the order (but after the date on which the inclusion of any term which is the subject of the order becomes unlawful by virtue of these Regulations).

Part II COLLECTIVE AGREEMENTS AND RULES OF UNDERTAKINGS

4

(1) This Part of this Schedule applies to—
(a) any term of a collective agreement, including an agreement which was not intended, or is presumed not to have been intended, to be a legally enforceable contract;
(b) any rule made by an employer for application to all or any of the persons who are employed by him or who apply to be, or are, considered by him for employment;
(c) any rule made by a trade organisation (within the meaning of regulation 18) or a qualifications body (within the meaning of regulation 19) for application to—
(i) all or any of its members or prospective members; or
(ii) all or any of the persons on whom it has conferred professional or trade qualifications (within the meaning of regulation 19) or who are seeking the professional or trade qualifications which it has power to confer.

(2) Any term or rule to which this Part of this Schedule applies is void where—
(a) the making of the collective agreement is, by reason of the inclusion of the term, unlawful by virtue of these Regulations;
(b) the term or rule is included or made in furtherance of an act which is unlawful by virtue of these Regulations; or
(c) the term or rule provides for the doing of an act which is unlawful by virtue of these Regulations.

(3)   Sub-paragraph (2) shall apply whether the agreement was entered into, or the rule made, before or after the date on which any term of the agreement or rule became unlawful by virtue of these Regulations; but in the case of an agreement entered into, or a rule made, before the date on which a term, or rule, became unlawful, that sub-paragraph does not apply to that term or rule in relation to any period before that date.

5

A person to whom this paragraph applies may present a complaint to an employment tribunal that a term or rule is void by virtue of paragraph 4 if he has reason to believe—
(a)   that the term or rule may at some future time have effect in relation to him; and

(b)   where he alleges that it is void by virtue of paragraph 4(2)(c), that—
    (i)   an act for the doing of which it provides, may at some such time be done in relation to him, and
    (ii)   the act would be unlawful by virtue of these Regulations if done in relation to him in present circumstances.

6

In the case of a complaint about—
(a)   a term of a collective agreement made by or on behalf of—
    (i)   an employer,
    (ii)   an organisation of employers of which an employer is a member, or
    (iii) an association of such organisations of one of which an employer is a member, or

(b)   a rule made by an employer within the meaning of paragraph 4(1)(b),

paragraph 5 applies to any person who is, or is genuinely and actively seeking to become, one of his employees.

7

In the case of a complaint about a rule made by an organisation or body to which paragraph 4(1)(c) applies, paragraph 5 applies to any person—
(a)   who is, or is genuinely and actively seeking to become, a member of the organisation or body;

(b)   on whom the organisation or body has conferred a professional or trade qualification (within the meaning of regulation 19) which the organisation or body has power to confer; or

(c)   who is genuinely and actively seeking such a professional or trade qualification which the organisation or body has power to confer.

8

(1)   When an employment tribunal finds that a complaint presented to it under paragraph 5 is well-founded the tribunal shall make an order declaring that the term or rule is void.

(2)   An order under sub-paragraph (1) may include provision as respects any period before the making of the order (but after the date on which the inclusion of the term or rule became unlawful by virtue of these Regulations).

9

The avoidance by virtue of paragraph 4(2) of any term or rule which provides for any person to be discriminated against shall be without prejudice to the following rights (except in so far as they enable any person to require another person to be treated less favourably than himself), namely—

(a)   such of the rights of the person to be discriminated against; and

(b)   such of the rights of any person who will be treated more favourably in direct or indirect consequence of the discrimination,

as are conferred by or in respect of a contract made or modified wholly or partly in pursuance of, or by reference to, that term or rule.

10

In this Schedule "collective agreement" means any agreement relating to one or more of the matters mentioned in section 178(2) of the Trade Union and Labour Relations (Consolidation) Act 1992 (collective agreements and collective bargaining), being an agreement made by or on behalf of one or more employers or one or more organisations of employers or associations of such organisations with one or more organisations of workers or associations of such organisations.

SCHEDULE 6 DUTY TO CONSIDER WORKING BEYOND RETIREMENT

Interpretation

1

(1)   In this Schedule—

"dismissal" means a dismissal within the meaning of section 95 of the 1996 Act;

"employee" means a person to whom regulation 30 (exception for retirement) applies and references to "employer" shall be construed accordingly;

"intended date of retirement" has the meaning given by sub-paragraph (2);

"operative date of termination" means (subject to paragraph 10(3))—
(a) where the employer terminates the employee's contract of employment by notice, the date on which the notice expires, or
(b) where the employer terminates the contract of employment without notice, the date on which the termination takes effect;

"request" means a request made under paragraph 5; and

"worker" has the same meaning as in section 230(3) of the 1996 Act.

(2)   In this Schedule "intended date of retirement" means—
(a) where the employer notifies a date in accordance with paragraph 2, that date;
(b) where the employer notifies a date in accordance with paragraph 4 and either no request is made or a request is made after the notification, that date;
(c) where,
(i)   the employer has not notified a date in accordance with paragraph 2,
(ii) a request is made before the employer has notified a date in accordance with paragraph 4 (including where no notification in accordance with that paragraph is given),

   (iii) the request is made by an employee who has reasonable grounds for believing that the employer intends to retire him on a certain date, and,

   (iv) the request identifies that date,

  the date so identified;

 (d) in a case to which paragraph 3 has applied, any earlier or later date that has superseded the date mentioned in paragraph (a), (b) or (c) as the intended date of retirement by virtue of paragraph 3(3);

 (e) in a case to which paragraph 10 has applied, the later date that has superseded the date mentioned in paragraph (a), (b) or (c) as the intended date of retirement by virtue of paragraph 10(3)(b).

Duty of employer to inform employee

2

(1) An employer who intends to retire an employee has a duty to notify the employee in writing of—

 (a) the employee's right to make a request; and

 (b) the date on which he intends the employee to retire,

not more than one year and not less than six months before that date.

(2) The duty to notify applies regardless of—

 (a) whether there is any term in the employee's contract of employment indicating when his retirement is expected to take place,

 (b) any other notification of, or information about, the employee's date of retirement given to him by the employer at any time, and

 (c) any other information about the employee's right to make a request given to him by the employer at any time.

Statutory right to request not to retire

5

(1) An employee may make a request to his employer not to retire on the intended date of retirement.

(2) In his request the employee must propose that his employment should continue, following the intended date of retirement—

 (a) indefinitely,

 (b) for a stated period, or

 (c) until a stated date;

and, if the request is made at a time when it is no longer possible for the employer to notify in accordance with paragraph 2 and the employer has not yet notified in accordance with paragraph 4, must identify the date on which he believes that the employer intends to retire him.

(3) A request must be in writing and state that it is made under this paragraph.

(4) An employee may only make one request under this paragraph in relation to any one intended date of retirement and may not make a request in relation to a date that supersedes a different date as the intended date of retirement by virtue of paragraph 3(3) or 10(3)(b).

(5) A request is only a request made under this paragraph if it is made—

(a) in a case where the employer has complied with paragraph 2, more than three months but not more than six months before the intended date of retirement, or

(b) in a case where the employer has not complied with paragraph 2, before, but not more than six months before, the intended date of retirement.

An employer's duty to consider a request

6

An employer to whom a request is made is under a duty to consider the request in accordance with paragraphs 7 to 9.

Dismissal before request considered

10

(1) This paragraph applies where—
    (a) by virtue of paragraph 6 an employer is under a duty to consider a request;
    (b) the employer dismisses the employee;
    (c) that dismissal is the contemplated dismissal to which the request relates; and
    (d) the operative date of termination would, but for sub-paragraph (3), fall on or before the day on which the employer gives notice in accordance with paragraph 7(6).

(2) Subject to sub-paragraph (4), the contract of employment shall continue in force for all purposes, including the purpose of determining for any purpose the period for which the employee has been continuously employed, until the day following that on which the notice under paragraph 7(6) is given.

(3) The day following the day on which that notice is given shall supersede—
    (a) the date mentioned in sub-paragraph (1)(d) as the operative date of termination; and
    (b) the date defined as the intended date of retirement in paragraph (a), (b) or (c) of paragraph 1(2) as the intended date of retirement.

(4) Any continuation of the contract of employment under sub-paragraph (2) shall be disregarded when determining the operative date of termination for the purposes of sections 98ZA to 98ZH of the 1996 Act.

Complaint to employment tribunal: failure to comply with paragraph 2

11

(1) An employee may present a complaint to an employment tribunal that his employer has failed to comply with the duty to notify him in paragraph 2.

(2) A tribunal shall not consider a complaint under this paragraph unless the complaint is presented—
    (a) before the end of the period of three months beginning with—
        (i) the last day permitted to the employer by paragraph 2 for complying with the duty to notify, or
        (ii) if the employee did not then know the date that would be the intended date of retirement, the first day on which he knew or should have known that date; or
    (b) within such further period as the tribunal considers reasonable in a case where it is satisfied that it was not reasonably practicable for the complaint to be presented before the end of that period of three months.

(3)   Where a tribunal finds that a complaint under this paragraph is well-founded it shall order the employer to pay compensation to the employee of such amount, not exceeding 8 weeks' pay, as the tribunal considers just and equitable in all the circumstances.

(4)   Chapter 2 of Part 14 of the 1996 Act (calculation of a week's pay) shall apply for the purposes of sub-paragraph (3); and in applying that Chapter the calculation date shall be taken to be the date on which the complaint was presented or, if earlier, the operative date of termination.

(5)   The limit in section 227(1) of the 1996 Act (maximum amount of a week's pay) shall apply for the purposes of sub-paragraph (3).

As amended by the Employment Relations Act 1999, s 34; Education Act 1997, s 51; School Standards and Framework Act 1998, s 140(1), Schedule 30 Para 183(a)(iii); Scotland Act 1998, s 48(6), s 87(1), Schedule 9; Education Act 2002, Schedule 22 Part 3; Ministry of Agriculture, Fisheries and Food (Dissolution) Order 2002/794; Fixed-term Employees (Prevention of Less Favourable Treatment) Regulations 2002/2034 Reg 11, Schedule 2 Part 1 Para 3(1), Schedule 2 Part 1 Para 3(7); Education Act 2002 (Modification and Transitional Provisions) (England) Regulations 2003/2045, reg 3; Employment Relations Act 2004, s 57, Schedule 1 Para 29, Schedule 2; Employment Equality (Age) (Amendment) Regulations 2006/2408 reg 2(4)(a), reg 2(4)(b), reg 2(6)(a), reg 2(6)(b), reg 2(6)(c), reg 2(6)(d); Employment Equality (Age) Regulations 2006 (Amendment) Regulations 2008/573 reg 5; Legal Services Act 2007 (Consequential Amendments) Order 2009/3348 art 23.

EU Materials

COUNCIL DIRECTIVE NO 98/59 ON THE APPROXIMATION OF THE LAWS OF THE MEMBER STATES RELATING TO COLLECTIVE REDUNDANCIES

SECTION I DEFINITIONS AND SCOPE

Article 1

1. For the purposes of this Directive:
    (a) "collective redundancies" means dismissals effected by an employer for one or more reasons not related to the individual workers concerned where, according to the choice of the Member States, the number of redundancies is:
        (i)   either, over a period of 30 days:
              — at least 10 in establishments normally employing more than 20 and less than 100 workers,
              — at least 10% of the number of workers in establishments normally employing at least 100 but less than 300 workers,
              — at least 30 in establishments normally employing 300 workers or more,
        (ii) or, over a period of 90 days, at least 20, whatever the number of workers normally employed in the establishments in question
    (b) "workers' representatives" means the workers' representatives provided for by the laws or practices of the Member States.

    For the purpose of calculating the number of redundancies provided for in the first subparagraph of point (a), terminations of an employment contract which occur on the employer's initiative for one or more reasons not related to the individual workers concerned shall be assimilated to redundancies, provided that there are at least five redundancies.

2. This Directive shall not apply to:
    (a) collective redundancies effected under contracts of employment concluded for limited periods of time or for specific tasks except where such redundancies take place prior to the date of expiry or the completion of such contracts;
    (b) workers employed by public administrative bodies or by establishments governed by public law (or, in Member States where this concept is unknown, by equivalent bodies);
    (c) the crews of seagoing vessels.

SECTION II INFORMATION AND CONSULTATION

Article 2

1. Where an employer is contemplating collective redundancies, he shall begin consultations with the workers' representatives in good time with a view to reaching an agreement.

2. These consultations shall, at least, cover ways and means of avoiding collective redundancies or reducing the number of workers affected, and of mitigating the consequences by recourse to accompanying social measures aimed, inter alia, at aid for redeploying or retraining workers made redundant.

   Member States may provide that the workers' representatives may call on the services of experts in accordance with national legislation and/or practice.

3. To enable workers' representatives to make constructive proposals, the employers shall in good time during the course of the consultations:
   (a) supply them with all relevant information and
   (b) in any event notify them in writing of:
       (i) the reasons for the projected redundancies;
       (ii) the number of categories of workers to be made redundant;
       (iii) the number and categories of workers normally employed;
       (iv) the period over which the projected redundancies are to be effected;
       (v) the criteria proposed for the selection of the workers to be made redundant in so far as national legislation and/or practice confers the power therefor upon the employer;
       (vi) the method for calculating any redundancy payments other than those arising out of national legislation and/or practice.
   The employer shall forward to the competent public authority a copy of, at least, the elements of the written communication which are provided for in the first subparagraph, point (b), subpoints (i) to (v).

4. The obligations laid down in paragraphs 1, 2 and 3 shall apply irrespective of whether the decision regarding collective redundancies is being taken by the employer or by an undertaking controlling the employer.

In considering alleged breaches of the information, consultation and notification requirements laid down by this Directive, account shall not be taken of any defence on the part of the employer on the ground that the necessary information has not been provided to the employer by the undertaking which took the decision leading to collective redundancies.

SECTION III PROCEDURE FOR COLLECTIVE REDUNDANCIES

Article 3

1. Employers shall notify the competent public authority in writing of any projected collective redundancies.

   However, Member States may provide that in the case of planned collective redundancies arising from termination of the establishment's activities as a result of a judicial decision, the employer shall be obliged to notify the competent public authority in writing only if the latter so requests.

   This notification shall contain all relevant information concerning the projected collective redundancies and the consultations with workers' representatives provided for in Article 2, and particularly the reasons for the redundancies, the number of workers to be made redundant, the number of workers normally employed and the period over which the redundancies are to be effected.

2.   Employers shall forward to the workers' representatives a copy of the notification provided for in paragraph 1.

The workers' representatives may send any comments they may have to the competent public authority.

Article 4

1.   Projected collective redundancies notified to the competent public authority shall take effect not earlier than 30 days after the notification referred to in Article 3(1) without prejudice to any provisions governing individual rights with regard to notice of dismissal.

Member States may grant the competent public authority the power to reduce the period provided for in the preceding subparagraph.

2.   The period provided for in paragraph 1 shall be used by the competent public authority to seek solutions to the problems raised by the projected collective redundancies.

3.   Where the initial period provided for in paragraph 1 is shorter than 60 days, Member States may grant the competent public authority the power to extend the initial period to 60 days following notification where the problems raised by the projected collective redundancies are not likely to be solved within the initial period.

Member States may grant the competent public authority wider powers of extension.

The employer must be informed of the extension and the grounds for it before expiry of the initial period provided for in paragraph 1.

4.   Member States need not apply this Article to collective redundancies arising from termination of the establishment's activities where this is the result of a judicial decision.

SECTION IV FINAL PROVISIONS

Article 5
This Directive shall not affect the right of Member States to apply or to introduce laws, regulations or administrative provisions which are more favourable to workers or to promote or to allow the application of collective agreements more favourable to workers.

Article 6
Member States shall ensure that judicial and/or administrative procedures for the enforcement of obligations under this Directive are available to the workers' representatives and/or workers.

COUNCIL DIRECTIVE NO 2000/43 IMPLEMENTING THE PRINCIPLE OF EQUAL TREATMENT BETWEEN PERSONS IRRESPECTIVE OF RACIAL OR ETHNIC ORIGIN

Chapter I GENERAL PROVISIONS

Article 1

Purpose
The purpose of this Directive is to lay down a framework for combating discrimination on the grounds of racial or ethnic origin, with a view to putting into effect in the Member States the principle of equal treatment.

Article 2

Concept of discrimination

1. For the purposes of this Directive, the principle of equal treatment shall mean that there shall be no direct or indirect discrimination based on racial or ethnic origin.

2. For the purposes of paragraph 1:
   (a) direct discrimination shall be taken to occur where one person is treated less favourably than another is, has been or would be treated in a comparable situation on grounds of racial or ethnic origin;
   (b) indirect discrimination shall be taken to occur where an apparently neutral provision, criterion or practice would put persons of a racial or ethnic origin at a particular disadvantage compared with other persons, unless that provision, criterion or practice is objectively justified by a legitimate aim and the means of achieving that aim are appropriate and necessary.

3. Harassment shall be deemed to be discrimination within the meaning of paragraph 1, when an unwanted conduct related to racial or ethnic origin takes place with the purpose or effect of violating the dignity of a person and of creating an intimidating, hostile, degrading, humiliating or offensive environment. In this context, the concept of harassment may be defined in accordance with the national laws and practice of the Member States.

4. An instruction to discriminate against persons on grounds of racial or ethnic origin shall be deemed to be discrimination within the meaning of paragraph 1.

Article 3

Scope

1. Within the limits of the powers conferred upon the Community, this Directive shall apply to all persons, as regards both the public and private sectors, including public bodies, in relation to:
   (a) conditions for access to employment, to self-employment and to occupation, including selection criteria and recruitment conditions, whatever the branch of activity and at all levels of the professional hierarchy, including promotion;
   (b) access to all types and to all levels of vocational guidance, vocational training, advanced vocational training and retraining, including practical work experience;
   (c) employment and working conditions, including dismissals and pay;
   (d) membership of and involvement in an organisation of workers or employers, or any organisation whose members carry on a particular profession, including the benefits provided for by such organisations;
   (e) social protection, including social security and healthcare;
   (f) social advantages;
   (g) education;
   (h) access to and supply of goods and services which are available to the public, including housing.

2. This Directive does not cover difference of treatment based on nationality and is without prejudice to provisions and conditions relating to the entry into and residence of third-country nationals and stateless persons on the territory of Member States, and to any treatment which arises from the legal status of the third-country nationals and stateless persons concerned.

Article 4

Genuine and determining occupational requirements

Notwithstanding Article 2(1) and (2), Member States may provide that a difference of treatment which is based on a characteristic related to racial or ethnic origin shall not constitute discrimination where, by reason of the nature of the particular occupational activities concerned or of the context in which they are carried out, such a characteristic constitutes a genuine and determining occupational requirement, provided that the objective is legitimate and the requirement is proportionate.

Article 5

Positive action

With a view to ensuring full equality in practice, the principle of equal treatment shall not prevent any Member State from maintaining or adopting specific measures to prevent or compensate for disadvantages linked to racial or ethnic origin.

Chapter II REMEDIES AND ENFORCEMENT

Article 7

Defence of rights

1. Member States shall ensure that judicial and/or administrative procedures, including where they deem it appropriate conciliation procedures, for the enforcement of obligations under this Directive are available to all persons who consider themselves wronged by failure to apply the principle of equal treatment to them, even after the relationship in which the discrimination is alleged to have occurred has ended.

2. Member States shall ensure that associations, organisations or other legal entities, which have, in accordance with the criteria laid down by their national law, a legitimate interest in ensuring that the provisions of this Directive are complied with, may engage, either on behalf or in support of the complainant, with his or her approval, in any judicial and/or administrative procedure provided for the enforcement of obligations under this Directive.

3. Paragraphs 1 and 2 are without prejudice to national rules relating to time limits for bringing actions as regards the principle of equality of treatment.

Article 8

Burden of proof

1. Member States shall take such measures as are necessary, in accordance with their national judicial systems, to ensure that, when persons who consider themselves wronged because the principle of equal treatment has not been applied to them establish, before a court or other competent authority, facts from which it may be presumed that there has been direct or indirect discrimination, it shall be for the respondent to prove that there has been no breach of the principle of equal treatment.

2. Paragraph 1 shall not prevent Member States from introducing rules of evidence which are more favourable to plaintiffs.

3. Paragraph 1 shall not apply to criminal procedures.

4. Paragraphs 1, 2 and 3 shall also apply to any proceedings brought in accordance with Article 7(2).

5. Member States need not apply paragraph 1 to proceedings in which it is for the court or competent body to investigate the facts of the case.

Article 9

Victimisation

Member States shall introduce into their national legal systems such measures as are necessary to protect individuals from any adverse treatment or adverse consequence as a reaction to a complaint or to proceedings aimed at enforcing compliance with the principle of equal treatment.

Chapter III BODIES FOR THE PROMOTION OF EQUAL TREATMENT

Article 13

1.   Member States shall designate a body or bodies for the promotion of equal treatment of all persons without discrimination on the grounds of racial or ethnic origin. These bodies may form part of agencies charged at national level with the defence of human rights or the safeguard of individuals' rights.

2.   Member States shall ensure that the competences of these bodies include:
— without prejudice to the right of victims and of associations, organisations or other legal entities referred to in Article 7(2), providing independent assistance to victims of discrimination in pursuing their complaints about discrimination,
— conducting independent surveys concerning discrimination,
— publishing independent reports and making recommendations on any issue relating to such discrimination.

COUNCIL DIRECTIVE NO 2000/78 ESTABLISHING A GENERAL FRAMEWORK FOR EQUAL TREATMENT IN EMPLOYMENT AND OCCUPATION

Chapter I GENERAL PROVISIONS

Article 1

Purpose

The purpose of this Directive is to lay down a general framework for combating discrimination on the grounds of religion or belief, disability, age or sexual orientation as regards employment and occupation, with a view to putting into effect in the Member States the principle of equal treatment.

Article 2

Concept of discrimination

1.   For the purposes of this Directive, the 'principle of equal treatment' shall mean that there shall be no direct or indirect discrimination whatsoever on any of the grounds referred to in Article 1.

2.   For the purposes of paragraph 1:
(a) direct discrimination shall be taken to occur where one person is treated less favourably than another is, has been or would be treated in a comparable situation, on any of the grounds referred to in Article 1;
(b) indirect discrimination shall be taken to occur where an apparently neutral provision, criterion or practice would put persons having a particular religion or belief, a particular disability, a particular age, or a particular sexual orientation at a particular disadvantage compared with other persons unless:
(i) that provision, criterion or practice is objectively justified by a legitimate aim and the means of achieving that aim are appropriate and necessary, or

(ii) as regards persons with a particular disability, the employer or any person or organisation to whom this Directive applies, is obliged, under national legislation, to take appropriate measures in line with the principles contained in Article 5 in order to eliminate disadvantages entailed by such provision, criterion or practice.

3. Harassment shall be deemed to be a form of discrimination within the meaning of paragraph 1, when unwanted conduct related to any of the grounds referred to in Article 1 takes place with the purpose or effect of violating the dignity of a person and of creating an intimidating, hostile, degrading, humiliating or offensive environment. In this context, the concept of harassment may be defined in accordance with the national laws and practice of the Member States.

4. An instruction to discriminate against persons on any of the grounds referred to in Article 1 shall be deemed to be discrimination within the meaning of paragraph 1.

5. This Directive shall be without prejudice to measures laid down by national law which, in a democratic society, are necessary for public security, for the maintenance of public order and the prevention of criminal offences, for the protection of health and for the protection of the rights and freedoms of others.

Article 3

Scope
1. Within the limits of the areas of competence conferred on the Community, this Directive shall apply to all persons, as regards both the public and private sectors, including public bodies, in relation to:
   (a) conditions for access to employment, to self-employment or to occupation, including selection criteria and recruitment conditions, whatever the branch of activity and at all levels of the professional hierarchy, including promotion;
   (b) access to all types and to all levels of vocational guidance, vocational training, advanced vocational training and retraining, including practical work experience;
   (c) employment and working conditions, including dismissals and pay;
   (d) membership of, and involvement in, an organisation of workers or employers, or any organisation whose members carry on a particular profession, including the benefits provided for by such organisations.

2. This Directive does not cover differences of treatment based on nationality and is without prejudice to provisions and conditions relating to the entry into and residence of third-country nationals and stateless persons in the territory of Member States, and to any treatment which arises from the legal status of the third-country nationals and stateless persons concerned.

3. This Directive does not apply to payments of any kind made by state schemes or similar, including state social security or social protection schemes.

4. Member States may provide that this Directive, in so far as it relates to discrimination on the grounds of disability and age, shall not apply to the armed forces.

Article 4

Occupational requirements
1. Notwithstanding Article 2(1) and (2), Member States may provide that a difference of treatment which is based on a characteristic related to any of the grounds referred to in Article 1 shall not constitute discrimination where, by reason of the nature of the particular occupational activities concerned or of the context in which they are carried out, such a characteristic constitutes a genuine and determining occupational requirement, provided that the objective is legitimate and the requirement is proportionate.

2.   Member States may maintain national legislation in force at the date of adoption of this Directive or provide for future legislation incorporating national practices existing at the date of adoption of this Directive pursuant to which, in the case of occupational activities within churches and other public or private organisations the ethos of which is based on religion or belief, a difference of treatment based on a person's religion or belief shall not constitute discrimination where, by reason of the nature of these activities or of the context in which they are carried out, a person's religion or belief constitute a genuine, legitimate and justified occupational requirement, having regard to the organisation's ethos. This difference of treatment shall be implemented taking account of Member States' constitutional provisions and principles, as well as the general principles of Community law, and should not justify discrimination on another ground.

Provided that its provisions are otherwise complied with, this Directive shall thus not prejudice the right of churches and other public or private organisations, the ethos of which is based on religion or belief, acting in conformity with national constitutions and laws, to require individuals working for them to act in good faith and with loyalty to the organisation's ethos.

Article 5

Reasonable accommodation for disabled persons
In order to guarantee compliance with the principle of equal treatment in relation to persons with disabilities, reasonable accommodation shall be provided. This means that employers shall take appropriate measures, where needed in a particular case, to enable a person with a disability to have access to, participate in, or advance in employment, or to undergo training, unless such measures would impose a disproportionate burden on the employer. This burden shall not be disproportionate when it is sufficiently remedied by measures existing within the framework of the disability policy of the Member State concerned.

Article 6

Justification of differences of treatment on grounds of age
1.   Notwithstanding Article 2(2), Member States may provide that differences of treatment on grounds of age shall not constitute discrimination, if, within the context of national law, they are objectively and reasonably justified by a legitimate aim, including legitimate employment policy, labour market and vocational training objectives, and if the means of achieving that aim are appropriate and necessary.

Such differences of treatment may include, among others:
(a) the setting of special conditions on access to employment and vocational training, employment and occupation, including dismissal and remuneration conditions, for young people, older workers and persons with caring responsibilities in order to promote their vocational integration or ensure their protection;
(b) the fixing of minimum conditions of age, professional experience or seniority in service for access to employment or to certain advantages linked to employment;
(c) the fixing of a maximum age for recruitment which is based on the training requirements of the post in question or the need for a reasonable period of employment before retirement.

2.   Notwithstanding Article 2(2), Member States may provide that the fixing for occupational social security schemes of ages for admission or entitlement to retirement or invalidity benefits, including the fixing under those schemes of different ages for employees or groups or categories of employees, and the use, in the context of such schemes, of age criteria in actuarial calculations, does not constitute discrimination on the grounds of age, provided this does not result in discrimination on the grounds of sex.

Article 7

Positive action

1.   With a view to ensuring full equality in practice, the principle of equal treatment shall not prevent any Member State from maintaining or adopting specific measures to prevent or compensate for disadvantages linked to any of the grounds referred to in Article 1.

2.   With regard to disabled persons, the principle of equal treatment shall be without prejudice to the right of Member States to maintain or adopt provisions on the protection of health and safety at work or to measures aimed at creating or maintaining provisions or facilities for safeguarding or promoting their integration into the working environment.

Chapter II REMEDIES AND ENFORCEMENT

Article 9

Defence of rights

1.   Member States shall ensure that judicial and/or administrative procedures, including where they deem it appropriate conciliation procedures, for the enforcement of obligations under this Directive are available to all persons who consider themselves wronged by failure to apply the principle of equal treatment to them, even after the relationship in which the discrimination is alleged to have occurred has ended.

2.   Member States shall ensure that associations, organisations or other legal entities which have, in accordance with the criteria laid down by their national law, a legitimate interest in ensuring that the provisions of this Directive are complied with, may engage, either on behalf or in support of the complainant, with his or her approval, in any judicial and/or administrative procedure provided for the enforcement of obligations under this Directive.

3.   Paragraphs 1 and 2 are without prejudice to national rules relating to time limits for bringing actions as regards the principle of equality of treatment.

Article 10

Burden of proof

1.   Member States shall take such measures as are necessary, in accordance with their national judicial systems, to ensure that, when persons who consider themselves wronged because the principle of equal treatment has not been applied to them establish, before a court or other competent authority, facts from which it may be presumed that there has been direct or indirect discrimination, it shall be for the respondent to prove that there has been no breach of the principle of equal treatment.

2.   Paragraph 1 shall not prevent Member States from introducing rules of evidence which are more favourable to plaintiffs.

3.   Paragraph 1 shall not apply to criminal procedures.

4.   Paragraphs 1, 2 and 3 shall also apply to any legal proceedings commenced in accordance with Article 9(2).

5.   Member States need not apply paragraph 1 to proceedings in which it is for the court or competent body to investigate the facts of the case.

Article 11

Victimisation

Member States shall introduce into their national legal systems such measures as are necessary to protect employees against dismissal or other adverse treatment by the employer as a reaction to a complaint within the undertaking or to any legal proceedings aimed at enforcing compliance with the principle of equal treatment.

Council Directive No 2001/23 On the Approximation of the laws of the Member States Relating to the Safeguarding of Employees' Rights in the event of Transfers of Undertakings, Businesses or Parts of Undertakings or Businesses

Article 1
1   (a) This Directive shall apply to any transfer of an undertaking, business, or part of an undertaking or business to another employer as a result of a legal transfer or merger.

(b) Subject to subparagraph (a) and the following provisions of this Article, there is a transfer within the meaning of this Directive where there is a transfer of an economic entity which retains its identity, meaning an organised grouping of resources which has the objective of pursuing an economic activity, whether or not that activity is central or ancillary.

(c) This Directive shall apply to public and private undertakings engaged in economic activities whether or not they are operating for gain. An administrative reorganisation of public administrative authorities, or the transfer of administrative functions between public administrative authorities, is not a transfer within the meaning of this Directive.

2.   This Directive shall apply where and in so far as the undertaking, business or part of the undertaking or business to be transferred is situated within the territorial scope of the Treaty.

3.   This Directive shall not apply to seagoing vessels.

Article 2
1.   For the purposes of this Directive:

(a) "transferor" shall mean any natural or legal person who, by reason of a transfer within the meaning of Article 1(1), ceases to be the employer in respect of the undertaking, business or part of the undertaking or business;

(b) "transferee" shall mean any natural or legal person who, by reason of a transfer within the meaning of Article 1(1), becomes the employer in respect of the undertaking, business or part of the undertaking or business;

(c) "representatives of employees" and related expressions shall mean the representatives of the employees provided for by the laws or practices of the Member States;

(d) "employee" shall mean any person who, in the Member State concerned, is protected as an employee under national employment law.

2.   This Directive shall be without prejudice to national law as regards the definition of contract of employment or employment relationship.

However, Member States shall not exclude from the scope of this Directive contracts of employment or employment relationships solely because:

(a)   of the number of working hours performed or to be performed,

(b)   they are employment relationships governed by a fixed-duration contract of employment within the meaning of Article 1(1) of Council Directive 91/383/EEC of 25 June 1991 supplementing the measures to encourage improvements in the safety and health at work of workers with a fixed-duration employment relationship or a temporary employment relationship (6), or

(c)   they are temporary employment relationships within the meaning of Article 1(2) of Directive 91/383/EEC, and the undertaking, business or part of the undertaking or business transferred is, or is part of, the temporary employment business which is the employer.

Chapter II SAFEGUARDING OF EMPLOYEES' RIGHTS

Article 3

1.   The transferor's rights and obligations arising from a contract of employment or from an employment relationship existing on the date of a transfer shall, by reason of such transfer, be transferred to the transferee.

Member States may provide that, after the date of transfer, the transferor and the transferee shall be jointly and severally liable in respect of obligations which arose before the date of transfer from a contract of employment or an employment relationship existing on the date of the transfer.

2.   Member States may adopt appropriate measures to ensure that the transferor notifies the transferee of all the rights and obligations which will be transferred to the transferee under this Article, so far as those rights and obligations are or ought to have been known to the transferor at the time of the transfer. A failure by the transferor to notify the transferee of any such right or obligation shall not affect the transfer of that right or obligation and the rights of any employees against the transferee and/or transferor in respect of that right or obligation.

3.   Following the transfer, the transferee shall continue to observe the terms and conditions agreed in any collective agreement on the same terms applicable to the transferor under that agreement, until the date of termination or expiry of the collective agreement or the entry into force or application of another collective agreement.

Member States may limit the period for observing such terms and conditions with the proviso that it shall not be less than one year.

4   (a)   Unless Member States provide otherwise, paragraphs 1 and 3 shall not apply in relation to employees' rights to old-age, invalidity or survivors' benefits under supplementary company or intercompany pension schemes outside the statutory social security schemes in Member States.

(b)   Even where they do not provide in accordance with subparagraph (a) that paragraphs 1 and 3 apply in relation to such rights, Member States shall adopt the measures necessary to protect the interests of employees and of persons no longer employed in the transferor's business at the time of the transfer in respect of rights conferring on them immediate or prospective entitlement to old age benefits, including survivors' benefits, under supplementary schemes referred to in subparagraph (a).

Article 4

1.   The transfer of the undertaking, business or part of the undertaking or business shall not in itself constitute grounds for dismissal by the transferor or the transferee. This provision shall not stand in the way of dismissals that may take place for economic, technical or organisational reasons entailing changes in the workforce.

Member States may provide that the first subparagraph shall not apply to certain specific categories of employees who are not covered by the laws or practice of the Member States in respect of protection against dismissal.

2.   If the contract of employment or the employment relationship is terminated because the transfer involves a substantial change in working conditions to the detriment of the

employee, the employer shall be regarded as having been responsible for termination of the contract of employment or of the employment relationship.

Article 5

1.   Unless Member States provide otherwise, Articles 3 and 4 shall not apply to any transfer of an undertaking, business or part of an undertaking or business where the transferor is the subject of bankruptcy proceedings or any analogous insolvency proceedings which have been instituted with a view to the liquidation of the assets of the transferor and are under the supervision of a competent public authority (which may be an insolvency practitioner authorised by a competent public authority).

2.   Where Articles 3 and 4 apply to a transfer during insolvency proceedings which have been opened in relation to a transferor (whether or not those proceedings have been instituted with a view to the liquidation of the assets of the transferor) and provided that such proceedings are under the supervision of a competent public authority (which may be an insolvency practitioner determined by national law) a Member State may provide that:

(a)   notwithstanding Article 3(1), the transferor's debts arising from any contracts of employment or employment relationships and payable before the transfer or before the opening of the insolvency proceedings shall not be transferred to the transferee, provided that such proceedings give rise, under the law of that Member State, to protection at least equivalent to that provided for in situations covered by Council Directive 80/987/EEC of 20 October 1980 on the approximation of the laws of the Member States relating to the protection of employees in the event of the insolvency of their employer (7), and, or alternatively, that,

(b)   the transferee, transferor or person or persons exercising the transferor's functions, on the one hand, and the representatives of the employees on the other hand may agree alterations, in so far as current law or practice permits, to the employees' terms and conditions of employment designed to safeguard employment opportunities by ensuring the survival of the undertaking, business or part of the undertaking or business.

3.   A Member State may apply paragraph 20(b) to any transfers where the transferor is in a situation of serious economic crisis, as defined by national law, provided that the situation is declared by a competent public authority and open to judicial supervision, on condition that such provisions already existed in national law on 17 July 1998.

The Commission shall present a report on the effects of this provision before 17 July 2003 and shall submit any appropriate proposals to the Council.

4.   Member States shall take appropriate measures with a view to preventing misuse of insolvency proceedings in such a way as to deprive employees of the rights provided for in this Directive.

Article 6

1.   If the undertaking, business or part of an undertaking or business preserves its autonomy, the status and function of the representatives or of the representation of the employees affected by the transfer shall be preserved on the same terms and subject to the same conditions as existed before the date of the transfer by virtue of law, regulation, administrative provision or agreement, provided that the conditions necessary for the constitution of the employee's representation are fulfilled.

The first subparagraph shall not supply if, under the laws, regulations, administrative provisions or practice in the Member States, or by agreement with the representatives of the employees, the conditions necessary for the reappointment of the representatives of the employees or for the reconstitution of the representation of the employees are fulfilled.

Where the transferor is the subject of bankruptcy proceedings or any analoguous insolvency proceedings which have been instituted with a view to the liquidation of the assets of the transferor and are under the supervision of a competent public authority (which may be an insolvency practitioner authorised by a competent public authority), Member States may take the necessary measures to ensure that the transferred employees are properly represented until the new election or designation of representatives of the employees.

If the undertaking, business or part of an undertaking or business does not preserve its autonomy, the Member States shall take the necessary measures to ensure that the employees transferred who were represented before the transfer continue to be properly represented during the period necessary for the reconstitution or reappointment of the representation of employees in accordance with national law or practice.

2.   If the term of office of the representatives of the employees affected by the transfer expires as a result of the transfer, the representatives shall continue to enjoy the protection provided by the laws, regulations, administrative provisions or practice of the Member States.

Chapter III INFORMATION AND CONSULTATION

Article 7
1.   The transferor and transferee shall be required to inform the representatives of their respective employees affected by the transfer of the following:
— the date or proposed date of the transfer,
— the reasons for the transfer,
— the legal, economic and social implications of the transfer for the employees,
— any measures envisaged in relation to the employees.

The transferor must give such information to the representatives of his employees in good time, before the transfer is carried out.

The transferee must give such information to the representatives of his employees in good time, and in any event before his employees are directly affected by the transfer as regards their conditions of work and employment.

2.   Where the transferor or the transferee envisages measures in relation to his employees, he shall consult the representatives of this employees in good time on such measures with a view to reaching an agreement.

3.   Member States whose laws, regulations or administrative provisions provide that representatives of the employees may have recourse to an arbitration board to obtain a decision on the measures to be taken in relation to employees may limit the obligations laid down in paragraphs 1 and 2 to cases where the transfer carried out gives rise to a change in the business likely to entail serious disadvantages for a considerable number of the employees.

The information and consultations shall cover at least the measures envisaged in relation to the employees.

The information must be provided and consultations take place in good time before the change in the business as referred to in the first subparagraph is effected.

4.   The obligations laid down in this Article shall apply irrespective of whether the decision resulting in the transfer is taken by the employer or an undertaking controlling the employer.

In considering alleged breaches of the information and consultation requirements laid down by this Directive, the argument that such a breach occurred because the information was not provided by an undertaking controlling the employer shall not be accepted as an excuse.

5.   Member States may limit the obligations laid down in paragraphs 1, 2 and 3 to undertakings or businesses which, in terms of the number of employees, meet the conditions for the election or nomination of a collegiate body representing the employees.

6.   Member States shall provide that, where there are no representatives of the employees in an undertaking or business through no fault of their own, the employees concerned must be informed in advance of:
— the date or proposed date of the transfer,
— the reason for the transfer,
— the legal, economic and social implications of the transfer for the employees,
— any measures envisaged in relation to the employees.

COUNCIL DIRECTIVE NO 2006/54 ON THE IMPLEMENTATION OF THE PRINCIPLE OF EQUAL OPPORTUNITIES AND EQUAL TREATMENT OF MEN AND WOMEN IN MATTERS OF EMPLOYMENT AND OCCUPATION (RECAST)

TITLE I GENERAL PROVISIONS

Article 1

Purpose
The purpose of this Directive is to ensure the implementation of the principle of equal opportunities and equal treatment of men and women in matters of employment and occupation.

To that end, it contains provisions to implement the principle of equal treatment in relation to:
(a)   access to employment, including promotion, and to vocational training;

(b)   working conditions, including pay;

(c)   occupational social security schemes.

It also contains provisions to ensure that such implementation is made more effective by the establishment of appropriate procedures.

Article 2

Definitions
1.   For the purposes of this Directive, the following definitions shall apply:
(a)   'direct discrimination': where one person is treated less favourably on grounds of sex than another is, has been or would be treated in a comparable situation;
(b)   'indirect discrimination': where an apparently neutral provision, criterion or practice would put persons of one sex at a particular disadvantage compared with persons of the other sex, unless that provision, criterion or practice is objectively justified by a legitimate aim, and the means of achieving that aim are appropriate and necessary;
(c)   'harassment': where unwanted conduct related to the sex of a person occurs with the purpose or effect of violating the dignity of a person, and of creating an intimidating, hostile, degrading, humiliating or offensive environment;
(d)   'sexual harassment': where any form of unwanted verbal, non-verbal or physical conduct of a sexual nature occurs, with the purpose or effect of violating the dignity

of a person, in particular when creating an intimidating, hostile, degrading, humiliating or offensive environment;

(e) 'pay': the ordinary basic or minimum wage or salary and any other consideration, whether in cash or in kind, which the worker receives directly or indirectly, in respect of his/her employment from his/her employer;

(f) 'occupational social security schemes': schemes not governed by Council Directive 79/7/EEC of 19 December 1978 on the progressive implementation of the principle of equal treatment for men and women in matters of social security whose purpose is to provide workers, whether employees or self-employed, in an undertaking or group of undertakings, area of economic activity, occupational sector or group of sectors with benefits intended to supplement the benefits provided by statutory social security schemes or to replace them, whether membership of such schemes is compulsory or optional.

2. For the purposes of this Directive, discrimination includes:

(a) harassment and sexual harassment, as well as any less favourable treatment based on a person's rejection of or submission to such conduct;

(b) instruction to discriminate against persons on grounds of sex;

(c) any less favourable treatment of a woman related to pregnancy or maternity leave within the meaning of Directive 92/85/EEC.

Article 3

Positive action

Member States may maintain or adopt measures within the meaning of Article 141(4) of the Treaty with a view to ensuring full equality in practice between men and women in working life.

TITLE II SPECIFIC PROVISIONS

Chapter I EQUAL PAY

Article 4

Prohibition of discrimination

For the same work or for work to which equal value is attributed, direct and indirect discrimination on grounds of sex with regard to all aspects and conditions of remuneration shall be eliminated. In particular, where a job classification system is used for determining pay, it shall be based on the same criteria for both men and women and so drawn up as to exclude any discrimination on grounds of sex.

Chapter III EQUAL TREATMENT AS REGARDS ACCESS TO EMPLOYMENT, VOCATIONAL TRAINING AND PROMOTION AND WORKING CONDITIONS

Article 14

Prohibition of discrimination

1. There shall be no direct or indirect discrimination on grounds of sex in the public or private sectors, including public bodies, in relation to:

(a) conditions for access to employment, to self-employment or to occupation, including selection criteria and recruitment conditions, whatever the branch of activity and at all levels of the professional hierarchy, including promotion;

(b) access to all types and to all levels of vocational guidance, vocational training, advanced vocational training and retraining, including practical work experience;

(c) employment and working conditions, including dismissals, as well as pay as provided for in Article 141 of the Treaty;

(d) membership of, and involvement in, an organisation of workers or employers, or any organisation whose members carry on a particular profession, including the benefits provided for by such organisations.

2.   Member States may provide, as regards access to employment including the training leading thereto, that a difference of treatment which is based on a characteristic related to sex shall not constitute discrimination where, by reason of the nature of the particular occupational activities concerned or of the context in which they are carried out, such a characteristic constitutes a genuine and determining occupational requirement, provided that its objective is legitimate and the requirement is proportionate.

Article 15

Return from maternity leave

A woman on maternity leave shall be entitled, after the end of her period of maternity leave, to return to her job or to an equivalent post on terms and conditions which are no less favourable to her and to benefit from any improvement in working conditions to which she would have been entitled during her absence.

Article 16

Paternity and adoption leave

This Directive is without prejudice to the right of Member States to recognise distinct rights to paternity and/or adoption leave. Those Member States which recognise such rights shall take the necessary measures to protect working men and women against dismissal due to exercising those rights and ensure that, at the end of such leave, they are entitled to return to their jobs or to equivalent posts on terms and conditions which are no less favourable to them, and to benefit from any improvement in working conditions to which they would have been entitled during their absence.

TITLE III HORIZONTAL PROVISIONS

Chapter I REMEDIES AND ENFORCEMENT

SECTION 1 REMEDIES

Article 17

Defence of rights

1.   Member States shall ensure that, after possible recourse to other competent authorities including where they deem it appropriate conciliation procedures, judicial procedures for the enforcement of obligations under this Directive are available to all persons who consider themselves wronged by failure to apply the principle of equal treatment to them, even after the relationship in which the discrimination is alleged to have occurred has ended.

2.   Member States shall ensure that associations, organisations or other legal entities which have, in accordance with the criteria laid down by their national law, a legitimate interest in ensuring that the provisions of this Directive are complied with, may engage, either on behalf or in support of the complainant, with his/her approval, in any judicial and/or administrative procedure provided for the enforcement of obligations under this Directive.

3.   Paragraphs 1 and 2 are without prejudice to national rules relating to time limits for bringing actions as regards the principle of equal treatment.

Article 18

Compensation or reparation

Member States shall introduce into their national legal systems such measures as are necessary to ensure real and effective compensation or reparation as the Member States so determine for the loss and damage sustained by a person injured as a result of discrimination on grounds of sex, in a way which is dissuasive and proportionate to the damage suffered. Such compensation or reparation may not be restricted by the fixing of a prior upper limit, except in cases where the employer can prove that the only damage suffered by an applicant as a result of discrimination within the meaning of this Directive is the refusal to take his/her job application into consideration.

Article 19

Burden of proof

1.   Member States shall take such measures as are necessary, in accordance with their national judicial systems, to ensure that, when persons who consider themselves wronged because the principle of equal treatment has not been applied to them establish, before a court or other competent authority, facts from which it may be presumed that there has been direct or indirect discrimination, it shall be for the respondent to prove that there has been no breach of the principle of equal treatment.

2.   Paragraph 1 shall not prevent Member States from introducing rules of evidence which are more favourable to plaintiffs.

3.   Member States need not apply paragraph 1 to proceedings in which it is for the court or competent body to investigate the facts of the case.

4.   Paragraphs 1, 2 and 3 shall also apply to:
    (a)   the situations covered by Article 141 of the Treaty and, insofar as discrimination based on sex is concerned, by Directives 92/85/EEC and 96/34/EC;
    (b)   any civil or administrative procedure concerning the public or private sector which provides for means of redress under national law pursuant to the measures referred to in (a) with the exception of out-of-court procedures of a voluntary nature or provided for in national law.

5.   This Article shall not apply to criminal procedures, unless otherwise provided by the Member States.

Chapter III GENERAL HORIZONTAL PROVISIONS

Article 23

Compliance

Member States shall take all necessary measures to ensure that:
(a)   any laws, regulations and administrative provisions contrary to the principle of equal treatment are abolished;

(b)   provisions contrary to the principle of equal treatment in individual or collective contracts or agreements, internal rules of undertakings or rules governing the independent occupations and professions and workers' and employers' organisations or any other arrangements shall be, or may be, declared null and void or are amended;

(c) occupational social security schemes containing such provisions may not be approved or extended by administrative measures.

Article 24

Victimisation

Member States shall introduce into their national legal systems such measures as are necessary to protect employees, including those who are employees' representatives provided for by national laws and/or practices, against dismissal or other adverse treatment by the employer as a reaction to a complaint within the undertaking or to any legal proceedings aimed at enforcing compliance with the principle of equal treatment.

Article 25

Penalties

Member States shall lay down the rules on penalties applicable to infringements of the national provisions adopted pursuant to this Directive, and shall take all measures necessary to ensure that they are applied. The penalties, which may comprise the payment of compensation to the victim, must be effective, proportionate and dissuasive. The Member States shall notify those provisions to the Commission by 5 October 2005 at the latest and shall notify it without delay of any subsequent amendment affecting them.

Article 26

Prevention of discrimination

Member States shall encourage, in accordance with national law, collective agreements or practice, employers and those responsible for access to vocational training to take effective measures to prevent all forms of discrimination on grounds of sex, in particular harassment and sexual harassment in the workplace, in access to employment, vocational training and promotion.

Other Materials

EHRC Code of Practice for the Elimination of Discrimination on the Grounds of Sex and Marriage and the Promotion of Equal Opportunity in Employment

Part I RECRUITMENT

12. It is unlawful: unless the job is covered by an exception: to discriminate directly or indirectly on the grounds of sex or marriage
    — in the arrangements made for deciding who should be offered a job
    — in any terms of employment
    — by refusing or omitting to offer a person employment

13. It is therefore recommended that:
    a) each individual should be assessed according to his or her personal capability to carry out a given job. It should not be assumed that men only or women only will be able to perform certain kinds of work;
    b) any qualifications or requirements applied to a job which effectively inhibit applications from one sex or from married people should be retained only if they are justifiable in terms of the job to be done;
    c) any age limits should be retained only if they are necessary for the job. An unjustifiable age limit could constitute unlawful indirect discrimination, for example, against women who have taken time out of employment for child-rearing;
    d) where trade unions uphold such qualifications or requirements as union policy, they should amend that policy in the light of any potentially unlawful effect.

GENUINE OCCUPATIONAL QUALIFICATIONS (GOQs)

14. It is unlawful: except for certain jobs when a person's sex is a genuine occupational qualification (GOQ) for that job to select candidates on the ground of sex.

15. There are very few instances in which a job will qualify for a GOQ on the ground of sex. However, exceptions may arise, for example, where considerations of privacy and decency or authenticity are involved. The SDA expressly states that the need of the job for strength and stamina does not justify restricting it to men. When a GOQ exists for a job, it applies also to promotion, transfer, on training for that job, but cannot be used to justify a dismissal.

16. In some instances, the GOQ will apply to some of the duties only. A GOQ will not be valid, however, where members of the appropriate sex are already employed in sufficient numbers to meet the employer's likely requirements without undue inconvenience. For example, in a job where sales assistants may be required to undertake changing room duties, it might not be lawful to claim a GOQ in respect of *all* the assistants on the grounds that any of them might be required to undertake changing room duties from time to time.

17. It is therefore recommended that: — A job for which a GOQ was used in the past should be re-examined if the post falls vacant to see whether the GOQ still applies. Circumstances may well have changed, rendering the GOQ inapplicable.

SOURCES OF RECRUITMENT

18. It is unlawful: unless the job is covered by an exception:
    — to discriminate on grounds of sex or marriage in the arrangements made for determining who should be offered employment whether recruiting by advertisements, through employment agencies, job centres, or career offices
    — to imply that applications from one sex or from married people will not be considered
    — to instruct or put pressure on others to omit to refer for employment people of one sex or married people unless the job is covered by an exception.
    — to publish or cause to be published an advertisement that indicates or might reasonably be understood as indicating an intention to discriminate unlawfully on grounds of sex or marriage.

ADVERTISING

19. It is therefore recommended that:
    a) job advertising should be carried out in such a way as to encourage applications from suitable candidates of both sexes. This can be achieved both by wording of the advertisements and, for example by placing advertisements in publications likely to reach both sexes. All advertising material and accompanying literature relating to employment or training issues should be reviewed to ensure that it avoids presenting men and women in stereotyped roles. Such stereotyping tends to perpetuate sex segregation in jobs and can also lead people of the opposite sex to believe that they would be unsuccessful in applying for particular jobs:
    b) where vacancies are filled by promotion or transfer, they should be published to all eligible employees in such a way that they do not restrict applications from either sex
    c) recruitment solely or primarily by word of mouth may unnecessarily restrict the choice of applicants available. The method should be avoided in a workforce predominantly of one sex, if in practice it prevents members of the opposite sex from applying
    d) where applicants are supplied through trade unions and members of one sex only come forward, this should be discussed with the unions and an alternative approach adopted.

CAREERS SERVICE/SCHOOLS

20. When notifying vacancies to the Careers Service, employers should specify that these are open to both boys and girls. This is especially important when a job has traditionally been done exclusively or mainly by one sex. If dealing with single sex schools, they should ensure, where possible, that both boys' and girls' schools are approached: it is also a good idea to remind mixed schools that jobs are open to boys and girls.

SELECTION METHODS

Tests

21.

a)   If selection tests are used, they should be specifically related to job and/or career requirements and should measure an individual's actual or inherent ability to do or train for the work or career.

b)   Tests should be reviewed regularly to ensure that they remain relevant and free from any unjustifiable bias, either in content or in scoring mechanism.

APPLICATIONS AND INTERVIEWING

22.   It is unlawful: unless the job is covered by an exception: to discriminate on grounds of sex or marriage by refusing or deliberately omitting to offer employment.

23.   It is therefore recommended that:
   a)   employers should ensure that personnel staff, line managers and all other employees who may come into contact with job applicants, should be trained in the provisions of the SDA, including the fact that it is unlawful to instruct or put pressure on others to discriminate;
   b)   applications from men and women should he processed in exactly the same way. For example, there should not be separate lists of male and female or married and single applicants. All those handling applications and conducting interviews should be trained in the avoidance of unlawful discrimination and records of interviews kept, where practicable, showing why applicants were or were not appointed;
   c)   questions should relate to the requirements of the job. Where it is necessary to assess whether personal circumstances will affect performance of the job (for example, where it involves unsocial hours or extensive travel) this should be discussed objectively without detailed questions based on assumptions about marital status, children and domestic obligations. Questions about marriage plans or family intentions should not be asked, as they could be construed as showing bias against women. Information necessary for personnel records can be collected after a job offer has been made.

PROMOTION, TRANSFER AND TRAINING

24.   It is unlawful: unless the job is covered by an exception, for employers to discriminate directly or indirectly on the grounds of sex or marriage in the way they afford access to opportunities for promotion, transfer or training.

25.   It is therefore recommended that:
   a)   where an appraisal system is in operation, the assessment criteria should be examined to ensure that they are not unlawfully discriminatory and the scheme monitored to assess how it is working in practice;
   b)   when a group of workers predominantly of one sex is excluded from an appraisal scheme, access to promotion, transfer and training and to other benefits should be reviewed, to ensure that there is no unlawful indirect discrimination;
   c)   promotion and career development patterns are reviewed to ensure that the traditional qualifications are justifiable requirements for the job to be done. In some circumstances, for example, promotion on the basis of length of service could amount to unlawful indirect discrimination, as it may unjustifiably affect more women than men;

d) when general ability and personal qualifies are the main requirements for promotion to a post, care should be taken to consider favourably candidates of both sexes with differing career patterns and general experience;

e) rules which restrict or preclude transfer between certain jobs should be questioned and charged if they are found to unlawfully discriminatory. Employees of one sex may be concentrated in sections from which transfers are traditionally restricted without real justification;

f) policies and practices regarding selection for training, day release and personal development should be examined for unlawful direct and indirect discrimination. Where there is found to be an imbalance in training as between sexes, the cause should be identified to ensure that it is not discriminatory;

g) age limits for access to training and promotion should be questioned.

HEALTH AND SAFETY LEGISLATION

26. Equal treatment of men and women may be limited by statutory provisions, which require men and women to be treated differently. For example, the Factories Act 1961 places restrictions on the hours of work of female manual employees, although the Health and Safety Executive can exempt employers from these restrictions, subject to certain conditions. The Mines and Quarries Act 1954 imposes limitations on women's work and there are restrictions where there is special concern for the unborn child (e.g. lead and ionising radiation). However the broad duties placed on employers by the Health and Safety at Work Act, 1974 makes no distinctions between men and women Section 2(1) requires employers to ensure, so far as is reasonably practicable, the health and safety and welfare at work of all employees.

Specific health and safety requirements under earlier legislation are unaffected by the act.

It is therefore recommended that: company policy should be reviewed and serious consideration given to any significant differences in treatment between men and women, and there should be well-founded reasons if such differences are maintained or introduced.

TERMS OF EMPLOYMENT, BENEFITS, FACILITIES AND SERVICES

27. It is unlawful: unless the job is covered by an exception: to discriminate on the grounds of sex or marriage, directly or indirectly, in the terms on which employment is offered or in affording access to any benefits, facilities or services.

28. It is therefore recommended that: all terms of employment, benefits, facilities and services are reviewed to ensure that there is no unlawful discrimination on grounds of sex or marriage. For example, part-time work, domestic leave, company cars and benefits for dependants should be available to both male and female employees in the same or not materially different circumstances.

29. In an establishment where part-timers are solely or mainly women, unlawful indirect discrimination may arise if, as a group, they are treated less favourably than other employees without justification. It is therefore recommended that: where part-time workers do not enjoy pro-rata pay or benefits with full-time workers, the arrangements should be reviewed to ensure that they are justified without regard to sex.

GRIEVANCES, DISCIPLINARY PROCEDURES AND VICTIMISATION

30. It is unlawful: to victimise an individual for a complaint made in good faith about sex or marriage discrimination or for giving evidence about such a complaint.

31. It is therefore recommended that:
    a) particular care is taken to ensure that an employee who has in good faith taken action under the Sex Discrimination Act or the Equal Pay Act does not receive less favourable treatment than other employees, for example by being disciplined or dismissed
    b) employees should be advised to use the internal procedures, where appropriate, but this is without prejudice to the individual's right to apply to an employment tribunal within the statutory time limit, i.e. before the end of the period of three months beginning when the act complained of was done, (There is no time limit if the victimisation is continuing.)
    c) particular care is taken to deal effectively with all complaints of discrimination, victimisation or harassment. It should not be assumed that they are made by those who are over-sensitive.

DISMISSALS, REDUNDANCIES AND OTHER UNFAVOURABLE TREATMENT OF EMPLOYEES

32. It is unlawful: to discriminate directly or indirectly on grounds of sex or marriage in dismissals or by treating an employee unfavorably in any other way. It is therefore recommended that:
    a) care is taken that members of one sex are not disciplined or dismissed for performance or behaviour which would be overlooked or condoned in the other sex;
    b) redundancy procedures affecting a group of employees predominantly of one sex should be reviewed, so as to remove any effects which could be disproportionate and unjustifiable;
    c) conditions of access to voluntary redundancy benefit should be made available on equal terms to male and female employees in the same or not materially different circumstances;
    d) where there is down-grading or short-time working (for example, owing to a change in the nature or volume of an employer's business) the arrangements should not unlawfully discriminate on the ground of sex;
    e) all reasonably practical steps should be taken to ensure that a standard of conduct or behaviour is observed which prevents members of either sex from being intimidated, harassed or otherwise subjected to unfavourable treatment on the ground of their sex.

Part II THE ROLE OF GOOD EMPLOYMENT PRACTICES IN PROMOTING EQUALITY OF OPPORTUNITY

33. This section of the Code describes those employment practices that help to promote equality of opportunity. It gives information about the formulation and implementation of equal opportunities policies. While such policies are not required by law, their value has been recognised by a number of employers who have voluntarily adopted them. Others may wish to follow this example.

FORMULATING AND EQUAL OPPORTUNITIES POLICY

34. An equal opportunities policy will ensure the effective use of human resources in the best interests of both the organisation and its employees, It is a commitment by an employer to

the development and use of employment procedures and practices which do not discriminate on grounds of sex or marriage and which provide genuine equality of opportunity for all employees. The detail of the policy will vary according to size of the organisation.

IMPLEMENTING THE POLICY

35. An equal opportunities policy must be seen to have the active support of management at the highest level. To ensure that the policy is fully effective, the following procedure is recommended:
   a)   the policy should be clearly stated and where appropriate, included in a collective agreement;
   b)   overall responsibility for implementing the policy should rest with senior management;
   c)   the policy should be made known to all employees and, where reasonably practicable, to all job applicants.

36. Trade unions have a very important part to play in implementing genuine equality of opportunity and they will obviously be involved in the review of established procedures to ensure that these are consistent with the law.

MONITORING

37. It is recommended that the policy be monitored regularly to ensure that it is working in practice. Consideration could he given to setting up a joint Management/ Trade Union Review Committee.

38. In a small firm with a simple structure it may be quite adequate to assess the distribution and payment of employees from personal knowledge.

39. In a large and complex organisation a more formal analysis will be necessary, for example, by sex, grade and payment in each unit. This may need to be introduced by stages as resources permit. Any formal analysis should be regularly updated and available to Management and Trade Unions to enable any necessary action to be taken.

40. Sensible monitoring will show, for example, whether members of one sex:
   a)   do not apply for employment or promotion, or that fewer apply than might be expected;
   b)   are not recruited, promoted or selected for training and development or are appointed/selected in a significantly lower proportion than their rate of application;
   c)   are concentrated in certain jobs, sections or departments.

POSITIVE ACTION

Recruitment, training and promotion
41. Selection for recruitment or promotion must be on merit, irrespective of sex. However, the Sex Discrimination Act does allow certain steps to redress the effects of previous unequal opportunities. Where there have been few or no members of one sex in particular work in their employment for the previous 12 months, the Act allows employers to give special encouragement to, and provide specific training for, the minority sex. Such measures are usually described as Positive Action.

42. Employers may wish to consider positive measures such as:
     a) training their own employees (male or female) for work which is traditionally the preserve of the other sex, for example, training women for skilled manual or technical work.
     b) positive encouragement to women to apply for management posts — special courses may be needed.
     c) advertisements which encourage applications from the minority sex, but make it clear that selection will be on merit without reference to sex.
     d) notifying job agencies, as part of a Positive Action Programme that they wish to encourage members of one sex to apply for vacancies, where few or no members of that sex are doing the work in question. In these circumstances, job agencies should tell both men and women about the posts and, in addition, let the under-represented sex know that applications from them are particularly welcome. Withholding information from one sex in an attempt to encourage applications from the opposite sex would be unlawful.

OTHER WORKING ARRANGEMENTS

43. There are other forms of action that could assist both employer and employee by helping to provide continuity of employment to working parents, many of whom will have valuable experience or skills.

     Employers may wish to consider with their employees whether:
     (a) certain jobs can be carried out on a part-time or flexi-time basis.
     (b) personal leave arrangements are adequate and available to both sexes. It should not be assumed that men may not need to undertake domestic responsibilities on occasion, especially at the time of childbirth.
     (c) child-care facilities are available locally or whether it would be feasible to establish nursery facilities on the premises or combine with other employers to provide them.
     (d) residential training could be facilitated for employees with young children. For example, where this type of training is necessary, by informing staff who are selected well in advance to enable them to make childcare and other personal arrangements; employers with their own residential training centres could also consider whether childcare facilities might he provided.
     (e) the statutory maternity leave provisions could he enhanced, for example, by reducing the qualifying service period, extending the leave period, or giving access to part-time arrangements on return.
     These arrangements, and others, are helpful to both sexes but are of particular benefit to women in helping them to remain in gainful employment during the years of child-rearing.

ACAS Code of Practice 2 – Disclosure of Information to Trade Unions for Collective Bargaining Purposes (revised 1997)

PROVIDING INFORMATION

9. The absence of relevant information about an employer's undertaking may to a material extent impede trade unions in collective bargaining, particularly if the information would influence the formulation, presentation or pursuance of a claim, or the conclusion of an agreement. The provision of relevant information in such circumstances would be in accordance with good industrial relations practice.

10. To determine what information will be relevant, negotiators should take account of the subject-matter of the negotiations and the issues raised during them; the level at which negotiations take place (department, plant, division, or company level); the size of the company; and the type of business the company is engaged in.

11. Collective bargaining within an undertaking can range from negotiations on specific matters arising daily at the workplace affecting particular sections of the workforce, to extensive periodic negotiations on terms and conditions of employment affecting the whole workforce in multi-plant companies. The relevant information and the depth, detail and form in which it could be presented to negotiators will vary accordingly. Consequently, it is not possible to compile a list of items that should be disclosed in all circumstances. Some examples of information relating to the undertaking which could be relevant in certain collective bargaining situations are given below:

   (i) *Pay and benefits:* principles and structure of payment systems; job evaluation systems and grading criteria; earnings and hours analysed according to work-group, grade, plant, sex, out-workers and homeworkers, department or division, giving, where appropriate, distributions and make-up of pay showing any additions to basic rate or salary; total pay bill; details of fringe benefits and non-wage labour costs.

   (ii) *Conditions of service:* policies on recruitment, redeployment, redundancy, training, equal opportunity, and promotion; appraisal systems; health, welfare and safety matters.

   (iii) *Manpower:* numbers employed analysed according to grade, department, location, age and sex; labour turnover; absenteeism; overtime and short-time; manning standards; planned changes in work methods, materials, equipment or organisation; available manpower plans; investment plans.

   (iv) *Performance:* productivity and efficiency data; savings from increased productivity and output, return on capital invested; sales and state of order book.

   (v) *Financial:* cost structures; gross and net profits; sources of earnings; assets; liabilities; allocation of profits; details of government financial assistance; transfer prices; loans to parent or subsidiary companies and interest charged.

12. These examples are not intended to represent a check list of information that should be provided for all negotiations. Nor are they meant to be an exhaustive list of types of information as other items may be relevant in particular negotiations.

RESTRICTIONS ON THE DUTY TO DISCLOSE

13. Trade unions and employers should be aware of the restrictions on the general duty to disclose information for collective bargaining.

14. Some examples of information which if disclosed in particular circumstances might cause substantial injury are: cost information on individual products; detailed analysis of proposed investment, marketing or pricing policies; and price quotas or the make-up of tender prices. Information which has to be made available publicly, for example under the Companies Acts, would not fall into this category.

15. Substantial injury may occur if, for example, certain customers would be lost to competitors, or suppliers would refuse to supply necessary materials, or the ability to raise funds to finance the company would be seriously impaired as a result of disclosing certain information. The burden of establishing a claim that disclosure of certain information would cause substantial injury lies with the employer.

TRADE UNIONS' RESPONSIBILITIES

16. Trade unions should identify and request the information they require for collective bargaining in advance of negotiations whenever practicable. Misunderstandings can be avoided, costs reduced, and time saved, if requests state as precisely as possible all the information required, and the reasons why the information is considered relevant. Requests should conform to an agreed procedure. A reasonable period of time should be allowed for employers to consider a request and to reply.

17. Trade unions should keep employers informed of the names of the representatives authorised to carry on collective bargaining on their behalf.

18. Where two or more trade unions are recognised by an employer for collective bargaining purposes they should co-ordinate their requests for information whenever possible.

19. Trade unions should review existing training programmes or establish new ones to ensure negotiators are equipped to understand and use information effectively.

EMPLOYERS' RESPONSIBILITIES

20. Employers should aim to be as open and helpful as possible in meeting trade union requests for information. Where a request is refused, the reasons for the refusal should be explained as far as possible to the trade union representatives concerned and be capable of being substantiated should the matter be taken to the Central Arbitration Committee.

21. Information agreed as relevant to collective bargaining should be made available as soon as possible once a request for the information has been made by an authorised trade union representative. Employers should present information in a form and style which recipients can reasonably be expected to understand.

JOINT ARRANGEMENTS FOR DISCLOSURE OF INFORMATION

22. Employers and trade unions should endeavour to arrive at a joint understanding on how the provisions on the disclosure of information can be implemented most effectively. They should consider what information is likely to be required, what is available, and what could reasonably be made available. Consideration should also be given to the form in which the information will be presented, when it should be presented and to whom. In particular, the parties should endeavour to reach an understanding on what information could most appropriately be provided on a regular basis.

23. Procedures for resolving possible disputes concerning any issues associated with the disclosure of information should be agreed. Where possible such procedures should normally be related to any existing arrangements within the undertaking or industry and the complaint, conciliation and arbitration procedure described in the Act.

EHRC Code of Practice on Equal Pay (revised 2003)

SECTION TWO: GOOD EQUAL PAY PRACTICE

INTRODUCTION

68 The loss to women arising out of the gender pay gap is well documented, but organisations also lose out by failing to properly reward the range of skills and experience

that women bring to the workforce. The most commonly recognised risk of failing to ensure that pay is determined without sex discrimination is equal pay cases being taken against the organisation. The direct costs of a claim can include not only any eventual equal pay award to the woman bringing the claim (see paragraph 67) but also the costs of time spent at a hearing, and the costs of legal representation. The indirect costs are harder to quantify, but include lower productivity on the part of those employees who consider that they are not getting equal pay and on the part of managers whose time is taken up in dealing with the claim.

69   Tackling the gender pay gap reduces the risk of litigation. It can also increase efficiency by attracting the best employees, reducing staff turnover, increasing commitment, and reducing absenteeism. Pay is one of the key factors affecting motivation and relationships at work. It is therefore important to develop pay arrangements that are right for the organisation and that reward employees fairly. Providing equal pay for equal work is central to the concept of rewarding people fairly for what they do.

THE ESSENTIAL FEATURES OF AN EQUAL PAY REVIEW

70   Employers are responsible for providing equal pay and for ensuring that pay systems are transparent. Pay arrangements are frequently complicated and the features that can give rise to sex discrimination are not always obvious. A structured pay system is more likely to provide equal pay and is easier to check than a system that relies primarily on managerial discretion. Acas, the employment relations' experts, provide basic advice on the various different types of pay systems and on job evaluation.

71   The advice given in paragraphs 39–46 on striking a balance between transparency and confidentiality are also relevant to equal pay reviews. The EOC has produced a guidance note that explains an employer's legal obligations when carrying out an equal pay review.

72   While employers are not required, by law, to carry out an equal pay review, this Code recommends equal pay reviews as the most appropriate method of ensuring that a pay system delivers equal pay free from sex bias. Whatever kind of equal pay review process is used, it should include:
*   Comparing the pay of men and women doing equal work. Here employers need to check for one or more of the following: like work; work rated as equivalent; work of equal value. These checks are the foundation of an equal pay review
*   Identifying any equal pay gaps
*   Eliminating those pay gaps that cannot satisfactorily be explained on grounds other than sex.

These features are the same whatever the size of the organisation and they are essential. A pay review process that does not include these features cannot claim to be an equal pay review. Moreover, an equal pay review is not simply a data collection exercise. It entails a commitment to put right any sex based pay inequalities and this means that the review must have the involvement and support of managers with the authority to deliver the necessary changes.

73   The validity of the review and success of subsequent action taken will be enhanced if the pay system is understood and accepted by the managers who operate the system, by the employees and by their unions. Employers should therefore aim to secure the involvement of employees and, where possible, trade union representatives, when carrying out an equal pay review.

VOLUNTARY EQUAL PAY REVIEWS

A model for carrying out an equal pay review

74   The EOC recommends a five-step equal pay review model:

STEP 1:   Deciding the scope of the review and identifying the data required

STEP 2:   Determining where men and women are doing equal work

STEP 3:   Collecting pay data to identify equal pay gaps

STEP 4:   Establishing the causes of any significant pay gaps and assessing the reasons for these

STEP 5:   Developing an equal pay action plan and/or reviewing and monitoring. The EOC Equal Pay Review Kit sets out the detail of the model recommended here and provides supporting guidance notes.

STEP 1: DECIDING THE SCOPE OF THE REVIEW AND IDENTIFYING THE DATA REQUIRED

75   In scoping the review employers need to decide:

- Which employees are going to be included? It is advisable to include all employees who are deemed to be in the same establishment or service (see paragraph 21)
- What information will be needed? Employers will need to collect and compare broad types of information about:
- All the various elements of pay, including pensions and other benefits
- The personal characteristics of each employee, that is, gender; full-time or part-time; qualifications relevant to the job; hours worked and when and where they work these; length of service; role and time in grade and performance related pay ratings
- It is particularly important to ensure that information is collected about part-time employees.

The information will vary depending upon the type of organisation, its pay policies and practices and the scope of the review.

- Who should be involved in carrying out the review? An equal pay review requires different types of input from people with different perspectives. There will be a need for knowledge and understanding of the pay and grading arrangements; of any job evaluation schemes; and of the payroll and human resource systems. It can also be helpful to have someone with an understanding of equality issues, particularly the effects of indirect discrimination in pay systems
- When to involve the workforce? Employers need to consider when to involve the trade unions or other employee representatives
- Whether expert advice is needed? Employers may also wish to consider whether to bring in outside expertise. Acas can provide practical, independent and impartial advice on the employee relations aspects of equal pay reviews.

The scope of the Equal Pay Review

In nearly three quarters of organisations, the review applied (or applies) to the whole workforce. In over half of all the cases it involved an examination of a job evaluation system to ensure that it was free of sex bias. Moreover, just under half of organisations had extended the review beyond pay and gender, to include other processes such as recruitment and selection; two-fifths had covered pay differences by ethnicity; more than a third had covered age and nearly a third had covered disability.

The scope of the Equal Pay Review

Percentage of organisations covering

Whole workforce 73

Examination of job evaluation system 55

Other HR processes 49

Pay differences by ethnic origin 40

Pay differences by age 36

Pay differences by disability 31

N = number of organisations 67

INCLUDE ETHNICITY AND DISABILITY IN THE REVIEW

76   This Code is concerned with an important, but narrow, aspect of sex discrimination in employment – the pay of women compared to men doing equal work, (or vice versa). It does not deal with comparisons on the grounds of ethnicity or disability. However, as a matter of good practice employers may also want to look at ethnicity and disability, or age. Before deciding to do so it may be helpful to consider the quality of the information available to the employer, and whether it is adequate for the purposes of carrying out a wider review. To ensure the relevant provisions of race and disability legislation are taken into account, it would be appropriate to seek advice from the Commission for Racial Equality and/or the Disability Rights Commission.

77   Public Sector organisations obliged by the Race Relations (Amendment) Act 2000 to adopt an Equality Scheme should ensure that their pay review deals with any pay gaps between workers from different ethnic groups as well as the gaps between men's and women's pay. Here too, advice can be obtained from the Commission for Racial Equality.

STEP 2: DETERMINING WHERE MEN AND WOMEN ARE DOING EQUAL WORK

78   In Step 2 employers need to do one or more of the following checks:
- Like work
- Work rated as equivalent
- Work of equal value.

These checks determine where men and women are doing equal work. They are the foundation of an equal pay review.

> **Example – determining where men and women are doing equal work**
> Human Resources and the unions met to agree which areas to examine. According to the HR manager, 'we already had an idea of where the discrepancies were'. Data collection was on the basis of figures from: the personnel database, the pay database, the performance pay database and the starters and leavers database. A small local consultancy had helped to introduce a new job evaluation scheme; however, the basis for making equal work comparisons was predominantly by existing grade. The organisation looked at global differences, differences by grade and differences by components of pay (basic pay, overtime and allowances).

79   Employers who do not have analytical job evaluation schemes designed with equal value in mind will need to find an alternative means of estimating whether men and women are

doing equal work. The EOC Equal Pay Review Kit includes suggestions as to how this can be done. Employers who do use analytical job evaluation schemes need to check that their scheme has been designed and implemented in such a way and at all times so as not to discriminate on grounds of sex.

STEP 3: COLLECTING PAY DATA TO IDENTIFY EQUAL PAY GAPS

80   In Step 3 employers need to collect and compare pay information for men and women doing equal work by:
  • Calculating average basic pay and total earnings
  • Comparing access to and amounts received of each element of the pay package.
To ensure comparisons are consistent, when calculating average basic pay and average total earnings for men and women separately, employers should do this either on an hourly basis or on a full-time salary basis (grossing up or down for those who work fewer, or more, hours – excluding overtime – per week than the norm).

81   Employers then need to review the pay comparisons to identify any gender pay gaps and decide if any are significant enough to warrant further investigation. It is advisable to record all the significant or patterned pay gaps that have been identified.

> **Example – data collection and analysis**
> The organisation had a well-established process for undertaking equal pay audits. Data were brought together and presented in tabular form by the data analysis section of the human resources department. The data were then reviewed, analysed and commented on by the head of employee relations, who shared the data with trade union representatives. Union and management worked together to develop action points arising from the data.

STEP 4: ESTABLISHING THE CAUSES OF ANY SIGNIFICANT PAY GAPS AND ASSESSING THE REASONS FOR THESE

82   In Step 4 employers need to:

  • Find out if there is a genuine and material reason for the difference in pay that has nothing to do with the sex of the jobholders
  • Examine their pay systems to find out which pay policies and practices are contributing to any gender pay gaps.

> **Example – finding out which policies and practices are contributing to the gender pay gap**
> The review showed a 23 per cent gap in the average basic pay of men and women across the organisation. In grades with a large enough number of staff to make a comparison, 50 per cent had variances of five per cent or greater in favour of either men or women. Starting pay was not found to be an issue, nor was performance pay. The key factor in grade inequalities was identified as long pay ranges and the impact of past restructuring. There was a body of staff (largely male), who had reached the upper quartile of their current pay range prior to the most recent restructuring. However, new appointees, who were increasingly female, and those who had taken career breaks, had little chance of progressing to this level. The other area of concern identified by the review was premium payments for working unsocial hours. These were paid at the rate of 20 per cent of basic salary to some grades. However, in 1998 these payments were restricted to existing staff. The period since 1998 had seen an increase in the number of female recruits into what were traditionally male areas. Due to the change in the

rules they were not eligible for the premium payments. The result was that overall in the eligible grades, men received on average two and a half times the amount of earnings from premium pay that women received.

83   Pay systems vary considerably. Pay systems that group jobs into pay grades or bands have traditionally treated jobs in the same grade or band as being of broadly equal value, either because they have been evaluated with similar scores under a job evaluation scheme, or because they are simply regarded as equivalent. However, recent years have seen a trend towards structures with fewer, broader grades or bands and greater use of performance pay and market factors. A single broad band or grade may contain jobs or roles of significantly different value because it encompasses a wide range of job evaluation scores. This, coupled with a wider use of other determinants of pay and more complex methods of pay progression, means that it is important for employers to check all aspects of the pay system from a variety of standpoints: design, implementation, and impact on men and women.

STEP 5: DEVELOPING AN EQUAL PAY ACTION PLAN AND/OR REVIEWING AND MONITORING

84   Where the reason for the pay difference is connected with sex, employers will need to provide equal pay for current and future employees.

85   Employers who find no gaps between men's and women's pay, or who find gaps for which there are genuinely non-discriminatory reasons, should nevertheless keep their pay systems under review by introducing regular monitoring undertaken jointly with trade unions. This will ensure that the pay system remains free of sex bias.

Example – developing an action plan
Following the review, an Action Plan looking at internal processes was developed. This is ongoing and is reviewed through partnership processes. The aim is to integrate equal pay issues into employee relations' work. Early action has been in relation to internal recruitment processes. This included looking at whether people were encouraged (or not) to apply for particular jobs. This lack of recognition of potential opportunities was closing off progression routes to some groups, and impacting on the organisational gender pay gap. The organisation also found that it had a body of staff (mainly women) that did not seek promotion. A challenge for the organisation was to encourage more women to aim for promotion, especially once they had fewer family responsibilities. The remuneration manager anticipated that the gender pay gap in the main staff would fall from the 13 per cent identified in the pay review to under five per cent over the following five years. A recent repeat of the review had already shown a fall, however, the decline in the gap might not always be maintained. This is because the company's pay system is highly market sensitive and a tightening of the labour market in areas in which men are in the majority (such as Information Technology) would have a negative impact on the downward trend.

SECTION THREE: AN EQUAL PAY POLICY

THE ORGANISATION'S INTENTIONS IN RESPECT OF EQUAL PAY

86   It is good equal pay practice to provide employees with a clear statement of the organisation's intentions in respect of equal pay. Evidence of an equal pay policy may assist an employer's defence against an equal pay claim.

87   It is recommended that an equal pay policy should:

- Commit the organisation to carry out an equal pay review and to monitor pay regularly in partnership with trade union/employee representatives
- Set objectives
- Identify the action to be taken
- Implement that action in a planned programme in partnership with the workforce
- Assign responsibility and accountability for the policy to a senior manager
- Commit the organisation to set aside the resources necessary to achieve equal pay.

88   Everyone involved in setting the pay of staff should be committed to and, if possible, trained in the identification of sex discrimination in the pay process.

A model equal pay policy
We are committed to the principle of equal pay for all our employees. We aim to eliminate any sex bias in our pay systems. We understand that equal pay between men and women is a legal right under both domestic and European law. It is in the interest of the organisation to ensure that we have a fair and just pay system. It is important that employees have confidence in the process of eliminating sex bias and we are therefore committed to working in partnership with the recognised trade unions. As good business practice we are committed to working with trade union/employee representatives to take action to ensure that we provide equal pay. We believe that in eliminating sex bias in our pay system we are sending a positive message to our staff and customers. It makes good business sense to have a fair, transparent reward system and it helps us to control costs. We recognise that avoiding unfair discrimination will improve morale and enhance efficiency. Our objectives are to:
- Eliminate any unfair, unjust or unlawful practices that impact on pay
- Take appropriate remedial action.

We will:
- Implement an equal pay review in line with EOC guidance for all current staff and starting pay for new staff (including those on maternity leave, career breaks, or non-standard contracts)
- Plan and implement actions in partnership with trade union/employee representatives
- Provide training and guidance for those involved in determining pay
- Inform employees of how these practices work and how their own pay is determined
- Respond to grievances on equal pay as a priority in conjunction with trade union/ employee representatives, monitor pay statistics annually.

EHRC: DISABILITY RIGHTS COMMISSION CODE OF PRACTICE ON EMPLOYMENT AND OCCUPATION (2004)

When is direct discrimination likely to occur?

4.7   Treatment of a disabled person is 'on the ground of' his disability if it is caused by the fact that he is disabled or has the disability in question. In general, this means that treatment is on the ground of disability if a disabled person would not have received it but for his disability. However, disability does not have to be the only (or even the main) cause of the treatment complained of – provided that it is an effective cause, determined objectively from all the circumstances.

4.8   Consequently, if the less favourable treatment occurs because of the employer's generalised, or stereotypical, assumptions about the disability or its effects, it is likely to be direct discrimination. This is because an employer would not normally make such assumptions about a non-disabled person, but would instead consider his individual abilities.

A blind woman is not short-listed for a job involving computers because the employer wrongly assumes that blind people cannot use them. The employer makes no attempt to look at the individual circumstances. The employer has treated the woman less favourably than other people by not short-listing her for the job. The treatment was on the ground of the woman's disability (because assumptions would not have been made about a non-disabled person).

4.9   In addition, less favourable treatment which is disability-specific, or which arises out of prejudice about disability (or about a particular type of disability), is also likely to amount to direct discrimination.

An employer seeking a shop assistant turns down a disabled applicant with a severe facial disfigurement solely on the ground that other employees would be uncomfortable working alongside him. This would amount to direct discrimination and would be unlawful.

A disabled woman who uses a wheelchair applies for a job. She can do the job just as well as any other applicant, but the employer wrongly assumes that the wheelchair will cause an obstruction in the office. He therefore gives the job to a person who is no more suitable for the job but who is not a wheelchair-user. This would amount to direct discrimination and would be unlawful.

4.10   In some cases, an apparently neutral reason for less favourable treatment of a disabled person may, on investigation, turn out to be a pretext for direct discrimination.

4.11   Direct discrimination will often occur where the employer is aware that the disabled person has a disability, and this is the reason for the employer's treatment of him. Direct discrimination need not be conscious – people may hold prejudices that they do not admit, even to themselves. Thus, a person may behave in a discriminatory way while believing that he would never do so. Moreover, direct discrimination may sometimes occur even though the employer is unaware of a person's disability.

An employer advertises a promotion internally to its workforce. The job description states that people with a history of mental illness would not be suitable for the post. An employee who would otherwise be eligible for the promotion has a history of schizophrenia, but the employer is unaware of this. The employee would, nevertheless, have a good claim for unlawful direct discrimination in relation to the promotion opportunities afforded to him by his employer. The act of direct discrimination in this case is the blanket ban on anyone who has had a mental illness, effectively rejecting whole categories of people with no consideration of their individual abilities.

4.12   In situations such as those described in the above examples, it will often be readily apparent that the disabled person concerned has been treated less favourably on the ground of his disability. In other cases, however, this may be less obvious. Whether or not the basis for the treatment in question appears to be clear, a useful way of telling whether or not it is discriminatory, (and of establishing what kind of discrimination it is), is to focus on the person with whom the disabled person should be compared. That person may be real or hypothetical (see paragraph 4.18).

Identifying comparators in respect of direct discrimination

4.13   In determining whether a disabled person has been treated less favourably in the context of direct discrimination, his treatment must be compared with that of an appropriate comparator. This must be someone who does not have the same disability. It could be a non-disabled person or a person with other disabilities.

A person who becomes disabled takes six months' sick leave because of his disability, and is dismissed by his employer. A non-disabled fellow employee also takes six months' sick leave (because he has broken his leg) but is not dismissed. The difference in treatment is attributable to the employer's unwillingness to employ disabled staff and the treatment is therefore on the ground of disability. The non-disabled employee is an appropriate comparator in the context of direct discrimination because his relevant circumstances are the same as those of the disabled person. It is the fact of having taken six months' sick leave which is relevant in these circumstances. As the disabled person has been treated less favourably than the comparator, this is direct discrimination.

4.14   It follows that, in the great majority of cases, some difference will exist between the circumstances (including the abilities) of the comparator and those of the disabled person – there is no need to find a comparator whose circumstances are the same as those of the disabled person in every respect. What matters is that the comparator's **relevant** circumstances (including his abilities) must be the same as, or not materially different from, those of the disabled person.

In the previous example, the position would be different if it were the employer's policy to dismiss any member of staff who has been off sick for six months, and that policy were applied equally to disabled and non-disabled staff. In this case there would be no direct discrimination because the disabled person would not have been treated less favourably than the comparator – both would have been dismissed. Nevertheless, there may be a claim for failure to make reasonable adjustments to the policy, for example by allowing disability leave (see paragraph 4.25). In addition, the employer's policy may give rise to a claim for disability-related discrimination (see paragraph 4.27).

4.15   Once an appropriate comparator is identified, it is clear that the situation described in the example at paragraph 4.8 amounts to direct discrimination:

In the example about the blind woman who is not short-listed for a job involving computers, there is direct discrimination because the woman was treated less favourably on the ground of her disability than an appropriate comparator (that is, a person who is not blind but who has the same abilities to do the job as the blind applicant): such a person would not have been rejected out of hand without consideration of her individual abilities.

4.16   The examples of direct discrimination in paragraph 4.9 also become clearer when the appropriate comparator is identified in each case:

In the example about the disabled person with a severe facial disfigurement who applies to be a shop assistant, there is direct discrimination because the man was treated less favourably on the ground of his disability than an appropriate comparator (that is, a person who does not have such a disfigurement but who does have the same abilities to do the job): such a person would not have been rejected in the same way.

In the example about the disabled woman who is not offered a job because she uses a wheelchair, there is direct discrimination because the woman was treated less favourably on the ground of her disability than an appropriate comparator (that is, a person who does not use a wheelchair but who does have the same abilities to do the job): such a person would not have been rejected in the same way.

4.17   The comparator used in relation to direct discrimination under the Act is the same as it is for other types of direct discrimination – such as direct sex discrimination. It is, however, made explicit in the Act that the comparator must have the same relevant abilities as the disabled person.

4.18 It may not be possible to identify an actual comparator whose relevant circumstances are the same as (or not materially different from) those of the disabled person in question. In such cases a hypothetical comparator may be used. Evidence which helps to establish how a hypothetical comparator would have been treated is likely to include details of how other people (not satisfying the statutory comparison test) were treated in circumstances which were broadly similar.

A disabled person works in a restaurant. She makes a mistake on the till and this results in a small financial loss to her employer. She is dismissed because of this. The situation has not arisen before, and so there is no actual comparator. Nevertheless, six months earlier a non-disabled fellow employee was disciplined for taking home items of food without permission and received a written warning. The treatment of that person might be used as evidence that a hypothetical non-disabled member of staff who makes an error on the till would not have been dismissed for that reason.

4.19 It should be noted that the type of comparator described in the preceding paragraphs is only relevant to disability discrimination when assessing whether there has been **direct** discrimination. A different comparison falls to be made when assessing whether there has been a failure to comply with a duty to make reasonable adjustments (see paragraphs 5.3 and 5.4) or when considering disability-related discrimination (see paragraph 4.30).

Focusing on relevant circumstances

4.20 As stated in paragraph 4.14, direct discrimination only occurs where the **relevant** circumstances of the comparator, including his abilities, are the same as, or not materially different from, those of the disabled person himself. It is therefore important to focus on those circumstances which are, in fact, relevant to the matter to which the less favourable treatment relates. Although, in some cases, the effects of the disability may be relevant, the fact of the disability itself is not a relevant circumstance for these purposes. This is because the comparison must be with a person **not** having that particular disability.

A disabled person with arthritis who can type at 30 words per minute (wpm) applies for an administrative job which includes typing, but is rejected on the ground that her typing speed is too slow. The correct comparator in a claim for direct discrimination would be a person not having arthritis who also has a typing speed of 30 wpm (with the same accuracy rate).

A disabled person with a severe visual impairment applies for a job as a bus driver and is refused the job because he fails to meet the minimum level of visual acuity which is essential to the safe performance of the job. The correct comparator is a person not having that particular disability (for example, a person who merely has poorer than average eyesight) also failing to meet that minimum standard.

A disabled person with schizophrenia applies for a job as an administrative assistant with his local authority, and declares his history of mental illness. The local authority refuses him employment, relying on a negative medical report from the authority's occupational health adviser which is based on assumptions about the effects of schizophrenia, without adequate consideration of the individual's abilities and the impact of the impairment in his particular case. This is likely to amount to direct discrimination and to be unlawful. The comparator here is a person who does not have schizophrenia, but who has the same abilities to do the job (including relevant qualifications and experience) as the disabled applicant: such a person would not have been rejected without adequate consideration of his individual abilities.

4.21 If (as in the above examples) a disabled person alleges that he has been refused the offer of a job on the ground of his disability, it is only appropriate to compare those of his circumstances which are relevant to his ability to do the job. It is not appropriate to compare other circumstances which are not relevant to this issue. The need to focus on relevant circumstances applies not only to recruitment cases of this kind, but also to any other situation where direct discrimination may have occurred.

A disabled man with arthritis applies for an administrative job which includes typing, but is rejected in favour of a non-disabled candidate. Because of his arthritis, the man has a slow typing speed and has difficulty walking. The job is entirely desk-based, and does not require the person doing it to be able to walk further than a few metres within the office. The comparator in a claim of direct discrimination would be a non-disabled applicant with the same slow typing speed (and with the same abilities to do the job – e.g., the same typing accuracy rate, and the same knowledge of word-processing packages) – but it would not be necessary for the comparator to have mobility problems (because the ability to walk further than a few metres is not relevant to the candidates' ability to do the job).

Relevance of reasonable adjustments to comparison

4.22 In making the comparison in respect of a claim of direct discrimination, the disabled person's abilities must be considered as they in fact are. In some cases, there will be particular reasonable adjustments which an employer was required by the Act to make, but in fact failed to make. It may be that those adjustments would have had an effect on the disabled person's abilities to do the job. But in making the comparison, the disabled person's abilities should be considered as they in fact were, and not as they would or might have been had those adjustments been made. On the other hand, if adjustments have in fact been made which have had the effect of enhancing the disabled person's abilities, then it is those enhanced abilities which should be considered. The disabled person's abilities are being considered as they in fact are (and not as they might have been if the adjustments had not been made).

A disabled person who applies for an administrative job which includes typing is not allowed to use her own adapted keyboard (even though it would have been reasonable for the employer to allow this) and types a test document at 30 wpm. Her speed with the adapted keyboard would have been 50 wpm. A non-disabled candidate is given the job because her typing speed on the test was 45 wpm with the same accuracy rate. This is not direct discrimination, as the comparator is a non-disabled person typing at 30 wpm. (But the disabled person would be likely to have good claims in respect of two other forms of discrimination – failure to make reasonable adjustments and disability-related discrimination – see paragraph 4.3.7.)

A disabled person with arthritis who applies for a similar job is allowed to use an adapted keyboard and types a test document at 50 wpm. A non-disabled candidate types at 30 wpm with the same accuracy rate. However, the disabled candidate is rejected because of prejudice and the other candidate is offered the job instead. This is direct discrimination, as the comparator would be a person not having arthritis who could type at 50 wpm.

Can direct discrimination be justified?
s 3A(4)

4.23 Treatment of a disabled person which amounts to direct discrimination under the Act's provisions on employment and occupation is unlawful. It can never be justified.

FAILURE TO MAKE REASONABLE ADJUSTMENTS – RELATIONSHIP TO DISCRIMINATION

4.24 For the reason given in paragraph 4.3, it may be necessary to consider whether an employer has failed to comply with a duty to make a reasonable adjustment in order to determine whether disability-related discrimination has occurred.

s 3A(2)

4.25 Irrespective of its relevance to disability-related discrimination, however, a failure to comply with a duty to make a reasonable adjustment in respect of a disabled person amounts to discrimination in its own right. Such a failure is therefore unlawful. Chapter 5 explains the circumstances in which an employer has such a duty, and gives guidance as to what employers need to do when the duty arises.

4.26 As with direct discrimination, the Act does not permit an employer to justify a failure to comply with a duty to make a reasonable adjustment (see paragraphs 5.43 and 5.44).

WHAT IS DISABILITY-RELATED DISCRIMINATION?

What does the Act say?
s 3A(1)

4.27 The Act says that an employer's treatment of a disabled person amounts to discrimination if:
- it is for a reason related to his disability
- the treatment is less favourable than the way in which the employer treats (or would treat) others to whom that reason does not (or would not) apply, and
- the employer cannot show that the treatment is justified.

4.28 Although the Act itself does not use the term "disability-related discrimination", this expression is used in the Code when referring to treatment of a disabled person which:
- is unlawful because each of the conditions listed in paragraph 4.27 is satisfied, but
- does **not** amount to direct discrimination under the Act.

4.29 In general, direct discrimination occurs when the reason for the less favourable treatment in question is the disability, while disability-related discrimination occurs when the reason relates to the disability but is not the disability itself. The expression "disability-related discrimination" therefore distinguishes less favourable treatment which amounts to direct discrimination from a wider class of less favourable treatment which, although not amounting to direct discrimination, is nevertheless unlawful.

When does disability-related discrimination occur?

4.30 In determining whether disability-related discrimination has occurred, the employer's treatment of the disabled person must be compared with that of a person **to whom the disability-related reason does not apply**. This contrasts with direct discrimination, which requires a comparison to be made with a person without the disability in question but whose relevant circumstances are the same. The comparator may be non-disabled or disabled – but the key point is that the disability-related reason for the less favourable treatment must not apply to him.

A disabled man is dismissed for taking six months' sick leave which is disability-related. The employer's policy, which has been applied equally to all staff (whether disabled or not) is to dismiss all employees who have taken this amount of sick leave. The disability-related reason for the less favourable treatment of the disabled person is the fact of having taken six months' sick leave, and the correct comparator is a person to whom that reason does not apply – that is, someone who has not taken six months' sick leave. Consequently, unless the employer can show that the treatment is justified, it will amount to disability-related discrimination because the comparator would **not** have been dismissed. However, the reason for the treatment is not the disability itself (it is only a matter related thereto, namely the amount of sick leave taken). So there is no direct discrimination.

A disabled woman is refused an administrative job because she cannot type. She cannot type because she has arthritis. A non-disabled person who was unable to type would also have been turned down. The disability-related reason for the less favourable treatment is the woman's inability to type, and the correct comparator is a person to whom that reason does not apply – that is, someone who can type. Such a person would not have been refused the job. Nevertheless, the disabled woman has been treated less favourably for a disability-related reason and this will be unlawful unless it can be justified. There is no direct discrimination, however, because the comparator for direct discrimination is a person who does not have arthritis, but who is also unable to type.

4.31   The relationship between a disabled person's disability and the employer's treatment of him must be judged objectively. The reason for any less favourable treatment may well relate to the disability even if the employer does not have knowledge of the disability as such, or of whether its salient features are such that it meets the definition of disability in the Act. Less favourable treatment which is not itself direct discrimination will still be unlawful (subject to justification) if, in fact, the reason for it relates to the person's disability.

A woman takes three periods of sickness absence in a two month period because of her disability, which is multiple sclerosis (MS). Her employer is unaware that she has MS and dismisses her, in the same way that it would dismiss any employee for a similar attendance record. Nevertheless, this is less favourable treatment for a disability-related reason (namely, the woman's record of sickness absence) and would be unlawful unless it can be justified.

4.32   The circumstances in which justification may be possible are explained in Chapter 6. However, it is worth noting that the possibility of justifying potential discrimination only arises at all when the form of discrimination being considered is disability-related discrimination, rather than direct discrimination or failure to make reasonable adjustments.

WHAT DOES THE ACT SAY ABOUT HARASSMENT?

s 3B(1)
4.38   The Act says that harassment occurs where, for a reason which relates to a person's disability, another person engages in unwanted conduct which has the purpose or effect of:
• violating the disabled person's dignity, or
•   creating an intimidating, hostile, degrading, humiliating or offensive environment for him.

s 3B(2)
4.39   If the conduct in question was engaged in with the intention that it should have either of these effects, then it amounts to harassment irrespective of its actual effect on the disabled person. In the absence of such intention, however, the conduct will only amount to harassment if it should reasonably be considered as having either of these effects. Regard must be had to all the circumstances in order to determine whether this is the case. Those circumstances include, in particular, the perception of the disabled person.

A man with a learning disability is often called 'stupid' and 'slow' by a colleague at work. This is harassment, whether or not the disabled man was present when these comments were made, because they were said with the intention of humiliating him.

A man with a stammer feels he is being harassed because his manager makes constant jokes about people with speech impairments. He asks his manager to stop doing this, but the manager says he is being 'oversensitive' as he habitually makes jokes in the office about many different sorts of people. This is likely to amount to harassment because making remarks of this kind should reasonably be considered as having either of the effects mentioned above.

An employee with HIV uses a colleague's mug. The colleague then makes a point of being seen washing the mug with bleach, which is not something she would do if anyone else used her mug. She also makes offensive comments about having her mug used by someone with HIV. This is likely to amount to harassment.

An employee circulates by email a joke about people with autism. A colleague with autism receives the email and finds the joke offensive. This is likely to amount to harassment.

A woman with depression considers that she is being harassed by her manager who constantly asks her if she is feeling all right, despite the fact that she has asked him not to do so in front of the rest of the team. This could amount to harassment.

6 JUSTIFICATION

INTRODUCTION

6.1 Most conduct which is potentially unlawful under Part 2 of the Act cannot be justified. Conduct which amounts to:
- direct discrimination
- failure to comply with a duty to make a reasonable adjustment
- victimisation
- harassment
- instructions or pressure to discriminate, or aiding an unlawful act is unlawful irrespective of the reason or motive for it.

WHEN DOES THE ACT PERMIT JUSTIFICATION?

6.2 Paragraph 4.27 explains that one of the forms of discrimination which is unlawful under Part 2 is disability-related discrimination. However, an employer's conduct towards a disabled person does not amount to disability-related discrimination if it can be justified. This chapter explains the limited circumstances in which this may happen.

s 3A(3) & (4)
6.3 Where less favourable treatment of a disabled person is capable of being justified (that is, where it is **not** direct discrimination), the Act says that it will, in fact, be justified if, but only if, the reason for the treatment is both material to the circumstances of the particular case **and** substantial. This is an objective test. 'Material' means that there must be a reasonably strong connection between the reason given for the treatment and the circumstances of the particular case. 'Substantial' means, in the context of justification, that the reason must carry real weight and be of substance.

A man who has severe back pain and is unable to bend is rejected for a job as a carpet fitter as he cannot carry out the essential requirement of the job, which is to fit carpets.

This would be lawful as the reason he is rejected is a substantial one and is clearly material to the circumstances.

6.4 In certain circumstances, the existence of a material and substantial reason for disability related less favourable treatment is not enough to justify that treatment. This is the case where an employer is also under a duty to make reasonable adjustments in relation to the disabled person but fails to comply with that duty.

s 3A(6)

6.5 In those circumstances, it is necessary to consider not only whether there is a material and substantial reason for the less favourable treatment, but also whether the treatment would still have been justified even if the employer had complied with its duty to make reasonable adjustments. In effect, it is necessary to ask the question 'would a reasonable adjustment have made any difference?' If a reasonable adjustment would have made a difference to the reason that is being used to justify the treatment, then the less favourable treatment cannot be justified.

An applicant for an administrative job appears not to be the best person for the job, but only because her typing speed is too slow as a result of arthritis in her hands. If a reasonable adjustment – perhaps an adapted keyboard – would overcome this, her typing speed would not in itself be a substantial reason for not employing her. Therefore the employer would be unlawfully discriminating if, on account of her typing speed, he did not employ her or provide that adjustment.

6.6 In relation to disability-related discrimination, the fact that an employer has failed to comply with a duty to make a reasonable adjustment means that the sequence of events for justifying disability-related less favourable treatment is as follows:

- The disabled person proves facts from which it could be inferred in the absence of An adequate explanation that:
  a. for a reason related to his disability, he has been treated less favourably than a person to whom that reason does not apply has been, or would be, treated, and
  b. a duty to make a reasonable adjustment has arisen in respect of him and the employer has failed to comply with it.
- The employer will be found to have discriminated unless it proves that:
  a. the reason for the treatment is both material to the circumstances of the particular case and substantial, and
  b. the reason would still have applied if the reasonable adjustment had been made.

CAN HEALTH AND SAFETY CONCERNS JUSTIFY LESS FAVOURABLE TREATMENT?

6.7 Stereotypical assumptions about the health and safety implications of disability should be avoided, both in general terms and in relation to particular types of disability. Indeed, less favourable treatment which is based on such assumptions may itself amount to direct discrimination – which is incapable of justification (see paragraph 4.5). The fact that a person has a disability does not necessarily mean that he represents an additional risk to health and safety.

An employer has a policy of not employing anyone with diabetes because it believes that people with this condition are a health and safety risk. A person with diabetes applies to work for this employer and is turned down on the basis of her disability, without regard to her personal circumstances. A stereotypical assumption has been made which is likely to amount to direct discrimination and is therefore unlawful.

6.8   Under health and safety law it is the duty of every employer to ensure, so far as is reasonably practicable, the health, safety and welfare at work of all employees. Part of this duty is a requirement for all employers to assess the risks to the health and safety of all employees in the workplace and then to put in place measures that reduce the risks to as low a level as can reasonably be achieved. Genuine concerns about the health and safety of anybody (including a disabled employee) may be relevant when seeking to establish that disability-related less favourable treatment of a disabled person is justified. However, it is important to remember that health and safety law does not require employers to remove all conceivable risk, but to ensure that risk is properly appreciated, understood and managed. Further information can be obtained from the Health and Safety Executive (see Appendix C for details).

6.9   It is the employer who must decide what action to take in response to concerns about health and safety. However, when an employer has reason to think that the effects of a person's disability may give rise to an issue about health and safety, it is prudent for it to have a new risk assessment carried out by a suitably qualified person. This is because:
   •   If an employer treats a disabled person less favourably merely on the basis of generalised assumptions about the health and safety implications of having a disability, such treatment may itself amount to direct discrimination – which is incapable of justification.
   •   Even where there is no direct discrimination, an employer which treats a disabled person less favourably without having a suitable and sufficient risk assessment carried out is unlikely to be able to show that its concerns about health and safety justify the less favourable treatment.
   A pilot develops a heart condition, and his employer asks him to undertake a risk assessment to be carried out by an appropriate consultant. This is likely to be justifiable.

6.10   Nevertheless, an employer should not subject a disabled person to a risk assessment if this is not merited by the particular circumstances of the case. A person with a learning disability has been working in a shop for many years, stocking shelves without any problems. A new manager is appointed who insists that a risk assessment is carried out for her but not for all the other shelf stackers. This is unlikely to be warranted – and indeed it is likely to amount to direct discrimination.

6.11   A risk assessment must be suitable and sufficient. It should identify the risks associated with a work activity, taking account of any reasonable adjustments put in place for the disabled person, and should be specific for the individual carrying out a particular task. It is therefore unlikely that an employer which has a general policy of treating people with certain disabilities (such as epilepsy, diabetes or mental health problems) less favourably than other people will be able to justify doing so – even if that policy is in accordance with the advice of an occupational health adviser.

6.12   A 'blanket' policy of this nature will usually be unlawful. This is because it is likely to amount to direct discrimination (which cannot ever be justified) or to disability-related less favourable treatment which is not justifiable in the circumstances – i.e., disability-related discrimination (see paragraphs 7.8 and 7.9).

6.13   Reasonable adjustments made by an employer may remove or reduce health and safety risks related to a person's disability. A suitable and sufficient assessment of such risks therefore needs to take account of the impact which making any reasonable adjustments would have. If a risk assessment is not conducted on this basis, then an employer is unlikely to be able to show that its concerns about health and safety justify less favourable treatment of the disabled person.

CAN MEDICAL INFORMATION JUSTIFY LESS FAVOURABLE TREATMENT?

6.14 Consideration of medical information (such as a doctor's report or the answers to a medical questionnaire) is likely to form part of an assessment of health and safety risks. In most cases, however, having a disability does not adversely affect a person's general health. In other cases, its effect on a person's health may fluctuate. Although medical information about a disability may justify an adverse employment decision (such as a decision to dismiss or not to promote), it will not do so if there is no effect on the person's ability to do the job (or if any effect is less than substantial), no matter how great the effects of the disability are in other ways. Indeed, less favourable treatment of a disabled person in a case where his disability has no effect on his ability to do the job may well amount to direct discrimination – which is incapable of being justified.

An employer requires all candidates for a job as a technician in a chemical plant to complete a medical questionnaire. Medical information about one candidate shows that she has a degenerative condition which is likely to affect her ability to walk. This is not relevant to her ability to do the sedentary job in question. It would be unlawful for the employer to reject her on the ground of her disability as her disability is irrelevant to her ability to do the job. This would amount to direct discrimination.

The same employer is looking for a technician to work on a specific project for two years. A medical questionnaire shows that a candidate has a degenerative condition which could mean that he would not be able to work for that long. Because of this, further medical evidence is requested from his doctor and this confirms that he would not be able to work for two years. It is likely to be lawful to reject this candidate if the two-year requirement is justified in terms of the work and if there are no reasonable adjustments that could be made.

6.15 In addition, where medical information is available, employers must weigh it up in the context of the actual job, and the capabilities of the individual. An employer should also consider whether reasonable adjustments could be made in order to overcome any problems which may have been identified as a result of the medical information. It should not be taken for granted that the person who provides the medical information will be aware that employers have a duty to make reasonable adjustments, what these adjustments might be, or of the relevant working arrangements. It is good practice, therefore, to ensure that medical advisers are made aware of these matters. Information provided by a medical adviser should only be relied on if the adviser has the appropriate knowledge and expertise.

An occupational health adviser recommends that an administrative assistant cannot carry on in her current job because she has been diagnosed with Repetitive Strain Injury. The employer has another member of staff who uses voice recognition software, and considers this technology may be of relevance. The employer asks the adviser to review his conclusion taking this into account. The adviser revises his opinion and concludes that, with appropriate software, she can continue in her role.

6.16 In any event, although medical evidence may generally be considered as an 'expert contribution', it should not ordinarily be the sole factor influencing an employer's decision on employment related matters. The views of the disabled person (about his own capabilities and possible adjustments) should also be sought. In addition, and subject to the considerations about confidentiality explained in paragraphs 8.21 and 8.22, other contributions could come from the disabled person's line manager (about the nature of the job and possible adjustments). It may also be possible to seek help from disability organisations or from Jobcentre Plus, who have staff trained to advise about disability issues in the workplace. Ultimately, it is for the employer – and not the medical adviser – to take decisions as to whether, for example, to reject a job applicant or to maintain a disabled person's employment.

An employer receives advice from an occupational health adviser stating simply that an employee is 'unfit for work'. In spite of this the employer must consider whether there are reasonable adjustments which should be made.

7 DISCRIMINATION IN THE RECRUITMENT OF EMPLOYEES

SPECIFYING THE JOB

How does the Act affect the way in which a job description or person specification should be prepared?

7.7   The inclusion of unnecessary or marginal requirements in a job description or person specification can lead to discrimination.

An employer stipulates that employees must be "active and energetic", when in fact the job in question is largely sedentary in nature. This requirement could unjustifiably exclude some people whose disabilities result in them getting tired more easily than others. An employer specifies that a driving licence is required for a job which involves limited travel. An applicant for the job has no driving licence because of the particular effects in his case of cerebral palsy. He is otherwise the best candidate for that job, he could easily and cheaply do the travelling involved other than by driving and it is likely to be a reasonable adjustment for the employer to let him do so. It would be discriminatory to insist on the specification and reject his application solely because he has no driving licence. An employer stipulates that employees must be "good team players", when in fact the job in question does not involve working in a team. This requirement could unjustifiably exclude some people who have difficulty communicating, such as some people with autism.

7.8   Blanket exclusions (i.e. exclusions which do not take account of individual circumstances) can also lead to discrimination. Indeed, such exclusions are likely to amount to direct discrimination, and so be incapable of justification (see paragraph 4.5).

An employer excludes people with epilepsy from all driving jobs. One of the jobs, in practice, only requires a standard licence and standard insurance cover. If, as a result, someone with epilepsy, who has such a licence and can obtain such insurance cover, is turned down for the job, the employer will have discriminated unlawfully in excluding her from consideration. An employer stipulates that candidates for a job must not have a history of mental illness, believing that such candidates will have poor attendance. The employer rejects an applicant solely because he has had a mental illness, without checking the individual's actual attendance record. This will amount to discrimination – and will be unlawful. An employer stipulates that anyone with an infectious disease cannot work in the food preparation area. It refuses to employ someone with AIDS in this area, believing him to be a health and safety risk. Whether or not the employer has a written policy to this effect, this action will amount to discrimination, as the employer has not considered the actual circumstances of the case.

7.9   In addition, stating that a certain personal, medical or health-related characteristic is essential or desirable can lead to discrimination if the characteristic is not necessary for the performance of the job. An employer would therefore need to ensure that any such requirements were genuinely essential to the job, and that it would not be reasonable to waive them in any individual case.

A television company requires all television engineers to have a high standard of hearing and vision. A woman with a hearing impairment is turned down for a job in the graphic design department because she does not pass a hearing test. If this standard of hearing is not necessary in order to do the particular job she applied for, the employer will have unlawfully discriminated against her by failing to make a reasonable adjustment to its policy of requiring job applicants to pass the test.

7.10 Likewise, although an employer is entitled to specify that applicants for a job must have certain qualifications, it will have to justify rejecting a disabled person for lacking a qualification if the reason why the disabled person lacks it is related to his disability. Justification will involve showing that the qualification is relevant and significant in terms of the particular job and the particular applicant, and that there is no reasonable adjustment which would change this. In some circumstances it might be feasible to reassign the duties to which the qualification relates, or to waive the requirement for the qualification if this particular applicant has alternative evidence of the necessary level of competence.

An employer seeking someone to work in an administrative post specifies that candidates must have the relevant NVQ Level 4 qualification. If Level 4 fairly reflects the complex and varied nature and substantial personal responsibility of the work, and these aspects of the job cannot reasonably be altered, the employer will be able to justify rejecting a disabled applicant who has only been able to reach Level 3 because of his disability and who cannot show the relevant level of competence by other means. An employer specifies that two GCSEs are required for a certain post. This is to show that a candidate has the general level of ability required. No particular subjects are specified. An applicant whose dyslexia prevented her from passing written examinations cannot meet this requirement. The employer would be unable to justify rejecting her on this account alone if she could show in some other way that she had the expertise called for in the post.

OFFERS OF EMPLOYMENT

7.32 Terms and conditions of service should not discriminate against a disabled person. In general, an employer should not offer a job to a disabled person on terms which are less favourable than those which would be offered to other people.

A person with a history of depression, is offered employment with a six month probationary period, even though other employees are only required to serve a three month probationary period. This will amount to direct discrimination and will be unlawful.

8 DISCRIMINATION AGAINST EMPLOYEES

TERMS AND CONDITIONS OF SERVICE

8.4 As stated at paragraph 7.32, terms and conditions of service should not discriminate against a disabled person. The employer should consider whether any reasonable adjustments need to be made to the terms and conditions which would otherwise apply.

An employer's terms and conditions state the hours an employee has to be in work. It might be a reasonable adjustment to change these hours for someone whose disability means that she has difficulty using public transport during rush hours.

8.5 Where the terms and conditions of employment include an element of performance-related pay, the employer must ensure that the way such pay arrangements operate does not discriminate against a disabled employee. If, on the ground of disability, an employee is denied the opportunity to receive performance-related pay, this is likely to be direct discrimination. Even if less favourable treatment of an employee in relation to performance-related pay is not directly discriminatory, it will amount to disability related discrimination unless the employer can show that it is justified.

8.6   If an employee has a disability which adversely affects his rate of output, the effect may be that he receives less under a performance-related pay scheme than other employees. The employer must consider whether there are reasonable adjustments which would overcome this substantial disadvantage.

A disabled man with arthritis works in telephone sales and is paid commission on the value of his sales. Because of a worsening of his impairment he is advised to switch to new computer equipment. This equipment slows his work down for a period of time while he gets used to it and consequently the value of his sales falls. It is likely to be a reasonable adjustment for his employer to continue to pay him his previous level of commission for the period in which he adjusts to the new equipment. A disabled home-worker, who is paid a fixed rate for each item he produces, has a reduced output rate because he does not have the right equipment to do the job to the best of his ability. It is likely to be a reasonable adjustment for the employer to provide that equipment, possibly with funding or advice from the Access to Work scheme, to improve the disabled worker's output and consequently his pay. A woman who has recently become disabled because of diabetes works for an employer that operates a performance related bonus scheme. When she has her annual appraisal, the woman is unable to demonstrate that she has met all her objectives for the year, unlike in previous years when she had in fact exceeded her objectives. The reason why the woman has not met her objectives this year is that she has been adjusting to her disability (attending hospital appointments, paying careful attention to her diet, taking regular breaks etc.). The disabled woman's employer is likely to be discriminating against her if, because she has not met her objectives for the year, it refuses to pay her a bonus.

Confidential information

8.21   The extent to which an employer is entitled to let other staff know about an employee's disability will depend partly on the terms of employment. An employer could be discriminating against the employee by revealing such information if the employer would not reveal similar information about another person for an equally legitimate management purpose; or if the employer revealed such information without consulting the individual, instead of adopting the usual practice of talking to an employee before revealing personal information about him. Employers also need to be aware that they have obligations under the Data Protection Act in respect of personal data.

8.22   However, as noted at paragraph 5.22, sometimes a reasonable adjustment will not work without the co-operation of other employees. In order to secure such cooperation, it may be necessary for the employer to tell one or more of a disabled person's colleagues (in confidence) about a disability which is not obvious. This may be limited to the disabled person's supervisor, or it may be appropriate to involve other colleagues, depending on the nature of the disability and the reason they need to know about it. In any event, an employer must not disclose confidential details about an employee without his consent. A disabled person's refusal to give such consent may impact upon the effectiveness of the adjustments which the employer is able to make or its ability to make adjustments at all.

In order for a person with epilepsy to work safely in a particular factory, it may be necessary to advise fellow workers about how they can assist the disabled worker to manage her condition. An office worker with cancer says that he does not want colleagues to know of his condition. As an adjustment he needs extra time away from work to receive treatment and to rest. Neither his colleagues nor the line manager need to be told the precise reasons for the extra leave but the latter will need to know that the adjustment is required in order to implement it effectively.

8.23   The Act does not prevent a disabled person keeping a disability confidential from an employer. But keeping a disability confidential is likely to mean that unless the employer could reasonably be expected to know about it anyway, the employer will not be under a duty to make a reasonable adjustment. If a disabled person expects an employer to make a reasonable adjustment, he will need to provide the employer – or someone acting on its behalf – with sufficient information to carry out that adjustment.

An employee has symptomatic HIV. He prefers not to tell his employer of the condition. However, as the condition progresses, he finds it increasingly difficult to work the required number of hours in a week. Until he tells his employer of his condition – or the employer becomes aware of it (or could reasonably be expected to be aware of it) – the employer does not have to make a reasonable adjustment by changing his working hours to overcome the difficulty. However, once the employer is informed he may then have to make a reasonable adjustment.

TERMINATION OF EMPLOYMENT

8.24   Where a disabled person is dismissed or is selected for redundancy or for compulsory early retirement (including compulsory ill-health retirement), the employer must ensure that the disabled person is not being discriminated against. It is likely to be direct discrimination if the dismissal or selection is made on the ground of disability (see paragraph 4.5). If the dismissal or selection is not directly discriminatory, but is made for a reason related to the disability, it will amount to disability-related discrimination unless the employer can show that it is justified. The reason would also have to be one which could not be removed by any reasonable adjustment.

It would be justifiable to terminate the employment of an employee whose disability makes it impossible for him any longer to perform the main functions of his job, if an adjustment such as a move to a vacant post elsewhere in the business is not practicable or otherwise not reasonable for the employer to have to make.

8.25   When setting criteria for redundancy selection, employers should consider whether any proposed criterion would adversely impact upon a disabled employee. If so, it may be necessary for the employer to make reasonable adjustments. For example, it is likely to be a reasonable adjustment to discount disability related sickness absence when assessing attendance as part of a redundancy selection scheme. Some employers use 'flexibility' as a selection criterion for redundancy (for example, willingness to re-locate or to work unpopular hours, or ability to carry out a wide variety of tasks). An employer should carefully consider how to apply this criterion to a disabled employee as it might be discriminatory.

8.26   Where the dismissal of a disabled person is being considered for a reason relating to that person's conduct, the employer should consider whether any reasonable adjustments need to be made to the disciplinary or dismissal process. In addition, if the conduct in question is related to the employee's disability, that may be relevant in determining the sanction which it is appropriate to impose.

A young man with learning disabilities asks if he can bring a friend to a disciplinary hearing, rather than a work colleague. It is likely to be a reasonable adjustment for his employer to allow this. A woman shouts at her line manager in front of work colleagues and uses inappropriate language. The employer would usually consider dismissal as a sanction for such behaviour, but takes into account the fact that she was in great pain on the day in question because of her disability and instead issues a warning. This is likely to be a reasonable adjustment to make.

EHRC CODE OF PRACTICE ON RACIAL EQUALITY IN EMPLOYMENT (2005)

THE RESPONSIBILITIES OF EMPLOYERS: EQUALITY OF OPPORTUNITY AND GOOD EMPLOYMENT PRACTICE

RECRUITMENT

Principles of good practice

4.4   The following principles apply to all aspects of recruitment for employment, including promotion, and training.
   a.   Recruitment policies, procedures and practices should meet all the terms and objectives of the organisation's equal opportunities policy and action plan.
   b.   All staff responsible for recruitment should receive training in the equal opportunities policy.
   c.   Opportunities for employment, including promotion, and training should be equally open to all eligible candidates, and selection should be based solely on merit (except where the positive action exception applies to training; see Appendix 1).
   d.   No applicant or worker should be placed at a disadvantage by rules, requirements, conditions or practices that have a disproportionately adverse effect on his or her racial group.

PLANNING

Person specifications

4.8   A person specification describes the skills, knowledge, abilities, qualifications, experience and qualities that are considered necessary or desirable in a candidate, in order to perform all the duties in the job description satisfactorily. It is recommended that employers prepare a written person specification to accompany the job description.

4.9   To avoid claims that a person specification includes potentially discriminatory requirements, criteria or conditions, employers need to make sure of the following.
   a.   The person specification includes only the criteria needed to perform the duties in the job description satisfactorily.
   b.   The person specification does not overstate the requirements; for example, by calling for 'excellent knowledge of English' (or Welsh in Wales) when "good understanding" is more appropriate, or by asking for higher qualifications than are actually needed to do the job satisfactorily.
   c.   The person specification makes clear the relative importance placed on each criterion, and whether it is necessary or desirable.
   d.   As far as possible, all the criteria are capable of being tested objectively. This means avoiding vague or subjective qualities. Attributes such as "leadership", which are widely used in the selection process, need to be precisely and objectively defined in terms of the measurable skills and qualities that contribute to it; for example, fairness, knowledge, diplomacy, imagination and decisiveness.

e.   The person specification makes clear that degrees or diplomas obtained abroad are acceptable, if they are of an equivalent standard to UK qualifications (see Appendix 5 for details of UK National Academic Recognition Information Centre).

f.   To reduce the risk of including criteria that reflect personal preferences rather than justifiable requirements, as far as possible, the manager responsible for the post obtains approval of the person specification from the person responsible for equal opportunities in the organisation (in smaller organisations, this might be the director or proprietor).

4.10 Employers should consider reviewing the person specifications they have used over a period of time, or a representative sample of them, as part of their equal opportunities review of the recruitment process, to make sure the requirements and criteria applied do not contribute to any significant disparities between the success rates for different racial groups.

The selection process

4.16 Employers are responsible for making sure their selection procedures are fair, and operate consistently, to ensure the appointment of the best person for the job, irrespective of race, colour, nationality (including citizenship) or ethnic or national origins.

Terms and conditions

4.37 It is unlawful for employers to discriminate, on racial grounds, in the terms and conditions of work they offer, including pay, hours of work, overtime, bonuses, holiday entitlement, sickness leave, and maternity and paternity leave.

4.38 It is recommended that employers make sure their rules and requirements on access to any benefits, facilities or services, such as luncheon vouchers, discount travel services or membership of a gym, do not unlawfully discriminate against a particular racial group (or groups) (see paras 2.9–2.13).

4.39 When employees' cultural or religious practices, such as those expressed in dress codes, conflict with an employer's policies or workplace requirements, it is recommended that the employer consider whether it is practicable to vary or adapt these requirements. Employers should consult staff, trades unions and other workplace representatives on practical ways in which they can accommodate workers' needs. Discrimination in the field of employment on grounds of religion or belief is unlawful under the Employment Equality (Religion or Belief) Regulations 2003. If the policy or requirement affects people from a particular racial group (or groups), it might also amount to unlawful indirect racial discrimination (see paras 2.9–2.13).

IN THE COURSE OF EMPLOYMENT

Language in the workplace

4.46 There is a clear business interest in having a common language in the workplace, to avoid misunderstandings, with all the risks these can entail, whether legal, financial or in relation to health and safety. It is also a matter of courtesy, conducive to good working relations, not to exclude people from conversations that might concern them, when they are present. In the main, English is the language of business in Britain and is likely to be the preferred language of communication in most workplaces (see Example 15 on p. 57), unless other languages are specifically required.

4.48 However, employers should make sure that any rules, requirements, conditions, policies or practices involving the use of a particular language during or outside working hours, for example during work breaks, do not amount to unlawful racial discrimination or harassment against a worker or job applicant (see Example 7, p. 22). Employers should be able to justify these as being a reasonable means of achieving a legitimate business end. Blanket rules, requirements or practices involving the use of a particular language are often unlikely to be justifiable. Even during working hours, most types of work permit casual conversation at the same time, for example while picking fruit, or filing papers. An employer who prohibits workers from talking casually to each other in a language they do not share with all colleagues, or uses occasions when this happens to trigger disciplinary or capability procedures or impede progress, may be considered to be acting unreasonably.

4.49   Employers should always consult workers, trade unions and other workplace representatives before drawing up any proposals on the use of language in the workplace.

4.50   Where the workforce includes people who are not proficient in the language of the workplace, employers should consider taking reasonable steps to improve communication (see Example I at para 4.58). These might include providing:

Example 15: Language
Shah v George Grassic t/a The Suite Factory [1995] DCLD 24
An Asian worker in a furniture factory (where there were eight Asians in a workforce of 40) came out of a disciplinary meeting onto the shop floor and, in the owner's presence, began to speak to other Asian workers in their own language. The owner instructed him to speak English, so that he knew what was being said. The worker refused and was warned that if he did not do as he had been instructed he would be dismissed immediately. The worker said he could speak in any language he wished and continued to ignore the instruction. He was then summarily dismissed. The tribunal dismissed the worker's complaint that he had been discriminated against on racial grounds, and ruled that, whether or not it is discriminatory to forbid people to speak in their native language depends on the circumstances: "If the worker had been told not to speak in his native tongue at all on any occasion at work, in any circumstances, then that, in our view, would clearly be a discriminatory instruction. . . . [but in these circumstances] It was not unreasonable for [the owner] to expect the common courtesy of being spoken to, or about, in a way in which he could understand."
a.   interpreting and translation facilities; for example, multilingual safety signs and notices, to make sure workers understand health and safety requirements;
b.   training in language and communication skills; and
c.   training for managers and supervisors on the various populations and cultures that make up Britain today.

Performance assessment
4.53   It is unlawful to discriminate against, or harass, a worker, on racial grounds in assessing his or her performance.

4.54   To strengthen their legal defence in any proceedings alleging unlawful racial discrimination, employers need to make sure that performance assessments are not used to pass judgments about the person, based on assumptions about their capabilities as members of certain racial groups. Employers will find it helpful to base all assessments on actual performance of specific tasks, measured by impartial and objective standards. This is particularly important when performance is linked to promotion or a benefit, such as pay or bonuses (see Example 16, p. 59).

4.55   It is recommended that training courses for managers on the equal opportunities policy (see para 3.20) should include guidance on objective performance assessment. Equally, any training on assessment methods should take the organisation's equal opportunities policy fully into account.

4.56 To be sure workers are being assessed fairly, and consistently, employers will find it helpful to monitor the results of performance assessments, by racial group (see paras 3.25–3.31), and use the data to inform their review of the organisation's policies, procedures and practices in this area. Any significant disparities in assessment marks between racial groups should be investigated, and steps taken to deal with possible causes.

Example 16: Performance assessment
Nasr v Salisbury Health Care NHS Trust, Case No. 3102492/99
A consultant of Egyptian origin was not awarded a discretionary point to take his salary above the standard, whereas his 12 colleagues, who were white and of British origin, had each been awarded at least one point. The tribunal upheld his claim of unlawful direct discrimination. It found that the members of the discretionary points committee did not independently record their assessment of each of the candidates against the appropriate criteria and guidelines. Nor were any notes kept of the discussions or the assessment process. The tribunal concluded that 'such a high level of subjectivity is anathema to the successful application of equal opportunity guidelines, since it works to the disadvantage of ethnic minorities, both in operation and perception'. The complainant was awarded £18,000 in exemplary damages.

Example H. A large-scale study of appraisal in 13 civil service departments in 2000 found that staff from white racial groups were consistently awarded higher marks than staff from other racial groups. This was true across grades, age groups, and length-of-service bands. The researchers found no evidence of significant differences in education or training between the groups that were likely to affect performance. Interviews with staff from all racial groups revealed common concerns about the appraisal system itself. Staff from 'non-white' groups were concerned that their performance reviews and appraisal markings reflected stereotyped attitudes about their racial groups. The researchers produced reports and made recommendations for each department. Departments are now acting on these and are themselves monitoring appraisal results and carrying out further investigations and analyses, for example of the language used in appraisal reports, depending on the racial groups concerned.

Promotion

4.60 It is unlawful for employers to discriminate against, or harass, workers on racial grounds in the way they make opportunities for promotion available, or by refusing or deliberately failing to make them available (see Example 18 below).

4.61 It is recommended that all promotion opportunities, including development opportunities that could lead to permanent promotion, should be advertised widely throughout the organisation, and filled in line with the organisation's equal opportunities and recruitment policies and procedures. This would mean using the organisation's standard job application form (if it has one) to fill all promotion and development opportunities, and making sure that selection is based strictly on demonstrable merit.

Example 18: Promotion
Dr Halim v Moray College, Case No. S/200267/02
The complainant, who was a lecturer at a college in Scotland, was twice overlooked for promotion, even though he was better qualified than those who were promoted. He believed this was because he had complained to the college principal that his line manager was racist and that he had given him unfair appraisals. The principal had advised the complainant to raise the matter directly with his line manager.

There were nine applicants for the first post, including the complainant and his line manager, and the panel included the principal. The principal's sole comment on the complainant was 'This man's not for shortlisting'. At the tribunal hearing, he said he did not consider the application to be 'a serious one' and thought it was all 'part of a sad ruse'. The complainant's line manager was appointed to the post. The panel for the second promotion included the complainant's line manager and the principal and deputy principal. This time he was rejected because the panel said he did not meet some of the essential criteria. The principal also told the tribunal that the complainant 'did not understand what the job was about'.

The tribunal found the college's explanations unconvincing. In upholding the complainant's claim, it took into account the following: unlike the shortlisted candidates, the complainant had met some of the essential criteria; the panel members had been aware of the complainant's grievance; and the person who was the subject of the grievance had been a member of the panel. The tribunal awarded £14,000 in damages.

4.62 Employers should avoid by-passing their recruitment procedures, unless a temporary promotion is absolutely necessary. In this case, the promotion should last no longer than the time needed to fill the post permanently, and openly, through the organisation's recruitment procedures.

4.63 Employers will find it helpful to build the following guidelines into their policies and procedures for promotion and career development.
   a.   Where posts are advertised internally and externally, the same selection procedures and criteria should apply to both internal and external candidates. Discussions about candidates, particularly internal candidates, should not be based on rumours or unsubstantiated opinions.
   b.   As far as possible, selection decisions based on performance assessments should be endorsed by the organisation's personnel department (if it has one).
   c.   No assumptions should be made about the eligibility of staff, based on their grade, current post or racial group, and information about all promotion and other development opportunities that could lead to permanent promotion, such as deputising and secondments, should be communicated to all staff; restricting applications for promotion and other development opportunities to staff at a particular grade or level could indirectly discriminate against some racial groups.
   d.   Records should be kept, by racial group, of who is taking up different types of opportunities, and who is not (see paras 3.25–3.31); who is successful, and who is not.

4.64 As part of their equal opportunities review of the recruitment process, employers should use the monitoring data on promotions to see if there are significant disparities between racial groups in the take-up of promotion and other development opportunities, success rates and length of time spent at a particular grade. If disparities are found, employers should investigate the possible causes in each case and take steps to remove any barriers.

Discipline and grievance

4.65 Employers must not discriminate on racial grounds in the way they respond to grievances, or invoke disciplinary measures. Disciplinary action is an extreme measure and should be taken fairly and consistently, regardless of the worker's racial group. Equally, allegations of racial discrimination or harassment must always be taken seriously and investigated promptly, not dismissed as "oversensitivity" on a worker's part.

4.66 All employers (irrespective of their size) must now have minimum statutory procedures in place for dealing with dismissal, disciplinary action and grievances in the workplace (section 3 of the Employment Rights Act 1996, as amended by the Employment Act 2002) (see 'disciplinary procedure' and 'grievance procedure' in the glossary at Appendix 7, and

ACAS in Appendix 5). These provisions apply only to employees (see the glossary at Appendix 7).

4.67 It is in the interests of employers to attempt, wherever possible, to resolve grievances as they arise, and before they become major problems, through mediation. Grievance procedures can provide an open and fair way for complainants to make their concerns known, and for their grievances to be resolved quickly, without having to bring legal proceedings.

4.68 It is recommended that employers monitor, by racial group, the number of workers who have brought grievances or been subjected to disciplinary action (public authorities with at least 150 full-time-equivalent workers have a legal duty to do this; see paras 3.32–3.34), and the outcomes of each case. It will also be useful to be able to match the data with information about the workers' grades, their managers and the areas of the organisation where they work.

4.69 If an investigation into a grievance or disciplinary matter finds evidence that the grievance was brought in bad faith, for example, to get another worker into trouble, the employer should take steps to make sure this does not happen again, either by recommending training or taking disciplinary action against the worker in question, as appropriate. However, employers must be careful not to punish someone for having made a complaint that proves to have been unfounded, but that was made in good faith, as that could amount to unlawful victimisation (see paras 2.14–2.15).

4.70 It is recommended that, before taking disciplinary action, employers should consider the possible effect on a worker's behaviour of the following:
a. racist abuse or other provocation on racial grounds;
b. difficulty in communicating with, or understanding, colleagues; and
c. different cultural norms.

4.71 As part of their equal opportunities review, employers should use the monitoring data on grievances and disciplinary action to see if there are significant disparities between racial groups, investigate the possible causes in each case, and take steps to deal with them.

Harassment

Example 19: Harassment
Milovanovic v Hebden Dyeing and Finishing Co Ltd, Case No. 29691/94 [1995] DCLD No. 24
A Serbian worker, who had lived in Britain for over 40 years, was one of 25 workers in a dyeing company. He complained in vain of persistent harassment based on his ethnic background, especially after the war in Bosnia began. He faced comments such as 'Go back to Bosnia or wherever you belong, and fight and die like a dog instead of our lads'; and 'If all foreigners and blacks go back to their own country, we will have a better environment in this country'. He handed in his notice and brought a successful claim of direct racial discrimination against the company (see para 2.16). The complainant was awarded around £4,000 in damages.

Example 20: Harassment
Mohammed Wahid Zia v Killermont Polo Club (Scotland) Ltd, Case No. S/105430/2001
A Muslim of Pakistani origin, who was employed as a part-time waiter in Glasgow, claimed that his employers, who were Indian Sikhs, harassed, humiliated and demeaned him on racial grounds, and that they also made derogatory remarks about his religion. The tribunal upheld his claims of direct racial discrimination (see para 2.16), victimisation and unfair dismissal. The application was made before 19 July 2003, when it became unlawful to treat a worker or a job applicant less favourably on grounds of religion or

belief. Since then, in similar circumstances, the case could have been brought on religious as well as racial grounds. The complainant was awarded a total of around £33,000 in compensation, including £22,000 for injury to feelings.

4.72 It is unlawful for employers to engage in, or condone, unwanted conduct that will violate the dignity of workers or job applicants, or create an intimidating, hostile, degrading, offensive or humiliating atmosphere for that person (see Example 7, p 22, and Examples 19 and 20 above).

4.73 It is recommended that employers introduce a policy for dealing with racial harassment. The policy could be part of a wider anti-harassment policy or the organisation's policies on discipline and grievance, or a policy covering dignity in the workplace. Whatever form the policy takes, it should make clear what is and what is not acceptable behaviour in the organisation (see the sample policy at Appendix 3).

4.74 To make sure the policy is effective, it is recommended that employers:
  a. publicise the policy through the organisation's websites, notice boards and other forms of communication, so that all staff know about it and understand why it has been adopted, how it will work and how it affects them;
  b. make both the policy for dealing with racial harassment and the equal opportunities policy standard components of all training, including induction and specialist courses; and
  c. offer an informal route to resolving a grievance as well as the formal one of an investigation.

4.75 If an allegation of racial harassment or discrimination is upheld, it is in the interest of good workplace relations for the employer to make sure that:
  a. the harassment has actually stopped, particularly if the parties continue to work together, and
  b. the complainant is not victimised for having brought the grievance.

Dismissal and termination of employment

4.76 It is unlawful for employers to discriminate against, or harass, workers on racial grounds, by dismissing them or subjecting them to any other detriment (see Example 21 below and Example 22, p. 66). Dismissal includes termination of a contract by the employer (with or without notice), and non-renewal or expiry of a fixed-term contract, unless a genuine occupational requirement applies (see para 2.36 and Appendix 1).

4.77 It is recommended that employers make sure the criteria they use for dismissal (including redundancies) are not indirectly discriminatory, and that their procedures are fair and objective, and are followed consistently.

4.78 Dismissal, or any other detriment – such as demotion or compulsory transfer – must always be fair and reasonable. Employers should make sure such decisions are based on a worker's actual performance or conduct during his or her employment, as reflected in any performance assessments. Any aptitude tests designed to select people for redundancy should be objective, and fairly and consistently administered (see paras 4.23–4.26). Wherever possible, employers should consult their workers, and trade unions and other workplace representatives, about proposed redundancies, and the criteria for selection.

Example 21: Dismissal
Birdi v Waites (1) and Waites Architecture (2), Case No. 37708/95 [1996] DCLD 30
A tribunal found that a firm of architects had a record of dismissing black and Asian professional staff after short service, and that this amounted to unlawful racial discrimination. It found that an Asian architect had been criticised without reason during his employment with the firm, marginalised and then dismissed after nine months, for

poor performance. He was the third consecutive ethnic minority worker to be dismissed in under 12 months.

Example 22: Redundancy
Sahota and ORS v Shareporter Ltd, [1983] COIT 1414/148
Three sewing machinists, each with less than a year's service claimed compensation for their selection for redundancy. Two were of Indian origin and the third was Italian. The machine room supervisor, whose views of black and Asian workers were known to be both strong and derogatory, had made the selection. The tribunal did not accept the company's claim that the machinists had been selected objectively, on the grounds of skill, as one of the machinists was a high bonus earner of some speed and reliability. The tribunal ruled that all three complainants had been dismissed in a redundancy situation because of their race.

4.79 Staff responsible for selecting workers for dismissal should be instructed not to discriminate on racial grounds, and trained in the organisation's equal opportunities policy, and how it might apply to dismissal and redundancy.

4.80 Workers who are eligible for redeployment should be given the chance to show they have the skills or abilities required in alternative jobs. Employers should use their normal recruitment policy to fill these jobs.

4.81 It is recommended that employers monitor all dismissals, by racial group (see also paras 3.25 and 3.31). They will find it useful to be able to match this data with information about the workers' grades, the areas of the organisation where they work, and their managers.

4.82 As well as the guidelines proposed in relation to disciplinary action (see paras 4.65–4.71), employers will find it helpful to:
   a. make sure the decision to dismiss is not made by one individual, but, as far as possible, in discussion with a senior member of staff in the personnel department (if the organisation has one);
   b. keep written records of all decisions to dismiss; and
   c. encourage leavers to give feedback about their employment.

4.83 Employers should use the monitoring data to see if policies, procedures or practices that might have been criticised in the feedback could be contributing to any significant disparities between racial groups, for example in performance ratings or promotion.

ACAS Code of Practice 1 – Disciplinary and Grievance Procedures (Revised April 2009)

4.   . . . whenever a disciplinary or grievance process is being followed it is important to deal with issues fairly. There are a number of elements to this:
   • Employers and employees should raise and deal with issues promptly and should not unreasonably delay meetings, decisions or confirmation of those decisions.
   • Employers and employees should act consistently.
   • Employers should carry out any necessary investigations, to establish the facts of the case.
   • Employers should inform employees of the basis of the problem and give them an opportunity to put their case in response before any decisions are made.
   • Employers should allow employees to be accompanied at any formal disciplinary or grievance meeting.
   • Employers should allow an employee to appeal against any formal decision made.

KEYS TO HANDLING DISCIPLINARY ISSUES IN THE WORKPLACE

Establish the facts of each case

5.   It is important to carry out necessary investigations of potential disciplinary matters without unreasonable delay to establish the facts of the case. In some cases this will require the holding of an investigatory meeting with the employee before proceeding to any disciplinary hearing. In others, the investigatory stage will be the collation of evidence by the employer for use at any disciplinary hearing.

6.   In misconduct cases, where practicable, different people should carry out the investigation and disciplinary hearing.

7.   If there is an investigatory meeting this should not by itself result in any disciplinary action. Although there is no statutory right for an employee to be accompanied at a formal investigatory meeting, such a right may be allowed under an employer's own procedure.

8.   In cases where a period of suspension with pay is considered necessary, this period should be as brief as possible, should be kept under review and it should be made clear that this suspension is not considered a disciplinary action.

Inform the employee of the problem

9.   If it is decided that there is a disciplinary case to answer, the employee should be notified of this in writing. This notification should contain sufficient information about the alleged misconduct or poor performance and its possible consequences to enable the employee to prepare to answer the case at a disciplinary meeting. It would normally be appropriate to provide copies of any written evidence, which may include any witness statements, with the notification.

10. The notification should also give details of the time and venue for the disciplinary meeting and advise the employee of their right to be accompanied at the meeting.

Hold a meeting with the employee to discuss the problem

11. The meeting should be held without unreasonable delay whilst allowing the employee reasonable time to prepare their case.

12. Employers and employees (and their companions) should make every effort to attend the meeting. At the meeting the employer should explain the complaint against the employee and go through the evidence that has been gathered. The employee should be allowed to set out their case and answer any allegations that have been made. The employee should also be given a reasonable opportunity to ask questions, present evidence and call relevant witnesses. They should also be given an opportunity to raise points about any information provided by witnesses. Where an employer or employee intends to call relevant witnesses they should give advance notice that they intend to do this.

Allow the employee to be accompanied at the meeting

13. Workers have a statutory right to be accompanied by a companion where the disciplinary meeting could result in:
     *   a formal warning being issued; or
     *   the taking of some other disciplinary action; or
     *   the confirmation of a warning or some other disciplinary action (appeal hearings).

14. The chosen companion may be a fellow worker, a trade union representative, or an official employed by a trade union. A trade union representative who is not an employed official must have been certified by their union as being competent to accompany a worker.

15. To exercise the statutory right to be accompanied workers must make a reasonable request. What is reasonable will depend on the circumstances of each individual case. However, it would not normally be reasonable for workers to insist on being accompanied by a companion whose presence would prejudice the hearing nor would it be reasonable for a worker to ask to be accompanied by a companion from a remote geographical location if someone suitable and willing was available on site.

16. The companion should be allowed to address the hearing to put and sum up the worker's case, respond on behalf of the worker to any views expressed at the meeting and confer with the worker during the hearing. The companion does not, however, have the right to answer questions on the worker's behalf, address the hearing if the worker does not wish it or prevent the employer from explaining their case.

Decide on appropriate action

17. After the meeting decide whether or not disciplinary or any other action is justified and inform the employee accordingly in writing.

18. Where misconduct is confirmed or the employee is found to be performing unsatisfactorily it is usual to give the employee a written warning. A further act of misconduct or failure to improve performance within a set period would normally result in a final written warning.

19. If an employee's first misconduct or unsatisfactory performance is sufficiently serious, it may be appropriate to move directly to a final written warning. This might occur where the employee's actions have had, or are liable to have, a serious or harmful impact on the organisation.

20. A first or final written warning should set out the nature of the misconduct or poor performance and the change in behaviour or improvement in performance required (with timescale). The employee should be told how long the warning will remain current. The employee should be informed of the consequences of further misconduct, or failure to improve performance, within the set period following a final warning. For instance that it may result in dismissal or some other contractual penalty such as demotion or loss of seniority.

21. A decision to dismiss should only be taken by a manager who has the authority to do so. The employee should be informed as soon as possible of the reasons for the dismissal, the date on which the employment contract will end, the appropriate period of notice and their right of appeal.

22. Some acts, termed gross misconduct, are so serious in themselves or have such serious consequences that they may call for dismissal without notice for a first offence. But a fair disciplinary process should always be followed, before dismissing for gross misconduct.

23. Disciplinary rules should give examples of acts which the employer regards as acts of gross misconduct. These may vary according to the nature of the organisation and what it does, but might include things such as theft or fraud, physical violence, gross negligence or serious insubordination.

24. Where an employee is persistently unable or unwilling to attend a disciplinary meeting without good cause the employer should make a decision on the evidence available.

Provide employees with an opportunity to appeal

25. Where an employee feels that disciplinary action taken against them is wrong or unjust they should appeal against the decision. Appeals should be heard without unreasonable

delay and ideally at an agreed time and place. Employees should let employers know the grounds for their appeal in writing.

26. The appeal should be dealt with impartially and wherever possible, by a manager who has not previously been involved in the case.

27. Workers have a statutory right to be accompanied at appeal hearings.

28. Employees should be informed in writing of the results of the appeal hearing as soon as possible.

Special cases
29. Where disciplinary action is being considered against an employee who is a trade union representative the normal disciplinary procedure should be followed. Depending on the circumstances, however, it is advisable to discuss the matter at an early stage with an official employed by the union, after obtaining the employee's agreement.

30. If an employee is charged with, or convicted of a criminal offence this is not normally in itself reason for disciplinary action. Consideration needs to be given to what effect the charge or conviction has on the employee's suitability to do the job and their relationship with their employer, work colleagues and customers.

Keys to handling grievances in the workplace

Let the employer know the nature of the grievance
31. If it is not possible to resolve a grievance informally employees should raise the matter formally and without unreasonable delay with a manager who is not the subject of the grievance. This should be done in writing and should set out the nature of the grievance.

Hold a meeting with the employee to discuss the grievance
32. Employers should arrange for a formal meeting to be held without unreasonable delay after a grievance is received.

33. Employers, employees and their companions should make every effort to attend the meeting. Employees should be allowed to explain their grievance and how they think it should be resolved. Consideration should be given to adjourning the meeting for any investigation that may be necessary.

Allow the employee to be accompanied at the meeting
34. Workers have a statutory right to be accompanied by a companion at a grievance meeting which deals with a complaint about a duty owed by the employer to the worker. So this would apply where the complaint is, for example, that the employer is not honouring the worker's contract, or is in breach of legislation.

35. The chosen companion may be a fellow worker, a trade union representative or an official employed by a trade union. A trade union representative who is not an employed official must have been certified by their union as being competent to accompany a worker.

36. To exercise the right to be accompanied a worker must first make a reasonable request. What is reasonable will depend on the circumstances of each individual case. However it would not normally be reasonable for workers to insist on being accompanied by a companion whose presence would prejudice the hearing nor would it be reasonable for a worker to ask to be accompanied by a companion from a remote geographical location if someone suitable and willing was available on site.

37.   The companion should be allowed to address the hearing to put and sum up the worker's case, respond on behalf of the worker to any views expressed at the meeting and confer with the worker during the hearing. The companion does not however, have the right to answer questions on the worker's behalf, address the hearing if the worker does not wish it or prevent the employer from explaining their case.

Decide on appropriate action

38.   Following the meeting decide on what action, if any, to take. Decisions should be communicated to the employee, in writing, without unreasonable delay and, where appropriate, should set out what action the employer intends to take to resolve the grievance. The employee should be informed that they can appeal if they are not content with the action taken.

Allow the employee to take the grievance further if not resolved

39.   Where an employee feels that their grievance has not been satisfactorily resolved they should appeal. They should let their employer know the grounds for their appeal without unreasonable delay and in writing.

40.   Appeals should be heard without unreasonable delay and at a time and place which should be notified to the employee in advance.

41.   The appeal should be dealt with impartially and wherever possible by a manager who has not previously been involved in the case.

42.   Workers have a statutory right to be accompanied at any such appeal hearing.

43.   The outcome of the appeal should be communicated to the employee in writing without unreasonable delay.

Overlapping grievance and disciplinary cases

44.   Where an employee raises a grievance during a disciplinary process the disciplinary process may be temporarily suspended in order to deal with the grievance. Where the grievance and disciplinary cases are related it may be appropriate to deal with both issues concurrently.

Collective grievances

45.   The provisions of this code do not apply to grievances raised on behalf of two or more employees by a representative of a recognised trade union or other appropriate workplace representative. These grievances should be handled in accordance with the organisation's collective grievance process.

Alphabetical Index

Chronological Index

Thematic Index